ECUMENISM
Theology and History

ECUMENISM

THEOLOGY AND HISTORY

by

BERNARD LAMBERT

Translated by
Lancelot C. Sheppard

HERDER AND HERDER

Distributed in USA and Canada by:

HERDER AND HERDER NEW YORK

232 Madison Avenue, New York, N. Y. 10016

Distributed in Great Britain and all other countries by:

BURNS & OATES LIMITED

25 Ashley Place, London S. W. I

Original edition:

"Le Problème Œcuménique"

(in two volumes),

Éditions du Centurion, Paris, 1962

Library of Congress Catalog Card No. 67-21091

First published in West Germany © 1967 by Herder KG

Printed in West Germany by Herder

CONTENTS

THE PROBLEM OF INTERDENOMINATIONAL RELATIONSHIPS: FROM THE CHURCHES TO THE CHURCH

THE DOGMATIC PROBLEM: THE ESSENCE OF CHRISTIANITY

CHAPTER V

THE PROBLEM OF THE CHURCH'S MISSION IN THE WORLD: RESPONSIBILITY AS A WITNESS OR MAKER OF THE WORLD TO COME?

CHAPTER VI

THE PROBLEM OF STRUCTURE: THE CHURCH OF THE APOSTLES OR THE CHURCH OF THE HIERARCHY

CHAPTER VII

THE PROBLEM OF WORSHIP:
THE IMPACT OF THE ECONOMY OF SALVATION ON THE CHURCH
AS WORSHIPPING COMMUNITY

CONTENTS

CONTENTS

CHAPTER XI

ISRAEL AND THE REUNION OF CHRISTIANS:
THE CHURCH OF JEWS AND GENTILES

CHAPTER XII

RENEWAL AND UNITY

PREFACE

I wrote this book thinking of those whom I know and have been pleased to meet, those who have helped me, inspired me, stimulated me in this world of the ecumenical movement and, more widely still, of those Churches and communions which, in the East and the West, lay claim to Christ's heritage.

Before I even put pen to paper my thoughts went out to my own Church, that venerable mother of inexhaustible wisdom, whom neither novelty surprises nor tradition weighs down, and to my friends of the other Christian communions, each one of whom reflects a school of thought, a history and a tradition. I questioned them once more in the common bonds of the *memoria amans*. I could see them, I still can, listening, questioning, answering. I see their faces again and once more I welcome their friendship. I know how they react when on my part there is slipped in some conviction in opposition to theirs, some interpretation which does not suit them. I admire their tact and humility and their hope that one day we shall understand one another. If they can derive some benefit from this work in the same way that I can take mine wherever it is to be found, it will make me glad and the Lord will already have been given glory thereby, for he knows how to change hope into achievement. This book is open to them. May they feel at home in it.

It is a particular source of pleasure for me to remember all those who are seeking the union of Christians, and those especially who devote their time, their hearts and their whole lives to it; earnestly I hope that in all Christian Churches and communions ecumenical vocations may spring up among pastors, professors, among those souls vowed to contemplation and among the laity in general without whom nothing will be accomplished, for the last word will remain with the local community: will they or will they not agree to accept, with the laity of other Christian Churches, that fellowship which their spiritual leaders have shown them as being the highest response to God's plan?

Ecumenical work calls on us to give a new dimension to the Christian virtues and, as a result, to rediscover, perhaps, certain aspects of them. The clear statement of our own beliefs and brotherly attention to those of others implies an ecumenical spirit, an ecumenical love. For to place the

1

Christian Churches and communions in one's heart, in short to discover oneself in and through the Church, means undertaking one of the most wonderful of explorations, for the Church is the perfect act of the Trinitarian revelation. Now if I ask: "What do I love in loving Love itself?" and if the answer is infinite, what will be the result if I seek to discover what the Church is, since the Church is a limitless vocation?

It is up to the Churches to decide whether the ecumenical movement will give new life to the Church Universal or whether it will only result in an alliance of partners whose influence is on the decline.

If the Churches are to respond to the challenge of a secularized society, they can do so only if they have the courage to forge new bonds of unity.

The widespread use of the term "ecumenical" in daily speech is an invitation to all to seek new ways. It is necessary to make a scientific study of the problem, so that the venture might not end in confusion.

In exploring the areas of this new discipline of the Church Universal the following method has been adopted. Each chapter is introduced by a precise statement of the problem treated in it. Then the various aspects of the problem are singled out for closer study. This is followed by an assessment of the present stage of the *rapprochement*. In the concluding part of each chapter the author indicates the lines along which progress can be achieved.

A second characteristic of the book is the ever recurring reference to the nature of the Church and of Christianity as the focus of the constituent aspects of the ecumenical problem: historical, doctrinal, missionary, structural, liturgical, psychological and sociological.

Finally, the conviction that ecumenism is indivisible has prompted the author to pay due regard to every partner of the ecumenical dialogue. The unity of the People of God is the common concern of Catholics, Orthodox, Anglicans, Protestants and Jews.

My grateful acknowledgement for help of all kinds must go to very many — to persons, places, books, institutions and associations. I shall not name persons, but their names, as they know, remain firmly before me; yet I must mention my special appreciation of institutions such as the Union Theological Seminary in New York for the help of its library, and more especially the Secretariat of the World Council of Churches at Geneva and the Institut oecuménique at Bossey, Switzerland.

The original French edition of this book was published in 1962. In the meanwhile the Second Vatican Council has taken place. The decisions of the Council have not necessitated any substantial changes in the book, but I have made a few minor adjustments in order to bring the English edition up to date. References to the documents of the Council have also been added in the footnotes.

Bernard Lambert, O. P.

CHAPTER I

Definition of the Ecumenical Problem

I. THE HISTORICAL OPPORTUNITY FOR UNITY

The ecumenical movement is definitely assuming the proportions of the greatest religious phenomenon of our times. No Christian denomination has remained outside it. An immense reality is coming into being. The wind now blowing is certainly that of the Spirit and its direction is towards new beginnings. What will be the shape of what is emerging in the search for a new expression of the command: "One Lord, one faith, one baptism" (Eph 4:5)? Is it not a miracle of grace that within the era of world revolution a period marked by the quest for unity should have come into existence?

As time passes it will perhaps be realized that the historical opportunity for the reunion of Christians, in suspense since the great divisions between East and West, occurred during our century and, precisely, during the period of some fifty years, between the conference of the movement for missionary co-operation, held at Edinburgh in 1910, and the Second Vatican Council. It was a decisive period in which can be seen the direction taken by each of the Christian communions to determine its course. Paths which were formerly parallel have begun to converge. The *rapprochement*, which began to take shape under Pius XI, obtained new emphasis under Pius XII, and became a veritable encounter under John XXIII. The Catholic Church has committed herself for the future in the first lines of the conciliar Decree on Ecumenism published on 21 November 1964: "Promoting the restoration of unity among all Christians is one of the chief concerns of the Second Sacred Ecumenical Synod of the Vatican."

1. What made the ecumenical movement possible in the Catholic Church?

We can take a brief look at the wonderful way in which the Holy Spirit has guided Christian people in our time. A movement of conversion—that is the appearance given by this continuous activity—firmly conducted over a long period, moving us, in accordance with our separate loyalties, to turn towards each other, as we seek with growing intensity to obey the Lord's summons to Christian people and the Churches. Christians—and this is the greatest grace of our time—have begun to look at each other mutually. In the communions that have arisen from the Reformation and in the Eastern Churches this has been called the Ecumenical Movement, and the Catholic Church has come out to meet this movement.

The Catholic ecumenical movement has only very recently received official approval in the Catholic Church. The first decisive act was that of the Holy Office, under Pius XII, on 20 December 1949.[1] The second was the institution, by John XXIII, on 5 June 1960, of a Secretariat for Christian Unity. And the third was the Vatican Ecumenical Council itself. These events set the seal on the end of an epoch; the era of the Counter-Reformation is over. The Church has taken the path towards a new age. No doubt it was necessary to make sure that everything had been prepared before setting the Church upon a new course. But her real reason for deciding to go forward was that this seemed to her the noblest way. A vigorous development is now in process. Things were done two years ago, six months ago; things will be done in six months, in a year, in two years, that would have been unthinkable only a short while ago.

In the Church it is often the case that what one man sows another reaps. The long and obscure labours, undertaken by individuals or groups, infinitely meritorious, because often misunderstood, labours that sought to awaken Christians to a full appreciation of what it means to belong to the Church and to Christianity, have at long last borne fruit. If there had been no ecumenical movement in Protestantism, and if Catholics had not joined in dialogue with it, the action of Pius XII and John XXIII would have been impossible. Every pope, it need hardly be said, is concerned with continuity. Some, however, are popes of a period of transition, of an active transition that can discover levers powerful enough to shift huge boulders. An age of integration requires means proportionate to it: the General Council and unity among Christians provide just that.

We must also take into account the remote preparations made by Providence in the last century. While in the Protestant world the outline of the ecumenical movement was gradually taking shape, and in the East

[1] Instruction *De Motione "Œcumenica"*.

the liberation of Christian peoples from the Ottoman yoke opened the way for some future dialogue with the Christian West, two main factors were preparing the entry nowadays of the Catholic Church into the movement. These factors were the renewal of ecclesiology and of exegesis.

The former originated with Möhler, whose inspiration and influence, adopted and extended by the activity of the Roman College, led to the schemes put forward for the definition of the Church at the First Vatican Council which were developed by Leo XIII (*Satis Cognitum*, 1896), and Pius XII (*Mystici Corporis*, 1943). What had made Möhler's synthesis possible was the positive confrontation which he initiated between the Catholic and Protestant conceptions of Christianity. He went beyond Bellarmine's valid, but inadequate idea, and re-integrated ecclesiology into its traditional setting of the Council of Chalcedon. In this way he linked up with an attempt made by pre-Tridentine German theology which, aware of the needs of the time and of the weak points of the opposing forces, was meant to go beyond the dilemmas and calm the conflicts.

Some eventualities legitimately call for an explanation, and we may well ask what the result would have been if the trend of pre-Tridentine German theology had been able to find an outlet in catechetical teaching, in the doctrine of the nature of the Church and in the pastoral ministry, instead of the Catholic position being solely concerned with controversy?

Everything, for instance, should have inclined Bellarmine to meet contemporary needs by developing a doctrine expounding the mystery of the Church. In his time the doctrine of the mystical body was far from being forgotten either by Catholic theologians or the Reformers. But circumstances intervened that led him to follow the path which ended in his becoming the champion of controversy.

During his residence in Louvain (1570–6) he commented on the *Summa* of St Thomas Aquinas. But just as he was about to deal with the question of Christ's "capital" grace, his grace as head of the Church, the locus classicus of the doctrine of the mystical body, he was called to the Roman College and for the next twelve years (1576–88) held the chair of Controversy in it,[2] thus originating the great series of Controversies and Conferences.[3]

If we are to judge this work fairly, we must take note of the place occupied in it by history. In his account of the nature of the Church Bellarmine's aim was to refute the famous "Centuries" of Matthias Flacius Illyricus and his collaborators of Mainz (Basle, 1560–74) which claimed to provide the historical justification for the religious revolution of the

[2] S. Tromp, "Conspectus chronologicus praelectionum quas habuit Sanctus Robertus Bellarminus in collegio S. J. lovaniensi et collegio romano", *Gregorianum*, XVI (1935), p. 101.
[3] *Disputationes de controversiis christianae fidei adversus hujus temporis haereticos* (1586–92).

sixteenth century. The Protestant controversialists wanted to demonstrate that it was the Reformed and not the Catholic Church that had kept continuity with the primitive Church. It was this basic importance of history in the religious controversy of the sixteenth century that compelled Bellarmine to enter the lists in the same field,[4] and this explains the incompleteness of his outlook.

He had no intention of expounding the mystery of the Church in all its fullness and inner reality. His purpose was to defend its historic and visible truth, and this was what he had been asked to do. His work, welcomed by the central government of the Church, set the general tone for the way in which the Church was conceived and for the Catholic attitude. Bellarmine's influence continued dominant so long as the circumstances to which it owed its origin remained. But there happened what is bound to happen when it becomes easier to go on repeating an established tradition than to weigh it in the scales against Christian truth as a whole. Ecclesiology was reduced to a branch of apologetics, and a restricted idea of the Church became institutionalized in the ordinary teaching of theology.

Today both sides deplore the fact that there was so much controversy. Perhaps we have even come to judge it too harshly. Where is the boundary of sincerity and truth to be drawn? Each party believed the conflict to be a legitimate defensive and offensive war. Perhaps, too, under our mutual blows we had some home-truths to administer to ourselves?

Even after the reform by the Council of Trent, the Catholic Church remained wounded. To many she appeared to be simply one denomination among others. Protestantism still protests that until she achieves a wider catholicity it will continue to be dissatisfied. And should we ever become reunited and this desideratum then be forgotten by the Church, a new Reformation would begin. Rather than regard this protest simply as an insult, we should see it as the terribly exacting requirement of a higher love that has been disappointed. The non-Catholic ecumenical movement sets us difficult questions that will allow us no rest, and we may no longer take refuge in silence. The answer must be given in terms of a catholicity regained. All Christians have been offered certain choices by the Holy Spirit which compel us to go forward. He has introduced new factors which call us to dialogue. He has led us by secret paths and suddenly brought us face to face with each other. It would be folly to imagine that we can turn back—the words of scripture "compel people to come in" (Lk 14:23) come to mind. Why should we be afraid, even though the door is narrow? We have been invited to the banquet of a wider, revi-

---

[4] P. Polman, *L'Élément historique dans la controverse religieuse au XVIe siècle* (1932); E. A. Ryan, *The Historical Scholarship of St Bellarmine* (1936).

talized catholicity, and to an immense celebration; our anxiety to see this come about should give us wings.

The renewal of ecclesiology in the Catholic Church marked one stage. The second was the renewal of exegesis that began at the turn of the last century. There also the dialogue between Catholic and Protestant scholarship, undertaken by pioneers, themselves unjustly suspected on occasion, was decisive, and continues to be so. But when the Church determined to restore its full value to the Bible she was admitting her willingness for it to react upon her own destiny. Speculative theology was compelled to give positive theology its rightful position, and the primacy of the sources of revelation regained its control. The entire life of the Church, in her liturgy, catechesis and pastoral ministry, has been deeply affected by the biblical movement.

2. New features in contemporary Catholicism

The essential features which increasingly define the shape of contemporary Catholicism may, it seems, be reduced to four principal ones.

First, the entire recentring of the principal manifestations of Christianity, under the primacy of the Word.

Dogmatically, the Church, without ceasing to be a visible, juridical, hierarchical society, is seen as the manifestation of the Word of God among men, and it is around this last aspect that all the images of the Church are co-ordinated.

In the liturgy we are witnessing a renewal of the meaning of the Word as the central point of what is called the liturgy of the Word and of the sacramental celebration. The Mass, the sacraments and sacramentals, the divine office and the liturgical year appear as a sacramental celebration of the Word which, in numerous ways, brings into existence what it proclaims.

In the sphere of evangelization, the Word also stands out as primary. It allows itself to be proclaimed by intermediaries whom it has chosen, and it has its own means of power of efficacy.

At the pastoral level the Church's action is grounded especially on faith as the foundation of salvation and justification and on the part it plays in evangelization, catechesis and pastoral work.

The missionary movement, the liturgical movement, the pastoral movement, the ecumenical movement are all indebted to the ecclesiological and biblical renewal.

The second characteristic feature is that the transcendent Christ is again seen as the centre of all things. We owe this especially to the restoration of the doctrine on the Church which has enabled the theology of the visible Church to be integrated into a far more extensive reality. The Church stands out, no longer as merely the Church of the earthly hierarchy, but in her majestic dimensions as the Church of the Trinity, the Church of the Word incarnate, the Church of the apostolic hierarchy, the Church of mankind. One result in particular is that the role of Peter and his successors has been replaced in a more appropriate setting.

We also owe this to the return to the written Word of God. The biblical movement has given us back the meaning of God's utterance which is the Word, Head of his Church, the primary and supreme summoner of man. As a result we have acquired a fresh realization of Christ's action in its entirety and of his supremacy. His action in the Church is twofold: first, interiorly, he communicates the life of grace; and then, externally, making use of the apostolic hierarchy, he directs men to the truth in belief and conduct.

It must be admitted that in the past some modes of expression gave the idea that Christ rules the Church like a constitutional monarch. Grace and the sacraments were too apt to be described as though they were part of a nobleman's vast wealth, controlled and distributed by his capable and industrious stewards. This explains why the importance of the Word came to be diminished, because, in the Word, the Lord's action cannot be foreseen, whereas in the sacraments, in principle, it can. By giving us back the meaning of the Word, the Holy Spirit has made us somewhat less complacent, but more attentive to his sovereign sway.

The third feature which marks an explicit growth in contemporary Catholicism is the clarification of the theology of her action in relation to Christ and the world.

How can we sum up the action of the Church? Is it simply that of a witness? Or, has she also a ministerial function? What precisely is her mission, and, in particular, that of her ministers? The answer given has been motivated by an acute sense of the need to break loose from an excessively juridical and administrative idea and practice, and by a resolve to overcome the vagueness about the laws of the Church's action. A theology of the Church's activity in the world is imperative. This must be based on a series of definite ideas and guiding principles. It is a corollary of the development of an ecclesiology that illustrates her mystery. It corresponds to a determination on the Church's part to acquire a more explicit awareness of her pastoral work as well as of her mystery.

Although it was not clear at the outset, at about the same time that ecumenical tendencies were beginning to take shape the Catholic Church was getting ready to answer the three main questions put to her by the non-Roman Catholic ecumenical movement: what do the Word of God, Christ and the Church mean to you?

By leading the Catholic Church to ask herself the very questions that lie at the heart of the reflection of the other Christian communions, the Spirit was preparing her for reconciliation; inevitably the day was coming when she would become conscious of ecumenism, and, in fact, this consciousness is the fourth feature of Catholicism in our time.

What are the characteristics of the ecumenical movement? In the realm of those communions that belong to the World Council of Churches it appears as an immense search for wholeness and unity on each of the planes that together make up the ecumenical problem: the Faith and Order movement is working for the restoration of unity in the spheres of doctrine, structure and worship. The Life and Work movement aims at the integration of isolated efforts with a view to unity of action in social and intellectual life. The missionary movement is trying to form a common front in the work of evangelization.

Among Catholics the first stage of development consisted of a re-appraisal of the true centre of Catholicism, and an examination of the chief questions which the non-Roman Catholic world was asking. This latter activity can be described as a way of drawing towards them, just as when the non-Catholic world asks the same questions as ourselves they are approaching us. This way of developing affinities is, by the power of the Holy Spirit, the primary means leading to subsequent dialogue. Official ecclesiastical relations were then lacking. As we know, they have now been established.

Although the Catholic Church has always been concerned with Christian unity, the credit for instituting the modern ecumenical movement belongs to the Anglican and Protestant communions. The Catholic Church at first greeted it coldly and with reserve, but as it increasingly gave signs and guarantees of being authentically Christian and pursued its inquiries with greater thoroughness, the Church began to take note of it in a kindly and encouraging way. For the Holy Spirit had inwardly prepared her to hear and appreciate this invitation, this speech, and now the Church's interest in this movement is rapidly increasing.

The main Christian bodies having thus approached each other, a valid dialogue between qualified persons can be established without danger of confusion, syncretism or eclecticism. Each side has opened out sufficiently to reconsider the other's point of view, to listen to it and question it.

3. New features in Protestantism

When judging any religious form, it is always extremely dangerous to view it only in the abstract, forgetting that a doctrine is lived by men who themselves form part of a group, a communion, a Church; it is equally dangerous to form a judgement only from the present situation without taking account of the stages that have preceded it.

A number of new religious features have come into existence; if these are not known there can be no just judgement and the opportunities for reunion will not be realized.

Among the Protestant bodies these new features call, first of all, for a renaissance of Protestantism and a conviction that it is not a proliferation of sects, but a world with its own unity and a living prophetic message.[5]

The human destiny of the Church is marked by the conflict between the forces of unity and disruption. The survival of Catholic unity can only be explained by a daily miracle. The same dramatic tension recurs in Protestantism, but with the difference that dogmatic trends have become transformed into sects and these, in due course, became Churches.

Today, however, there is a desire for this tendency to be reversed in the direction of the essential unity accepted at the Reformation. This is the normal theme of ecumenical literature and of the great ecumenical conferences. Protestantism, we are assured, is not naturally self-divisive. At its origin, it aimed at unity and union. The idea of the Church, as held by the Reformers, was ecumenical, and the present movement is not an exotic development; it springs from the very nature of Protestantism. If the original ecumenical intention did not materialize, this was due to extrinsic causes, to the secularism of the princes, for example, who were only too glad to take over the Reformation for their own advantage, and also to the continuance of certain Catholic ideas in the minds of the Reformers, particularly those of the union between Church and State, and the desire to provide a doctrinal basis, a fixed creed, as the setting for their teaching. The union between Church and State in England, Germany, Geneva and elsewhere led to national and religious partition; on the other hand, creeds taken as a starting point led the reforming trends into distinct Churches. In this twofold way the fundamental and most real purpose of the reformers was distorted. They neither wanted to found Churches, nor a new Church; their aim was primarily the reformation of the "one" Church.

Contemporary Protestantism intends to take up the work of the Reformation, but to avoid what it considers to be the errors of the Reformers. Its motto would be: Back to the Reformers, but transcend them.[6]

Is it a return to the Reformation or a new reform? Unquestionably, both. It is, first, a return to the Reformation, for the various denominations and trends, in Europe as in America, are rediscovering themselves

[5] John T. McNeill, *Unitive Protestantism* (1930).
[6] Martin J. Heinecken, *Christ Frees and Unites* (1957); Walter M. Horton, *Toward a Reborn Church* (1949); Charles C. Morrison, *The Unfinished Reformation* (1953).

by going back to their origins. But it is also and equally, a new reformation. There is not to be a return to the Reformers on all points; what they achieved historically is to be surpassed, what they were unable to achieve, though it belonged to their essential intention, is to be fulfilled. There is not to be a number of Reformations, but one unified Reformation, not another Church, but a single Church, the one Body of Christ, and that would be the great united and reformed Church.

Herein lies the dangerous predicament of any reform; it easily becomes ambivalent and its balance is precarious. On several points, the purpose of the Reformers' revolt was to restore to prominence and esteem principles and truths which their brethren were unwilling to admit. Did not the remedies prove to be more hazardous than the ills they set out to heal? The sixteenth century Reformers had no desire to produce a divided Christendom, but their movement carried them further than they had intended, and when the Catholic reformation had been sanctioned by the decrees of the Council of Trent the two sections of Western Christianity could see the gulf that separated them. The Christian world must remember this example. Should the extraordinary movement of self-reformation, which is at present permeating Protestantism, "go beyond" the Reformers, that is, further than the idea of a unified Protestantism, it would have gone too far. There are moments in history when everything remains possible so long as situations have not developed to a point of rigidity. The goal will not have been reached, and so danger can still be averted. But should the movement really reach this position "beyond" the Reformers, would there be any alternative to a new counter-Reformation?

This initial characteristic of contemporary Protestantism is accompanied by others which are called the search for unity as the Lord's commandment, the building of an "evangelical Catholicity", or, if the expression is preferred, of an "ecumenical Church", and lastly, the formation of an ecumenical spirit adequate to a unified religious world.

Contemporary religious activity is endeavouring to meet the needs of a world that has never been more one, but whose unity has never been more threatened. Are we to regard the movement for Christian reunion as a sociological repercussion of the trend towards the unification of the world,[7] an attempt to be effective out of self-interest? Both these ideas have some truth in them, but the really dominant factor is that of a new realization of our Lord's purpose to give unity to the world for the healing of the divisions among the nations.

The rediscovery of the Church's note of unity is paralleled by that of catholicity. If there is one title which is claimed today by denominations other than the Roman Church, it is certainly that of catholic. Orthodoxy

[7] Robert Lee, *The Social Sources of Church Unity* (1960).

has always proclaimed it as exclusively her own. Anglicanism has always resisted assimilation with continental Lutheranism or Calvinism. The other denominations, too, are now asking themselves why they have relinquished the title Catholic to Catholicism for so long. This claim must not be considered as an absolutely new conviction, but as a revival, in reaction against the Protestant ethos of the last century: Christianity is not worthy of the name unless it is universal, catholic. We should realize, however, what kind of catholicity is meant: it is an evangelical, not a Roman catholicity.

It is difficult to decide which element in this aim is the more dramatic: its immense ambition or its startling danger. The ecumenical cross-current has set itself as the incoming of hope against the seemingly unending process of fission with its inevitable disintegration. Protestantism looks optimistically to its future; far from being moribund it is on the way to that decisive hour decreed by Providence for its message to be at last delivered. The very divisions which it experienced contributed to its maturity, enabling it to understand the human schism more thoroughly. To this divided world it would bring the doctrine and the form it so greatly needs, and in the consciousness of this mission it feels a renewed vitality, and has rediscovered its solidarity in multiplicity. In our time it seems that the doctrine of the Reformation, with whatever errors may be due to the Reformer eliminated, will have its chance to evangelize the world. It could bring a new kind of catholicism to a politically divided world. It could offer the separated Christian denominations a rallying point in the idea of a Church that is essentially invisible, whose visible unity—admittedly indispensable, though not essential—would be ordered in such a way that the characteristic features of each of its component parts would be safeguarded.

According to this idea of "evangelical catholicity", any group which expresses total allegiance to our Lord in its doctrine, and in its members provides a living testimony to Christ's Spirit, is ripe for the production of the fruits of the Holy Spirit, and as such must be recognized as belonging to the Catholic Church. There is no reason for the attribution of the term "Catholic" to the Roman Church alone. Any group may claim it, provided it displays the two fundamental conditions: doctrinal allegiance to Christ and an expression of Christianity in its members' lives. For it is Christ who is the Catholic par excellence, the timeless and transcendent centre of catholicity. One becomes a Catholic not by belonging to a privileged Church, but by belonging to Christ. It is Jesus Christ himself who, through the belief and the way of life he created in those claiming to be his disciples, in the last resort decides the membership of the One Holy Catholic Church. Just as faith determines salvation, so it also provides the criterion for catholicity.

But many obstacles block the road leading to this catholicity. The first of them arises within Protestantism itself. The enthusiasm following the great meeting in Amsterdam in 1948 has now died out. Its place has been taken by a more sober and critical examination of the concrete possibilities of union, and hence of the chances of success for the theory of evangelical catholicism. As yet the future is by no means certain. Will the various denominations be willing to lose their own individuality? What will be their function in this coming catholicity? What sort of visible unity will they provide as an expression of that inner invisible unity which many of them assume as the starting point? No answer can be given in advance. It has been stated that it will be formulated gradually day by day.

In contemporary Protestantism there are a number of other major characteristics. These are all related to the rediscovery of the Church as an institution or to a more thorough appreciation of that idea.

Protestant teaching on the Church can no longer be generally described as dominated by that liberal Protestant interpretation, which prevailed during the last century and until about 1915, and which was influential enough to make both Protestants and Catholics believe that it was also the teaching originally held by the Reformers. In the nineteenth century the Church was usually regarded by Protestants as merely a religious association and not as the *Ecclesia,* in the strict sense. According to this idea what came first was the believer. He and his fellows are united in a free association in order to produce a congregation. The Church is simply the sum of congregations of this kind. The idea of the Church was thus always individualistic, democratic and atomistic. The Church of the New Testament was interpreted in sociological and humanitarian terms.[8] Since then, however, a more accurate notion of the Church has appeared. "It has come to be realized that in the mind of the New Testament the Church comes into existence from above and not from below, and that its origin is in God, not man. The one universal Church is primary and a local Church is an expression of the life and unity of the whole. This, in fact, was the original interpretation. The Church was seen as a universal reality, and each section of it was a 'church' to the extent it was a miniature of the whole. Thus the Church is a body made up of men and women in which the unity of each part corresponds to the unity of the whole, repeats it, represents it, in fact *is it.*"[9]

There is a similar renewal of interest among Lutherans, especially in the German and Swedish High Church, and in the denominations that have sprung from Calvinism, namely the Reformed Church and Presbyterianism. Even the forms of radical Protestantism of the evangelical type like the

---

[8] W. A. Visser 't Hooft and J. H. Oldham, *The Church and its Function in Society* (1937), p. 23.
[9] Visser 't Hooft, *op. cit.,* p. 24; Claude Welch, *The Reality of the Church* (1958).

Methodists and Baptists have undergone this influence. In exegesis, in ecclesiology, in the life of the Protestant denominations and in the movements towards reunion stirring within them, we are witnessing a reassessment of the Church as an institution in striking contrast—as was noted above—with the idea of Protestantism which, looked at from the outside, had long seemed normal. Visible realities are increasingly believed to be both signs and means of inner communion. Experience has demonstrated once again the weakness of a purely inner and individualistic allegiance to our Lord, the poverty of an ethereal ministry and the absence of visible community discipline and institutions.

Looked at from every aspect, the Church as an institution is being rediscovered structurally, or at least a fresh appreciation of it is being attempted. First of all it is a fresh appreciation of tradition, for there is an increasing realization that scripture originated in the ecclesiastical community, that it existed among a group of human beings before it was written down and became a canonical norm. The community of the Church, in its life, doctrine, worship and its ideal, was God's word *lived*. Studies on the formation of the Bible and the history of the Church in its origins have overthrown the judgements still maintained by some outdated exegetes in opposition to the general trend of Protestantism.

Then, experience has shown that the principle of *scriptura sola* provokes division because it sanctions the indefinite multiplication of creeds, and consequently the continuance of sects which tend to become parallel, if not rival, Churches. This has led to a state of mind that is willing to return to the idea of "Scripture (interpreted) within the Church", but without the infallible magisterium, the principle of the collective agreement of the various denominations takes its place as the criterion of certainty.[10] In a sense, therefore, there has been a return to the early idea of tradition: to the criteria of Vincent of Lérins: universality, duration, agreement *(Quod ubique, quod semper, quod ab omnibus).* These criteria are re-interpreted in Protestant terms: that is, without any teaching authority, but admitting that as a body the Church is infallible because the Holy Spirit dwells in her. There is even a return to the apostolic tradition: the apostles as a body increasingly came to be seen as the collective norm of belief, even though a clear division was made between them and their successors. A norm in the past is acceptable, but not a living apostolic norm. The principle of *scriptura sola*, long considered as a principle of unity and a focal point for every Protestant denomination, has led finally to division and chaos in the denominations. If the ecumenical re-alignment is to continue to make good headway, it would seem to need to be balanced by a measure of return to tradition.

[10] Albert C. Outler, *The Christian Tradition and the Unity We Seek* (1957).

Here again must be acknowledged the advantages effected by the ecumenical movement. The continuous development of sects into so many autarchic Churches reduces dogmatic orthodoxy to chaos, but as soon as the movement towards unity makes itself felt, the quest for orthodoxy is one of its first results.

The rediscovery of doctrinal orthodoxy is a central fact which has therefore not concluded its work of producing surprises in Protestantism. It is penetrating into the great world federations of the denominations, the national, regional and urban councils of the churches, and the great inter-denominational agencies. This movement endeavours to lessen differences, and to rediscover the bonds of unity, lost amid tortuous denominational bypaths. This is the excellent work being achieved by the Faith and Order movement. The Life and Work movement led to the strong conviction that any collaboration in depth in the domain of applied Christianity *must*, sooner or later, find or establish common principles with the essence of Christianity as their foundation.

It is true that significant results can be obtained in the domain of applied Christianity even though a single absolute creed has not previously been agreed upon. As an example may be quoted the National Council of the Churches of Christ, in the United States, which incorporates more than thirty-five Protestant and Orthodox denominations and represents about thirty-five million Christians. This body, formerly known as the Federal Council of Churches, has, since 1908, been able to carry out a task on the basis of a unity depending explicitly on applied and not on doctrinal Christianity. However, since the Assembly of Evanston, in 1954, there has existed in the National Council of the Churches of Christ, in the United States, a department of Faith and Order in dependence upon a combined commission of the National Council and the World Council of Churches. This may be a sign of a development towards a common orthodoxy. The National Council appreciated both its utility and its danger. Generally speaking, if this search for a common orthodoxy does not advance as speedily as we should like, the delays cannot be attributed to deliberate dogmatic ignorance. Often an empirical approach or an agreed minimum of commonly held evangelical social convictions offers the sole possibility of gaining access to the denominations which fan out from the Eastern Churches, at one extreme, to radical Protestantism on the other. It is difficult to know which to admire the most: the results obtained, or the fact that this body was not only able to come into existence, but also to grow and to create an ecumenical vocabulary by stimulating its members to collaborate on practical issues and then to extend this activity to considerations of doctrine.

This rediscovery of dogmatic orthodoxy may travel far before it meets the boundary which Protestantism cannot allow itself to cross, and which

15

is called the infallible magisterium. If it can achieve an agreement on doctrine the result would be admirable enough. But will this, in fact, be possible without what protects, supports and completes it? We shall attempt to forestall the answer. Protestantism cannot itself pronounce a final judgement on what it will ultimately become, for, as it develops, its new position will make possible judgements and standpoints that would earlier have been premature. Twenty years ago, who would have dared to talk about an ecumenical theology? Today it is in everybody's mouth.

This ecumenical theology might be described as an attempt to interpret Christianity on the basis of the common essence of Protestantism. It does not offer itself as the official or even as the binding theology of the ecumenical movement; it does not even claim to correspond to a commonly accepted agreement. It is, rather, an exploratory operation to discover meeting points.[11] Where will it end? Some Protestants even question its possibility. They say that it would be incompatible with the independence necessary for free examination. Other exegetes and theologians, however, have produced works that are serving as leads in this direction.

At the heart of the problem of the Church is that of worship. The Church is a liturgical assembly. The rediscovery of the Church as an institution has brought with it a restoration of community worship. Reinhold Niebuhr's severe criticism of the poverty of some forms of Protestant worship is well known.[12] Liturgical decline is the inevitable result of the division into sects and of their proliferation as Churches which desire to be organically autonomous. Each division cuts a piece from the common patrimony and makes it its own. Fruitful dialogue between the part and the whole is replaced by an exhausting monologue conducted by the part with itself. Symbols are thrown overboard. A parish cannot be exhorted to adopt a religion of the spirit and be expected to remain faithful to it, if it is forgotten that the radical condition of Christianity is to be an incarnate religion. In all ages, worship and the sacraments have been the central means around which Christian initiation has normally developed. The sacred mysteries transmitted in public worship provide a way, common to God and mankind, and make possible a living, concrete

[11] Daniel T. Jenkins, "Is an Ecumenical Theology Emerging?", *The Presbyter* (October 1944), pp. 4–6; H. P. Ehrenberg, "There is an Ecumenical Theology", *The Presbyter* (August 1945), pp. 18–21; Wilhelm Pauck, "The Prospect for Ecumenical Theology Today", *The Journal of Religion* (1945), pp. 79–97; John C. Bennett and others, *The Journal of Religion* (1945), pp. 274–9; Louis Matthews Sweet, "Towards an Ecumenical Theology", *Christendom* (1941), pp. 377–88; Carl Keller, "Das Problem einer Ökumenischen Theologie", *Evangelisches Missions-Magazin* (September 1947), pp. 148–58; W. A. Visser 't Hooft, *Misère et Grandeur de L'Église* (1943); pp. 67 ff.; Walter Marshall Horton, *Christian Theology, An Ecumenical Approach* (1955); R. Paquier, "Des théologies confessionnelles à une théologie œcuménique", *Verbum Caro*, II (1948), pp. 3–14.
[12] *Essays in Applied Christianity* (1959), pp. 57–66.

and complete relationship between them. The sacred mysteries impart doctrine to the soul and equip it with the faith that can assimilate it. Without their presence the assembly of the faithful becomes lifeless for want of symbols.

This new approach to worship is another definite result of the movement to unity.[13] As the denominations draw together, mutual comparisons are inevitable, and exchanges and borrowings occur; no union between them is possible without the preliminary question: what form of worship will be adopted? The principal interdenominational agencies have begun campaigns on an urban, regional and national scale, to promote religious practice and have encouraged member-denominations to devote certain days to communal worship. Special commissions of the World Council of Churches have produced noteworthy studies on worship, its forms and origins. Could it be said that an ecumenical form of worship is in process of formation? If by that is meant a form of worship corresponding to organic union, the least that can be said is that this is not the most cherished idea; during the last thirty years it has not been organic union that has headed the list in denominational unions. Nevertheless, an idea has been introduced that has prophetic significance. What solution will at length be adopted? The existence within Roman Catholicism of twelve different rites and with eight liturgical languages shows that plurality of liturgical forms is the most flexible way of leading men to pray without at the same time jeopardizing unity. Both experience and human psychology show this to be true.

In connection with worship, as with many other matters, the usual idea that Protestantism is a purely "spiritual" religion, must be revised. Contemporary Protestantism has itself passed judgement on a form of worship whose forms are excessively free. It is no longer accepted that this is the essential and typical feature of Protestant worship. Our judgement of Protestant life must therefore follow this development.

A related trend deserving mention is the extraordinary spread of religious orders and institutes that has occurred since the nineteenth century. This increase remained steady between the two wars and continued after the second.[14] The Anglican Communion is in the lead both as regards the old orders and new foundations. Wherever it exists religious orders are to be found. In the United States today there are eleven religious congregations of men and fifteen of women.[15] More than a third of the religious congregations of men and the majority of those of

---

[13] Friedrich Heiler, "Die liturgisch-sakramentalen Erneuerungsbestrebungen im Protestantismus", *Eine Heilige Kirche, Zeitschrift für ökumenische Einheit* (1953–4).

[14] Peter F. Anson, *The Call of the Cloister, Religious Communities and Kindred Bodies in the Anglican Communion* (1955).

[15] *The Episcopal Church Annual* (1959), pp. 129 ff.

women are American in origin. Lutheranism, in Sweden, Germany, the United States and in the Reformed Church of France, and in Switzerland, exhibits a similar but far less developed phenomenon. One conclusion may be drawn: the rediscovery of the Church has either introduced or renewed the understanding of the traditional mission of the religious orders in the life of the Church: to be, namely, prophetic witnesses of the Church to come.

Historically, the factor underlying the movement giving rise to these remarkable characteristics was the rediscovery and the amazing development of the sense of Christian responsibility to the world. This impulse is called Evangelism, the incarnation of the Gospel. No sphere has been untouched by this contemporary evangelical fervour: religious observance, education, pastoral work, social service, spiritual direction, leisure, the attitude to social problems, political activity, etc. have all been influenced by it.

Evangelism and the missionary spirit are one and the same thing. Evangelism has operated in the "missions of the interior", that is, within the secularized and paganized Western world, to bring it back to the Gospel, and the "foreign" missions, whether in strictly pagan lands, or even in places where the majority are Catholics or Orthodox.

Were it not for the Evangelical Alliance, formed in London in 1846, with a missionary purpose, for the youth movements, the Y. M. C. A. (1878) and the Y. W. C. A. (1894), for the Student Christian Movement (1895), which came about as movements for the defence of Christian principles, and were it not also for the missionary movement, the modern ecumenical movement would probably not have existed.[16] The youth movements provided an international nursery for leaders who later appeared at the head of the ecumenical movement. And it was through the establishment of the universal conference of Protestant missionary societies in pagan or Moslem lands, in Edinburgh, in 1910, that Christian work in social problems (Life and Work) and the inquiry into doctrine were brought into being and enabled to develop to such an extent that it became necessary to form a body representing the Churches: and this was called the World Council.

It was this same concern for the evangelization of the world that led to the founding, in 1908, of the Federal Council of Churches, in the United States, that has since become the National Council of the Churches

---

[16] W. Wilson Cash, *The Missionary Church, a Study in the Contribution of Modern Missions to Ecumenical Christianity* (1939); H. Meyer, "Evangelism, the Driving Force in the Ecumenical Movement", *Ecumenical Review* (July 1954), pp. 425–9; Clarence Prouty Shedd and others, *History of the World Alliance of Young Men's Christian Associations* (1955); William Richey Hogg, *Ecumenical Foundations: A History of the International Missionary Council and its Nineteenth Century Background* (1952).

of Christ, in the United States. This Council, the most important of its kind in the world, has served as a prototype for the national councils of Churches in several countries.

One of the most extraordinary religious experiments in the world, a source of hope for all Christians, thus became possible when Protestantism allowed the virtue of unity to spread within it.

When we consider this rediscovery, re-assessment, or at least, new emphasis on the fundamental elements of Catholicism within Protestantism—on such factors as unity, the institutional nature of the Church, orthodoxy in doctrine, the ministry, worship, the spiritual life, the catholic spirit, the evangelization of the world—we may well ask whether Protestantism is developing towards Catholicism. Paul Tillich's radical and negative reply to this question is well known. [17] These various tendencies, he says, are alien importations, principally from Catholicism. In his view it is not they which will deliver Protestantism from the dangers threatening it; rather will it be energetic, more authentically Protestant and liberal groups diffused as widely as possible.

It seems more accurate, however, to accept the judgement of contemporary Protestantism as whole, and see these new developments not as something exotic, not as a desire for imitation, or to play a trick on Catholicism, but as a return to the inherent principles of Protestantism. The trend towards division had been dominant for so long that the impression emerged that nothing else could be expected. But the contemporary movement is set in the opposite direction. Indeed, had this effort been contrary to the nature of Protestantism, it would certainly not have a century of progress to report. To state the matter clearly, we have here an immense activity of self-reformation, which, based on a fresh appreciation of origins, is seeking to spread itself to the whole body of Christians. A certain liberal wing, supported by some famous names, is at present fighting a rear-guard action. Protestantism, however, has felt instructively that its hoped-for renewal does not lie there. But where, precisely, does it lie?

4. What direction are these developments taking?

Has the non-Roman ecumenical movement any clear idea of where it is going? As a movement of re-integration, it endeavours to take into account the hopes and expectations of Anglicanism, classical and radical Protestantism and Orthodoxy as well. If it was right to talk of the ideal of establishing an evangelical catholicity it must also be admitted that this

[17] *The Protestant Era* (1948), chapter xiv.

same notion is troubled by the attraction of another—that represented in the World Council of Churches by the Eastern Churches. The latter's insistence on an uncompromising affirmation of the Orthodox position in their reports at the Assemblies of the Council and in comparative studies issued by the permanent Commissions for Studies compels the inquiry to remain open to additional aspects, to a fullness with which it is as yet unacquainted.

It is a gripping experience to watch these forces in tension, even in conflict. They explode in an outburst of co-operative energy, and then their vehemence dies down. There are moments of recoil, of hesitation, and long periods of waiting. Once it has been recognized, it becomes impossible not to feel the splendour of the dynamism that has let these Christian nebulae loose upon the world through the great divisions, and that now, by a mysterious force of attraction, are seeking a central nucleus to which they may again adhere. The non-Roman ecumenical movement is in an exploratory stage. It knows where it comes from, but not where it is going. Compelled to remain open, it is trying to define itself, but at the same time it experiences the fear of coming to an end.

Must we describe some of the visions which present a picture of a promised land, as utterly unpractical, for example "the Great Church",[18] a "world Christian Fellowship",[19] a "world Christian Community",[20] "world Christianity",[21] a "world-wide Christianity",[22] a "united Church",[23] "the Super-Church"?[24]

What would be the fundamental principles of such a Church? To begin with it must be pointed out that every statement on this subject is con-jectural. The reality in question is not something given at the start, but something in process of being discovered. Also, the ideas of the leaders are not necessarily those of the congregations. Nor does there exist any official doctrine of an organism that could enunciate such fundamental principles. The World Council is not a super-Church and it has no inten-tion of compromising the member-Churches. Finally, there is no ecumenical agreement on this matter, representing an official standpoint of all the denominations. The World Council does not even feel itself called to set up the framework of the Church of the future. It is there to promote the idea of that Church, to make it possible, and then to disappear.

[18] Theodore O. Wedel, *The Coming Great Church* (1945).
[19] Kenneth S. Latourette, *Toward a World Christian Fellowship* (1938).
[20] Idem, *The Emergence of a World Christian Community* (1949).
[21] Henry P. Van Dusen, *World Christianity* (1947).
[22] Stephen Neill, "The Union of the Churches" in *The Coming of Age of Christianity* (1951), chapter vi.
[23] Winfred E. Garrison, *The Quest and Character of a United Church* (1957).
[24] W. A. Visser 't Hooft, "The Super-Church and the Ecumenical Movement", *Ecumenical Review* (July 1958), pp. 365–85.

Any statement about this Church in process of development depends on the personal interpretation made by writers thoroughly at home in the ecumenical problem and who may be described as representatives of their own denominations.

From these, certain conclusions may be drawn which, though not being irreformable, do enable us to envisage the ideal of the "Great Church" and the kind of Christianity to which non-Roman ecumenism is tending. The matter is important because the main factor governing the divisions among Christians, as well as what may perpetuate them, is the whole conception of the Church.

We may consider as characteristic the accounts given by Bishop Stephen Neill, and Winfred E. Garrison.

The former, whilst fully admitting the contingent nature of a task of this kind, thinks that he can discern seven conditions necessary for a world-wide "Great Church".[25]

(i) It must be firmly based on the Bible as the Word of God, but the rights of Tradition must also be fully accepted. A conflict between the Bible and Tradition is largely groundless, because the Bible originated in the life of the people of God.

(ii) A united Church must have a ministry that is accepted by each party: it seems certain that this would be impossible unless the historical episcopate is allowed its place in the ministerial order of the Church.

(iii) A unified Church of this kind must have certain means by which the authority of the Church as a whole may be expressed. The way in which such authority is exercised by the Church of Rome will never be acceptable to those Churches that have upheld a different tradition of freedom in their constitutional structure. How then can this authority find expression? A difficult question. It may be that when the time comes, the great Councils of undivided Christendom will ultimately be found to provide a formula that can be utilized whenever the different stages of the Church's life call for it.

(iv) A united Church must, always and everywhere, be conscious of its unity as the Body of Christ. But this must be a unity of love, not of coercion. The external forms and expressions of unity are valid only insofar as they serve to maintain that inner unity which is the work of the Holy Spirit.

(v) Within this united Church there must be room for great variety in the spheres of organization, worship, the relations between Church and State and between the Church and the nations, in the style and special characteristics of each, following, in fact, the example of the status of the Uniates in the Catholic Church and the relationship of intercommunion between the Anglican and Old Catholic Churches.

---

[25] Neill, "The Union of Churches", *loc. cit.*

(vi) A Church of this kind must allow extensive experimental freedom in the manners of bearing witness, the forms of Christian life and of service. The Holy Spirit has often manifested himself through other paths than those of responsible officials of the Church. The failure of these latter to respond has been one of the most fruitful causes of schisms.

(vii) We must humbly realize that human wisdom, even when helped by God, will certainly not always be able to preserve the Church from heresy and schism. We must hope for union and strive for it, but we must also keep in mind that there are no mechanical means for maintaining it.

Bishop Neill concludes by pointing out that this extremely vague outline shows how far we still are from even the initial concrete realization of the ideal envisaged.

The history of Christianity is a quest for Unity, and an attempt to preserve it. What, in the view of W. E. Garrison, would be the characteristics of a single united Church, such as is needed in our modern world? [26]

On the path to unity certain methods, which have been repeatedly tried, have only led to further failures. Did not the decrees of the Council of Trent, and the earlier excommunication of Michael Cerularius in 1054, really establish division in the Church? The Councils of Ephesus in 431 and Chalcedon in 451 were ruthless, but with what results? The dissentients were thrown out and obliged to set themselves up as Nestorian and Monophysite Churches. Even before Nicaea, was the Church really one? W. E. Garrison replies that it was neither one, nor divided. Whenever an attempt was made to impose unity by force, the only result was to transform disagreement into division.

The same thing occurred again in Protestantism. Consider Luther's repression of the Anabaptists, or Calvin's order that Michael Servetus should be executed, or the repudiation of "dissenters" by the established Church in England and Scotland and by the Puritan groups of the first colonies of New England. The history of Christianity is permeated by a long series of dissensions that have been met by corresponding coercive measures for the sake of unity. But the repudiating body never recovers those whom it has repelled and condemned. Separation becomes established as division.

Therefore, says Dr Garrison, in our time, we must not attempt to unite the various denominations on the basis of doctrine, ecclesiastical government or uniformity in worship. Denominationalism must persist, but as a secondary element in the wider framework of the universal Church, the brotherhood and witness-bearing assembly of all Christians. Freedom, loyalty, mutual love and the recognition of a shared common responsibility form the only basis and the only essential characteristics of this

[26] Garrison, *op. cit.*

Church. The divided state of Christians is a fact. That must be admitted. Two approaches to it are possible, either the very points on which Christians are disunited may be changed into points of agreement; and this would lead to a relatively homogeneous Church. Or else the points of divergence may retain their status as opinion, personal convictions, and practical realities, without being allowed to act as barriers between Christians.

The first solution corresponds to that kind of unity which is imposed by force. It is a method whose success is contradicted by history. The Church, he says, has never achieved even approximate uniformity without recourse to violence. Imposed uniformity has never failed to lead to persecution, to the Inquisition, to outbreaks of violence.

Have better results been obtained by the application of civil liberty within religion? On the contrary, legal protection granted to the right of freedom of opinion and separatism, has only meant that sects have flourished and multiplied. The aim was to avoid uniformity, the result was sectarianism, that is the repetition, this time in fragmentary form, of compulsory uniformities. This way leads to separation repeated *ad infinitum*. Now, if some methods have proved to be impracticable, why should not others be tried? The kind of unity which to some extent existed before the Renaissance can never be restored. Has not the time come to attempt a fresh start? Why, asks Dr Garrison, should we not now try something else, that is, freedom "within" the Church? This could be the formula of the future; it is midway between the two others and transcends them, and thereby it should be possible to unite separated Christians in one universal Church, union among Protestants coming first, and among the Churches afterwards.

For the moment judgement can be suspended on this supposedly new formula which approaches the problem of unity through the essential issue of the relations between authority and freedom in the Church. Suffering, we may think, often exerts pressure on experience, on the content of belief, and even on the Lord's commandments. At any rate we must remember the facts of history. Perhaps we should see how deeply Christians are divided before seeking for the means by which they may be united.

These two solutions represent a widespread expectation and demand.

5. Has the die been cast?

Is it true that we are faced by Christian worlds which, having drawn closer together, and looked on each other with a mixture of surprise, embarrassment and love, will tomorrow turn away once more as strangers to each other, entrenched within their own frontiers leaving the world to cry death beneath the Cross of Christ split asunder?

No, for all is not definitely settled, in the first place in non-Roman Catholic Christendom. Many of the appeals to the "Great Church", objectively unacceptable to Catholicism, spring from hearts moved by an unconscious attraction towards the one true Church. The Lord will make the final choice and he well knows what can be put to the credit of unity.

Explicit appeals for unity with Rome may be exceptional, yet can there not be perceived a certain avowal in the form of expressions of bitter regret, the signs of love frustrated and hope deceived?

The ecumenical movement is still at the exploratory stage: it has not yet found the Promised Land. Even those who try to dream of the outlines of a catholicity according to their heart's desire realize that this is a far-distant prospect. How long will the wandering in the desert go on? Succulent grapes, it is said, have been brought back from Canaan, but has the coveted land been conquered?

Protestantism today is undergoing a quite exceptional experience. The immense work of self-reformation in which it is involved cannot be achieved in the enclosed circle of its own life: it must be combined with Orthodoxy and a missionary outlook on the world. The dialogue which provoked it has been the means of its own resurrection, and it is understandable that some Protestant bodies, fearful of too strong a leaven, have been unwilling to join the World Council of Churches. At the very time when it was being set up in Amsterdam, an anti-ecumenical body, the "International Council of Christian Churches" was set up in the same city, as a protest against the ecumenical movement whose tendency was considered to be too Catholic.

And yet Protestantism has really determined its course, the course of self-reform. The change dates from that moment. The new spirit does not desire purely and simply to repeat the Reformation. The present leaders of the new phase of the Reformation are experiencing the same anxieties as the first reformers. They look back to their ancestors for enlightenment, and also to ask them if the causes which, on the Catholic side, provoked the revolt of the first reformers still exist.

Why should we not approach the issue by going to the heart of the matter which is the nature of the Church and of Christianity? For it is there that occurs the dramatic encounter with Christ and his great unity which grips the Christian, torments him, will not let him rest, and makes him root out everything in his being that is alien to the soul of the Church. Here Catholics, Protestants, Anglicans and Orthodox come together, pilgrims scrutinizing each other in the uncertainty of their hearts. Our Lord will forgive those who have fallen in the uncertain light that has led them on.

Is everything in Catholicism and the Eastern Churches not in communion with Rome definitively settled? Is the Catholic Church as immovable as she is accused of being?

Suppose that reunion has been achieved. As a result there would exist, as at present in the East, wide liturgical, ritual and disciplinary differences, even in the West, but in the unity of one same faith. Suppose, again, as present trends predict, increased local initiative by dioceses under their bishops, provinces under their metropolitans, of national Churches and extensive areas of the world under councils largely endowed with self-direction, while unity with the centre is balanced by a new method of representation of local Churches at that centre. Consider again that there had been a solemn definition of the nature and mission of the laity in the Church and the world, a question dear to the heart of Protestantism; suppose that theological discussions between East and West had been renewed, after the way had been prepared by a rediscovery of the Fathers, and of Christian origins, for a wider presentation of the revealed message in the form of biblical theology in those parts in which, as a consequence of differing traditions, the scholastic account was contrary to habits of thought. Lastly, take it that between the Churches of the East and West, at last reunited, a genuine communion of life had come into existence—would the final result be that we could say that the Catholic Church had ceased to be catholic? The face of the Church would be different from that which we know. New features would have sprung from her eternal youthfulness, but would the essence and life of the Church have been thereby compromised?

6. The hesitations of history

As in every great period of the Church's history, men, Christian men, are hesitating in the face of too many possibilities that seek their way before committing themselves, that first deny and then accept, or having rejected again take up what they had previously cast aside, that produce tentative developments like evolutionary branches whose destiny is to flourish and then pass away. But the thrust of the sap finds a way elsewhere, and there the promise lies.

It is certainly true that the history of Christianity is at present undecided in many hearts today.

7. What is at stake for success?

Consider what is at stake in the success or failure of reunion. We can make two hypotheses. Suppose that no encounter takes place. In that case two things are possible: either the world will become increasingly more deeply divided into two huge Christian bodies, each conscious of its individuality, its resources and its mission. At best, the formula which would prevail would be that of co-existence in intensified isolation. To what distant age would the reunion of Christians be deferred? What Christian communion could congratulate itself on such an arrangement?

Or else the ecumenical movement among non-Roman Catholic Christians may come to an abrupt termination: the Catholic Church would then remain alone in its unity, while elsewhere the process of division would begin again with the added weight of the bitterness and frustration of hope deceived. Could this be interpreted as a victory for Christianity and the Catholic Church? Certainly not. The Catholic Church does not play in the world the part of a secular power which with self-confidence awaits the collapse of its opponents in order to reap a harvest of triumph and glory from a field of ruins. She has nothing to gain from a world with its religion in dissolution. She believes that it will always be much easier for a world, which though a different frontier, is still Christian, to be converted rather than for an embittered, secularized and irreligious world. Every sincere move towards God is an approach towards a reality whose secret intent is to reveal itself in the end. It is growth in loyalty to Christ that makes possible a dialogue in which the language of one Christian ceases to be completely incomprehensible to another.

It may, perhaps, be argued that we should distinguish between non-Catholic denominations considered as bodies and the Christians who compose them. On this view the failure of the bodies would be desired in order that their members should be set free. The Catholic Church could not indulge a desire of this kind without also wishing for the destruction of certain ecclesial realities which she must recognize wherever they are to be found. She also realizes that the experience of an imperfect realization of communion may serve as education towards complete realization, and that a tendential belonging to the Church does not always proceed from the lowest degree to complete membership at one bound. The rediscovery and the return to the origins of so many realities of the Church provides an unhoped-for opportunity for a mutual encounter which has not been possible since the separation occurred.

But consider the second hypothesis: that the movement towards reunion succeeds. What would result? Corporate Christianity would regain its membership; the expansion of Christianity would attain untold proportions; one and the same Catholic spirit would penetrate from one end of the world to the other, and form the surest foundation of an authentic international community; harmony between the ministers of the Gospel in face of the rest of the world, which would make that world more ready to believe; a commonly accepted doctrine, definite and all embracing, which would flow from the abundant riches of the liturgical mysteries; a common worship, one in substance, multiple in expression, leading mankind to the unity of worship in heaven; a single bridge-structure between earth and heaven; as between civilization and the Church, acting as the needful preparation for the eschatological advent of a single kingdom; one same essential transmission of the Word, incarnate in the flesh, in literal reality, in the community of mankind, a transmission, a tradition, in which the world would infallibly accomplish its return to the Father, the source of its salvation; one same image of the Lord refracted in a world wherein the Father would recognize the features of his Son. In short, a true springtide of the Church and the world.

If there is a vision towards which we should go forward, why should it not be this one rather than an anaemic ideal which is defeatist but claiming to be realist?

Division leads nowhere: neither for oneself nor for anyone. No man in exile is free. No Christian value, outside its one true orbit, can fulfil the promise of its origin, develop in an orderly way, or attain its fullness.

For a long while now, we have lived within our respective fortresses, taking no notice of each other, and hoping perhaps that one or other would end in collapse. But contrary to a number of predictions, for home consumption, neither Protestantism, Orthodoxy, Catholicism nor Anglicanism has yet died. And if we can foretell the future from experience of the past, the history of either Roman or non-Roman Christianity is not yet concluded.

Has not the time arrived when Christians, conscious of the fact that what is lacking to Christ, to the Body of Christ, is also lacking to each of his members, ought to make their voices heard above their divisions, and let it be known how grievously their separation affects them, that the absence of their fellows constitutes a running sore, and moved by a common desire for unity, look for means of healing, and allow love and faith to discover, to create, ways that would lead each to the other? If it is true that a deadlock must simply be left to produce what it can, it is also true that once its possibilities have been exhausted, a new must be found. What a confession of weakness to make no attempt! May the divisions among Christians which have come to be accepted as almost definitive prove to be only in fact a phenomenon of a certain period of Christian history.

It may even be said that the miracle of the healing of the Christian body is already beginning now that the Christian communions have set themselves to obey the Lord's command: "Rise and walk" (Mt 9:5). All things begin to be possible when men agree to start out towards each other. There will be no reunion without a preliminary journeying towards a mutual encounter. At this point it is necessary to find agreement on the meaning of the phrase so often used; the "return of the dissidents".

8. Return or reconciliation?

There is a way of interpreting the phrase which will never get us out of the impasse. The expression is ill-sounding to the ears of other Christians who instinctively refer it to the historical circumstances of the separation, and it is against these that they are still protesting. They are also afraid lest several centuries of development of their traditions might be obliterated by an unqualified return to Catholicism. When Catholics assure them that their values will not be forsworn but fulfilled, by the fact of their return, this promise seems to them too much a matter of words. They ask whether in fact the Catholic Church has ever succeeded in concluding any kind of union with Protestantism or Anglicanism which approaches the status of the Uniate Churches of the East. In addition, since they have long been outside the development of Catholic tradition, they find it hard to understand this Church which though maintaining its own identity from the beginning, has, like every living being, developed during the course of its existence.

So, the word "return" provokes fear. It seems equivocal, negative, retrograde. In a sense what counts is not so much what the Catholic Church means by this word but what ideas Protestants, the Orthodox and Anglicans draw from it. As a remedy for this psychological handicap, why should we not use rather the expression "the reconciliation of Christians?" It expresses the contribution which the Catholic Church and the other Christian communions must make corporately as Churches, in the progress towards reunion as Christians. Experience has shown that, in the past, the definition of a truth has never been sufficient to ensure an automatic return to unity. Should the Catholic Church be restored to new splendour, would this lead infallibly to worldwide adherence to her? Whenever a division has occurred, the Church has afterwards experienced such an outbreak of new life, but where can we observe the achievement of any significant reunion?

Therefore, it is not enough for the Church to define the truth, to open her gates, extend her arms, adorn herself, become resplendent. In a sense she must also go outside herself, take the lead and search the highways. She must go out to meet those whom she wishes to encounter. The grace, the measure of being a Christian, is not the obligatory accompaniment of a passive, narrow and monopolizing attitude which takes no account of the Good Shepherd's generously prevenient wisdom.

We should surround the historical opportunity for Christian reconciliation with the possibility of work in common. Let each of us, on both sides, resolve to do our part of this task, and, above and beyond our divisions, to carry on a dialogue in spite of every obstacle. What is there that still prevents us from beginning a dialogue that is down-to-earth

28

and offers continuous development? Is it not true that the vital condition of bodily life is an ability to give and receive? Would not the interchange of lofty purposes lead at length to the mutual sharing of a single loaf?

II. ECUMENISM AT THE SERVICE OF RECONCILIATION AMONG CHRISTIANS

To draw nearer together as a result of interior evolution is an important step forward. But the great difficulty is to effect a meeting at fundamental level and to unite. Ecumenism can therefore be regarded as the instrument of creative relationships. It is a mystique, a theology, a method, a mode of action. Thus it supplies a universal need. Unilateral ecumenism is inescapably condemned to remain shut in upon itself. If the Catholic Church had not decided to commit herself to the work of ecumenism, the entire non-Catholic movement would have remained semi-ecumenical: it would either have failed to interest the rest of the world or have allowed it to remain completely outside its own perspective. To the non-Roman ecumenical movement must now correspond the Catholic ecumenical movement. We have drawn closer together: ecumenism in depth must now be the connecting link.

1. The meaning of the word "ecumenical"

As a preliminary, the two words "ecumenical movement" need to be explained.

The word "ecumenical" has received various meanings in the course of history. 1. It denotes the inhabited surface of the globe and whatever relates to it: see, for example, Acts 17:31. 2. What refers to the Roman Empire considered as a unity: example, Luke 2:2. 3. What belongs to the whole Church or represents her: for example, the ecumenical councils, so called because they assembled the bishops from the entire Roman Empire, the *Oikumene*. Even today the Greek Orthodox Patriarch of Constantinople is called the Ecumenical Patriarch, in honour of Constantinople, which, for many centuries, was the capital of the *Oikumene*. 4. What has universal ecclesiastical validity: for example, the Eastern Church speaks of three ecumenical "doctors"; in the sixteenth century the three main creeds were termed ecumenical for the first time. 5. What refers to the relations and the unity between two or more Churches or between Christians of different denominations. This is the modern meaning of the word. It first acquired this sense with Count Zinzendorf, the father of the renewed Moravian Church of the eighteenth century. (The Moravian Church had, from its origins, when the Reformation began, been a body with union as its aim.[27]) The spread of this meaning is presumed to be due especially to the activity of the Universal Evangelical Alliance during the last century. 6. Lastly, the phrase designates the awareness of belonging to a world Christian "fellowship" and indicates a desire for union with other Churches. This final meaning dates from the first twenty years of the nineteenth century when it was used as an explanation of the presence of representatives of many different Churches at the Conferences of Stockholm and Lausanne. It was continued in the Oxford Conference of 1937.[28]

The most contemporary meaning, the one that would obtain the most acceptance in every Christian communion, is that of Christian interchange and the quest for Christian universality.

The meaning of the word, like the ideas and things connected with it, has thus undergone development.

It is this sense of Christian interchange that explains the nature of the World Council of Churches. In his statement on 27 January 1960, in reply to the summoning of the ecumenical council by Pope John XXIII, Dr Visser 't Hooft recalled it once again: "The World of Churches has always kept to the method—and always will keep to it—that enables the Churches to come together and hold discussions in order to reach agreement on the measures to be taken with the reunion of the Churches as the goal."[29]

What does the word "movement" mean? It combines the ideas of tension, need, quest, dynamic trust, and also receptivity, obedience, acquiescence in the impulse that directs us and in the goal which draws us on.

Is the ecumenical movement a theory, a system, a plan systematically carried out? It first appeared as the response to an anxious expectation, the expression of a need, the manifestation of a faith endued with a new creative energy which, trusting in the inspiration of the Holy Spirit, open and subject to his commands, set out to fulfil a purpose as vast as the Spirit himself.

So the phrase "ecumenical movement" denotes an immense activity undertaken by every Christian communion, which by means of dialogue, co-operation, integration, and individual and institutional union, aims at drawing Christians together and reconciling them, healing their damaged traditions, and, in short, bringing the mystical Body of Christ to its perfect fulfilment.

[27] J. R. Meinlick, *Count Zinzendorf* (1957).
[28] W. A. Visser 't Hooft, *The Meaning of Ecumenical* (1953), pp. 5–6.
[29] *S. Œ. P. I.* (January 1960).

A man may be said to have or not to have the ecumenical spirit according to his spiritual sympathy with other Christians or his lack of it. Ultimately the ecumenical spirit and the spirit of catholicity are one, for both signify universality. There are three levels at which catholicity is manifested: one of them is concerned with the expansion of Christianity in the non-Christian world; the second, with its expansion in that part of the world that is already Catholic; and the third, with that part of the world that is already Christian. It is this third aspect which is precisely the field of ecumenism.

To be involved in ecumenism means being involved in the totality of ideas, principles, problems, activities and institutions which together account for the origin and development of the ecumenical movement.

2. Common agreement on the nature of the ecumenical movement

Is it possible to perceive a common measure of agreement in the Christian world on the nature of the ecumenical movement? All are agreed that it can be defined as a movement dedicated to a quest for integrity and unity, of reconciliation and healing, by dialogue, mutual encounter, co-operation and integration.

There is also unanimous agreement that ecumenism cannot be a movement of spiritual coercion, of pressure (however disguised) brought to bear on consciences to move them to oneself. Real ecumenism is a proclamation of unity. It will try to show that unity in its splendour, but it will also hold the ways of the Lord in reverence, and respect freedom of conscience. Catholics, Protestants, Anglicans and Orthodox have all, at some time in their history, used force in the service of faith. And even today not every mutual grievance on this score has passed away.

Ecumenism is at the service of authentic faith, and the weapons of faith are not those of force or intolerance. The central committee of the World Council of Churches recalled this fact at its meeting at St Andrews in Scotland in August 1960. The Catholic Church, for her part, has no desire to bring pressure on any Church, communion or denomination in order to draw them to herself.[30] Ecumenism is not something to be made use of for some other end, even if that end is the noblest of causes, namely, the spread of the faith throughout the world. It is a sacred reality which we serve, the very cause of unity. Thus, for the Catholic Church, ecumenism is not an exceptionally subtle way of rallying the rest of the Christian world to herself. Not that we are indifferent to our Lord's desire to gather the people of every race and nation together, even numerically,

[30] A. F. Carillo de Albornoz, *Roman Catholicism and Religious Liberty* (1959).

but we do not believe that the *compelle intrare* (Lk 14:23) implies spiritual coercion, or any insidious machination, even "for the greater glory of God".

Is it a movement of conversion? There is complete agreement in emphasizing the difference between proselytism and ecumenism. But the work of conversion aims at answering the immediate and individual needs of souls. These need truth, and the task of bringing it to them cannot be put off.

Ecumenism primarily envisages corporate bodies and traditions and not individuals and immediate situations. It is because these two aspects were so long confused, or rather, because too little attention was paid to the second, that the ecumenical movement took such a time to become established in the Catholic Church. If we see the ecumenical problem primarily in terms of conversion, then the Protestant world will be trying to convert the Catholic and Orthodox worlds; the Orthodox world will be engaged in converting the Catholic and Protestant worlds; and the Catholic world will be similarly occupied with regard to the Protestant and Orthodox world. Such an attitude would lead nowhere; its result would simply be to isolate the great Christian bodies by reducing their mutual relationships to that of laying siege to each other, and of each taking from the other what it could.

We should therefore keep the two aspects clearly distinct. Ecumenism, which is a long term process, offers no solution to the immediate and individual needs of souls in trouble. They cannot be advised to await the unknown day when Christians will have reunited. They must be given an answer as soon as possible. But does this mean that conversion and ecumenism are opposed to each other? Not if by conversion we mean the turning towards each other, and the turning of all Christians directly towards God, towards the essential and authentic reality of Christianity and catholicity. For in that case it surely implies a general movement of conversion, a conversion of corporate Christian bodies to Christ, the norm and model of catholicity. It is the mutual encounter between traditions that have suffered distortion, the drawing together of separated brethren, the healing of communities that have been injured, the integration of all Christians in the *Una Sancta*.

Ecumenism does not lay the emphasis on spiritual coercion, but on illumination. It is not interested in proselytism, but in the conversion of corporate bodies. It therefore implies mutual acceptance. But how far does this go?

It must be admitted in all honesty that each Christian communion hesitates at the idea of the acceptance of other Christian groups for fear that a positive response might entail a dogmatic judgement which it could not conscientiously give. The whole history of Christianity is filled with the record of the resistance of Catholicism to Protestantism and vice-versa; of Orthodoxy to Protestantism and Catholicism, and vice-versa. Some facts relating to this do, however, demand consideration. Our actions of corporate mutual rejection in the fourth, the eleventh and the sixteenth centuries did not succeed in ending the existence or development of any communion and there is nothing to indicate that the end of Catholicism, Protestantism or Orthodoxy is at hand. And, so far as we can see, none of the Christian divisions has the power to eliminate or subjugate the others, or even to make the rest of the world believe that it alone is the true representative of Christianity. Christians of every denomination have periodically announced the extermination of other Christians by the Angel of God. But the survival of the Christian communions leads us to think that our Lord did not ratify their desires, and that in his plans he reserves a part of their development to himself. This moves us to ask whether we should not more genuinely enter into his purpose if we chose other means. All of us are to some extent in the ridiculous position of wanting the present situation to be altered without first accepting the fact of our reciprocal existence. We are not asked to change our denominational allegiance, nor to pass a dogmatic judgement upon other communions, but to consider ourselves as all members of a scattered family in search of healing and the recovery of its unity.

But does mutual acceptance end with a tolerant juxtaposition, with the co-existence of positions that contradict each other, sometimes on essential points?

A love of peace is certainly necessary, and for this, mutual acceptance is an elementary condition. But would not a status quo, even though cordial, really amount to no more than a mutilated ecumenism, for ecumenism aims at the re-establishment of order among the sons of the Father's House? In other words, if mutual acceptance is to be truly ecumenical, it must be understood in a dynamic, creative sense.

A further conviction that becomes increasingly imperative is that the solution to the divided state of Christians is not to be found in eclecticism, syncretism or the least common denominator. For Catholicism and Orthodoxy the thing is excluded *a priori*. As a witness to the Protestant attitude, we may take the *Responses of the Churches to Lund* in 1952.[31] In this document it is repeatedly declared by denominations belonging to the classical or radical tradition that nothing will satisfy them apart from the pure and integral Word of God, however great the patience this demands.

There are indeed other trends which consider that difficulties arising from doctrinal contradictions can be eliminated by using general formulas

[31] Published by the World Council of Churches in 1952.

33

which would leave each believer, each denomination, and above all, our Lord, with the task of giving, to each case, the meaning which they respectively ascribe to them. But there is a serious objection to any arrangement of this sort. The intention of doing one thing or another is so weakened that either nothing definite is effectively done, or else if it is done, it is done by a kind of magic, an activity clean contrary to the mind of the Reformation. This solution is not, therefore, a satisfactory ecumenical method.

Would more support be gained for the idea of a super-Church, or a federation of Churches that would ultimately come under the presidency of the pope, analogous to a kind of ecclesiastical world government reuniting Churches, sects and denominations?

The result would certainly be more organization, but it is not obvious that more unity would be attained. Effective union must no doubt be preceded by a certain amount of practical collaboration between the various communions under a spiritual leadership, but the solution of a super-Church or of a federation is only semi-ecumenical. The unity of the Church is not the result of mathematically adding up everything which bears the name of Christian, as though God's Holy Church was merely the sum of the separated branches again brought together. In their state of separation, Churches, communions and sects have each developed along the lines of its own view of what a loyal adherence to Christianity means. How can such development be harmoniously adjusted to unity? Christian reunion involves adaptation, and sometimes healing of past wounds.

But when we speak of the healing of mutilated traditions, should we be thinking of Anglicans, Protestants and Orthodox only?

It would be a great illusion to imagine that the absence of Catholics is a loss to other Christians, but that their absence is no loss to us; and that although we are ready to welcome them, we could, strictly speaking, do without them. The truth is quite different. The break between East and West in the Middle Ages, as well as the separation between the Catholic Church and the Reformed bodies was a real mutilation for all concerned and we have suffered from it ever since. It is only very recently that, as a whole, we have regained sufficient strength to want to heal our wounds.

For the wounds of the Church and their healing can be considered in two ways. One is canonical, the other pastoral. These two ways are not opposed to each other. The canonical way has a pastoral concern. It is at the service of charity and truth in the Church. The canon law of the Catholic Church explicitly warns us against the temptation of separating the two aspects (canon 2214).

However, it happens that the canonical point of view comes to be divorced from the pastoral. It then turns to legalism, to juridicism. According to this way of looking at things, heresy and schism, as external sins, incur the censures assigned to them in the code of canon law; the precise canon is applied, the operation performed, and the object of trouble cut off from the Church. The Body of Christ, it is assumed, recovers its health. There is no longer any problem, and all is well.

Nevertheless, this is not the pastoral and evangelical point of view. When the Good Shepherd loses a sheep, he leaves the ninety-nine others and goes in search of the hundredth. In the parable of the prodigal son, the father is not satisfied with leaving the door open in expectation of his son; scanning the distance as far as he can see, he keeps watching for his return; he jumps up and runs out to meet the young man on his return.

If, up to now, the state of the dismemberment of Christ's Body has been accepted straight away, it is because the legalistic spirit has prevailed over the pastoral and evangelical spirit in the way in which Christian divisions have been regarded. Such an approach was all the easier as it could be justified by legal reasons. But justice must be the expression of just relationships within a given order of reality. It only attains an equilibrium in symbiosis with truth and charity, as it does in God.

Others, believing that the protest made at the Reformation forms a necessary element in the vitality and sound development of Christianity, have suggested that there should be an integration of Protestant bodies within Catholicism that would safeguard both their incorporation and their own special mission.

Even if this suggestion was expanded into the idea that the Church of Christ is a dialectical unity enclosing a plurality of Christian worlds, each of which represents only a single aspect of Christian truth, it would only introduce a confusion between conflict and tension, dualism and duality. There are grounds for believing that unity could not persist or even come into existence under the influence of an idea of this kind. For it would lead to an ecumenism based on the theory of a Church composed of various branches, forgetting that in ecumenism what counts is not so much the assembling of men, as their integration, not merely drawing them together but also healing them, not merely organizing them, but also bringing them within a vital order.

Still others have suggested that we should proceed as if unity already existed, and take action accordingly. But, as Visser 't Hooft justly comments, [32] even though "to proceed as if" may have been necessary for a time in order that the ecumenical movement might be enabled to begin in religious bodies only too well aware of their differences, the formula

---

[32] *Les Exigences de notre vocation commune* (1960), chapter i: "Comment croître dans l'unité".

cannot go on being used indefinitely. Once exalted to the level of a principle, the risk would be that we should forget the real goal to be reached. And in any case, it would soon run into concrete problems that cannot be left unheeded.

Would it be more realistic to proceed as if the divisions of the third, fourth, eleventh and sixteenth centuries had never existed? It would be highly desirable if it were possible, but facts would soon bring us back to realities which only real ecumenical courage would enable us to confront.

In ecumenism false starts must be avoided. Some of these offer many attractions; others, despite their good intentions, lack the necessary breadth of vision and penetration. In both cases, the result is confusion rather than progress.

Much will be gained by a critical elucidation of a general agreement on the principal features of what is and what is not genuine ecumenism. Did I go too far by pointing out that it seems to most people that ecumenism is made up not of spiritual coercion, but of illumination, not of proselytism, but of corporate conversion, not doctrinal indifference, but dynamic acceptance of Christian differences, not juridical self-sufficience, but an effort to heal traditions that have been impaired?

A lofty profession of ecumenism may at times conceal a subjective pietism, whereas fraternal love ought to be accompanied by a courageous adherence to the truth. Others barely escape liberalism when they put their trust in some practical common front, and treat doctrinal differences as matters of merely academic interest. Conversely, it is laid down by some that a common declaration of principles is an essential prerequisite to any reciprocal activity among Christians.

If we took this line, however, should we not be forgetting that although we first become ecumenical through an attitude of mind, we must also at the same time express this in the concrete by definite ecumenical activity. Idea and action mutually assist and control each other.

But can we travel without knowing where we are going? Can we engage in ecumenical co-operation if we are unaware of the goal which explains the means we use?

This goal, however, is in fact not unknown to Catholics, Protestants, Orthodox or Anglicans. It is clearly indicated in the Gospels. It is the unity of all Christians. What we do not agree about is how this unity ought to be expressed and what means should be taken to achieve it. And this is why, although there is an ecumenical problem, very fortunately also there exists an ecumenical movement.

3. Differences of view on the nature of the ecumenical movement

Do Catholics, Anglicans, Protestants and Orthodox give exactly the same meaning to the ecumenical movement?

On the day when all Christians give the same meaning to it, the ecumenical problem will disappear; for complete understanding will have been reached. An ecumenical problem exists because in fact misunderstanding exists, but there is an ecumenical movement because there is a determination to achieve it.

Although the great Christian communions are not in agreement on every point, they all admit that the ecumenical movement may be defined as a search for integration and unity: for reconciliation and healing through mutual acceptance, drawing together, encounter, dialogue, reconsideration, co-operation and mutual adaptation.

Why do we not all give exactly the same meaning to the ecumenical movement? It is because we do not share the same idea of what ecumenism really is. This is the heart of the debate. Our criteria of the nature of the ecumenical reality are different.

The various meanings of the word *oikumene* have been mentioned. Geographically, it denotes the entire inhabited world. Politically, it meant the Roman Empire which, through its extent, came to symbolize the empire of the world. It appears that it was St Ignatius of Antioch[33] who, about A.D. 100, first used the word *katholikos*, later adopted in the Nicene Creed, though it occurs nowhere in scripture, as the equivalent of the pagan *oikumene*. It was only after the conversion of the Roman Empire that the word ecumenical came to be accepted by the Church in the same sense as Catholic, as a designation of one of the characteristics of the universal Church, namely, orthodoxy, in opposition to whatever is partial, heretical, schismatic or sectarian. Just as the Empire was a system that extended a single, universally valid rule of law throughout its dominions, so the ecumenical councils were the expressions of a single law and a single belief, a single norm whose frontiers coincided with those of the Empire, the political *oikumene*. In this way the word ecumenical acquired its third, ecclesiastical and religious meaning. It then came to mean the integral content of Christian truth, the quality which is common to the whole Church, concerns the whole Church, includes the whole Church.

After the separation between East and West in the Middle Ages there came a long period which has not yet reached its end. During it the word "ecumenical" was appropriated by both sides as the symbol of orthodoxy. The Orthodox Church reserves it to herself as being the equivalent of

[33] *Epistola ad Smyrnenses*, 8, 2.

orthodox doctrine, while the Catholic Church uses it to denote the general councils that bring all Catholic bishops together in order to establish norms that are valid for the whole Catholic body.

For a century now this word has enjoyed a singularly successful career among Protestants, but its meaning has changed. It no longer designates what is valid for the visible Church as a whole, since it is only too obvious that there are a great number of Christian communions. Instead, it designates Christian universality—what concerns all Christians, what they have in common, what is believed by them, what includes all Christians. In this way it becomes, therefore, the expression of a general interest in everything Christian, of a sense of solidarity among Christians, of a desire to be present wherever anything that affects all Christians is decided.

As a result of this evolution of the modern sense of the word, induced by a growing awareness of the solidarity of all Christians and of a desire for world-wide reunion, some Protestant and even some Orthodox bodies were somewhat upset by the announcement of a Catholic ecumenical council. It seemed to them inconceivable that the Catholic Church should presume to hold ecumenical sessions behind closed doors. In their view, if they had no part in them, then, however ecumenical in intention, these would be no more than meetings of one local Church. It was in order to satisfy this feeling that the special Secretariat for Unity was instituted to act as an intermediary between the council and other Christians. This was the first move towards recognition of the modern development of the word ecumenical in its sense of an awareness of the solidarity and responsibility of all Christians towards the whole world, the modern *oikumene*.

But is it possible to go further than this? We have reached the decisive issue: the difference in the idea of the nature of ecumenism and in the criterion to apply to it.

What was it that enabled the primitive Church, confronted by heretical and schismatic sectarian tendencies, to establish its idea of catholicity and ecumenicity, that is, to establish the rule of orthodoxy and truth for the universal Church? It was the unanimity of the apostolic testimony as received in every region, from the beginning, by everyone. At a later date St Vincent of Lérins expressed this in the words *Quod ubique, quod semper, quod ab omnibus*. As long as the apostles, the decisive and fundamental witnesses of Christian truth, were alive, their preaching acted as the living norm of the community's faith. The Church felt, however, the need to provide herself through the apostles, by means of her living tradition, with a written "rule of faith". In this way the Gospels appeared as witnesses and norms of the belief received by all men, everywhere, since Christ. The ecumenical creeds, in their turn, appeared as abridgements of the "rule of faith", intended to make the apostolic testimony more accessible to the entire body of believers, especially at their baptism.

Therefore a statement was considered to be catholic and ecumenical if it correctly expressed the Christo-apostolic testimony as having been the common possession of the Churches from the beginning, always believed by them, their corporate concern, and including them all without exception. Catholicity and ecumenicity signify the substantially identical extension of an undivided totality of beliefs, symbols and attachments held in common. Catholic and ecumenical orthodoxy, as expressed in the New Testament writings, the creeds, the ecumenical councils and the life of the Church in the early centuries, is at the opposite pole to every separatist movement, whether heresy, schism or sect.

It follows that what is authentically apostolic can be truly catholic and ecumenical. But the testimony of the apostles cannot be separated from the written or experienced Word of God. Hence only what is truly scriptural and traditional can be genuinely catholic and ecumenical. The heart of the apostolic proclamation is the announcement of the Good News incorporated in Jesus Christ. Thus genuine ecumenicity is evangelical. Finally, the apostolic testimony in scripture and tradition must be the criterion of authority until the end of time. Consequently, what is validly catholic and ecumenical is valid for ever.

It may therefore be said that as regards Catholicism the following chain of reasoning holds good: catholic-ecumenical-universal = apostolic-traditional-scriptural-visible-permanent.

Among Protestants, however, these terms are interpreted in conformity with an idea of the Church as the invisible communion of saints of every age and all peoples, known to God alone. Hence, for them, catholicity, ecumenicity and apostolicity are essentially inner and spiritual realities. They exist beforehand in God, in Christ, and only need to be made manifest by signs of external unity.

There are therefore three fundamental factors which separate us in the understanding of what ecumenism means: these are the historical continuity of the Catholic *oikumene*, the sacramentality and visibility of the Church. Both the problem and the ecumenical movements thus acquire their concrete definition from the way they correspond with the respective standpoints of the Christian communions.

What is the essence of the ecumenical problem? In the Protestant view there exists an essentially invisible form of Christianity which stands above all the Christian communions and unites them despite their divisions. The inner form of world Christianity is hidden in the Lord; its external form is unhappily at the mercy of the incoherence of its divisions. There is the Catholic Church, the Orthodox Eastern Churches, the Anglican Communion, the Protestant denominations, the sects. Not one of them is the Church. All of them are the Church. The Church that is within them must be enabled to be made clearly manifest as the result of reunion.

For Catholicism, on the other hand, the form of world Christianity already exists substantially. This is the Catholic Church. She proceeds from Christ and has done so without any interruption in her history from the time when she first came forth from his flesh and blood. She also proceeds from him in the present through the continuity established between heaven and earth by the power of the resurrection and ascension and Pentecost which ensures that Christ's transcendent presence in heaven shall not fail to be at the same time an immanent presence in his Church. From this point of view, the ecumenical problem would not consist in re-making the substance of the Church's visible unity, for it already exists, but in bringing it to perfection; not in re-creating, but in restoring it through the union and reconciliation of Christians. The Church is one and unique, but in the other Christian communions there exist elements of the Church, in different degrees of worth and wholeness. Through reunion these elements must be enabled to regain their fullness and completion.[34]

The Orthodox world makes her own what the Catholic Church affirms about herself. The existence of the Church as a unique reality, even today and in spite of the existence of a number of Churches, brings us to the claims of the Greek Orthodox Church, who declares that she alone possesses the right to be this one Church, through her uninterrupted historical continuity with the undivided Church. This claim means that the undivided Church was an undoubted continuation of the apostolic Church, at least until the ninth century. The dispute between East and West led to the formation of the Roman Catholic Church as a new Church, as a consequence of innovations repudiated by the Greek Orthodox Church. Thus, wherever the Greek Orthodox Church continued to exist she remained undivided, but that part of the West that had broken with her became a new separated Church. Later, when large sections of this new Church separated from her at the Reformation, further new separated Churches came into being. These latter took no account of the unchanged part of the Church which still persisted, and they have gone further than the Roman Church herself in the introduction of innovations.[35]

What is the essence of the ecumenical movement at the present time?

In the Protestant view the essence of the movement lies in "the setting out together (of the Churches) for, and their commitment to, the crusade to deliver the Church from her captivity within the Churches by con-

---

[34] Second Vatican Council, Decree on Ecumenism, chapter i: "Catholic Principles on Ecumenism".

[35] Hamilcar Alivisatos, "The Holy Greek Orthodox Church" in R. Newton Flew, ed., *The Nature of the Church* (1952), pp. 46–7.

fronting all the Churches with the Church described to us in scripture." [36] C. C. Morrison prefers to define it as "the re-emergence in Protestantism of the unfinished task of the Reformation." [37]

It is difficult to obtain a clear idea of what the Orthodox Churches consider to be the essence of the ecumenical movement. There is no declaration or explicit statement of their common standpoint. Most of them have entered late into the movement. All things considered, it is still the Patriarchate of Constantinople, with its delegate to the World Council of Churches, which best represents their collective opinion. In so far as any general conclusions may be drawn, it seems that among the adherents of the Patriarchate two theories hold the field. On the one hand, the essence of the ecumenical movement is the union of the Catholic, Orthodox, Protestant and Anglican Churches on the basis of communion and *de jure* equality; and on the other hand that the essence of the movement lies in the union of the Catholic Church and the Protestant communions with the Orthodox Church as their centre. [38]

For Catholicism the essence of the movement lies in universal reconstitution of the body of Christians, by the restoration, the diffusion, the sharing in common and the enrichment of a Christian unity which, despite the clouds and shadows that have obscured it and the wounds that have impaired it, has not ceased to exist visibly on earth.

Should the expression "ecumenical movement" no longer be used in Catholicism on the grounds that it is given a different interpretation elsewhere? In its Monitum of 20 December 1949, the Holy Office was the first to accept it in an official although indirect way. There was, therefore, no reason to substitute the term "unionism" for it. In any case, if the logic of meaning is to be taken to the limit, what word should we use instead of "Christ", "the Church", "God" and so on because ostensibly others interpret them differently? It is a question of the definition of terms.

No useful purpose would be served by allowing it to be supposed that there is complete agreement on the goal, the method, and the activity of ecumenism. Since, by definition, method is the kind of procedure taken in a movement towards an end, it follows that the nature of the end will determine the nature of the method.

It must be asked, however, whether radically different ideas of the ultimate unity of faith do not make ecumenical activity useless from the start. Or, to put it clearly, can ecumenical activity have any meaning for

[36] Visser 't Hooft, *Misère et Grandeur de L'Église*, p. 67.
[37] *The Unfinished Reformation*, p. xi.
[38] N. Zernov, "The Eastern Churches and the Ecumenical Movement in the Twentieth Century" in Ruth Rouse and Stephen Neill, ed., *A History of the Ecumenical Movement* (1954), pp. 645–77, 717.

the Catholic Church if Protestantism, for example, claims that unity of faith is not to be sought in the direction indicated by the Catholic Church? Conversely, has that activity any meaning for Protestantism if the Catholic Church claims that the unity of the Church as desired by Protestantism is unacceptable to her?

These two different kinds of the theology of unity underlie two different approaches to ecumenism. In the abstract, therefore, the following conclusion is inevitable: these two worlds, with their different approaches towards a goal, may perhaps draw nearer to each other, may have some contact with each other at one point or another, but they will never reunite. Why should they even set out on the journey? And since the goal is different, shall we not find in the field of action and method a repetition of the same difficulty which already exists as to the goal? Is it worth the trouble of setting out towards each other, if as the result of divergent aims it cannot be foreseen that any meeting is possible? Here, the last word is not with logic, reason and evidence, but with faith, love and hope.

4. A radical choice

Ecumenical work and investigation are not carried on under a cloudless sky. The thrill of joy when unity has been discovered may be abruptly followed by disappointment in the face of obstacles. But difficulties and moments of darkness must be accepted; they must be seen to be inevitable. They will surely come, and often amount to a deadlock.

Our Christian virtues must now learn to adapt themselves to ecumenical needs. Have not our defects contrived to flourish in the field of inter-Christian relationships?

Often the best way to free ourselves from what divides us is to turn back to what unites us. The light and heat proceeding from the factors of unity will absorb the solid elements of division. Did not a Protestant, William the Silent, say that it is not necessary to have hope in order to begin a task, nor to succeed in order to persevere? Does the present record of our relationships reveal only setbacks?

We must, therefore, go forward, and perhaps the great success of the ecumenical movement is that we are making our way towards each other, although at the outset so many different directions were taken.

Ultimately, a fundamental choice must be made: do we really wish to meet or not? Have, or have we not, the faith and hope that one day this meeting will take place? If not, then it is certain that our different convictions about the end and the method will infallibly produce not just a course running parallel, but an increasingly clearly marked separation. The Christian world will remain divided into several bodies, each with its own increased internal cohesion, but developing as strangers to each other until the end of time.

Only if we make the radical choice of accepting each other as sharing in a common destiny, with the prophetic hope that the break in unity may be overcome, and with faith in the Holy Spirit's power to reconcile, can we come to agree that although our diversities are many, we will take steps to draw together.

This simple decision is sufficient to establish the generous characteristics of an attitude shared by all. And yet, if we are to meet one day, must we not in a sense be already united? If division, schism and heresy originate in a division within the soul, then it is within the soul that the motivating principle of reunion must begin to live. But how are we to incorporate each other in our heart, our mind, our life? We must first create between us a relationship of goodwill, sympathy and love. Then we must learn to know each other, as we are at present, as we once were.

Christians will be reconciled by piety not pietism, by genuine integrity and not by integralism, by truth and not concordism, by openness, not narrowness of mind.

5. Ecumenism as a theological discipline and as a spirit

Need it be said that Christian unity cannot be left to chance, to mere goodwill, enthusiasm and improvisation? Christians may have been drawn together by some instinctive urge; their union will not follow automatically. A well thought-out and methodical effort will be needed, and this is attained by seeking out principles and laws, that is, through scientific research. This is the task of a theology of ecumenism, the inspiration and the guide of apostolic activity. It will take note of the various movements that have led the main Christian bodies to draw together, and then it must define the problems raised by the encounter between Christians and their union. One of its functions is negative: to control uncritical ecumenical activity and thought. But its main function is positive: to show that between God's activity in the general economy of salvation and in the gathering together of divided Christian bodies, there is an essential continuity. The latter, of course, is not in every respect an entirely new development. Many authors in the Church, beginning with St Cyprian, have written on the unity of the Church and worked for it. What they have done should move us to do likewise.

Its mystique, method and mode of action are those of unity, and unity not simply as a "note" of the Church, but unity in depth, unity, therefore, in intimate relationship with the subject of theology, which is God. Its essential idea is that of a healing process at work in the Christian world as a whole, of God's self-revelation in history, through signs, actions, events, gifts and through a covenant. This idea may seem too vague because it is really applicable to the cure of every kind of error or defect. But the necessary specific qualification can at once be added: the cure and the reconciliation which we are concerned with has as its object the impaired traditions of Christian bodies as such, whether this is the result of communion being broken off or of the creation of new Christian communions, and whatever the responsibility each must bear.

This new discipline, very different from previous apologetics, has secured a foothold in the syllabus of the ecclesiastical teaching of every denomination. Ecumenism may be defined either as a science or as an art. As a science it forms part of theology; as an art, it is the putting into apostolic and pastoral practice of its reality as a science.

Ecumenism as a science must include two parts: a descriptive part, concerned with the study of the origin, constitution, beliefs, life and activity of the Christian communions and their mutual relationships; secondly, a synthesis which answers the questions: what is the nature of the unity and universality of the Church? What specific problems are involved? What ways and means are appropriate for the achievment of unity among Christians and the fullness of the Church?

Ecumenism forms part of the doctrine on the Church because it is a function of the Church. It is a distinct part, for whereas the special object of the doctrine of the Church is the mystery of the Church considered intrinsically, ecumenism is concerned with the relations between the Church and other Christian communions. It is a *de facto* situation, resulting first from the appearance of sects and heresies, and then of the Nestorian and Monophysite Churches, the religious separation between East and West, the coming of the Reformation and of new Christian communions; it is this situation which compels us to consider the relationship between the Church and the Churches. Thus ecumenism obviously has its own special object, and this distinguishes it from ecclesiology and apologetics. It follows from this that normally it must have a treatise of its own, varying in extent according to needs.

Theology is at the service of the Church's life. It must, therefore, correspond with the needs of that life. Sometimes it happens that theology lags behind developments in the Church; this is explained in part by the fact that life in general, and the life of the Church in particular, raise many problems and lead to situations with which systematic theology finds difficulty in keeping up. In addition, because its method is partly deductive, theology is inclined to become isolated in abstraction. Such facts as those of divided Christendom, the existence of Christian communities opposed to each other, and the very concrete nature of the Church's life, provide an indication to theology that it should extend its interest to other fields.

In our time, however, new facts, the facts of ecumenism, are inviting theology to more explicit, more co-ordinated, more methodical, that is, more scientific developments, in order to meet the contemporary needs of the Church now engaged on the work of Christian reunion.

Among Protestants, it is clear, great hopes are set on ecumenism both as a science and an art. It has been pointed out that the coming of the universal Church, in idea and in reality, has given rise, in Protestant circles, to a new science, namely ecumenism. Ecumenism is the science of the universal Church, of its nature, functions, relationships and strategy. In the religious sphere it corresponds to geopolitics in the secular sphere.[39]

It may well be that ecumenism is called to play a no less important part in the Catholic Church. For what else is it about than the restoration of unity among Christians, the healing and regaining of impaired traditions, the integration of all Christians in the mystical Body of Christ? We, in our turn, may also say: ecumenism is the science of and towards this universal Church, in its nature, functions, relationships and strategy.

Shall we ever attain visible unity? The Protestant dialectic of the simultaneity of righteousness and sin, of division and unity, leads to the view that this can be no more than an eschatological hope; it seems that the utmost we can do is to proclaim the signs of unity received in Christ, and the signs that are the fore-runners of ultimate unity. A pessimistic outlook, Catholics will say: a realistic outlook, Protestants will reply.

On all sides, therefore, the importance of establishing this science is evident—the science of ecumenism which deals with unity in its every aspect.

How can we form an exact definition of Catholic ecumenism as a science? It is a part of theology[40] whose object is the study of the unity and universality of the Church in its relationships with the present separation and ultimate reconciliation of the Churches and Christian communions.

As a part of theology, ecumenism is focussed on God, in whose service it endeavours to repair, in the Christian world taken as a whole, the breaches made in the communication of himself by the Triune God in his covenant. In this way apostolic and pastoral activity with Christian

---

[39] John A. Mackay, "Protestantism" in Edward J. Jurji, ed., *The Great Religions of the Modern World* (1946), p. 366; *cf.* Visser 't Hooft, *Misère et Grandeur de L'Église*, pp. 67 ff.; G. Thils, *La Théologie œcuménique: Notions, Formes, Démarches,* Bibliotheca Ephemeridum Theologicarum Lovaniensium, vol. XVI (1960); *Consultation sur l'Œcuménisme et la théologie œcuménique,* August 25—30, 1960.

[40] In the terms of Thomist theology, a potential part. The expression a "potential part" indicates both the idea of actual belonging to Christ and a potential tendency or movement towards the Church of all Christian traditions, of all Christians, of all Christian bodies situated outside the juridical frontiers of the Church, whatever their actual state.

reunion as its object finds its foundation and its traditional theological control.

The method peculiar to ecumenism is the normal theological method qualified by the special needs that flow from its object and its aim.

Its method is theological because its whole procedure is governed by reason illuminated by faith. [41] The subject matter, principles and goal of ecumenism are provided by revelation, the faith and the Church. In its advance towards unity, faith makes use of reason and of everything that co-operates with that purpose: the history of symbols, doctrines, denominations and Churches, psychology, sociology, etc.

There is a single goal, the unity of the Church, and this goal dictates the method. In a complex problem such as this it is essential for the method to be clearly defined. In this case, the method is initially historical and comparative. For to disregard all knowledge of the origin of the Christian denominations leads inevitably to losing ourselves in the labyrinth of derivations, relationship between bodies, the constant evolution of religious forms.

Some sort of psychological method is also required to grasp the interplay of relationships between the various Churches and communions, and a sociological method to understand the organic life of different bodies.

If we restricted ourselves to the dogmatic point of view alone, it would mean reducing the ecumenical problem to one of its component parts, even though it is the principal one. The theological method is the more efficacious to the extent that it is based on a descriptive account and an analysis of Christian problems and communions.

The various aspects of the ecumenical method converge in the method used by the Church to carry out her mission. It is a method of conversion; the conversion of hearts to mutual love; the conversion of minds to the unity of the same faith; the conversion of what is partial to the fullness of catholicity.

Ecumenism is a basic factor in the Church's work, for like everything alive, she is driven to safeguard her existence and to repair whatever damage is done to it. When any separation occurs it inflicts a wound not only on those who leave but also on those who stand firm, because the Church is a family, a home. She fulfils her mission to the communions separated from her by assuming spiritual responsibility for them, accepting them as brothers, by her concern for them, drawing near to them, entering into a dialogue with them, collaborating with them, and finally achieving reunion.

Ecumenism, therefore, as a theological discipline is the study of the mystery of the Church from the point of view of the integral recovery

[41] First Vatican Council, Session III, chapter iv.

of that Trinitarian communication which has been impaired by the withdrawal of the Churches and by the creation of dissident Christian communions. The principal means to such an integral recovery can be stated to be the reconciliation between Christians who are heirs to a patrimony which they possess in various states, as exiles from it or as their native land, as a vestigial element of what it once was or in its fullness.

The ecumenical movement in the Church proceeds from the unity of heart and soul between Christ and his mystical Body.

In this way, through contemplation of the mystery of sin, of predestination and salvation, in individuals and communities, ecumenism is at the very centre of the Christian mystery itself. It becomes the most relevant and moving form of contemplation because its object is the mystery of the union between Christ and his Body in its suffering, humiliated or glorious life, according as it is broken by divisions or is restored by reconciliation.

The recovery and restoration of impaired traditions, of the inheritance of grace in Christian bodies, is the proximate end which ecumenism pursues in order to reach the ultimate fullness of the Body of Christ. [42]

Where have these wounds been inflicted? On the historic continuity of the Church, on revealed doctrine, on the interpretation of the Church's mission to the world, on her structural formation, on the way the sacred mysteries are celebrated, on the ecumenical spirit and the unity of Christendom. The wounds of the Church, in fact, constitute the ecumenical problem. There is no element in the Church, which has not suffered from them; there is no Christian of any communion who has not been afflicted by them.

Ecumenism's initial task is to define the ecumenical problem; and definition of the ecumenical problem means recognizing that it exists, circumscribing its boundaries, grasping its essence. In the next place comes the work of healing in all the spheres in which unity has been impaired.

6. The ecumenical problem and ecumenical problems

To obtain a definition of the ecumenical problem we must approach it in different ways and consider it from a number of different aspects.

There is an ecumenical problem and there are ecumenical problems. They are a result of differences of interpretation of continuity in relation

[42] O. Tomkins, *The Wholeness of the Church* (1949); E. L. Mascall, *The Recovery of Unity* (1958); H. P. Douglass, *Church Unity Movements in the United States* (1934), p. 146.

to Christ, of differences of attitude in respect of communication between religious groups, differences of belief, differences concerning the Church's mission, structure, worship, psychology and organic life. The ecumenical problem is the sum total of all these individual problems.

Can ecumenical work be undertaken with the idea that it is the future that counts, and that the past can be forgotten? What denomination would agree thus to relegate its traditions and origin to obscurity in this way? And yet the problem of how the transition from the Church to the Churches occurred must be faced. There is, therefore, a historical problem.

At the present time we must take the path from multiplicity to unity. A choice has to be made between various forms of ecumenism. This is the problem of inter-denominational relations.

At the doctrinal level, also, a choice must be made between conceptions of the essence of Christianity. Christianity is a single reality, but it finds and must find its expression in a number of different ways when varieties of belief become incompatible with the unity of faith. This is the dogmatic problem.

This same question of the relations between plurality and unity recurs in the problem of the Church's mission, constitution and worship, and in the psychological and sociological elements which condition the unity of the Church and of Christians: from these arise so many essential variants of a same problem.

Perhaps investigation of the ecumenical problem requires a realization of the extent of our divisions and of the depth of our unity. The deeper we penetrate the more thoroughly open we shall become; the more exact our knowledge, the greater our appreciation of the implications of wholeness; and love will know how to adjust what must be accepted after the mind has concluded its investigations. After all, what more does it amount to than a renewed and deepened understanding of our common calling into one Church, in which we acknowledge our errors, forgive each other and share together both greatness and sorrows as we mount the steep path to the truth of Christianity?

III. THE PURPOSE OF THIS BOOK

No inquiry into ecumenism can lead far or be right unless it is systematically based on typology, that is, on a scientific study of the character of the forms of Christianity, enabling them to be compared and classified. "Protestantism" is an abstraction. What exists are various forms, various types of Protestantism. It should also be realized that the Eastern Churches are divided into several rites, each with its own character.

In the first place there must be taken into account the formative action of history upon all these types, and it must be constantly kept in mind. As the ecumenical problem comes to display definitely new aspects—interdenominational, dogmatic, missionary, structural, liturgical, psychological and sociological—we can watch it step by step assuming distinct forms and an altered shape.

But what is the vital spirit of these religious forms? The question introduces us to the factor that is co-ordinate with the analysis of these types—that is, the life that exists within these clear-cut demarcations, these species and forms. We must distinguish between what ought to be and what actually is. For instance, there are denominations which, according to their original principles, ought to have a liturgy of a certain kind, ought to have one definite method of evangelizing, ought to have a particular form of constitution, but for various reasons have, in all these matters, something quite different. We should remember this if we are concerned with providing a serviceable account of things as they are.

It must also be noted carefully that in every instance, when a typology has been established, a schematic account produced, when the very heart of the religious forms has been revealed then we are dealing with an abstraction. This should never be forgotten. There is a phrase in English, "tentative proposal", which is both moderate and exact. Criticism has the inherent right to endeavour to do better, and in any case there is nothing which prevents a first trial or endeavour from producing a definitive solution. Each must be considered on its own merits. The necessary abridgements in such accounts, the inevitable distortions, also make their contribution to a sounder appreciation of the reality. The science of ecumenism must constantly return to consideration of its object.

The definition of problems and knowledge of our relationships are urgent tasks; solutions also must be sought.

Each chapter-heading is followed by the central question corresponding to it. In most cases this is expressed in terms of a conflict. Thus the drama of divided Christendom is revealed. And yet, are the positions always contradictory? Is reconciliation between them impossible? For example, must a choice be made between the Church's mission in this world and her mission in relation to life after death, between the Church of the apostles and that of the hierarchy, between the liturgy of the Word and that of the sacrament? Obviously, opposing, contrary and contradictory attitudes must give way to those of healing, conversion and reconciliation. Where could we find a better starting point for the solution of our common ecumenical problem than in a return to thorough study of the doctrine of the universal Church? Our Catholic view of Christianity is governed by a permanent structural reality, a fundamental schematic approach which reappears in every aspect of the ecumenical problem.

My use of it as an illustration comes from no desire to cast into outer darkness the doctrine held by Christian communions like the Churches of the Anglican Communion, the Old Catholic and the Orthodox Churches. I have no intention of implying that their points of agreement with us have escaped my attention. Let it be clearly understood at this point, and if I do not repeat it throughout the book, it is not through forgetfulness or repudiation. If it is useful to remember our points of agreement, we should not lose sight of what remains to be done and is the most arduous. It hardly needs saying that it is not on our points of agreement that there is an ecumenical problem. The subject of the present study is not so much the agreements that have already been reached as those that are now being sought with trouble and anxiety of heart and often with confusion of mind. We are concerned here not with what has been established but with what remains to be established.

Ecumenical good will has brought all Christians together round a table to discuss the problem of their unity. Once we have defined and clearly marked out the essential and authentic aspects of our disagreements by that very fact, we shall have settled half of our problems, for the beginning of unity is enlightenment.

Who are those confronting each other? They are the Catholic Church, the Churches of the Christian East, the Churches of the Anglican and Protestant communions. The first category is clear. The second includes not only the Orthodox, but also the representatives of the other Eastern rites, and we do not forget the indispensable part that must be played in the ecumenical dialogue by the Eastern Churches in union with Rome.

The Anglicans may be allowed to describe themselves. The Lambeth Conference laid down that the Churches of the Anglican Communion are Catholic as understood by the English Reformation. They are Catholic, but reformed; they are reformed, but Catholic. [43]

Shortly before this, the Committee on the Unity of the Church had declared during the same conference: "The type represented by Anglicanism includes a harmony between Catholic and Protestant factors which exists in no other communion. It is conscious of both these aspects simultaneously". [44]

Obviously, therefore, the Anglican Communion holds a distinctive position with respect to Protestants, Roman Catholics and Eastern Christians, and this position also indicates the direction of its affinities.

There remain the numerous Protestant bodies. Their interest depends upon their complexity. To take this into account is not to imply that the ecumenical movement is solely a Protestant affair. How can we forget

[43] *The Lambeth Conference, 1948. Report of the Committee on the Anglican Communion* (1948), p. 83.
[44] *Ibid.*, p. 78.

the merits and activities of the Churches of the Anglican Communion and of some Orthodox Churches in this sphere? An eloquent account of them has been produced. There is no need to repeat it, or to draw up an honours list.

Bishop Stephen C. Neill describes the embarrassment which he and Miss Ruth Rouse experienced when they were preparing their *History of the Ecumenical Movement, 1517–1948* (1954), because this history often seemed to be almost a history of the ecumenical efforts of Anglicans. From the Edinburgh Conference in 1910 until today, the Churches of the Anglican Communion have been distinguished by the extent and persistence of their work for Christian unity. But how can we fail to recognize also the immensity of the ecumenical activity undertaken by the Protestant world, and the growing importance of the Protestant problem within the general problem of Christian reconciliation? If Catholics, Anglicans and the Orthodox are in agreement on many points, let them give thanks to the Lord, for there will be fewer problems to deal with! Together let them apply themselves to this great work of reconciliation with the Protestant world. Through its numbers, through the extent and variety of its activity, and the complexity of the movements which it includes, that world holds an immense position in the whole ecumenical problem. Would a union which included Catholics, the Orthodox, Old Catholics and Anglicans, but left the Protestant world on one side, be an ecumenical success?

It would be contradictory to the very purpose of ecumenism if any Christian body was for any reason forgotten or excluded. Churches which are proud of their inheritance should not despise their brethren who come to them out of spiritual poverty; they should not crush the weakest, but rather, approach them with a greater love; they should not look with a contemptuous glance upon those denominations whose doctrine they find so vague and uncertain, but remember that, in spite of everything, these are the ways along which souls make their journey to God. They should rather thank the Lord who has given them bread which no flesh and blood has purchased, and since love obliterates all blemishes, let them approach these denominations and say: come, brothers, what is ours is yours.

While we Christians are discussing our own reunion, a hidden questioner is watching us: I refer to Israel. If it is a mistake, an error, to have introduced into this work a chapter on "Israel and the reunion of Christians", it has been done with premeditation. Christianity and Judaism are linked together in the ecumenical problem, because they are linked together in the Church and in unity. Christianity is the religion of the covenant: from Sinai to Calvary, God's plan is one. When heresy and schism tear that covenant apart, Christ's purpose for the Church becomes obstructed by the Churches.

51

CHAPTER II

The Historical Problem:
From the Church to the Churches

I. DEFINITION OF THE PROBLEM

Although there are principles at the basis of ecumenical work, there are also facts. These facts are odd, difficult and inter-connected. Governmental censuses, reports by U.N.O., official documents of religious denominations, the statistics of international information agencies, all record the great number of forms assumed by Christianity, and the religious division of the Christian world.[1] In the United States, for example, it is easy to point to the existence of more than two hundred and fifty officially registered religious bodies.[2]

Religious pluralism, however, is obviously not confined to Europe and America. It is to be found wherever the Christian denominations are concerned in missionary activity.[3]

---

[1] *World Christian Handbook*, published by *International Review of Missions* (1952); *A Christian Year Book* (1941 ff.; 5th edition, 1950).

[2] *Yearbook of American Churches*, 1961; Frank S. Mead, *Handbook of Denominations in the United States* (1961); Leo K. Rosten, *A Guide to the Religions of America* (1955); Jan Karel van Baalen, *The Chaos of Cults* (1961); Charles S. Braden, *These Also Believe: A Study of Modern American Cults and Minority Religious Movements* (1949); E. T. Clark, *The Small Sects in America* (1949); Ralph Lord Roy, *Apostles of Discord: A Study of Organised Bigotry and Disruption on the Fringes of Protestantism* (1933); *List of Orthodox, Other Eastern Churches, Polish National Catholic Church* (1958); J. L. Neve, *Churches and Sects of Christendom* (1952); H. Mulert and E. Schott, *Konfessionskunde, Die Christlichen Kirchen und Sekten heute* (1956); E. Royston Pike, *Encyclopedia of Religion and Religions* (1958); K. Algermissen, *Christian Denominations* (1946); John B. Gobb, *Varieties of Protestantism* (1959); Einer Molland, *Christendom: the Christian Churches, their Doctrines, Constitutional Forms and Ways of Worship* (1959).

[3] *Protestant Churches of Asia, The Middle East, Africa, Latin America and the Pacific Area:* a revision of *The Younger Churches, Some Facts and Observations*, published by Union Theological Seminary, New York, in 1959.

A glance at the Middle East will show that a multiplicity of different Churches is not a phenomenon exclusive to Protestantism. There are Eastern Churches in union with Rome that are better called united Eastern Churches than uniates. There are Nestorian Eastern Churches that separated from the Catholic Church after the Council of Ephesus, and Monophysite Eastern Churches that broke away after the Council of Chalcedon. And then, since 1054, there have been the Greek and Russian Orthodox Churches etc.[4]

A survey of the religious statistics of the great cosmopolitan cities such as New York, Chicago, London, Paris, Montreal, or of the great historic sees such as Antioch with five patriarchates, and Alexandria with three, or a mere walk along the streets of some great American, English, German or Canadian city, will bring us face to face with the ecumenical problem. The general impression is that of being confronted by a religious world blown to atoms and whose secret of cohesion has been lost. But can it be rediscovered?

A superficial observer will see Protestantism in its various forms, Orthodoxy and the Eastern Churches, as absorbed in one deliquescent mass. But the major trends and typical forms of both Protestantism and Orthodoxy must be perceived and kept distinct. However developed the system of branches, there must be a trunk which supports it. The outgrowth retains something of the original essence. A structure exists with a definite unity, and it is this that enables us to follow the winding tracks of the circulating life and makes a reintegration into unity possible.

Ecumenism has established its position as a science. It is composed of phenomenological descriptions, history and theology. It starts from a wide experience of actually existing forms. It traces and describes their shape. It looks for relationship between them, compares, contrasts and defines them. It abstracts an essence, and with this essence as a guiding principle, it re-examines the existing forms. It tries to assess the results and the course of events through the memory which each denomination preserves of its history and its origins. It studies the alterations which each separate body has undergone. Above all it pays attention to their approach towards unity.

We must, therefore, learn to appreciate the different origins of religious bodies, the relationship between their characteristic elements, the way they become interdependent, their features, types and forms. For the sake of treating this extremely complex matter in orderly fashion, the following procedure will be adopted:

[4] Donald Attwater, *The Christian Churches of the East* (1948), vol. I: *The Churches in Communion with Rome,* vol. II: *The Churches not in Communion with Rome;* Adrian Fortescue, *The Lesser Eastern Churches* (1913); *The Uniat Eastern Churches: The Byzantine Rite in Italy, Sicily, Syria and Egypt* (1923); R. Janin, *Les Églises orientales et les Rites orientaux* (1955).

First, the terms will be defined: religious bodies, denominations, the Church, confessions, communions, sects, movements, conferences. Then the major trends which have given rise to the various denominations, sects, religious bodies etc., will be distinguished. Thirdly, a division according to types will be established. Lastly, we shall consider the central issue involved in the historical problem, namely, the continuity between the Church and Christ.

The presuppositions to all this are an acquaintance with the general history of the reunion of Christian bodies[5] and a knowledge of the most important problems encountered during the course of the relationships effected between the denominations. In this chapter, therefore, we shall be engaged in elucidating the fundamental components which are present in every aspect of the ecumenical problem. It will be helpful to keep them in mind.

1. The different terms

(a) *Religious body.* The term "religious body" is the widest. The inquiry conducted by the "Bureau of the Census" in the United States in 1936 on religious bodies[6] covers every religious form which is legally incorporated in any kind of collective association. This could equally well be a Church, such as the Catholic Church, a sect such as the Jehovah's Witnesses, an association or conference such as the Lutheran Synod of Missouri, or a Jewish, Mohammedan or Buddhist religious community. "Religious body", therefore, denotes a group of people understood to be a religious entity, with a definite structure, and publicly known by a definite title. Clearly there are not as many religions as there are religious bodies or denominations.

(b) *Denomination.* These are distinct Christian entities, whose titles, whether legally registered or not, express a communal belief, worship and discipline.

It is a term of broad connotation. A religious denomination may be either a Church, such as the Catholic Church and the Orthodox Churches, or simply a community such as the Unitarians, or an association such as the Synodal Conference of Missouri. It can also be a separated body to which the term sect cannot always be applied, for example, the Northern and Southern Baptist Conventions. Sometimes, however, a denomination possesses the true characteristics of a sect, for example, "The Disciples of

---

[5] Rouse and Neill, *op. cit.;* Caius Jackson Slosser, *Christian Unity: Its History and Challenge in All Communions and All Lands* (1929).
[6] *Religious Bodies, 1936. Selected Statistics for the United States by Denominations and Geographic Divisions,* published by the Dept. of Commerce, Washington, in 1941.

Christ" in relation to Presbyterianism or the Methodists in relation to the Church of England.

Primarily, therefore, the term suggests the idea of a special title expressing the character of some distinctive feature, or the essential nature, of some group. It is based upon an independence and autonomy in the spheres of doctrine, worship, discipline and administration, and in this there can be infinite variation. It does not necessarily denote a religious body which differs from others by distinctive notes from the dogmatic, structural and liturgical points of view. Several denominations may closely resemble each other and together form a single confessional family. Thus, for instance, there is not only one Methodist Church, but a Methodist family; not one Baptist Church, but a Baptist family; not one Lutheran Church but a number of Lutheran bodies. The members of these families retain their allegiance to their original source, but their mutual relationship are complex; these may be hostile, independent, autonomous, intimate, ecumenically minded etc.

Not all denominations have their own "creed". In principle, the oldest of them possess one, and the families that have issued from the major denominations do not. Consider, for example, the case of Methodism. The Anglican Church from which it originated has an authoritative expression of its belief, the Book of Common Prayer, but Methodism is far from possessing a formula of belief endowed with a similar authority, and the members of the Methodist family have, in their turn, divided up their common heritage.

The characteristics of an important denomination can generally be explained, but they have also often been the result of some particular event. In the latter case, the nature of the new denomination must be discerned by reference to the common history.

On account of its original meaning of "appellation" the term "denomination" implies no assertion of religious truth or falsehood. From this essentially statistical point of view, the Catholic Church is one denomination among others. It is true that sometimes the word is a synonym for a sect. But it is principally the expression of a common name and can be used to cover with equal validity either the great historical confessions or the sects that originated in the radical or anthropocentric movements produced by the Reformation.

It will be helpful to retain this characteristic of generality in the definition of "denomination", enabling it to be used to include many religious bodies, and this is the meaning it will be given in this book.

It seems that the word has a different meaning in the United States from that obtaining in England. In England, as a result of the position of the Established Church, any other body is considered to be a denomination, that is, basically, a "sect". In the United States, where the system of the established Church for a time hovered like a sinister shadow, the term "denomination" does not suggest the idea of a sect, or at least, if it does suggest it, then the implied meaning is in accordance with the derivation of the word sect from *sequi* (to follow) and not from *secare* (to separate), so that in America to belong to a denomination means to follow some religious conviction incorporated in a fellowship that is more or less distinct from others. It does not imply the idea of a dissenting religious body because, as already observed, America has never experienced a situation in which a Church has been established or Church and State have been united. The position has always been that of the equality of all religious bodies before the law.

(c) *Church*. If we keep to the biblical use of the term, the word 'Church' in the New Testament has only two meanings: the Church is the body organically one with Christ; the Church is the local manifestation of this one body. Those communities which have arisen from heresy and exist outside this one Church are not Churches, but sects. This, moreover, is the unanimous opinion of the Fathers.

Before the decree of the Second Vatican Council on ecumenism (21 November 1964) the official documents of the Catholic Church gave the title of Church to communions separated from her only in the case of the Eastern Orthodox Churches. For the Catholic Church a Church is only really such where there is an authentic Eucharist. The specific character of the Eucharist is to unite the Church, so that if there is no real Eucharist there cannot be substantially a Church. Nevertheless, Paul VI in his homily on Maundy Thursday, 1964, called the Anglican Communion a Church. But we do not deny the existence of vestiges of the Church as Church in those bodies originating at the Reformation in the sixteenth century, for wherever the Word calls and gathers men together the Church is manifested. It is for this reason that the decree on ecumenism (chapter iii, second part) calls those communions that originated at the Reformation ecclesial communities, or Churches, in order to stress that the Catholic Church considers that the mystery of the Church is present in these communions in an inchoative state that exists in the various denominations in differing degrees. For the substance to be present the genuine sacrament must be joined to the authentic Word. And for the Church to be fully realized, in addition there must be unity of communion; this postulates the link with the centre of visible unity (*cf.* Constitution on the Church *Lumen Gentium*, chapter III, and Decree on Ecumensim, chapter I).

In the non-Roman Christian world, however, the divisions of Christendom have given rise to three other notions of the Church which have a varying legitimacy. Thus the word Church is used to express (a) the territorial organization, for example, the Lutheran Church of Norway, or the

United Church of Canada; (b) the particular denomination or confession, for example, the Reformed Confession, as the designation of the Presbyterian Church in Scotland; (c) the international organization of a confession, for example "the Anglican Communion", the fraternal association of the Anglican Churches spread over five continents.[7]

The idea underlying these three notions is that no Christian communion can at present claim to be the Church. Every Christian communion can, however, legitimately call itself a Church, if it possesses the ecumenical consciousness of belonging to the one Catholic Church. "Only those bodies which have preserved the ecumenical consciousness of belonging to the one Catholic Church of which they form only a part, can lay claim to the name of Church".[8] Any denomination which put itself forward as the true and only Church, by that very fact cuts itself off from the true Catholic Church, even if it calls itself the Catholic Church, for the fact is that the true Church exists wherever there is communion in the Spirit of Christ. Any denomination which loses or repudiates this ecumenical consciousness of being a part of the Church of Christ and declares that it is itself that Church, thereby reduces itself to the level of a sect.[9]

This is a new concept of the Church: the one, universal and *invisible* Church is the only true Church. In a sense—through the local fragmentary expressions which represent it— it is also visible.

It follows that it is this term "Church" which offers the most difficulties; because it raises the problem of the relationship between the Church and the Churches. Is the Church a hidden universal reality? Or is it a reality that is already visible? Two different concepts confront each other: the Church as the communion of saints and the Church as an organic community that is simultaneously visible and invisible.

In Protestantism, the Church primarily signifies the communion of saints; in Catholicism its primary meaning is that of an organic communion, an embodied alliance between God and man, a visible, unique and universal reality.

It is in accordance with the idea of the Church that is prevalent among them that the Protestant denominations consider it lawful to call themselves Churches. All of them do so, as their official registration,[10] and their taking part in the National Council of the Churches of Christ in the United States or the World Council of Churches plainly shows. The most radical denomi-

[7] O. S. Tomkins, "Les Communautés territoriales et confessionnelles au sein de l'Église universelle" in *Rapport d'Amsterdam*, vol. I, p. 199.
[8] Mathew Spinka, "Christianity and the Churches" in O. Frederick Nolde, ed., *Toward Worldwide Christianity*, The Interseminary Series, vol. IV, p. 2 (1946).
[9] *Ibid.*
[10] *Yearbook of American Churches*, published by the National Council of the Churches of Christ in the U.S.A., New York, in 1965.

nations do not form part of these two councils; nonetheless they bear the title of Church, for example, the Church of the New Jerusalem (Sweden-borgians); the Unitarian Church; the Church of the Latter Day Saints (Mormons); the Catholic Apostolic Church (Irvingites).

The Protestant denominations, however, have not always been called Churches. The name seems to have become generalized about a century ago. This was due to the activity of Hugh Price Hughes (1847–1902), a Methodist leader in England. Previously the term had been reserved to the Established Church. Indirectly, the Catholic Church may have contributed to the spread of this practice. In England, only one Church, the Establishment, was recognized. No other religious body had the right to have churches, but only chapels. Numerically, and in relation to the Established Church, the Catholic Church had had the appearance of a sect of the same kind as those of the Free Churches. But when in 1850, the Catholic hierarchy was restored in England, the Catholic Church felt herself in a better position to call herself the Church. The Free Churches, beginning with the Methodists, followed suit. The Protestant denominations in the United States, without the handicap of an established Church, have found it natural to act in the same way. It has now become the normal practice. It has even crossed the frontiers of Christianity. There are Buddhist and even Jewish "Churches". In these two latter instances, it seems clear that this is a way of describing themselves in accordance with the thought forms of the West.

What then does the word Church ultimately imply? In the Protestant denominations it is frequently used in a sociological, juridical and adminis-trative, rather than a dogmatic sense, in order to designate a religious body, distinguished from other bodies by its history, its form of worship, its belief and its government. In this way it becomes practically equivalent to de-nomination, and it follows the latter's vague and unsettled contours.

The World Council of Churches has explained what sense of the word it accepts as the basis for its relationship and labour. "The term Church denotes the denominations that are composed of autonomous Churches established in some definite territory. Apart from an acceptance of the basic pronouncement of the World Council of Churches, necessary if a request for admission is to be taken into consideration, the following criteria will be applied: (i) *Autonomy:* to gain admission, a Church must give proof of its autonomy. It will be considered to be autonomous if, together with its acceptance of fellowship with other Churches and especially with those of its own confession, it depends upon no other Church for its own existence, that is, as regards the formation, ordination and upkeep of its ministers, its recruitment, the function of its laity, its preaching, its inter-ecclesiastical relationships, the use it makes of its resources, whatever their origin. (ii) *Stability:* a Church can be admitted only if it provides evidence of a stability acceptable to its fellow-Churches and has a programme for corporate development and evangelization. (iii) *Numerical importance:* the question of the numerical importance of a candidate Church will also be taken into account. (iv) *Relationships with other Churches:* when a Church is seeking admission, the quality of the relationships it maintains with the other Churches will be examined.[11]

(d) *Confession.* Are the terms "church", "denomination", "confession", synonymous? They are sometimes used in this way. For example, if I say: "I belong to the Presbyterian, Anglican or Reformed Confession", this means that I belong to the corresponding denomination or Church. In this case a Confession signifies a religious organization, which, like a Church, a denomination or a communion, is recognized by some distinctive profession of faith.

In a more exact sense, it refers to a formulary of faith, a normative body of doctrine, which expresses the belief of a given denomination or Church. The title of the book *The Creeds of Christendom* by Philip Schaff[12] does not refer to the great creeds of the Church of early centuries, such as the Apostles' Creed or the Nicene Creed, etc., but to the different interpretations given to Christianity, codified in a body of doctrine considered as the norm of faith and of the public expression of faith, in the Churches and denominations of Christendom.

When, therefore, a Church or denomination is designated by the term "confession", it is with reference to a given interpretation of revelation considered as normative and regulative of the belief of a given Church or denomination. But not every denomination has its own profession of faith. In England, the Reformation movement drew up a profession of this kind, and became incorporated in a Church with clearly defined characteristics. Methodism, on the other hand, produced no "creed" in any precise sense. The twenty-five articles drawn up by Wesley (The Methodist Articles on Religion, 1784) are more in the nature of a spiritual guide than of a normative synthesis of a particular interpretation of Christianity. In their turn, the sects that originated in Methodism also did not produce any official and organized "creed". Their doctrinal character is essentially directed towards social activity. We cannot, therefore, speak with accuracy of a Methodist confession.

Lutheranism was given its own definite credal expression by Luther and Melanchthon, although it did not become a single Church. In matters of ecclesiastical organization and liturgy it adopted a great many forms. But all Lutherans of every Lutheran Church or communion, whether "established" or not, give their allegiance to the Lutheran confession: Luther's

---

[11] *Rapport d'Amsterdam,* vol. V, pp. 265–6.
[12] First published in 1877; 6th edition, 3 volumes, 1931.

catechism, 1529; the Confession of Augsburg, 1530; the Formula of Concord, 1577; the Visitation Articles of Saxony, 1592.

Calvinism also did not become a single Church. Membership is of the Reformed Church, but not of the Calvinist Church. Calvinism is a theology, not a Church. A number of different reformed, evangelical Churches exist in Switzerland, Germany, France, Belgium, Holland, Scotland, Italy and the United States. Congregationalism, a near relation of Presbyterianism, follows in the wake of Calvinism, and like Presbyterianism, has drawn up various confessions of faith.

The group of Free Churches—Methodist, Baptist, Quaker, Congregationalist—is of special interest. These sects had their origin in England, either as products of tendencies within the Established Church or in opposition to it. Each of them has its own confession.

The modern ecumenical movement by leading to the formation of new groupings has occasionally given rise to new confessions of faith. This can be seen in the case of those organic unions between denominations that have sprung from dissimilar trends, for example, the United Church of Canada (1925); the Congregationalist Churches and the Christian Churches (1929). But there are other instances of a similar kind that have produced no new "creed", for example, the Church of South India (1947).

Lastly, when denominations that are already related, unite, a common declaration of faith suffices and this is frequently not a new confession.

We must take note of a considerable difference that exists between the two major types of Protestantism: the classical and the radical types. Philip Schaff points out that, with the Presbyterian declaration of Westminster (Confession 1646; Catechism 1647), the era of the production of "creeds" ended.[13] This classical type of the reformed faith differs widely from the radical type. The latter, as expressed in its anabaptist, anti-trinitarian and the purely spiritual forms, produced no great confession of faith. Even the group of the Free Churches, closely connected with this type, does not have the same theological depth and scope. The classical denominations spoke of "creeds", as the means of expressing their faith. The new ones prefer the words "covenant" (Congregationalists); "confession" (Baptists); "mystical" spiritual expression (Quakers). The declarations of faith made by these denominations—with the exception of the Savoy declaration (1658) and the Baptist confession (1688) which contain the substance of the Westminster Confession—are limited in scope and characterized by generalization, in contrast to the older confessions that came out of the great theological controversies of the sixteenth century. They contain much less theology and leave a wider margin for individual judgement.

---

[13] *Ibid.*, vol. I, p. 187.

(e) *Communion*. Whereas the term "denomination" signifies the special title and characteristics of a religious body, the term "confession" its interpretation of the Christian faith, the term "Church" its organic aspect, "communion" primarily expresses the aspect of the connection, the bond, the spiritual community existing between the members themselves and with the body as a whole. If we refer the term to the Eucharist its meaning is evident. A communion is a religious fellowship, a fraternal association of Christians who take part in a common Christian reality and share a common life of faith, thought, feeling, concerns and activity.

The term may be used in order to designate a body of greater or less extent. Thus we speak of the Anglican Communion as the designation of those Churches throughout the world that are regulated by the Anglican system and mutually affiliated under the nominal direction of the Archbishop of Canterbury.

Communion is obviously connected with union. Religious bodies that are more completely unified feel more at home in using the term than do those whose unity is uncertain.

Today we are witnessing its gradual restoration to a position of repute, doubtless due to the renewed appreciation of the Eucharist in a number of Protestant denominations. It may also be due to a feeling that the word "church" as the designation of every denomination seems excessive. "Communion" has the advantage of expressing the bond of unity between the members of a denomination without giving the impression that every denomination intends to play the part which belongs to the Church.

(f) *Sect*. This term designates a group of people who in the sphere of faith or in the field of action, or even in both, are distinct from some other group of like nature. The adherents of a sect have their own special way of understanding some central point of Christianity and this makes them dissenters with respect to a religious body admittedly endowed with doctrinal or historical authority.

There can, of course, be different interpretations, opinions, and even parties, according to people's attitude of opposition to or sympathy with a given doctrine, practice or person, without thereby endangering the essential and organic unity of a denomination. A sect only comes into existence when a group attaches itself to a leader whom it follows into dissent, both with regard to communion and to doctrine. Two factors contribute to the formation of a sect: one of them is related to the unity of communion from which the group has withdrawn, and the other to the unity of doctrine out of which a choice is made that substantially modifies it, or introduces a serious alteration in its structural integrity.

It seems, however, that the word sect does not mean exactly the same thing in Europe as it does in the United States. In the latter, where, save for brief attempts in certain States, there has never been an established Church, the word sect is normally derived from *secare* and not from *sequi*.[14] The idea is that of a Christendom cut in sections which are democratically equal, and it may be the case that a group which began as a sect succeeds in winning its patent of nobility and attains the rank of a Church.

In Europe, on the other hand, the word sect is considered to be derived from *sequi,* as in fact it is. The first Christians who followed Jesus were described as a sect (Acts 24:5; 28:22). Once the infant Church had acquired autonomy, the situation demanded special supervision by the Apostles in order to avert dissension (2 Pet 2:1; Gal 5:20; 1 Cor 2:19). We can best obtain an idea of the meaning of a sect from the history of early Christianity. In heretical Gnosticism, for example, in Montanism and Millenarianism, we can observe the emergence of features that became permanent characteristics. First, we note the resolve to appeal from a moribund orthodoxy, or from one regarded as such, to an idea of the Gospel held to be purer. The protesting group, always few in number, rather than agree to remain as the leaven in the lump, increasingly breaks away from the community of believers in the name of a mission which it sees as loftier than that upheld by the body as a whole. Secondly, it displays a tendency to add to those elements accepted by the community others concerning organization, teaching, recruitment, spirituality, and the observance of religious and penitential practices. In each of these matters, the sect tries to show that its own position is in accordance with scripture, and it does this with fanatical energy. Thirdly, it endeavours to show itself visibly and tangibly as a congregation of those who have truly been regenerated. In addition, other minor characteristics may be present: a restless and excessive proselytizing zeal, a systematic rejection of certain civic obligations on the grounds of fidelity to the Gospel.[15]

When the Reformation was established on the continent of Europe, it was described as a sect. This was the name given to the Lutherans at the Diet of Augsburg held under Charles V in 1530. But in 1555, in the treaty of religious peace of Augsburg, the "adherents of the Confession of Augsburg" were allowed the status of Church on the same footing as the Roman Catholic Church. Calvinists, Anabaptists and Socianians, however, were not included in this privilege. It was only at the conclusion of the Thirty Years' War, in 1648, that these reformed bodies were accepted as Churches. In England, the Church became the Established Church without any question of its first being a sect.

When the dissenters appeared in England—Presbyterians and Congre-

[14] H. H. Lyon, *A Study of the Sects* (1891); H. C. McComas, *Psychology of Religious Sects* (1912); Charles W. Ferguson, *The Confusion of Tongues* (1929); Clark, *op. cit.*
[15] Cf. Neve, *op. cit.,* pp. 32—35.

gationalists first and then Quakers, Baptists and Methodists—they were first called Non-conformists, a polite word to avoid calling them sectarians, while on the continent the Mennonites and Moravians, arriving after the early denominations which had graduated to the title of Church, were regarded as sects. New sects periodically appeared, several of which in due course became "Churches". They first appear as a challenge to the older denominations. Some of them manage to continue; many vanish. But those which reach the rank of Church can only do so after they have to some extent acquired the customs, style and institutions of a Church. Consider, for example, the difference between Baptists and Jehovah's Witnesses. The latter are definitely a sect, but the Baptists describe themselves as a Church, although when they were first established in England they were regarded as a sect.

The question of the distinction between Church and sect is difficult and delicate. A denomination will feel insulted if it is allowed to believe that it is not considered to be a Church. But can there really be several Churches? Where is the dividing line between Church and sect? Is the frontier changeable and subjective? Consider the case of Luther and Calvin. They had no intention of founding a new Church, but only of reforming the old Church. At first their movement assumed the characteristics of a sect. But it was not long before their adherents formed themselves into a Church.

Consider also a book like *The Nature of the Church*,[16] an inquiry in preparation for the Lund Conference in 1952. Is it not surprising to find that along with the great historic Churches, like the Catholic and Orthodox Churches, or Protestant denominations of the classical type, there are other denominations, for long considered in the Protestant world as sects, but which now, having acquired the name of Church, are bent on discussing the nature of the Church?

The ecumenical problem is precisely due to this extraordinary anomaly: the Church and the Churches. Can there be several Churches? When is an individual Church an authentic representative of the universal Church? What judgement must be passed on the prevailing habit in contemporary Protestantism of most denominations calling themselves Churches and acting as such?

(g) *Conference*. This term in its religious sense can have two meanings:

In the first place, it designates the internal organization of a denomination. In Congregationalism, a conference is a local organization representing the Churches of a district; in Methodism, it denotes one or more orders, meetings of ministers and laity: the annual, general and district conferences. In the Anglican Communion it denotes the meeting of bishops,

---

[16] Cited above in chapter i, footnote 35.

invited by the Archbishop of Canterbury, in order to discuss subjects of common interest. It is held about once every ten years in Lambeth Palace. The Lambeth Conference is neither a synod nor a council. It has no canonical existence and is based on no constitution. But it is a fact.

Secondly, conference may acquire a wider meaning and become the equivalent of denomination. For instance, the "Synodal Conference of North America" (Missouri Synod) is the name given to a Lutheran association formed in 1872 in the United States which is an expression of a strict interpretation of Lutheranism.

(h) *Movement or trend.* A movement or trend is neither a Church, a denomination, a sect, a conference nor a communion. It is a series of actions, events, dispositions, in the doctrinal or moral order, that are all directed to some end. Christianity was a movement before it became a Church. The Reformation was a movement in England, Germany, Switzerland, Scandinavia, before it separated out into various trends from which the denominations emerged.

A movement does not always result in an institution in the form of a Church. The Calvinist reform did not give rise to a Calvinist Church. The Reformation was a movement in which Calvin and other reformers played their part: there are Presbyterian Churches and Reformed Churches. Similarly, in England, the Independent movement led to Congregationalism, and the eighteenth-century revivalist movement to Methodism. The Anabaptist movement in Germany and Switzerland did not find expression in an Anabaptist Church, but in a number of sects: Mennonites, Baptists, Quakers. The movement towards union in Protestantism has not yet led to a united world Protestant Church, but only to various unions between denominations.

2. Trends and movements at the Reformation from which denominations, Churches, sects, confessions etc. originated

If we see Luther as the sum total of Protestantism and the Reformation, we unduly simplify matters, both doctrinally and historically. Luther is the great champion of the Protestant tradition; he is neither its source, nor the complete expression of its numerous aspects. By taking no account of this primary fact we run the risk of making no progress at all in ecumenism. Before Luther, there were Wycliffe and John Huss. Contemporary with him, and more or less in sympathy with his views, were a number of other reformers, some of them not too startling, but all having a decisive influence on the direction taken by the Reformation: Melanchthon who to some extent altered Luther's own outlook; Bucer who had a direct influence on Calvin and the English Reformation. The Reformation was not the work of any one man, nor was it the result of a single line of thought or a single tradition, and a mere synthesis of Luther's doctrine leaves much unaccounted for; it is a most extensive and complex phenomenon. It existed in too many countries for it to be attributable to one or two leaders only. It created a general explosion because it had a general cause. It spread to many places, not as proceeding from a single centre, but as the result of an explosion provoked by the same reasons. The men who were the leaders of a common movement were first borne along and raised up by it. To begin with, they felt and experienced an obscure and confused yearning for reformation in the Church. Their genius, temperament, mutual relationships, circumstances and the mystery of their free will did the rest. They became the leaders of a movement which they succeeded in moulding according to their personal character, the bent of their experience and their environment.

The word Reformation is thus an abstract word that covers a number of different types of reform, each of which is conscious of its relationship with the others, without any desire to be identified with them. There are the classical types of reform: Lutheran, Calvinist, Anglican. There are also the radical types—puritan or non-conformist—such as the Congregationalists, Baptists, Methodists; and there are the humanitarian or anthropocentric types, such as the Unitarian, Adventist, Christian-Scientist, etc.

3. Ecumenical survey of the principal trends and movements [17]

(a) *Lutheranism and Calvinism.* Lutheranism and Calvinism will be considered here as spiritual trends and they will be considered comparatively. There can be no question of giving an account of their origin and history. Too many excellent studies exist for there to be any need to go over the work again. In any case one would be hard put to it to select one of them in preference to another. There are countless books on Luther and Calvin and the subject is far from being exhausted, especially as a consequence of the inevitable readjustment called for by the ecumenical movement. Moreover, owing to the fact that the angle of approach in the present inquiry is principally that of the incidence of the various spiritual trends

[17] Two special chapters, chapter x, "The Place of the Eastern Churches in the Una Sancta" and chapter xi, "Israel and the Reunion of Christians" complete this ecumenical sketch. Solely the necessity of introducing gradually all the essential aspects of the problem has governed the present mode of presentation. In addition, it hardly seems necessary to repeat that this book is not a history of the ecumenical movement, but a definition of various constituent aspects of the ecumenical problem, valid, with the necessary adaptations, for all, whether they be Catholics, Orthodox, Anglicans, Protestants or Jews.

upon ecumenical problems, attention will be concentrated on the weight, the tendencies, and the characteristics of the forces confronting each other.

Three decisive factors must be underlined. First, the separate stages that contributed to the formation of Lutheranism and Calvinism. In both cases, we encounter a system of thought, reconsidered, rethought, constantly corrected. Luther and Calvin, originally Catholics, developed towards the outlook of the Reformation by degrees and only gradually became Protestant. It was not until the days of their maturity that their ideas assumed a final form. The Reformation certainly had its forerunners, but in itself it was something profoundly original and new. It was so extensive an achievement that it covered the whole area of Catholicism itself and of necessity had to be completed piece by piece, according as the facts, life, circumstances and needs took shape and raised questions which the reformers had to tackle. It was not a system worked out in the calm of some quiet retreat, but a body of ideas that emerged in the throes of a long conflict and in the course of a heart-searching protest. It contains reconsiderations, repetitions, contradictions, improvisations. It was a quite definite, but uncompleted body of ideas, a dialectic in tension, in movement. Once Luther and Calvin had died, however, this interpretation of Christianity, together with its defects and its virtues, its certitudes and off hand opinions, was canonized and became the norm of orthodoxy for all who wanted to make this heritage their own. To be a Lutheran, Luther must be followed; to be a Calvinist, Calvin must be followed. The Protestant denominations exchanged criticisms of their respective founders, but each of them held its own to be, so to say, infallible.

Although the creative intuition of the Reformation appeared during the time when Luther and Calvin were still outwardly members of the Catholic Church, it only disclosed itself gradually. It follows from this that there are two ways of obtaining an understanding of these two spiritual trends. These two ways are complementary. The first is to try to grasp the intuition which contains the synthesis of all the elements involved. The second is to make an analysis of the various stages of their development. In this latter case, three stages need to be clearly distinguished: first, Luther's and Calvin's transference from Catholicism to Lutheranism or Calvinism, that is, the growth of their ideas until the time when these became a distinct body of thought; secondly, the development of Lutheranism or Calvinism towards Protestantism, that is, the open declaration of dissent from the accepted idea of the nature of Christianity; and thirdly, the attainment of Lutheran or Calvinist orthodoxy, that is, the systematic and normative establishment of the new belief with its own confession and credal books and the setting up of a distinct Church.

The ideas with which the Reformers began must not be confused with those with which they ended. What they had in mind in their early days was not a different Church but the same Church with a difference, the foundation of a reformed but not a new Church. This distinction between the different stages is of the greatest importance if we are to appreciate the present positions and attitudes existing in the Lutheran and Calvinist world. The characteristic features of the phases in the development of Luther's and Calvin's thought reappear in the doctrine and thought of their heirs, so that we can say that there now exist as many trends as there were phases in the development of the reformers' thought. It would not be difficult to attach to these tendencies the names of Lutheran and Calvinist pastors, theologians, and even religious communities who belonged to this or that period of the life and thought of Luther and Calvin: either more or less close to Catholicism or to the establishment of a separate Church. Therefore, there are several different modes of being a Lutheran, Calvinist or member of the reformed Church. It was necessary to say this to dispel the illusion cherished by some Catholics who imagine that reunion has been achieved whenever a Lutheran or Calvinist follows the teaching of Luther or Calvin of a period when either of these was closer to Catholicism and also to calm the fears of those extreme Lutherans or Calvinists who cannot believe that it is possible to be a Lutheran or Calvinist in any other way than their own.

The second feature to be noted is that of the complicated origin of the Lutheran and Calvinist traditions. Although Luther and Calvin occupy a predominant position in the Lutheran and Calvinist traditions, they were not their sole authors. Luther was much indebted to his collaborators, notably to Melanchthon. In the Calvinist tradition a debt of this kind is even more evident. Calvin is its greatest name, but together with him we find Farel, Bucer, Zwingli, Oecolampadius, Bullinger, Beza, Cranmer and Knox. The position of Calvinism can best be described by saying that by using the name of "reformed" it desired to be clearly distinguished from Lutheranism by the fact that it went further in the reformation of the Church, and in a definitely Puritan direction. Theologically, one may be a Calvinist; institutionally, one is a member of the Reformed Church. But one is a Lutheran because one belongs to the Lutheran Church. The Calvinist reformed tradition took different forms according to its development in Switzerland, Geneva, France, Scotland, Holland and the United States. It is not exactly the same thing to be a Calvinist, a Presbyterian, or a Remonstrant, but to be any one of these is to be not a Lutheran, but a member of the Reformed Church. If a comparison be made between three reformed confessions—the Gallican confession of faith, drawn up by Calvin and his disciple De Chandieu, in 1559; the Scottish confessions of faith of 1560 and 1580; the Belgian confession of faith composed by Guy de Brès in 1561, for the Reformed Churches in Flanders and Holland—the concern for adaptation to different peoples with different temperaments at once becomes evident.

The Lutheran world, also, includes perceptible differences. In Germany itself Lutheranism displays a significant variety of structural and liturgical forms. Comparison of German Lutheranism with that of Sweden, Norway and Finland shows this to be truer still. In the Scandinavian countries the outward forms are Catholic; their content is Lutheran.

The third point concerns the respective importance of Lutheranism and the reformed tradition.

There is no question here of determining whether Luther or Calvin was the most original and most powerful religious thinker. What is at issue is to set out the historical development.

Lutheranism, at first in the vanguard of the Reformation, was soon, and decisively, overtaken by Calvinism. Today, in spite of the importance of Lutheranism, evidenced by the Lutheran World Federation with its seat alongside the World Council of Churches, the dominant inspiration in the Protestant world is still not that of Lutheranism, but of the Reformed Church. This can be gathered from the subjects studied by the department of Faith and Order. One of its leading ideas is that of an inquiry into the nature of our Lord's sovereign rule, a specifically Calvinist predilection. The dynamic notion of the Church's mission in the world is also Calvinist, not Lutheran, in character.

This supremacy of the Reformed tradition in Protestantism is due to several causes. Firstly, there is its power of assimilation and its international relations. In its initial phase Calvinism was the spiritual offspring of Lutheranism, but it very soon acquired a personality of its own. In early Protestantism it quickly became the rallying point and the focus for the integration of the manifold trends of the Reformation. Through Bucer it assimilated something of the inspiration of the Anabaptist movement, that is, practical social development in the local congregation. It made a sympathetic approach to Zwingli in the question of liturgy. It tried to come to an agreement with Anglicanism by concessions in issues of secondary importance. Later, it exhibited receptivity to the influence of Pietism and Methodism, but it did not fail to influence them in return. It was not content merely to accept some of the elements of Lutheranism; it reacted and caused Lutheranism to share to some extent in its own life and in Christian social activity. It also exercised a decisive influence on American life, on the National Council of the Churches of Christ in the United States, and *ipso facto* on the denominations which compose it. Right from the beginning, Calvinism developed in every direction: Germany, Switzerland, the Low Countries, France and England. Calvin had only one desire: to unite all the branches of the Reformation in a single Protestant body. The resistance of German Lutheranism and the independent attitude of Anglicanism prevented this happening. Calvinism, which began as a spiritual movement and not as a Church, was obliged to become a Church. The Calvinist inspiration became embodied in various national religious structures.

The appearance of the contemporay ecumenical movement is to a very large extent a revival of Calvin's ecumenical spirit. From the point of view of the history of civilizations, it may be said that Calvinism has done more to mould Protestant man than any other denomination derived from the Reformation.

It was the very essence of Calvinism that made it the most dynamic factor in the Reformation, surpassing Lutheranism. By nature it is active, powerful, constantly expanding, open to international contacts. It has resources in plenty for forming it into religious bodies which, while being each very distinctive, yet share in a spiritual nature common to them all. Its driving energy impels it to penetrate the world of politics and economics, to influence national and international life, spheres which early Lutheranism had abandoned to the secular power, putting its trust in the Christianity of princes. It is not surprising, therefore, that on the threshold of the modern world, Calvinism undertook what Lutheranism, with its individ-ualist and introverted nature, felt powerless to attempt and what Cathol-icism in a state of paralysis could not comprehend and did not know how to set about: this was to give the new Western world the Christian inspi-ration for a new era. In the absence of a serious body of Catholic thought able to direct the political, economic and social issues of the coming world, one man opted for Christianity and that man was Calvin. His decision, together with that of the political, social and economic forces, contributed to endow Western man with characteristics which would not have come into being had Calvin never existed. This is why reunion has implications of such importance: the history of civilization itself and the character of a special human type are involved in it equally with the Christian religion.

(b) *Anglicanism.* The English Reformation is to be understood not by approaching it from the continent, but from England. It has its own char-acteristics, its own logic and its own destiny.[18]

The judgement passed by a Church on itself is not necessarily one which

[18] Paul Elmer More and F. L. Cross, compilers and ed., *Anglicanism: The Thought and Practice of the Church of England, Illustrated from the Religious Literature of the Seventeenth Century* (1st ed., 1935; 2nd ed., 1951); Cyril Garbett, *The Claims of the Church of England* (1947); E. R. Morgan and Roger Lloyd, ed., *The Mission of the Anglican Communion* (1948); Leonard Elliot Binns, *The Early Evangelicals: a Religious and Social Study* (1953); S. C. Carpenter, *The Church in England, 597—1688* (1954); Philip Hughes, *The Reformation in England* (3 vols., 1950–4); H. A. Hodges, *Anglicanism and Ortho-doxy, A Study in Dialectical Churchmanship* (1955); David M. Paton, ed., *Essays in Anglican Self-Criticism* (1958).

God or the other Churches will ratify. But in the ecumenical dialogue courtesy demands that every person being questioned must be allowed the occasion to explain himself. This, in any case, is only common sense. If two persons are to be brought together, is it not essential to begin from the original position of each of them?

An accurate assessment of everything said and done by the Church of England since its break with Rome would show that in its view the true Catholic Church in England is not the Roman Catholic Church, but the Church of England. Christianity came from the apostles. It spread to England through the activity of monks who came from Rome. An English Catholic Church, the "Ecclesia Anglicana" as it is called in Magna Carta (1215), came into being and formed part of the universal Church. In the sixteenth century it became obvious that reformation was needed. The Anglican Church was reformed but it did not cease to be Catholic. "The Churches of the Anglican Communion are Catholic as understood by the English Reformation. They are Catholic, but reformed; they are reformed, but Catholic." [19]

We are thus asked to understand that the Churches of the Anglican Communion do not form a sect, and did not originate in the sixteenth century. They are genuine parts of the universal Church, and in all essentials go back to the Church of the apostles.[20] The Anglican Church is the Catholic Church reformed. These two attributes, "Catholic" and "reformed", applied to it, must be correctly understood. "Reformed", in this case, means the Reformation as understood in England. The English Reformation, unlike that of the continent, did not develop on the basis of a theological intuition which was later extended to the whole Christian order, but on a point of view that was primarily a concrete and practical one.

The English Reformers had no idea of establishing a different Church, but a Church that was different. This explains why in the Churches of the Anglican Communion tradition occupies so important a position alongside the great creeds, the episcopal constitution, the sacraments, the liturgy, the testimony of the saints and the consensus of the laity (consensus fidelium). The official formularies—the Thirty-Nine Articles, the Book of Common Prayer, the Ordinal and the ecclesiastical canons—must be seen as belonging to this whole body of tradition. They should not be considered as a compact body of doctrine, the source of all later Anglican teaching. They are the reflection of various influences, but they are not the complete expression of the thought, belief and doctrine of the Anglican Communion.

The concrete question that faced the Catholic Church in England in the

---

[19] *The Lambeth Conference*, 1948, p. 83.
[20] *Ibid.*, p. 78.

sixteenth century was not whether, but how, the Church must be reformed. Scripture was regarded as the primary norm to be referred to. Some of the reformers accepted the interpretation given to it by the Fathers and early bishops; others read it through the eyes of the continental reformers. The Anglican preoccupation with incorporating, as a Church and simultaneously, both Catholic and Protestant elements, dates from this time. The report on the unity of the Church at the Lambeth Conference of 1948 roundly declares that Anglicanism incorporates a harmony of Catholic and Protestant factors which is not found in any other communion.[21] Have we really grasped the spirit of Anglicanism if we describe it as a doctrinal compromise between Lutheran, Catholic and Calvinist elements, an eclectic formula of reform? This way of interpreting the *via media,* the middle way, which, since the Elizabethan settlement, it has made its own, as a rejection both of Rome and Geneva, is too negative and does not do justice to Anglicanism's own idea of itself. It sees itself as a reform within Catholicism, most anxious to preserve the traditional Catholic heritage, but open to the "protest" made by the continental Reformation. In short, it claims to hold the Catholic faith in its entirety, but "shorn of the deformities, exaggerations, and excessive definitions of both the Protestant left and the extreme right of Tridentine Catholicism".[22]

It is this that explains why Anglicanism, although incorporating a number of Protestant features, cannot be assimilated either to the continental Reformation or to English Protestantism. The English Reformation, especially in its early days, was tempted by Puritanism: for a century and a half, from Henry VIII to James II, it was stirred to the depths by conflicts between the Catholic and Protestant parties, but in the end it achieved stability and became the orthodoxy of the *via media.* For this reason, in this book Anglicanism and Protestantism, whether English or not, will be distinguished from each other.

But a difficulty springs to mind: how can a Church, qua Church, incorporate Catholic and Protestant elements simultaneously? In Anglicanism this was attempted by "comprehensiveness", that is, by trying to unite all the Christians of a nation within a single Church. This was certainly no easy ideal to attain. A number of means were employed: a calculated absence of precision in definitions, combined with breadth of outlook; constraint but also toleration; unity over a wide field, but also the tension of internal dialectic; explicit standpoints but also confidence in what remains implicit.

History, however, is meant to help; it must not be allowed to become a handicap. In this inquiry we have had the development of forms and

---

[21] *Ibid.*
[22] Stephen C. Neill, *Anglicanism* (1958), p. 119.

facts constantly in mind. The light thrown by the past on the present must not be neglected, but when everything has been said and pondered, when justice has been done to long-standing grievances, one question, and that the most important, still remains: what is to be done about reunion?

Perusal of the reports of the Lambeth Conferences since 1865 enables us to follow the course of the development of the Anglican Communion. Anglicanism has distilled its own experience and become universal. The word "Anglican", in its widest sense, is no longer restricted to its original meaning as simply denoting the Church of England. Several Churches of the Anglican Communion, for example, those of China, Japan and India, do not even bear its name. The fact that the Church of England is still united to the State, that the Anglican Communion is called "Anglican", and that the formula which unites them orignated and was fashioned in England, is seen today as entirely accidental in relation to the essence of Anglicanism. The local connotation of the word "Anglican" has vanished; its present meaning is ecclesiastical and doctrinal. The factor that has been transmitted from the Church of England to the other Churches of the Anglican Communion is the principle of ecclesiastical organization on a territorial basis, that is, ecclesiastical self-government, each Church being on an equal footing with the others; the principle that the Church is incarnated in the human reality of each nation; the principle of a Church both Catholic and reformed, reformed and Catholic; and the principle of belonging to the universal Church.[23]

Today the Anglican Communion appears as a fraternal association of Churches of a special type, historically and spiritually united, called by God to serve the nations. Autonomous, but independent, influencing each other, buth each having its own national mode of expression, they are united by the bonds of a common faith, structure, loyalty to our Lord, and evangelizing activity. "The Anglican Communion is like a river with many branches, each of which is coloured by the earth through which it flows, and yet gives the best of itself to the main stream which is on the way to the ocean, symbol of the greatest of all encounters, wherein the Anglican Communion would be able to become once more a part of reunited Christendom."[24]

Together with the major movements of Lutheranism, Calvinism and Anglicanism, there have been from the start three other movements, not to be confused with them. These are Anabaptism, the sects of 'the religion of the spirit', and the Antitrinitarian sects.[25] Poorer in doctrine, historically

[23] *The Lambeth Conferences (1867–1948)* (1948), pp. 173–4.
[24] *The Lambeth Conference, 1948,* p. 83; John William Charles Wand, *The Anglican Communion: A Survey* (1948).
[25] Cf. Fritz Blanke in Guy F. Hersberger, ed., *The Recovery of the Anabaptist Vision* (1957).

less striking in their activity than the major movements, they have nonetheless played an important part in the formation of the general Protestant tradition. From the outset they gave rise to several sects, some of which still exist, after undergoing considerable changes. Mention can be made of the Mennonites, for instance, who began as Anabaptists; the Schwenkfeldians (originating in the "sects of the spirit"); and others, more or less connected with them, for example the Unitarians (connected with the Antitrinitarians).

Immigration has not lessened their numbers, and they largely account for the host of denominations in the United States. If numbers were an infallible criterion, some of these denominations would reduce the "classical" denominations to the rank of sects. In the United States, for instance, Baptists are more numerous than the Lutherans, Calvinists, Anglicans and the Orthodox Churches.

In spite of their limited numbers, some sects, Unitarianism for example, have exercised a decisive and enduring influence on the second period of American culture. The present methods of American education would be incomprehensible without Emerson.

These three trends, to which may be added the Independent and Adventist movements, have exercised considerable influence on classical Protestantism. Their presence has compelled recognition to the point that without taking them into account no accurate idea of the Protestant tradition can be obtained and no assessment made of the forces that confront each other in the field of ecumenism.[26]

The nature of the denominations originating in these trends complicates the task of ecumenism. Their requirements, their traditions, have impressed themselves on the other denominations which have had to give way on certain points for the sake of mutual encounter and collaboration. The future of interdenominational relationships cannot depend upon the decision of classical type Protestant communions alone; the radical denominations are making their voices heard with equal power.

(c) *Anabaptism.* Anabaptism[27] may be divided into the movement of the Swiss Brethren, the Hutterite Brethren in Moravia, the Melchiorites and Mennonites.[28]

---

[26] C. Dillenberger and C. Welch, *Protestant Christianity* (1955).

[27] Fritz Blanke, "The First Anabaptist Congregation, Zolligen, 1525", *M.Q.R.*, XXVII (January 1953), p. 33; R. J. Smithson, *The Anabaptists* (1935); Robert Friedmann, "Anabaptism and Protestantism", *M.Q.R.*, XXIV (January 1950), pp. 18–19; Hersberger, *op. cit.*

[28] C. Krahn, *Menno Simons, 1496–1561 (1936)*; C. Henry Smith, *The Story of the Mennonites* (3rd edition, revised and enlarged by Cornelius Krahn, 1950).

The essence of Anabaptism lies in its idea of the Church. "The real debate between Anabaptist and the other contemporary reformers lay in deciding what type of Church should replace the existing one."[29] Indeed, while the reformers only wanted to reform the existing Church in accordance with the Bible, the radicals wished to construct a new Church out of the Bible. It can be said that it is in this way that the classical or conservative type of reformers may be differentiated from the radical reformers. Although the Catholic Church regards every form of dissent due to heresy as a sect, nonetheless a distinction must be made between those reformers who desired to reform the Church in a way that would lead to a different, but not a new Church, and those who deliberately set out to create a new Church. In other words, the tendency to become a sect is a phenomenon that normally belongs to radical Protestantism. The tendency to remain in the Church as reformed corresponds to the aim of classical Protestantism. This is the dividing line effecting a major distinction within Protestantism. This is the basis for any understanding of the complex developments and especially for avoiding confusion of the various trends into one indeterminate and unrecognizable amalgam.

(d) *The sects of the "religion of the spirit"*. There are four principal representatives for this trend: Andrew Carlstadt, Thomas Münzer, Sebastian Franck and Kaspar Schwenkfeld. It is rooted in the mysticism of the end of the Middle Ages.

What is the difference between classical Protestantism and these "spiritual" sects? The latter are characterized by their opposition to fixed dogmas in the name of personal experience, and by their obsession with eschatology.

How is this difference to be explained? Münzer and Carlstadt were originators, reformers of a practical turn of mind. The great creative theologian who took up and recast the leading ideas of the "spiritual" movement was Kasper Schwenkfeld.

In comparison with the "spirituals", Luther, Zwingli, Melanchthon, Oecolampadius, Calvin, Beza, Bucer, Cranmer and Knox were all conservative. They did not question the fact that God had revealed himself through the scriptures. But while they were developing this line of approach, a different theology was in the making. This may be called the theology of the "inner light"—whence the term "spiritual". It refused to accept scripture as such, that is as the written Word of God. The Bible is no more than the empty letter. The Spirit must be its Master, its teacher, the one who reveals its meaning. The Bible only becomes the "Word" if man can read it with a certain "spiritual" preparation. In short, the "Word" was considered as having its existence *within man:* the emphasis was put on per-

[29] Smithson, *op. cit.*, pp. 14–15.

sonal experience. Christ's sufferings, for example, as recorded in the Gospel, can only help man on condition that when he suffers he does so in the spirit of Christ. The sacraments are regarded as empty ceremonies, at the most capable of symbolizing baptism by the Spirit in the case of baptism, or inner communion with Christ in the case of the Eucharist. In addition, the doctrine of original sin must be discarded because it tends to enfeeble human effort. The true Church is in the realm of the Spirit. The outward forms of the Church, its corporate worship, the functions of its ministers, must all be put aside. Infant baptism was regarded as a magical rite too closely resembling the practice of the Roman Church.

The "spiritual" and Anabaptist trends are at one on many points, and some authors include them both under the heading of Anabaptism.[30] But Fritz Blanke, professor of history in the University of Zurich, considers that they should be distinguished.[31] At all events, the fact remains that these two trends inaugurated a new reformed tradition in Protestantism, independent of the tradition of classical Protestantism. It is to this new tradition that the Free Churches belong. The theory of the Church as the product of a free association or of the Church as the "religion" of the Spirit also originated in it, and it forms the basis of the Baptist, Congregational and even more completely the Quaker denominations.

In the Protestant world much confusion has resulted from the clash of these two traditions. The Lutheran, Reformed and Anglican traditions have regarded the "spiritual" tradition as a manifestation of anarchy. But the other tradition maintained that it is only taking the Reformation to its logical conclusion. Even today when, as a result of the ecumenical movement, the "classical" denominations have restored some of the "Catholic" elements retained by the first Reformers and included in the corresponding credal books, but subsequently relegated to the background through the influence of radical Protestantism, they often find themselves accused of venturing too close to "Catholicism".

It is not surprising that several Catholic interpreters of the Reformation attribute to Luther and Calvin characteristics that properly belong to the other tradition.

But is the distinction between the two traditions always unmistakably clear? At the extremes, it is: Calvin and Luther on the one hand, Münzer, Carlstadt etc. on the other, clearly manifest through their respective modes of action, the difference that divides them. And yet, though on the peaks there is this difference, between the two traditions communication exists. G. D. Henderson declares that "there were two attitudes that Calvin sought to avoid: that of Rome and that of the Anabaptists; both seemed to him

[30] Dillenberger and Welch, *op. cit.*, pp. 58–66.
[31] Blanke, *loc. cit.*

to dissociate wrongfully the Spirit from the Word. He does not appear to have been concerned with the distinction between the Bible and the Word of God in the Bible, which we are nowadays inclined to make. In his view, Holy Scripture was the Word of God to be regarded as having come down from heaven (Inst., 1, 7, 1)".[32]

At the same time, however, the emphasis was strongly laid on the Holy Spirit as the interpreter of the Word. "Holy Scripture can only yield a saving knowledge of God when its certitude is based on the inner convincing power of the Holy Spirit (Inst., 1, 8, 13), that is, the hidden convincing power of the Holy Spirit seems to indicate, in a sense which we might term sacramental, that he so transforms the literal meaning of the Bible that the Word becomes available to our faith."

Calvin was not unaware that no one is truly a person unless he lives in society and that no one has a real identity except in and through reactions towards others. This perhaps exhibits Bucer's influence to some extent; it is anyhow very different from Luther's teaching on justification by faith which, despite Holl's assertions, is emphatically individualistic. In his doctrine of the Church, Calvin follows St Cyprian: "For those to whom God is a Father, the Church must also be a Mother." Thus in his whole system a definite priority is evident.

Although Calvin was profoundly dissatisfied with the ideas of Rome, he was far from completely accepting those of the Anabaptists. These latter seemed to him to put too much stress on the importance which the Reformation attributed to the individual and to the religion of the spirit, to individual experience as opposed to official dogma, to freedom in contrast to authority. Individualism is not the sole constructive feature in the Protestant system, even though it is an important element in it. Calvin was thoroughly conscious of the fact that uncontrolled private judgement meant subjectivity, eccentricity, anarchy, in fact all the dangers associated with Münzer. Like Luther and Zwingli, he too was impatient with the Anabaptists. The Quaker's "inner light", the Buchmanite's "inner guide",[33] the mystic's contempt for ways and means—all this Calvin would have condemned. Interpretation (of the scriptures) must be safe-guarded by the relationship between the individual and the religious collectivity, instructed and organized, under the guidance of the Spirit. But Calvin also knew as well as anyone that saving faith is the property of the individual and that it is his sins that are forgiven. In his view, one of the great things rediscov-

[32] G. D. Henderson, "Calvin's Doctrine of the Church" in *World Conference on Faith and Order. The 1947 Meeting of the Continuation Committee held at St George's School, Clarens, Switzerland, August 28 — September 1, 1947.* Issued by the Committee, Christchurch, Oxford, England, and St John's Rectory, Washington, Connecticut, U.S.A., no. 102.
[33] Buchmanism or Moral Rearmament.

ered by the Reformation was that the individual Christian could be in direct communion with God. He held firmly that neither God's grace, nor the Holy Spirit, is tied exclusively to the sacraments or to other external elements of an organized form of Christianity, but can act directly without the help of intermediaries of this kind.[34]

Henderson notes Calvin's fear of breaking the unity of the Church; this was what he dreaded most. In that case, what was it that assured him that he was right to persevere in the course he was taking? It was a principle very much akin to that of Anabaptism: "the religion of the Spirit". "In this matter the only possible test is individual and subjective, and Calvin had to confess that it *is God alone who, by illuminating our minds, enables us to grasp his Truth, who imprints it on our souls through his Spirit, and by the indisputable testimony he assigns to it makes our consciences steadfast*" (*Corpus Reformatorum* 5, 405–6). "If the whole range of Calvin's thought is considered, and if we take into account his presuppositions, his implications and his somewhat contradictory emphasis, it may be said that, in his view, the definitive test is not the letter of Scripture, but the Word of God; that, on the one hand, he gives pride of place to the potent influence of the Spirit-guided community and the authority of the Church, and on the other, to the independence of the Spirit-guided individual. In this way he allowed for the element of truth in both extremes, although he pointed out their dangers."[35]

(e) *Antitrinitarianism.* In the early days of the Reformation, Anabaptism, the "spiritual" sects, and the Antitrinitarians must be seen as separate bodies. But this must not be allowed to conceal the relationships that existed between them.[36] As time went on, they became more separate and their differences more evident. But among the early "spirituals" there had been Antitrinitarians, for example, H. Denck and S. Franck, and the first Socinians owed something to Anabaptism.

The chief Antitrinitarian theorist was Fausto Sozzini (1539–1604) who inherited this approach from his uncle Lelio Sozzini († 1562). Socinianism had been a doctrinal movement, not a denomination. Unitarianism was the name adopted by Socinianism in Transylvania, where, as in Poland, Italian Antitrinitarian theologians had sought refuge. The original Socinian doctrine is contained in the *Catechism of Racov,* issued in 1605. It is a peculiar combination of supernaturalism, rationalistic humanism, and ideas that are alien to historical Christianity. The Bible is accepted, though the Old Testament is treated with indifference. The New Testament alone is the

---

[34] Henderson, *loc. cit.*
[35] *Ibid.*
[36] Neve, *op. cit.,* chapter xii: "The Rationalist Group: Unitarians, Universalists"; vol. II, chapter viii: "The Old Socinians or Unitarians".

source of revelation, but only what can be proved by reason may be claimed as Christian truth. By this criterion, the Trinity, the Incarnation and the two natures in Christ are eliminated. It is a return to monotheism: Christ is only a man of a higher quality than other men. Saving faith is obedience to the commandments, and religion is moral behaviour.

Socinianism or Unitarianism developed in explicit opposition to Roman Catholicism. It occupies a position within the Protestant Reformation as a whole, but it has its own special characteristics. Later, in England and the United States, Unitarianism allied itself with illuminism and anthropocentric humanism. The great Unitarian names, Emerson, for example, appear. But in Emerson's case, the elements of the greatest significance were due not to Unitarianism, but to the "inner light" which he borrowed from the Quakers.

Unitarians are to be found in local or national Protestant councils. But their presence is due to their interest in social rather than dogmatic activity. For them religion is essentially good conduct in the service of man.

(f) *The Independent Movement.* Between early and modern Protestantism a movement of great importance must be located: that of the Independents. It was from them that the Free Churches in England originated: the Congregational, Baptist, Methodist and Presbyterian Churches, and the Society of Friends (Quakers). These denominations form the historical body of dissenters or of non-conformity.[37]

The importance of these denominations may be gathered from the introductory words by Horton Davies in which he said that he did not intend to stress the negative attitudes of the Free Churches, branded by such expressions as "the disagreements of dissent", but to record the many positive contributions which these Churches have made to national and religious life.

In personal religion and culture, in the doctrine of the Church and politics, in social welfare and missions, in education and liturgy, the Free Churches of England have contributed to the life of England, the Commonwealth and the United States in an exceptional way.[38]

We must observe, to begin with, that these denominations have been influenced by other movements. The Congregationalists, for instance, are now substantially the same as the Presbyterians. The only difference is that, in principle, they uphold the autonomy of the local Church.[39] The Presby-

[37] Henry Townsend, *The Claim of the Free Churches* (1949).
[38] Horton Davies, *The English Free Churches* (1952).
[39] George T. Ladd, *The Principles of Church Polity* (1882); R. W. Dale, *History of English Congregationalism* (1907); Malcolm K. Burton, *Destiny for Congregationalism. A Constitution for Congregationalism* (1953).

terians themselves are the combined product of English Puritanism and the presbyteral form of government taken over from Calvinism.[40]

The Baptists, as we have seen, are connected with the Anabaptist Movement. They originated in various countries; those of England were an offshoot of Dutch Anabaptism.[41] The Quakers likewise formed part of the "spiritual" movement contemporary with Anabaptism.[42]

The term "Independent movement" may legitimately be used to denote the convergence of several different tendencies to produce the same result. Although these tendencies were similar, they were not identical. The movement was made up of several trends. Of these the chief was the Puritan trend, to which Presbyterianism belonged and the Independent section, whence came Congregationalism, which was the extreme left wing of Puritanism. The Puritans were advocates of a national Church which they hoped to cleanse and reform, and rescue from its Catholic features, in conformity with Calvinist principles. Salvation is to be obtained from God without the mediation of any action by a Church.

The Independents upheld the sovereignty of the local Church, and they separated themselves from the Established Church. (Hence their name "separatists".) They also insisted that the local Church should have the right to express its opinion in the selection of ministers, in the government of the Church and in the adoption of Confessions of Faith. The Presbyterians stood for a form of government by representative chambers (courts).

The first Baptists in England appear as an offshoot of the general movement of independence away from the Established Church. But, whereas Congregationalists demanded autonomy only for the local Church, the Baptists, who were themselves organised on the Congregationalist principle, went still further and claimed independence for each individual.

[40] Leonard Bacon, *The Genesis of the New England Churches* (1874); J. Gregory, *Puritanism in the Old World and in the New, from its Inception in the Reign of Elizabeth to the Establishment of the Puritan Theocracy in New England, a Historical Handbook* (1896); W. H. Frere and C. E. Douglas, ed., *Puritan Manifestos. A Study of the Origin of the Puritan Revolt, with a reprint of the Admonition to the Parliament and Kindred Documents, 1572* (1907); C. E. Whiting, *Studies in English Puritanism from the Restoration to the Revolution, 1660–88* (1931); William Warren Sweet, ed., *The Presbyterians, 1783 to 1840: A Collection of Source Materials* (1936); William Haller, *The Rise of Puritanism, or the Way to the New Jerusalem as set forth in Pulpit and Press from Thomas Cartwright to John Lilburn and John Milton, 1570–1643* (1957); Harry Grant Plum, *Restoration Puritanism: A Study of the Growth of English Liberty* (1943); Conrad Wright, *The Beginning of Unitarianism in America (The Revolt against Calvinism in 18th Century New England)* (1955); Perry Miller, ed., *The American Puritans, their Prose and Poetry* (1956).
[41] Duke McCall, ed., *What is the Church?* (1958); Edward Starr, ed., *A Baptist Bibliography, being a Register of Printed Material by and about Baptists, including works written against Baptists* (6 vols., 1947–59).
[42] Robert Barclay, *An Apology for the True Christian Divinity* (1701); John Skyes, *The Quakers: A New Look at Their Place in Society* (1958).

What was the background to all this? Under Cranmer's influence came the first influx of continental Protestantism. With his two Prayer Books and the Thirty-Nine Articles evolution in the direction of Lutheran Protestantism was accelerated. In 1560, Presbyterianism was introduced into Scotland by John Knox who had drawn his inspiration from Calvin in Geneva. Between 1569 and 1603, Presbyterianism was brought to England by Thomas Cartwright, a disciple of Calvin's successor, Theodore Beza. From 1587 onwards the Puritan agitation stirred up by Cartwright and Walter Travers, reached its peak, and Anglicans watched with dismay the development of the dissenting party. Conflict between the two parties increased. James I, who succeeded Elizabeth I in 1603, and who tried to impose bishops appointed by the Crown on Scotland, and harassed the Puritans in England, provoked the dissenters to rebel. The memory of James's action against the Scottish Presbyterians has persisted down to our own times. It explains the refusal by the Presbyterian Church of Scotland, in 1959, to accept the plan for union with the Anglican Church. Under Charles I, Anglicanism was in serious danger of being dislodged. Up to then, Puritans and Independents had only wanted to be an influential section in the nation, bent on reforming the national Church on the lines of the original purity of the Gospel. But during the Long Parliament (1640–53) it looked as though Presbyterianism was about to become the national religion. The legislation was voted, but as the result of a conflict between the Presbyterian party and Parliament, it was not carried out. Parliament was intent on retaining its complete control over the nation, while the Presbyterians desired a Church free to govern itself. By a hair's breadth, therefore, England escaped becoming Presbyterian. In 1659, after Cromwell's brief spell as "Lord Protector of the Republic of England", the country returned, with Charles II, to monarchy, the episcopate and the liturgy. The king was converted to Catholicism on his deathbed in 1685. His brother James II was converted in about 1670. But in the revolution of 1688 he lost the throne, and the crown passed to William of Orange. In 1690 the Toleration Act became law and the Presbyterians were granted freedom to organize themselves and to preach according to their conscience.

In reflecting on the difficulties inherent in the reunion of Christian denominations, we must remember that history weighs heavily upon the decisions men make. What the denominations which owe their origin to the Independent movement fought for so long will not be easily forsaken by them.

The last group of Free Churches is that of the Methodists, linked with the name of two Wesleys, John and Charles. Yet though these were the protagonists of Methodism, they were not its sole creators. It is indebted partly to the evangelical movement of the eighteenth century whose source was William Law, the leading spirit of the Oxford Methodists, and partly to the Moravians, who were the means of leading the Wesleys to their experience of justification by faith alone. The Wesleys' personal allegience was to the High Church party in the Church of England, and when the movement began, they had no thought of seceding from that Church. Their aim was to make contact with the masses of the indifferent, and to go out and look for them in their own environment. They adopted a method of preaching that spoke directly to lay people and they organized a system of conversion in the form of classes open to those interested.

The first reaction of the Established Church was to refuse communion to the Wesleys' converts. Charles Wesley declared that he was ready to make every possible concession to the Established Church, provided that it did not interfere with those elements he considered essential to his "society", namely, lay preaching, open-air sermons, personal experience of justification. And yet, despite the attitude of the Established Church towards the new society, he long refused to sanction the administration of the sacraments by ministers without Anglican episcopal ordination, and for a considerable time he hesitated before he felt himself authorized to ordain.

These facts account for the constituent features of Methodism. Its general aspect is democratic and of a definitely popular tendency. Bishops are optional, and a hard and fast system of theological doctrine is not insisted on. Today, at least in America, the concern of Methodism has moved from the salvation of the individual to that of society. It has become above all the leader in social action and the herald of the "social Gospel".

Need it be added that Methodism believes that it has a special mission in the work for Christian reunion? Its social interests provide it with a basis for practical activity in which Christians can learn collaboration. Its unexacting doctrinal teaching does not present acute difficulties that could prove embarrassing to dialogue.[43]

(g) *The Adventist Movement.* This movement illustrates an extreme and eccentric form of a fundamental aspect of Protestantism. But Protestantism, especially in its classical type, is not prepared, and rightly, to acknowledge in the Adventism as interpreted by the Jehovah's Witnesses[44] and the Seventh Day Adventists that authentic eschatology which is an essential

[43] C. H. Hopkins, *The Rise of Social Gospel in American Protestantism* (1865–1915) (1940); Alexander C. Zabriskie, ed., *Anglican Evangelicalism* (1943); John M. Moore, *Methodism in Belief and Action* (1946); H. E. Luccok and Paul Hutchinson, *The Story of Methodism* (1949); Richard M. Cameron, *The Rise of Methodism, A Source Book* (1954); Mack B. Stokes, *Major Methodist Beliefs, those that are distinctly Methodist as well as those that are held in common with others* (1956); *Doctrines and Disciplines of the Methodist Church, 1956; (The Methodist Episcopal Church; The Methodist Episcopal Church, South; The Methodist Protestant Church)* (1957).
[44] Marley Cole, *Jehovah's Witnesses* (1955); G. Herbert, *Les Témoins de Jéhovah* (1960).

dimension of Christianity. This modern Adventism contains a materialistic and chronological interpretation of Christ's return, and, at least for the Jehovah's Witnesses, Christ is not the Son of God.

Adventism appeared as a derivation from the Anabaptist movement to which it is distantly connected by way of the Baptists. One of the features of Anabaptism was precisely an exaggerated eschatology.

The name "Adventism" originates in the central importance attached to Christ's second coming: his visible return is expected in the near future.

William Miller (1782—1849) was the founder of this movement. In his youth a sceptic, he was converted and became a Baptist minister. Through reading the scriptures, especially the prophetical books, he became convinced that the customary way of propagating the Gospel did not correspond with the truth. The preaching of Christ's imminent return in order to establish his kingdom on earth for a thousand years would alone be able to bring about the conversion of the world. When Christ comes, the triumph of the Gospel will begin. The distinguishing mark of Adventist belief in Christ's second coming is the mode in which it is held. Chronological calculations are essential to it. The Adventist believes, as the result of chronological calculations and the symbolic meaning of the numbers given in the Bible, that he has found the secret of the end of time. It is true, of course, that Christians have always been fascinated by the numbers given in the Bible; St Augustine himself exercised his ingenuity in deciphering them. When the Adventists are reminded that Christ said that no one knows the day or the hour of his return (Mt 24:36), they reply that he also said: as soon as the fig tree puts forth its leaves you know that summer has come (Mt 24:32). Signs that are forerunners of his coming do therefore exist.

Chronological calculations, however, tend to become embarrassing, especially when Christ's return has been announced for a definite date, and it does not occur ... All that can then be done is to begin the calculations over again, or, if the criticism has been too crushing, to found a new sect whose calculations will naturally be infallible. Strictly from the point of view of the ideas involved, the systematic chronological constructions in which, in the order of their occurrence, all the events that separate us from the end of the world find their place can well be described as phenomenal. These seekers are the watchers on the tower who flash the signals to the people, calling them to get ready for Christ's coming. But since Christ is soon to be on his way, the old order has outlived its purpose: Churches, societies, States, as we know them, no longer have a place in the order of things. This is the reason for the Adventists' hostility to every Church without exception and their neutrality—the word a euphemism—towards national interests.

(h) *Twentieth-century sects*. It is not only in Catholicism, but in Protestantism also, that much is heard today about an "offensive" being waged by the sects.[45] They are to be found everywhere, in every continent and country, even in the remotest islands and on the most inhospitable shores. The arrival and expansion of these modern sects, Adventist, Pentecostal, "holiness", etc. at a time when ecumenism is drawing Christians together is a striking phenomenon.

What are their characteristics? First of all should be noted their propensity to depart from the central positions of historical Christianity. They constitute a genuinely centrifugal movement, increasing in speed and power. Their importance must not be gauged solely by their rapid numerical growth, but also by their claim to be creating a new world side by side with that of Catholicism, Orthodoxy and Protestantism. They assert that they are taking the place of the older denominations, because these are bankrupt.

A second characteristic is their appeal to the masses, to the most poverty-stricken and uncultivated peoples. These sects are rediscovering the miraculous power of the evangelization of the poor (Mt 11:5) as a sign of the coming of the Good News.

It might be asserted that, as time goes on, the older denominations begin to lose their capacity to extend their influence to the humblest persons on the circumference of society, and turn their attention to those classes that sociologically are better situated. Without deliberate intent, they are led to lose interest in "the little ones" and these latter in the end feel like strangers. This is the point when the new sects take over with their offer of immediate and attractive personal salvation. They provide the disinherited with the means of expressing the state of their souls and their religious needs. They give them a voice. In the Pentecostal and "holiness" bodies, and to some extent among the Adventists, considerable freedom of emotional expression is allowed in their meetings for worship. Anyone can shout out "Alleluia" if he is moved to do so, or pray aloud while the minister is leading the service. What is important to them is the discovery of personal salvation, a religion in which they are no longer on the circumference.

The success of these sects is due to a number of causes. In the first place, it may be regarded as a reaction against uncertainty and insecurity. A great deal of religious information finds its way into magazines, but quantity prevails over quality. There are so many convictions, so many beliefs. The

---

[45] Ch. Chéry, O.P., *L'Offensive des Sectes* (1954); E. van Hoff, *L'Église et les Sectes* (1951); Horton Davies, "Centrifugal Christian Sects", *Religion in Life* (Summer 1956); Charles S. Braden, "Centrifugal Christian Sects, Adventists and Pentecostal", *Religion in Life* (Summer 1956).

discoveries of archaeology raise difficult problems even for the most learn-ed. Ordinary folk only gather a harvest of confusion from them. Since everything is queried, where is certitude to be found? This leads us to the third characteristic which is personal experience.

In these new sects, the duty of bearing witness has been shifted from the corporate body to the individual. Personal evangelism is the means employed. Every member becomes a missionary. He goes from door to door. His purpose is not the limited one of inducing people to come to church; first and foremost he tries to promote personal adherence to Christ. What argument is used? It is the witnessing to what the Gospel has done in him who proclaims it. Thus these sects lay their emphasis on what has happened to their individual members, on stories of conversion and of the experience of justification by faith. In the Pentecostal and "holiness" sects, worship tends to culminate in outbursts of emotional excitement when the baptism of the Holy Spirit is received: vehement elation, speaking in tongues, dancing, loud shouts, the experience of ecstacy. These pathetic phenomena in the eyes of the adepts constitute the confirmation of the presence of the very essence of Christianity in its purest state in the gift of the baptism of the Spirit, accompanied by the reappearance of miracles and the mystery of Pentecost. How can the faith of a man who has under-gone an experience of this kind be shaken?

Another feature is that of the resolute requirement of perfection. Their spirituality aims at keeping them unspotted by this world, held to be perverse, wicked and condemned. Their eyes are strained to the vision of a world renewed in which the Lord will reign without hindrance to-gether with them, the Righteous, the little remnant described by the proph-ets. They despise luxury, wealth, everything which the modern world finds pleasurable, everything that flatters vanity. For them there is no problem of Christian culture or civilization. This world is but passive, it will be shattered by the world that is on its way. Why waste one's time? Christ and civilization are antagonists. For the same reason the question of Chris-tian citizenship does not arise; their true citizenship is in heaven. The State and society are necessary and inevitable evils, in essence already committed to the flames. What alone matters, therefore, is personal holi-ness, the experience of the eschatological gift of the Spirit, the burning expectation of what that gift will bring. From all things else men must keep themselves unspotted, not only from the things of the world, but also from those of the ancient Churches which have become huge systems of compromise with the world.

The final aspect of these sects is their biblical simplicity. The Bible is their all. But their subjective approach, unprotected from danger by the counterbalance of a tradition, moves them to complete the silence of the Bible on certain subjects with their personal inventions. Their favourite books are Daniel and the Apocalypse. It is always amazing to find how many people of the lowliest culture know the Bible practically by heart! It is true that they expound it with an assurance incredibly sealed against a questioner's point of view.

What will these sects become? We know that several denominations that now hold positions of respect were considered to be sects when they began. Contemporary sects are embittered and anti-institutional. But as they grow in stature, they will find it necessary to include some of those elements which hold a Church together. We may foresee that their criticism of the old denominations will become less harsh, and that they will equip themselves with a body of ministers possessing a sounder theological and exegetical training. They will then acquire a number of significant elements of the Bible and the Church which they now lack, and learn that although the world must be made Christian there is a right way of doing it. When the day dawns in which some of them—in the case of the Pentecostals a beginning has been made—decide to join the World Council of Churches, they may be led to realize the truth of various matters which they now reject. It is another field for ecumenism to incorporate. In any case, ought we not to recognize the elements of Christian truth which the teaching of these sects contains? In Adventism one aspect of Christian eschatology is present; the "holiness" groups bring out the fact that Christianity is the real remedy for sinful man; the Pentecostals bear witness to the truth that here and now the Church's essential life is drawn from the Holy Spirit.

What reply must be given to the "offensive" of these sects? An easy answer would be to mobilize the whole ecclesiastical armoury to denounce and crush them. Certainly we ought to be aware of what they are teaching and protect the unsuspecting from its dangers. But condemnation and warning signals may be deceptive. The finest and most genuine pastoral approach will be to say: a sect exists; very well; it may be that someone on the circumference has been forgotten. The natural intermediaries best suited to lead these sects to truer appreciation of historical Christianity may well be the Baptist and Methodist denominations.

(i) *The unionist trend.* So far we have only discussed those tendencies or movements whose action has been separatist. But since the Reformation began, another trend, that towards unity regained, has pursued its course: the names of Dury, Calixtus, Comenius, Ussher, Stillingfleet, Grotius, Baxter, Leibniz, etc. mark its progress. Contemporary ecumenism is not something utterly new, a completely new beginning.[46] The history of Christianity is often presented in terms of conflict and separatism, but is it not true that the striving for unity has also been a constant factor? Non-Roman

[46] Cf. Rouse and Neill, *op. cit.,* chapters i–iii.

ecumenism can turn to decisive gestures in its past history that provide encouragement for what it is doing today.

The "classical" reformers had no intention of creating a new Church; their aim was to reform the old one. They remembered the unity in which all of them once had shared, and they were quick to realize that their own work was in need of unification. From the start Luther, Melanchthon, Zwingli, Bullinger, Calvin, Bucer and Cranmer can be observed trying to establish contact. Luther and Zwingli tried to unite the various sections of the Reformation in Germany; Cranmer tried to unite the Church of England with continental Protestantism; Calvin wrote to Cranmer that whatever the cost and difficulty, his ambition was to bring the reforming movements together in unity. He was even willing to accept the Confession of Augsburg.

Their dream of unity was, for various reasons, never realized. It was frustrated by the determination of rulers to make use of the Reformation for their own advantage; by the deceptive phrase "union between Church and State" which in fact subjected the Churches to external control; and by the adoption of Confessions of Faith whose rigidity shut the door to other currents of opinion. As a result, the general movement of the Reformation was split up into individual reformed bodies, essentially identified with a nation, which remained as a whole separated from each other so long as the nationalist principle prevailed.

In discussing the trend towards union we must not think of some group intrinsically devoted to union, in the way that some other may be Anglican, Lutheran or Calvinist. It has been rather a general frame of mind which has been active since the Reformation began; it has based itself on those passages in scripture where unity is described as our Lord's command and as an essential element in the structure of his Church. If the Reformation is regarded solely from the point of view of its separatist tendencies, something of its total purpose has been missed.

In our time the trend towards unity, the ecumenical movement, exerts the greatest influence and extends far beyond the boundaries of Protestantism. Its dream is the reunion, if possible, of every Christian denomination.

4. Typological division of Protestantism

Any consideration of the ecumenical problem in its historical aspect must start from the fact of the extraordinary number of denominations that actually exist, even though we must not regard every religious body with a juridical status as a denomination clearly marked off from all the rest. For there are, in fact, families or constellations of denominations gravitating, more or less independently, around some central body. Therefore, to consider each denomination as inevitably a new brand of religion would be a gross error.

During the last four centuries Protestantism has found expression in two types, the classical and radical.

By classical Protestantism is meant the major ecclesiastical systems resulting from the Reformation which, while they rebelled against Roman Catholicism, desired to retain their own version of Catholicism. This is the "classical" type of Protestantism; Lutheran, Calvinist, Zwinglian and Moravian. They deserve the title "classical" not only because they have a historic ancestry, but also on account of the importance and authority of their credal books. "Classical", in this sense, means the new orthodoxy as conceived by the Reformation. Compared with radical Protestantism classical Protestantism is conservative. It insists on the fixed nature of doctrine. The written Word is the voice of God. It maintains the visible forms of the Church as expressed in worship and ministry.

Radical Protestantism is more akin to sectarianism in Protestant history. It originated in the one-sided emphasis given to some aspect of the Reformation by individual groups or schools of religious thought which followed certain leaders. What characterized radical Protestantism is "non-conformity"; in general it is of a more advanced type than is classical Protestantism; its aim is to be more thoroughly reformed, purer, truly Puritan. Unlike the classical type, it does not hold a general view of the Church as a whole. It is concerned not so much with a changed Church but with a new Church. It insists on personal religious experience. The principle of the "inner light", driven to its ultimate conclusions, has led to all the excesses of private judgement. Eschatology has often become "eschatologism". Hostility to the visible structure of the Church led to hostility to the very idea of a Church as such. Luther and Calvin's judgement of the Anabaptist and "spiritual" movements is worth recalling, and also the attitude of the Established Church in England to those new trends which were to end in the creation of the Free Churches.

Radical Protestantism has found expression in two principal forms: the evangelical and the humanist. The first is characterized by its "nonconformity", that is, its extreme independence and its absence of any fixed ideas on the nature of the dogma, structure and liturgy of the Church and Christianity. Baptists, Congregationalists, Quakers and Methodists belong to this group. The use of the word 'evangelical' to describe this type of Protestantism must not be confused with its use as a description of the German Evangelical Church. Protestantism in its entirety would claim to be evangelical in the sense of a return to the Gospel. But this particular group of Protestants, in contrast with its more "established" branches, is characterized by a more fervent and literal "return".

The second group of radicals consists of tendencies, sects, highly secularized bodies, whose characteristic feature is the attempt to harmonize the Word of God with reason, revelation with culture, Christianity with the world and the temporal order, making reason, culture and the temporal order the ultimate criterion of truth. This humanist and anthropocentric trend is really an anticipation of liberal and modernist Protestantism: as examples of it we may mention the Unitarians, the Universalists, the Church of the New Jerusalem, the Christadelphians, Christian Science.

There are, therefore, three fundamental categories of religious groups in Protestantism, although the boundaries between them cannot always be clearly defined. The various denominations may be classified as follows:

(A) Classical Protestantism
Lutheran, Calvinist, Zwinglian, Moravian Protestantism.
(B) Radical Protestantism
(i) *Evangelical:* Baptists, Congregationalists, Quakers, Methodists.
As a derivation from the Baptists appeared the Adventist type.
(ii) *Humanitarian*
Anthropocentric: for example, Christian Science, the Church of Christ Scientist.
(C) Mixed Groups
Antitrinitarian: Unitarians, Universalists etc. belonging partly to classical Protestantism and partly to radical Protestantism. These groups always arise as a consequence of an ecumenical intention, for example, the Disciples of Christ (U. S. A., 1810—13) to be placed midway between Presbyterians and Baptists.

Unless these categories are kept in mind the complex development of the movement towards contact and reunion within Protestantism cannot be understood. They must also be remembered when, in this book, the question arises of whether there is a single essence common to all forms of Protestantism, or of what are the points of cleavage on structural, liturgical and evangelical matters between the various denominations.

II. THE MOVEMENT TOWARDS DISINTEGRATION OF CHRISTIAN UNITY

This is the crux of the ecumenical problem in its historical aspect. Each separate Christian communion offers its own theory to explain the break-up of unity, and some regard this as detrimental, while others call it progress. The pure Gospel and loyalty to it were the constant watchwords of those who remained in the undivided Church of early days, and later in the Catholic Church. Nestorian, Monophysite, Orthodox, Protestant and Anglican Churches, which set out on their own, made the same claim. These latter bodies did not, however, believe that they had parted with unity, for each in turn was convinced that it was itself the focus and the refuge of orthodox truth in the world. Innovation has always been taken as the criterion of the abandonment of the truth of Christianity. But there are two ways of innovating: either a really new element may be introduced, or an element judged to be alien to the Gospel may be suppressed. The Catholic Church, for example, was condemned by the Christian East on account of positive innovations, while Protestantism appeared as an innovator at the very time when it was suppressing what it thought to be excessive in the Catholic Church, and the Orthodox Churches were reminding themselves that until at least the eighth century, they themselves had accepted the "innovations" of the undivided Church.

Novelty has always and everywhere been regarded with horror. But this horror has not proved an obstacle to the break-up of Christian unity!

We must carefully consider this ecumenical problem while looking at the general picture of the separated Churches and the various Christian communions.

1. Origin of the divisions of Churches and dissident communions

Various diagrams can be drawn to present a general conspectus of the principal divisions of Christianity. One could be constructed under the heading of "Judeo-Christian bodies", another would include the Eastern Churches, and a third might be limited to Protestantism. As Judaism and Orthodoxy are considered later, the necessary supplementary information can be postponed until then.

On whatever principle a diagram of the divisions among Christian bodies is drawn up, it is always unjust in its simplicity. To begin with, it necessitates a choice. In this matter the adoption of any one starting point implies the rejection of several others. But it is also the source of profound reflections. It raises the question of what circumstances make division possible, imminent or inevitable. In what circumstances does unity become attainable? What bounds can be set to either unity or division?

A certain logic can be discerned in the long path towards separation. One thing occurred because of another. Are the dogmatic factors alone responsible? Of course not; we know that other factors play their part: migrations, political institutions, social outlook, differences of culture, nationality, race, economic situation, historical tradition etc. It happens that some of these are concealed beneath others, and that those put forward are not the basic reasons or the most deep-rooted.

Then, it must be remembered that all Christians share in a common destiny. Whether our list of the separated Christian bodies begins with Jerusalem, Constantinople, Moscow, Canterbury, or any other place in the world regarded as the fount of Christian orthodoxy, this tree must have branches, these scattered members must be members of a body. The fellowship of all Christians is, therefore, an inescapable reality. In the economy of salvation we all share in a single destiny. It must be admitted that we shall all be judged by God, according to a twofold criterion: our relationship with our brethren with whom we are in communion and the absence of relationship with our brethren from whom we are separated.

It is also true that although a list of the divisions in Christendom reveals the ways in which Christians have become separated, it can also be a pointer in the opposite direction, the path to unity.

Every Christian, according to his denomination, Orthodox, Protestant, Anglican or Catholic, will obviously account for the origin of religious dissent in his own way. If he is a Nestorian or a Monophysite, he will say that the true form of Christianity is Nestorianism or Monophysitism, from which the Catholic Church broke away at Ephesus (431) or Chalcedon (451). If he is a member of the Orthodox Church, then Orthodoxy will be true Christianity, from which the Roman Catholic Church officially departed in 1054.[47] If he is a Protestant, there are several possible positions he might adopt. He might claim, for instance, that it is Protestantism which is a true return to Christian origins at an earlier stage than that represented by Catholicism, Orthodoxy and the Eastern Churches of the fifth century.[48] Or else he might say: Christianity has split into three major forms: Catholicism, Orthodoxy and Protestantism. There has been a schism within the Church, but no schismatic Church. It would, therefore, be pointless to claim that any particular body represents the original truth. Each has its own share in that truth.

I shall now explain why the Catholic Church is taken as the historical root of Christianity. It is because the whole tradition of this Church is identical with that of the English Church before the Anglican Reformation; with that of Calvin before the Calvinist Reformation; with that of Luther before the Lutheran Reformation; with that of the Orthodox Church before the separation; with her at the Council of Florence (1439); with the Monophysite Churches before Chalcedon; with the Nestorian Churches before Ephesus.

All of us, therefore, agree in confessing what our common creeds proclaim: "I believe in the Holy Ghost, the Holy Catholic Church" (Apostles' Creed);

---

[47] Alivisatos, "The Holy Greek Orthodox Church", loc. cit., pp. 47–8.
[48] Lettre synodale de L'Église Réformée des Pays-Bas (1950); What is the Difference? Protestant and Roman Catholic Beliefs Compared (1954).

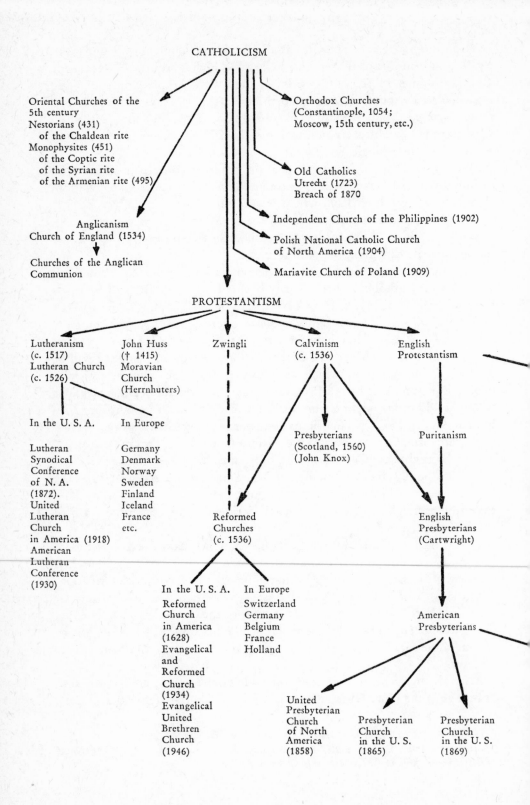

CATHOLICISM

Oriental Churches of the
5th century
Nestorians (431)
    of the Chaldean rite
Monophysites (451)
    of the Coptic rite
    of the Syrian rite
    of the Armenian rite (495)

Orthodox Churches
(Constantinople, 1054;
Moscow, 15th century, etc.)

Old Catholics
Utrecht (1723)
Breach of 1870

Anglicanism
Church of England (1534)

Churches of the Anglican
Communion

Independent Church of the Philippines (1902)

Polish National Catholic Church
of North America (1904)

Mariavite Church of Poland (1909)

PROTESTANTISM

Lutheranism
(c. 1517)
Lutheran Church
(c. 1526)

John Huss
(† 1415)
Moravian
Church
(Herrnhuters)

Zwingli

Calvinism
(c. 1536)

English
Protestantism

In the U. S. A.

In Europe

Lutheran
Synodical
Conference
of N. A.
(1872).
United
Lutheran
Church
in America (1918)
American
Lutheran
Conference
(1930)

Germany
Denmark
Norway
Sweden
Finland
Iceland
France
etc.

Presbyterians
(Scotland, 1560)
(John Knox)

Puritanism

Reformed
Churches
(c. 1536)

English
Presbyterians
(Cartwright)

In the U. S. A.
Reformed
Church
in America
(1628)
Evangelical
and
Reformed
Church
(1934)
Evangelical
United
Brethren
Church
(1946)

In Europe
Switzerland
Germany
Belgium
France
Holland

American
Presbyterians

United
Presbyterian
Church
of North
America
(1858)

Presbyterian
Church
in the U. S.
(1865)

Presbyterian
Church
in the U. S.
(1869)

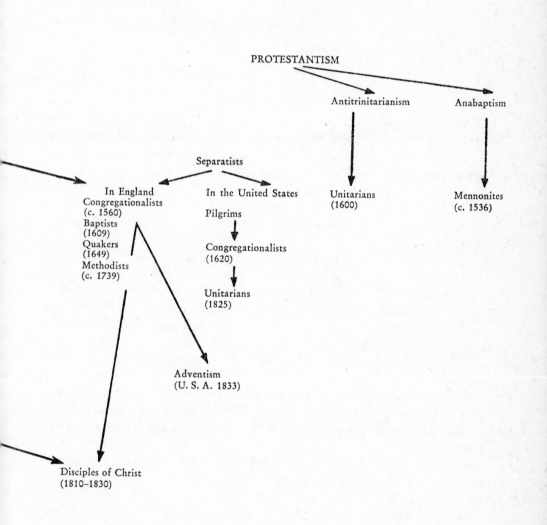

PROTESTANTISM

Antitrinitarianism

Anabaptism

Separatists

In England
Congregationalists
(c. 1560)
Baptists
(1609)
Quakers
(1649)
Methodists
(c. 1739)

In the United States

Pilgrims

Congregationalists
(1620)

Unitarians
(1825)

Unitarians
(1600)

Mennonites
(c. 1536)

Adventism
(U. S. A. 1833)

Disciples of Christ
(1810–1830)

in "One Holy, Catholic and Apostolic Church" (Niceno-Constantinopolitan Creed).

No later deviations from the commonly accepted definitions of Ephesus, Chalcedon and Florence, during the centuries when corporate Christian life was undivided, can ever efface what has been proclaimed with a single heart and a united faith, outside the realm of all conflicting issues. For when, through God's grace, we affirm his reality, we are gripped by something greater than ourselves. The glory of the Spirit grips the Church composed of men, it takes possession of the believer and makes him one with the Spirit of God. The essence of Christianity is a garden enclosed only to be entered by affirmation. What has been given to him abides and it cannot be taken away. But we can take ourselves away from him.

2. The problem of historical continuity

If Bossuet returned to this world, he would have many things to add to his celebrated *Histoire des Variations*—some developments that would not surprise him and others that he could not have foreseen. For instance, he would not be surprised to find that the tendency to become a sect has been transformed into a tendency to become a Church. But he would be truly asthonished to find that the very Protestantism whose fragmentation leading to inevitable extinction he had foretold, as the result of unbridled individualism, has in fact proved itself able to recuperate, renew and reform itself.

In a century and a culture which both formed a zenith in human history, and when the Catholic order contained the unity of the world in its scope, Bossuet could only half understand the meaning of Protestantism which had more affinities with the baroque than the classical spirit. The classical social order was self contained, self possessed within the boundaries of its achievement. Baroque culture, on the other hand, in this anticipating Romanticism, was restless, anxious, unstable. It existed in a state of tension, of self-examination, of unending reform. Not that the Baroque detested what is steadfast and definite, but what is fixed. It was not hostile to clarity of statement, but to what cannot be reconsidered. It did not set itself against authoritative pronouncements, but only against what excludes dialogue and the sometimes devious excursions of freedom. Its presentation of the unshakable structure of reality, of its inexhaustible content, differs from that of the classical period. Is it destructive? It has a passion for analysis, but only to create a new synthesis. It objects to our thinking that history has concluded before God himself brought it to its end. It feels that everything is always reaching out to a reality beyond itself. It cannot tolerate that a temporary stage should be taken as a golden age; in its eyes that would mean the acceptance of twilight and of a merely academic peroration. It is the religion of the Word, and why should speech be silenced?

Bossuet observed Protestantism in its beginnings. He observed the shaping of its outlines, its expansion, the formation of its various branches. He realized that it was endangering the order without which his world would be unthinkable. He watched its development, and put his finger on its weaknesses and incoherences. But not every aspect of history can be foreseen, and it happens that some doctrinal truth, present, though hidden, comes to an unexpected flowering.

Bossuet was an ecumenist, ahead of many others. He understood the importance of the unity of the Church and of Christians for the unity of the world. But, ironically enough, the *Histoire des Variations,* by its undue pessimism, counted for much in holding Catholics back from concerning themselves with the reunion of Christians. In addition, complacency in the conviction that absolute truth was on the Catholic side and absolute error on the Protestant, adopted the *Histoire des Variations* as further corroboration of the established position, immunizing it from any chance disturbance. In this way, Bossuet the apostle and the bishop was forgotten, and only the historian was considered. As a historian the field of vision of his faith was inevitably narrower than that of the pastor.

But does all this mean that the problem is reducible to variations on the theme of separation in the past and on that of unity in the present? In what precisely does the historical aspect of the ecumenical problem consist?

To summarise an aspect of such proportions is not easy. But one central theme dominates it and is the factor linking together all the others; it is that of the historical continuity of the Church.

When we say that every denomination makes an unmistakable claim to have an historical connection with Christ, we are giving expression to a fundamental and elementary conviction, common to them all. The very names of a number of them show an awareness of the need to be rooted in this way. And if the reality of an historical connection with Christ is to be judged solely by the name adopted by a Church or a denomination, then a particular religious body, the "Disciples of Christ", the "Church of Christ", the "Apostolic Church" etc., may express this relationship more explicitly than the name "Catholic", nowhere mentioned in the Bible, and only making its first appearance about 100 A.D. in a letter from St Ignatius of Antioch to the Church of Smyrna, or than that of "Orthodox" which, as the exclusive attribute of a Church, only came into use at a much later date.

A denomination desiring to be Christian without any historical relationship with Christ is a living contradiction in terms. If an attempt is made to interpret and describe Christianity, leaving historical continuity with the Incarnation on one side, it would end inevitably as a mere idea and an organization without substance, in which the corporate reality of a Church would soon be dissolved into subjectivism and rationalistic criticism. If for any reason, and whatever the form assumed, the historical fact of the Incarnation is given up, what foundation, what prototype, what goal can be assigned to Christianity?

This theme of an obligatory historical continuity with the Incarnation, which pertains to the denominations of Christianity, is one of the most promising meeting points in ecumenism, but also one of the most difficult. Much may be hoped from it, precisely because it is the way from the Church to Christ. But the path is strewn with obstacles. Each denomination firmly proclaims that it is loyal to one or all of the following points which preserve continuity with the Word Incarnate: the proclamation of the primitive teaching of the Gospel; the administration of baptism; the celebration of the Eucharist; a specific ministry; a relationship with the mysteries of the passion, resurrection and Pentecost, or with those forms instituted by the apostles; with the age-old forms of Christian living, with missionary zeal etc. We should observe the divergences, but also note a common conviction: the conviction of the need to be linked with the Word Incarnate.

But what are the requisite elements if a genuine form of continuity is to exist? Must there be a continuity of essence? Would a Church still be Christian if its continuity was only in non-essentials? Are the mere traces of continuity sufficient? Is there one perfect mode of continuity? Where is it to be found? What will be the relationship between it and the others? To what precise extent does an imperfect mode still share in the authenticity of the perfect mode? Or, is there, in fact, only one, essentially unique, mode of continuity, while all the rest are inadequate? Are the Protestant and Eastern denominations to be placed on the same level of historical continuity? And must not the Protestant denominations be differentiated according to the various types of Protestantism?

Historical continuity is broken if we admit the existence of a number of Churches, each claiming to be complete, organically one and practically universal. The contradiction between various self-sufficient ecclesiastical units and our Lord's desire to found only one Church is an intolerable disorder based on the human will trying to substitute itself for the divine.

The most vehement critics of denominationalism have come from Protestantism itself. Denominationalism is a scandalous and uncontrolled waste of Protestant resources. It hampers missionaries in heathen lands; it frustrates the work which Protestantism, as a Church of Christ, must attempt in spreading abroad social Christianity; it places it in a position of inferiority in competition with well-organized and aggressive Roman Catholicism. It produces Chauvinism and pettiness, in contrast with Catholic largeness of spirit. It fosters a subtle and corrosive moral insincerity among Protestants. It prevents the local Church from taking advantage of the universality proper to the Christian reality, and to which it could aspire if it fully shared in the wide vision, the spiritual inspiration, the riches of that fellowship, promised as its birthright to every local Church which has its part in the universal Church. Denominationalism, again, condemns its ministers to unworthy methods and procedures, unfitted to the self-respect of one who has been called to a lofty vocation. Lastly, under the pretext of exalting a kind of freedom, which is in fact erroneous, denominationalism only succeeds in rejecting the freedom that has been won in Christ.[49]

The Church must, therefore, be delivered from the limitations of denominationalism which prevent it from showing itself in its catholicity. The true nature of the Church must again be freed from that which conceals it, just as, in the sixteenth-century, the Reformers effected a similar grand ecumenical awakening. The ecumenical Church must be freed and brought forth from behind the ramparts erected by human hands.[50]

These same critics point out that ultimately it is not denominationalism but "ecclesialism" which is reprehensible; it is this which has corrupted authentic denominationalism. Hundreds of "Churches" ought to return to the status of denominations: they should give up "ecclesialism" which is the factor really responsible for the fragmentation of the Church, and has led to that multitude of religious bodies, all anxious to be autonomous, self-sufficient, and independent, all considering themselves as Churches. Every denomination, in one way or another, accepts the name of Church. In addition they take upon themselves the performance of these collective and community actions which, by right, belong to the one universal Church, namely, baptism, the Eucharist, ordination, missionary expansion, Christian education, corporate worship, a system of ideas corresponding to their own confessions of faith.

Each of them, for example, makes use of baptism as a means of incorporating members into itself, instead of primarily into the Church of Jesus Christ. It ordains a minister to the ministry of a particular denomination, instead of to the ministry of the universal Church. It sends out missionaries, but these introduce their converts into their own body, instead of into the universal Church. It gives children a Christian formation, but is it a formation in the perspective of the Church? Will these children become adults primarily belonging to a denominational "Church", or to the Church as a whole? Does not public worship remain worship confined to a sect, rather than something offered in union with the universal Church? Is not the Eucharist restricted to a sectarian celebration, rather than being the gathering of the community to share in the one common loaf?

---

[49] Morrison, *op. cit.*, pp. 28–29.
[50] *Ibid.*

Belief expressed in some particular confession of faith amounts, therefore, to a claim to be a doctrinal formula commanding the allegiance of all Christians, whereas in fact it is merely a distorted ray from a truth which is intrinsically one and undivided. In short, an organization of restricted range arrogates to itself that character of organic unity which can belong to the universal Church alone.[51]

The criticism is evidently absolute: denominationalism has been guilty, at every level, of usurping a title, functions, a nature, and the means of expression which are the sole property of the universal Church. Nor has this deviation occurred blamelessly, for the denominations have presumed to domesticate, for their own purposes, holy and universal things meant for the entire community of the Church of mankind. As a result, a whole system of man-made structures has been superimposed upon that of the Church. Internal schisms have split the unity of the Church, and thereby obscured the verification of its existence. Thus the Church has been pushed back towards the frontiers of its invisibility.

This judgement, Protestant in origin, raises several awkward questions. Did the Reformation in Germany, Geneva and England cease to be true to its original intention when it began in each case to express itself in so many separate Churches? Have all the Churches that have appeared since that time been mere substitutes for each other?

We have reached the most decisive issues. Are not the one universal Church and the denomination that has become a Church mutually exclusive? Is the suggestion of reducing "ecclesialism" to a moderate denominationalism really valid, if no authority can ever prevent a denomination from usurping afresh the status of a Church? Unless indeed this authority is presumed to be that of free consent; even so, it will be necessary to await its formation.

There is no need to insist unduly on the difficulties encountered by the Protestant ecumenical movement, difficulties which it is confronting courageously. The progressive analysis of the components of the ecumenical problem in its historical aspect has led us to the question: How has it happened that during the course of Christian history the necessary historical continuity with the Word Incarnate has become obscured? In what way will the scattered elements now be brought together again?

The distinction increasingly being made between two kinds of continuity—the historical and the transhistorical—is undoubtedly sound. The first springs from the Incarnation; the second from the relationship with the ascended Lord. And yet agreement has not been reached as to how the two are related, nor on the degree of acceptance which must be given to each. Would we be drawing the right conclusion if we said that the first is after all accidental and that the second is the one that counts? Karl Bath's message

[51] Morrison, *op. cit.*, chapter iii.

to the Amsterdam Assembly is really an expression of this point of view. But it has two disadvantages: it unduly minimizes the significance of the Incarnation; and its interpretation of the intentions of the first reformers is far too free. For they realized with great clarity the continuity which must exist between the Church and Christ. Once that continuity is broken, there is no longer any Church. At the very time when they were intent on reforming the Church, it was this continuity that they wanted at all costs to preserve. They had no intention of displacing the historical by the trans-historical continuity. They wanted to preserve them both; their aim was not to discover some new form of historic continuity, but to achieve a modification of that already existing. All we have to ask is whether what they succeeded in doing went beyond their original intention. It is time to remind ourselves of the conditions that a genuine reformation would demand.[52]

Any reflection on the characteristics of the future "great ecumenical Church" must inevitably dwell on the nature and the extent of this twofold continuity and their mutual relationships.

[52] Y. M.-J. Congar, O.P., *Vraie et Fausse Réforme dans L'Église* (1950), part II: "Conditions d'un réformisme sans schisme".

CHAPTER III

The Problem of Interdenominational
Relationships: from the Churches to the Church

I. DEFINITION OF THE PROBLEM

1. Dimensions of the ecumenical movement

It would be a mistake to suppose that the whole ecumenical movement can be reduced to the organization of the World Council of Churches alone, and even worse to confuse this institution, despite its leading nature, with the end pursued by the ecumenical movement as a whole.

It is understandable that, impressed by the annual sessions of the central committee of the World Council, by the periodic meetings of its general assembly, people may be tempted to think that it is the ecumenical movement itself; conducive to this opinion, of course, is the fact that the World Council is the ecumenical movement's most remarkable expression or its peak and climax, coming at the meeting-point of no less than seven movements which are ecumenical in approach and have combined to form it and that today it is the means of co-ordination in the departments of Faith and Order, Life and Action, World Mission and Evangelism.

In reality, however, the World Council is merely a result—it might almost be called an epiphenomenon—of an infinitely wider movement, one arising from the dynamic elements of the Reformation and from the intrinsic power of Christianity. Its driving power, what controls it, is the quest for, the vital need for that without which permanency in being is impossible, namely unity. It has no meaning save within a greater movement and a greater problem.

2. The method to be used

There are two ways of approaching the problem of interdenominational relationships. In the first place they can be followed in geographical order. The movements towards unity may then be studied in regions, countries and continents. Concern for ecumenism, indeed, varies greatly in different places, and, as a consequence, the history of the relations between Churches and denominations is governed by a whole set of special and unique circumstances which are likely to modify everything relating to Christian unity from one country to another.

In this connection may be mentioned: H. Paul Douglass for the United States;[1] E. Lloyd Morrow for Canada;[2] Robert Adams[3] and J. R. Fleming[4] for Scotland; Bengt Sundkler for India;[5] G. K. A. Bell for England;[6] A. Keller and G. Stewart for Europe as a whole.[7]

The second method is closely related to the first. It consists of a study of the movements towards unity regarded from the point of view of the central attitudes of the different churches and denominations. Auguste Senaud,[8] and Henry R. T. Brandreth,[9] may be taken as representatives of this approach. Their general method consists in consideration of each one of the series of Christian denominations—the Catholic Church, the Eastern Orthodox Churches, the Anglican and Episcopalian Church, the Protestant and Old Catholic denominations—taken in turn as the basis of comparison.[10]

Between the history of the movements towards reunion and the theology of unity, a typology of union occupies a privileged position. Ecumenical experience in different countries and among different Christian bodies makes it clear that the approaches to unity are multiple, and the modes of meeting and collaboration between denominations varied. A graduated

---

[1] Douglass, *Church Unity Movement in the United States;* J. Robert Nelson, ed., *Christian Unity in North America* (1958).

[2] *Church Union in Canada, its History, Motives, Doctrines and Government* (1923).

[3] *The Scottish Church, 1500–1920: A Graphic Chart* (1923); *The Presbyterian Church of Scotland, 1560–1929: its Divisions and Unions, a Chart* (1929).

[4] *The Story of Church Union In Scotland: Its Origins and Progress, 1560–1929* (1929).

[5] *The Church of South India: the Movement towards Union, 1900–1947* (1954).

[6] *Documents on Christian Unity* (3 vol.: 1924, 1930, 1948).

[7] *Protestant Europe: Its Crisis and Outlook* (1927).

[8] *Christian Unity, a Bibliography. Selected Titles Concerning Relations between the Churches and International Christian Movements* (1937).

[9] *Unity and Reunion. A Bibliography* (1st edition: 1945; 2nd edition, with supplement: 1948).

[10] Ruth Rouse and Stephen C. Neill, in their *History of the Ecumenical Movement,* cited above, have sought to unite these two ways of regarding the problem of interdenominational relations.

scale could be established that would enable the various stages to be marked off in the movement's development. Unity, when achieved, will not be something uniform or simple, but a highly complex reality.

The typological analysis of interdenominational relationships, which is the purpose of this chapter, aims at being a contribution to the practical methodology of ecumenism through an examination which excludes no aspect but includes them all. It will also serve as a guide to testing the steps to be taken to restore the unity of Christendom and to reintegrate the Churches and denominations into the Una Sancta.

Protestants prefer to speak of the manifestation of unity already given to Christians in Christ rather than the regaining of unity.[11] There is no question, they say, of creating a unity; despite Christian divisions, it is already in existence. Do not Christ's redemptive death for all men, the part that all men have in the Holy Spirit, the fellowship of all Christians in Christ's Body, and the unity of God's family, justified by the blood of Christ and reconciled with the Father in Christ, constitute so many bonds of real unity? The conviction prevails, therefore, that, despite appearances, unity exists, concealed beneath defective forms from which it must be freed. It is this unity which is seeking to shake off shackles, to become clear for all to see. One day it must be revealed. Every prayer, every effort towards Christian unity, relies upon this fact as a presupposition given by God. By their divisions, Christians have introduced a contradiction between their Church life and the fundamental nature of the Church. They have publicly rejected what, by God's grace, they are. The Church is called to show herself outwardly as the visible form of God's assembly of mankind, of the reunion of God's scattered children effected by Christ, so that every man may be enabled to say: this is my home, my Father's house, which I left through sinning and to which his love has brought me back.[12]

The quest for unity pursued by the ecumenical movement has three characteristics. It is dynamic, drawing us towards Christian unity through action, through the practice, even if only in the humblest way, of some form of union. It is optimistic. It trusts in the light shed by active work and exploratory measures: a merely abstract study of unity cannot yield all the necessary knowledge. It advances gradually; unity will be effected by the necessary stages. It involves a long process of training, an education. Moreover, although primarily it is a gift of God, it must be

---

[11] P. S. Minear, ed., *The Nature of the Unity We Seek* (1959), p. 257; J. E. Leslie Newbigin, "Address", *Minutes of the Uniting General Synod of the United Church of Christ, Cleveland, Ohio, June 25–27, 1957*, p. 97; W. A. Visser 't Hooft, "Various Meanings of Unity and the Unity which the World Council of Churches Seeks to Promote", *Ecumenical Review* (1955), pp. 17 ff.

[12] Newbigin, *loc. cit.*

recognized that for God to achieve his purpose, there is a sense in which he needs mankind and human history. Or, more accurately, the Churches and Christians prove their grace of unity in Christ by their practical efforts towards the attainment of visible unity. After all, what reality could inner unity possess if it failed to be operative?

The various methods of the works for unity within the ecumenical movement may be described. They extend from the simple meetings to organic union, and between these two extremes there are the various kinds of approach: negotiations, all the kinds of co-operation between individuals, groups, denominations and Churches, federations, intercommunion, mutual recognition, complete union. What are the forms and types of Christian unity in the view of non-Roman ecumenism?

It is useful to know that these are enumerated in different ways. H. Paul Douglass, for example, mentions three kinds of objective unity: 1. The unity of co-operative action. 2. The unity of mutual recognition. 3. Corporate union.[13] Henry P. van Dusen describes eight kinds of Christian fellowship and co-operation: 1. The association of persons of different communions. 2. Conferences between members of different denominations. 3. Non-denominational associations. 4. Interdenominational conferences of representative officials. 5. Interdenominational organizations (often these organizations do not represent communions, but are rather offices or agencies of communions). 6. World denominational associations. 7. Federations of Churches. 8. Unions between Churches.[14] Bishop Stephen Neill, in an official document proceeding from the Commission on Faith and Order, of the World Council of Churches, gives a survey of the progress towards union in 1937–1952, on lines similar to those of Douglas.[15]

In the *History of the Ecumenical Movement*, published under the direction of Ruth Rouse and Stephen C. Neill in 1954,[16] in an appendix to chapter 10 will be found a table of the projects for union between 1910 and 1952. In particular, the following are mentioned: 1. The mergers which imply full organic union at the intra- and trans-confessional levels. 2. Intercommunion, either complete or limited. 3. Federal unions involving less than full organic union. 4. Negotiations with a view to closer relationships without going so far as organic union. 5. Conversations with a view to better understanding or mutual recognition.

Lastly the report of the Conference on Faith and Order, held at Oberlin

[13] *A Decade of Objective Progress in Church Unity, 1927–1936* (1937).
[14] *World Christianity*, pp. 84–100.
[15] *Toward Church Union, 1937–1952: A Survey of Approaches to Closer Union Among the Churches* (1952); see also Robert S. Bilheimer, *The Quest for Christian Unity* (1952), pp. 36, 86–7.
[16] Pp. 496–505.

in 1957, mentions that at least four types of union must be recognized.[17] 1. The dynamic sense of the fraternal association of all Christians. 2. Co-operation in witness and service. 3. Agreement on ideas or practice—or both—with regard to certain essential issues. 4. Organic union. These four types of union are not, however, mutually exclusive.[18]

The following table is an attempt to provide a general survey of the extent of the ecumenical movement. It begins with the basic elements in which all Christians are united and ends with complete organic union, that is, union in its most integrated form.

3. Typology of the forms of union

(1) The fundamental union resulting from the subjective relationship to Christ and from the objective meeting in the common elements of Christianity.

(2) Union through conversations and special meetings.

    A. Conversations:

      the result of individual initiative

      officially authorized

      Propaganda through agencies or associations for the promotion of unity.

    B. Special meetings:

      Exploratory proposals:

      unilateral

      bilateral

      Discussions

      Negotiations over specific points

(3) Union through co-operation.

    A. Non-denominational: agencies or associations not directly ecumeni-cal in aim, for example, the National Council of Christians and Jews in the United States.

    B. Intra-confessional: between groups that are members of the same confessional family.

      (i) National Councils, for example, The Lutheran National Council.

      (ii) World Federation, for example, The Lutheran World Federation.

    C. Trans-confessional:

      (i) Specialized intermediary agencies of unrelated denominations in co-operation together.

---

[17] Already mentioned in *Report 1 of the Commission on the "Meanings of Unity", Faith and Order Conference* (1937).

[18] Minear, *op. cit.*, p. 257.

(ii) Councils or Federations:
- a) of parishes or a town, for example, The New York Council of Churches.
- b) of a region, for example, Southern California Council of Churches.
- c) of a State (of the United States) for example, Massachusetts Council of Churches.
- d) of a nation, for example, The National Council of the Churches of Christ in America.
- e) of several nations. The World Council of Churches.

(4) Union by Federation.

(5) Union through mutual recognition, leaving the way open to intercommunion.

Partial or complete intercommunion, either intra-confessional or trans-confessional.

A. On the national level

B. Internationally.

(6) Organic union:

A. Intra-confessional = between denominations of a single confessional family.

B. Trans-confessional = between unrelated denominations.

II. FROM THE CHURCHES TO THE CHURCH

Having set out the method of examining the forms taken by union in the course of its history, we shall now be able to follow the ecumenical movement along its various paths.

1. The fundamental union given by God

A distinction must first be made between Christian unity and the unity of the Church. The former idea has a wider connotation than the latter. Christian unity underlies all the forms of ecclesiastical unity; but it does not find direct expression in institutional terms. It is the factor that makes every pursuit of Christian unity possible.[19]

Every Christian must acknowledge a certain fellowship, a certain relationship common to all, from the very fact of a sincere subjective tending towards a common goal, Christ, "the reconciler of Christians".

[19] *Report 1 of the Commission on the "Meanings of Unity", Faith and Order Conference,* Edinburgh, 1937 (1938).

Differences in ideas and allegiance do not completely impede the ultimate reality, which is one and the same, from communicating itself to men in various ways. As a result of this approach towards the same final reality, there is also present an objective meeting-point in some of the common elements of Christianity, for example, the Bible, some of the sacraments, belief in the Trinity, belief that God is love, self-committal to Christ, the search for the Kingdom of God, the acceptance of the Church, at least in some of its aspects, the love of one's neighbour, and so on. It is, therefore, correct to speak of a kind of basic Christian unity. This is different from the unity of the Church, which is a perfected unity at every level. Therefore, we shall call the former a unity of all Christians in their approach to Christ and of a common possession of Christianity either in its plenitude or in its vestiges.

2. Union through conversations and special meetings

This initial form of Christian unity penetrates through the divisions between denominations or Churches. However imperfect it may be, it is a dynamic fact and its desire is to find its completion in a perfect form of Christian unity, in the unity of the Church.

It finds expression in various ways: first as love, shown as open-heartedness, a welcoming spirit, a will to agree, a wish for increased unity. This will be followed by mutual interest, a concern to come together, an attempt to discover activities that will create connecting links, Christian readiness to act as mediators for each other, the desire to build bridges between Christians, transcending their divisions, so that the great prayer for unity may be proved to be true.

These inner attitudes must come first. Essentially, it is a matter of education: an education in method on the basis of a given reality. External action cannot be improvised, or at least, if they are merely external, they will not last long. The inner form of Christian unity is expressed initially in the union achieved through encounter, and it begins with conversation. It is an exchange, although not necessarily an agreement. We may recall the part played by this very simple act of conversation in the relations between the apostles, at the time when all the Churches were in touch with each other, and when all the apostles took the necessary steps to remain in communion with each other. When Peter and Paul, for example, came into conflict, James acted as moderator. When Paul was suspected of departing from orthodoxy, he was able to make his voice heard. When Peter seemed to hesitate, Paul, while recognizing his authority, rebuked him. No one was condemned on hearsay, or without hope of an opportunity to justify himself. No one was dismissed without having himself been heard. Has the manner of apostolic conversation been lost? Who had a fuller realization of its worth, than the apostles, coming as they did from the source of unity, with their relationships derived from the Lord himself? If there is one tradition which the Churches must cherish, is it not bound to be that which preserves the apostolic way of life as the model for the Church's life?

When this minimum of union formed by conversation becomes normally absent between Churches and denominations, we can see how far the "will to non-union" or at least indifference about union, can go.

On the other hand, we can estimate the quality of the "will to union" when conversation is not only not refused, but welcomed, accepted, pursued in spite of obstacles, taken up again in spite of being broken off, maintained as the expression of a love, determined, despite disagreements, not to let itself be rebuffed.

In the ecumenical movement conversation has been promoted to the rank of an institution. Some conversations have been begun through private initiative. These exist in every country; they take place between all Churches and denominations. They form the starting-point for greater achievements.

There are also officially authorized conversations. In this case two or several denominations or Churches appoint representatives whose task is to make themselves acquainted with the respective positions. Official conversations exist, for instance, between Anglicans and the Orthodox, Anglicans and the Free Churches, etc.

Conversations can also become meetings of a special kind. The appointed emissaries explore the possible points of agreement. They try to discover points of contact and to extend them. They may put forward proposals for investigation. The discussions will bring out the opposing points of view. There may be either a unilateral or bilateral proposal. The conversations may then develop into negotiations offering definite terms. An agreement may follow, but if one of the parties is unprepared to commit itself, the official conversations may be indefinitely suspended. Even if a positive conclusion is reached, a period for mutual adaptation and deepening agreement will usually have to intervene.

Negotiations will vary according to the kind of union sought: action that will lead to co-operation; federal union; mutual recognition; intercommunion; organic union. They will also differ in as much as they take place between communions that belong to the same family of denominations or not.

In its Instruction of 20 December 1949,[20] the Holy Office accepted the importance of the exchange of points of view, and outlined a series of

---

[20] *Acta Apostolicae Sedis* (January 1950).

constructive regulations. Unhappily, few Catholic dioceses have considered taking advantage of them.

We must also include in this sphere of conversations the work of those agencies, associations or institutions of propaganda, specially set up to promote the cause of unity, for example, the Christian Unity League and the Christian Herald Institute, in the United States; the Friends of Reunion, in England; the Conference on Anglican Initiative, in China; the Syrian Union of Fellowship, in India; and, among Catholics, the Una Sancta in Germany, the Catholic Secretariat for Promoting Unity, etc.

The propaganda for unity conducted by these associations by meetings and conversations leads to the same object as that with which pastoral work and evangelization is concerned: the human person. Thanks to them, we are enabled to reach that very simple, elementary, practical, but too often neglected truth, that the positions, theories and doctrines, which from one's own point of view may be called dangerous or even monstrous, do not exist in some remote world of abstraction: they exist *in man*. How many Catholics and Protestants only know the Reformation and Catholicism from the contents of Denzinger's *Enchiridion Symbolorum*? Not that we deny the value of Denzinger, but when we meet Christians in whom the life of the Reformation or of Catholicism is a reality, we are experiencing something very different from knowing other Christians often by means of a few words only. Is it not a fact that many judgements are passed on men, social situations, Churches, from a merely notional and abstract acquaintance with them? Is it allowable to confuse a summary, even a true one, with a man, a denomination, or a Church? Personal contact brings the ecumenical problem on to the existential, human, living and evangelical plane.

3. Union through co-operation

A. AT THE NON-DENOMINATIONAL LEVEL

The reference here is to associations without a directly ecumenical aim which are open to all denominations. Their purpose is to obtain a better mutual understanding and an improvement of social relations. A typical example is that of the National Conference of Christians and Jews, in the United States, in which Catholics, Protestants and Jews collaborate. A similar organization exists in Canada, England and, at world level, in Geneva. Their governing idea is that of brotherhood on the local, national and international plane under the Fatherhood of God.[21] This organization

[21] James E. Pitt, *Adventures in Brotherhood* (1955); *National Conference of Christians and Jews, Program Manual, Policy, Provisional Issue* (1957).

is independent of any control by Church or synagogue, but it closely watches everything that has to do with relations between religious bodies and especially those of an ecumenical character. In its own way, and in addition to its own work, it acts as a valuable agent, in bringing men of different beliefs together.

B. AT THE INTRA-CONFESSIONAL LEVEL

Secondly, there are several organizations whose purpose is to secure co-operation between related bodies within the same confessional family.

Union through co-operation of this kind can exist on two levels: *national* and *international*. The regular go-between for co-operation is an agency. Consider, for example, the case of Lutheranism in the United States. It has a National Lutheran Council which acts as an agency for most of the Lutheran bodies.[22]

On the international level, there is also a World Lutheran Federation, which in 1959, represented sixty-one Churches and about fifty million Lutherans of thirty-two countries.[23]

Any attempt to acquire a concrete understanding of contemporary Lutheranism must certainly take the Lutheran World Federation into account. This organization has a worldwide concern for social matters. Its departments include those of education, missions at home and abroad, international affairs, world social service, the function of the laity in the world and in the Church. In this way, modern Lutheranism thus responded by deeds to the many social preoccupations occurring in Luther's thought. The size and character of this organization represents, in theological terms, an interpretation of the Church's mission in the world. In general, the same sort of organization can be observed in the other parts of the Protestant world today.

Most of the confessional families now possess world agencies of this kind.[24] They are more or less organized. Their significance depends upon the number of those taking part and on the degree of autonomy or independence of the Churches attached to it. They are first and foremost at the service of the member-Churches of a denominational family; and their work may be described as a kind of confessional or interdenomina-

---

[22] The United Lutheran Church, The American Lutheran Church, The Augustana Lutheran Church, The Evangelical Lutheran Church, The Lutheran Free Church, The Finnish Evangelical Church.

[23] *Directory of the Lutheran World Federation* (1959).

[24] On account of the character and structure of the Churches composing it, the Anglican Communion, which is a particular type of a world union of Churches, is to be distinguished from the Protestant world unions which have just been mentioned.

tional ecumenism. They keep in touch with the other great agencies concerned with ecumenism, for example, the World Council of Churches, but they do not form part of them. The World Council is a council of Churches and not a council composed of either the councils of Churches or of World Federations of Churches.

These world agencies have increased rapidly and their organization continues to improve. This is a new and very important development in ecumenical affairs. They may presage the establishment of unified Churches formed out of those at present diversified within the boundaries of a single denomination, at the national or international level. In the future, for example, there may be a single Lutheran Church, perhaps on the lines of the Anglican Communion. The World Council of Churches could continue to serve as an agency mediating between the Churches during the time that these were trying to achieve one of the various forms of unity—that of co-operation; federation, intercommunion, or organic union—among themselves.

The idea of international agencies between denominations or Churches belonging to the same kind is far from having exhausted all that it can yield. It will have significant repercussions on the development of the ecumenical movement, the World Council of Churches, the national councils of Churches, the member-denominations.

To the extent that it makes the confessional families more aware of themselves, and better organized, will it, in the long run, promote union or division? Or will it lead to a renewed and more thorough dialogue between the forces working towards union and those of disruption?

One of the most interesting developments at present is precisely the consideration being given by the confessional world alliances to the contribution made by each of them to the ecumenical movement, and to the significance of that movement for each of them.

C. AT THE TRANS-CONFESSIONAL LEVEL

It is in this sphere that the widest range of co-operation occurs.

(i) Church agencies or intermediary societies

First may be noticed the existence of Church agencies, which co-operate together among themselves, or of intermediary societies. Their purpose is mutual assistance, in matters accessible to all, concerning the testimony which Christianity and the Church must give to the world in the fields of missionary endeavour, education and charity.

The action of these bodies is not directly ecumenical. But the history of the ecumenical movement bears witness to all that the World Council and ecumenism as a whole owes to the Y. M. C. A., to the missionary movement and to the Federal Council of the Churches of Christ.

It is principally through the establishment of the Church councils that ecumenical activity becomes immediately measurable.

(ii) Church councils

(a) Parochial, urban, regional and national councils, including those of the American States

These councils are commonest in the United States, but they are also found in the other Anglo-Saxon countries. There are local councils of parishes and towns, for example, in New York, Chicago and London. There are also regional councils of Churches, for example, the Southern California Council of Churches; and councils of individual American States, for example, the Massachusetts Council of Churches. In the United States there are over eight hundred councils of this kind. The vast majority of them are concerned with issues of practical rather than doctrinal Christianity: with Life and Work, rather than Faith and Order. Some State Councils, however, which have the advantage of retaining theologians of distinction among their members, have recently produced doctrinal works of real value. The Massachusetts Council is a case in point.[25]

The theory underlying the creation of these councils has been explained in a book entitled: *Growing together. A Manual for Councils of Churches.*[26] The American State Councils have adapted it to their own needs.[27] A council of Churches is not a Church. Unlike the major denominations, it will have no creed of its own. It claims no right to decide what is theologically true or false, nor to administer the sacraments. It aims at being no more than an officially approved and constituted agency of a group of Churches and communions which wish to extend their field of work through co-operation.[28] The nature of these councils is summed up in the phrase: "American Co-operative Christianity".[29] Their form of government is based on both the congregational principle of autonomy and the democratic principle of representation. Authority is accepted, not imposed. Each retains its freedom within the boundaries of this voluntary association. The idea of collective responsibility, given as the criterion of mature churchmanship, acts as a counterpoise to local authority.

[25] *Towards Christian Unity,* a paper prepared by the Central Study Group of the Massachusetts Council of Churches, Boston, 1958.
[26] Published by the National Council of the Churches of Christ in the U.S.A., New York, in 1955.
[27] *Handbook for Local Council of Churches in Massachusetts* (1955).
[28] Wilbur C. Parry, "What is a Council of Churches?" in *Growing Together,* p. 18.
[29] J. Quinter Miller, "Philosophy" in *Growing Together,* p. 22.

The structure of collective action is established in them on a functional principle, and its application varies according to local needs. The function determines the structure, not vice versa.

Co-operative work is organized by means of committees, divisions and sectors. Its units are combined with each other by related committees entering into a relationship within a higher committee.

The Church councils, therefore, are neither supra-Churches, nor Churches alongside the existing Churches. Even so, they do express a kind of emergent agreement on the nature of Christianity as understood in the United States. Christianity is social and co-operative. The nature of the Church is such that it is constructed from its base to its summit by degrees of representation. Authority exerts no other compulsion than the worth of its plans for action, and the impact which its deeds make upon society: it is service not power, it is a moral guide, and its strength is that of persuasion, attraction and spiritual leadership. Those who "rule" it, do so by delegation. Their authority results from the co-ordination of the freely given consent of the contracting parties, and from the belief in a co-operative responsibility in which the laity as a whole fully share.

Development of Church councils in the United States will be watched with interest. The formula is clearly "Free Churches". They stand for agreement, consent, and they exert a growing influence in the consolidation of a spirit of a particular type of Christianity. Their influence will be considerable in the future growth of ecumenism. In the United States, so far, the prevailing form of ecumenism has been co-operative in character. American Protestant Christianity has attained powerful and distinct means of expression; it is co-operative, social, missionary, eager to speak to every department of human life.

The disparity between the member denominations has led to questions of Faith and Order being left in the background, and to the main emphasis being laid on those of Life and Action, or on the witness, through life and work, to Christ's saving power at work in society. With regard to any situation that has been experimentally analysed, it is asked: What must be done if we and our Churches are to submit ourselves again to God's judgement; if we are to respond to his summons and to the mission he has committed to Christians and the Churches? What must be done to bring Christ before society so that all men accept his sovereign rule?[30]

[30] H. Paul Douglass, *Church Comity, a Study of Cooperative Church Extension in American Cities* (1929); *Protestant Cooperation in American Cities* (1930); R. B. Guild and Ross W. Sanderson, *Community Programs for Cooperating Churches* (1933); J. Quinter Miller, ed., *Experiences in Cooperation,* prepared by the Inter-Council Field Department; idem, *Plan-book; American Cooperative Christianity,* prepared and published by the Inter-Council Field Department, New York (1945); idem, *Forward Together — Church Cooperation Services,* prepared by the Inter-Council Field Department for use by state and local denominational and interdenominational agencies of the Churches (not dated).

(b) The National Council of the Churches of Christ in the United States

The United States is not alone in possessing a national council of Churches. In Britain there is the British Council; in Canada, the Canadian Council, in India and Japan, the National Councils, in France, the Protestant Federation of France; in Indonesia, the Indonesian National Council, etc. The structure of these councils is practically the same throughout the world.

Of all the national councils, the one that is most noteworthy, and which has exerted the greatest influence on the others, and also on the World Council, is that of the United States.[31] In 1950 it replaced the Federal Council of Churches set up in 1908. It includes over thirty-three denominations and represents more than forty-five million members, that is, roughly the same proportion of the population as American Catholicism.

What is true of Church councils at the urban and regional level, is even truer of the National Council of the Churches of Christ in the United States.

Up to the present it has been almost exclusively occupied with "practical Christianity". Like most other councils, the National Council of Churches has always confined itself at the theological level to a few essential principles, such as those mentioned above. It has always been careful not to act like a Church, not to provide itself with a creed, and especially not to act as a super-Church. It is an agency for action between the Churches and denominations. Its structure is democratic and representative. It draws its strength from the principle of co-operative responsibility, from the freely given consent of the member Churches to collaborate under a common direction. The member Churches remain autonomous. They can reject whatever they find unacceptable, and apply what is offered to them as it seems best to them. The higher authority is regarded as a service. It considers that it has neither the right nor the power to lay an obligation on the member Churches. Its power is that of a moral guide, of a source of evangelical and prophetic inspiration.

---

[31] Elias B. Sandford, *Church-Federation, Inter-Church Conference on Federation, New York, September 15–21, 1905* (1906); *Origin and History of the Federal Council of the Churches of Christ in America* (1916); Clarence R. Athearn, *Inter-Church Government* (*circa* 1925); Charles S. MacFarland, *Christian Unity in Practice and Prophecy* (1933); *Christian Unity in the Making, The First Twenty-five Years of the Federal Council of the Churches of Christ in America, 1905–1930,* published by the Federal Council of Churches, New York, 1948; John A. Hutchinson, *We Are Not Divided; A Critical and Historical Study of the Federal Council of the Churches of Christ in America* (1941); idem, *Christian Faith in Action,* Commemorative Volume, *The Founding of the National Council of the Churches of Christ in the United States of America* (1951); idem, *Triennial Report, 1957,* National Council of the Churches of Christ in the United States of America (1957).

With regard to the expression of social beliefs the Council has also consistently refrained from dogmatizing. There exist general directions, definite views, a tradition represented mainly by the seniors. But it would be difficult to elaborate any kind of synthesis of its social creed. If desired, it might conceivably be done, but this would involve the danger of imposing an artificial unity on a body accustomed to a far greater freedom. In any case, a glance at the variety of its constituent members would show that in practice it would be an impossible task. Any attempt to come to grips with the complexity of the ideas in question would have to take into account all the different statements made in the sections on missions at home and abroad and on education. Support might also be had from the various theses worked out by authors of distinction; these would serve as pointers. [32]

The National Council of the Churches might be termed the higher council of co-operative Christianity in the United States. On the lowest rung, there are the local councils who lay the foundations for Christian co-operation; higher up there are the regional or State councils. The National Council is not a council of councils, but of Churches. Its members are Churches.

The numerous denominations that make up the council belong to both the classical and radical types, and in addition, most of the Orthodox, Greek, Russian, Rumanian, Syrian, Serbian, and Ukrainian Churches, are members. So, too, is the National Polish Catholic Church of America.

The National Council originated in the meeting of twenty-nine Churches and nine general agencies, [33] and a multitude of local and State councils.

Its aim is to bring the Christian witness into the arena of life and work, covering every aspect of human activity: education, social and public relations, missions, pastoral work, and worship. It is an all-embracing evangelical mission; nothing is to be left aside. Business and leisure, culture and the arts, all are to be made Christian. Youth, adults, family life, must be included. Social welfare, race relations, international affairs, must be borne in mind. There is the work of evangelism to be done among the laity of the member Churches in the United States, and among the millions

[32] Harry F. Ward, *The Social Creed of the Churches* (1914); "After Thirty Years, A National Inventory in Terms of the Social Ideas of the Churches", *Information Service*, N. C. C. A. (20 June 1942); "The Social Ideals of the Churches" (collective position adopted in 1912), in *Christian Unity at Work,* a document of the Federal Council of Churches, New York (1912), pp. 174–5.

[33] Federal Council of the Churches of Christ in America, Foreign Missions Conference of North America, Home Mission Council of North America, International Council of Religious Education, Missionary Education Movement, National Protestant Council on Higher Education, Student Volunteer Movement for Christian Missions, United Council of Church Women.

who are attached to no Church at all. There is also the work of the foreign missions.

If anyone cares to take the trouble to form a true estimate of this immense effort, its analyses, initiatives and successes, the conclusion that it must be founded upon saints, apostles and prophets, and has its place in the establishment of the Kingdom of God, seems inevitable. The National Council is a huge reality in progress. It endeavours to keep infinitely close to whatever needs to be evangelized. From year to year, it corrects and adjusts the plan of its administration in order to meet current needs. It is not afraid to welcome influential factors which it knows will in due course modify its own position: it has given a welcome of this kind to the Orthodox Churches, and it is now opening out to Faith and Order. It originated in concrete and practical necessities, and hence it is committed to social work, and it makes this work more thorough through sociological studies and meditation on the Bible. It is open to all the major ecumenical trends. Together with Faith and Order, it has just taken a further step towards unity.

In thinking of the future of Christianity in the United States, we must necessarily take into account not only some particular Church, however numerically significant, but also the practice of Church councils, and most especially the part played by the National Council of Churches. For this council is an additional major characteristic of American Protestantism. Its structure is that of the Free Churches and it is the representative of "practical Christianity". It stands for a programme of Christian cooperation and conciliarism. It is dynamic, welcoming, missionary and prophetic. It must be reckoned with if the future of ecumenism is to be appreciated. The present direction of ecumenism in the United States is not towards interdenominational organic union. But no final judgement should be passed. That is something America loathes.

(c) The World Council of Churches

The account given of Church councils in general will serve as an introduction to the meaning of the World Council. It is not a super-Church, nor a new Church alongside the others. Neither is it the visible framework of the universal Church. And finally, it is not the preliminary sketch of what has been called "the future great Church".[34] What it really is merits the description of an agency between Churches and denominations, worldwide in extent.[35]

[34] Outler, *The Christian Tradition and the Unity We Seek*, p. 161.
[35] W. A. Visser 't Hooft, *The World Council of Churches: Its Nature, its Limits* (1945); *The World Council of Churches: Its Process of Formation, Minutes and Reports of the Meeting of the Provisional Committee of the World Council of Churches held in Geneva*

(aa) The nature of the Council

There has been some uncertainty and even conflict over the nature of the World Council. Matters have been cleared up, although there are still issues that will doubtless be dealt with later. Visser 't Hooft's idea of the Council, at least in reference to the period of its foundation, seems to differ from that of the Central Committee. He believed that sometimes, on momentous occasions, when events of ecumenical significance occur, the Council could attain to the rank of a Church. The Church as an act of God could stand revealed, becoming perceptible and visible in the Council, when the member-Churches have met in General Assembly and have corporately put themselves under the rule of God. Visser 't Hooft's idea should be compared with that expressed by Karl Barth at the Assembly of Amsterdam.[36] The Secretary-General's view tended to go beyond the idea of an agency and reach out to that of a Church. If the Church is an Act-Event, will it not be present when Christians of all denominations have met together at the summons of the Word of God? The great ecumenical meetings will thus provide an opportunity for the bright light of the Event to irradiate among divided but now reunited men. He admitted, however, that the Council could not be truly a Church, since the essential and traditional notes of the Church are lacking, and also because as a result of the diversity of its members, the Council does not possess the principal characteristics of the Koinonia that are mentioned in the Acts and the Epistles: common witness and sacraments. On the other hand, the Council cannot be a merely higher council of religious administration. The Conferences of Stockholm (1925), Lausanne (1927), Oxford (1937), Edinburgh (1937), etc., without meaning to speak in the name of the Churches, claimed that even then they were a manifestation of the unity of the Church of Christ. *A fortiori*, why could not the World Council make manifest, at least in special circumstances, the essential unity of the Church of Christ, the final unity already acquired in principle and present in Christ, the head of the Church, communicating itself to the rest of his Body? The Council will sometimes be the Church, sometimes not, but it must always and with increasing intensity aim at being so.

This solution which attempts to take two ideas into account—the

from February 21st to 23rd, 1946; The Constitutional Documents of the World Council of Churches with an introduction by W. A. Visser 't Hooft (1946); "Various Meanings of Unity and the Unity which the W. C. C. Seeks to Promote", *Ecumenical Review* (October 1955), pp. 18–29; "The Super-Church and the Ecumenical Movement", *Ecumenical Review*, vol. X, no. 4 (July 1958), pp. 365–85; Leslie E. Cooke, "The Significance of the World Council of Churches for the Member Churches", in *Proceedings of the Eighth Assembly of the International Congregational Council* (1958), pp. 69–79.
[36] "L'Église, congrégation vivante du Seigneur Jésus", report of the Assembly, vol. I: *L'Église universelle dans le dessein de Dieu* (1949), pp. 95–107.

Council is occasionally the Church, the Council is not the Church—might seem to reconcile all the various opinions. But it has theological implications, and, therefore, identifies the Council with a particular theological standpoint. In a sense, it contradicts other standpoints accepted by Anglicans, the Orthodox etc.

The Central Committee, composed of representatives of the major denominations in the ecumenical movement, at its meeting in Toronto, 1950, brought the explanation of the Council's nature back to a less committed position, one more representative of the general view. The Council, it was declared, is not based upon any particular idea of the Church. It must not take the problem of the nature of the Church as settled from the start. On the contrary, every aspect of that problem demands investigation. Any Church may form part of the Council; its own idea of the nature of the Church will not conflict with the nature of the Council, for the latter is not committed to any special theory of the Church, and does not consider itself to be a Church.

The statement, therefore, implies that the Council is a world trans-confessional agency, the perfect medium for a dialogue between the Churches and about the Church, but it refuses to become the instrument of any particular confession or of any theological school. It is open to all traditions and its aim is to enable them to communicate with each other, but it does not identify itself with anyone of them. Does this mean that therefore its position is eclectic and relativist? Surely not; it simply means that it refuses to become anything different from what it essentially is: an agency that will not pass judgement on the worth, in terms of its significance as a Church, of any denomination, and which is dedicated to the furtherance of unity.

The answer given initially by Visser 't Hooft amounts to a premature reply to the central problem, as yet not even clearly perceived by most members of the Council: what is the nature of the Church? The position adopted by the Central Committee, though less lofty, is closer to the facts. It confines itself to the statement: "The member Churches of the ecumenical Council recognize that in the other Churches, elements of the true Church exist." [37] These traces, these "vestiges of the Church" must be followed up: they are pointers towards true unity and the nature of the Church; one day things will be illuminated afresh.

Does this new interpretation indicate an absolute refusal to take a definite standpoint with regard to the nature of Church? It cannot imply absolute neutrality for, in this sphere, that is impossible. Each member starts from some position, some particular belief, some choice. The Council has tried to find a middle way by refraining from the adoption of a creed

[37] Document of Toronto, section iv, 3.

118

of its own, but it could not help being influenced by the essential principles of Protestantism. In short, it has followed the course that seemed natural to it, that of being a higher ecumenical agency generously open to the expression of every conception of the Church, and worthy of receiving the first impact of the truth which they contain.

At this point, numerous analogies between the World Council and the National Council of the Churches of Christ in the United States appear. Its structure is democratic and representative. The authority of its leaders comes, not from any kind of power originating in divine or canon law, but from a consent that draws its strength from a sense of collective responsibility with regard to the world and Christianity. The member Churches remain autonomous—and this recalls the Congregational principle—but tempered by the fact of belonging to a world Christian fellowship. The World Council's attractive power is due to its prophetic, evangelical and missionary significance, in its capacity for spiritual and moral guidance. It makes no claim to possess either the right or the power to exercise authority over a member Church. Its power is persuasive and indicative, not jurisdictional and imperative. It serves as an excellent medium for consultation, moral enlightenment, dialogue, project research, and for the interpretation of the views of the member Churches to the great humanitarian or political world organizations, etc. But it also differs from the National Council of the Churches of Christ in many ways. Their main concern has to do with problems of "Life and Action"; the World Council is increasingly occupied with those of "Faith and Order". The National Council is confined to one country: the World Council is open to the Oikumene. The National Council interprets the Church's mission in national terms; the World Council sees it in the perspective of the whole world.

These differences and likenesses may be judged from the following table which shows the most striking influences that affected the World Council when it began. A number of important movements, for example, that of the Bible Society, the associations aiming at the achievment of a relationship with the Orthodox, must be taken into account in any statement claiming to be exhaustive.

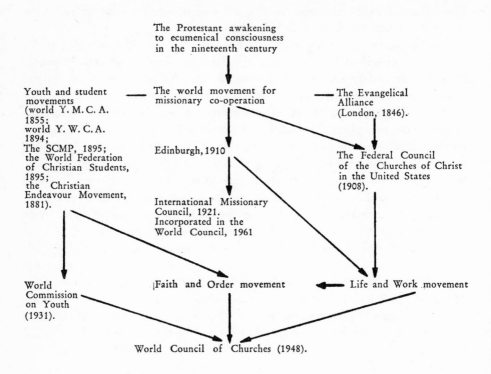

A schematic table of this kind can only be the merest sketch of all that the World Council owes to its sources.[38] It is indebted to remarkable men

[38] For the contribution of the various trends to the formation of the World Council of Churches and to the development of ecumenism in general: Cash, *The Missionary Church, a Study in the Contribution of Modern Missions to Ecumenical Christianity;* Charles H. Hopkins, *The Rise of the Social Gospel in American Protestantism, 1865–1915* (1940); William Adams Brown, *Toward a United Church: Three Decades of Ecumenical Christianity* (1946); Ruth Rouse, *The World's Student Christian Federation, a History of the First Thirty Years* (1948); William Richey Hogg, *Ecumenical Foundations; a History of the International Missionary Council and its Nineteenth-century Background;* Rouse and Neill, ed., *op. cit.;* John T. McNeill, *Modern Christian Movements* (1954); H. Meyer, "Evangelism, the Driving Force in the Ecumenical Movement", *Ecumenical Review* (July 1954), pp. 425–9; Clarence Prouty Shedd and others, *History of the World's*

such as Archbishop Nathan Söderblom,[39] Bishop Brent,[40] John R. Mott, etc., as well as to various societies that have worked for the cause of unity, although not acting officially in the name of any particular Church. The Youth and Student Movements are cases in point. These have been seedbeds of leaders in the ecumenical movement.

The structure of the World Council was inspired by the example of the Federal Council of the Churches of Christ in America which was itself modelled on the American Constitution.[41] This Constitution, as is known, chiefly is inspired by the Congregational principle.

Several Churches,[42] notably those of the Anglican Communion, were also influential in the formation of the World Council. Episcopalians, for instance, were responsible for the organization of the Christian Unity Foundation of New York, whose aim was to promote Christian unity throughout the world by undertaking inquiries and conferences. This was the first attempt by any denomination to set up on its own authority a system of exchanges intended to provide a friendly interpretation of some other denomination, with no polemical or critical motive. Again, in Cincinnati, 19 October 1910, at the general Convention of the Episcopalian Church, a commission was appointed to hold consultations with regard to the holding of a world conference on the problem of the Faith and Order of the Church. After seventeen years work it took place in Lausanne, 1927. Anglican and Episcopalian activity has been directed towards the issues of doctrinal Christianity: that of the denominations of the Free Church type has been mainly concerned with "practical Christianity".

Alliance of Young Men's Christian Associations (1955); Gustave Thils, *Histoire doctrinale du Mouvement œcuménique* (1955).

For what concerns the contribution of the Evangelical Alliance (World Evangelical Alliance), the reports of the general conferences must be consulted: 1851, London; 1855, Paris; 1857, Berlin; 1861, Geneva; 1867, Amsterdam; 1873, New York; 1879, Basle; 1884, Copenhagen; 1891, Florence; 1896, London; 1907, London (diamond jubilee); 1923, Westminster.

[39] J. G. H. Hoffmann, *N. Söderblom, prophète de L'Œcuménisme* (1948).

[40] Alexander C. Zabriskie, *Bishop Brent, Crusader for Christian Unity* (1948).

[41] Athearn, *Inter-Church Government.*

[42] J. L. Neve, *The Lutherans in the Movements for Church Union* (1921); E. R. Morgan and Roger Lloyd, ed., *The Mission of the Anglican Communion* (1948); Anders Nygren, "The Basis of Ecumenicity in Lutheran Theology", *The Lutheran World Review* (5 January 1949), pp. 15–18; "The Task of the Lutheran Church in a New Day", *The Lutheran World Review*, vol. I, no. 1 (July 1948), pp. 6–19; R. N. Flew and Rupert Davies, *The Catholicity of Protestantism* (1950), p. 38; Burton, *Destiny for Congregationalism;* Cook, *loc. cit.;* Jacob Marcellus Kik, *Ecumenism and the Evangelical* (1958).

(cc) The Council and the quest for unity

The World Council is aware of the scope of the issues now opening up before it and before the Churches.[43] Its own function lies in the sphere of the common vocation of the Churches, in that order of things that has to do with the Church's life and mission, and where individual Churches can only take adequate action if united. Unity, therefore, is its own special field of vision, its centre of interest and concern. Its activity concentrates upon showing the place of unity in the Church's vocation, demonstrating the urgent need of unity in the common work of evangelization, and letting it be seen that both unity and the Church's mission belong to the Church's essence.

Unity is its goal: it is also its method. The Churches learn the meaning of unity by practising it together, by fraternal correction, by expressing a common conviction with regard to problems of vital importance to the world, by mutual assistance in the work of evangelization. The World Council is the supreme connecting link in this collaboration. It is the spur to the formation of an ecumenical conscience; it lends itself to educational projects; it summons world assemblies; it supports the study of plans or subjects of common interest; it puts forward the common point of view on decisive world issues; it draws Churches out of their isolation and gives them a sense of collective fellowship; it takes the initiative in the name of all, in works of social help and charity. In short, it is the link and the servant of the Churches. Its misson is a combination of witness, communal action and service.

Although it is not a Church and is not developing into a Church, it cannot be said to be without any of the factors that constitute a Church. For is it not true that some element of a Church is present wherever men have met together through the action of the Word of God to bear witness to God's great deeds of deliverance? Wherever men have assembled in brotherly communion in the Lord's presence? And wherever they manifest their faith in the Word and their communion in the same love by mutual service? And if this is true of the most insignificant gathering of church-men, must it not be *a fortiori* true of the World Council of Churches? Ecumenical education must teach us to discover, respect and reverence every constituent element of a Church in any place where it may be found.

It is sometimes opportune to recall one of the incidents in the Gospel. John had said to the Lord: "Master, we saw a man casting out demons in your name, and we forbade him, because he does not follow with us."

[43] W. A. Visser 't Hooft, "The Scope of the W. C. C. Programme" in *Minutes and Reports of the Eleventh Meeting of the Central Committee, Nyborg Strand, Denmark, August 21–29, 1958.*

But Jesus said to him, "Do not forbid him; for he that is not against you is for you" (Lk 9:49–50).

What are the World Council's prospects for the future? Its second Assembly at Evanston in 1954 declared, in the conclusion of the Document of Toronto: "The moment it became clear that the purpose of the Council was not to be a federation, nor to become a world Church by incorporating the doctrines and methods of the member Churches in a synthesis, its constant aim, of necessity, was to decrease in the future, so that the unity of the Church may increase and be made manifest.[44]

If the Council is not a Church and has no function save that of being a world agency for the service of the Churches, then negotiations on unity must *de jure* belong primarily to the latter, because they hold, either vestigially or in their fullness, those essentially constituent elements of the Church which the World Council, not being a Church, does not possess. So the Council has no overseer's powers with regard to negotiations on unity, but, of course, it will be realized that the member Churches feel bound to respect the canons of loyalty and mutual respect, especially when the cause is one that ultimately affects the destiny of them all.[45]

4. Union through federation

So far we have examined three fundamental forms of union: that of a subjective approach to Christ and of objective encounter in common elements of Christianity; that of conversations and meetings for a special purpose; and that of co-operation. The highest point, on a world level, of union through co-operation between Churches and denominations in the ecumenical movement, is the World Council of Churches. We now reach a form of union that is still a type of co-operation, but midway between co-operation and organic union based on the unity of recognition.

In federal union the autonomy of the Churches taking part is retained, but they delegate some of their authority to a central bureau which, in the name of all, carries out a special function in clearly defined spheres, such as that of missionary activity. Examples are the Federation of Swiss Protestant Churches, or the Federation which includes the Congregational Church and the Churches of Christ in the United States. A similar form has been adopted in Spain, Germany, China and Great Britain.

Federal unity may occur either between members of a single confessional

[44] *Deuxième Assemblée du Conseil œcuménique des Églises, Evanston, 1954* (1954), p. 42; see also the official report of the Fourth World Conference on Faith and Order, Montreal, 1963.

[45] Oliver Stratford Tomkins, "The Nature of Ecumenical Cooperation", *The International Review of Missions* (1954), pp. 301–5.

family or between different confessions. In the United States there have been (and still are) several different proposals with regard to federal union, for example, that put forward in Philadelphia in 1920 for the establishment of the United Church of Christ in America, and later, the United Church of Christian America, or the project for federal union supported during the last fifteen years by Stanley E. Jones. This latter proposal would allow the Churches or denominations to retain their autonomy, but would unite them in a federal system copied from the American Constitution in which the central government is responsible for all the issues of interest to all the States. [46]

The plans for federal union have had little success on the transconfessional level in America. Union between the members of individual confessional families has been more welcomed. It is clear that in the United States, as elsewhere, the denominations have found it easier to create organic unions between communions that are alike than between those that belong to different forms of confession.

The idea of federal union may perhaps win wider support in the future, when the great confessional families have first re-arranged themselves and the thought of reunion naturally suggests itself. The Methodist, Lutheran and Presbyterian Churches of America are cases in point.

5. Union through mutual recognition open to intercommunion

This type of union is characterized by reciprocal admission of identity, or of substantial identity in the sphere of visible realities such as the creeds, the sacraments, the ministry and the form of government.

Intercommunion should not be confused with the union of mutual recognition. The former, as the word suggests, refers to the sacrament of the Eucharist and, through the Eucharist, to corporate communion. The term intercommunion came into use as the result of the separation between Christians and their organization into distinct Churches after the Reformation. In the early days of the Church, communion or non-communion were the terms used of Christians: heresy or schism involved the rupture of communion; reabsorption involved the restoration of communion, that is, primarily, partaking of the same Eucharist, the sign and the cause of the unity of the Church, of the same orthodoxy and of the common life. The fragmentation of Christianity led to a number of ecclesiastical communions, each different in its idea of the faith, in its structure and in its corporate worship. The word intercommunion stands for a series of attempts to bring all Christians back to the communion of one Church.

[46] George L. Hunt, *A Plan to Christian Unity* (1958).

Is intercommunion a well defined type of union like, for example, the federal and the co-operative? There is no doubt that it produces union of a kind. But its position belongs to the order of means or effects. It may prove to be a path leading to a greater union. It may also be the sign that such union has been achieved. The question is much disputed in the World Council today. The Orthodox Churches, for example, assert that communion cannot be used as the means for the attainment of a greater union, unless substantial agreement on the faith, the ministry and the Eucharist has been reached beforehand. But other member Churches of the Council would be willing to accept communion as a means, provided that some degree of mutual recognition was present already.

Churches may well achieve intercommunion or even complete communion, without going so far as organic fusion or administrative centralization.

Plenary communion indicates agreement between Churches in the spheres of Faith, Order, and the forms of Christian life. It is in this way that various Churches which are the components of the Catholic Church are in communion with each other, and similarly in the case of the Churches of the Anglican Communion and the Orthodox Churches.

Intercommunion may be either partial or complete. Partial communion is limited to agreement on some particular, and as a rule, exceptional issues. A noteworthy instance is that of the reception of Holy Communion in those Churches which, having recognized the validity of the sacrament given by each of them, make no difference between those who come to receive it. Complete intercommunion exists when mutual recognition of each other's mode of expressing the faith and of the validity of each other's ministry, having been declared, the laity of the Churches concerned are admitted to Holy Communion, whatever differences may still remain. Partial intercommunion has been practised during several ecumenical conferences, and it is a growing custom, at least between some denominations of a special type. A representative example of it may be seen in the relationship between the Anglican Church and the Church of Sweden.

In 1888 official conversations began. In 1911, an Anglican commission declared that episcopal succession had been uninterruptedly maintained by the Church of Sweden and that its idea of a bishop's office was authentic. The office of a priest was also understood correctly as a divinely instituted instrument for the ministry of the Word and the Sacraments, and this notion had been transmitted throughout the history of the Church of Sweden. [47]

The Commission made several recommendations, for example, that the

---

[47] *The Lambeth Conferences 1867–1948,* p. 134.

laity of the Church of Sweden be allowed to receive Holy Communion in Anglican churches; that permission be granted for Swedish ministers to preach from time to time in an Anglican church; that in places where no Swedish church is available, Anglican churches may be used for marriage ceremonies and funerals.

At the Lambeth Conference in 1920, the sub-committee on the relations between Churches of episcopal structure and on their reunion accepted the conclusions of the Anglican commission on the significance of the episcopate and the priesthood in the Church of Sweden, and it suggested that the recommendation previously put forward should be accepted. It also said that, in its opinion, the time had come for Anglican bishops to be ready to answer affirmatively a possible invitation to take part in the consecration of Swedish bishops.

Next, we may quote an example of complete intercommunion, not involving corporate and administrative fusion. In 1931 an agreement was reached between the Anglican Communion and the Old Catholic Church of Utrecht, with the possibility of an exchange of bishops for episcopal consecrations. The following basic principles of intercommunion were laid down:

1. Each of the communions recognizes the Catholicity and independence of the other and maintains its own.

2. Each of the communions agrees to admit the members of the other communion to take part in the sacraments.

3. Intercommunion does not necessitate in either communion a complete acceptance of the doctrinal views, the sacramental devotion or the liturgical practice characterizing the other. [48]

Other projects have been put forward that are not, strictly speaking, forms of intercommunion, but steps intended to lead to it. These include such measures as "economy", interim agreements, supplementary ordinations.

The principle of economy indicates the exceptional acceptance of the sacraments of the Eucharist and Baptism in another Church when the ministry of one's own Church is defective. This kind of limited agreement does not imply the recognition of the substance of each other's doctrine. It has occurred between the Anglican Communion and a number of other Churches, for example, the Orthodox Churches of Constantinople, Jerusalem, Cyprus and Rumania.

An example of an interim arrangement is that concluded between the Anglican Communion and the Lutheran Churches of Finland, Lithuania, and Esthonia. By virtue of this understanding, an Anglican bishop could be invited to take part in the consecration of a bishop in these countries,

[48] *The Lambeth Conference, 1948,* p. 73.

and these three Churches agree that their members may receive Holy Communion in Anglican churches.

The third proposal to be considered is that of Supplemental Ordination. A typical example is the plan put forward in 1940, involving Australian Anglicans, Methodists and Congregationalists. These denominations would contribute to each other whatever was needed to make their ordinations equivalent or identical. The essential procedure would be the laying on of hands on the ministers of other denominations, together with the words: "Receive the Holy Spirit for the extension of your ministry." This agreement in no way implies the acceptance of the theory of ordination held by any of the contracting parties. It only means that the significance of ordination is accepted as having an intrinsic and extended meaning for all concerned; Christ's ministry, it is believed, is above and beyond any theological interpretation of it. [49]

6. Corporate union

This type of union accepts the principle of fusion as its ideal. Communions, denominations and Churches engage in negotiations; the outcome may be a single Church. This Church may represent the unification of the different sections of one confession, or a union effected between different confessions as a whole. This unit will have one structure, one ministry, one government, one creed. It may be complete or incomplete.

Complete corporate union implies identity in belief, structure and ministry. Its incomplete form includes every kind of union that is below complete corporate union but above federal union. It takes place either in transitional situations in which sections of the same family are moving towards unity, or between different denominations. In the latter case the approach to corporate union is gradual. It begins with matters concerning the ministry and communion, and then deals with structure and doctrine. Lutheranism in the United States provides an example. A mixed commission for Lutheran unity was set up, representing four branches of Lutheranism, and this, through various stages, led to the formation, in 1960, of the Evangelical Lutheran Church in America. In the same country, a similar project is being worked out for three Presbyterian communions. [50]

---

[49] F. de Witt Barry, *The Australian Proposals for Intercommunion* (1948); *The Lambeth Conference, 1948*, pp. 64–6.
[50] *The Plan Providing for the Union of the Presbyterian Church in the United States of America and the Presbyterian Church in the United States and the United Presbyterian Church of North America as the Presbyterian Church of the United States*, issued in 1954 as revised in November 1953.

Plans for corporate union are a periodic phenomenon in the United States. The Greenwich plan may be cited among the most recent. Those who have taken part in the discussions are the Disciples of Christ, the Evangelical and Reformed Church, the Presbyterian Church in the United States, the Presbyterian Church in the United States of America, and two Methodist Churches—the Methodist Church in the United States of America and the Christian Methodist Church. The first conference on Church Union was held at Greenwich in the State of Connecticut in 1949. The Greenwich plan aims at incorporating three types of constitution: Congregational, Episcopal, and Presbyterian, within the constitution of a united Church. This is the first time that a scheme for a united Church included so many disparate elements.[51] The latest idea is that of Dr Eugene Carson Blake (1961); he aims at uniting twenty million members in a single body: Episcopalians, Presbyterians of the north, most of the Methodists, and the United Church of Christ. In short, the Congregational, Presbyterian and Episcopal principles would be made to work together.

Incomplete and complete corporate union can be achieved on a national or international scale. It may take place between the divisions of a single confession or between different confessions. The United Church of Canada and the Church of South India are examples of the latter. The comparison between these two Churches belongs exclusively to the general type of corporate union.

The various forms of corporate union between the divisions of a single confessional family are of considerable interest. During the last fifty years these have been taking place at an ever increasing rate. Between 1911 and 1948 twenty-six such unions have been arranged in a great many countries: the United States, Scotland, England, France, Holland, Switzerland, Italy, Central Africa, South Africa, Madagascar, India, China, Korea, Mexico, Brazil. The denominations involved in these unions were Presbyterians, Baptists, Methodists, Congregationalists, Calvinists, Lutherans and Evangelicals.[52] The five Anglican dioceses constituting the Church of South India should be added to these.

That the families of Protestant confessional bodies should combine into complete forms of corporate union presents little difficulty. Spiritual relationship, common origin, similarity in constitution—these provide a

---

[51] Ivan Lee Holt, *The World Methodist Movement* (1950); Ivan Lee Holt and E. T. Clark, *The World Methodist Movement* (1956).

[52] Douglass, *A Decade of Objective Progress in Church Unity, 1927–1936; "Ecumenicity in America"* in Nolde, ed., *Towards Worldwide Christianity*, pp. 169–223; Neill, *Towards Church Union;* Bilheimer, *The Quest for Christian Unity;* J. Robert Nelson, "Survey of Church Union Negotiations", *The Ecumenical Review,* vol. VIII, no. 1 (October 1955), pp. 76–93; Keith Bridston, "Church Union Negotiations 1957–1959", *The Ecumenical Review* (January 1960).

common starting point. Is it unreasonable to predict a union between different confessions within a single nation, for example, the national incorporation of the Methodist or Lutheran denominations in the United States and in other nations? There can be no certainty about it. In the United States it is this type of union which is the most frequent.

Will this development extend still further? Shall we see the formation of a single communion of some particular confession at the international level? A world Lutheran communion, a world Methodist communion? It looks indeed as though the various world agencies of the different denominations may be called to play a part similar to that of the World Council of Churches and serve the Churches as an agent which gradually effaces itself as union is achieved. At the end of this evolutionary process, the different denominations will still exist, but they will exist in a consolidated state. What will be their mutual relationship within a world union? The Study Group of the Massachusetts Council of Churches has suggested a plan for the formation of uniat Protestant bodies which would enable some of them that have developed their own traditions, but desire to join a larger entity, to combine intercommunion and diversity.[53]

A project of the same nature may perhaps be put forward in the future enabling the consolidated Protestant confessions to keep their own special forms of Christianity within a wider structure that still does not constitute complete corporate union.

Various hypotheses may be envisaged on the basis of certain principles. The definitive conclusion obviously cannot now be drawn. Christians are engaged in heart-searching reflection. Periodically the impression is given that one formula will prevail, at other times it will be another. Projects for union between the various sections of one confession run parallel with those for corporate union between different confessions. Between 1910 and 1948 fourteen unions of this latter kind were achieved. They occurred in the following countries: the United States, Canada, Rhodesia, India, Siam, China, Japan, the Philippines, Guatemala, Porto-Rico. The bodies which took part in them were Presbyterians, Baptists, Methodists, Congregationalists, Calvinists, Anglicans, Evangelicals, United Brethren, Christian Churches and some "United Churches". In addition, a series of negotiations for the furtherance of corporate reunion between different denominations is in progress.

Although the latter development is less frequent than corporate union between the different sections of a single confession on account of the difficulties and risks involved, it is nevertheless a phenomenon of the ecumenical movement that demands constant attention. Its results may

---

[53] *Toward Christian Unity*, a paper prepared by the Central Study Group of the Massachusetts Council of Churches, Boston, 1958, p. 16.

be more costing, but they are more important than unions effected between sections of a single confession precisely because they indicate that the obstacles offering the most resistance have been overcome. It has led to union between differing radical denominations, differing classical denominations, and between radical and classical denominations.[54]

These results call for careful scrutiny in each case. The instances of corporate reunion effected between bodies of a radically Protestant type were, after all, between denominations already very near to each other. Union between Protestant bodies of the classical type, on the other hand, was often beset by serious conflict. In Germany, for example, where the union between the Reformed (Calvinists) and the Lutherans was effected by absorption, the ultimate was later reduced to a federation. Again, corporate reunion between denominations of the classical and radical types does not follow an absolutely identical pattern. The Church of Christ in Japan, for example, and the United Church of Christ in America, primarily represent a functional unity. The two most typical instances are certainly those of the United Church of Canada, and especially the Church of South India. The latter provides a superlative instance of a pilot scheme for those countries in which a similar situation exists. Its plan for union, involving as it does the retention of the episcopate, needs to be carefully distinguished from all the others. The same reservation applies to every project that includes the Anglican Communion.

Conversations or negotiations aiming at corporate reunion are taking place between, for example, the United Church of Canada and the Anglican Church of Canada: the Presbyterians, Methodists and two Anglican dioceses in Nigeria; the Methodists, Baptists, Presbyterians and Anglicans in Ceylon.

---

[54] As an example of the first case can be quoted the union of the Christian Churches with the Congregational Churches to form in 1931 in the U. S. A. the Congregational Christian Churches. As a type of union between denominations of the classical type we can quote the union of the Calvinist and Lutheran communions in Germany whence emerged the Evangelical and Reformed Church.

As an example of union between denominations of the radical and classical type can be quoted the United Church of Canada (1925: Methodists, Congregationalists and Presbyterians).

The Church of Christ in Japan (1941): Congregationalists, Disciples, Evangelical United Brethren, Methodists, Presbyterians, Calvinists, Baptists, Holiness.

The Evangelical Church in the Philippines (1944): Presbyterians, Congregationalists, Evangelical United Brethren, Methodists, Disciples.

The Church of South India (1947): Methodists, Presbyterians, Congregationalists and five Anglican dioceses.

The United Church of Christ: Congregational Christian Churches and Evangelical and Reformed (U. S. A., 1958).

The Protestant denominations have begun on a large-scale process of drawing nearer to each other, of co-operation and of every kind of union. Reconciliation and co-operation exceed expectation. But with organic union, especially at the trans-confessional level there is far less enthusiasm. Several years must pass before any definite conclusion can be drawn. We must see whether any one line of action emerges clearly, or whether several emerge on a more or less equal basis. [55]

III. CONFLICT OR DILEMMA BETWEEN VARIOUS FORMS OF ECUMENISM

If we pause to reflect on the meaning of these immense developments that are unfolding in the quest for unity, the question arises whether God is not leading these Christian communions through a kind of catechumenate towards that goal. The drawing closer which springs from an awareness of common ties; initiatives undertaken locally by Christian bodies; the establishment of agencies for co-ordinating denominational co-operation; the increase in the quality and extent of common enterprises; unified missionary planning to bring into the Church the masses that are outside; the unification of agencies concerned with ecumenism; the integration of national ecumenical movements into a single world movement; inter-communion—all these factors are the intermediary stages, the practical and theoretical apprenticeship of unity. Each stage crowned with success, each obstacle overcome, marks a fresh root in unity. Unity stands out with increasing clarity. It hallows the efforts made by men and gives them for this reason the highest sanction. It would be difficult for the generations that have grown up in this atmosphere to return to separatism.

There is also the problem of the form which unity will take. It has

[55] The Lord Bishop of Madras, "The Church in Southern India", *The Review of Churches*, vol. I, 1924, pp. 485–95. *Report of the Joint Doctrinal Commission appointed by the Ecumenical Patriarch and the Archbishop of Canterbury for Consultation on the Points of Agreement and Differences between the Anglican and the Eastern Orthodox Churches, Report Only* (1932); Cyril Charles Richardson, *The Sacrament of Reunion, a Discussion of the Proposed Concordat between the Presbyterian and Protestant Episcopal Churches* (1940); *Scheme of Church Union in Ceylon*, published by the Negotiating Committee (1949); *Church Relations in England, being the Report of Conversations between Representatives of the Archbishop of Canterbury and Representatives of the Evangelical Free Churches in England* (1950); Sundkler, *op. cit.; Plan of Church Union in North India and Pakistan* (3rd revised edition, 1957); *Proposed Scheme of Church Union*, prepared by the Nigeria Church Union Committee representing the Anglican, Presbyterian and Methodist Churches in Nigeria and the Cameroons, April 1957 (including draft basis of Union and Constitution of the United Church); *Conversations between the Church of England and the Methodist Church, An Interim Statement* (1958).

been much discussed, and up to now three tendencies have prevailed in the ecumenical movement. The first insists that matters of doctrine should predominate in the quest for union; the second lays stress on the co-ordination of structures; the third puts foremost the Christian way of life.

The experience gained through ecumenical relationships has shown that it is not possible to limit unity to "practical Christianity", to the field of charity and apostolic collaboration alone. Problems of belief and doctrine sooner or later assert themselves. Questions arising from an understanding of the plan of the economy of salvation cannot be for ever avoided. The moment we face the purpose of the Church's mission—man in history, in the world as it is—is also the moment when the doctrinal issues regarding the revealed plan of the economy of salvation become apparent.

And yet it was also felt to be extremely difficult to envisage the problem of unity by taking the dogmatic or doctrinal aspect as the starting point for reconciliation. Every such approach to the problem that attempted to exclude other avenues has led to retrogression and failure. At the same time it is now fully appreciated that the installation of the Kingdom of God in the world and the proclamation of the faith need a certain structure.

One conclusion emerges: catholicity is a complex whole whose parts are co-ordinated within the unity of an order that can suffer no substantial change or diminution without endangering the catholicity, and therefore the unity, of the whole. And unity is the best and basic element in Christianity, the hardest thing to preserve or to restore.

The fate of the ecumenical movement will be decided on the basis of five major formulas of union—spiritual union, union in co-operation, union by federation, union by mutual recognition open to intercommunion and organic union: five major formulas of unity and, as a consequence, five kinds of ecumenism.

The first could be called a spiritual ecumenism. Relying on the encounter in the same Christ of all Christians of good will, and on the presence of Christianity either in a vestigial or fuller state, spiritual ecumenism cultivates in the hearts of Christians those dispositions favourable to reconciliation and communion.

Will these good dispositions lead to any exterior manifestation? At this point occurs the union effected by conversations and encounters with an ecumenical purpose. We can divide the forms of ecumenism into two principal classes, spiritual ecumenism and organic ecumenism. By the latter is meant the attempt to make visible, to organize the union of Christians in one sole body of Christ. Union by conversations and ecumenical encounters forms the intermediate agency between the promotion of spiritual ecumenical attitudes and the concrete process of gathering Christians together and their reconciliation.

Dialogue, conversations, mutual intercourse and meetings may create real bonds of unity, but they obviously cannot be ends in themselves, as would happen if such association degenerated into an "ecumenical club" made up of friends belonging to different confessions, well "adjusted" to each other through frequent discussions of a superficial nature and not really concerned with the achievement of practical reunion.

Spiritual ecumenism must be transformed into corporate ecumenism, with a constitution resembling that of a living organism or a social body. As the result of ecumenical experience four different formulas [56] have emerged: union through co-operation, federation, intercommunion and corporate reunion. This means that there are four distinct types of ecumenism. Co-operative and federal ecumenism are alike conciliar in form. Intercommunion and corporate reunion seem to us to correspond most closely to authentic ecumenism. They presuppose the best elements in the other types, and incorporate them in the revealed notion of the Church: the Body of Christ.

[56] C. A. Briggs, *Church Unity, A Study of Its Most Important Problems* (1909); *Christian Unity: its Principles and Possibilities* (1921); Charles Ewing Brown, *A New Approach to Christian Unity* (1931); Kenneth MacKenzie, ed., *Union of Christendom* (1938); H. L. Goudge, *The Church of England and Reunion* (1938); L. S. Thornton, *The Common Life in the Body of Christ* (1942); H. Burn Murdoch, *Church Continuity and Unity* (1945); S. Bolshakoff, *The Doctrine of the Unity of the Church in the Works of Khomjakov and Moehler* (1946); Angus Dunn, *Prospecting for a United Church*, The William Henry Hoover Lectureship on Christian Unity, University of Chicago, 1946 (1948); J. J. Willis, J. W. Arthur, S. C. Neill, G. W. Broomfield, R. K. Orchard, *Toward a United Church* (1947); K. L. Garrick Smith, *The Church and the Churches, a Book on Christian Unity* (1948); Horton, Toward a Reborn Church; G. K. A. Bell, *Christian Unity, The Anglican Position* (1948); Kenneth MacKenzie, ed., *Truth, Unity and Reunion* (1948), a sequel to *Union of Christendom;* idem, *The Approach to Christian Unity, Sermons preached before the University of Cambridge, 1951* (1951); L. A. Zander, *Vision and Action, The Problem of Ecumenism* (1952); William Nicholls, *Ecumenism and Catholicity* (1952); Hans W. Gensichen, *The Elements of Ecumenism* (1954); Anthony Hanson, *The Meaning of Unity, a Study of a Biblical Theme* (1954); *The Unity of the Church, Papers presented to the Commission on Theology and Liturgy of the Lutheran World Federation* (1957); G. W. Bromiley, *The Unity and Disunity of the Church* (1958); E. L. Mascall, *The Recovery of Unity, A Theological Approach* (1958); Michael Bruce, ed., *Barriers to Unity* (1959).

CHAPTER IV

The Dogmatic Problem:
The Essence of Christianity

I. THE DEFINITION OF THE PROBLEM

1. Method to be used

There are two ways of approaching the question. The first consists in making an analytic and comparative summary of the great doctrinal systems which are in confrontation. The second consists in bringing out and following to its conclusion a central synthetic view which governs the present and can lead us to the point which the ecumenical problem has reached in its dogmatic aspect. Here the principal features of the first method will be suggested and, in accordance with the general plan of this book, emphasis will be laid on the second, namely, by bringing knowledge of the past to bear on the evolution of the present.

(a) The analytical and comparative method

This method is based on a long-standing tradition. The great names of Johann Christoph Koecher (1699—1772),[1] Philipp Konrad Marheineke (1780—1846)[2] and Georg Benedikt Winer[3] are well known in this connection.

[1] *Io. Christoph. Kocheri d. Bibliotheca Theologiae symbolicae et catecheticae, itemque liturgica, concinno ordine disposita, variisque observationibus theologicis et litterariis instructa atque illustrata* (Guelpherbyti, apud Io. Christoph Meisnerum, 1751).

[2] *Christliche Symbolik, oder Historischkritische und dogmatisch-komparative Darstellung des katholischen, lutherischen, reformierten und sozinianischen Lehrbegriffs, nebst einem Abriss der Lehre und Verfassung der übrigen occidentalischen Religions-partheyen, wie auch der griechischen Kirche* (1810–13), vol. III; S. Mathies and W. Vatke, ed., *Christliche Symbolik, oder komparative Darstellung des katholischen, lutherischen, reformierten, sozianischen und des Lehrbegriffes der griechischen Kirche, nebst einem Abriss der Lehre und Verfassung der kleineren occidentalischen Religions-partheien* (1848).

[3] Georg Benedikt Winer, *Comparative Darstellung des Lehrbegriffs der verschiedenen*

The fundamental credal books of each confession are compared on each major doctrinal point, but without criticism, judgement or controversy. This method is solely expository.

But is it enough to confine investigation to the official creeds or doctrinal declarations of the various confessions? Confrontation of the credal books on the central doctrinal points inevitably leaves out of account part of the richness and special flavour of each confession. For example, a precise idea of the dogmatic position of the Scottish Presbyterian Church can be obtained by reading the *First Scottish Confession* (1560) and the Second Scottish Confession (1581),[4] but a better understanding of its real character will be gained by reading, for example, the sermons of Robert Bruce on the Eucharist.[5] The same is true of Lutheranism if the *Augsburg Confession* (1530), the *Formula of Concord* (1576) and the *Articles of the Visitation of Saxony* are completed by reading the works of Luther.

The official confessions, creeds, official doctrinal declarations were never intended to be anything else but summaries, standard explanations deriving from preaching and teaching. There is some advantage, then, if we combine study of them with that of the more general sources whence the diversity of beliefs has arisen.

Insufficiency of method can only add to the present deadlock. It may be displeasing to Protestants that the Catholic Church and the Orthodox Church give such great importance to tradition. But the criterion of adequate knowledge and objective interpretation is not the sources which we would like to have for each denomination but those which it actually possesses. Should the intention of reaching objectively a matter for study in the ecumenical field contradict the method adopted by every scholar as an elementary principle of research, namely subjection to the object in view and the intention of letting nothing pass?

In that case, the comparative method by the use of tables, like those of Winer's, which fills a need by making known the connections between doctrines in their normal form, must be surpassed and integrated into a more adequate general view elaborating the shades of differences, the shapes, the origins, the kernel of thought, the soul of a doctrine.

The method, which is excellent at the analytical level, is inadequate at the organic level. Knowledge of the dogmatic dimensions of the ecumenical problem cannot, as for far too long was the case in apologetics, whether Catholic, Protestant or Orthodox, or even in the dogmatic

---

christlichen Kirchenparteien nebst vollständigen Belegen aus den symbol. Schriften derselben (3rd edition, 1866), E. T.: *A Comparative View of the Doctrines of the Various Communities of Christendom* (1873).

[4] Cf. Philipp Schaff, *op. cit.*, vol. III, pp. 437–80.

[5] T. F. Torrance, ed., *Sermons on the Sacrament* (1958).

treatises, be based on the arid and fragmentary enunciation of a doctrine classed "heretical teaching" or "doctrine of heretics or schismatics" or "doctrine of enemies of the faith". Analytical knowledge of doctrines is necessary, but we should be well aware of its inadequacy.

(b) *The organic method*

This method is based on the principle that there is a central intuition governing the unfolding of each organic interpretation of Christianity. Where is the key to be found? Only an organic method of interpretation will enable us to find it. As an example we shall take here John Adam Moehler's *Symbolik*.[6] This is how he introduces his work: "The first idea of this work was suggested, we ought to say, by the opponents of our faith. For a long time past, in almost all the universities of Germany, Protestants have given public lectures on the doctrinal differences dividing Christian Europe. For our part we have always approved this kind of teaching, and we formed the plan of introducing it into the Catholic sphere."[7] The governing idea of the *Symbolik* is that the differing interpretations to be found in the Christian world amount in fact to different ideas about the essence of Christianity. Each system forms one whole propelled by a logical living impulse towards what it believes to be true. The central intuition may be false, but it possesses a certain balance, a certain unity. It is not that there is intuition and, by its side, what is false; but there is this or that intuition which exists in a state of falsity.[8]

But where is this central, essential idea given expression? In varying degrees and, according to the character of each denomination, in the creeds, the great theological classics, in the whole body of traditional, patristic or conciliar texts, in current teaching, in pastoral practice, worship, spirituality and ecclesiastical discipline. In a word, in the living totality of each denomination, in its genesis, in its life, past and present. And so we must seek the living soul which has found expression in a body and has been endowed with means of expression, a form of life, and a spirit.

Moehler's method is not perfect from every point of view. The phenomenological basis for information on the global reality of each prominent denomination was wanting. In addition, he depended too exclusively on documents which had received public and official sanction. Nevertheless, his general method was right: to form a thorough idea of the

---

[6] *Symbolik, oder Darstellung der dogmatischen Gegensätze der Katholiken und Protestanten nach ihren öffentlichen Bekenntnisschriften* (1832).
[7] *Ibid.*, p. vii.
[8] L. Bouyer, *Du Protestantisme à l'Église* (1959).

unity of each confession and the connection between the various trends of the Reformation. Thus a further step is needed.

(c) *The global method*

The most adequate method incorporates the two other stages and adds its own characteristic, which is to be inclusive. Every denomination should be seen as a whole in which thought, action and life are not separate but are bound up together as body and soul with a special destiny.

Even a superficial examination of the present organization of the Protestant denominations, for example, at least of those which are of some importance, will show that each one regards itself as an organic and living whole. Lutheranism, Anglicanism, etc., are not merely abstract propositions; they are a form of Christian life. The World Lutheran Federation, the Anglican Communion study every world problem—peace, evangelization, the missions; they seek to influence events, society, man. And it is the same with every other prominent denomination. It is almost unbelievable that serious-minded people should think that they had understood all about Protestantism after the summary enunciation of what has been called the material principle and the formal principle of Protestantism, or, indeed, of Catholicism, by the mere mention of the dogma of the primacy and infallibility of the pope. If hitherto the *rapprochement* of Christians has been so slow, could it not be attributed very largely to a defective method? We should all ask to be understood in accordance with the inner logic, the organic and inclusive expression of our life.

2. Conflict or dilemma?

There is, from the Catholic as from the Protestant point of view, a way of looking at the dogmatic problem which will never lead anywhere at the ecumenical level. It consists in placing between the two such disagreement that opposition becomes an insoluble dilemma. According to this view Catholicism and Protestantism so differ from each other that they are mutually and completely exclusive. Thus there is no common ground between them, but complete and objective difference as between one thing and another.

We can see how this operates at different levels. At the personal level the individual must give his allegiance to this or that communion. The conflict leads to dilemma. It is impossible to be Catholic and Protestant at the same time, since the Christian must take sides to a vital degree. And for the same reason it is completely unacceptable that a Church should be Catholic and Protestant at the same time, for that would mean placing on an equal footing, at the level of the complete commitment of the Church, Catholic principles which, on the other hand, contradict Protestant principles. The Catholic Church cannot allow herself to enter into communion with a Church which claims to incorporate both Catholic and Protestant elements and does so in the name of a higher, more comprehensive catholicity. Such a position is a snare, and no authorization for it is to be found in scripture or tradition. An effort must be made, of course, to achieve a spiritual and psychological comprehensiveness, but organic comprehensiveness of elements which are mutually contradictory cannot be the principle of true catholicity.

For us Catholic teaching is clear. The object of faith is to be embraced integrally. If on some point a Catholic refuses to give his assent to what is of faith, by that very fact he destroys his virtue of faith and is no longer a Catholic.[9]

But if it is a question of comparing the respective doctrinal content of beliefs, can it entail always conflict even to the point of dilemma?[10] There are numerous fields of encounter: scripture, tradition and, to differing degrees, a certain common *ethos* of Christian civilization. It is often a matter of really substantial portions rather than of mere traces. If then opposition between Catholicism and Protestantism is allowed to crystallize, as between black and white, the question has been wrongly put and there will be no way out of the dilemma. Protestantism has been placed wholly outside Catholicism in such a way that it can never return; it is forced to turn in upon itself, and to deny increasingly its points of contact with us; it is emptied of its Catholic values to the degree that they are absolutely foreign to it. The history of our conflicts shows us clearly the oppositions between the two: those of contradiction, contrariety, deprivation. But is it right to reduce them all to the strongest among them? Protestantism cannot reach understanding of itself if it attempts to do so independently of Catholicism.

What is authentic in Protestantism has its place in Catholicism. If the essence of Christianity could only be defined by one aspect in each of the following pairs: invisibility-visibility, event-institution, eschatology-temporality, actualism-mediation, freedom-authority; and if one or other of these aspects was represented by Catholicism or Protestantism, there would be a dilemma from which there was no issue. In reality, the problem is far more complex and for this reason: Catholicism must recognize in Protestantism, Anglicanism and Orthodoxy certain Catholic

[9] Thomas Aquinas, *Summa Theologiae*, II a II aa, q. 5, a. 3 *c*; Leo XIII, *Satis Cognitum*, in Cattin-Conus, *op. cit.*, no. 631.
[10] T. Strotmann, *Conflit jusqu'au dilemme?* On H. Van de Pol's *Christian Dilemma* see *Irénikon*, 22 (1949), pp. 276–82; the same idea is held today by an American Lutheran, Jaroslav Pelikan, in *The Riddle of Roman Catholicism* (1959).

values, of varying importance, it is true, and Orthodoxy, Anglicanism and Protestantism must also allow that certain values which they possess also exist in Catholicism. A Catholic, for example, must refuse to believe that Protestantism is so far to be identified with eschatology that it has wholly absorbed it and there is nothing of it left for Catholicism, or that Orthodoxy means theophany to such a degree that Catholicism has no other mission in the Christian world than to represent the visible and the human even though it is subject to grace. For the same reason, Protestantism can claim certain aspects of visibility, institution and historicity. The greater realization of the importance of these matters nowadays is one of the most encouraging events in the Christian world. Centuries of controversy, of misunderstanding, of withdrawal, had led to an oversimplification in our ideas about each other, often, to cap it all, accompanied by designations that were no more than caricatures. Today, the Christian communions are making progress towards greater integrity. They are refusing to allow themselves to be deformed. They reject those simplifications whose only contribution is a deceptive clarity. Christianity is a complex reality and so it must be defined in complex terms.

Catholicism is often accused of being a vast system of contraries, a *complexus oppositorum*.[11] This criticism can well be held to be grounds for pride. Can the Christian religion be regarded as adequate unless it is a special synthesis of elements which belong to time and eternity, nature and supernature, human and divine? If Christianity is derived from all the mysteries of Christ—and this must be a postulate allowing no discussion—must it not unite the two aspects: that of the historical descent of the Incarnation with that of the Ascension which transcends time? This unity is necessarily complex. Every denomination which desires to be Christian must necessarily situate itself in terms of this complexity. The Reformers did not become Protestants because they abolished a series of terms of the series of contrary pairs, but because they changed the balance and the nature of the relationship between the two. The period of exclusive choice of one series of terms began with radical Protestantism.

Maintenance of the complexity between opposite terms must not therefore be regarded as a weakness or cause for shame for anyone, since, on the contrary, it belongs to the very nature of Christianity. The history of the conflicts which led to the great divisions between East and West, and then to those in the West, merely bears witness to the constituent presence of elements in tension. Every case of dissidence that occurred did so on the grounds of reclaiming lost or misunderstood values. The whole tragedy has come from the fact that the tensions have been exacer-

[11] Friedrich Heiler, *Der Katholizismus, seine Idee und seine Erscheinung* (1923), p. 76.

bated into conflicts during which, and as a direct result of which, a new balance has been sought at the expense of a series of aspects equally essential to the internal complexity of Christianity.

The Protestant and the Orthodox problems become false problems and, on that score, insoluble problems, if one is led to pose them outside the fullness and the orbit of catholicity. The Reformation, the schisms of the East, were, in the first place, cases of crisis within the Catholic Church. The Reformation and the oriental schisms will come to an end when they have no longer any reason to exist, and that will occur when we have, I do not say approved their positions, but have answered the questions which they raised.

Catholicism must endeavour to rethink Protestantism, Anglicanism and Orthodoxy within her own universal fullness; Protestantism, Anglicanism and Orthodoxy must do the same for Catholicism and for each other.

If we seek a very general summary of the ecumenical problem in its dogmatic aspect, we shall find that there are two quite distinct interpretations of the essence of Christianity: the Protestant conception and that of Catholicism and Orthodoxy. Catholicism and Orthodoxy are here considered together, because in substance they are identical. They really differ only in their mode of approach, in their emphasis on different aspects, more than their acceptance of fundamentals. But between Catholicism and Protestantism the interpretation of the essence of Christianity is far more divergent. To express it briefly, it may be said that the difference between Catholicism and classical Protestantism lies in a shift in the centre of gravity, whereas between Catholicism and radical Protestantism the difference leads increasingly to the disappearance of a series of terms held together in tension. With liberal Protestantism this disappearance becomes complete.

Does Anglicanism offer a conception of the essence of Christianity specifically distinct from those of Catholicism and Protestantism? The answer to this question is to be found in the general account which the Anglican Communion gives of itself, as being both Catholic and reformed, reformed and Catholic, a communion with a unique position among Christian bodies, and incorporating both Catholic and Protestant elements. The Anglican approach to the dogmatic and other aspects of the ecumenical problem is in line with this position. It is neither Roman Catholic, nor Protestant, but Anglican. Its basis is a unity of dialectical tension between its Catholic and Protestant elements. From a Catholic point of view, the criticism of this standpoint is not that it tries to understand the Protestant point of view, but that it accepts it within its own life, and yet intends to remain Catholic. In his Encyclical on the unity of the Church, *Satis Cognitum*, Leo XIII quotes the following words of St Augustine: "On many points they are with me; in some only, they are not

141

with me. But on account of these few points on which they are separated from me, all the others on which they are with me avail them nothing." And he adds: "Nothing could be truer; for those who take from Christian doctrine only what they want, are relying on their own judgement and not on faith." [12]

3. The adequate principle for a definition of the essence of Protestantism

Some consider that the essence of Protestantism could be deduced from Luther alone. Protestantism would then appear as a kind of developed, systematized, dogmatized Luther.[1] It is a view not without an element of truth, but it oversimplifies matters. Classical Protestantism cannot be summed up in Luther alone. Nor can radical Protestantism be reduced to classical Protestantism. An adequate comprehension of the Protestant tradition must be defined from its fundamental characteristics taken as a whole.

Is there in fact an essence of Protestantism, and in what does it consist? Is there really anything in common between classical and radical Protestantism? In what way is Congregationalism akin to Methodism? Lutheranism to Anabaptism? Adventism to Pentecostalism? The Mennonites to the Presbyterians? etc.

If we try to solve the problem from within the realm of feelings and appearances, the difference will inevitably seem impossible to overcome. And yet, whether we like it or not, there *are* elements in common. In any case, the modern ecumenical movement would have been impossible, had these bodies been unable to come together on the basis of agreement on some fundamental points. It is these common elements that make integration possible.

Since Protestantism began, there have been a number of attempts to create "harmonies" between the Protestant "creeds" and to bring out the points in which they agree and disagree. In 1581 Theodore Beza, in collaboration with Salnar and Daneau, produced a Harmony of the Confessions. This was issued in Latin in Geneva, and in English in 1586, 1643 and 1844, with additions by Peter Hall.[2]

In 1612 a harmony of the Reformed confessions was published in Latin. In 1654 it was reissued with corrections added by the Synod of Dort (1619), together with the Confession of Cyril, Patriarch of Con-

---

[12] Text in Cattin-Conus, *op. cit.*, p. 353.
[1] Karl Adam, *Vers l'unité chrétienne* (1949), p. 50.
[2] *The Harmony of the Protestant Confessions exhibiting the Faith of the Churches of Christ Reformed after the Pure and Holy Doctrine of the Gospel, through Europe* (1844).

stantinople, and the General Confession of the Reformed Churches of Poland, Lithuania and the provinces annexed following the decisions of the assembly of Thorn.

In 1808, B. Porteous published a collection of Reformed confessions, and this was reissued in 1827. During the same year, J. C. William Augusti published a collection of Continental confessions.[3] In 1835, the Rev. Steward produced *The Scriptural Unity of Protestant Churches,* and in 1837 the Rev. John Cumming issued *The Unity of Protestantism, being Articles of Religion from the Creeds of the Reformed Churches.* Three years later, the *Collectio Confessionum in Ecclesiis Reformatis* was published by Dr H. A. Niemeyer. In 1923 an English translation of Forbe's *Irenicum* was produced by E. C. Selwyn.[4] And examples could be multiplied.

The general purpose of these collections and harmonies which appeared on the continent was to show, through comparison with each other, the unity of the Protestant "creeds", and to refute the accusation that Protestantism is a mere chaotic mass destined to disintegrate. Those published in England were meant to convince the nation that, thanks to its agreement with the other Protestant confessions, Anglicanism could rightly remain what it was, and had no need to return to Roman Catholicism.[5]

II. THE HEART OF PROTESTANTISM

What constitutes the vital essence of the Reformation? Is it the principle of private judgement? A careful examination of the history of Protestantism will show that the practice of free-examination must not be considered as an absolute sanction of individualism. It may certainly lead to it; and it has certainly succumbed to it. And yet, for the sake of accuracy, it must be said that on the whole, classical and even radical Protestantism has always held that scripture must be interpreted according to the peculiar tradition of each denomination. Today this point is emerging with increasing clarity in Protestantism. The Bible has been given to the Church; it must be read in community. The Spirit speaks through it to the Churches. It cannot contradict itself since it is one and unalterable. It must, therefore, guide those it teaches to similar conclusions on essentials.

Protestant theologians are sometimes startled when asked what lies at

[3] It was entitled: *Corpus Librorum Symbolicorum, qui in Ecclesia Reformatorum Auctoritatem Publicam obtinuerunt.*
[4] *Irenicum* Joannis Forbesii (Aberdoniae, 1624).
[5] Slosser, *op. cit.,* p. 362.

the heart of the Reformation and what the essential principles of Protestantism are. This is because "Protestantism", as such, does not exist. It only exists in its various embodiments. And yet, family features shared by even the most dissimilar denominations, the common conviction of being Protestant and not Catholic or Orthodox, the very existence of the World Council of Churches, all bear unmistakable witness to elements held in common.

It is these elements, these principles that we must try to define. We shall not forget that they are the result of an abstraction. They must be considered as pointers to the complete reality, and not as that reality itself.

The spirit of the Reformation as expressed in its faith and its way of life is commonly reduced to two great principles, one called the formal, the other the material principle. These are the supreme authority of the Word of God and justification by faith.

This simplification, however, seems too schematic; it fails to do justice to the complexity of the principles of the Reformation. In the present work the heart of the Reformation will be considered as expressed in the three following principles:

1. The supreme authority of the Word of God.
2. The immediacy and transcendence of Christ's action over the Church, the soul and the world.
3. The nature of the Church as witness.

Every Protestant or anyone whose position approximates to Protestantism will feel at home in these principles, even though he may interpret them in terms of his own denomination.

1. The supreme authority of the Word of God

The primacy of the Word of God in Protestantism is a fact, a climate, a dogma. It belongs to the whole Protestant tradition, right from its manifold origins. It holds the title role in every denomination, without exception. It is a prerequisite to their activity, their thought, their life. It is the measure, the norm and the regulating principle of Protestant orthodoxy. It has an equal authority over official and individual thought. It is the inspiration for a way of life and for the organization of human life.

It must always be remembered that if we wish to know the idea which Protestantism holds about the structure, mission and nature of the Church, the principles it considers to underlie evangelization and the part that Christians must play in the world, its conception of worship, prayer, devotion, and pastoral authority, how it understands the conditions required for the ecumenical dialogue, the characteristics it looks for in what is called "the future great Church", the "ecumenical Church", the "universal Christian fellowship" which it believes to be the meeting point for all Christians, then on all these issues, we must start from the absolutely fundamental principle of the primacy of the Word of God. Entry must be through this door if Protestant psychology is to be understood.

(a) How Catholics understand the Word of God

It is correct to say that when contemporary Protestantism discusses the meaning of "the Word of God", it has a better understanding of its significance than the first reformers had. Not that the new appreciation contradicts the old, but it is more complete, more extensive, more certain and penetrates more deeply. It owes this to the increasing information acquired by exegesis, and especially to a more thorough knowledge of biblical psychology.

It is an unfortunate fact that the slight contribution made by the Semitic world to Christian thought, and in particular the absence of Israel from the Church, has led to an imbalance in favour of Greek thought. There has been a great temptation to abstract a single element from the wealth of meaning contained in the biblical phrase "the Word of God", to reduce it to a philosophical concept, and to make it the equivalent of only those constituents of revelation which can be intellectually communicated and perceived.[6] The concept of revelation became simplified to that of a divine utterance which was merely a verbal expression on the part of God. A great part of the content of revelation was thus pared away. Many of our ecumenical difficulties have arisen from these sins of omission on both sides. This does not mean that the categories of Greek and Scholastic philosophy are to be despised, but it does mean that through the reduction of the biblical outlook to philosophical notions, a part of the Christian mystery has been lost sight of. The word "mystery" has had its significance renewed;[7] and now the same process is taking place with regard to the meaning of *the Word* of God.[8]

Need we point out that the origins of the Bible lie in the Semitic and not in either the Hellenic or the Latin world? Does not the value of a method spring from the harmony between it and its subject matter?

The Semitic mind has its own way of approaching reality. It seeks the concrete, the perceptible, the living being. It is intuitive; it does not make our precise distinctions between cause and effect, the symbol and

---

[6] J.-Ph. Ramseyer, "Parole" in *Vocabulaire biblique* (1st edition, 1954; 2nd edition, 1956).
[7] K. Prümm, "Mystère" in *Dict. Bibl.*, suppl. VI, fasc. XXX (1957), col. 1–225.
[8] E. g. Divo Barsotti, *La Parole de Dieu dans le mystère chrétien* (1954); L. M. Dewailly, *Jésus-Christ, Parole de Dieu* (1945).

the thing symbolized. In the effect, it sees cause and effect together; in a person's actions it sees his soul; in words it understands not merely a statement, but the expression of their living source. Its method is not to go back from effect to cause as though the one could be detached from the other, but by an apprehension that surrounds them both, that is total and simultaneous. Its way of approaching both the concrete and the abstract differs from that of the Greeks, the Latins or any other races. It seeks the totality of a being, and it reaches it in an all embracing way, by a slow process, in which both the senses and the intellect have an equal share.[9]

When we read in Genesis that God created heaven and earth by his Word, when the prophets say that the Word of God was addressed to them, when St John tells us that God reveals himself in his Word, or when in the Acts (4, 29, 31) it is stated that God directs the development of the Church's history through the proclamation of his Word—it is obvious that we must attribute a wider meaning to the noun "Word" than that of a communication made explicit in a sentence, or of knowledge conveyed by concepts. At least four different meanings are involved: the act of creative power, an element of intellectual knowledge, a theophany made manifest in the person of the Word incarnate, and the witness borne to a living reality which acts with sovereign power at the very moment when its messenger proclaims it.

It is the presence in both the Old and New Testaments of these two elements of knowledge and dynamism, sometimes separately, sometimes in combination, that prohibits us from restricting the meaning of "the Word" to that of a verbal or conceptual expression alone.

The Word, therefore, indicates an act, an event, a deed done by God, through which he reveals his purpose and writes the history of salvation. It is a thing of power, energy and radiant life. It is a concrete entity, filled with glory and supreme reality. It is a break through by God into time, his direct summons to mankind, now enabled to respond to it, an inner witness within the human consciousness. It is a sign, a sacrament, a symbol, a miracle, a striking deed. It also contains an element of knowledge, for it involves instruction in wisdom and understanding about God, man and the universe. It has a didactic purpose; to men who do not know the truths of salvation, it reveals the existence of the super-natural realm.

As a message of truth, a verbal or written expression, a theophany

---

[9] W. W. Robinson, "Hebrew Psychology" in A. S. Peake, ed., *The People and the Book* (1925); J. Pedersen, *Israel, Its Life and Culture*, vol. II (1926); Max Kadushin, *Organic Thinking, A Study in Rabbinic Thought* (1938); Thorlief Boman, *Hebrew Thought Compared with Greek* (1st English edition, 1960).

made manifest, an act of God's glory: no single phrase can be an adequate rendering of the full meaning of "Word" of God. Its content is the whole history of salvation, for that history is simply the solemn Word which God addresses to the world, summoning it to existence and redemption. To preach the Word does not mean repeating propositions, however noble; reiterating phrases, even though revealed; drawing up arguments to support some human conclusion. It is to call down upon the world the cataclysm of God's power in its creative and illuminating strength; it is to fling the gates of his luminous and active presence wide open, so that it brings into existence what it reveals in symbols. It means making room for that Word which is God revealing himself, for this Word never exists without the presence of the One who utters it. This is the first characteristic of the Word in the Bible, and this is its essence.

Its second characteristic is its vital and dynamic relationship with God. Israel did not separate the written or spoken Word from its Author, nor the event willed by God from its Agent, nor the symbol chosen by God from the reality he meant to symbolize by it. Word and Deed accompany each other. Symbols, events, signs, miracles, prophecies, all these were seen by Israel in their vital, intimate, contemporary relationship with God. The Word has no meaning save as the Word of God, as God actually speaking, as the living Word in action, as an event (Heb 4: 12–13). In short, it is God's absolute presence. It is his presence, either illuminated or veiled, either quiescent or in action, communicating itself to men through words, images, signs, deeds, miracles, and even silences, that arouse the soul's attention. The Word will not allow itself to be confined by any human account of itself. There is no substitute for it. Hidden in the human words spoken in God's name, there is the Word. Nor will it allow itself to be reduced to the communication of a sealed up message, even if carried by a faithful messenger. On the contrary, it is present in the message, fully charged with its vital power, a power that transforms both the messenger and those to whom it is addressed, whether it be the course of history, human consciousness, mankind or the world.

The third characteristic of the Word is its existence in time. When I say that I believe in God because he has spoken, I am expressing the formal motive of my faith, the authority of God's self-revelation. But what is the concrete meaning of the Word as God's self-revelation? Should we say that this is solely the Word as a statement in the order of abstract truths? This would depreciate the meaning of the authority of God's Word as the formal motive of faith, for that concerns the Word in its concrete historical manifestation, and in the economy of salvation, culminating in the Word incarnate. Faith cannot dispense with God's revelation in history, for the God of faith is the God of Jesus Christ, "the God of Abraham, Isaac and Jacob" (Exod 13, 6), the God whose

147

Word is living tradition. The Word of God became an event in time. It is, therefore, impossible to make ones way to God without travelling along the road of his incarnate Word.

What is the fourth characteristic of the Word? The living and active Word of God is essentially a Word in eschatological tension. The purpose of the revealed and revealing Word is not to exist in a self-subsistent order of Platonic truth, suspended above men, unknown by them, and, as it were, running parallel to their existence. For the Word is in fact, the ultimate, the conclusive reality, the Eschaton. The Word at whose fiat, the world, mankind, history, the Church, comes into being, is related to them as the last and final centre and end of the whole universe, the focus of attraction from which nothing can escape. The cyclical idea of time is shown to be false. The Word postulates an order, a termination to the seemingly unending recurrence of things. But this terminal characteristic must not be understood as only a final chronological point, in the way that a meeting may be said to be the end of a journey. Its eschatological nature must also be seen as a presence already here that grapples with history and demands an account of its stewardship. Time is wholly encircled by the Word which enlightens it, presses upon it, calls it to obedience, and moves it to abandon itself in it as in its deepest and most sublime reality.

This fourth characteristic involves as a corollary the aspect of personal relationship. It is addressed to mankind, the world and the Church. It is spoken to a listener, and that listener must answer. It is direct, immediate, radically purposive. It is to man that God speaks. His Word is not uttered in a void of everlasting silence. It is an act of shattering power. No man is beyond its reach. Wherever a man may go, it will pursue him, even into the bowels of the earth. Sooner or later, weak and breathless, he will have to yield. "Thou art stronger than I" groaned Jeremiah (Jer 20:7), and St Paul confessed that the Word had taken him captive (Phil 3:12).

Because it is the supreme initiator, the Word is the supreme organizer of an order of life, of communal existence, of human destiny. This indeed is another of its characteristics. The Word which in its eternal wisdom has foreshadowed the beauty of a multitude of brethren in unity, and loved the splendour of that image radiating from its essence, has become sheer mercy towards them. It has summoned them, justified them, drawn them together, and glorified them. "And the Word became flesh" (Jn 1:14), in order "to gather into one the children of God who are scattered abroad" (Jn 11:52).

The Word also includes a sacrifical dimension, and this is its final characteristic. "He came to his own home, and his own people received him not" (Jn 1:11). The prophets, martyrs and apostles showed in their lives that the Word meets opposition. The age-long history of the covenant records that although the Word "conquered kingdoms, enforced justice, received promises, stopped the mouths of lions, quenched raging fire" (Heb 11:33–34), it also "suffered mocking and scourging, and even chains and imprisonment"; it was seen "wandering over deserts and mountains, and in dens and caves of the earth" (Heb 11:36–39). The Word "of whom the world was not worthy" (Heb 11:38)! Together with festive celebrations of the covenant, there have also been betrayals and disloyal deeds, hours of crucifixion when the Word traversed the world with the appearance of the Suffering Servant and of the Lamb of God. The blood of the Word is shed and sacrificed, and it is then that it becomes redemptive.

But whether it is glorified or immolated, the Word is always present and at hand, and therein lies its victory. The hour of Calvary marks the most paradoxical incident in the life of the Word; it was the hour when it was identified with silence and death. And it was at this very time, when, so to say, the Word re-entered the Father's bosom, that it rose again in the brightness of the Holy Spirit. It is this immolated, glorified, risen Word, that has given itself to the Church as real food and drink (Jn 6:56).

Why was it that so large a part of the Christian world allowed the eucharistic realism of the Word to disappear, and that having proclaimed the great return to the Word in its fullness, it still does not draw out all the consequences from it?

If Protestantism had been merely an abstract declaration of theoretical truths, a method of evangelizing that used the Bible as an arsenal of revealed propositions, merely a witness (even if a faithful witness) to the truth of a revelation contained in a book which is called the scriptures, it would have vanished long ago from the face of the earth. When Catholics have been faced, as happens frequently, with the enthusiasm and effectiveness of the preaching of a Protestant missionary or minister, they have wondered where such things originated. Where could the undeniable success of these apostles reside, whose only resource lies practically in the Word of God alone? The question ignored the fact that it is the Word that precisely constitutes their power. Had they looked at the Bible with an unclouded vision, they would have been able to see the sacramental significance of scripture as the instrument of that eternal Word which brings the cosmos into existence and overthrows the universe, "destroys, overthrows, builds and plants (cf. Jer 1:10). Had they realized this, they would have known that the Word never returns to its emissary without having produced its effect. These Protestants had only this, but they had it and how powerful it is!

One can appreciate the immense enthusiasm of the Reformation, the kind of earth-shaking illumination that suddenly gave a meaning to what had been a mass of chaotic indifference, when the first reformers made their own discovery of *this* supreme biblical truth: Scripture is the Word of God and its power is infinite. What was it then that separated them from Catholicism? It was their very passion for the scriptures alone, *scriptura sola*. Through this they shut themselves off from some of the aspects of the Word that are no less authentic than what they proclaimed. The Reformation was led further than its object while it continued to contain truth.

(b) The primacy of the Word of God in Protestantism

When the first reformers came to regard the Bible as a kind of sacrament, and proclaimed scripture and the Word to be inseparable, they were, perhaps, more truly heirs of the Middle Ages and witnesses to the central Christian tradition than they imagined. For the idea of the Bible as a sacrament of the Word is in complete accord with the idea of the Word incarnate as the fundamental sacrament of the Father, and with the idea of the Church as a sacramental reality resulting from the connection binding the Mystical Body to its Head.

Since the Reformation, the distinction between scripture and the sacraments has been exaggerated. In practice, it seems that we have been content too long to leave the Word to the Protestants and neatly confine ourselves within the seven sacraments. The contemporary rediscovery of the sacramental nature of the Church was bound to lead to a reconsideration of the idea of scripture as a sacrament of the Word and, like the seven sacraments, endowed with the power of sanctifying mankind.[10]

In a sense, and if considered only in its material composition, the Bible is a dead monument. It comes alive when God makes it a contemporary reality to the human mind. A wonderful union is then produced between the heavenly element, the Word, and the earthly element, the letter, a union that is truly sacramental in character. The Bible is seen as the sacrament of the Word, the sacred sign which sanctifies mankind. The "Word" of scripture does not mean the words taken in their material reality, but these same words filled with the soul of the Word incarnate, with the breath of God's Spirit. It is, therefore, a message of knowledge and love, not simply of ideas, but filled with the power and energy of the relations between the Persons of the Trinity. Scripture is only materially the Word of God; it becomes that Word formally, when through it God actually speaks to man. It is then that the living Word of God makes itself heard. The material of the scriptures is made resplendent with the heavenly presence which sees in them its own face. In a recollected soul, scripture becomes a

[10] H. Schillebeeckx, "Parole et Sacrement", *Lumière et Vie* (January–March 1960), pp. 24–5.

theophany of immense attraction which delights in the revelation of the different aspects of the divine presence. The soul is made joyful in its Creator, in God its Saviour. Scripture is seen to be in truth the sacrament of the Word, because through it "the Holy" comes into the world and makes men holy.

In spite of this the Reformation led to Protestantism. We must take great care to grasp the exact meaning given by the Reformation to the primacy of the Word of God in scripture. Here, as in many other matters, the error of the Reformation does not spring from the kind of truths it affirms; it is due to those it has denied or omitted.

Its interpretation has been principally vitiated by the fundamental transference to the Bible of something which rightly belongs to the sphere of mediation by the Christian community. Scripture becomes *the* sacrament, the only sacrament in the true sense of the word. It becomes the fundamental mediation,[11] the immediate mediation between God and men. This is the heart of the Protestant idea of the Church. Scripture is the one true sacrament. All the others are relative to it, and are only outward expressions of its inner reality. Now it is held that in Protestantism this inner event is the central act of Chritianity. We can see in this the emergence of the idea of a Church that is essentially an event hidden in the heart of God.

We are not in any way suggesting that the sacramental significance and the mediatory role should be rejected, but simply that over-statements need correction.

Keeping in mind the difference between "Protestantism" in the abstract, and its concrete forms, we shall try now to delineate the characteristics which belong to the primacy of the Word of God in Protestantism.

Primarily and quite simply it means that the Word of God comes before all else; before the authority of tradition; before that of the Church, before that of an infallible magisterium. Primacy, in this case, means an absolute anteriority. Tradition and the Church will in the end be allowed to possess authority, but it is posterior to that of the Word.

Protestantism is unable to see that the Church's infallible magisterium and tradition may also be modalities of the one undivided Word.

In the second place, primacy means supremacy. The authority of God's Word exercises a supreme primacy over all lesser authorities, the supremacy of a ruler over his subjects. It is endowed with its own infallibility, transcendent, unshared. The others are only authoritative in as much as they are external but faithful witnesses in relation to the absolute authority of the Word. The position is somewhat like that of John the Baptist, the Precursor, the Witness, who pointed out the Lord, the only Lord.

Catholic criticism has shown that this standpoint ascribes a purely

---

[11] John Baillie, *Our Knowledge of God* (1939), pp. 178–201.

external character to the witness borne to revealed truth by the Church, whereas, on the Catholic view, the magisterium functions in a sacramental relationship to that of Christ.

Lastly, in Protestantism, primacy implies transcendence. The Word of God is not tied to any lesser authority that may utter it, proclaim it, use it as a witness, or bears witness to it. The Word of God cannot become a part of any combination with created reality. It is unique and unadulterated. A man may utter the Word, but he must know that he always does so with impure lips, because he is a sinner and so remains when imputed to be justified.

Protestantism is thus unable to accept the fact that the transcendent Word might be able to ally itself with the created word through some grace given to the latter which makes it sacramental. And yet our Lord told his apostles: "whatever you bind on earth shall be bound in heaven" Matt 18, 18). In short, in Protestantism, scripture is accepted as the sacrament of the living Word of God which brings the letter to life, but those other manifestations of the revelation of the Word, called tradition, the sacraments, the magisterium of the Church, are not accepted, even though these also are truly the Word shown forth. Therefore, what separates us is not the primacy of the Word of God as such, nor its perfection, nor its present power of universal influence, nor its absolute supremacy. It is the refusal to accept the fact that the human word had been enabled, through a special calling of grace, to share in the transcendence of the divine Word, as expressed in the infallible magisterium. This ultimately implies a rejection of the total sacramental nature of the Word.

(c) Scripture and tradition

What is the relationship between scripture and tradition? Is scripture all that is needed by the Church? Does it contain the whole of revelation? Newman said that after the Council of Trent it might be thought that scripture contains, at least implicitly, everything that has been revealed. How are we to interpret the Council's words: "Revelation is contained in the sacred books and in the unwritten traditions"?[12]

According to J. R. Geiselmann,[13] the Council of Trent explicitly excluded the idea that revelation was contained only partially in scripture and partially in tradition.

[12] Denzinger, *Enchiridion Symbolorum*, no. 784.
[13] "Das Missverständnis über das Verhältnis von Schrift und Tradition und seine Überwindung in der Katholischen Theologie", *Una Sancta* (September 1956), pp. 131–50; "Un malentendu dissipé: Écriture et Tradition dans la théologie catholique", *Istina*, no. 2 (1958). See also the Second Vatican Council's Dogmatic Constitution on Revelation. The Council has closed no door. On the contrary, it has provided a good basis for a further dialogue.

152

Fr G. H. Tavard, A. A.,[14] follows J. R. Geiselmann; and Fr M. J. Congar, O. P., in a review of Fr Tavard's book takes a favourable view of this interpretation.[15] But Fr H. Lennerz, S. J.,[16] and Fr Bévenot, S. J.,[17] reject it as against the evidence.

What is meant by the conjunction "and" in the words quoted from the Council? Does it mean "partially in scripture and partially in tradition", so that scripture and tradition have each a different content? Does it mean that there is only a single and identical revelation, communicated through two sources, two avenues? Or, is it not more likely to mean that revelation is contained simultaneously in the source and in the stream that issues from it and makes its content explicit in a homogeneous way?

In the first case, scripture is not all sufficient. Revelation is considered as bipartite. In the second, scripture and tradition repeat each other, but in a different way. In the third, tradition is regarded as the homogeneous development of the source under the influence of the Word.

It is abundantly clear that the problem is not an easy one. The word tradition evidently has several different meanings.

One fact should draw our attention. The Protestant rejection of tradition was accompanied by a similar reaction against the doctrine of the Eucharist, against several other sacraments, against the acceptance of a particular structure of the Church, against even the number of inspired books, against the recognition of the Ecumenical Councils, etc. And yet the Reformation was brought about in the name of the primacy of the Word of God. Is scripture, therefore, in fact all sufficient?

Another factor to be kept in mind is the ambience in which it is read.

If it is agreed that revelation is to be found in its entirety in scripture, at least implicitly, must it not also be agreed that not everything in scripture is clear and comprehensible, that something apart from it was necessary in order to settle its canon, to decide on the structural forms of the Church's constitution, to reach an understanding of the nature of the sacraments and their correct celebration?

The age-long experience of Protestantism in its divisions, in its very reunification, provides clear proof that if we start from the principle of scripture alone, we shall never arrive at the Catholic or Orthodox view of things. Had tradition been of no account in Christianity, Christendom would not have become deeply divided in doctrine at the Reformation. Agreement that the Word of God exists in scripture, is therefore not enough. Agreement must also be reached as to its meaning.

[14] *Holy Writ or Holy Church: the Crisis of the Protestant Reformation* (1959).
[15] *R. S. P. T.* (April 1960); see also Fr Congar's *La Tradition et les traditions* (1960).
[16] *Gregorianum*, XL (1959), pp. 38–53.
[17] *Heythrop Journal*, I (1960), pp. 34–47, and *Theological Studies*, III (1960), pp. 484–5.

What name must be given to that other factor, which is not scripture, but discloses its meaning, and which either brings out or confirms in explicit terms those truths and facts which scripture expresses only in subtle hints or with extreme brevity, when it goes so far as that?

It is tradition that has shown the Western as well as the Eastern Church to celebrate the one Eucharist in a legitimate diversity of liturgies, to understand the Church as the great sacrament of Christ whose own deeds and words are sacramentals, to accept the institution of the hierarchy as a revealed fact originating in the indivisible totality of the revelation given by Christ and the apostles. It is tradition that has led to the clarification of a number of obscure truths and facts in scripture.

In the ancient creeds, the apostolic canons, the decrees and canons of local or ecumenical councils, the early liturgies that owe their origin to the apostles and the Fathers, the acts of the martyrs, the early histories of the Church, the writings of the Fathers, the doctors and the saints, the liturgical books, the catechesis, the pronouncements of the papal magisterium—in all these it is the voice of tradition that makes itself heard. It proclaims that the message was not revealed to men in order to remain, as it were, suspended above their heads; it was entrusted to a living community. In both the Old and New Testaments the revelation was given by God, through Christ, in a total and living way: in a total way, in the shape of a series of truths and also of facts, as doctrine and as history, as teaching and as things done; in a living way, because before being written down, the message was transmitted to a living tradition, to a corporate body which carries it and wherein it dwells, a body it transforms and whose substance it at the same time incorporates into itself. It is connatural to tradition to be incarnate. How else could it take hold of man's whole being, how else could man grasp it in its fullness? Let us be clear then as to the import of the word tradition: in one sense, tradition includes scripture in itself; in another, it is less than or different from scripture, although never in opposition to it.

We must, therefore, assert that in conjunction with scripture, the teachings of the faith and of religion, and the sacramental rites, are preserved in the Church by means of tradition which, like scripture, is an authentic mode of the expression of divine revelation.

Is it a different mode, or the same mode expressed differently? As a general rule, tradition and scripture may be considered as the letter and its interpretation; but this is not always the case. For not everything that the Lord said and did has been consigned to the books accepted as the canon of scripture. In relation to this, we speak of tradition in the restrictive sense: this or that tradition. It is not wholly true to say that tradition expresses the affirmations of scripture in a different way, if by that is meant that an opposition exists between scripture and its defined authentic meaning. Nor is it wholly true to say that everything is implicitly contained in scripture, if by that is meant that the complete and exact meaning of scripture can be strictly ascertained without any reference to tradition.

If we are to understand tradition, it is of the utmost importance to observe that what has been revealed and transmitted is not something abstract and conceptual. There are also deeds, facts, events, examples, "typical" forms of activity, that foreshadow future realities, a history. Scripture certainly contains an historical as well as a doctrinal order, but before revelation came to be written down, it was given, laid hold of and lived in deeds, signs, symbols, images, practical rules, doctrinal instructions. And even when it was written down, it did not become alien to its environment. Everything that was implicit in it, was brought to completion through the practice of living it. Scripture is like the history of the tradition of the people of God, the written memory which the Christian community gave itself, in order to fix the history of the birth and life of its Head, of its own birth and its own life, and to be able to recall them to future generations.

It is on account of the complexity of revelation—a combination that is both doctrinal and practical; a message vitally given by the Word of Truth, eternal and incarnate; a manifestation of the mystery of God through words, deeds, events, examples, facts—that we must be careful to put no opposition between scripture and tradition, tradition and Church. Scripture dwells in a living community as in its own environment, and it is natural that the exchanges proper to life should develop between it and its environment.

We know that the commandment given by the Lord to the apostles chosen to be the official guarantors of revelation was of a twofold order: that of doctrine and that of action. It was an order of doctrine, for transmitting the truth about the Saviour's nature and life, about the history of salvation and the people of God; and an order of action, for the apostles had to perform certain actions of the kind the Lord himself had done, and whose prototype is the "Do this in remembrance of me" (Lk 22:19; 1 Cor 11:24). Scripture often affirms, with reference to Jesus, the connection between these spheres of doctrine and action (Acts 1:1; Mk 6:30; Mt 7:24; Mt 5:19). Revelation and its transmission thus entail an aspect that has to do with deeds and facts, equally with the aspect that is concerned with doctrine and is non-temporal in character. We read of what Jesus said, and that must be said again; we read of what he did, and that has to be repeated by deeds, actions, signs, symbols, rites, sacraments, by a Christian individual and a community life built up in imitation of him. Lacking anything of this there would be a failure to transmit the fullness of the revelation of the Word of God in whom everything is sacred: words and doctrine, life,

155

deeds and examples. Revelation is a tradition which is transmitted by practice, by vital incorporation. A man, a community, a Church carry it on, and accomplish it. In every age of the Church, tradition, understood in its full extent, has always been the most important instrument in the formation of the Christian soul. Through a combination of doctrinal teaching, moral rules, sacramental rites and disciplinary canons, that is, through a body of truths and facts, it incorporates men in the history of salvation and enables them to share in the coming of the Word of God into the world and in what he did. Initiation into Christianity is not merely an initiation into a doctrine, but into a total life: that of the Church, with its past, present and future hope. In this sense tradition is identical with the life of the Church from the time when it began, from the time when it became true that the Church was in existence within the reality of its mystical Head.

How was a revelation of this kind, a revealed Word of this kind to be transmitted? And how can it be done so that what is transmitted is as complete as what was originally given? Jesus answered this problem by choosing a group of twelve to be with him, to share his life, see how he worked, what he did, and the way he revealed. These chosen witnesses, these official guarantors, were to be the educators of the new mankind. Their task was to bring the whole reality of Christ into existence in this new people by means of words, instruction, actions, signs and examples, which being grafted in those of Christ, and filled with the Word's own power, would create the presence of the Word of Truth, and of the Word-as-Action in its entirety in their midst.

Tradition does not only imply the transmission of ideas; it also includes the concrete, factual, practical and operative transmission of what has been given. It demands not only the adhesion of faith, but also performance in the realm of action. Tradition is transmitted through words, writings, deeds. These are the truths of tradition; these form its dogmatic teaching. There are also the facts of tradition; these belong to the sphere of law, dogma and ritual. Together they constitute the deposit of the revelation given by Christ and the apostles. The integral Christo-apostolic revelation is a body of teaching words, deeds, facts, events. It is a history, a doctrine, a life.

When, therefore, the presence of the Kingdom began to make its appearance in space and time, it raised up a people among whom it dwelt as in a living community. From within this tradition, scripture, of both the Old and New Testaments, came into existence as the illustrious witness of the infallible presence which made its permanence manifest through wondrous deeds. Scripture was first a continuity, a reality experienced within a living tradition, before being committed to writing. To make an opposition between scripture and tradition is to create a false problem which should be avoided. The living tradition is anterior to scripture, and any kind of contradiction between them is rendered impossible by the fact that it is one and the same revealed infallible living Word that was first received in the tradition and later re-echoed in scripture. The latter itself bears witness to tradition, but this does not mean that tradition thereby ceases to be a witness to the Word. If there is a difference between the two, it is due to the fact that tradition represents in an organic, historical, concrete condition, and as interpreting it by life and made incarnate, the same reality which scripture expresses in literary form. Any supposed dilemma between them is really a false problem, for in both of them there is one Word only. Scripture originated in the living tradition, and if its full meaning is to be discovered it must be immersed in that tradition again. Separated from the living tradition, scripture easily loses its coherence, as the increase in the number of sects has shown.

Does this mean that tradition has its total expression in scripture? Consider a similar problem: can even the best history of a kingdom and a king provide a complete account of the life of either of them? Does life find its complete expression in scripture? Does history yield all its content in a narrative, even if that narrative is inspired? Can the whole of its practical aspect, the aspect governed by human decisions, the aspect concerned with customary behaviour and deeds done, concrete and existential reality, what is taken as understood, or is only implicit, be contained in a literary memorial otherwise than as an abridgement? Scripture is the greatest witness of the living tradition, but the living tradition, which contains scripture, is greater than that part of itself which is called scripture. The Father uttered a Word in time, and that Word burst forth into innumerable shoots of life. "There are also many other things which Jesus did; were every one of them to be written, I suppose that the world itself could not contain the books that would be written" (Jn 21:25).

Must scripture be given precedence over tradition as a whole? There can only be one answer: the primacy of the Word of God expressing itself through both scripture and tradition.

Must it be said that revelation is to be found partially in scripture and partially in tradition? Or that what scripture says in one way, tradition says in another? The element of truth in each these positions should by now be clear.

But is this the whole truth about tradition? The hidden source of the living tradition has already been suggested: it is the presence of the creative Word of God which swells like a river of life, keeping true to its own nature from the beginning of revelation until its final consummation. The essence of tradition consists in its being the homogeneous evolution of a single source under the impact of the creative Word.

The mutual relationship between tradition and scripture has been established. We turn now to consider what are the constituent elements of the idea of tradition in Catholicism.

(d) The Catholic idea of tradition

A number of different factors contribute to the idea of tradition: memory, inner realization and awareness, infallibility and authority.

The *memoria amans* continues its petition for love as the steady development of an inner realization unfolds itself, and in the power of this ideal kept bright in its heart, it grows in likeness to the beloved object. What we have no secret motive for imitating, holds our thoughts no longer, for the love that would bind the image to our heart, and activate the movement to identify ourselves with it, has passed away.

It is the Three Persons who are ultimately responsible for tradition in the Church, and each in accordance with his own personality: the Father as the source of continuity; the Son as the living head of the enduring reality; the Holy Spirit as *memoria amans,* the memory which retains its object, is eager to return to it and to embrace it in his love. It is the Holy Spirit who closes the circle of unity in God. He dwells in the Church in order to remind her of everything Christ said and did. His function is to complete the circle of history and to bring it to its consummation in God.

As a communal memory, the Church transmits the whole of the Christian revelation held by her in remembrance from the time when it became true that the Son of God was to become incarnate.

Tradition, in its full extent, is all that has ben given, received and must be integrally transmitted until the end of the world; its mission is to bring history, mankind and the universe into conformity with their destiny in the Church. It includes everything preserved by the Church as the memory of the community; everything that must be integrally maintained until the world's end, when it must be recognizable as the same as that given in the beginning.

What has been given and received, what must be preserved is Christ in his mysteries, given to the Church and dwelling in her, his teaching through words and deeds, all the means of salvation which he instituted, the apostolate of the Twelve, the sacraments from the first time of their celebration, prayers and worship adopted from the Old Testament as he showed his disciples the way to pray, the new elements which he introduced, the realization that from Abraham's day until our own one family has existed, and, finally, the mystery of the Spirit given to the Church.

The Church must always be seen as the point where two streams meet and intersect: through one of them the Trinity bestows itself on man; through the other, men give themselves to God.

At the midpoint of this meeting stands the memory, the consciousness of the past which in the Church is something belonging to mankind and to the Trinity. In the Church we are of the same blood, the same race and the same seed as the apostles, prophets, patriarchs, doctors, and pontiffs, for we constitute one single body, with members in heaven, on earth and in purgatory. Thus there exists a mysterious persistence of awareness of the Church's past from the remotest ages, when she was only being prefigured, foretold and prophesied, until she entered time historically, through her shared life with Christ, ascended into glory, at the right hand of the Father.

In this way the Church, as a communal memory, preserves in the communion of saints of all periods, the living remembrance of the different stages through which God's plan has come to be established.

We still keep the memory of those early events which foreshadowed the shape of things to come; the candour of man's first response to God in the earthly paradise; God's presence in the burning bush still makes its impact on our soul; we feel the dread and the exaltation experienced by the prophets; we go with Israel on the long journey into exile. The Church still hears resounding in her heart, Mary's *fiat*, and the despair of the *consummatum est*. It was not only in a former age that the Church spread out from Jerusalem; she does so today; in those great waves stirred up by the Spirit, and known as the apostolate of the Twelve, the conversion of the barbarians, the evangelization of other lands. The Church is a community of memory. Her members need only to probe into their hearts, that is, into the heart and consciousness of the Church, in order to find all past things present. This does not mean that anything due to the finger of God in history, to the breath of the Spirit who spoke through the prophets, or to the resounding voice of God's Word may legitimately be withdrawn from it.

But the Spirit also makes Christ, "the tradition" of the Father, an inner reality in the Church. The Spirit enables Christ's words and deeds to penetrate into the apostles and pastors, into the flock and through the flock into the whole of history, into cultures and civilizations, into mankind and every nation. The insight which he provides into Christ's words and deeds implies also that he incorporates us into the living Christ; Christ lives within us. The apostles enjoyed a special relationship with the Spirit; he makes use of them as forerunners to mark the progress of the renewal of history. They stand as the outposts of the world's recapitulation. They are themselves the Twelve Gates of the City.

Tradition is also consciousness. History is called to realize, through the Church, the inner meaning of its reality in the mystery revealed by Christ and the apostles. Tradition is the self-awareness of history. It selects what is significant and keeps it alive. It is the means by which history is gathered into unity, time redeemed, the harvest stored, the world recapitulated in the Lord.

It transforms the ancient era, the era of sin, into the new age, the era of redemption. Every day, by means of it, everlastingness penetrates a little further into the world and brings it towards that simultaneity and coherence in which eternity consists: the possession in God's presence of endless life whole and perfect at a single moment.

When eternity penetrated into human history the new age had thus begun. History, the world, the harvest were already reintegrated prophetically in the vision of Christ and the apostles. Tradition unfolds revelation. It constitutes the bond of unity between the origin and the end, between the grand design and its fulfilment. It issues from the Ultimate Being and opens out into eschatology, like a river into its ocean, there to be lost, there to be consummated, there to achieve its fullest identity, in God's presence. When all is over, when all the wealth of the nations has gone in through the Twelve Gates that open on to the Lord, then tradition will be transformed by being fulfilled. *Civitas tota simul:* the City will be filled with all the wealth of earth and heaven. The period of the apostolate, dependent on the Lord, will be closed. This will be "the eighth day".

Yet there is no contempt for history here. Tradition, which gives significance to time by denying that it is eternally recurrent, will not throw contempt on such future as remains, precisely when it is projecting upon the world the unchangeable image of a new heaven and a new earth.

Tradition is also homogeneity, infallibility, authority. Did the Word of God who made provision for revelation, also provide for the guidance and regulation of the human minds in which it is received? Or was it content for the truth of God to be splintered by human judgement?

Those who uphold the sacred deeds of tradition are in reality guarding something more than these deeds: they are also guarding the symbols of the Alliance. Those who preserve the sacred truths of tradition are in reality maintaining something more than these truths; they are guarding the Word of the covenant.

The history of Christian divisions amply shows that though the meaning of revelation may have been propounded, this is no guarantee that it will be preserved, and that regret for its loss provides no assurance that it will be regained.

We have mentioned homogeneity, but can all traditions be placed on an equal footing?

In Protestantism two series of traditions are distinguished: apostolic tradition from which scripture issued, and human ecclesiastical tradition, which is post-apostolic. The former is divine and is identical with Christ's infallible revelation. The latter belongs to the same sphere as the visibility of the Church, that is, it is useful, necessary for the well-being of the Church, but human, external and fallible. It is on a very different level from the former.

In Catholicism, three levels of tradition are recognized. First, that which comes from Christ and from his teaching, either in public, or privately to the apostles (Acts 1, 3). Secondly, that which comes from the apostles, but in which Christ and the Holy Spirit intervened, immediately after the Ascension. Thirdly, there are the post-apostolic ecclesiastical traditions of the Church: doctrinal definitions and canonical decrees given for the guidance of the Church's members.

We hold, with the Protestants, that the tradition of the apostles and the revelation given by Christ are binding for ever. We also agree that with the death of the last apostle revelation was closed, and that all that the Church is to do is to transmit the apostolic deposit. But agreement ends when we come to the mode of this transmission and to the authority equipped to transmit it.

Is the apostolic deposit transmitted like a sealed letter? Or is it rather a living reality, incorporated in a community? Is it transmitted with the possibility of its being lost, or are the necessary means of protection guaranteed to it?

To posit a break in continuity between the Church of the apostles and the post-apostolic Church would, in the Catholic view, amount to the admission of so profond a change in the Church's life that her nature would have become essentially changed. The true Church would have ended with the death of the last apostle, and another would have taken her place. It would be to admit that, to begin with, there was a living tradition, which was the vehicle of scripture, but that at a given moment it ceased to be accepted. At the start the Church would have been a community assisted by the Spirit, but not forever. The apostles would have declared the authoritative meaning of revelation within the living community of the Church, but the reasons which, in the Lord's mind, sanctioned their position as living, infallible guarantors of revelation would have ceased to count. And so we should be led to the paradoxical conclusion that the nearer to the origins of the Church, the greater the need for an authority to ensure that revelation would remain homogeneous with itself, but the further those origins were left behind, the less necessary this became. The Church's continuity would, in fact, have been broken in two.

What is the truth of the matter? The apostles died, and yet surely it was essential for their function to continue. Only thus could the community of the Church escape being separated from its source. And since in the doctrinal authority of the successors of the apostles we see one more of the manifold manifestations of the Word, we do not shrink from proclaiming that Christ is the Lord of tradition, and that there is no other.[18]

Would an ineffective primacy of the Word still remain a primacy? Would sovereignty over a divided family still be sovereignty? Would a transcendent power that appeared to have lost all concern for the affairs of the Church still be absolute?

Richard Paquier does not see how it can be denied that the apostles must have chosen their successors, first elders, then bishops. In as much as the apostolate was a wittness by eye and ear to the events and deeds of our Lord's life, it was unique and could not be transmitted. But that living authority and unifying control represented by the apostles did not in any way cease to be neccessary to the Church of Christ. It is true that the Church had collected the apostolic writings into a doctrinal canon of scripture. But if she had merely possessed a literature which contained the apostolic writings and not also a general ministry to ensure the safeguard of this good "deposit", she would have been like a country endowed with a first-rate written constitution and yet having no government with the power to apply it and make it respected.[19] Shortly afterwards he adds: "No more appropriate means than the episcopal succession has been discovered to make the Church clearly evident throughout time as an institution, an organic body, the Body of Christ, while Holy Scripture and the confessions of faith received with finality, ensure her identity as a community vivified by Christ's Spirit."[20]

The successors of the apostles were selected to be witnesses of the original witnesses so as to safeguard their testimony. Christ's action in choosing the apostolic college as corporate guarantors of the realities of his life and mysteries was bound to seem to the apostles as an act that created tradition. Revelation, we should remember, is not a matter of truths only: it also includes deeds, facts, "typical" happenings that foreshadowed future realities. The institution of the apostolic college is a "typical" happening of this kind: it was both a present revelation and the beginning of the tradition of the future.

This work of safeguarding the mystery present in the world and of maintaining it in homogeneity to the end by assimilating what is akin to it and rejecting alien elements, belongs to the function of the hierarchic apostolate in general. Is this a usurpation of God's rights? No, it is an instrument at the service of revelation. And it is because the apostles and

[18] O. Cullmann, *La Tradition* (1954); K. E. Skydsgaard, *One in Christ, Protestants and Catholics; Where They Agree, Where They Differ* (1957), chapter III: "Scripture and Tradition".

[19] "L'Épiscopat dans la structure institutionnelle de l'Église", *Verbum Caro*, 49 (1959), p. 42.

[20] *Ibid.*, p. 47.

their successors must be equipped with the means of reaching their goal and of carrying out their mission that they have a share in our Lord's infallibility. The function of the magisterium is not to add anything whatsoever to revelation, but to extend the Divine Word and its infallibility to the entire community of the Church. The magisterium's own idea of itself is that of a minister and servant of the Word. Far from introducing a new revelation, it confines itself to declaring whether or not the reflection on her faith pursued throughout her history is in conformity with the message of Christ and the apostles.

The infallibility of the magisterium is not a substitute for either the interior testimony of the Spirit or the authority of scripture. The inner testimony serves as an inner authentification of scripture, bringing it to life in the mind. The magisterium, on the other hand, is an outward authentification of the revealed Word within the community of believers.

In the object and the act of faith there is God alone. The magisterium intervenes from the outside as the indispensable condition for an authentic entry into the fullness of that inheritance reserved for men from all eternity. It discards what is unworthy, and welcomes into the City whatever befits its nature.

The apostle lives on in the authority of his successors. What then is the meaning of authority?

The true idea of authority combines a number of elements: origin, initiative, creation, juridical guarantee, dignity, perfection, official recognition, the right to be accepted with respect, and to serve as a model, a guide, a rule.

The authority of the apostles first comes to them, therefore, from their position as an origin. Who was closer to the source of revelation than they?

It also comes to them from the guarantees which they offer. Who, more than they, has received the Holy Spirit for a mission and has given so many proofs that the Holy Spirit dwells in them?

Thirdly, their authority is based on their works. These men who, in the Holy Spirit and through contact with the Word, acquired a mysterious maturity equipping them to be the stewards of the Kingdom and the dispensers of the mysteries of God for the whole world and all time, became, under our Lord's authority, "authors" of the Church.

Servants of the Word, witnesses of the great deeds of God, heralds of the Good News, summoners of mankind to submit to the Lord's sovereign rule, ministers of the faith and of the sacraments—these are the attributes with which the apostles appear before us. What authority has ever been less despotic or masterful? It is the authority of holiness and contemplation, of divine election, of direct contact with the Master, of the outpouring of the Spirit, of responsibility and of the Church's mission, and it is the authority resulting from good works performed.

No other source of authority exists in the Church, and it could be expressed in no other way, without contradicting the very foundation of the Church.

The successors of the apostles base themselves upon the apostles whose message they transmit, like an unbroken chain, until the end of the world. This is the apostolicity of origin. They have received from the Spirit, through the laying on of the apostles' hands, the charism which makes continuity certain. This is the apostolicity of guarantee.

Nothing in scripture permits the supposition of any difficulty in the transmission of the appropriate charisms from the apostles to elders and then to bishops. Since the Church is founded on witness and authority, it follows that public recognition of the particular men appointed by the apostles and the Spirit—as the apostles themselves had been appointed by Christ and the Spirit—to be witnesses and ministers of revelation is essentially self-evident.

Is there any hope that Catholicism and Protestantism will reach an agreement on this, the most radical issue that divides them, in the interpretation of the essence of Christianity?

It is most important to seek the utmost fidelity to revelation: imperceptibly, this will decrease the distance between the two sides. When scripture, tradition, the magisterium and the sacraments are all seen more clearly as existing under the primacy of the Word, we shall be able to turn to our brethren and say: what is ours is yours; here is your home; you will take nothing when you claim your own. We have but one desire—that you should claim it all. In it you would rediscover yourselves, and, through union with your brethren, something greater than yourselves.[21]

[21] Karl Barth, *The Word of God and the Word of Man* (1928); *The Doctrine of the Word of God* (1936), chapter i, "The Word of God as the Criterion of Dogmatics"; *Church Dogmatics* (1956), vol. I, *The Doctrine of the Word of God*, chapter iii, "Holy Scripture", chapter iv, "The Proclamation of the Church"; H. H. Rowley, *The Authority of the Bible* (1950); H. Strohl, *La Pensée de la Réforme* (1951); Alan Richardson and W. Schweitzer, ed., *Biblical Authority for Today* (1951); E. Ortigues, "La Tradition de l'Évangile dans l'Église d'après la doctrine catholique", *Foi et Vie* (July 1951), pp. 304 to 322; Rupert E. Davies, *The Problem of Authority in the Continental Reformers, A Study in Luther, Zwingli and Calvin* (1946); Ellen Flesseman-Van Leer, *Tradition and Scripture in the Early Church* (1954); J. K. S. Reid, *The Authority of Scripture, a Study of the Reformation and Post-Reformation Understanding of the Bible* (1957); Raymond Abba, *The Nature and Authority of the Bible* (1958); Jean Bresch, Theobald Süss, Roger Mehl, René Blanc, in *Positions luthériennes*, 3 (1958), number on Tradition; Sergii, Bishop of Staraya Russa, "Holy Tradition" in H. Waddams, ed., *Anglo-Russian Theological Conference, Moscow, July 1956* (1958), pp. 31–6; Paul de Voogt, "Écriture et Tradition d'après les études catholiques récentes", *Istina*, II (1958), pp. 183–96; J. R. Geiselmann, *Die lebendige Überlieferung als Norm des christlichen Glaubens* (1959); J. Betz and H. Fries, *Kirche und Überlieferung* (1960); *La Réforme, servante de l'unité* (1960).

2. The immediacy and transcendence of the relationship between Christ, the Church, the soul and the world

(a) The eschatological question

When the apostles met Jesus and believed in him they all suddenly realized that now finally they had entered into the events of the last days, those astounding realities whose dawning had been heralded by the prophets. Jesus told them: "The Kingdom of God is in the midst of you" (Lk 17:21).

The New Testament overflows with irrepressible joy produced by the overwhelming evidence that the absolutely new reality had entered into the world, that history had no further surprises in store, because the unbelievable and decisive Event had come in person. He had come in the simplest and least ostentatious manner, in the silence and humility of Nazareth and Bethlehem. And henceforth everything was virtually at an end. The coming of Jesus had shown that the last days had begun and that history must bow before its ruler. It meant a revaluation of all values, and that history must confess its master: "He has put down the mighty from their thrones, and exalted those of low degree; he has filled the hungry with good things, and the rich he has sent empty away" (Lk 1:52–53).

The great news proclaimed to the world was that mankind had been liberated through the power of those ultimate realities that had penetrated into time.

Man continues in his obedience to Caesar, and he does so all the more willingly, now he knows that Caesar would have no power had he not received it from God; he still goes on living amid the myths which the world fashions from age to age, but the Spirit shows him that they are but dust; he knows that he must die, but whether he dies by a tyrant's hand, in prison, or in any other way, matters little, for he is a free man. What does the sky, the earth and the sea, gold and power, the State and its might, signify to the new man who in comparison with them has suddenly acquired so eminent a stature, that of deliverance in the Lord, and power of such a kind that he has learnt the exact worth of things, their limitations, their entirely limited status in the economy of the divine plan? The magic spell of the earthly creations has been broken. We now know its content; and its alluring mystery, which moved us to believe that it held the secret of all things, has disappeared. It vanished quickly, in the few months that divided the *fiat* of the annunciation from the birth in Bethlehem. Henceforth many things ceased to matter. We are free, with a freedom no one can take from us. Pettiness, envy, despotic pride, sin, death and hell, all these enslaving potentates have lost their grip, for they are the attributes of the "old" man who may still persecute and torment the "new" man, but not deprive him of the secret of his freedom.

Christianity cannot escape the dominance of the power and splendour of eschatology, that is, certitude about the end of the world, and faith that the End of Time has come in person.

History is moving towards its End, but the End has already intervened in person, and his intervention continues; he has come into history, never again to leave. Henceforth he is the ultimate Presence that presides in the world over the activities of men and the development of empires, directs them to his own purposes, weighs and judges them.

Our trust, therefore, is unshakably based on three great conclusive series of facts: History has an end; the New Man is a reality existing now on earth; the End in person is at the heart of time, and Eternity has inserted its supreme and immutable activity amid all that is transitory and changeable. These three significant series together make up the eschatological dimension of Christianity. It is not a minor dimension of either Christianity or theology. In addition, revelation, the Incarnation, the Church, grace, the sacraments, receive from it their highest illumination. As the actual presence of the Ultimate in time, and as the culmination and end of time itself, it affords the most embracing insight into the truths of revelation; it clarifies their exact position, and is the best indication of their real significance.[22]

It is a matter of extreme importance. Once again we are at the centre of Christianity, and hence at the starting-point of the logical differences between Christian bodies. For what ultimately divides us most is the way the presence of meta-history, or of the ultimate realities in relationship to history, is interpreted. How does this presence exist in history? How does it act there? Is the relationship between them external and transcendent? Is it immanent and yet still transcendent? Is it merely alongside? Is it dynamic? Is it simply the contact between two natures, or something deeper? And what is our own position in relation to it? Are we just witnesses? Do we merely provide opportunities for God to act? Are we free persons created in God's image? And is the Church no more than a sign, the sacraments no more than a symbolic memorial, sealing the Promise, anticipating future reality, or are they more than this?

In short, are the relations that unite men, the Church and the ultimate realities, tangential, haphazard, external, parallel, or do they involve a real and deep intercommunion, a vital participation?

Each type of answer gives rise to a different doctrine on the Church, a

[22] P. Galot, "Eschatologie", *Dictionnaire de spiritualité*, fascicles XXVIII–XXIX (1960), col. 1020–1059; F. X. Durwell, *La Résurrection de Jésus, mystère de salut* (2nd edition, 1954), preface; Dogmatic Constitution of the Second Vatican Council on the Church, chapter 7: "The Eschatological Nature of the Pilgrim Church and her Union with the Heavenly Church".

different idea of the essence of Christianity. If we say that the communication between the ultimate or eschatological realities and men is by way of a memorial, a seal, a fore-telling, we arrive at one idea of Christianity. But if we say that these relations are such as to mark a real beginning of our share in the ultimate realities from above, we arrive at a different view. In the former case, the nature of the Church will be that of a sign, fore-running, foretelling, but tangential; in the latter, she will be, here on earth, a real beginning of the Kingdom of God. Two doctrines on the Church thus make their appearance: in one of them divine reality is only imputed; in the other, there is a real participation in the nature of God.

The Reformation did not invent this problem! It has existed since Christianity began. In the Incarnation and Ascension an element of ultimate reality came to us, but not completely. How do we possess it, and how much of it do we lack? What is the relation between this having and not-having?

Reading the works of the Reformers, we encounter a titanic effort to think out the meaning of Christianity as a whole, in a new way in accordance with a new interpretation of eschatology. This effort assumed the proportions of a revolution; it involved the central issue of the Reformation. Luther and Calvin were almost immediately engaged in it, and throughout their lives they were constantly reconsidering and re-examining it, and making it the organic centre of their entire system. In 1536, when the first edition of the *Institution of the Christian Religion* was published, Calvin had already written *Psychopannychia*, a treatise on eschatology, in 1534. This was re-issued in 1536, and again in 1542; and the subject occupied a foremost position in his preaching and writing until his death.[23]

It would, therefore, be completely incorrect to think that eschatology is a comparatively recent theory in Protestantism, or that it has only been discussed during these last few years, that is, since the appearance of the theory of "consequent" eschatology. It has formed the tissue of Protestant thought since its beginning. The centre of the great classical tradition of Protestantism is eschatology and the way that the ultimate realities produce their effect in time.

From the outset the classical and radical traditions of the Reformation were divergent in their interpretation. This divergence still continues, although the convergence of opinion now tends to be concentrated an the views shared by different communions, rather than in those of particular communions only. It is expressed in the various theories of consequent

---

[23] Fr. Wendel, *Calvin, sources et évolution de sa pensée* (1950); Walter E. Steuermann, *A Critical Study of Calvin's Concept of Faith* (1952); T. F. Torrance, *Kingdom and Church; A Study on the Theology of Reformation* (1956).

eschatology, demythologized eschatology, fulfilled eschatology, and anticipated eschatology.[24]

Need we repeat that the difference between Protestantism and Catholicism does not consist in the fact that the former is eschatological, and the latter not! Nor is it true that the chief concern of Protestantism is with the movement towards the final outcome of all things, whereas Catholicism is mainly interested in things as they are. The fact is that in Protestantism eschatology is wholly concerned with interpreting man's present condition in order to understand what he has become through redemption, how he came to be redeemed, and what consequences for time and eternity follow from it. The essential difference, therefore, does not lie in either the rejection or acceptance of eschatology, but in two fundamental ways of interpreting it.

According to the Protestant view, Christ, through his death, resurrection and ascension, did deeds that were decisive, final and absolute. From them nothing may be withdrawn or added. They can in no way be repeated. The accomplishment was total; and it was done once for all time. All that has to be done now, is to declare its power, bear witness to it, proclaim it, explain its meaning. This implies that any created activity giving the least impression of anything lacking in the perfection of the deeds done by Christ, or permitting the idea that these absolute deeds could in any sense be repeated, or, even worse, that any element could be taken from them and committed to human control, is utterly excluded.

Catholics must be most careful to ascertain the exact source of the attitude taken by Protestants which regarded to certain matters—Mary's part in the redemption, the function of the priesthood and the hierarchy, etc.—which is ultimately due to a particular eschatological standpoint. The logic of Protestantism, which is derived from a special view of God's transcendence, claims that since Christ is God and infinite, and since his saving activity was perfect, it can have no need of the visible mediation of the Church to be associated with it.[25]

What is the essence of the Catholic position? It holds that the Church is the Kingdom of God on earth, in a rudimentary stage; she is on pilgrimage, but she really is that Kingdom. Her present share in God's grace means that even now she has a real part in the life of glory, one day to be revealed

---

[24] P. Prigent, "L'Eschatologie dans le Nouveau Testament", Église et Théologie, 66 (1959), pp. 26–39; Galot, "Eschatologie", loc. cit.; William Manson, G. W. Lampe, T. F. Torrance, "Eschatology", Scottish Journal of Theology, Occasional Papers, no. 2 (1953, 1957); Neill G. Hamilton, "The Holy Spirit and Eschatolgy in Paul", Scottish Journal of Theology, Occasional Papers (1957).

[25] J. J. von Allmen, "Pour un prophétisme sacramentel" in L'Église et les Églises, vol. I (1955), p. 314; T. F. Torrance, "The Eschatology of the Reformation" in "Eschatology", Scottish Journal of Theology, Occasional Papers, no. 2 (1957), p. 37.

in its fullness. The divine presence, the ultimate and absolute reality, really dwells in her.

Protestantism, however, considers that the historical Church, the Church as we see her, is not the Church of faith. That Church is hidden in Christ. Eschatology transcends, surpasses history, and in whatever way it comes into contact with it, and is present to it, it never influences Christians except in a tangential and extrinsic way, for human nature, corrupted by sin, cannot be inwardly renewed by grace. The presence of the ultimate realities has its effect upon Christians, but the contact is always external. God acts, man is moved, the infinite and the finite come into contact; the two realities become contiguous and that is grace.

This notion loses sight of a number of revealed statements which show in how many ways God is trying to give himself to men, to move and transform them, not in the way that one sphere takes the place of a smaller one, but like a Father whose munificence can bestow his gifts, while safeguarding both his own transcendence and our own weakness.

The difference between us, therefore, turns on the way God's gifts are communicated. We hold that the Catholic approach is in accordance with tradition, as it has been handed down since the Church began, and, what is more, we regard it as the logical outcome of the prophetic statements in the Old Testament, on the outpouring of the messianic gifts, when the Kingdom of God should become visible at some future date, in the person of the King's Son. It is tradition that has obviously clarified the meaning of scripture, and any interpretation, which discards tradition from the start, is logically bound to arrive at different conclusions.

If we make allowance for the various explanations of eschatology to be found in Protestantism, does it remain possible to expound a coherent doctrine with sufficient scope and precision to qualify as the second essential principle of Protestantism?

For, among the Reformers there are differences in emphasis. Foremost in Luther's teaching is the *"theologia crucis"*, whereas the reformed (Calvinist) tradition centres upon the Resurrection, the Ascension and Pentecost. Lutheran doctrine lays its stress on the nothingness of man, on death and judgement; Calvinist theology is principally concerned with the ascended Christ in glory who, from his exalted position, sends forth the Holy Spirit. In Lutheranism, therefore, we observe a kind of unconcern about transforming the world, whereas this has pride of place in Calvinism. We may say that here are two eschatologies, in one judgement predominates, in the other love.[26] For Calvin, Christ's lordship expresses an aspect that differs from that of his work as Saviour; for Luther, the two ideas are

[26] *Ibid.*, p. 40.

identical. These different outlooks are influential in the World Council of Churches today, but the Calvinist tradition is predominant.[27]

(b) The essence of the second principle

If we take every aspect into account, it seems that, in the perspective of Protestant eschatology, the second main principle of the Reformation may be said to be that of the transcendence and immediacy of Christ's action on souls, on the Church and the world. We mean by this, that according to Protestantism, the relationship uniting Christ with men is completely, directly, and exclusively in Christ's power alone, and that no mediation of an ecclesiastical kind may be interposed between Christ's Spirit and his Church.

The way salvation is attained, Christ's authority over his Church and over the world, the norm of Christianity, the sources of Christian activity in the world—all this interpreted in the light of these principles and, in conjunction with the absolute primacy of the Word of God, gives us the essence of Protestantism. Its third main principle is simply an added corollary.

If we express the primacy of the Word in terms of the second central principle, we shall see that Jesus, through his Spirit, is God revealing himself in the Bible as redeeming truth. This principle unfolds itself into secondary principles: Jesus, and he alone, imputes righteousness by his activity; he alone saves. He alone is the supreme Lord of the Church and the world; he alone, as described in the Gospels, is the norm that regulates salvation, and, when risen, he became replete with such power that, in himself alone, he is the permanent, total and sufficient source of the energy needed for Christian activity in the world.

It should be noted that this principle of the transcendence and immediacy of Christ's action takes on a somewhat different mode according as it is applied to classical or radical Protestantism. Interpreted absolutely and rigorously, it would lead to an extreme form of puritanism. And that in fact is what it has done. The difference between classical and radical Protestantism is that the latter applies the central principles of the Reformation with greater rigidity. The tendency to puritanism characterizes radical Protestantism: it means a more single-minded and thorough determination to secure a more radical deliverance from institutional survivals considered to be too mediational, too Catholic, and hence, insufficiently reformed.

[27] For example, *La Seigneurie du Christ sur l'Église et sur le Monde,* report of a meeting at Arnoldshain, Germany, 5–8 July 1956, document A 1956, document B 1957 (1957). A Catholic counterpart, "La Seigneurie du Christ sur l'Église et le Monde", was published in *Istina,* April–June 1959, pp. 131–66; H. G. Wood, C. H. Dodd, Edwyn Bevan, Eugene Lyman, Paul Tillich, H. D. Wendland, Christopher Dawson, *The Kingdom of God and History,* a study prepared in view of the Oxford Conference, 1937.

Since, however, variation in intensity does not cause a specific difference in the nature of things, it may be concluded that the principle of transcendence and immediacy is valid, other things being equal, for all forms of Protestantism. It would, therefore, not seem to be disloyal to the Protestant tradition as a whole to present this principle explicitly as a synthesis of principles in which the Lutheran and Calvinist mood is plainly evident. There are four such subordinate principles; they must not be regarded as a static synthesis, but as a synthesis existing in a state of tension. The first is Lutheran and Calvinist; the second is Calvinist; the third is Lutheran and Calvinist; the fourth is Calvinist. Even a comparatively modest acquaintance with the documents of the World Council will bring them to light.

(i) Jesus, and he alone, through his work of imputing righteousness, is the one who saves

The word "imputation" expresses the relation between the present visible condition of sinful man and his eschatological condition wherein, as a newly created being, he is hidden in Christ. The word expresses the Protestant standpoint on eschatology in its relationship to time, considered in its activity here and now.

Man is a sinner; on account of original sin he is essentially incapable of entering into relationship with God. And yet, by an act of mercy, God looks upon him as righteous, and this sheerly gratuitous act is an eschatological act, having its roots in Christ's death and resurrection. Justification is called forensic (pertaining to the forum, the tribunal of God), because it is grounded on the act of God the Father in judgement of Christ on the Cross, judging and forgiving us in Christ, who has fulfilled all the requirements of "justice" for our sakes. When God regards us as just (or righteous), he is anticipating the revelation of the final result of his judgement on Christ's second coming.[28] The concept of imputation thus holds both aspects of justification together: its aspect as a reality already active and yet still on the way; its aspect as a gift, external and yet transcendent.

The axiom "sola fide", through faith alone, is the phrase that expresses that everything is from God and that salvation is not in man's power, even when assisted by grace. It marks the profound opposition between Protestantism and Catholicism. It is faith alone that justifies—this is what Protestants claim. It is faith "informed" by charity that justifies—this the Catholic affirmation. Faith, even without charity, is the root of justification, so Catholicism declares. Faith is no more than the knowledge of the new way in which God regards us; this is the Protestant view.

Neither Luther nor Calvin would agree that man takes any part whatever in his salvation, even if that part, through a supernatural gift expressed

---

[28] Gordon Rupp, *The Righteousness of God* (1953).

171

in an act of love, was divine in origin. And, in order to promote God's justice and splendour, they did their utmost to limit man's part in his salvation: man is justified by faith alone, but this faith is *trust,* faith which hands itself over, yields and capitulates to the transcendence of God's action that motivates it; faith which is an awareness that the sinner, while still remaining essentially a sinner, has become an object of benevolent regard on the part of God, who agrees to take no notice of his sins.

This faith, which justifies a man, thus seems to be simply the knowledge of the new relationship between God and man, and in the concrete its nature is declaratory, since it corresponds to a judicial act of God. What change has taken place in man through the knowledge of this new relation? It must be admitted that something has certainly changed, for God's action comes into real contact with the sinner. Something is also changed because the hope of salvation implanted in the sinner involves a modification in his outlook. Philip Maury is right in drawing attention to this point, often overlooked by Catholic observers, who interpret forensic justification as though it involved no change in man.[29] Something is indeed changed as the result of this knowledge and this hope, but it does not imply the beginning of a partaking of God's nature. In the Catholic view, charity cannot be left outside the scope of that justification which saves mankind. But for Protestantism, salvation is essentially the work of God alone. Faith is an act of God in us, that is, the testimony he induces in our minds that his attitude towards us has changed. In the Catholic view, justification is a theandric work. Protestants admit that faith leads to a new kind of behaviour and action, but for all that, it does not implant in human nature the radical principle of a new existence. It is essentially concerned with the change that has taken place in the Lord's attitude to mankind. But Catholics hold that, through "living" faith, the real principle of a new existence does enter into human nature.

What, according to Protestantism, does faith indicate? It indicates that our being has been enclosed within Christ's "justice", and taken up with him into heaven. In this way, the Christian has been introduced into the new age, the age of "justice". But it is essential to realize what this exactly means. He has been introduced there through an eschatological transference which leaves him essentially a sinner while declaring him to be "just" in God's sight. Something in the human condition on earth has changed, and this is man's knowledge of his new relationship, but there has been no change in the depths of his nature. He is essentially a sinner declared to be "just"— hence the expression *simul justus et peccator.* To believe, to have faith, is to possess the certitude of our "justice" in Jesus Christ. Justification,

---

[29] *Qu'est-ce que l'Eschatologie?* (1960); E. H. Wahlstrom, *The New Life in Christ* (1950); J. F. Thomas, *Christian Ethics and Moral Philosophy* (1955).

therefore, concerns the position of a sinner in God's sight. It is a change in the relationship between him and ourselves.[30]

In this way, the Reformation intended to proscribe every human attempt to claim some responsibility in the work of justification.

Here lies the deepest difference between Protestantism and Catholicism; in the former, the transcendence demanded by the relationship between God and man is so accentuated that it is made absolute on God's side; in the latter, God's transcendence is maintained, but the theandric principle is associated with it. For Luther and Calvin, man's association with God is exclusively on the part of God. In Catholicism, this association essentially depends on God, but man has a vital part in it, through the supernatural gift of charity, which God inserts in his nature. From this there follow two ways of raising man to the plane of the divine holiness: one of them makes the whole operation God's; the other declares that God's holiness is powerful enough to give a new vitality to man.

What, in fact, is the relationship between justification and sanctification?

By its nature, justification differs from sanctification, although the two are connected. By its nature, justification precedes sanctification. Man is declared "just" before God's tribunal, and, through his faith, he accepts this. But now he must live as a pardoned and acquitted person. Sanctification is concerned with the continual and gratuitous renewal which the Holy Spirit effects in us, in order to deliver us from the stain of sin, to transform our nature in God's image, and to enable us to do good works.

We must, however, thoroughly understand that the Holy Spirit's action is direct and immediate. The idea of grace as an ontological entity, even if wholly dependent in origin and actuality upon the Holy Spirit, is unthinkable in Protestantism. If a justified man lives in a holy manner, this is because the same Spirit of God is working directly and continuously in him and on him. Christ, therefore, is said to dwell in our hearts through his inherent power and the force of his illumination, but not through a real partaking of his nature, by grace understood as a specific ontological reality, constantly flowing from its uncreated source.

These are the two poles in opposition to each other; one of them stands for transcendence and immediacy; in the other transcendence has become presence, communicated by way of a living, personal and immanent gift.

[30] Anders Nygren, "The Task of the Lutheran Church in a New Day", *The Lutheran World Review*, I, 1948, pp. 6–19; Charles Hauter, "Quelques considérations sur la déité de Dieu et l'humanité de l'homme dans la formule de la justification par la foi" in *World Lutheranism Today* (a tribute to Anders Nygren, November 15th, 1950), pp. 137–58; Calvin, *Institutes*, III, chapter xii, 9; J. de Senarclens, *Héritiers de la Réformation, le point de départ de la foi* (1956).

(ii) Jesus alone is the sovereign Lord of the Church and the world

Jesus, the Word of God, the sole Saviour of the world has, through his Ascencion, become universal Lord. Christ's Lordship places him in a transcendent realm. God has put all things under his feet, and it is to him that the Church and the world owe obedience. The Lord himself guides the Church directly and immediately. He associates Christians with him in the fight against the evil powers of the world; through his Word he reveals his plan to them; through his Spirit he enables them to understand its present and permanent bearing upon history; and it is to the complete fulfilment of God's plan, the establishment of his Kingdom, that he is leading the Church and the world.

Christ's eschatological Lordship is, therefore, already in action. He manifests his power in the holy lives of Christians, in the way they show their love for men, in their struggle for the transformation of the world, in their fight against the powers of evil, in the witness of every kind that they bear to the fact that the end of time has come. Christians must, therefore, realize that this present world is already judged, and they must decipher this divine judgement as events occur and explain it to mankind. A missionary task is thus obligatory upon them. Jesus has become universal Lord, and through the witness borne by Christians, the news must be spread to the ends of the earth. Jesus conquered sin, death and hell. Christians must bear witness to the world of this final victory which transcends history. The battle has been won. The conflicts that remain to be fought are rearguard actions only. Through his Lordship, Christ has given a meaning to the history of the world. It is the work of Christians to make known to history this meaning of which it is unaware, and to show that it is impossible for anyone to escape his regal power, for he is able to utilize even men's disobedience.

We should note a central difference. In Protestantism, Christ's Lordship is proclaimed, for, in a transcendent and eschatological way, it is already a fact. In Catholicism, it is proclaimed as virtually accomplished, and yet as being also in process of constant real accomplisment in history, with the visible Church exercising a mediating function in that work.

(iii) Jesus, as described in the Gospel alone, is the normative rule for human life and salvation

Here we meet again that fundamental insistence on the relationship of immediacy between Christ and men. Where must a man who wishes to lead the good life find the model and rule for his activity? In some treatise constructed on the idea of human nature, or in the concrete example of our Lord? Where must he try to learn what it means to lead a holy life, and how to join in the combat waged by God against the powers of evil? The answer is to be found completely in the Gospel. For a Christian the concrete and total norm is scripture. The moral teaching he finds in it assumes the form of a direct dialogue between Christ and God. So it will be in the relations between men and our Lord. God calls and man replies. The summons to faith and to a holy life is a question. Man must answer, and Christ teaches us how to do so, in a way acceptable to God. Could a Christian find a better norm elsewhere? He sees in the Gospel that the Father accepted his Son's human life and judged it perfect. He also exalted the Son and brought him to share his power in heaven.

Protestant moral teaching, in harmony with this view, is endowed with unquestionable grandeur. It is a morality of imitation, association and dialogue. Some fundamental differences from the Catholic view should be noted. For the latter, the moral life finds expression in the new life, centred in grace, with the virtues as its detailed expression. For Catholics, to live in a Christian way, means taking, through Christ's grace, as full a part as possible—given our situation on earth—in Christ's holy mind and will. This moral teaching is certainly one of imitation, of personal responsibility, of response and association, but it also implies man's inner transformation, in a communion of grace with the Lord.[31]

(iv) *The risen Jesus is by himself alone the supreme force necessary for all activity*

Here again we cannot avoid perceiving the principle of transcendence and immediacy, and this time almost in its pure state. Nothing comparable to the eschatological power of God brought into the world could be so capable of transforming it. In Protestantism, Christians rely on the power bestowed on Christ as the result of his Resurrection. Christ has become life renewed, Spirit, God's perfect "Justice". A Christian has only to equip himself with the power of the Resurrection and, protected by it, he can go forth into the world, not with the strength of his own human resources, but with that of God. In this way, Christ will extend the influential power of the Resurrection. Is it not also clear that the Resurrection is the source of the dynamism of the apostolate? In the faith of the Resurrection, and conscious of being witnesses to it, the apostles set out to conquer the world and to begin the work of extending the Kingdom of God.

A Christian, therefore, who places his reliance upon the eschatological act of the Resurrection, is all powerful. In reality, it is God who exerts his power in him. For Christ is the Living One. Sinful man is dead, but Christ gives him the certainty that one day his being will be filled with the new life. And even now, the sinner experiences the first glimpse of the dawning of that Resurrection which awaits him. The Holy Spirit, the seal of justification, enables him to perform deeds proclaiming the

---

[31] B. Häring, *La Loi du Christ*, vol. I (1955), introduction, pp. 13–19, and 1st section, "L'Idée-mère de la morale chrétienne", pp. 29–47.

perfect eschatological life. As yet his life is not the renewed and risen life, but it is the sign and foretaste of it. Sinful man is sure that the perfect life will come, because the judicial sentence of God's tribunal has acquitted him for ever. He must await the end. Does this mean that he must be a quietist? No, because justification involves joining the ranks of those engaged in the work of God's "justice". Men are called to be witnesses of the Resurrection. If they have been justified, they must be really bent on giving signs of their election and salvation. Since the eschatological power of the Resurrection drives them to be God's witnesses, is there anything they should be incapable of doing?

Once more we must point out the difference which, in this instance also, divides Protestantism from Catholicism, and extends throughout all the sacraments. This difference is due to two ways of regarding the operative work of the Resurrection. According to Protestantism, the power of the Resurrection is infinite, because it fulfilled all things once for all, and at a single stroke. The Church's work is to proclaim it and allow it to act. For Catholicism, the eschatological power of the Resurrection acts not only through its being declared as a fact, through the proclamation which gives admission to it, but also through the exercise and propagation of its action in the course of history by means of the visible mediation of the Church. According to the outlook of each side, the general sacramentality of the Church is either rejected or accepted.

The great eschatological view of things holds a dominant position in Christianity. Eschatology, need we repeat, does not only mean a striving on the part of Christianity towards its perfection at the end of time. It also denotes a relationship to those ultimate and decisive deeds which are in some way present to history, to Christians, to the Church and the world. It is on the meaning of eschatology and on the way that it exists in time that Christians are divided.

3. The nature of the Church as witness

What then is the meaning of the Church in Protestantism? Her nature is wholly dependent upon the two principles of the absolute primacy of the Word and of the immediacy of the relationship between God and man.

We may take as typical the explanation given by Karl Barth: "The Church, the living congregation of Jesus Christ, the living Lord".[32]

[32] World meeting of the World Council of Churches, Amsterdam, 1948, official report, vol. I, *L'Église universelle dans le dessein de Dieu* (1949), pp. 94–107.

First, what is it that the Church is not? "The Church is neither the community, nor the visible body of those who believe in Jesus Christ, nor the organ representing them in a monarchical, aristocratic or democratic form. She is not an idea, nor an institution, nor a pact. She is the event which gathers two or three together in the name of Jesus Christ, that is, through the power of his summons to them, and the mandate with which he entrusts them. The structure of the Church is only meaningful in relation to this event: the living congregation" (pp. 102–3).

The essence of the Church thus consists in being event and history, dialogue and response, act and continuous creation. The Church is the event which gathers the congregation together by means of the Word and Spirit of Jesus Christ, her living Lord.

"The congregation is *the event,* occurring in the last days, through which is effected the gathering together *(congregatio)* of the people *(fidelium)* whom Jesus Christ, the living Lord, has decided to elect and qualify, as witness of the victory he has won, and as announcers of its final and universal manifestation.

"The congregation is the event which specifically distinguishes some men from all others and unites them together. Through Jesus Christ, these men all find themselves brought together to the knowledge of the divine grace which judges, and of the divine judgement which pardons, all summoned to acknowledge God and serve their neighbour, all charged, in this sense, with a mission to the rest of the world.

"The congregation is the event through which the complete sovereignty of Jesus Christ—Lord of the Church, but also Lord of the world—meets its response and its correspondence in the completely free obedience of the men he has qualified, elected, joined together and summoned to acknowledgement and service.

"The congregation is the event through which men who have recognized in the work of Jesus Christ, reconciling the world with God, a manifest and obligatory word, unite together before the world, in order to share its wretchedness and its hope.

"The congregation is the event which makes the prophetic-apostolic testimony given in the Scriptures on Jesus Christ, present, active and fruitful, and which visibly manifests the authority of this testimony amid the successive attempts made by men to fathom, explain and preach it.

"The congregation is the event through which the communion of the Holy Spirit, by the power of the word of Jesus Christ, heard in common in the testimony of the Bible, also creates through divine power, a human communion: a harmony between faith and its profession, between love and its activities, between hope and its certainties; and this harmony is true for all men.

"The congregation is the event through which Baptism, man's intro-

177

duction to the riches of Jesus Christ, and the Lord's Supper, a man's support in his new condition as beneficiary and debtor, exert their power in favour of many whose lives now depend upon it alone.

"The congregation is the event through which the preaching of the word of Jesus Christ, the call to believe in him, and also the intimation of the temporal, political and social significance of the salvation made manifest in him, makes known and bears witness to the divine mission of Jesus Christ in the non-Christian world (for which he also most truly died and rose again)" (pp. 96–7).

The Church, therefore, has her position pre-eminently with God and depends upon him at every moment, in the way an event depends upon the person producing it. It is the Lord who created her, sustains her, owns and governs her. The Church "draws *her life* from that of the Lord alone, and her *reality* solely from the origin assigned to her" (p. 95). She has no other essence and no other existence than the act "of drawing her own life from the action of her living Lord" (p. 95). On God's side her security is *guaranteed* and she must always endure. "She is *guaranteed (perpetuo mansura est)* by the indestructible life of her Head, the Lord Jesus Christ risen from the dead, by the conclusive character of the work he accomplished once for all, by the power of the Word and the Spirit which he retains, by the impossibility of exhausting the testimony borne to him by the prophets and apostles, by the well-grounded nature of baptism and the Lord's Supper, signs he instituted, by his own unwearying fidelity to his congregation" (p. 98).

But the Church, guaranteed from above, is threatened from below. She is in danger. She may be led into temptation and succumb to it, "for the life of the congregation of Jesus Christ, in its nature and in the forms in which it is expressed, is that of a created being; it cannot be kept from falling back into unbelief, heresy, egoism or from despair, disintegration and death, in any absolute way, but only by the contingency of the event—that event through which the action of Jesus Christ predominates over human sin" (p. 98).

The being of the Church is, therefore, variable. Her life is constantly fluctuating from existence to non-existence, according to whether she keeps in vital continuity with her source or not. When she yields to temptations from below, she ceases to be "the event"; she is no longer a living being. What still goes by the name of Church is only the Church in a merely nominal fashion. The sovereign divine act, no longer having anything to work upon, the current of life no longer flows. "The history, the movement, the action inaugurated by Jesus Christ, the first subject, are not carried on in the second subject, in the congregation. On the contrary, they come to a standstill and remain immobile" (p. 100).

Could it happen that that event which is the Church should completely disappear from the earth? Karl Barth argues that we cannot exclude this possibility; it hangs above the Church like a warning threat. Since the Church is a created reality, she is not absolutely indefectible. The relationship uniting her to the Lord is tangential and forensic and, therefore, does not make her immortal. It is certainly true that in some of her aspects, in some spheres of her existence, in some local congregations, the Church-as-event ultimately collapses into death and destruction when she becomes faithless and apostate. If the evil in her fails to become general, the Church owes this to the sovereignty, the fidelity and patience of the Lord who, in his mercy, saves her in extremis. But when she yields to temptation, she ceases to be a Church and becomes a pseudo-Church. "She is then an ecclesiastical substitute endowed with all the outward characteristics of the living congregation, but without their inner substance" (p. 100). Thus the Church on earth as a whole looks like a land laid waste where only a few lights still shine. The living congregations persist; others are dead. Between these latter, unity has ceased to exist, for unity is a sign of the common life.

Is it possible for a dead congregation to come to life again? It is, as the result of the Lord's supremely effective initiative, and of the overt hostility that must be shown to it by a living congregation in order to move it to become faithful again. The Church becomes possible once more in this congregation, provided the latter agrees to become again the authentic event which it essentially is. The Church then shines with renewed splendour in every region. "The renewal of the living congregation, which at once implies its unity, is the work of its living Lord: it is the new light and strength of his word, attested by the Bible; it is the new strength of his Spirit; it is his new presence in the liturgy, in baptism and the Eucharist. He alone is exempt from all danger. He alone, privileged by his imperishable life, so predominates over the guilt of that criminality to which Christian and ecclesiastical life succumbs, that he is able to keep that life in existence and save it. He alone is the hope of the Church" (p. 102).

What is the relationship between the ecclesiastical structure and the event? Although the local congregation is "the primary, regular and normal form of this event" (p. 103), it still remains true that its structure is no more than the form taken by a human attempt to serve the Word. The true Church which is the Church of the free congregation—that is, the living congregation, engaged in dialogue and answering—of the free word of God—that is transcending every kind of structure—is consonant with structural variety, so long as the essence of the Church-as-event is safe-guarded. "The structure of the Church is no more an end in itself than is the Church herself. It is a human attempt to serve the Word of God, in conformity with that Word itself, by setting in motion, in face of the

danger to the Church, the maximum of understanding, courage and efficiency, so that the immediate meeting and communion between Jesus Christ,
the living Lord, and his congregation should be produced again. The
event itself does not depend upon human initiative. But the removal of
inevitable obstacles does depend upon that initiative. This is the meaning
of the structure of the Church" (pp. 105–6). The criterion which determines the worth of any structure is its usefulness in preserving the freedom
of the Word of God for the congregation and in preserving the freedom
of the congregation for the Word of God. Karl Barth sees in the principle
of congregationalism—the free congregation of the free Word of God,
not in the way Congregationalism at present exists—the principle that
can ensure the ecumenical unity of the Church (pp. 106–7).

But the explanation of the idea of the Church in terms of *a congregation*
is only significant and fruitful when it is understood as a *living* congregation, originating in the event of its assembling, as described in the para-
graphs above. That congregation, and that alone, is the decisive element
in the final relations between God and man. And it is this history which
constitutes *the essence* of the Church (p. 97).

What does this all amount to? What does the Church-as-event ultimately
mean? What is the Church's inner nature? In this context, a living congregation essentially means one that is constituted through God's sovereign act, summoning it and gathering it together, as a speaker in conversation with him. The Church is seen to be by nature a dialogue and a
response. Her very being consists in waiting upon, hearing and responding to the Word. She is the Word's witness, in conversation with God.

Karl Barth's is *one* representative account of the essential idea which
Protestantism has formed of the nature of the Church. The Protestant
world will not publish any disagreement with it, although in the event of
its being declared to be *the* perfectly representative account, it would feel
authorized to do so. The idea of continuity implied in the Church's designation as 'body of Christ' is compelling Protestantism to do justice to
the institutional aspect of the Church's constitution.

Is the being of the Church to be found solely in the part she takes in
"the event", or is it also institutional? Protestant doctrine on the Church
prefers as a rule to answer this question not in ontological terms, but in
terms of life and action. It is explained that the Church's life presents
three aspects: testimony through the proclamation and exposition of the
faith; testimony through common life *(Koinonia)*, in which the Church,
especially in her worship, gives thanks to God and adores him; and
thirdly, the service through which Christians make known their love for
each other.

These three ways in which the Church's life is expressed, are activities
that correspond to *the* Action, *the* Event, by means of which God is con-

stantly sustaining the Church in the world, enveloping her in his almighty Word. Primarily, therefore, in her very essence, she is a witness. Her life witnesses to God's grace, to his judgement and his sovereignty. She is indeed the Body of Christ, but, according to Protestantism, she is his Body, not through a real participation in the divine nature, but through an external imputation of God's "justice".

We must always come back to the central problem of the ecumenical debate: what is Christianity?[33] Each individual Church, each Christian communion, must ask this question when it examines itself, its history, its ecumenical relations, its belief, mission, structure, liturgy and organic life, and when it renews its consecration to the sole service of the glory of the Lord with its whole heart and mind.

[33] J. A. Mackay, *Protestantism* in Edward J. Jurgi, ed., *The Great Religions of the Modern World* (1947); Anders Nygren, *The Faith of the Christian Church* (1948); G. Florovsky, J. Leenhardt, R. Prentner, A. Richardson, C. Spicq, O. P., *La Sainte Église universelle* (1948); Flew and Davies, *The Catholicity of Protestantism*; H. Strohl, "La Notion d'Église chez les Réformateurs", *Revue d'Histoire et de Philosophie religieuse* (1936), pp. 265–319; W. H. van de Pol, *The Christian Dilemma* (1952); Anders Nygren, *Christ and His Church* (1956); F. J. Leenhardt, *Catholicisme romain et Protestantisme* (1957); R. Mehl, *Du catholicisme romain, approche et interprétation* (1957); Claude Welch, *The Reality of the Church* (1958).

CHAPTER V

The Problem of the Church's Mission in the World:
Rosponsibility as a Witness
or Maker of the World to Come?

I. DEFINITION OF THE ECUMENICAL PROBLEM
IN THE LIGHT OF THE CHURCH'S MISSION

Everything today urges us to rethink the mission of the Church.

In the first place the day of Protestant, Anglican, or Catholic missions as we have known them till these last few years, will soon be altogether done, not as if there were no more non-Christians to convert or a territory ceased to be mission country in any respect on the establishment of a native hierarchy, but because the young self-governing Churches have joined the Church's general mission and because many of the problems they face are the same as those which more ancient Churches have.

Vast changes in the conditions that prevail in former missionary countries necessarily mean re-interpreting the mission of the Church in the light of the new circumstances. In most of the former mission territories the Church is a minority. These countries have now achieved independence. Their governments and most of their people profess religions that are not Christian. The result is that a good deal of the Church's mission must be carried out in collaboration with non-Christians, through witness, community life, and service. In other words, the Church's mission is developing common features, and the distinction between mission territories and Christian territories is becoming blurred. We must think more and more in terms of a missionary Church to the whole world.

It is, therefore, not enough to say that the aim of the Church's mission in missionary countries is the *plantatio Ecclesiae*—setting up the Church's organization among non-Christians, though that is certainly the central aim; for the Church being the living environment of the Christian, her action remains tentative and incomplete until her structures are firmly enough established, enabling her to lead an autonomous life.

In the second place we have the de-Christianization and secularization of the world, to which must be added the massive entrée of temporal values furnished by modern technological civilization. No Church can protect itself against new influences by clinging to the status quo and to isolation. The era of isolation is over and change is accelerating. So the Church is forced to set to work, taking stock of the modern world's problems and confronting them with her universal mission.

Finally, we are brought to re-examine the nature of the Church's mission by the total confrontation which the ecumenical movement has entailed. Given one world to save, should there be various conceptions of the Church's mission?

1. What the problem involves

The question put here therefore applies to the essential mission of the Church. There is only one Church and she is missionary, because she is apostolic and apostolicity means mission. The Church is missionary because she is one, holy and catholic. The Church's mission is one, and it is to the Christian world, the non-Christian world, and the world that once was Christian. Long-established use of the term "missionary" to designate apostolic work among unbelievers gave us the idea that it applies only to that kind of apostolate; and so a whole area of the Church's apostolic being was left in the shadows. Then with the secularization of the world the old Christian countries emerged as mission territories and we had to speak of the internal mission when referring to this new missionary apostolate. Little by little the whole missionary reality of the Church had to reappear.

Obviously several questions are involved here: the mission of the Church, valid for every age; the mission of the Church specialized according to its several aims; and the way or ways in which this mission can be suitably carried out in our time.

We shall try to single out, in terms of the ecumenical problem, the Catholic features of the Church's universal mission.

This mission must be understood to transcend interpretations Western and Eastern. Let no one misunderstand us: Catholicism is one; there are neither two Catholicisms nor three; but there are different expressions of the same universal religion. Every culture, every national temperament tries to express it and none does so adequately. The Latin spirit, the Oriental spirit, the Asian spirit, or any you like — all are of the earth and have its limitations. Catholicism belongs to another order of universality, and always in some way surpasses even the noblest expression of itself. So if we desire the mission of the Church to unite us all one day, in the West and in the East, we must determine what each of our expressions is and what the mission of the Church is as such: the mission of the Church must be understood in its catholicity beyond Eastern or Western interpretations, as a plenitude that embraces both.

Catholicity in expression and catholicity in time. The history of Christianity has been one long debate, an oscillation between two poles: renouncing the world, and the pursuit of earthly values. What is the world worth? Must one avoid its defilement? Is it commendable to give up the world through asceticism? Can one lawfully work in it? Should one labour to transform it, to prepare it for its eschatological state? Evidently many answers are possible: the world, a place and occasion for asceticism, the world, ambiguous place where good and evil strangely mingle; the world, God's creation worthy of attention because of its place in the divine plan. How will the Church make her choice? Will she make only one choice? Whether she accepts or rejects the world, how many different ways will she do it in?

The ecumenical solution to the difficult problem of the Church's mission in the world cannot be a selective compendium of the major explanations given by the Christian world as a whole. And if that were desirable, it would be impossible.

One begins to realize how tremendously complex a task it is to recover the full sense of the Church's mission in the world. It means no less than achieving unity on a matter that has always given rise to divisions and schisms, and still causes the commonest difficulties with regard to the action of the Churches and the Christian communions. The Churches would have been too present in the world, the communions too absent from it. The Churches would have unduly relaxed the tension which must exist between the present world and the world to come, becoming vast compromises; the communions would have left the world to its fate, preferring peace and quiet or merely saving the individual soul. Some, under cover of effecting the Christian transformation of economic, political, and international life, would have sought power, and on the pretext that the kingdom of God had come would have tried to practise a spiritual imperialism; while others out of spiritual selfishness, or to avoid defilement, would have deliberately held themselves back from temporal affairs, thereby debasing man still further.

The idea of the Church's mission has become fragmented as the result of the divisions among Christians.

The ideal seeking fulfilment, through the effort to heal these divisions, is that of the united mission of the Church seen as a common undertaking in a world in search of unity.

The ecumenical problem from the aspect of the Church's mission consists precisely in unravelling the chain of the various conflicts and in the universal recovery of the full meaning of the Church's mission, leading to the integrated activity of Christians and Christian communions in the world.

The problem as a whole can be envisaged from three schematic summaries of what may be called the system of Catholicism, Orthodoxy and Protestantism. These provide the essential data in each instance. Useful for comparison, they need to be completed by the concrete and individual variations that exist in the living realities.

There seems no reason to consider the interpretation of the Church's mission held by the Anglican Communion as a fourth major position with an originality of its own. In the words of the Lambeth Conferences, it has two characteristic features: it is traditional and it aims at being as comprehensive as possible. It is traditional because it is based on the idea of the Church as the Body of Christ, and as the community of people associated in his mystery. The Church's mission is carried out by both clergy and laity acting in a communal and hierarchical way. The nature of the mission is derived from the nature of the Church: a universal mission for the redemption of mankind, of the material universe, time and society. The Lambeth Conferences provide an admirable expression of the answer which the Churches of the Anglican Communion propose for contemporary needs and of the extent of their committal to them. Youth, the family, economic and industrial transformation, the problem of peace, human rights, the responsibilities of the State, education—all these are subjects of their case.

This stress on Catholicity is accompanied by the desire of entering as widely as possible into communion with other denominations. Can the Anglican Communion and the Christian communions in general be said to be fulfilling the Church's mission perfectly so long as the Churches and denominations are divided? Obviously not. The concept of "comprehensiveness", expressing the Anglican approach to every aspect of the ecumenical problem, recurs again here. When the Churches of the Anglican Communion have been absorbed in a wider Communion, the latter will be ready to carry out the Church's mission more completely—as both Catholic and Reformed.

2. Schematic images of the Church's mission

A. THE ORTHODOX CONCEPTION

We may picture the Eastern Orthodox conception in the form of two concentric circles, the inner circle being the Church; the outer, the nation and the State. The State represents Christ's kingship; the Church primarily represents his priesthood. The bond binding the body (the nation, the State) with the soul (the Church) is ensured by the prophetic ministry, and the goal is the final unity of the Church triumphant. The whole constitutes the Christian social order.

The idea is that of an organism. The Church is the soul and consciousness of the body, which is the nation and the State, and she is, necessarily, at the centre of Christian society. She is the point where the eschatological realities come down to the earth, and from which men rise up to the realities above. She is a hierophany, a spiritual emanation from heaven, the sacred enclosure wherein the heavenly realities constantly moving between the Church on earth and the Church in heaven so harmonize as to tend to lose their separate identity. In principle, the Church on earth has no other tasks than those pertaining to her as the soul of the Christian society. She must radiate the eschatological power and grace to the entire Christian society. She must above all "seek the Kingdom of God", all the rest being simply additional. The liturgy, the sacraments, the word, ecclesiastical customs represent the Church's specific tasks and spheres. The remainder does not directly concern her. She is the leaven, the inspiration, the projection of heaven upon earth, the eschatological realities refracted in the world. It is not her special task to take on the Christian organization of the world. It is enough for her to be present in it as Church, and that means, to be the soul of the world. What pertains to the body is not her special sphere. The Christian people, the laity, the emperors, should take the responsibility for that.

The characteristics of this spirit can be understood more clearly when compared with the activity of the Catholic Church and the Protestant communions in connection with the worldwide application of Christianity. In the Orthodox Church, it would be useless to look for any detailed teaching, or even any dynamic conviction about the Church's presence in the economic, political and technological world, or in that of science, public health, culture or leisure. It would be vain to look for a specific synthesis of faith and science, of revelation and historical development, or an integration of mathematical-scientific knowledge with subsistent Truth. Not that in Orthodoxy there is no Christian idea of culture and historical development, and no concern of this kind, but it is of a different nature from that in the West, partly no doubt because monasticism has always played a fundamental part in Orthodox spirituality. And yet the importance of monasticism is, itself, a result of a general point of view on the function of the Church as the soul of the social body. The Church's outlook is undifferentiated and general; in principle she does not give specific answers to particular problems: she deals rather with mankind as a whole, and it is for individual men and nations to draw the conclusions that follow from the situation of the New Man. The Church, as such, does not try to create a civilization, produce social programmes, or Christian States. She accepts tasks that are specifically religious, but she is not committed to the establishment of any Christian social order. She achieves that additional element of the Kingdom—a living and

187

homogeneous Christian order—circuitously, through the depth of the faith and the transformed lives of the Christian people, so that although the laity provide the element of normal contact between the Church and the world, her spirituality remains more that of an inspired dynamism than an explicit doctrine, more monastic than lay.

Some tendencies are becoming apparent today among the young Orthodox in Greece, Syria, the Lebanon and the United States, that aim at broadcasting the Church's presence and making it more explicit and detailed. Preoccupations such as these formed part of the programme for reunion put forward by the representatives of the Eastern Churches at Rhodes in 1961. The attempt is being made, naturally, to find an answer in the spiritual resources of Orthodox thought itself; the mere existence of ascetic and monastic testimony does not suffice to cope with the enveloping movement of atheistic humanism and materialism.

B. THE CATHOLIC CONCEPTION

The Catholic system may be pictured as an ellipse with two foci, one of them being the State, the other the Church. The Church is the Kingdom of God on earth, although she is not that Kingdom as perfected and concluded, but as its beginning and on pilgrimage. Essentially, she is the only, the unique Church, existing in two different states. Thus she is both an organization aiming at heaven and the Kingdom of God on earth. The relation between this world and the new world above is based upon a relation between nature and supernature, intrinsic to the Church. The Church exists in the nation and the world, but she is greater than the nation, the State and the world, and, in fact, she contains them. But there must be no confusion between the Church and the State. Each has its own part to play. The Church holds no *de jure* supremacy over the State or any nation, for her Kingdom is not of this world. She does not share in all Christ's regal prerogatives. The sphere of action of the hierarchic Church includes all strictly ecclesial tasks: the Word and the sacraments. It also extends to the "mixed" sphere, comprising such things as education and public charity, and also to the whole of secular life, but only in its bearing upon salvation. With regard to the State, the Church holds the position of a "perfect" society, autonomous and independent of the State. She has authority to judge it from her religious point of view, and the right and responsibility to be its inspiration. She is not a State, but she possesses the attributes of a "perfect" society, that is, legislative executive and judicial power. Contact between the Church and the world, between the Church and the State, principally occurs through the magisterium or prophetic ministry; but in so far as the authority of the hierarchy has a jurisdiction over the secular power, and to the extent in which the sacraments are bridges between heaven and earth, the Church affects and envelops the world in a prophetic, regal and priestly way. The sphere of her activity is not limited to that of the Word, the liturgy and the sacraments. She does not, of course, assert that it is the clergy who must themselves ensure that Christianity is present throughout the temporal and secular order. For historical reasons she has sometimes had to take over additional functions to those properly her own, but the fact remains that while the clergy have their special attributes, the laity also have theirs. For the laity, too, are authentically the Church, and in their order they have an irreplaceable part to play. Through their collaboration, clergy and laity together, bring out and express the Church's entire mission on earth.[1] Through them the Church can become the consciousness of the State and nation, and achieve the two aspects of her mission: the immediate aspect—the unification in Christ of all things on earth (Eph 1:10); the ultimate aspect, heaven. The laity have an immense field of activity before them: problems of the family, education and society; the spheres of science and art, literature, the press and radio; the domain of political obligation and of economic development.

The metaphor of an ellipse is to be understood of an inclusion of the world, nations and States, not through temporal and political control over them by the Church, but through her catholicity. If she is the point where the eschatological realities come into contact with this world, then she is the matrix of the world to come. She accepts all cultures and civilizations, and transforms them to the image of the Lord.

C. THE PROTESTANT CONCEPTION

There are two spheres that are different in size, outside each other, but contiguous: the smallest of these is that of the Christian people; the larger is that of the eschatological realities—it contains Christ, the Eschaton, the glorious Head of renewed mankind who sits at the right hand of the Father. In him the true Church, the invisible Church, the communion of saints, is to be found. Outside this sphere, there is the world and nature, subject to sin. God selects certain men, through his Word, and gathers them into a new community. The reality of a Christian is hidden in Christ and will be revealed only on the last day. For the time being, the justified sinner, living in time and the world, is covered by God's "Justice". This contact produces certain real effects: the small sphere is moved by the principal one, through the latter's transcendent grace. Its movements are signs of either grace received or grace to come. Only when the life of

[1] Y. M.-J. Congar, *Jalons pour une théologie du laïcat* (1953), English translation: *Lay People in the Church* (2nd edition, 1963).

189

an individual or a collectivity has ended, will the extrinsicism dividing God's "justice" and man's sin be over.

The actual contact between the two spheres takes place essentially through the Word and the prophetic ministry. The Word is the dynamic presence of Christ the Eschaton. It is the act which sets men, Christian men, in motion, for Christ is the personal Presence of activity in action. In Christ Jesus, Word and Power, Word and Act are one and inseparable. Christ is the Word, the Power, the dynamic Energy. Since he is the ultimate reality, his coming into the world marked the entry of the eschatological realities into history, and although, through the Ascension, he ceased to be visible to us, he still remains infinitely present and active. The Ascension did not indicate the withdrawal of the eschatological realities that had once been manifested: these continued to be present in the world, to listen to and question it, to move it to supply an answer, to cover it with the power of salvation. The Kingdom of God is, therefore, present whenever the dynamic power of the Word produces justification, and it does this directly, without mediation. One has only to come into its sovereign presence and submit to its omnipotent action. Scripture as God's Word is the means of contact between the two spheres; it also approaches as near as possible to the eternal and non-material Word; and it is an embodied reality and can be reached by man. Together with the prophetic ministry, other links exist, those, for example, of communal life and mutual service, but they are not on a level with the basic link, the Word of God. The Church's mission, therefore, is to be the witness of the Word through the sacraments, communal life and mutual service.

What is the Church's position in relation to the civil power? The Confessions and Declarations of Faith of the fifteenth and sixteenth centuries that expound it, still presuppose the existence of a Christian social order, and they sound strangely in our secularized world. In general, the magistrates (rulers and judges) are regarded as God's vicars. The justice they administer is a dim reflection of God's holiness, but in spite of its inadequacy, it remains valid. The highest function of the State is to promote the preaching of the faith and good conduct. The State is a kind of extra-territorial bishop for the Church.[2]

The internal adjustment of these common principles, differed, however, according to each Reformer. Zwingli, for instance, saw the relations between Church and State as forming a unity of compenetration.[3] Luther,

---

[2] The Sixty-seven Articles of Ulrich Zwingli, A. D. 1523, art. xxxiv–xxxvi, in Philip Schaff, *The Creeds of Christendom,* vol. III, p. 203; The First Helvetic Confession, A. D. 1536, art. xxvii, in Schaff, *op. cit.,* p. 229; The Scottish Confession of Faith, A. D. 1560, art. xxiv, in Schaff, *op. cit.,* pp. 474–6.

[3] H. Schmid, *Zwingli, Lehre von der göttlichen und menschlichen Gerechtigkeit* in the series *Studien zur Dogmengeschichte und systematischen Theologie,* 12 (1959).

who for a long time vacillated over this problem, ended by surrendering all authority over social life to the prince. Calvin's theocratic view of society led him to subordinate the State to the ecclesiastical power.[4] In practice, the relations between Church and State, among Lutherans and in the Calvinist Churches, were settled in as many ways as local circumstances demanded, and they varied from complete union between Church and State to complete separation, and these differences remain today. The Protestant world as a whole is deeply divided on this matter, not only within its radical tradition as well.

Similar disagreements recur with regard to the Church's social mission. Protestantism in general is divided into two opposing camps. The first holds that the social transformation of the world is a matter of urgency; the second shows indifference to it, on account of the eschatological hope. Precise classifications are difficult, because the boundaries marking off the different convictions do not necessarily coincide with confessional allegiances. The Lutheran denominations of the United States, for example, are much closer to Calvinist views than are the French Lutheran bodies. The Calvinist Churches and Methodism decided from the start to work for the transformation of the world, and it is their influence that inspires the social activity of the National Council of the Churches of Christ in the United States and of the World Council of Churches.

Lutheran thought on the matter of the social mission of Christianity has always been uncertain. Indeed, it may be asked whether Luther had any special teaching on this subject at all. But at least some principles are surely implied in the secularization of monastic property, the abolition of the monastic life, the assignation to the secular power of the responsibility for judging questions that until then had been subject to ecclesiastical interpretation, such as those of usury and the just price. Moreover, the abolition of the monastic life entailed the disappearance of monastic spirituality which, until the Reformation, had been influential in the spirituality of lay people. The Church took on the appearance of a great company of the laity, and a new spirituality became inevitable. Calvin had a clearer grasp of this than Luther, doubtless for personal reasons. Troeltsch[5] considers that Luther, in the view he took of the economic order, remained essentially a man of the Middle Ages when ascetic interests predominated. Work, Luther held, is a remedy for sin, a duty, a result of original sin. We must give ourselves to it because God has instituted it as a means through which he educates and disciplines us. In this world man must labour; the part he has to play is determined

---

[4] W. A. Mueller, *Church and State in Luther and Calvin* (1954).
[5] *The Social Teaching of the Christian Churches* (1st edition, 1931; third edition, 1950), vol. II, p. 554.

by considerations of faith and love, in acceptance of God's will.[6] Luther thus remained at one with the monastic tradition, even though the principles he put forward and the actions he undertook pointed in other directions.

What Luther would or could not do, Calvin accomplished. Monastic spirituality was ill-suited to the era of the Renaissance, and when the priesthood and the monasteries were suppressed, it lost the reason for its existence. Christians involved in the temporal order needed something different. A Church that had become a company of layfolk would have to have a lay spirituality. A world expanding socially and economically required a new theological interpretation of progress.[7] In his theocentric convictions, Calvin remained a man of the Middle Ages, but he brought the idea of God's glory (central to his thought) down to the economic and social spheres. Work, he considered, is not merely a remedy for sin; it contributes to God's sovereign control of the world, and it promotes his glory. Each man accepts it in a different way, according to the wealth of the callings God has implanted in the world. The idea of a calling, a vocation, hitherto reserved to the summons to the religious life, was extended at the Reformation to the Christian people as a whole, in accordance with the position assigned to the Word by Protestantism. The Word is a call from God directed to every individual in his concrete situation. Since to every situation there was a corresponding call, the hierarchy of such situations and the whole social order constituted a world of vocations. Both Luther and Calvin shared this doctrine of the calling, the direct, particular, personal summons, which made the Church a people of the called, and her mission a vocational system. But each accepted this from his own point of view. Luther put his trust in God, but mistrusted man; he connected work with expiation for sin; other matters he was content to leave to the civil authority considered as the social aspect of the organism of the Christian society, and he relied on the Christian spirit of that authority. Calvin, on the other hand, tried from the start to incorporate in the Gospel the civil authority with its responsibility for the secular world.

D. LIKENESS AND DIFFERENCES

It will have doubtless been observed that there are similarities between the Catholic and Protestant positions, and between the latter and the

[6] G. W. Forell, *Faith Active in Love: an Investigation of the Principles underlying Luther's Social Ethics* (1954).
[7] André Bieler, *La Pensée économique et sociale de Calvin* (1959); Richard Tawney, *Religion and the Rise of Capitalism* (1926); Jean-Marcel Lechner, *Le Christianisme social de Jean Calvin* (1954).

Orthodox conception. A certain lack of interest, particularly in early Lutheranism, on the subject of the transformation of the world, bears a resemblance to the indifference of the Orthodox to the same matter. It is true that the basic reasons are not the same. In Orthodoxy, it is because this world is nothing in comparison with heaven, whereas in Lutheranism, it is because the world is fundamentally corrupt.

The prophetic link between the two spheres of the divine and human offers a further instance of likeness. In Orthodoxy, the link between the Church-soul and the Nation-body is supremely the prophet; hence the extraordinary importance of monks in the Eastern world as witnesses of heaven and heralds of the last things, so that even the bishops are always selected from the ranks of monks, or at least they must have taken monastic vows before becoming bishops. A bishop, in fact, is a prophet because he is a successor of the apostles, the prophets of the new law. One of the keys to the understanding of the Eastern world is this amazing diffusion of Greek, Coptic, Slav, Armenian and Syrian monasticism, which has spread into Palestine, Egypt, Cappadocia, Constantinople, Georgia, Mount Athos and the Meteores in Greece, the islands of Lake Tana in Ethiopia, the Slav countries, and wherever Orthodoxy is represented. Monasticism occupies a central position because the prophetic idea is present at the meeting-point between earth and heaven, between the soul and the body of Christian society.

In Protestantism, it is impossible not to see that the centrally important position occupied by the prophetic idea is due to the position assigned to the Word and its proclamation. The kerygma, in the sense of the proclamation and its content, is the link between heaven and the Christian people, between the final realities and this present world. It is mainly, and almost solely, by its means that the divine sphere moves and transfigures the world. Whether it is only delivered from time to time, or whether it is bound up with some regular function, it is the kerygma that enables the two spheres to come into contact. Hence the importance of preaching in Protestantism, for preachers are the successors of the apostles and prophets in their function as heralds of God's Law; they are the witnesses of the link binding time with eternity, the heralds of the mysterious reality of the New Man hidden in Christ, which sometimes visits the world like a lightning flash.

The Protestant conception, however, does not escape being marked by some decidedly Western characteristics. Although eschatological ideas predominate, nevertheless it is a preoccupation with human destiny that holds the central position in Lutheran and Calvinist inquiries. The East is less interested in power than adoration, and when the eschatological realities are disclosed to its soul, they feel them to be so great that all other things disappear from sight. Moreover, since these realities are so absolute, how could they fail to take care of mankind? (Mt 6:25–34). Although the Christian West, whether Catholic or Protestant, puts the pursuit of the ultimate realities above everything, it still continues to ask what God's power, made manifest in the Word and the sacraments, represents in the concrete with regard to the world. It loves to contemplate God's glory, but perhaps it is primarily attracted by the fact of being acted upon by that glory.

Looking back on the characteristics of the three great bodies, we observe that Catholicism, Orthodoxy, and Protestantism, each represents a system of relations between the Church and the world, and between this world and heaven. What differentiates them is not a reference either to earth or heaven, but the way their relations are adjusted.

In Orthodoxy, the form is organic and eschatological. By organic we mean the type of union existing between soul and body, and by eschatological the fact that the Church is essentially an organization with heaven in view, and devoting herself to the corresponding tasks.

In Catholicism, the form is hierarchic and maximal. By hierarchic we mean an order, intrinsic to the Church, naturally subordinate to supernature. The word maximal is used to indicate the plenary nature of the Church's active responsibility for the world, not only by way of bearing external witness, as in Protestantism, but principally through the incorporation of all values in herself and through the amendment which she effects in the world.

In Protestantism, the form may be described as that of an extrinsic association and of a tangential relationship. The former term denotes the extrinsic and forensic nature of the relationship between the Church on earth and the eschatological realities hidden in Christ. The latter indicates that the realities between God and mankind are analogous to those between two spheres differing in size and quality: the smaller is ruled by the larger, by whom it is activated. The contacts are real, but tangential.

The Orthodox conception depends upon the Platonic theory of emanations or likenesses; it makes this world an epiphany of the spiritual world; the Catholic conception is based on the principle of the raising of the natural to the supernatural order; and the Protestant conception on that of the corruption and restoration of nature.

These three systems of relations are each exposed to specific difficulties and temptations. The difficulty which the Orthodox East always has to face is that Caesar may stifle or enslave the Church, the nation's soul. In Catholicism, the special sphere of our difficulties is the area of "mixed" problems, in which both Church and State have each a share in responsibility for them. At all times and everywhere, there has been (and there will continue to be) the conflict between the Priesthood and the Empire, whether "the Empire" is called emperor, king, dictator or politician. In

Protestantism, the particular danger is the relinquishment of the world to the conscience of the prince. When that conscience ceases to be Christian, then Christians, the Church and Christianity itself, are endangered. Caesar may become master in the Church, legislate on religious matters, enslave the prophets. Worse still, if the world is abandoned to its own resources, that abandonment will, through the unhallowing of the Christian people, rebound upon the Church and Christianity.

The specific temptations inherent in these three systems are, for the East, that the Church may become Quietist and the pursuit of the eschatological realities may cause history and this world (whose every part is in need of salvation) to be forgotten; for Catholicism, the distinction between the natural and supernatural order may be transformed into a separation and history and heaven may become strangers, even if militant secularism does not raise its head and move against Christianity; for Protestantism, that either the world and history may be rejected in the name of the eschatological realities, or the natural order may be separated from the supernatural. Such is the irony of things that Protestantism, which to some extent holds a position between Catholicism and Orthodoxy, in fact shares the difficulties and temptations of both.

The experience of our respective setbacks shows clearly that no single Christian approach is sufficient automatically to ensure the world's salvation. The triumph of Christianity always lies ahead. Nothing has been permanently won, and a new beginning is always imperative. It would be futile to attempt to stay the development of history, even if the whole world had become Christian.

Western Christianity, equally with that of the East, has its crises. The present crisis of Western civilization has been examined from many points of view by historians of civilization, theologians, sociologists and ministers of religion. From their analyses it is clear that the trouble springs not from religion itself, but from the obstacles that hinder its influence. The heart of our Christian civilization has always been the dynamic influence of Christianity over social life and institutions. But now Christian civilization has been secularized; and this phenomenon is as widespread in Protestantism as in Catholicism. On the one side there is the Christian religion, and on the other, a technical, scientific and secular order which exists in a moral and spiritual void. [8]

The world of Orthodoxy is also experiencing spiritual crises. Since the revolution in Russia, as the result of the establishment of atheist political regimes, several Orthodox Churches have lost their traditional function as the conscience of the State, and, to a considerable extent, the soul of the nation. And yet a situation of this kind is not something absolutely

[8] Christopher Dawson, *The Crisis of Western Education* (1961).

new in the general history of Orthodoxy. The patriarchate of Constantinople, the Balkan Churches and those of the Middle East, had undergone something similar under the Turks. In the grip of adversity, the Orthodox Church had endeavoured to remain the Christian soul of the people, and she is continuing the effort now. Behind the iron curtain the Churches are confident that it is they and not atheism who will have the last word. Marxist materialism represents an extreme form of Western secularism, and because it is Western and secular, it is certain ultimately to be overthrown through the inherent vitality of the Eastern Christian tradition, over which the temptation to secularism would have no power, were it not imposed by violence.

But this will not put an end to a critical situation, for even when the Orthodox Churches are again in a position to resume their traditional role, they will have to carry it out among peoples who have been formed by a materialist philosophy based exclusively on the values of this world; and it is doubtful whether monastic spirituality alone will be able to satisfy their special needs.

We should remember that the problem is that of the recovery, throughout the Christian world, of a realization of the Church's mission which has been either distorted, fragmented, or diminished as the result of the divisions among Christians. It has become too Western, even though still Catholic; too Eastern, even though still traditional; split up into a number of disconnected interpretations among Protestants; endeavouring to combine Catholic with Protestant elements, in Anglicanism, to regain the unity of the Church's mission, but rejecting infallibility as the guarantee that that mission will remain authentic and in action.

Catholicism, Orthodoxy and Anglicanism have much in common as regards the Church's mission. The main problems to do with the recovery of its integral meaning are to be found in Protestantism, and this fact demands further consideration.

3. Protestant ideas on the Church's mission

A. THE PRINCIPLES BEHIND THE IDEAS

The idea of the Church's mission depends upon the idea that has been formed of her nature. It follows that there are as many ideas of her mission as of her essence.[9]

[9] Hans Jochen Margull, *Église et Mission, Positions luthériennes* 3 (1959), pp. 115–27; *Theologie der missionarischen Verkündigung, Evangelisation als ökumenisches Problem* (1959); T. A. Kantonen, *The Theology of Evangelism* (1954); Julian N. Hartt, *Toward a Theology of Evangelism* (1954); Visser 't Hooft and Oldham, *op. cit.*, paper prepared

This inital approach inevitably follows the historical sequence of the various kinds of denomination originating in the Reformation. It provides a precise account of the idea of the Church as it exists in both the classical and radical Protestant bodies; it brings out the primarily inner nature of the Lutheran idea; the dynamic thoroughness of that of the Calvinist group of Churches; passing on to the Nonconformist and humanist bodies, it indicates the note of free evangelization in the former, and the reduction of Christianity to a mere instrument of human development in the latter.

B. THE FACTS BEHIND THE IDEAS

The second approach studies the phenomena. It attempts to trace back the typical lines of thought that run across confessional divisions and permeates the activity of the Protestant bodies. It thus provides concrete information about the idea of the Church's mission in contemporary Protestantism.

It is not always the idea that *de jure* ought to be held that is held *de facto*. Through the pressure of needs, geographic and social environments, of different periods, of ecumenical and social intercourse, Christian bodies may give up some of their convictions and practices and accept others that do not always seem to follow from their principles. In addition, the different ideas on the Church's mission should be considered either in a descending line according to the constituent elements of each communion, or in a horizontal line according to the phenomenological cleavage, established independently of particular frontiers.

Methods of evangelizing should not be confused with types of interpreting the Church's mission. Revivalism, for example, is a method, and it would be difficult to see it as a special interpretation of that mission. There is, of course, nothing wrong in mutual and tacit borrowing of methods by Christian bodies of whatever kind, provided there is no sacrifice of principle. And, in fact, there seem to be three main types of mission shared by contemporary Protestantism. The first concentrates upon witness; the second on communal life; the third on service. The division does not imply that some only devote themselves to the witness of the Word while others are exclusively concerned with service *(diakonia)* or communal life *(koinonia)*. Concrete existence is more complex. It is the varying proportion of each type in the mixture which marks the difference.

(i) The mission of witness by the Word

First of all, this means preaching, and secondly, the spreading of the Word by the community of lay people. On account of the importance it attaches

in view of the Faith and Order Conference at Oxford in 1937 on the theme "Église, Communauté et État".

to the Word, Protestantism is compelled to make sure of its renewal through this permanent and indispensable witness. An increased development of preaching in all its forms, and the great number of publications on preaching (many of them noteworthy) is a characteristic feature of all Protestant denominations today.

The witness of preaching is extended through its communication to the world by the laity. The Word of God can only acquire its full dimensions by being transmitted from place to place, in the family, social life and the State, that is, in the environment as a whole, and by continuing to question and awaken people in every walk of human life. The people perform this function, when each individual feels called to be a missionary of the Word.

(ii) Mission by means of community or koinonia

Witness by the Word, then, goes far beyond the boundaries of religious buildings. It is borne to all those to be evangelized wherever they are. Since the end of the Second World War Protestantism has tried a number of experiments; among these have been factory chaplaincies, associations of Christian workers, the work of religious communities like those of Taizé and Iona, the creation of cells of Christian activity to penetrate the organizations of the modern world, evangelization through the Christan's identification with his milieu, developments in spiritual counselling, pastoral advice and so on. These various activities are connected with the second type of the concrete exercise of the Church's mission, that is, the mission by means of community or koinonia.

How does the community as such become a worthy instrument to express the Church's mission?

The incidents in the gospel that support this idea are the selection of a group of disciples, the formation of a koinonia, a common brotherhood with our Lord, the sending of the Holy Spirit to the apostolic community. The creative power of this community is to be judged from the fact that the Holy Spirit was given to it *as a corporate body*, to be with and in it, in order to transform the world. "A city built on a hill cannot be hidden" (Mt 5:14): when a lamp is lit it inevitably shines (Mt 5:15). The Lord has placed his confidence in a gathering of all Christians into a single body, rather than in a number of isolated individuals.

The entire community is an expression of the Church's mission by demonstrating to the world that if the community becomes divided the mission becomes impossible. It continues to fulfil its mission by showing that the root as well as the flower of the mission is unity, and that Christian perfection is attainable only in the Body of Christ.

(iii) The mission expressed through diakonia or service

Christians needed a long initiation before being convinced that the era of individualism and merely subjective religion is over, and that God can only be genuinely served when he is rediscovered by man, in man. Love has developed into action; faith has become operative in works of charity; the Church's mission has taken the form of service, a diakonia. And, in truth, is not the very existence of the Church a kind of service of grace to the world?

The Church's work of service is expressed in three ways: action of the Church as a Church; action taken by individual Christians; specifically Christian action in society.

The national councils of Churches, the world unions of the denominations, and the World Council of Churches have assumed responsibility for a number of spiritual and corporal works of mercy: help to refugees, to the poor and those in distress, and to the underdeveloped countries, the disinherited Churches. They have fought for social justice, and for the development of a social system with that justice at heart.

A Christian carries out his mission as an individual when he fulfils his calling in the world. The Protestant doctrine of "election", which involves the corollary of the idea of obedience to God and of service to God in the world, has been thoroughly refashioned and reorientated to the needs of the modern world. But it has not been considered sufficient to recall its meaning. Groups connected with the Church have become centres of instruction and meeting points where members may acquire interest and guidance for pilot experiments that express the Christian calling in our time.

Individual Christian living has expanded into Christian social action in the spheres of everyday work, professional and corporate life. In a pluralist world, such as ours, Christian activity has found it necessary to cross the boundaries of its own denomination, and even those of the Christian world as a whole. In countries where non-Christians are in the majority, or where they control the State, a Christian will fulfil his mission of service by contributing to the human and temporal development of his country, by combating tyranny, by making an effort to preserve areas open to the eschatological realities. In those countries where Catholics or Orthodox are in the majority, he will fulfil that mission by giving his service to the construction of a common Christian ideal.

(iv) The goals that command these three kinds of mission

What are the goals whose attraction governs these three types of mission in the Church? They may be described in different ways; they may vary from a point of view which presupposes the complete sanctification of human life to a mere imputation of "justice", including all the stages between these extremes; or they may change from an historical to an eschatological outlook—in the World Assembly at Evanston this alternative again became evident, some communions and some theologians emphasizing the Church's mission as related to this world, while others stressed its relation to heaven[10]—this relation covering all the intermediary stages—realized eschatology, eschatology in process of realization,[11] or anticipated eschatology.[12]

But the two most important goals would appear to be those of the Institution and the Event: that is, an idea of the Church's mission as either an institution or an event. These are at opposite extremes. In no denomination is either of them completely realized, and it is by their mode of realization that one denomination differs from another.

The Protestant world is still divided between these two opposites in its teaching on the Church: the Church as Institution and as Event.[13] In the same way, it alternates between two ideas of the Church's mission: one of them rooted in a mediating institution, penetrated by the mission of the Event; the other, a mission directly accomplished by Christ, the missionary and evangelist. Or, to express it differently, the gospel in the setting of the Church, and the gospel as event.

The most modern representative of the idea of the Church's mission as Event is J. C. Hoekendijk, who has radically re-examined the idea of the Church as Event and applied it to contemporary issues.[14] Just as the Church is essentially Event and has being and existence only as Event, so she is essentially a missionary Event, and exists only through her missionary commitment.

At this point we are reminded of Karl Barth's words at the Assembly of Amsterdam: "The Church, the living congregation of Jesus Christ, the living Lord".[15] It needed only one step further to advance from the idea

[10] Karl Barth, Connaître Dieu et le servir (1945); L'Humanité de Dieu (1956).
[11] C. H. Dodd, The Interpretation of the Fourth Gospel (1953).
[12] O. Cullmann, Le Christ et le Temps (1953); E. T.: Christ and Time (1951).
[13] J. L. Leuba, L'Institution et l'Événement (1950).
[14] J. C. Hoekendijk, "The Call to Evangelism", The International Review of Missions, 154 (1950), pp. 162–75; "The Evangelization of Man in Modern Society", The Ecumenical Review 2 (1950), pp. 133–40; "La Mission et l'Œcuménisme", Le Monde non chrétien 19 (1951), pp. 327–340; "L'Église dans la pensée missionnaire", Le Monde non chrétien 20 (1951), pp. 415–433; "A Pantomime of Salvation", Social Progress (June 1959), pp. 13–19; "Neue Wege christlicher Verkündigung", Junge Kirche (1 July 1959), pp. 356–9; "Plan d'étude sur la théologie de l'Évangélisation et de la Mission", Revue de l'Évangélisation 84 (1959), pp. 227–41; Hans-Werner Gensichen, "Grundfragen der Kirchenwerdung in der Mission (zum Gespräch mit J. C. Hoekendijk)", Evangelische Missions-Zeitschrift (February 1951), pp. 33–46.
[15] Rapport général, vol. I, L'Église universelle dans le dessein de Dieu.

of the Church's essence and unity as Event, to that of her mission as convertible with her being as that same Event. Hoekendijk has made explicit what was implicit in Karl Barth's thought.

At the same time, it would be incorrect to believe that this is the one and only interpretation of the Church's mission in Protestantism, and to conclude that in Protestantism the Church's mission and essence are held to be identical. The idea that the Church is merely functional, a missionary "event", that her mission is her essence, is not the only idea prevailing in Protestantism.[16] For, in fact, together with the view that the Church's nature and mission must be measured by the fact of the "event", another doctrinal line of thought exists which includes the institutional aspect of the Church's mission. The Church is the Body of Christ, and this means that "the event" is not a passing moment, but endures, that it is in continuity with Christ, that its constitution is a bridgehead of the Kingdom that never fails.[17] This last standpoint is in no way alien to a number of pronouncements made by the International Council of Missions and the World Council of Churches.

4. The essence of the Church's mission from the point of view of the essential principles of Protestantism

Is it possible to single out one distinctive idea of the Church's mission that may be said to flow from the essence of Protestantism? Since we found that this could be done with regard to the central principles of the Reformation, it would seem to be no less possible with regard to the Church's mission. It is an abstraction, but that does not involve untruth; it is simply a means of reaching one aspect of the truth. On such a view, we may ask, what becomes of the principles of the absolute primacy of the Word of God, of the immanence and transcendence of the relationship between Christ and mankind, and of the Church's nature as witness, when we consider their bearing upon the Church's mission?

A. THE WORLD MADE ONE BY THE WORD OF GOD

The significance of the first principle lies in the fact that the Church's basic mission is the proclamation of the Gospel and the unification of the world through God's Word. Through the kerygma, the Church proclaims that the living Christ, the Eschaton, continues after his Resurrection and Ascension to "do and to teach" (Acts 1:1), as he did and taught before

[16] M.-J. Le Guillou, *Mission et Unité, les Exigences de la Communion* (1960), vol. I, p. 254.
[17] W. Andersen, *Towards a Theology of Mission,* International Missionary Council Research Pamphlet, no. 2 (1955), pp. 48–49.

he was crucified. In her proclamation of the kerygma, the Church is the annunciation used by God to break through the barriers of time, and to contact mankind. The Church exists in order that the eschatological presence of the Crucified and Risen Lord may act in the human situation to judge, test and save it. The Church's kerygmatic action resembles a sacrament at the service of the Christ-Eschaton in the way that the collection of the scriptures is a sacrament at the service of the Word. But just as the Spirit illumines our minds in order that we may understand the Word, so it infinitely surpasses the material proclamation made by the Church. It draws men, scripture, and the community of the Church in its wake, casts a heavenly light upon them and gives them a foretaste of the age to come. The primary aspect of the Church's mission, acting under the primacy of the Word, is therefore that of a kerygmatic mission. The Church proclaims that the era of the ultimate events has come about. She declares their presence, makes men aware of them, and effaces herself before their vivid reality, inevitably predominant, because the Lord, through his Resurrection, is utterly abounding life. When Jesus came into the world, he worked miracles in order to awaken faith. He did something which was not yet faith, but led to it. So it is when the mystery of salvation is preached. It is like a miracle which prepares the way for the sudden arrival of the Saviour who comes when the faith is proclaimed.

Catholics should take careful note of the precise significance of this position. It is based on deeds done by Christ with complete finality; their absolute value transcends the course of history. Everything that matters has been achieved. What we have to do is to preach it, reveal it, proclaim it. The sacraments have meaning through their relationship to this proclamation; but they are merely signs; they commemorate, and declare. Their purpose is controlled by the unification of the world by the Word. They effect nothing new, or at least only a new way of making the same proclamation.[18] It follows therefore that our disagreement with Protestants is profound; for we hold that the sacraments effect what they signify; intrinsically they contain the divine presence.

The evangelical interests of Protestants and Anglicans have resulted in some admirable definitions of evangelization. John R. Mott has made a collection of the best of them.[19] The conference in Geneva in 1947 on evangelization, which practically succeeded the Anglican committee of inquiry on the Church's evangelizing task,[20] produced an excellent report:

---

[18] T. F. Torrance, *Conflict and Agreement in the Church*, vol. I: *Order and Disorder* (1959), p. 209.

[19] *Evangelism for the World Today* (1938).

[20] The Archbishop's Committee of Inquiry on the Evangelistic Work of the Church, 1918. Cf. Bryan Green, *The Practice of Evangelism* (1951), p. 16.

Evangelization, it says, is the proclamation and presentation of God's Good News in Jesus Christ in a way that through the power of the Holy Spirit will lead men to put their trust in God, and in Jesus Christ, who saves them from guilt and the dominion of sin, who calls them to follow him and to serve him as their King and Lord, within the brotherly fellowship of the Church and through the manifold callings of the common life.

B. CHRIST AS THE FIRST AND SOLE EVANGELIST

This definition is inspired by the second essential principle of Protestantism: the immediacy and the transcendence of the relationship between God and man. Expressed in terms of the Church's mission, this principle implies that between the Church and Christ the distance is infinite. Just as a miracle that draws man's attention to the divine power is not yet faith in the Word, but the sign that points the way to the entrance into faith, so the Church effaces herself when confronted by the Lord's transcendence. She is like the Fore-runner, who is not the Lord, but points him out. She is like the miracle, the sign which beckons, attracts and calls men to believe, and yet never crosses the threshold of the divine transcendence. Between the Church's mission and that of the Lord, there remains a radical difference, which is due to the corruption of human nature. The Church may be the herald proclaiming that the final realities have come into being; she may be the Lord's Fore-runner, who comes suddenly and pulls down the barriers between time and eternity. But as a sign, she is, like every sign, an event, a contingent happening, a Church-that-comes-to-be, the earthly shape taken by the "event" of Christ, as it moves towards its own activity. Between Christ and the Church there is not, there can never be, an identity of mission, any more than there can be a real communication through any common sharing of the divine nature. The Church is the sign of the place where God meets the world, the place where the Word still becomes incarnate in the world. But the sign is transitory. It has no reality as an incorporation of the kingdom of heaven on earth. The Incarnation of the Word first needs the Church and then dispenses with her. It needs her in order to create the conditions necessary for its presence; but once it has become a present reality, it moves the Church away, takes her place, or, if it allows her to remain, it maintains a difference between itself and her that can never be overcome. The Church can never say: through God's grace my mission is theandric. The most she can say is that she reflects the brightness of her Lord, rather like an usher who announces the approach of a great personage, effaces himself before him who comes, but retains some reflected glory from the name he has uttered and from the man who has passed close to him.

203

Thus the Church, who carries out her mission of proclamation in the world, exists like a miraculous sign, given a new value through the radiant power of the risen and ascended Christ. The Church is not intrinsically filled by the Presence, for the Presence is imputed to her. But she is, quite literally, charged with her mission. It compels her, drives her on and she always has an added dimension due to that tangential contact which sent her out into the world. This, then, is the mystery of the Church's mission: the mystery of the missionary God has its ground in the Church; it makes her feel its weight, its dynamism, its drive to the ends of the earth. And yet, however intimate this contact may be, it is never anything more than tangential and extrinsic. The Church and the Lord, the Church the Lord's Apostle and Witness, form a unity in their mission, but this does not involve an essential communion between them; it simply means that they are contiguous and that they work together. Christ is the first and the sole evangelist: that is the Protestant view. Catholics, on the other hand, hold that the Church's mission is theandric; in it the Body of Christ which is the Church has a vital and inward relationship with the proclamation of salvation to renewed mankind.

C. THE NATURE OF THE CHURCH IS THE WITNESS OF A PEOPLE: THE LAITY

The most characteristic and the deepest idea which Protestantism has formed with regard to the Church is that of a people, the laity. The Church is the Church of mankind, and as such, excludes the hierarchic and sacerdotal Church. It is the body of all believers which makes up the priestly and prophetic kingdom. The Church's mission is the mission of this laity, who in all the variety of their callings in which they give themselves to every kind of service, are a people of prophets, priests and kings, in equal measure. Since the Church is a company of men and women called to bear witness to the act of salvation effected in Christ, her mission is seen to be involving precisely the duty of witnessing. As a fellowship of witnesses, she bears witness to the present activity of the Holy Spirit, to the work done by Christ long ago, to the immediate activity of the Lord Jesus in every man, and to the complete disclosure of our new manhood in heaven.

There is a phrase which is the controlling factor in this idea: it is "once for all" (Heb 9:12). Christ won the final and conclusive victory. Therefore, all that remains for the witnesses to do, is to transmit the news from generation to generation, to climb the ramparts and declare it to the combatants.

In Protestant thought, the eschatological realities will remain a world distinctly on its own until the end of time. They make contact with us, they exert their attraction by miraculous signs such as the kerygma, baptism and the Eucharist, active analogies of the Word,[21] that is, dynamic signs of the process through which God draws us to himself. These active analogies are charged with the power of the ultimate realities, but, a point that must not be forgotten, there is nothing intrinsic about this; no divine "energy" is transmitted through them, as is the case in the Catholic idea of the sacraments. They bear and support the ultimate realities, and this is what is meant by saying that they are charged with them. For the Church to bear witness means that she delivers this burden to the world.

In these essential principles of Protestantism we therefore meet a new way of looking at the Church's mission in the world; or, more correctly, these principles give rise to a number of new ways of looking at it.

II. ECUMENICAL RECONCILIATION IN THE SPHERE OF THE CHURCH'S MISSION

1. In non-Roman Catholic Christianity

Since the ecumenical movement came on the scene, there has been a persistent development towards unification in the activity of Christian Churches and communions. Work concerned with the Church's mission, that had been scattered, divergent and often contradictory, is gradually being transformed into missionary activity freed from competitive rivalries between the denominations and duplication.

Some Catholic critics who reduce the whole ecumenical problem to a single dogmatic aspect, have failed to realize the implications of this question as discussed at Edinburgh and Stockholm. They denounce the pragmatism and activism, but they forget that everything has to have a beginning, and that in actual fact no other course was possible. Besides, experience has shown that action taken in common has led to reflection on the sources of that action.

Conversion to the appreciation of what the complete idea of the Church's mission really means, began with self-criticism about the apostolic value of the service given to the world. The Churches and communions had to realize that if they were caught in an impasse, the fault was their own. They had been too slow in grasping what was involved in the development of modern society. They had rarely ventured beyond the habitual limits of their activities, and had remained attached to out-dated social institutions. They had believed their own world to be the whole world, and as a result their language had gradually become foreign to their

---

[21] T. F. Torrance, *Conflict and Agreement in the Church*, vol. II, *The Ministry and the Sacraments of the Gospel* (1960), p. 146.

hearers, who had been swept towards new ideas by the development of the modern world. There was one conclusion that no one could avoid: an "established" Church, accepted by the world, becomes a kindly and inoffensive body, a Church largely identified with the world's structures and standards, blessing and sanctioning the established order, without comparing it with what the Gospel demands. In short, a Church filled with the illusion of being at the heart of the world, but in fact, being far from it.

How can the Church be restored to the world, and the world to the Church? The meaning of the solidarity binding the Church to the world must be rediscovered, a way must be found to make the summons to redemption heard once more, and it must be made clear what the decisive problems really are. There must be an end to assertions that the Church has the answer to every human need, unaccompanied by a reply to any one of them in particular. There must be an end to men being considered as things; to their problems being treated as "cases", and their situations as dossiers. Human beings must be rediscovered, Christian persons, men and women of destiny! The pastor must again become the shepherd who knows each member of his flock, and each member must know him once more. The Church must reclaim her position as the spearhead of the Kingdom compelling the world to look up and recognize its coming. The sense of being on pilgrimage must be regained, and, in short, there must be a new beginning. [22]

The movement of approach in the sphere of the Church's mission between Protestants, Anglicans and Orthodox had its initial development in the context of missionary action. It was continued through Christian commitment to social action. Then an attempt was made to integrate unity of action and unity of belief. Lastly, the idea of the Church's general mission and that of her unity have increasingly tended to combine. Mutual concern about the question of the mission, has led towards unity, and now unity is giving its blessing to the mission. We may gladly agree that an immense result has already been achieved: the Church's mission has been explicitly expressed in universal terms. A study such as that of Dr W. A. Visser 't Hooft, [23] which attempts to establish an equilibrium and harmony between the various standpoints on the Church's mission, is careful to guide minds gently to a conclusion, and yet it may be taken as an example of the progress so far accomplished. A transition has been effected from the position of "let us act as if" unity of action at the

---

[22] Rapport général de l'Assemblée d'Amsterdam, report of the second section: "Le dessein de Dieu et le témoignage de l'Église"; Heinrich Kraemer, The Christian Message in a non-Christian World (1947).

[23] The Pressure of Our Common Calling (1959); Les Exigences de notre vocation commune (1960).

service of the Church's mission exists, to that of an inquiry into the foundations of effective unity. It has come to be seen that all share in a common calling: it is that of witness, communion in Christ and service.[24] Now these three forms of mission are connected with Christ's three functions—those of prophet, priest and king. Witness is connected with the first of these; communion with the second; service with the third. This indicates a notable development: Christian action and the Christian mission are searching for their roots in Christology.

A better equilibrium between the two aspects of the Church's mission is now established, and it marks a return to the traditional positions of Christianity. Instead of making too exclusive a choice between social transformation or the eschatological realities, an increasing effort is being made, and has even reached the stage of an accomplished fact, to follow the guidance of the principle of the constant interconnection between temporal and eternal concerns.[25]

The Churches and Christian communions have had to face the same basic facts: the end of the *corpus christianum*, secularization of the world and the advent of the new "post-Christian" man. And they have had to make their choice. They had either to turn away from the problem of mankind's salvation, and thus make the uselessness of their activity, and their own disappearance, certain; or else rediscover the significance of the universal applicability of Christianity and, in this way, gain renewed depth in the understanding of their mission.

Real life, the analysis of the same social realities, the same problems, often the same solutions, have produced more results in mutual relationships than would have an abrupt discussion of the principles of belief. Something similar occurs when the parents of families act at odds with each other, terminate all relationships and yet their children become members of the same sports club at the university. Which of them is in the right, parents or children? The children, with their trust in life, are led by some half-realized intuition, to see that to be alive means to be reconciled, while the parents hold that some principles are more important than life itself.

Does this mean that youth is always right? It may well be that last century it was the youth movements—the World Alliance of the Y. M. C. A. and the World Federation of Christian Students—that made the ecumenical movement possible. They believed that there are areas of

---

[24] "Une réflexion théologique sur le travail d'évangélisation", special number of the *Bulletin des Études*, V, 1 and 2 (November 1959).

[25] Ray C. Petry, *Christian Eschatology and Social Thought* (1956); Edward Duff, *The Social Thought of the World Council of Churches* (1956). See also the four volumes on *The Church and Society*, published by the World Council of Churches in preparation of the World Conference on Church and Society, Geneva 1966.

common ground, wherein the various forms of Christianity can undertake a dialogue that would yield results.

What has been accomplished within these Christian bodies must now be followed up from their ranks to those of Catholicism. On neither side has there been sufficient study of their common origins, nor a comparison made between their principal concerns and the way in which these can be adjusted. Through doctrine and history they have become strangers, although perhaps not to such an extent as is believed. If, therefore, the immense effort to understand the modern world and its problems, made in Catholicism as elsewhere, goes unobserved, it will be a mutual loss. Disagreements there may be: need these always amount to an unbridgeable dilemma? Ought not the elements we share in common be allowed their due position?

2. Meeting points with Catholicism

While in the other Christian communions a great process of reform on the subject of the Church's mission has been taking place, the Catholic Church herself, especially since the last war, has felt the need to return to a full understanding of the essence of her mission in the world. The war and its aftermath, international disturbances, world revolution and general de-Christianization, have faced her with problems which have often turned out to be identical with those encountered by the religious bodies originating in the Reformation and by the Orthodox Churches.

This mutual approach springing from inner convictions due to a kind of spiritual conversion to the heart of unity, has, most fortunately gone beyond the mere juxtaposition of the main interests of the various Christian bodies. From the very fact that these bodies have had to define their attitude to world problems, there followed the welcome discovery that on many issues they shared a common approach. A form of spiritual osmosis has occurred between their different ideas of responsibility, and occasionally insights have been exchanged. The renewed understanding of the Church's mission may thus serve as an avenue to a meeting point. It could happen that the same phenomenon which appeared in the reformed Churches—the understanding of the Church's mission leading to unity— may be reproduced on a scale that will cover all the Christian Churches and communions.

On this common ground of agreement—the resolve to save our modern world—several major meeting-points emerge, which, if logically developed, could play a large part in Christian reconciliation.

The first of these is the restoration of unity between religion and life. We are living in a secularized atmosphere: the State, legislation, politics, education, philosophy, science, leisure activities, public charity—nothing remains outside the new climate that has transformed the landscape of the human soul. We need to rediscover the idea of the sacred, the vital element of religion and of human destiny.

The second point where Christians have an opportunity of meeting is the restoration of the true order of all things by Christianity. Christianity is in the world to bring about the Christian revolution in a way that will endure until the end of the world, when everything will be taken up into eternity. Is the Kingdom of God a reality in this world, or does it belong exclusively to heaven? Absolute optimism is the expression of a secularized mind. On the other hand, absence from this world's affairs, in the name of absolute eschatology, seems to imply a lack of faith.

In what does the Christian revolution consist? It is a refusal of evil in the world; it is a discernment between good and evil, the promotion of the works of the Kingdom. Christianity exists in the world in order to ask the world a searching question, to disturb it in its false security, to confront it with a problem in its very heart, to make it realize that, in the things beyond its material eyesight, there is something truer and more vital than is to be found in its everyday experience. To reason about sin and righteousness, holiness and transcendence, freedom and mystery, that is its function.

Power to reject, to perfect, to transcend, that is Christianity. It is a force of opposition to the world's evil deeds; a principle of selection, purification and advancement amid the ambivalence and ambiguity of its works: a presence producing an acceptance of death to self in order to rise again to life in the Kingdom. It is more than a merely final perfection bestowed upon the natural order; it is something quite beyond them. It is more than a reality on the same level as human activity; it is a criticism, a judgement, a new direction.

Its revolutionary power lies in its ability to indicate that the realm of immanence in which man lives is not the whole of reality, but that there remains also transcendence; it causes what is transcendent to enter into the human situation in order to shatter the fabric of this world and its boundaries and, in faith to guide this world, earthbound by nature, construction and existence, towards an invisible magnetic pole.

The third point offering grounds for agreement is the formation of the features of Christ in the matrix of the world.

Christ's mysteries have an essential bearing upon the transformation of the world. The Church militant looks upon Christ as the sacrament of the future. When that has been finally and fully achieved, it will bring with it the perfect actuality of those Messianic realities prophesied as the adjuncts of the Kingdom. If we speak of the world becoming Christian, we mean that it will "put on" Christ, adopt his attitude to life, his mentality, be drawn in and with him to work for the completion of the new mankind. There is but one likeness of Christ, and it follows that the image of the Christian world cannot, if it is to be authentic, exhibit contradictory features.

The deep reflection which is now taking place throughout the whole Christian world has produced a great number of different points of view. From them it has become evident that the Church's mission must consist of witness and evangelization; of inter-communion and union; service and charity. There is a preference for joining it to Christ's three functions, as King, Priest and Prophet; and it is seen as the continuation of Christ's own mission of reconciliation and redemption, of recapitulation and salvation. But others prefer to express it differently: it is, they say, a mission that brings the realities of the last age before mankind, proclaims them, and is their sign. It is also a mission of witness like that of the Suffering Servant.

These different ideas of the Church's mission obviously need to be harmonized.

III. THE MISSION OF THE UNIVERSAL CHURCH ACCORDING TO CATHOLICISM

Since the concept of the Church governs the interpretation of her mission, the meaning of the word "Church" must first be ascertained.

Its fundamental meaning is that of a congregation that has been summoned. The Church is the "convocation", the body "convoked" by the Trinity. It is formed by the Father in the Spirit, who spoke by the prophets: by Christ, the Father's herald; by the Apostles, the bishops and the other members of the Church. Its purpose is to gather all men and the material universe into a "congregation" and into a single body of salvation.

The Church may therefore be defined with reference to four relationships: that is, as related to mankind, to the apostolic hierarchy, to the incarnate Word and to the Trinity.

In relation to the Trinity, the Church is the mystery of the summons to mankind made by the Three Persons, and by the heralds chosen by the Trinity, in order that the universe as a whole may be gathered into it.

In relation to the incarnate Word, the Church is the mystery of the divine and human nature of Christ sacramentally penetrating history; that is, the mystery of the theandric life of the Church.

In relation to the apostolic hierarchy, the Church is the mystery of Christ-the-Apostle, continued in the Twelve and their successors, to gather in unity the Church of mankind.

In relation to mankind, the Church is the mystery of the "election", the "convocation", the "congregation" and the communal life of the people of God.

Every aspect, therefore, leads to the heart of the mystery, for what makes the human community one? Is it not the community of the Trinity, the circumincession of the Three Persons? What makes the communication of the Trinity to mankind possible? Is it not the sacramental nature of the Word incarnate (the Church of the Word Incarnate)? What makes possible the structural form of the Church of mankind able to represent the "structure" of the Trinity? Is it not the apostolic hierarchy (the Church of the hierarchy)? Every aspect, every degree, reveals the essential significance of the Trinity. The hierarchy is the prophet of the last things, of the stage when the Trinity is "all in all". The sacraments, proceeding from the Word incarnate, are the way leading to the Trinity; community of life shared among men is the result. The image of the Trinity is reproduced in mankind through its conformation to the Son. He who sees the Church sees the Son and, seing the Son, sees the Father.

1. Is the Church the Church of the Incarnation or the Church of Glory?

The Catholic Church deduces the logical consequences following from the definition of her mystery, and discovering there the true proportions of her nature, she understands also the laws of her activity and of her mission in relation to time and eternity.

Central to the explanation of the mystery of the Catholic Church there is a definite eschatological point of view, and at bottom, it is the specific eschatological point of view that governs the specific idea of the Church's mission. There are as many ideas on the Church's nature and mission as there are ideas on eschatology.

Christianity is a new life in Christ. As the canon of the Mass for the Ascension in the Roman Church explains: for us all "the substance of our human frailty" has been taken up with Christ into heaven. It is the same idea that underlies St Paul's statements about our death, resurrection and ascension in Christ. Differences between Christians all spring from the way in which the relation between our earthly being subject to sin and that "substance of our human frailty" taken up with Christ into heaven, is interpreted. The Orthodox Churches interpret it as a form of communion, illumination and transfiguration. Protestants regard it as that of two realities in contact, and to that extent united, but in their essence still separate, and merely related tangentially. Catholicism, on the other hand, holds that an inner continuity exists between the earthly and heavenly situations, between grace and glory. "The substance of our human frailty" is even now, in this world, really united to Christ's substance in heaven.

The Orthodox and Catholic views are ultimately in agreement; they lead to the same conclusion—the transfiguration and deification of the world. Their difference lies in the way they express this, in their mode of approach. In Orthodox teaching, redemption means the emanation of divine "energies" which, by means of the Incarnation, lead to the transfiguration and illumination of the world. Grace is more a beam of glory and a reflection of it than a source of activity. In Catholicism, especially in its Western form, redemption is considered mainly as a cleansing from sin and a raising to the supernatural order. In Protestantism, it is the complete and instantaneous restoration of human nature to its perfect state, through Christ's vicarious expiation. What exists in Christ is transferred to men in an external though real manner, so that they may be enabled, in a state of life wherein they obey God, to fulfil the obligations incumbent upon them.

The standpoint of the Catholic Church is dictated by a view of the eschatological realities as present and active in the historical Church which is also the Church of faith.

The Lord's Incarnation, death, Resurrection and Ascension, are eschatological deeds. The mission of the Holy Spirit is an eschatological event and his presence in the Church where he is the source of grace, brings her into the centre of the eschatological order. When we say that a Christian is a son of God, we mean that his eschatological reality as a "new man" is already present, not indeed perfectly developed, but in the degree possible, while man is still in the uncertainties of his pilgrimage.

The Church is eschatological through her undeviating advance towards her consummation in heaven, and on account of the Three Persons, from whom she originates and who dwell in her. The Church is partly in this world, and yet her whole being proclaims that she is infinitely closer to the fellowship of the Trinity than to any human society. Her whole being speaks to us of the divine presence and—according to an idea much to the mind of Orthodox Christians—makes us see it as a heavenly hierophany: the liturgy, prayer, the proclamation of the Word, fraternal love, the religious life, the impregnation of the world by the spiritual presence of Christianity. When our Lord said that the gift of a glass of water was a gift to him (Mt 25:35–46), that when Saul attacked the Church, he was attacking him (Acts 9:4), was he not explaining that the Church is fundamentally an eschatological reality, containing the divine presence within her?

This is the very crux of the disagreements among Christians. For Protestantism, the historical Church and the eschatological realities are two things which encounter and touch each other, but remain for ever separate. For Catholicism, the Church is the Kingdom of God, in its initial stage, and on pilgrimage, but real.

Thus the Church's mission is governed by the way she understands the ultimate realities present within her: the Trinity, the happiness of everlasting life. And it is this which establishes the equilibrium of her action, as well as her obedience in the work of saving men in the totality of their nature, for time and eternity.

No Church or Christian body is ever exempt from temptation. There is no churchman who does not sometimes fall. But the eschatological realities already present in the Church are a restraining factor holding her back and a lode star that guides her. They constitute her norm, her rule, her measure. It is they that move her to labour for the world's transformation, but at the same time keep her from being ensnared in an earthly Messianism. They remind her that the transformation which the world must undergo is principally to become conformed to the divine presence. The conquest of space and the discovery of the last secrets of the atom, are nothing if they are not in some way brought into relation with the deliverance wrought by the Kingdom.

The comparison between the Church and Christ, her exemplar, in his earthly life, must be drawn once more. Like him, she is at once divine and human, incarnate and transcendent. She belongs to the realm of things done and of things still to be done. She exists together with what is final, absolute, terminal and eternal. But she also belongs to the realm of what is in need of perfection, the relative, the developing and the terminal. She is present in the infinite and boundless, and also in the localized and finite. In her Head, and in her soul, she is beyond the disturbance of the passions, and yet in that element of her condition which has not attained to perfect joy, she lives in sorrow. In heaven she is everlastingly alive, but here she is still subject to the sting of death. In her Head, she has been restored and he has brought her into the being of God, and yet at the same time she strives for the reconciliation of mankind, of material reality and of all creation, with God.

All the arrows of history pierce her. Every sorrow afflicts her. And yet she remains brimful of inexpressible joy. She ascends from earth, but descends from heaven. She was begotten in time, and yet she is older than creation (The Shepherd of Hermas, vision 2). She is evidently visible and discernible, but, at the same time, we can see that she fits perfectly into the mystery of God. She is on the same plane as the Saviour's humility and manhood, but she also springs from God's glory.

She is the Church of the Incarnation, and of the Ascension; of the Cross and the Resurrection.

She is without blemish and untained, and yet not without sinners.

Her way lies among the realities of today, and, in this living present, she transcends herself in Christ, who is her deepest self, her abiding consciousness, the synthesis of past and future, her memory now of what she was before the creation of the world, the Wisdom that gives unity to the plan of salvation.

She has her place in the development of history. She is subject to its influences, its variations, repercussions and its violent disturbances. But she dominates it with gentleness. She incorporates it. The world provides her material basis, but ultimately it is she who leads the world to the eschatological realities. The world thinks it knows where it is going, but it does not know who in reality is directing it, nor the goal to which it is being guided. The Church even now is ready to welcome mankind's final achievements, for she herself has reached the goal in which history finds its consummation.

That goal had been reached already in the life and ministry of Jesus. He is the revelation of the last word, the final summons and appeal addressed by heaven to the world. As the revealer of the Omega and the Absolute, he discloses the eschatological realities at work in time, and time is fundamentally directed to eternity. Throughout the Gospel the "last things" are visibly and mightily in action, hastening to fulfilment. Terms like Lamb of God, bread of life, light of the world, the vine, the Good Shepherd, are eschatological; they herald the perfect, shared life with God. [26] When John sent to ask Jesus whether in fact he was the Messiah, Jesus answered that this was beyond doubt, because his works were disclosing the activity of the Ultimate reality in time. Where the infinite presence of God becomes evident, we may see a sign of the end foretold by the prophets.

The same thought recurs in the Joannine teaching on God's judgement already active in the world; in the eschatological discourse with which Mark opens his narrative of the Passion that accomplished the final and everlasting covenant; in the glorification bestowed on Jesus in his Passion; above all, in the Resurrection which is the special work of the Father, who made Jesus the One who lives for evermore (Acts 2:24–34; Rom 6:9); and lastly in Pentecost and the spread of the Church to the ends of the earth. The Church is God's last word to the world.

In the thought of Jesus and the evangelists, this series of events is evidently considered to be the fulfilment as well as the revelation, of an eschatological purpose. Someone and something is at work in the temporal order to bring about happenings that would have an absolute significance. The Messianic King has come: the Word has made itself heard. He has adopted Moses and the prophets and incorporated them in his teaching, with an authority that transcended them. What they had figuratively proclaimed and begun, he brought into the world of reality. The eschatological meaning of God's law is now disclosed: it is a community of life and action with the Trinity.

[26] J. Jeremias, *The Parables of Jesus* (1954).

214

Jesus was seen to be the revealer of the ultimate development of all reality. As the high priest who offers the perfect sacrifice that will endure for ever, he gathers the Church around him, as the final Temple, the worshipping community that celebrates the imposing liturgy of the Lamb (Rev 21:22). Wherever priesthood now exists, therefore, wherever there is a ministry in the Church, it has come down from heaven.

The Kingship of Jesus, also, is disclosed in its eschatological meaning. The risen Christ has become both "Lord and Christ" (Acts 2:36), to reign everywhere for ever. All regal power in the Church, all jurisdiction, is therefore grounded in the Resurrection and Ascension.

Lastly, eternal life itself consists entirely in the knowledge of the Father, Son and Holy Spirit (Jn 17:3), an everlasting existence in communion, in identity of thought with God. But it is Jesus, the Revealer of the Father, the absolute master of all that pertains to religion, who is the bringer of every form of knowledge needed for eternal happiness. It follows that all teaching authority now vested in the Church comes down from the supreme teaching authority of the Lord, and its infallibility is derived here and now from heaven precisely because of its eschatological character.

It is because the Church's priesthood, regality and teaching authority are essentially eschatological that Jesus conferred the most significant forms of authority upon the apostles only after his Resurrection: the authority to forgive sins (Jn 20:22–23), the mission and authority to teach the whole world (Mt 28:19–20), Peter's regal authority as primate, which thus clearly manifests the eschatological meaning of this primacy (Jn 21:15–18).

We can now see how through the activity of the eschatological realities present in the Church, the transformation of the world has already begun.

2. The formation of the Church; her prefiguration and transfiguration

Two major stages may be distinguished in the formation of the Church: one of them extends inclusively, from the moment of the Incarnation until Christ's death; the other from the Resurrection until the Church attains her final perfection. The two phases need not be separated any more than they were in Christ. Christ's existence and that of the Church are concurrent. Where he begins to be, the Church begins. She is a participant in all his mysteries. With him she was born, grew, died, rose again and now reigns, even though she is still on earth in union with him. She came forth from the old Covenant as he did; she was transformed into the new Covenant when he died and rose again.

If, then, the history of Christ can be seen in two stages—up to his death and then the transfiguration of the Resurrection-Ascension—the Church also can be seen thus in two constituent phases: that extending from the Incarnation to the Cross, and that from the Resurrection to the consummation. The first phase leads from the figures of the Old Testament to the reality of the Church created on the cross. The second phase bursts forth like a transformation.

The Fathers are unanimous in holding that the Church was born on the Cross; she was mysteriously drawn from Christ's side, as Eve from Adam's. But with the Resurrection, there began, both for Christ and the Church, a transformed existence. More accurately, the Church's ultimate and eternal mode of existence began, her heavenly, transformed existence. It is within this transformed sphere that the bestowal of authority on the apostles one evening after the Resurrection, and of the primacy on Peter, must be regarded, for the former structure of the Church was superseded, and with it, those responsible for assembling the people. Within this same sphere the mission of the magisterium entrusted to the apostles was also established. They were the true prophets of the absolute, of that final era which in a sense is no longer a reality to come, since it is already present. The former prophets, foretelling the Messianic kingdom to come, prefigured these new prophets of that kingdom there present in that Church. She was visible, but with a visibility transformed from the start.

A peak must first be surmounted, the further slopes of death must be traversed by the transition of the Passover. Grace, the partaking of grace, thenceforth itself springs from the same transformed sphere.

But what is grace? It is not a self-subsistent reality, an intermediary between God and man, a substitute for him, a fluid separable from its source, and able to be retained for a while on its own. Grace is Christ himself, actively redeeming. It is his presence, illuminating, acting, transforming. It is the transformed Christ actually transforming mankind and the world. His presence does not leave man unchanged; it is not a mere matter of contact. When the Lord "passes over", men are left with the intrinsic result of his favour which is grace. The Lord's grace abides with them.

The mystery of God acts through a great many symbols endowed with a practical power deriving from the full force of the Lord's power, present in them and most literally in action. This presence surmounts man's activity; it awakens and heals him; and man, raised above himself by the divine "energy", becomes a partner in the Lord's transforming work. This is so, because the Church is the Body of Christ, and a body cannot exist or act apart from its head.

This doctrine, as a whole, may be summed up in the following idea: Christ, in whom the transformed unity exists, has brought mankind into the unity of the Trinity. The ultimate realities have been communicated to

216

mankind. This share in the unity of the Trinity is given in the sacramental form of the Word of God incarnate in the scriptures; in the Church, Christ's mystical Body; in the Eucharist, his sacramental body.

3. East and West

The Church's mission has two poles: time and eternity. The value of each must be recognized, but a hierarchy must exist between them. Whether the expression of Catholicism be Eastern or Western, one fact remains: the essential structure of Christianity is relational and hierarchical, and eschatological realities have been here in the midst of time since Christ came on earth. But the East draws different conclusions from those of the West. Since eschatology has already begun, the West says, and we are living in the last days, we must hasten to make straight the ways for the coming of the Lord (Lk 3:4). We must labour to restore all things in Christ. God's kingdom must spread in the life of society as well as in personal life, in the life of conscience as well as in national life, in legislation, the arts, science, the whole order of profane values. For the Orthodox East it is enough for the Church to be the soul of the nation. Since eschatology is already present in the world, the Church must not be distracted by anything less than the absolute.

The Orthodox conception regards itself to be the more authentic one because it is more patristic. It points out, besides, that in the Acts of the Apostles, the Epistles of St Paul and St John, we do not find the Church offering immediate answers to particular problems which the world poses, or trying to modify the prevailing civilization, but responding to everything with faith, charity, baptism, and the Eucharist. The Church figures as the leaven in the meal, the salt of the eath, the light of the world. She seeks to christianize man, and by this interior work lays the indispensable foundations for a social and national life befitting the definitive reality of the new man God has made. By studying to convert hearts and minds she grapples with human problems at their very roots, causing divine truth, love, and all the virtues — the basis of Christian life for all peoples — to flow out from within.

Thus in the Orthodox East the conception of the Church's mission remained exactly what it was in the first period, even through the great Christian civilization of Byzantium. The Church exercises her mission above all from within; she does not offer solutions to the world's immediate problems; she responds to them with faith, love, baptism, the Eucharist, and thus transforms individuals, court, and emperor; and when evil rules the State or society, she is not directly involved. So the persecutions she suffers now are not those which attach to active ecclesiastical efforts to transform society.

217

Catholicism goes into more precise detail than the Orthodox East about the mission of the Church. It pictures a single end with a hierarchically ordered duality of aspects; the immediate aim is to usher in and establish the kingdom of God on earth; the ultimate aim is the kingdom of God in heaven. These two stages of a single end are not treated as two autonomous or parallel ends. They are inwardly linked by a continuity like that which leads from grace to glory. If the energies of the kingdom are present on earth, how can they not tend to transform the whole world? So the mission of the Church must fit into the total order of time and eternity.

The fact that the Church was forced, until the official recognition of Christianity by the Edict of Mila in 313, to rest content with an imprecise and interior transformation of the world, does not mean that her mission has no other aspect. For if that position was plainly evangelic, it is also evangelic to declare that since the eschatological presence of the kingdom has descended into time all things must be brought under its rule and summed up in Christ. Christianity is universally applicable, but it must also be universally applied.

In the mind of the Eastern Church the single end of salvation and heaven are more autonomous, as it were exclusive, since this world is transitory and the world to come where there is no sin or blame, can be possessed here and now. All the same the East is not indifferent towards the establishment of a Christian civilization: that will come by way of superabundance as a by-product of seeking the kingdom. But it is not sought in itself as a necessary step towards the universal establishment of the kingdom.

Accordingly there are two ways, consistent with the Gospel, of envisaging the arrival in time of eschatological power and of submitting to its sway.

The spirit of the Orthodox Church and the spirit of the Catholic Church are different. In principle they are akin, even though nine centuries of separation have sharpened the difference. For the sake of ecumenical relations we must carefully ascertain those points where they agree and disagree.

But these expressions of Christianity envisage religion as a religion of salvation which delivers man from sin and death and brings him to eternal life through faith in Jesus Christ and obedience to his law. But at once we encounter differences. Eastern Christianity stresses the eschatological character of redemption; Western, the beginning of the life of salvation in this world. For both, the Beyond is the goal of redemption and the essence of redemption is the disclosure of saving power in history; but in the East saving power is not so much the power which vanquishes sin as that which triumphs over the ephemeral condition of the world and over death, whereas the West emphasizes the consequences which heavenly beatitude already has on earth. The presence in time of eschatology, or rather of the Eschaton, is felt in the East to be an expression of glory, to snatch men from their present condition and transport them into the Beyond, rather than a power that transforms creation and the world here and now: glory rather than dynamic power, an inner change of heart rather than invitation to social action, spiritual conversion rather than Christian law, more for the adoration of God than for the service of the world. In short the West, whether Catholic or Protestant, sees word and sacrament as a power for transforming the world, even though it also sees in them the presence of God which he adores. The West has developed the theology of the redemption more than the theology of the Incarnation. In the East more stress is laid on divinity made man than on man divinized. The West is taken up with the remission of sins and with salvation in this world. The East is not uninterested in these things, but its own concerns are less anthropological.

We find the same spirit in the realm of liturgical and sacramental life. For Catholics and Orthodox alike the liturgy and the sacraments are the heart of religious life. In principle there are no differences, for we share the eucharistic mystery and the same sacraments, though the rite varies. But the Eastern Church stresses the fact that we are preparing for the Beyond, lifted to a higher plane, transported into the eschatological kingdom. The Eastern Christian at Mass feels lifted above the earth towards heaven; he has a foretaste of heavenly things. The sacrifice goes on behind the iconostasis, in an atmosphere of mystery. One could well say that heaven descends to earth, time vanishing in its presence. In the Western Church, by contrast, the explicit culmination on which everything converges, architecture as well as men's attention, is the sacrifice that blots out sin. Hence the prominent position of the altar and the importance of the consecration. No one denies that celebration of the sacred mysteries is a theophany, but the word strikes a Western mind as exotic. What is stressed is sacrifice to blot out sin rather than a celebration at which one experiences the ineffable — more the healing of the soul than selfless adoration of God. Never is the glory divorced from its temporal implications. If we are exalted to heaven, we do not forget to lay hold on precise spiritual goods. At times the establishment of a life conformed to God's law overshadows mystical preparation for the Beyond. Perhaps we think too much of power and too little of glory. Only consider the terms used in speaking of the sacred liturgy which constantly recur: satisfaction, expiation, justice, propitiation, penalties due to sin, merit, demerit, obtaining heavenly favours, power to act. Others, those most used in the East, are much more rarely met with.

It would be interesting to compare the evolution of liturgical piety in East and West, at least since the separation. We should doubtless discover that certain features of the Western or Eastern mind were finally taken to convey the whole of Christianity. Yet none of them is alien to the spirit of the Gospel. The only error is the lack of communication between Eastern mind and Western. Have not the Eastern Churches in communion with Rome a mission of reconciliation here?

The different Western and Eastern views on the connection between eschatology and time appear again in the realm of Christian life. In the Western Church a Christian must, besides saving his soul, devote himself to conquering the world for God. He knows he is engaged in a battle which must bring everything good and holy into profane life. He has not been delivered from evil solely for his own personal benefit. Once redeemed, he cannot forget about the world: he must draw it into his own liberation. So, strong in the power of eschatology, he boldly undertakes to subject all things — spiritual, social and profane — to the Lord's sovereign rule. In Eastern Christianity the laymen's position comes closer to the monastic ideal than to a spirituality for a Christian in the world. *Mutatis mutandis,* his ideal retains the main features of the monastic approach: the monk expects nothing of this world, he knows it to be fleeting and deceitful, he tries to remain undefiled by it, asking only that it help him contemplate even now the heavenly realities to come. Why should one struggle to subject the world to God when there is one's soul to save? What are the most dazzling of successes compared with the presence of those eschatological realities which man already knows in symbols? Must one not make a choice in accordance with the absolute scale of values? What is this world compared with the next? Is not adoration of God infinitely better homage than the efforts one might make to transform the economic and social order? The world passes away: our destiny is elsewhere. And so the idea of a lay vocation in the temporal order sounds bizarre and irreligious to the Eastern Christian. The organizing energy and conquering aggressiveness with which the Western Christian sets about changing the world and subjecting it to God are a violent contrast with the compassion for the world, the melancholy, the disinterested outlook of the Eastern Christian who lives according to his faith.

Obviously it is no small matter to strike a balance. We may be permitted to see the frightful reaction of Marxist materialism in Orthodox countries as a kind of absolute vindication of the layman's temporal vocation against a certain absenteeism.

The mission of the Church must embrace the State and the nation. But how? The Church is the mother of believers, the guardian of tradition, the interpreter of the Christian inheritance. But at once differences emerge. A Church conceived of as a perfect society seems to Orthodoxy to be too similar to a State or a kingdom. It cannot picture a Church and a State facing each other as one power faces another. The Church can be neither a State nor an empire. She is a spirit, she is a leaven, she is the salt of the earth. She is the deathless soul of the nation and the eternal conscience of the State. The soul has no business to be the body. The ideal, indeed, would be for the soul to dispense with the body so far as possible. True, the Church cannot be indifferent to the body, the nation, since Christians are in the world.

But she gives them what she is in a position to give them, and those things belong exclusively to the religious order. It is not for her to translate into social terms the moral impulses she communicates to men. That is the business of laymen. The Church gives us a general orientation in view of ultimate realities. Christian heads of State must accept it and govern accordingly. Occasionally the hierarchical Church will intervene public affairs in a prophetic capacity, but never as one sovereign power addressing another.

On the other hand, the Western Church defines herself as a perfect, self-governing society independent of the State, which would never on any account accept absorption in the State, as the tremendous struggles between Papacy and Empire have shown. The Church is in the nation, in the world, but she is more universal than the nation and the world. The Church holds that it is her mission to recapitulate all things in Christ, bringing all peoples, cultures, and civilizations under her dominion. And to do so she must have complete freedom of action and the appropriate means at her disposal. Such is the very logic of her catholicity. While remaining specifically distinct from State and nation, she spiritually receives them into her bosom to begin on earth the realization of the universal final kingdom, by giving man his supernatural education and completely transforming the human condition.

The Western Church has defined the relations between Church and State in her own terms. There is more of a distinction than many suppose. We must consider the logic of each system: in the West, there are two powers facing each other; in Orthodoxy, the Church is the soul of the nation. Judging either position in terms of the other would mean misinterpreting the facts and ending with a caricature of the true situation: spiritual imperialism on the one hand, confusion between Church and State on the other.

Similarly the Eastern Church has explained in its own way the part the Church must play in the world: leaven, conscience, soul, inspiration, prophecy. Many Western judgements, which dismissed Orthodoxy as sheer absenteeism, have to be revised. Had the influence of the Orthodox Eastern Churches been as negligible as some say, Eastern Christendom would long ago have become a thing of the past. The invasions of Seljuks, Tartars, and Turks, and Communist pressure today, would have left no trace of Christianity behind. We must salute our brethren in the faith who for two thousand years have manned the outworks of the Christian world and who the moment they are given a brief respite bring life from death in the power of their traditional Christianity. We have found three fundamental formula for the Church's mission: being witness, as in Protestantism generally; being the soul and conscience of the nation and the State; and finally the most universal formula, which makes the Church at once God's witness in the world, the conscience of the nation and the State, and the matrix of the world to come.

Perhaps three words sum up these differences; for Catholicism, especially in the West, recapitulation; for the East, epiphany; for Protestantism, witness. Each indicates a conviction that Christianity can be applied to every aspect of the world. There is nothing in the world that cannot be recapitulated in Christ. There is nothing in the world that cannot be transfigured. There is nothing in the world that falls outside the scope of the salvation Christ has won us. Recapitulation would have Christ all in all; transfiguration would divinize man; witness would proclaim the universal salvation won in Christ. The Protestant thinks of a work done at once, definitively, which then needs only to be signified, proclaimed, bodied forth in the world. The Orthodox sees salvation as a hierophany. The Catholic sees the salvation accomplished in Christ as something that has not only been effected but that is actively at work within man here and now.

Shall we say that these differences represent a conflict between the Platonic spirit and the Aristotelian? That for the first few centuries the Church led a Platonic life, that then the Aristotelian spirit conquered the Western Church while the East remained faithful to Plato and Plotinus,[27] and that afterwards the Reformation, especially the Lutheran Reformation, brought about a return to the Platonic spirit?

All things considered, the Western Church has attempted a synthesis between the two aspects which are seeking the world to come and developing the kingdom of God on earth, assigning created things an end of their own: the establishment of the kingdom, and preparation of the new heavens and the new earth.

4. St Augustine and the Church's mission

In the undivided Church, a difference in spirit between the Eastern and Western Churches soon became manifest. St Clement of Rome, Tertullian, Novatian, St Hilary of Poiters and St Ambrose are Latin. Clement of Alexandria, the Cappadocian Fathers, St Athanasius and St Basil are Eastern.

There was, however, one man, during the period of the undivided Church, who managed to achieve a synthesis between the spirit of East and West, and to define the twofold mission of the Church. This man was St Augustine. Of all the Fathers, and perhaps of all Christian thinkers, he is the one from whom the Catholic Church derived most vitality. He was a man of two races and two mentalities, a Latin and a Berber. Peter the Venerable, abbot of Cluny, described him to St Bernard as "the greatest

[27] A. v. Harnack, *Grundriss der theologischen Wissenschaften, Dogmengeschichte*, part IV, vol. III: *Der Geist der morgenländischen Kirche im Unterschied von der abendländischen* (5th edition, 1914), pp. 157–83.

teacher of the Churches after the apostles" (*P. L.*, 182,405). He assimilated the Christianity of the East, influenced by Plato and Plotinus, and he combined this system of thought with that of the West, nurtured by his own experience of salvation and of the order of the world. In the *City of God* he provided a perennial definition of the Church's mission, with its twofold direction towards heaven and towards the establishment of the Kingdom of God on earth. The two directions of his thought, mankind's salvation and the intrinsic significance of this world—are combined in a synthesis of the Church's mission in time and eternity, of the utmost grandeur and harmony. As regards the understanding of her mission, the Catholic Church owes more to him than to anyone, more even than to St Thomas Aquinas.

Protestantism itself is not without its debt to him. The Augustinian origins of Luther's and Calvin's ideas should be carefully noted. The Augustinian monk was neither a Thomist nor an Aristotelian; nor was Calvin. Both of them were Augustinians; and therefore, both were medieval, for the Middle Ages did not draw its sustenance principally from Thomas, but from Augustine. Luther and Calvin looked to Augustine as their master, and in his teaching they received a portion of the spirit of Plato and Plotinus. Luther's eschatological interests were quick to draw his attention from this world, and this brought him closer to the mentality of the East. But it was the same eschatological concern that committed Calvin to the transformation of the world.[28] This makes him thoroughly Western and Augustinian. And yet both of them were only partially faithful to the spirit of St Augustine.

Ernst Troeltsch, in his great book,[29] is largely responsible for the accusation of Aristotelian unilateralism, which Protestants so easily make against Catholicism and St Thomas Aquinas.

A different criticism of the Catholic Church comes from the East. The Orthodox Churches are essentially Platonic and Plotinian in spirit. They rebuke Catholicism for choosing St Thomas as its "common Doctor"; they say he was in essence a Christian Aristotle, who was responsible for the inability of Catholicism to understand.

A great deal is attributed to St Thomas, and rightly.[30] But it is forgotten that he was a man of tradition. Protestants in their criticism are mainly concerned with the Catholic idea of Christianity as hierarchical and relational which is unacceptable to Protestantism on account of the Reformers' interpretation of man's original state. Now in fact the funda-

[28] E. B. Warfield, *Calvin and Augustine* (1956); Jean Boisset, *Sagesse et Sainteté dans la pensée de Jean Calvin* (1959).
[29] *Op. cit.*
[30] W. A. Visser 't Hooft and J. H. Oldham, *The Church and its Function in Society*, chapter vi, "The Church and the World", section II: "Nature and Supernature". Compare

mental theory of the relations between the Church and the world, or of the Church's mission in the world, was taken by St Thomas Aquinas from St Augustine and from the Christological formula of the Council of Chalcedon.

Two important works, published since 1939,[31] have shown beyond dispute that Plato and Plotinus are much more thoroughly incorporated in the synthesis of St Thomas than had hitherto been suspected. These two studies are philosophical, but they apply also to the theological aspect of Thomist thought. According to Fr. Geiger, the characteristic of the Thomist system is a synthesis between two kinds of participation: participation through likeness or through strict hierarchical degrees, as in the Platonic scheeme of things; and participation resulting in a composite reality, according to the Aristotelian view. All things considered, it is the Platonic and not the Aristotelian idea of participation that prevails in the Thomist synthesis.

St Thomas began his intellectual career in the tradition of medieval Augustinianism. He took over the Augustinian synthesis of the position of the diverse elements in the Church's mission, but he did so in the style of the major scholastic thinkers. Personal experience and the drama of individual life are absent. His description is objective, and its details more philosophical. The ideas of Plato and Aristotle are expressed impersonally. And yet the same Augustinian spirit is present. Augustine rather than Aristotle is Thomas's master with regard to the adjustments of the relations between the Church and the world. Thomas made use of Aristotle, but only to the extent in which his contribution was useful.

The practical result of Christian experience in both East and West illustrates the fact that there is no one ideal theory that best expresses the relationship between the Church and the State and the world, between time and eternity, that shields the Church from every problem, and automatically ensures the Christianization of the world. In the end, it is not those who cry Lord, Lord, who will enter into the Kingdom of heaven, but those who do the Father's will (Mt 7:21). Historically, there are two major points of view which have found expression in Christianity, one of them Eastern, the other Western. Each has suffered setbacks, but in spite of this they have managed to maintain or to restore Christianity in those parts of the world where they have established themselves. Their yield has been abundant, and it continues. We must therefore judge each tree by its fruits, remembering the storms which each has had to weather.

this with three documents of the Second Vatican Council: the Pastoral Constitution on the Church in the Modern World, the Decree on the Apostolate of the Laity and the Decree on the Church's Missionary Activity.

[31] C. Fabro, *La Nozione metafisica di participazione secondo s. Tomaso d'Aquino* (1939); L. B. Geiger, *La Participation dans la philosophie de s. Thomas d'Aquin* (1942).

CHAPTER VI

The Problem of Structure: The Church
of the Apostles or the Church of the Hierarchy?

I. DEFINITION OF THE PROBLEM

1. The ecumenical problem in relation to the Church's structure

The subject of this chapter may be suitably defined by relating it to the movement of Faith and Order, whose purpose, it need hardly be said, is the quest for unity in the two spheres expressed by its title.

By "unity of faith" is meant harmony in the belief and doctrinal expression of Christianity. Christianity expresses its faith in two general ways: in the form of creeds and confessions; and through liturgical modes which are the concrete symbols of belief. The other expressions of its faith are systematized around these two main forms. Some general types of Church government are expressions of belief; and there are also factual realities that have a dogmatic significance—the institution of marriage, the institution of their successors by the apostles, etc. Faith also finds expression in the concrete way in which it is lived. It is not solely or exhaustively expressed by symbolic ideas. There are deeds as well as words of faith.

What does the word "order" mean in the phrase "Faith and Order"? What kind of unity is sought in the sphere of "order" in the ecumenical movement of Faith and Order? Sometimes this phrase is understood to mean the faith and the constitution of the Church, or else the doctrinal development of Christianity. But both of these expressions are defective; for the faith is itself part of the Church's constitution, and also the word "order" does not refer exclusively to her doctrinal aspect. By "order" we understand ministry, sacraments, worship and discipline, that is the "order" of the Church,[1] or, what amounts to practically the same thing;

[1] Francis J. Hall, *Christian Reunion in Ecumenical Light* (1930), p. 9.

the word "order" denotes: worship, discipline and government. It is, therefore, better not to translate "Faith and Order" by faith and constitution, or by doctrinal Christianity.

The Faith and Order movement signifies, therefore, the quest for unity in both the sphere of the symbolical expression of the faith, and in that of the ministry, the sacraments, worship, and the Church's government.

The word "order" has thus a twofold meaning. With reference to structure, it expresses the form of the Church's government, and with reference to worship it denotes all the functions and all the means that make up the Church's worship. In the phrase "Faith and Order", the word order clearly indicates its relationship with the Church. It is the order of the Church, that is, the structure of its government and worship; it is the arrangement of the members of the Church in a unified fashion, with a view to serving the Church as a social body—that is the task of government—and with a view to the service owed to God by the Church as the Body of Christ—that is the task of worship. There is a right way, in the exact sense, an order, of carrying out these tasks and of performing these functions. The Church's order, therefore, may be summed up as the coordination of the communal and liturgical life of the Church at the service of God's glory in the world. The sacrament of Holy Orders is that participation, in a special degree, in Christ's threefold Messianic power as King, Priest and Prophet, that ensures the harmonious coordination of the Church's life as a praying, missionary and militant community on pilgrimage.

In the chapter on the dogmatic problem, the question of the unity of faith was considered. It was looked at from the point of view of its relationship with the Word, for it is the Word which ultimately produces the unity of Christianity. The first part of the expression "Faith and Order" has been studied. The second, that of order, remains to be considered, and this will be done in its two aspects of structure and worship. It will be seen that the Word is in the background of these two aspects also, for Christ as Word is Prophet (the aspect of faith); he is King (the aspect of government); he is Priest (the aspect of worship). In this chapter the structural problem will be examined, that is, the problem of the forms of the Church's government. The second aspect of the word order, that of worship, will be discussed in the following chapter.

To begin with, the nature of the ecumenical problem in its structural aspect will be defined. What is involved is the regaining of the unity of apostolic ministry, broken up, disintegrated and scattered among the numerous Christian bodies. It is a question of particular difficulty because Catholicism, Orthodoxy and all Churches that possess an apostolic, hierarchical structure, believe that there is a necessary connection between unity of faith and unity of structure. They hold that there is a continuity between the Word of God, or the Word incarnate as Prophet, King and Priest. It follows that for them it is not a matter of indifference whether unity of structure in the Church exists or not. The Protestant bodies, on the other hand, take a wider view, precisely because they have a different interpretation of the Word as an eschatological reality in action in the world. Within the Christian world, there is thus a division in depth on the matter of the Church's government, because there is a similar division on the interpretation of the Word and on eschatology.

Three questions present themselves: what is the reality resulting from the present state of division? Are there any signs of re-integration? What is the faith of the Catholic Church on the question of structure?

The only way to grasp the problem is to see it as it actually is in its typical forms.

2. Typical structural forms in Protestantism

First, we must make up our minds about the meaning of a word. In Protestantism, the word "democratic" is widely used to express the nature of certain forms of government. Orthodoxy sometimes adopts the same expression in order to indicate the equality of the Churches in the autocephalous system.

It need hardly be pointed out that this word occurs nowhere in scripture as a description of the structure with which Christ endowed his Church. In the early Church can be observed a communal structure denoted by the word *koinonia*. There are good grounds for thinking that the use of the word "democratic" to describe the structural nature of the Church of Christ springs from the intrusion of non-theological, in fact of sociological and psychological factors. Those Protestant circles today which are most concerned with being true to the real originality of the Christian religion prefer to employ a terminology more akin to that of scripture. But since the democratic principle has made its way into the structure of several Protestant bodies, mention must be made of it in any typological survey that aims at respecting the facts.

Secondly, we must observe the area covered by these types. There is no Protestant body in our time that does not admit the importance of some form of organized structure in the expression of Christianity. Even a doctrine of the Church centred upon the idea of the Church as "event" finds itself obliged to allow room for an institutional structure, although, as in Congregationalism, this may only be in the most attenuated form. A Church as a mere "event" is a phantom; it would no longer be the Church, but the atomisation of the Church, and its reduction to the most concealed and subjective individualism. The institution, at least some form of institution, is, therefore, inescapable. We shall accept it as one of the poles of those forms which the construction of the Church may assume. The only possible opposite pole is that of charismatic government. In Protestantism, every form of ecclesiastical government has its position between these two poles.

The theory of a charismatic organization of the Church[2] is probably only found today in Pentecostalism and in some of the Adventist sects.

The plurality of institutional structures in Protestantism:

(i) The democratic principle

According to the democratic idea, the necesssity of a social authority without which no society can endure is accepted as in every other system. There is, however, a difference in the view which it holds as to the origin of power and as to the way in which it acts.

It maintains that the proximate subject of all social rights is the community itself, that is, its members as a whole, equally sharing those rights. The members exercise their rights either immediately, in a common assembly, or mediately, through individuals whom they elect and depute to carry out certain social functions in the name of the communal authority and with its power.

If, as a result of this, there follows some inequality in social rights, this is because the autonomous will of society has decided to remit, as a whole or in part, the power that it cannot or will not exercise on its own, to a moral or physical person to exercise in its name.

The functions thus delegated may be altered, restricted, abrogated by the community which created them, and the person to whom a function of this kind has been committed must give an account of his administration to the community; he must surrender his post if the time fixed for its exercise has expired; should he be found wanting, the community may dismiss him at will.

Some hold that it was this kind of constitution that governed the early Church. On this view, Christ committed plenary authority to the early community, permitting it to use it either in a common assembly (1 Cor 11:18), or by means of special functions instituted by it for the administration of communal property, for teaching or for leading the community. Such functions would therefore be proximately human in origin, and so belong to human law, subject to the changes of time, and to the law of development which produces new forms and institutions as circumstances demand.

[2] R. Söhm, *Wesen und Ursprung des Katholizismus* (1913).

As against the charismatic principle of the Church's government, there stands the whole series of institutional forms, included in the Congregational, Presbyterian and Episcopal types.

These three types need to be interpreted according to the Protestant theory of the universal priesthood of all believers. The Church is composed of a people of layfolk with diverse callings and functions, but undivided by any hierarchical differentiation, whatever system, Congregational, Presbyterian, or even Episcopal, may unite them. We take the word "Episcopal" in the sense given to it by some Protestant bodies and not by the Anglican Communion.

In reality, however, according to the spirit of scripture, the principle of Christian equality has nothing in common with the democratic principle. Each belongs to a different order of reality; one of them belongs to that of the structure of religion, and the other to that of the secular sphere. The democratic principle, moreover, belongs to a period before that of the Christian revelation. The words of scripture refer to the equality of men as new creatures in Christ. It is from this principle that the Church must be understood, not from that of democracy. Admittedly there is some likeness between the two principles, and this explains the confusion.

The difference between them does not alter the undeniable fact that the principle of Christian equality has been well and truly interpreted in the light of the democratic spirit. This is so true that one of the greatest difficulties that Protestantism finds, as it rediscovers the exact revealed meaning of the Church's structure, is precisely the attitude of mind created by a long tradition of such interpretation. Grotius,[3] Pufendorf,[4] Böhmer,[5] Heineck,[6] etc. were its main originators.

In order to explain the Protestant idea of the Church's structure, it is necessary, therefore, to take both principles and facts into account. The Congregational, Presbyterian and even some of the Episcopal systems certainly seem to have been to some extent handicapped by a democratic interpretation which gives status to the democratic principle as existing in the Church and tends to make ministers representatives of men rather than of God, their authority springing more from the congregation than from above.

In the Catholic Church, in the Anglican Communion and in Orthodoxy, on the other hand, it is held that although bishops represent their people, they are first and foremost the representatives of God who bestows their authority upon them. All Christians are equal in the blood of Christ, but

[3] *De Jure Belli ac Pacis* (1st edition, 1646), Bk. I, chapters i and ii, no. 2.
[4] *De Habitu religionis Christianae ad vitam civilem* (5th edition, 1713), section 2, 28.
[5] *Jus parochiale* (5th edition, 1738), Bk. I, chapter i, section 46.
[6] *Elementa juris naturae et gentium*, Pastromi, s. d., I, p. III, no. 183 ff.

grace produces a diversity of callings, since the Church is an organic body. It would be a difficult process to untie the knot which binds the Protestant position on eschatology, in its structural aspect, to an explanation, democratic in character, which has intruded upon the principle that Christians are equal because they are new creatures in Christ.

(ii) The three types of strutcure

A. THE CONGREGATIONAL PRINCIPLE

In essence, this principle is that of the covenant or alliance. Historically, it originated among the bodies of Independents in Great Britain, as a reaction against the unbending creeds and authority of the Established Church. It is this original hostility that explains why the Independents and Baptists refused from the start to produce any formal creed. Instead they used a kind of declaration of faith which—called a covenant and not a creed—expressed loyalty to Christ and his Church.

Accordingly the dissidents settled on a day on which, after prayer and fasting, united in a common purpose of seeking God's face, they formed a circle with joined hands, and each declared his faith and his repentance, and commending their union to God, they agreed to walk together in God's ways, as revealed in the past, or as they might be revealed in the future.[7] Hence the name of Congregationalist bestowed on the members of this new denomination.

But the principle of the covenant did not seem to be acceptable to all Puritans. The Presbyterians never made use of it. The Baptists themselves at first opposed it. The Baptist Church of Longsworth was the first, in 1656, to be established on the principle of the covenant, but it was not before the end of the seventeenth century that the Baptists reached agreement among themselves to follow the principle.

Several denominations have made the congregational principle their own. It is to be found among the Adventists (except those of the Seventh Day?), the Disciples of Christ, the Plymouth Brethren, the Darbyists, the Unitarians, the Universalists, some Lutheran bodies (the Synod of Missouri) and naturally the Congregationalists themselves.

What are the principles involved? Firstly, that of individual equality, and of each member's personal control over his own religious life and that of his congregation. Secondly, that of the autonomy—not necessarily the independence—of the local Church, balanced by that of communion between the local Churches. Thirdly, that of the preservation of the results

---

[7] Champlin Burrage, *The Early English Dissenters in the Light of Recent Research* (2 vol., 1912); Horton Davis, *The English Free Churches.*

230

of the communal experience, balanced by that of progress through individual investigation. [8]

It was observed above that the influence of the congregational principle has extended far beyond the numerical importance of the Congregationalist bodies. From the point of view of the doctrine of the Church it is also important to remember the biblical principle on which it is based—the idea of the covenant.

B. THE SYNODAL PRINCIPLE

The structural principle midway between that of episcopalianism and that of congregationalism is normally denoted by several different names: synodal, connectional, presbyterian, presbyterian-synodal.

A whole series of denominations have a similar structure: the Calvinist Churches—obviously including the Presbyterians; the Evangelical Church; the Methodists in Great Britain, the Mennonites, the Dunkers, some Lutheran bodies, at least those of the United States.

This governmental system is based on the union between local congregations through elected representatives (although sometimes, as formerly in the Lutheran Church of Prussia, these were appointed by the government), who are delegated to the central assembly. This assembly is known by different names: the General Assembly (Presbyterian); Synod (Lutheran); General Conference (Methodist); Consistory (Calvinist, Lutheran). It holds the chief responsibility over all the congregations in the spheres of doctrine and discipline. The basis of authority, therefore, is the concerted voice of all the bodies represented by their delegates. The local congregations, independent in their activity, are nevertheless considered as being organically related to each other. No congregation has the right to undertake any important action without the consent of the others. Thus the central assembly, under whatever name, acts as a centre for mediation in the cooperative work of the local congregations.

All things considered, the term "connectional" or "synodal" is the most suitable for covering all these related forms of government. But there seems little doubt that its most typical form is Presbyterian. The category of ecclesiastical structural forms that lies midway between those of Congregationalism and episcopacy is often simply described as Presbyterian. This indicates the importance of the line of Calvinist Churches from which this kind of government is derived, just as the Congregationalist line is derived from the Independents.

What is the internal organization of the Presbyterian structure? Today

[8] Ladd, *op. cit.; Proceedings of the Eighth Assembly of the International Congregational Council* (1958).

it includes four stages. First, the consistory of the elders (of the local congregation), made up of the pastor and the elders. This is the "Kirk session". It acts as the controlling authority for the local Church. The next stage is that of the regional consistory (presbytery) made up of all the pastors of a region and of an equal number of elders elected by their peers. This consistory exercises episcopal responsibility collectively. The third stage is that of the regional synod, and this varies in importance in different countries and regions. Fourthly, there is the national synod or general assembly which, like the regional synod, is made up of an equal number of elders and pastors; the moderator is the name given to its leading minister.

It will be seen, therefore, that this system of government is based on the consistory of the elders and on that of the region. The structure of the Presbyterian Church is fashioned from the bottom upwards. The share of responsibility allowed to the elders is the result of the theological importance which scripture attributes to the partnership between the presbyters and the apostles in the administration, control and government of the Church. The function of the elders is, exactly like that of ministers, spiritual; these latter have the Word and the sacraments for their special work; and the elders are, together with the minister, presbyters in the full sense. The consistory of the elders (Kirk session) is a homogeneous body made up, as we have seen, of the minister or pastor and the elders. Minister and elders do not form separate orders within an ecclesiastical hierarchy. There is a difference in their callings and functions, but no hierarchical, let alone sacramental, difference. Neither the pastor or minister, nor the elders, have received any form of the sacrament of Holy Orders. It should be noted, moreover, that the Scottish Confessions of faith are most careful to exclude any such idea. Every notion of corporate separation or of opposition between pastors and elders is excluded at every level: that is, in the consistory of the elders (Kirk session), the regional consistory, the synod and general assembly. The principle followed is that exemplified in the apostolic age which shows us different gifts and functions, some being apostles, others elders. And yet, in the Presbyterian system, a minister is not the equivalent of an apostle, because the Twelve constituted an order in the Church that cannot be repeated. A minister or a pastor is not a successor of an apostle in the sense in which this is understood in Catholicism and Orthodoxy, but as a witness entrusted with a special calling within the Church, that does not, however, involve any specific differentiation from that of the elders. In other words, it is the whole Church which succeeds the apostles, and not any particular class on any special grounds. A pastor has a ministerial function; an elder's function is both governmental and pastoral. Each elder is put in charge of a district; he regularly visits it and has pastoral responsibility for it, and with the full authority of a presbyter, he shares with the ministers a position of privilege in ecclesiastical meetings, during which everyone is allowed to express his point of view and to vote on matters concerning doctrine, worship, government and discipline.[9]

Whenever the question of reunion between denominations arises, the principle of the homogeneity of the consistory as an intangible principle in the presbyterian system must be most carefully observed. The Church comes down from the apostles and originated with them. In this sense it is the Church of the apostles, but the apostles do not in any way carry on any permanent function in the Church today. All ecclesiastical functions are equal with respect to their position as "sucessors" of the apostles. The apostolic institution existed once only, once for all, and then perfectly. Such continuity as exists between the special office of the apostles and that of present-day ministers of the Church is one of relationship and of spiritual inheritance; it is not functional.

It should be noted, however, that in Presbyterianism there is no opposition, on principle, to the use of the word "bishop". The Presbyterians of Hungary employ it. Calvin observes that it is mentioned in scripture and, therefore, may be adopted by the Church. But, in fact, chiefly for historical reasons, it has been rejected up to now, and any willingness to accept it would be due only to the fact that it is considered to be identical with presbyter. In addition, it was quickly pointed out that on the supposition that the regional consistory (presbytery) collectively exercises the episcopal function, it is superfluous; within the college of presbyters there can be no need to bestow the title of bishop on any particular member.

John Knox installed Presbyterianism in Scotland after his formation under Calvin's direction in Geneva. Following the democratic principle of adapting the Church's constitution to territorial needs, there are certain differences between the Presbyterian Churches and other Churches that are Calvinist in origin. Substantially, however, they are the same.

Calvin had instituted four classes of ministers: pastors entrusted with preaching the Word, administering the sacraments, interceding with God, leading the laity, exercising discipline; "doctors" to whom the task of teaching in the Church, and especially the formation of youth was committed; the elders, appointed to assist pastors in governing the Church and forming a kind of court of discipline, with the task of seeing that the precepts of the Gospel were duly observed; and finally, the deacons whose work was to visit the sick, meet the needs of the poor, and collaborate in administering Church property.

[9] *Constitution of the Presbyterian Church in the United States of America, 1956–7; Glasgow Speaks, a Reply to the Joint Report on Anglican-Presbyterian Relations* (1959); H. J. Wotherspoon and J. M. Kirpatrick, *A Manual of Church Doctrine according to the Church of Scotland* (revised and enlarged edition, 1960).

Calvin found these four classes in scripture and he retained them. The rest of the Church's organization was left to human initiative. Accordingly, Calvin set up two "deputations", the "venerable company" made up of ministers and "doctors", entrusted with doctrine as a whole and with instituting ministers; and the "consistory" composed of ministers and elders, and responsible for government and discipline.

It has been observed that, for Calvinists, there are ultimately two kinds of ministers: the *ministri docentes*—teaching ministers, pastors and "doctors"; and the *ministri ministrantes,* ministers who administer—elders and deacons who form the presbyterial college around the minister.[10] The division into pastors, elders and deacons, to which, usually, but not always, the "doctors" are added, exemplifies an attempt to restore the threefold ministry of the early Church: that of bishops, presbyters and deacons. Of these, unquestionably the most essential is that of pastor. From the outset the reformers hesitated about the name to be given to the one responsible for this function. Should he be called a priest, a word of biblical origin? For reasons easily to be understood the word pastor, also occurring in the Bible, was adopted.

One important point of relevance to the ecumenical dialogue should be indicated. Nowhere in the Calvinist or Presbyterian Churches is any difference made between a bishop and a presbyter. Who, then, carries out the work of a bishop? In the Presbyterian system, this is done by the regional consistory, including the pastor, acting as a single unit. But, on the continent, the Calvinist Churches tend to attribute episcopal functions to the pastor: the pastor of a parish is, in fact, a pastor-bishop. J. J. von Allmen explains this difference by a divergence between the adoption at the ecclesiological level of the traditional difference between Church and parish without a corresponding distinction at the ministerial level.[11] Thus there are no bishops over a Church as such; their place is taken by classes or synods; but there are as many bishops as there are parishes. The pastoral ministry, therefore, was made episcopal, but the parishes were not made churches. In Catholicism and Orthodoxy, on the other hand, there is a proportion between function and community; the local Church or parish is not fully a Church; the name Church is properly ascribed only to that body over which a bishop presides. It is not a question of number, but of plenitude.

One of the deficiencies of the Reformation is here to be seen. The Reformers established new norms, but with the traditional Catholic system

---

[10] H. L. J. Heppe, *Die Dogmatik der Evangelisch-reformierten Kirche dargestellt und aus den Quellen belegt* (1935), p. 530.

[11] "L'Autorité pastorale d'après les confessions de foi réformée", *Verbum Caro* 55 (1960), p. 204.

as their inspiration. Under the strain of events, pressed from all quarters to answer every question, engaged on a complete revision of Christianity as a whole, the Reformers frequently had to improvise, and since they had received their initial formation in Catholicism, they were unable to rethink Christianity in a way that was detached not only from their past, but also from the surviving influences on their general ambience. After their death their ideas were canonized and became dogmas, but with their deficiencies as well as their intuitions. And it is on this, taken as a whole, that the Protestant world is based.

The Reformation, at least in its early stages, was willing to admit that within the body of pastors there could be varying degrees. But historical reasons and a narrowing of doctrine which occurred after the original Reformers contributed to the reduction of all pastors to the same level within their homogeneous consistory or group of ecclesiastical functions.

C. THE EPISCOPAL PRINCIPLE

It is difficult for Protestantism to leave out of account the existence in scripture of the name and office of a bishop; when it keeps silent about the name, it still retains at least some aspects of the office, even though it is hesitant about the moral or physical persons to whom this office is to be attributed. In the case of the Presbyterian and Calvinist Churches the position is clear. Would it be going too far to put forward the hypothesis that in the Congregationalist system, in which the local Church is the true Church, it is the congregation as a whole that, in contrast with Catholicism and Orthodoxy, corporately carries out the work of a bishop? On this view the community has absorbed the episcopate and reduced it to each of its members. This formula contradicts the great rule laid down by St Cyprian in the phrase: "The bishop is in the Church and the Church is in the bishop" (*Ep.* 66, 8, 33), which means that a bishop sustains and recapitulates his Church; he is the mediate source of its life and its unity; it is he who ensures that a local congregation shall be a genuine Church with the same nature and qualities as the Church as a whole. The dissolution of the episcopal principle into a collective office has immediate repercussions on the Church that absorbs it; the most serious of these is that this Church cannot be an authentic Church, even if it possesses certain of its features.

Would it be forcing the issue to say that Protestantism, which in general rejects the episcopal principle as a personal office of apostolic origin, has even so retained it, although eliminating what was its heart and soul—the apostolic succession? The network of episcopacy spread throughout the Protestant world can easily be seen: in one place the local congregation is its own bishop; in another it is the presbytery, the synod, the general assembly; or elsewhere it may be a person in the central administration of a communion, to whom the title bishop and some of the official powers corresponding to it, excluding, of course, the apostolic succession, are ascribed.

The episcopal form has been adopted among Protestants, by Lutheranism (to some extent in Europe, not in the United States); by Methodism (in the United States, not in Great Britain); by the Moravian Brethren who are also called the Church of the Unity of the Bohemian Brethren; by the Churches of Sweden, Finland, Norway, etc.

EPISCOPACY AND LUTHERANISM

Luther consistently declared that the Church's unity is not created by uniformity of constitution and liturgy; nor is it broken by their variety. Why? It is because the Church is the Body of Christ. What does this expression mean? The word "Christ" denotes the Head who guides and governs the Body, his members, by his Spirit. The word "Body" denotes all those, known to God, who have faith: this is the communion of saints. To be guided by Christ and to have faith is to be a member of Christ's Body and of the communion of saints.

The Church is simultaneously visible and invisible. She is visible because Christians are visible and are interconnected by outward signs; she is invisible because faith in the human heart cannot be seen. Now the Church is made up by men who have faith and these are known to God alone. The Church, therefore, is essentially invisible. She may be defined as the fraternal fellowship of all countries and every denomination, known to God alone, in whom the Holy Spirit, where and when God wills, creates faith through the Word and the sacraments.

By these words "where and when God wills" (Confession of Augsburg, art. 5), Luther meant that if God does indeed mean to make use of the Word and the sacraments, he will do so at his own good pleasure.

The Church, therefore, is created; she is alive; she dwells in human hearts. Believers exist and through them it can be seen that the Church exists. Her existence is indicated to the outside world by the fact that the people hear a sermon; someone preaches; the congregation celebrates the Eucharist; baptism is administered, etc. The invisible Church, therefore, has external "notes" or marks that can be discerned distinctly, for the Word and the sacraments are verifiable realities. The ministry of the Word is related to the ministry of the *Verbum Dei* in souls. The sacraments, in their turn, are a Word made visible. The Word is preached and heard; it produces its effect. The sacraments make the proclaimed Word visible; they confirm it; they place God's seal on his promises.

Is preaching or the administration of the sacraments sufficient to create

236

faith? If these are to produce real faith and a truly believing Church, they must possess certain qualities: they must be true and pure. But what is true and pure doctrine? What are true sacraments? They must be essentially the same realities that the apostles received from Christ. If this is so, then true faith can be created by preaching and truly confirmed by the sacraments. It becomes the same as that of the apostles.

The problem, it will be seen, reduces itself to that of apostolicity. The authentic Church is the Church which is truly apostolic. How can a Church be truly apostolic otherwise than through succession? This is the heart of the matter. For the expression "apostolic succession" can be understood in various ways. It may mean the succession of bishops appointed *ad hoc,* for a see or a diocese: in which case it refers to succession in a see, not to succession through ordination. Secondly, it may refer to ordination or consecration. Thirdly, it may mean succession in the work and doctrine of the apostles.

It was this third sense that Luther made his own. He rejected the second, and only superficially accepted the first. It may be said, therefore, that apostolic succession, in his mind, meant essentially that men become Christians, and, up to a point, successors of the apostles, by sharing the apostles' faith. True faith is created by the Word and the sacraments in the form in which these were given to the Church by the apostles. Wherever the Word is preached and the sacraments administered in this way, the true Church, the true apostolic succession, the true Body of Christ, exists, whether there is episcopal consecration or not. Wherever true doctrine and true sacraments do not exist, there the apostolic succession is broken, despite the presence of consecrated bishops.

The key to Lutheran teaching on succession is the idea that the Gospel is itself the succession. We give credit to a bishop, Luther said, not because he is the successor of a bishop in a given locality, but because he teaches the Gospel correctly.[12] Essentially, therefore, succession means succession in doctrine, the work, the spirit of the apostles.

But what on this view becomes of the doctrine of Holy Orders? Luther replies: where the authentic Word and the true sacraments exist, there the Church is also; and where the Church exists, there too will be all those rights that have been bestowed upon her, and especially the right to ordain. For if the notion of apostolic succession denotes succession in the doctrine, work and spirit of these apostles, the power of ordination belongs in principle to all, in the same way as the apostolic succession belongs to the whole Church, provided she is the true Church. For, says Luther, it is unlikely that the reformed bodies could have all the great gifts of the Church, the Word of God, Christ, the Spirit, baptism, the Eucharist, the

[12] H. H. Kramm, *The Theology of Martin Luther* (1947).

keys, the ministry, and not also have the least of the Church's gifts—the power to call particular persons to administer those gifts.

It follows from this that the ministry is the possession of the congregation as a whole. But it is also true that no one may presume to take it upon himself without the consent of the congregation.

Luther retains the universal priesthood of believers and the ministry on an equal footing. The former does not make the latter useless. Theological science, special formation, and personal qualities which befit a man for the ministry, are not to be found in every believer. Nor is the Church to be transformed into a market place on the pretext of the universal priesthood of believers. But it is principally because it is God himself who has instituted the ministry that the Church is authorized by divine command to call upon specially appointed individuals.

The changing circumstances amid which Luther had to develop his teaching had their influence on his different standpoints. To begin with, in reaction against priests and bishops, he proclaimed the universal priesthood of baptized believers, but later, pressed by certain illuminist enthusiasts, he was obliged to take back a part of what he had rejected. God, he said, instituted a ministry, and in ordinary circumstances, the minister alone has the right to preach and administer the sacraments. In a city, all are citizens, and yet not one of them may, because of this, appoint himself mayor. He must be elected. A mayor does not become a citizen as the result of his election. He was already a citizen, and he takes his citizenship into his new office. So it is with a believer. He is of equal standing with a priest, but he may not arbitrarily assume the exercise of those functions that pertain to an elected minister. It is the community that must delegate to one of its fellows the power of administering those rights that are common to the Christian community. A Christian who is thus elected does not become a priest through his election to the ministry or through his ordination. He was this already through his baptism, but his election now gives him the right to exercise the functions of the divinely instituted ministry, granting the fact that these are meant to be reserved to a single minister.

During the last years of his life Luther laid still more stress on the authority of the ministry. He taught that God decides to give the Holy Spirit only to those who receive him through the Word and the ministry. He included the position and work of a pastor in his description of the Church: the Church is a body of baptized and believing Christians in the care of a pastor. He also held that the true Church can be known outwardly by the fact that she calls and ordains bishops, pastors and preachers. He taught, too, that to become a pastor an outward in addition to an inner call is necessary, and that it is God who moves the congregation or the Church's government to call and ordain some particular person to

238

the ministry. In proof of this he can be given a document as an official recognition that he is qualified to carry out his duties. But ordination was not considered to be a sacrament. It is a vocation. To ordain, Luther said, is to call; and the call to the ministry is the most important part of ordination. It is, on the one hand, the public confirmation, on the part of the legal authorities of the Church or of the pastors of the neighbouring congregations, that the ordinand has been called to the ministry in due legal form; and, on the other, it is the official declaration that he is qualified to preach the pure Gospel and to be a true successor of the apostles. In Lutheranism, ordination has always been accompanied by an examination, which, like ordination, is an act of the Church, and no outside diploma can be a substitute for it; for the Church alone has the requisite responsibility for declaring that the candidate has the doctrinal qualifications necessary for the ministry.

When he accepts the ministry, a candidate accepts certain obligations. In the early days of Lutheranism, an ordinand was reminded that he was being entrusted with a duty. Some years later it was decided that he must take an oath committing him to preach the Gospel and to reject all heretical teaching. Finally, he was required to take an oath (and sometimes to sign a document) promising to carry out his ministry in conformity with the principles set forth in the Bible and as interpreted by the Confession of Augsburg.

According to Lutheran teaching, ordination does not imprint an indelible "character" in the soul of its recipient. The rights granted to him may, for a grave reason—for example, in the case of immoral conduct, ineptitude, heresy—be revoked by the legal authority of the Church, but not by the congregation itself.

Luther does, however, admit that a situation may arise when a local congregation could itself ordain a man. If a group of people are shipwrecked on a desert island, they could elect and ordain one of their members who seemed most suitable for the ministry and this man could lawfully administer the sacraments. His reason for this is again based on the fact that it is the congregation of believers who have the apostolic succession. But as a general rule, the ministry is transmitted from minister to ministers. The congregation plays its part only by cooperating in the election.

Luther went still further than this: he said that a layman could validly perform the functions of a minister, even if he was not ordained. He could administer the sacraments, hear confessions, and give absolution. He added, however, that, except on occasions of urgency, this would be illicit and a great offence against God.

Thus the ministry produces no specific difference between ministers and non-ministers. Nor are there degrees or ranks within the ministry—and

239

this is a matter of divine institution. What is to be thought then about the traditional distinction between bishop, priest and deacon? Luther's view was that in scripture and the earliest writings of the Church, "bishop" and "priest" were practically synonymous terms, and that at any rate evidence to the contrary was lacking.

If the three degrees of the ministry are to be retained, this can only be for practical reasons; a well-tested tradition deserves retention. Episcopacy, however, is not necessary for the true apostolic succession, nor for valid ordination, but only pure doctrine. If a choice has to be made between doctrine and the episcopate, it is the latter that in an emergency must be dropped. In conformity with this principle, when in a diocese the bishop remained Catholic and the majority of the people became Protestant, Luther organized his Church in this diocese in a non-episcopal form. He did this without the slightest scruple, because in his view world unity in liturgical practice and Church order were wholly secondary matters. The most varied types of ecclesiastical constitution and of ordination and liturgy had no necessary connection with the unity and authenticity of the Church.

Thus he accepted an episcopate, but only as a human institution. In principle, all priests are bishops. And yet he admitted that an individual pastor could not have ultimate authority in the Church. The Church must have some means of controlling the doctrine and work of the pastors, their formation, examination, their vocation and ordination. Since God has not laid down how this is to be done, it falls on the Church to discover the way. It will vary in form in different periods, countries and circumstances. Authority to control may be given to a group of Christians, to a committee of ministers and laymen, to the theological faculty of a Lutheran university, to a council of pastors, or even to a kind of super-minister, a "pastor pastorum". The title of this latter matters little; it is a question of taste. Several Lutheran Churches have retained or re-introduced the term "bishop". Luther preferred it, but he had no objection to that of superintendent. At the present time the chief pastor is called indifferently general superintendent, *Landesoberintendant, Oberhofprediger, Senior, Landesbischof*. But there is no difference between this pastor and the other ministers in respect of ordination, but only in relation to the kind of work.

Will a Church have an episcopal structure or not? Luther considered that each territory will decide the answer for itself, according to the circumstances prevailing in each case. Personally, he preferred to retain the episcopate; what he wanted, he said, was not to abolish, but to reform it. He hoped indeed that throughout Germany the episcopal constitution might be preserved under the primacy of the Archbishop of Mainz as head of an independent German Church. But the primate refused, and the different attitude of each bishop made Luther's plan impossible. In those territories where the bishops were hostile to the Reformation, Luther had to introduce appropriate kinds of constitution. He was not himself a bishop, and yet he consecrated the bishops of Naumburg and Merseburg. He did not see why he should not do so; he was a priest and he held the pure doctrine.

In Lutheranism, therefore, a considerable structural variety exists. Its Churches may accept or discard episcopacy. Hanover, Bavaria, Württemberg, and Saxony have had bishops for the last thirty years. Sweden has kept its episcopal structure since 1527 when Lutheranism became the official religion without, however, giving any external signs of a break with Catholicism; in fact it is held that in Sweden the historical apostolic succession has been preserved. Finland has returned to the episcopal succession after an interval of "priestly succession": at the beginning of the nineteenth century the Finnish Lutheran bishops had almost all disappeared; the Russian government was opposed to the arrival of a foreign Lutheran prelate for the consecration of a new bishop; and so it was decided that an ordinary pastor should hold the position. This resulted in a regime of "priestly succession". When Finland regained her independence, episcopal succession was restored by the Archbishop of Uppsala.

Lutheranism, therefore, is compatible either with episcopacy or its absence, and with a unitary or plural episcopate. A plural episcopate indicates that a congregation or a diocese may have several bishops.

The title of bishop may be maintained, and some of his functions. The apostolic succession may even be considered to have been preserved. But the meaning of the episcopal principle in the Lutheran communions has now been made clear.

3. The structure of episcopacy in the Churches of the Anglican Communion

There are three degrees in the ministry: bishops, priests and deacons. These have existed from the earliest days and their continuance is thus desirable. No one is admitted to the ministry who has not been ordained in the way that the ordinal prescribes, or who has not received episcopal ordination or consecration.

Legitimate episcopal consecration requires the laying on of hands by three bishops who have been duly consecrated and whose apostolic succession is undisputed. A bishop must first have been a deacon and a priest.

The canonical duties of bishops are similar to those in Catholicism:

they have to govern their dioceses, preside over diocesan assemblies, visit the parishes every three years, administer confirmation, receive candidates for Orders, ordain deacons and priests, induct priests in their parishes, take part in the consecration of bishops.

A priest's duties are to preach, administer the sacraments, prepare candidates for confirmation, celebrate marriages, take funerals, administer the various affairs of the parish. In addition, they consecrate Churches.

A deacon assists priests in public worship, reads the scriptures and the homilies, baptizes children in the absence of a priest, preaches when the bishop allows it, seeks out the sick, the poor, the infirm, assists and helps them in their needs.

Lay readers read the Gospel and Epistle; they do not belong to the ministry. They must be licensed by the bishop.

Legislative control is exercised by two convocations. Both consist of two "houses"; an upper house of diocesan bishops: a lower house of representatives of the clergy and of some individuals appointed *ex officio*.

The Churches of the Anglican Communion have certain individual characteristics: the Church of England, for example, has a juridical link with the Crown and Parliament, but its position, in this respect, is wholly different from that of Anglicanism as such: its communions throughout the world illustrate this fact. The Anglican Church in the United States, officially entitled the Episcopal Church, also has some special characteristics that are due to its American environment.

The Anglican Communion holds that between its own and Protestant ordinations there is a radical difference. Its own it considers to be Catholic.

We shall abstain from discussing the course of the controversy between Catholics and Anglicans on this matter. It has been tortuous and is still a sensitive spot. The arguments on both sides have been set forth clearly and are well known.[13] But at a time when reconciliation is much desired, is it not fitting to inquire whether on a final analysis there is no solution to the deadlock? Has there been no change at all since the pronouncement by Leo XIII (*Apostolicae Curae*, 13 September 1896)?

By the Agreement of Bonn, 1931, the Church of England established

---

[13] *Anglican Orders. The Bull of His Holiness Leo XIII, September 13, 1896 and the Answer of the Archbishops of England, March 29, 1897* (1954); A. J. Mason, *The Church of England and Episcopacy* (1914); E. C. Messenger, *The Lutheran Origin of the Anglican Ordinal* (1931); Edward R. Hardy, ed., *Orthodox Statements on Anglican Orders* (1946); K. E. Kirk, ed., *The Apostolic Ministry, Essays on the History and Doctrine of Episcopacy* (1946); More and Cross, *Anglicanism;* Francis Clark, *Anglican Orders and Defect of Intention* (1956); C. Hoare, *The Edwardian Ordinal* (1957); A. L. Peck, *Anglicanism and Episcopacy, a Re-examination of Evidence* (1958); W. Jardine Grisbrooke, *Anglican Liturgies of the Seventeenth and Eighteenth Centuries* (1958).

relationships of intercommunion with the Old Catholic Churches of the Union of Utrecht, and most of the Churches of the Anglican Communion have followed this example. In 1946, the Episcopal Church in the United States concluded a similar agreement with the Polish National Catholic Church which is in communion with the Old Catholic Churches of Europe. Bishop S. C. Neill observes that in 1958 about half the Anglican episcopate had the Anglican episcopal succession together with that of the Old Catholics, and that before long all Anglican bishops would have it. He thinks that Rome might now reconsider the decision of Leo XIII's encyclical. [14]

It needs to be seen whether the decree of Pius XII on ordination has any application in this case. [15] Three bishops are normally required for episcopal consecration and all three are truly consecrators. But one alone will suffice. What happens, then, if out of the three consecrators only one is admitted by Rome to be in possession of the apostolic succession? Would the candidate become a bishop, and would the priests whom he ordains be validly ordained priests? (It should be remembered also that Anglicanism has for some time reverted to the rite of ordination as it was before the alterations introduced under Edward VI.)

It will be objected that according to the Catholic canon law now in force, it is not possible to proceed to the episcopate without having first received priestly ordination. But the solemn teaching of the Catholic Church in the third chapter of the conciliar Constitution on the Church, promulgated on November 21, 1964, lays down that the episcopate is the fullness of the sacrament of orders and it is known that from the second century until the end of the ninth century no less than thirty-four popes were certainly or very probably consecrated bishops of Rome directly without previous ordination to the priesthood. [16]

Do these historical and doctrinal factors offer any basis for an approach towards reconciliation? Even if it is accepted that they do, there remains the difficulty that in the Catholic Church the episcopate in communion with the pope is held to be infallible, a view which Anglicans do not accept.

In addition, it is difficult to know exactly the extent to which episcopal consecration has spread as the result of these unions, agreements and intercommunion. In 1948, for example, three American Anglican bishops consecrated three bishops of the Independent Philippine Church which had restored episcopacy although it lacked regular episcopal succession.

[14] "Hierarchie, anglikanische", *Weltkirchen Lexikon, Handbuch der Ökumene* (1960), p. 551.
[15] *Acta Apostolicae Sedis*, annus XXXVII, series II, vol. XII (1945), p. 132.
[16] Mgr M. Andrieu, "La Carrière ecclésiastique des papes et les documents liturgiques du Moyen Age", *Revue des Sciences Religieuses* (1947), pp. 90–120.

These new bishops consecrated others, and thus this Church holds the Anglican succession. But, it should be noted that this gesture of the Anglican Church of the United States was a purely personal initiative, taken without consulting the other Anglican provinces, and these have so far made no pronouncement on its significance. The Anglican succession is also enjoyed by the Church of South India, and further projects for other unions have been studied. We realize that the Churches of the Anglican Communion intend to use this means as a method of healing the wounds of Christendom. But the attitude of the Catholic Church on the validity of Anglican Orders implicitly raises the question of the acceptance of the extension of the episcopate brought about by the Churches of the Anglican Communion.

4. The essence of Protestantism from the point of view of the Church's structure

Is there in Protestantism an essential common standpoint with regard to the Church's structure, or, if the phrase is preferred, her forms of government?

The account given above of the kinds of institutional forms showed clearly that though most various, they can be reduced to a few typical structures. But in what sense do these forms conform to the logic of a single structure?

Any answer to this will necessarily be the result of an abstraction, as in the other examples of the fundamental aspects of the ecumenical problem. This abstraction does not take the whole of the reality into account, but it has the advantage of centralizing the problems, and in view of the fact that the concrete forms are more numerous, the method becomes all the more necessary. An ecumenical dialogue that based itself upon the supposition that each Protestant denomination is a world on its own would surely end up in a maze. Forget the types, and you are lost. But we must draw even closer to the issue, and examine the essential principles of Protestantism in their bearing on denominational structures. In addition, there is no solution to the problem of any particular denomination to the exclusion of that of others. The ecumenical problem is a unity, and when any one case is considered, the question of the essence of the whole must be invoked. Otherwise one would have to begin again each time, as if an absolute novelty had to be dealt with.

How are the governmental principles of the Church envisaged from the point of view of the fundamental principles of Protestantism?

A. THE ABSOLUTE PRIMACY OF THE WORD AND THE LOSS OF ALL VISIBLE STRUCTURE IN THE WORD

Unless the Protestant spirit as expressed in the form of the Church's government is first seen in the light of the Word, it will be extremely difficult to understand.

In Protestantism the Word stands out as the power which is the inner source of the Church's constitution and government. Before every institution, whether it be human or even divine-and-human, the most pure Word of God exists, and it is this Word that sounds in men's hearts, calling them to believe. Its call is manifold, and results, therefore, in a gathering together, in a Church. Only God knows those who are his; this is the invisible Church, the Church based on the faith that cannot be seen. And it is the Word who has called each and all; knows them in the secret recesses of their hearts; knows which of them is a true believer; and maintains them in the *forma fidei* in its presence. The Word, therefore, has the privilege of absolute anteriority over every other summoning power. No minister, no pastor can act as a substitute for what only the Word can do. The minister, the pastor, give their assistance as it were from the outside; they are witnesses; they have a position of responsibility in the visible order of the Church; but their part is not comparable with the infinite area covered by the Word's governmental activity, for the Word is the supreme Providence of his Church. He knows the plan of salvation; he is able to direct the course of events and the lives of men according to the scheme of his purpose. On him, therefore, the Church is entirely grounded. She is lost in him, and in him she is to be regarded as hidden.

Being perfect and preceding every other summoning power, to which it appeals solely as witnesses, it could, in principle, dispense with human help. The radical nature of the "spiritual", Anabaptist and liberal Protestant movements pushed the logic of this principle to an extreme and unilateral conclusion. For if, they said, the Word is perfect, the supreme governing principle, and infallible Providence, then why should it need the visible structure of a Church? God leads; he is king and sovereign; let us submit to his government and that will suffice.

We have noted that the Lutheran reformation was, to begin with, clearly committed to the logical application of the principle of the Word's absolute perfection, but that, gradually, Luther was compelled to make room for the visible constitution of the Church. Calvin's development was similar. With the new editions of his *Institutes* he gave back to the constitution what he had previously taken away. Experience forced the Reformers to recognize that although the Church is immersed in God, she is also in some way incarnate. This means that the Word which sounds in the secret of men's hearts is the same Word which sounds among visible

245

mankind. Thus, in a sense, the Word itself becomes visible. Is the Word present in the congregation of the faithful in the Church? In the preaching of the pastor? In baptism? In Christian living conformed to the Gospel precepts? The answer must be yes and no. For the Word may equally well be there as not there, for how can we tell whether any individual really has the faith, that baptism is well and truly administered, that a preacher holds pure doctrine, that the Christian living of this or that person is any more than a façade? On the other hand, all these things may be true and authentic, and be like a Word of God made visible. God alone can separate the true from the false. But this amounts to saying that the Word's absolute perfection must not be considered unilaterally. The exact expression will therefore be: the Word is of such perfection that it is able to penetrate even into the outer, physical, visible life of the Church and into that of every Christian in order to lay hold of everything that is its own, and of that alone. What else remains it abandons, for this is not its own; it is sin, dissolution, corruption.

Finally, the Word, preceding everything it has instituted, perfect in its power to shape the religious experience of all men, is also supreme in the present influence of its universal government throughout mankind. According to Protestantism, the structure of every ecclesiastical institution must be seen as the reflection of the eschatological realities in the world of today. These enter into relationship with time, as with a reality of some ontological significance and a corresponding element of dynamism. Protestantism and Catholicism differ profoundly on this point. For the former it is a question of contact, of power influencing at a meeting-point, of touch at a tangent. For the latter, it is an influence producing, through the visible institution, a vital participation, and gives it a dynamism which incorporates human initiative with the work of the Kingdom.

B. THE IMMEDIACY AND TRANSCENDENCE OF THE RELATIONSHIP BETWEEN CHRIST AND THE CHURCH, AND CHRIST AS THE PASTOR AND MINISTER OF THE CHURCH

In Protestantism it is an axiom, commonly accepted as beyond discussion, that the supreme and single head of the Church is Christ alone, and that it is he alone, through the word of scripture, who regulates the visible order of the visible Church, that is, everything that has to do with worship, teaching, discipline and government.

It is Christ also who determines that some men should enter the ministry that calls the world under the transcendent and immediate authority of the Word. And the Church, guided by the Spirit, recognizes them as duly qualified. She sets them apart for their special activity, and ordains them for the work of the ministry.

The essential order of the Church, that is, the disposal of her members in a relationship for unity for the service of the Church, as a social body and for serving God, is based upon Christ himself. The ministers, the pastors, and all who have some official part to play in the Church are the external instruments, adjutants in the Christological order of the Church. They work in hallowed association with him, but their function is always extrinsic to his. There is never an inner and vital participation between Christ's ministry and that of the Church's ministers. The essential Order of the Church literally cannot be shared, for that Order is Christ, and it is perfect. A man given the vocation of service in the ministry does not receive a spiritual "character" in his soul equipping him to perform some spiritual activity implying a real part in the Order of Christ.

Christ is the fundamental, perfect and transcendent Order of the Church. He is her Head, with the sole primacy over her, spiritually supreme, with the power of universal influence. As the sovereign Word, he can teach all things; as the sovereign priest, he offered a perfect oblation; as universal king, the ends of the earth are reached under the sway of the influx of his power. In the Church, therefore, there is a single magisterium, a single priesthood, a single jurisdiction, and these are Christ's. He owns them and exercises them without intermediary. Ministers and pastors are the witnesses and heralds of his magisterium, priesthood and jurisdiction. They summon men to obey, but their role is extrinsic. In Protestantism, the teaching authority is that of a witness; ordination to holy things is not a sacrament, but commemorative and intercessory; jurisdiction for the guidance of souls and the government of the Church is not to give commands but to suggest. [17]

C. THE CHURCH'S NATURE AS A WITNESS AND THE PART PLAYED BY MINISTERS AND PASTORS AS WITNESSES OF CHRIST, THE UNIQUE MINISTER OF THE CHURCH

The Protestant idea of the Church's constitution is not that of a void or an absence. No Protestant body, particularly in our time, fails to recognize the importance of the visible aspect of the Church as an institution. The essential difference between Protestantism and Catholicism lies in the notion each forms of the relation between Christ, the Omega reality, and the Church, or, to express it differently, in the relation between the eschatological realities and time. Christ came to this world and was seen as the minister of salvation, the supreme pastor, the perfect leader of the new

[17] "Rapport de la Commission théologique pour la recherche de l'unité, Fédération protestante de France, Bièvres, 15–16 juin, 1954", *Positions luthériennes,* 3rd year, no. 2 (April 1955), pp. 104–8.

mankind. Therefore, says Protestantism, all ministerial activity has been accomplished, all pastoral work done, and the work of recapitulation is complete. All that remains is to bear witness to this, announce it, make it known. The various ministries in the Church are thus ministries of witness, activities whose purpose is to proclaim everything which Christ, as the perfect minister, vicariously fulfilled for all men who are to be drawn to salvation.

Catholicism, on the contrary, holds that Christ's presence as minister, pastor and perfect leader is a reality which, without ceasing to be transcendent, has also become immanent, that is, Christ is and remains in the Church as the one who inspires all ministerial and pastoral work, and all work for souls. The eschatological realities substantially keep their identity, but are committed and shared, and the actions through which this is done, endow those who profit from it with a special gift of grace, enabling them to cooperate, in a divine and human way, with the work of salvation.

What then is meant by a pastor in Protestantism? It is a pity that no definite answer can be given, but, unfortunately, such an answer based on unanimous views and ideas, is impossible. In spite of the Protestant emphasis on the pastor, his position retains an element of ambiguity. At the Reformation, the pastor was first the successor of the Catholic priest, and then took his place as the head of a parish. Is a pastor, then, purely and simply, a layman? What authority does he possess? What is his work? What is the precise nature of his calling? Does he hold an indispensable position in the Church?

The most accurate notion is probably that he is a spiritual guide. In his congregation he is like a spiritual trainer, the leader of a line. His special vocation, that of self-devotion to the service of God and of souls, has been officially recognized by his Church. He has received an appropriate formation. He may act as an evangelist, a teacher of doctrine, a schoolmaster, a counsellor, a sacred minister, in short, a specialist in the things of God. The authority he exercises among his people springs from his vocation, ordination, and his standing as a witness. A spiritual leader, a specialist in the things of God, a religious trainer—these attributes describe him. But any idea of priestly mediation between the congregation and God must be eliminated from the picture.

What do Protestant ordinations signify? Almost all Protestant bodies have some form of ordination. Its form differs, and it can be more or less solemn. Essentially, however, it is the same, and conforms to Luther's definition: to ordain is to call. The Church ordains a man when she calls him to exercise, in her name, ecclesiastical activities as a spiritual guide. An ordained man is sent, given a mission by God and the community, to carry out a religious work among Christian people. He is given an "order", that is, a command. But Protestant ordination is never considered as an act which shapes the community of believers into an organic body within the Church.

The ordination of a Protestant pastor must be understood as a direct operation of the Word. A pastor is directly ordained and hallowed by God, as Moses was by Yahweh, and the apostles under the new law.[18] It is literally an eschatological act. A pastor or a minister is ordained in the way that the Church or the apostolic ministry was hallowed. All Protestant ordination is grounded on this basic hallowing and is included in its scope. It is, in fact, simply an act which proclaims, recalls and signifies the hallowing of the Church once for all in the Lord, and which now requires only to be witnessed. Every form of ministry has been fulfilled in Christ's which incorporated that of the apostles in itself; it now only requires to be proclaimed. Protestant ordination is a commemoration, a recalling, an anamnesis of the hallowing accomplished beforehand, of the perfect ministry vicariously exercised once for all by Christ and the apostles and enduring until the end of time. When a Protestant denomination ordains a man, it intends nothing more than a reminder of these original and perfect actions that cannot be repeated.

Here, once again, the difference between Protestantism and those Churches that have retained the priesthood becomes apparent. With the latter, the priesthood is not merely a reminder of that of Christ, a commemoration of a hallowing done before, an anticipation of the end, in the eternal offering of Christ, the hierarch of the liturgy in heaven; it is also a sacramental presence of Christ among men. In fact, it is this word *presence* that provides a key to our differences. Catholics believe that Christ's priesthood is really present in his priests; but Protestants hold that the presence of his priesthood among its pastors and indeed among the faithful in general is one of continuity, contact, dynamic power transmitted tangentially to men. The eschatological realities and the fact of presence are again seen to be the central question.

Does this mean that a pastor's ordination bestows nothing upon him? He is given a ministerial grace, in the sense that Christ's dynamic power is extended to him, equipping him with the ability to do his work well. Has Protestant ordination no sacred significance? The rites of the laying on of hands, the administering of the oath, and the declaration of faith which accompany it, obviously have a religious import. Is a Protestant minister no more than a layman? He may not be a priest, but he is permanently distinct from the laity because he is ordained to proclaim, recall and signify the total hallowing of the Church, and to bear witness to the ministry accomplished by Christ and the apostles. But his ordination does not mark him with an indelible "character".

---

[18] T. F. Torrance, *Conflict and Agreement in the Church,* vol. II, p. 39.

We have indicated the different standpoints adopted by the Churches and denominations produced by the different movements of reform from the fifteenth century onwards, with regard to the Church's constitution. Three fundamental principles emerge: the principles of congregationalism, presbyterianism and episcopacy.

The ecumenical problem in its constitutional aspect is that of integrating these three principles so as to form a single Church. If the local Church or presbyteral body absorbs the bishop, there can no longer be a genuine Church, because a bishop is the principle of the Church's visible unity. In St Cyprian's phrase: the Church is in the bishop. It may also be said that a bishop is in a Church as the keystone of her constitution and to ensure her organic unity.[19] He must not be dissolved in her. Church and bishop are inseparably united. If he becomes meaningless, so does she, and the immediate corollary is the break up of her unity. It follows that there will be as many constitutions, all alien to each other, as there are ideas about the Church's nature. The unity of the Church will be restored in Protestantism when the three constitutional principles, now existing apart, again come to be integrated, that is, when the local congregation again accepts the principle of the priesthood, and the principle of the priesthood is again incorporated in that of episcopacy. This means that there must be pastors who are truly priests and bishops whose office genuinely corresponds with their title. This without question is Catholic unity.

II. ECUMENICAL FULFILMENT IN ITS CONSTITUTIONAL ASPECT

1. Within Protestantism

If simplification is synonymous with a certain drawing closer together, it can be said that there is a certain structural coming together both within Protestantism and also between Protestantism and Catholicism.

The vast upheaval effected by the ecumenical movement has produced a new centrality, and it has led to the elimination of constitutional forms that displayed a certain eccentricity. Denominations with some roots in common have tended to adopt similar constitutions; the unions that have taken place within a single confession or between different confessions have led to increased uniformity; and the spread of the spirit of ecumenism has worked towards concentrating upon the main types of constitution.

A number of non-theological factors have played their part in this development. In Protestantism on the European continent, the new estimate

[19] J. A. Moehler, *L'Unité dans l'Église* (1938).

of the Church's constitution has been largely the result of the abandonment by the State of the "episcopal" role either given to it at the Reformation or usurped by it.

An equally important factor in producing a new relationship between
constitutions, and to which we have already referred, has been the re-
introduction of various episcopal activities as if by a kind of compensation or as the result of the logic of an institution: for example, the
general control of a Church's life; supervision to see that its doctrine
remains true; the communal organization of charitable, evangelical and
missionary work; the establishment in the name of the community as
such, of intercommunion or discussions with other religious bodies.

It is a fact that can be interpreted in various ways. Is it an example of
self-healing? It may be. What does seem indisputable is that these are
activities which, according to scripture and tradition, belong to the episcopate. It matters little, from the point of view of the problem we are
attempting to solve, whether these are exercised by the consistory, the
synod, the central assembly, the general superintendent, or even by someone
with the title of bishop.

This leads to an inevitable conclusion: when Protestantism began to
turn its back on doctrinal liberalism, it was necessarily brought back if
not to the episcopate in its fullness—which would contradict its essential
principles—but at least to some of its aspects which it practises in a
democratic, communal way, and sometimes with even an element of
hierarchic emphasis.

The entire problem is to know whether further advance is necessary.
This is the great debate. Those who hold that the episcopate does not even
form part of the *bene esse* of the Church see no need for development.
Others agree that though the episcopate is not an indispensable factor
of the Church's *esse*, it is a part of her *bene esse*, and that this kind of
structure should be welcomed on account of its power to create unity in
local congregations and to maintain continuity in the life of the denominations. A third group considers that the episcopate is necessary for the
plene esse of the Church, for her fullness; she can do without it, but it
contributes to her perfection, her wholeness, and it completes her.

2. Is there a fresh approach between Catholicism and Protestantism with respect to the Church's constitution?

Any account of the ecumenical attempts to bring both points of view closer
together must point out the extent of the activity undertaken by the
Churches of the Anglican Communion to restore unity to the ministry
and constitution of the Church. Their unique position moves them to act

251

as a bridge Church between bodies with an episcopal constitution and those without.

The two main difficulties which confront the Catholic Church with regard to the apostolic succession in the Anglican Communion, those, namely, of the validity of its episcopal succession and infallibility of the episcopal body, do not prevent an appreciation of the significance involved in the testimony given by the Anglican Churches to the Protestant bodies on the essential position of the episcopate in the Church's constitution. We may instance their influence in the Churches of Sweden, Norway, Finland, Latvia, and Esthonia; the part played in the formation of the Church of South India; the plans and negotiations being pursued on a broad front of Christian denominations; the establishment of intercommunion with Churches that have the apostolic succession beyond dispute. All this illustrates the fundamental importance which the Anglican Communion attributes to the historical episcopate in any project for reunion. The Lambeth Conferences constitute the solemn expression of this conviction.

The Churches of the Anglican Communion, the Church of England in particular, take especial care to treat each case on its own, and to refrain from establishing a mutual relationship that would depreciate the Anglican succession, and they try to create such a relationship in a way that is as prudent as it is persevering, following the lines laid down by the Lambeth Conference of 1888, in a series of propositions known as the Lambeth Quadrilateral.

When conversations have taken place between the Anglican Communion and groups of Presbyterians, it is interesting to note what the latter put forward as the grounds for an approach to Churches with an episcopal constitution. The Calvinist Churches would be ready to reach an agreement with the Anglican Communion on a number of points, provided the Anglicans would admit the truth of a position acceptable to them, namely, that of an episcopate realized in the regional consistory (presbytery) and based on the identity between presbyter and bishop. A special function would be admitted to belong to whoever ultimately bore the name of bishop, although not the apostolic succession. In other words, the historical and the corporate episcopate would be mutually adjusted. Neither form, it was asserted, would lose anything, for each would be completed by the other. In the Church of Scotland, for example, the regional consistory (presbytery) would remain what it is, but for its Moderator it would have a "personal bishop in the consistory", whereas in the Church of England the bishop would become integrated in his college of priests, acting among them as the president of a committee of priests; there would thus be Presbyterian bishops and elders who would be bishops.[20]

[20] T. F. Torrance, *Conflict and Agreement in the Church,* vol. I, pp. 141–2.

But, on the one hand, it is difficult to imagine that the Anglican Church would give up positions it has so much at heart, and, on the other, Presbyterianism considers that its fidelity to Christianity depends upon the identity between presbyter and bishop. Its programme can provide a constitutional meeting point for all denominations except those who lay claim to the apostolic succession.

The real division is that between the Reformed and the Catholic theory. The Reformed are ready to consider any concession, except that of making the episcopate an essential ministry, heir of the apostles, to which the other forms of the ministry would be intrinsically inferior. Some even go so far as to accept the institution of the episcopate as an undeniable reality, precisely because its purpose is to make the identity of the Church as the organic body of Christ manifest through the ages. But they only affirm this on the understanding that the episcopate is essentially identical with the presbyterate. If this is granted, it can then be affirmed: "The Bible ensures the Church's identity, but it cannot form new communities or ordain, nor can it guarantee the Church's catholicity. That function belongs to a living ministry for which no written work can be a substitute."[21]

But, apart from this or that particular issue, is it possible to affirm any approximation between the constitution of Catholicism and that of Protestantism? If we consider the development of the Catholic Church and of Protestant bodies during the last forty years, an affirmative answer may be truly given. The Church's constitution is composed of three principles: the episcopal, presbyteral and congregational. Now, in the Catholic Church, the coming of Catholic Action, and of all the various movements of the apostolate; the increase in works of social service; and the growing realization of the responsibilities of lay people in the world—these together have meant that the "congregational" principle has been given renewed vitality; in parishes, dioceses, in the Church in every country and throughout the world, there are laymen who have become major witnesses of Christianity, who have made its mission their own, who carry it out efficiently and with great distinction, and who do a work outside the scope of priests and bishops. In the early Church these men would have been called elders, not necessarily on account of their age, but because of their ripe experience, their faithful witness and wide vision. In the Catholic Church, the idea that a bishop is a monarch, a man of universal competence, deciding everything himself, no longer corresponds with the facts. Today a bishop governs his Church more and more with the aid

---

[21] R. Paquier, "L'Épiscopat dans la structure institutionelle de l'Église", *Verbum Caro* 49 (1959); T. F. Torrance, *Le Sacerdoce Royal* (1958), pp. 96–7; "Royal Priesthood" *Scottish Journal of Theology, Occasional Papers* (1955).

of his "presbyters", among whom ecclesiastical advisers and specialists are preeminent, and also with lay advisers, consultants and specialists who are engaged in general apostolic work, social service and in embodying the Church's social teaching in economic life, etc. These latter provide a further example of "elders" who, in their own order, collaborate with priests and bishops.

In the Anglican Communion the government consists of two Chambers: an upper chamber of bishops; a lower chamber of clergy and lay representatives.

Ceteris paribus, we may observe certain parallels between the national, regional or international conferences of Catholic bishops, and the upper Chamber or the Lambeth Conference, in the Anglican Communion; and also between the permanent Catholic councils of the general apostolate or of charitable works that include clerical and lay advisers and authorities, and the Anglican lower Chamber. The point of the comparison obviously lies in the need to integrate the episcopal, presbyteral and congregational principles within the Church.

Turning now to the Protestant denominations, we may observe a further resemblance. How can it escape notice that the regional or national synods, the national assemblies, the regional or national Councils, and even the World Council of Churches, do, in fact, carry out some of the functions of the episcopate, for example, collective responsibility for evangelization, the promotion of foreign missions, the organization of works of charity and assistance on a communal scale, the spiritual formation of the Christian people, and the establishment of intercommunion with different Churches. These activities belong, in principle, to the episcopate, and in the Protestant denominations they are carried out by the community. Even congregationalism has been compelled to develop in this direction.

As a result a better balance, a more inclusive incorporation of the essential elements of the community, has been developed. It would not be far from the truth to say that today all Christian bodies accept in a general way the three integrating principles of the episcopate, the presbytery and the congregation. All Christians have been moved to take this line, through the implications of their own life and through the impulse of the Holy Spirit; and when we pay more attention to the present than the past, or when the fog that divides us suddenly vanishes, we see that unconsciously we have drawn together.

Our differences depend upon the way in which the three principles are integrated; in Catholicism, the bishop belongs to the order of presbyters, but is not identified with it; the order of presbyters is within the congregation or local Church, but is not identified with it; the local Church belongs to the order of presbyters, but is not wholly contained within it; and the order of presbyters belongs to the order of the episcopate, but priests and bishops are not identical. The Church is in the bishop and the bishop in the Church. The difference is due to the apostolic succession and the priesthood. But all Christians are in a sense priests, and, in a sense, they are even bishops, in as much as they share in the Church's scrutiny of the world to be evangelized. But as regards their share in Christ's unique priesthood, it differs in mode, nature and degree.

The constitutional problem in the Catholic Church is inseparably bound up with her dogma, her mission and her unity. A concession on one point would at once involve results on every level. But even more than the fear that her whole structure might crumble, the decisive factor in her attitude is her doctrine on the relation between the Word and her visible existence.

III. CATHOLIC DOCTRINE ON THE CHURCH'S CONSTITUTION

1. The problem of presence within the mystery of that constitution

Our problem is profound, and Protestantism shares it: how does the presence of Christ, risen and ascended, with the fullness of the Spirit in his humanity, continue to influence the world and the Church? The answer depends directly upon the way in which the eschatological realities and their relationship with the Church's duration is interpreted.

It is a problem in ecumenism connected with that of worship: how is the "mystery" made present in the course of the Church's worship? Is Christ's action exercised only in a transcendental way, or does it make use of intermediary signs rendered effective by his presence?

In Protestantism, the sacraments are held to bestow practically nothing that has not already been bestowed by the Word, and the ministry is held to do practically nothing that was not done once for all by Christ the sole minister of salvation. It is a doctrine of the Church that considers commemoration, sign, proclamation, as existing under the transcendence and immediacy of the Lord's presence, acting upon or alongside them.

In Catholicism, one idea predominates: it is that of the Lord's real presence; and it is this idea that explains the need for the Church's mediation and also accounts for the presence of the Lord's action then and there by means of it. An ecclesiology of the Lord's real presence is an ecclesiology in which God really effects something in the centre of man's being: baptism is a real new birth; the Eucharist is the sacrament of the Lord really present; the laying on of hands in Holy Orders is the sacrament through which the Lord personally equips a man with the vocation to the apostolate and gives him the corresponding "character"; a priest's absolution is the sacrament of the real forgiveness of human sin in heaven. In a doctrine of this kind, God's presence cannot be simply a matter of external contact; it must be truly sacramental; it will not be restricted to being recalled, proclaimed, signified; it must be communicated, spread abroad, given; and when it becomes immanent, it remains transcendent.

Catholicism is a coherent whole in which the various elements mutually support each other. Some of them can be directly demonstrated; others are justified by the logic, the coherence of the whole. Many problems are solved within the life, order, faith and tradition of the Church, whose demonstration would be difficult on historical or exegetical grounds. Human reason cannot account for everything. When it cannot, our faith is corroborated by tradition, which maintains and safeguards continuity in the interpretation of the meaning of scripture, for tradition is the present and living consciousness, the loving memory of every element in Christianity, especially of what is best in it, its order. We can see that order in which each part has its appropriate position. We may be able to explain, present and describe it, but we cannot justify it completely on the historical or exegetical level. The insight of faith and what it consequently accepts come first. Reason, history and theology merely attempt to provide understanding and illustration. Faith provides its own illumination—if one is a believer. We may be tempted to try to discover in the historic past insights which are equal to the clarity which faith gives us in the present. But this is not wholly possible. We are living within a tradition which goes back to the beginning of the Church, and the apostles who were there at the start did things which even they could only imperfectly explain, for their actions were performed within the sphere of the Christian "mystery". What they did was literally within a realm of "mystery" beyond the historical facts of time and space. And since they were the fundamental witnesses of Christianity, what they established at once assumed the status of norms.

Tradition originated in this concern to preserve the deeds, the acts and utterances of the apostles. That is why it consists of documents, but also of concrete deeds, repeated patterns of thought, and oral explanations that crystallized into customs, later expressed in the writings of the early Fathers. An element of life as a whole was transmitted; it contained concealed realities that were connected, but unexpressed. There was, for instance, correspondence between the nature of the Eucharist and the kind of ministry involved; between the way Christ is present in the sacraments, and in the mystery of the Church; between the Lord's action in the individual soul and in the Church as a whole; between the constitution of the Church and the theandric nature of the incarnate Word. Does the Church come down from heaven? If she does, this must truly affect her worship and her constitution, and every aspect of her being. This is what is called the "order" of Christianity: in it every part contributes a partial interpretation of the others.

The Catholic Church has a definite standpoint with regard to the Church's constitution. She regards it as a vital element in the living centre and contemporary reality which we call presence.

2. The Church comes down from heaven

The Church's descent from the realms of glory was verified in a series of events. It began on Sinai, and was continued in the Incarnation and on the Cross when the Son began to be glorified, and finally in the Resurrection and Ascension. These manifestations follow a plan of divine wisdom; they are linked together and each is more explicit than the previous one. Those that came first prepared the way for their successors; and these in turn formed their predecessors into a unified whole, brought them to completion *and* took a step beyond them. The Resurrection and Ascension represent the highest peak before the last and absolute culmination of all things is reached. In them the mystery of the Church is centred; the Body of Christ is taken with him, its Head, into the orbit of the Trinity. Christ's manhood, made perfect, is filled with the Holy Spirit, and, in a sense, all mankind accompanies him, for he is the new Adam, and the source of life that will bring the new mankind into being. God's glory descends upon the manhood of Jesus, and thence upon all men united *in ecclesia* with Christ, its Head.

The Church, therefore, in the truth of her present existence, in her ultimate reality, exists in this heavenly glory. There, in the mystery of the union between Head and Body in the Trinity, her mystery is fully accomplished. Christ's life, renewed, and now limitless, flows from its union with the Godhead into his human soul that has set itself right with God, and become preeminently the source of grace for all men. It is true, of course, that this same "hypostatic" union existed from the moment of his Incarnation, and its fullness overflowed into the holiness of his soul, and thence into his mystical Body. Even so, he lacked the completion of the Resurrection.

When we think of the Church, it is upon this supreme moment of the fulfilment of her mystery that we must concentrate. In the heavenly glory of the Ascension and Resurrection, the Church lives with Christ. The meaning of her mystery, therefore, is this: Christ's life, in the glory of heaven, unites men with each other and with the Trinity.

It is in that realm, therefore, that the mystery of the Church's being and life has its origins, its roots, its unfolding: a mystery of unity, holiness, catholicity and even of apostolicity. It is in that realm that the Church first becomes a fact, an existing reality. And the reality thus produced comes down to earth in the form of a "mystery". The Church on earth is the point where the Church in heaven touches the world; she is the sign and symbol of that Church, its consequence, its image and sacrament. She points to it, proclaims it, fulfils it. She is the outstanding sign, the meeting point, the "event" on earth of that ever enduring actually which is in heaven, for Christ, there, is everlasting and total actuality.

Catholic unity is the presence on earth, in an appropriate form, of that unity which exists in the glory of Christ, the originator of the new mankind.

The Church's holiness is the overflow of that perfect unity present in Christ at his Ascension. It issues from that heavenly unity, integrity and spiritual anointing which the Spirit imparts to Christ's ascended manhood.

The catholicity of the Church is the expression in space and time of the unity already existing in heaven between Christ the Head and his Body. The coming of Christ's manhood into heaven was the origin of catholicity and the source of its development. His manhood was mysteriously brought into the divine unity and that mystery has been extended into this world; *because* it reached that realm it necessarily became a reality here. The introduction of the world into Catholic unity is due to the impact made by that catholicity which is expressed and signified by catholicity on earth; earth receives its impact, develops and spreads it abroad. It also indicates it as a promise: "that they all may be one, as you and I are one" (Jn 17:22).

The same holds good for apostolicity. It was, we should note, after the Resurrection and Ascension that the primacy was conferred on Peter and the final powers upon the apostles. This was because the ministry has a twofold foundation: the Incarnation and the Ascension. Together these provide an explanation of the structure of the sacraments: the Incarnation, the visible and invisible, the divine and human, in combination: the Ascension, representing earth's part in the reality of heaven, a part made evident by signs which show forth on earth the communication between the Head and the Body in the glory of heaven. They are signs that effect what they signify, that, being themselves the descent of the Church in heaven to the Church in time, are the very means by which it descends. In the process, they prefigure and make way for the ultimate completion. They are sacraments of that supreme actuality which surmounts the whole present life of the Church on earth. They bring forth that life and direct it aloft.

It is a sacramentalism, therefore, for which the past is vividly actual; it is also turned towards the future, intrinsically related to the ultimate reality already achieved in heaven. Preeminently, too, it is a presence which makes use of and transfigures the visible mediatorial activity of the Church.

Thus the Church is to be regarded as coming down from glory. Her decisive moments were Sinai, the Incarnation, the Cross, the Resurrection and the Ascension, leading to the final consummation.

The Resurrection and Ascension represent the peak: Peter's primacy and the authority of the apostles surround it. The ministry and the apostolic succession are rooted *in caelestibus:* they owe their reality to the glory of Christ, and are not simply human in origin. Apostolicity originates in Christ, the Apostle of the Father: in him it is utter glory. The glory of the Church is a reflection of his. Christ the Apostle communicates its fruits to Peter in the primacy and to the other apostles in their respective powers.

3. Christ's presence as head of the apostolic body

The Church's foundations lie in the mystery of Christ's presence. What particular aspect of that presence is responsible for the constitution of the Church?

It is unfortunate that little importance is usually attached to the position of Christ as the Apostle of the Father, which expresses the inner meaning of his mission in the world, and is the primary source of every apostolic mission. It is from this event and institution that the Church's apostolicity draws all its reality, dynamism and meaning. She depends upon it not only as upon a starting point in a bygone age, but as on a fact that endlessly endures. Christ was, is, and for ever will be the Father's Apostle. At his Incarnation he was seen to be the Apostle entrusted with a mission of redemption. Once that mission was accomplished, he became the Apostle in glory, and that glory was extended to the Church, and first to his immediate witnesses, the apostles, upon whom the clear light of the apostolic Spirit with which he was filled through his Resurrection and Ascension was shed. And it is this which explains why the ultimate and most important commissions entrusted to the Church for her future were only given her after the Resurrection, that is, when Christ received the power of his mission in its fullness. At his Ascension, with his mission completed, the Apostle of the Father sent his Spirit to the apostles. The eschatological realities were therefore present at that time, and its presence accounts for the mission with which the apostles were endowed. Christ, the absolute Apostle, sent forth his Spirit to the Twelve whom he had appointed as apostles. But, until Pentecost, they lacked a quality that only Christ, the Eschaton, could imprint on their souls with the sending of the Holy Spirit as the personal seal of the apostolicity of the Incarnate Word. With the imposition of that seal upon the "college" of the Twelve, Christ confirmed the unity that must reign between himself and his witnesses, and the Church became wholly incorporated within the boundaries of his own apostolicity. By what means was this achieved?

Christ is the Apostle of the Father (Heb 3:1). As such, he is the leading Apostle, or to express it accurately, the Head of the apostolic body. Head and body together form a single reality, and accordingly Christ the Apostle and the apostolic body together constitute a single whole.

The characteristics attributed to Christ as Head of the Church are applicable to him analogically as Head of the apostolic body. They are three in number: order, perfection and power *(virtus)*.[22]

As Head of that body he holds the primacy with regard to the Church's mission, her commission and her testimony. This means that through him the new and definitive apostolic lineage began. The grace bestowed on him as an apostle was that of the one first called and sent, who as the originator virtually contains all the others and can, therefore, summon them and endow them with a mission to the apostolate.

An apostle is a man chosen to be an official guarantor of the essential facts of the order of salvation. He has been sent to give authoritative testimony to what he has seen and heard, and his testimony is able to command unqualified assent from those to whom his mission is directed. Now, Christ saw all things, heard all things, knew everything that is in the Father. His presence in the Father is the guarantee of the truth he reveals. His self expression is in the name of the Father with whom he forms a unity, and his testimony is authoritative. The testimony, the apostolicity of the Son was the point at which the godhead inserted itself into the world. The Son was sent as the Father's Apostle. He is the archetype of the apostolate, the perfect Apostle. It is with the characteristics of an apostle that he is primarily looked upon by his Father, and when the Father contemplates the Church, he sees her primarily in the unity through which she is wholly conformed to the primordial Apostle. The Church is apostolic because her Head is the Apostle par excellence. The unity between Christ and the Church, his Body, cannot be other than apostolic. The Church's order and constitution are necessarily apostolic, and they are grounded in the manifestation of the ultimate realities in the form of the mission first of the Word and then of the Spirit.

The second characteristic that belongs to Christ as Head of the apostolic body is perfection. This means, in the first place, that the apostolic mission existed in him in its fullness. Everything that is to be found fragmented in the Twelve and their successors exists as a coherent whole in him. The apostles and their successors are included in the Lord's perfection and grace. If there is any one who is the "universal form" of the apostolate, it can be he alone. He it is who makes every mission authentic and forms

[22] St Thomas Aquinas, *Summa Theologica*, IIIa pars, qu. 8, art. 1.

them all into a synthesis, who recapitulates and incorporates them into his own mission. Each individual mission has its climax in the consciousness of the first apostle. All that each individual apostle loved, desired, thought of, hoped for, with regard to the kingdom; all that Peter, Paul, John, Augustine, Ambrose, Hilary, Cyril, Basil, Chrysostom, the popes, the bishops of East and West, in all ages and places, personally lived in the consciousness of being sent by God—all this was perfectly alive in the mind of Christ and absorbed in the fullness of his mission. Christ is the total perfection of all the apostolic activity that has been pursued throughout the ages. He is the perfect source of the grace with which the Church of the apostolic hierarchy is endowed. In him the synthesis is perfect, because every mission is recapitulated in him. He is its perfect consciousness, because he is the consciousness and the apostolic awareness of the Church of the apostolic hierarchy. He constitutes her resources, because the Church of the apostles and of the hierarchy draws all her gifts from him. He is her life, because her apostolic mission owes its entire existence to what Christ underwent when he was sent as the Suffering Servant and then as the envoy of glory. The Church's life can be no other than apostolic.

Christ is the Church's first Apostle. He is the perfect Apostle. He is also the active principle which promotes the apostolate in every aspect of its driving force, power, dynamism, and onward march. When we think of Christ the Apostle it is in actual communication with the apostles that we see him. The apostolate signifies being sent. The apostles must be regarded as existing under the rule of Christ, the Apostle. Christ is the centre from which they move and are governed. He coordinates and brings every apostolic work and every missionary activity to its appropriate end.

Christ's mission as the Head of the apostolic body exercises its influence in a twofold direction: internal and external. Internally, Christ spreads abroad everywhere energy, light and the grace of missionary activity; he sends forth the summons, the apostolic calling; he provides what is necessary for understanding God's plan and the world's needs. He inspires the apostles and their successors with the most adequate means for bringing Christianity to the world.

Externally, Christ also exercises a universal influence. He it was who chose apostles who could be seen. He it was who led them to perform those actions which had the power to ensure the permanency of the Church's apostolic constitution. He directs those who lead the Church. He is the ultimate coordinating centre of the apostolic power in its outlook, actions, desires, plans and functions. The spiritual resources of each individual Church and of the Church as a whole are derived from his universal mission. Every individual mission has its climax in him, because its existence depends upon him.

261

The shape of the Church, her inner reality, her life, her being, everything in her, comes before us with the mark of apostolicity. She cannot be other than apostolic. There is not one reality which is the Body of Christ and another which is apostolicity. The Body of Christ is apostolic in its entirety. On account of this it follows that the episcopal and primatial constitution is not something superficial and accidental in the Church. It belongs to her very essence. The quality of being apostolic marks Christianity in depth, and it is because they are modes of apostolicity that Romanitas, or if for the sake of precision we may coin the words "Petrinity" and "episcopality", form part of the Church's inmost constitution. The quality of being Peter affects the universal Church. The quality of being a bishop also effects the whole Church through the medium of each individual Church.

Finally, what other meaning can apostolicity have than that it is the Word of the Father sent into the world, there to become visible as an apostle, communicating itself to a Body in order to make it apostolic and give it an apostolic constitution? The condition of being incarnate that pertains to Christ, the Father's Apostle, discloses a fundamental law of the Church's being: visible apostolicity is the link between her two aspects—the historical and the transhistorical. It springs from the very nature of Christ and from the institution of the apostles. And his paradigm was so clear, basic and inescapable in the eyes of the apostles, that they required it to be continued as long as the Church is in this world. Scripture gives no account of any lengthy deliberations on the occasion of choosing successors to the apostles. At most we observe somewhat differing forms in different places, but these do not affect the essential elements. It matters little that the bishop, in the exact form in which he is known to us at the beginning of the second century, represents the end of a development, in the course of which the "episcopos" appears as a connecting link. Nor does it matter that in some places the episcopate was collective and in others unitary; nor that to begin with a bishop was not the bishop of a diocese, but of a local Church—we might say, of a parish. Nor, finally, is it of importance that it took some time for the nature of the episcopate to be clearly seen in its relation to the apostolic succession. Ultimately this is secondary. What does matter is that a principle had been established through the Incarnation of Christ, the Father's Apostle; a paradigm had been revealed as expressing the fundamental way in which the Christian religion exists: the apostles themselves had experienced it as determining their own destiny; Christ's example and their own showed one thing only; apostolicity for ever forms part of the Church's very being, and visible apostolicity is the link between her historical and trans-historical aspects. The twelve apostles could pass away, but the principle they represented could not end with them, for if it had ended with them, the

Church would have ceased to be apostolic. She would have been apostolic for a time, and then a different Church would have come on the scene. In short, the Church's continuity beginning with Christ and going on into the future would have been broken. The Church would be of apostolic origin, but would not be wholly apostolic now. Could a Church that was apostolic merely by attribution be really so?

The apostles and the early Church found in the exemplar of Christ, the Father's Apostle, the revelation of the principle that the link between the historical and the eschatological aspects of the Church is the visible apostolate. Now, as long as the Church is in this world, she must maintain the connection between time and eternity. She had no other choice to make than that which was in front of her—the visible apostolate. It followed with complete logicality that apostolicity must be permanent, not indeed with those privileges that were strictly personal to the apostles and came to an end when they died, but with what was essentially enduring in it as the link between time and the realities of heaven.

Without long debates and with a certain personal freedom of interpretation, such as befitted the world-wide mission of each apostle, the principle was put into practice through successive adaptations. How was this actually done? The point is still under discussion. The books of the New Testament, which do not describe this development fully, do at least give us the principle, and the principle is clear: the Church, derived from Christ the Apostle, is and remains apostolic through the visible apostolicity whose purpose is to maintain the link between her historical and trans-historical aspects.

Other landmarks help us to grasp the continuity that links Christ the Apostle with the bishops, by way of the Twelve and the *episcopes.*

The four fundamental points which account for the nature and purpose of the apostolate and have been transmitted to the episcopate are substantially the same as those that exist in the apostolic mission of Christ: the revelation of the Father's love; the revelation of God's personal presence in the Church on earth; the revelation of the communion between God and men; and lastly the revelation of the hidden things of God.

In relation to charity, an apostle was the official witness of Christ's and the Father's love. Christ's love was made plain to him in a thousand ways: by personal help, by miracles, friendship and the gift of his life. An apostle had also a mission of his own to carry out in the sphere of divine love. He had not only to bear witness to Christ's love as an official witness with a mandate and an obligation to do this, but like Christ himself he was given a communal mission of divine love. Just as Christ had been, so he too was like the presence of God's love within the Church. Charity, divine love, is the source and origin of unity. An apostle had a special relationship with that love. The apostolate and later the episcopate, are a form of communal love which has a real part in building up the Church. The example of the early Church shows clearly that this kind of love comes into existence not in a moral person but in real individual persons, in Peter, Paul, John, etc. An apostle, a bishop, represent the form taken by divine love in the community of the Church.

This initial aspect of love as a structural force is completed by the effective bringing of Christ's love into the routine of daily life. An apostle and a bishop organize, spread abroad and administer the charity of God. In the early Church, which held all things in common, we can see the apostles definitely engaged in this activity. The administration of "charity", which was originally the concern of the apostles, is a landmark that explains the continuity between the apostles, the *episcopes* and bishops. In the present organization of the Church, on the diocesan level as well as universally, the administration of charity exists as an eminently episcopal function. The charitable work of the papacy may be taken as only one example. Another that may be instanced is the detailed administration in a diocese like that of New York as it is recorded in the diocesan directory.

Presiding over the liturgy provides the second reason that explains the transition from the apostolic body to the episcopate. Christ came into the world as the supreme pontiff. He gave his apostles the power to perform the Eucharist, that is, to celebrate his real presence among his people—the purpose of his Incarnation. The apostolic body was closely bound up with that presence and the Eucharist truly forms the link between the Church's historical and trans-historical aspects. The permanence of the Eucharist as the memorial of Christ's presence in his Church, and even more as his personal presence *in mysterio*, is a further factor leading to the permanence of the apostolic function in definite individuals.

Christ, the Father's Apostle, stands out as the bond and source of unity. The apostles, too, formed such a bond. Their mission, like Christ's, was to reveal and bring about communion between God and men. Christ and his apostles lived a life aimed at bringing about the communion, the summoning and assembly of men *in Ecclesia*. The mission of an apostle was to bear witness to the communion achieved in Christ between God and man. But it was not only to bear witness to it; it was also to effect it. An apostle was the link between the historical and trans-historical communion in the Church. It is an undeniable fact that in the early Church there were definite individuals who provided the key to communion, and these were the apostles. Once again we meet with a revealing paradigm with regard to the nature of the Church, and one, therefore, destined to be permanent.

Lastly, the apostolic body of the Twelve needed to be continued in definite individuals for the sake of the unity of the faith.

The Church's apostolicity implies the spirit of succession and continuity. Christ was the revealer of the hidden things of God. He left us with an image of God that must remain unchanged until the consummation of the world. It can allow of no alteration, for it concerns the shaping of mankind into the image of the divine revealed person. Is such a thing possible without tradition? And who can be the guardian of tradition? In the first instance, it is certainly the Word. And yet why did the Word join the apostles with himself, unless it was to make them the norms of faith? The apostles died, but apostolicity remained. The problem of apostolicity is that of identity; the unity first given with revelation must be maintained unchanged until history ends. We do not deny that scripture unifies the Church in depth and preserves her identity. We do not deny that Christ and his Spirit maintain her unity. But what Christ did is sufficient to show that the Church is based on a twofold continuity: the interior continuity of faith, the testimony of Christ and the Spirit in the soul; the external historic continuity in obedience to the primacy of the Word. This historic continuity demands that apostolicity, that is, the episcopate, shall be permanent, not only as a symbol, a sign, but also as the necessary means and effective sign of continuity in obedience and loyalty to the revealed Word. In addition, since Word and Sacraments are inseparable, the Word continuing itself sacramentally, continuity in obedience to the Word calls for continuity in obedience to the sacramental word. The Church's identity, from beginning to end, rests on this twofold historic continuity. No better way has yet been found of preserving this continuity than that of the apostolic body and episcopal succession.

4. The apostolic hierarchy as the ministry of the Presence

Through the apostolic hierarchy, Christ, the ultimate reality of the Church, reaches out to everything which lies between his two comings.

The purpose of the magisterium is to be the permanent presence of the teaching of Christ and the apostles; the purpose of the priesthood is to preserve permanently in the Church on earth the real presence of Christ in glory; the purpose of the Church's government is to maintain Christ's presence as grasping the world in order to recapitulate it in himself.

The prophetic, priestly and regal functions of the Church must be seen in relation to the Ascension as well as to the Incarnation.

There is, in fact, a frequent anomaly in the way these three functions are presented. They are considered as related to the Incarnation, and this is correct, but the mystery of the Resurrection and Ascension are neglected. Practically, it is the mystery of the Incarnation leading up to the Cross that is alone taken into account, and the fact that after Pentecost the

Church derives her life from the Ascension and the Resurrection is forgotten. Why should these additional mysteries have occurred if they were not meant to have been considered with the others?

The true reason why some of Christ's mysteries have been neglected is, doubtless, the fact that too narrow a view of the Incarnation has been adopted. It has been endlessly repeated that the Church is the extension of the Incarnation, but almost as though the Incarnation ended with Christ's death. And afterwards? The disregard of these facts has led to the omission of some eschatological events which are central to the Church's mystery. Christ who sent the Holy Spirit at Pentecost, who sits at the Father's right hand, who is risen, does not cease to be the Word incarnate. To consider the Church as the Church of the Word incarnate only so far as the Cross, is to allow the fullness of the mystery of Christ the Eschaton to be lost. It is from this mystery that the Church now derives her life, and it contains every aspect of his life in suffering and in glory. It is in the totality of Christ in glory that the Church is rooted today, and not in some vague survival of the Incarnation, situated practically apart from him and continuing to make its effect felt in a way that is quasi-independent of his final state of perfection. Christ is risen; he is at the Father's right hand; he is the Eschaton. Therefore, it is on him, as he finally became, that the Church depends. She draws her existence on earth from his primacy; his perfection and the influx of his eschatological power. In the ascended Christ, "the age to come" is an accomplished fact; the present age is seen to be within his compass; and "the age to come" makes its entry into time.

In other words, because Christ is risen and ascended, the mysteries of the Incarnation and Redemption do not reach us in themselves, abstracting from Christ's total life in heaven: they reach us from Christ himself in glory. Each of his mysteries has, of course, an eschatological dimension, since they are final deeds done by the Word of God; but because Christ is a single and unique person, it is in his perfect eschatological achievement that he reaches us, by giving to each of his deeds and mysteries its own special effect. There was not one Christ at the Incarnation, another on the Cross, and yet another at the Resurrection. There is only a single second Person of the Trinity whose experience forms a continuity. In the infinite unction which the sacred manhood of the glorified Christ receives from the Holy Spirit, each earlier aspect of his mystery acquires its fullness, and it is as such, in this eschatological fulfilment, that it continues its effect on earth. The Church, therefore, must not be understood as the extension of the Incarnation in too restricted a manner. She must indeed be considered as its prolongation, but including the eschatological fulfilment which the Ascension entails. Thus, for example, when it is said that in the Eucharist, the Word is made flesh, this must be seen to be the glorified flesh whose suffering is over; or, when it is said that the apostolic and hierarchic constitution of the Church militant is the sacrament of Christ the Apostle, it must be realized that this refers to Christ the Apostle in glory who had already been sent on earth. It is Christ in his perfect state in glory who becomes present in the Church on earth under this or that aspect of his mystery. There is extension of the Incarnation, but this involves no abstraction from Christ's last mysteries; it involves following the course of his mysteries up to their triumphant consummation. And it is from that position that we must see how the eternal Christ is present in scripture, in the Eucharist, in the apostolic ministry, and in the Church in general.

Eschatology is thus the keystone of the Church. It enables us to understand the nature of the Church's ministerial constitution. The latter is the sacrament of heavenly realities; it serves them as their instrument; it reveals them as their sacrament. And by revealing them, it enables men to understand the inner order of the Trinity—an existence wherein the Father gives a mission to the Son, and the Son and the Father together give a mission to the Spirit. The apostolic constitution of the Church is in the image of the divine "missions" from which it proceeds. When the whole course of Christ's apostolic mission from eternity to time and from time to eternity had been accomplished, it was made present on earth in a structure which endures from the Church's beginning to her end. And this is the apostolic structure whose purpose is to maintain intact, identical with herself, the revealed presence in whom the world's salvation is contained.

Christ the Apostle is in contact with the whole Church from her beginning to her end in the form of prophetic, apostolic unity. That is the magisterial aspect of the Church of the apostolic hierarchy.

He is also in contact with her in the form of sacramental apostolic unity. And that is the priestly aspect of the Church of the apostolic hierarchy.

Again, he is in contact with her in the form of the unity of apostolic government. This is the aspect which expresses her part in his kingship.

In this threefold unity, apostolicity is regarded as a single whole, that is, the apostles and their successors are seen as forming part of one essential mission. Their magisterium is substantially one and the same; so too is their priesthood and government. Some of the apostles' privileges were exceptional and could not be transmitted. But the structural work of the apostolic body had to be carried on by individuals, for visible apostolicity is the link between time in its full extent and the eschatological events and eternity.

We must now examine the meaning of apostolic unity in each instance.

A. THE PROPHETIC AND APOSTOLIC UNITY

The revelation contained in scripture and tradition is God's prophetic word, valid for all time. It was completed with the death of the last apostle, and is in process of realization until the end of all things. The abiding magisterium of the Church is the means by which the revealed prophetic word is made a reality in the present; it is scripture in action, tradition in action.

Revelation is seen to be wholly apostolic in character. The apostles had a lofty prophetic understanding of all Christian truth to the end of time, although this was not expressed in our dogmatic terms. It can and must be said that they and their successors, from the beginning to the end, form a single body. Their successors are mystically incorporated in them, built into them as into the foundation. We may say that the apostles live again in their successors, but it would be more correct to say that the apostolic body is mystically one, with Christ as its Head, just as the popes are one with Peter who is one with Christ.

The original apostolic body, therefore, was in prophetic contact with all things "from the beginning to the end". It grasped history as a unified whole. It incorporated all its successors in a prophetic unity, so that bishops are not so much new apostles as, mystically, the apostles themselves: *non novi apostoli, sed iidem noviter.* They make the prophetic unity of revelation real and present in each period of history.

The entire structure of the Church is essentially prophetic in intent. Far from being concerned with binding the Church to the world, its aim is to draw her from it, to perfect her in a higher unity, that of the ordered society of those whose bliss is the Trinity. It is essential for the Church militant to have an episcopal constitution, for it is only in this way that the encounter between Christianity and the world can be effected. But at the same time, the whole meaning of the episcopate is to be found in its prophetic character. It does not labour to build an abiding city here below, as though that was its goal; it labours here to build a city of pilgrims.

Although the Church's prophetic character is most evident in the apostolic body, a prophetic (magisterial-prophetic) body, this note penetrates the Church militant in its entirety. The Church militant is a prophecy; she is prophecy; the proclamation of what the Church will be when she has reached her goal.

B. THE SACRAMENTAL APOSTOLIC UNITY AND THE CONSECRATION OF THE WORLD

History is the carrying out of the divine plan of recapitulation which God brings about in the world through the progressive triumph over those of its elements that are still undetermined and which become fewer as mankind draws near its end. The marks of Christ are now more evident than they were when he came into the world. When the world turned from paganism to Christianity, it was given a stamp that the Church is always repeating, making more profound and extending.

What can this progressive hallowing of the world be called, save a sacramental movement? For, on the one hand, the world of "the age to come", the world of the "mysteries" won by Christ in glory, penetrates into this world in order to select, lay hold of, direct and hallow its elements, and to become present to them, and, on the other hand, as a result of this, what has been laid hold of and hallowed, becomes determinate, ceases to be fluctuating and purposeless, and is caught up into a network of the divine meanings of sacred signs that enlighten it and bring it into relationship with Christ's coming.

This must certainly be what it signifies, since the Word incarnate is the great sacrament of the Father, and because it is in him that the plan of universal recapitulation is carried out. Since Christianity originates in Christ, it can only be an immense sacramental whole, out of which those more determinate and determining centres, the sacraments, emerge. These, however, do not exhaust the wealth of the Church's sacramental mystery. This idea was so profound a source of life to the early Church that there was never any inclination to lay down precisely how many sacraments there are. The theological reflection on the sacramental mystery of the Church, which led to the defining of this matter during the Middle Ages, can be fully understood only if it is seen against the background of Christ and the Church as the fundamental sacraments.[23]

The sacraments exist in relationship to the fundamental sacramentality of the mystery of Christ as memorial, presence and anticipation: as memorial because they commemorate the sacramental Incarnation of the Word; as presence, because the Word is continuously active in them; as anticipation, because they move towards their consummation.

Now, who is it that was first chosen, reached, and grasped in the Incarnation? Who is it in this world that gains deliverance, and is hallowed? Who is it that first enters into the dominion of the sacraments? Surely mankind. And in mankind who was it that was most especially reached, grasped and hallowed? Surely the twelve apostles. From the beginning of the Lord's ministry, they were chosen, called, integrated into a unity whose centre was Christ. An apostle was one with him who sent him.

---

[23] E. H. Schillebeeckx, *De Sacramentele Heilseconomie* (1952); E. T.: *Christ, the Sacrament of Encounter with God (1960)*. See also the key documents of the Second Vatican Council: the Dogmatic Constitution on the Church, chapters i and iii, and the Decree on the Bishops' Pastoral Office in the Church.

All the apostles were one in Christ's apostolicity. And from Pentecost onwards, they themselves can be seen exercising the power to choose, summon, gather together and hallow. They chose the world for God; they reached, grasped, delivered and hallowed it. They acted as a Church and a Sacrament.

How did they do this? First of all, by the proclamation of the kerygma. In the Epistles of St Paul, preaching is literally understood as a sacramental action through which the mystery of the Kingdom, hidden to past ages, now fulfilled in Christ in glory, is revealed to the men in whom his life is to be continued.

This aspect of preaching, as forming part of the general sacramentality of the Church, was rightly reaffirmed by the Reformers who regularly added an account of the function of preaching to their exposition of the sacraments.[24] In these accounts preaching is described as the supreme sacramental action of the Church. The other sacraments continue the sacramental action of the Word and confirm it. They succeed in making it visible, present and effective. There is, however, a profound difference between Protestantism and Catholicism in this matter: for the latter, a sacrament effects what it signifies, whereas for the former it is only another mode of a single proclamation.

The mystery of the Kingdom becomes incarnate in the Church's life. It does not merely just touch the world, it reaches right into it, is incorporated in it, becomes flesh in it. It has but one object—to take complete possession of it, so that one day Christ may be all in all. The two means of achieving this are the ministry of the Word considered as a sacrament, and that of the other sacraments. Word and sacraments are the fundamental means by which the occupation of the present age by the power of the "age to come" is effected: through them the sacramentalization of the world is achieved. In scripture this work is disclosed as a unified activity occurring in the interval between Christ's two comings. The duration of the Church is the time set aside for the hallowing of the world through sacramental action.

The apostles corporately were the leaders of the sacramental action by which the elements of this world are chosen, called and integrated into the Kingdom. Scripture clearly discloses a fundamental paradigm, of a sacramental type, according to which the eschatological realities are made present to this age, and act on and in it. It also explicitly indicates the

---

[24] Luther, *De Captivitate Babylonica*, Clemen edition, vol. I (1933), p. 510; Guy de Bres, "La Confession de foi des Églises réformées wallones et flamandes" (1561), Schaff, *op. cit.*, III, art. 33; "Le Catéchisme de Heidelberg" (1563), Schaff, *op. cit.*, III, pp. 65–67; Henri Bullinger, "La Deuxième Confession Helvétique" (1566), Schaff, *op. cit.*, III, chapter xix.

true position of the apostolic ministry in this action, and it shows that the work of giving a sacramental character to the world, to be continued until the end of history, is envisaged under the form of enduring apostolic action. This truth must have quickly become evident to the apostles. Did not Christ's person offer them the prototype of the sacramentalization of mankind? In him, human nature had been chosen, delivered and hallowed. The apostles knew that this work must go on producing its effect until the end of time. In Christ, the Father's Apostle, they saw the hand of God taking hold of the world. They themselves had been chosen in order to be one with the Apostle who sent them. In short, the apostolic work of hallowing the world must be continued. As persons the apostles could pass away, but their function must remain until the mysterious conclusion of the period fixed for the world's sanctification.

C. APOSTOLIC JURISDICTIONAL UNITY AND THE RECAPITULATION OF THE WORLD IN CHRIST

The coming of the Word into the world amounted to a real grasp of the world by the Word, a laying hold of the created order by his sovereignty, a massive act of recapitulation of the universe in his person. In short, through his Incarnation, the Word visibly established his regal jurisdiction in the world. This world is now no longer abandoned to the prince of darkness. Christ let this be clearly seen. His statements on this matter are the expression of a real claim of total jurisdiction over the universe. From the beginning to the end of his mission, Christ carried on a struggle for the reconquest of his Kingdom (Jn 12:31; 14:30; 16:11). St Paul gave a wonderful development to the ideas on this aspect of Christ's dominion over the world. The Gospel as a whole repeats the same doctrine, not always in explicit terms as in St Paul, but by means of facts, concrete events, definite attitudes, deeds that had the significance of prototypes.

The doctrine of Christ's universal sovereignty is common to Catholicism and Protestantism. But Catholics take a different view with regard to the way it comes about, because their idea of apostolicity is different. In Protestantism, it is a question of proclaiming Christ's sovereignty that has already been accomplished. In Catholicism, it is a question of a reality which though accomplished, takes effective possession of time by means of the unity of apostolic government. Christ did not intend to communicate every aspect of his regality to the Church, but certain aspects of it only, so as to make them the sacrament of his presence, taking hold of the world in order to recapitulate it.

St Paul expresses the great law of universal recapitulation in Christ as being that which governs God's activity, the ordering of his ways and the working out of his plans (Eph. 1:10). The result and the purpose of all the hidden activity which is unfolded in the mystery of either Christ or the Church is recapitulation. This recapitulation takes place on different levels.

There is the recapitulation which the Church as a whole effects, through bringing men "into Christ". There is the recapitulation effected by the laity, especially through bringing the material creation "into Christ and the Church". There is the recapitulation effected by the bishops, through bringing men and civilizations into the Church. There is the recapitulation effected by the pope, through bringing the laity, the bishops and human activities "into Christ and the Church".

The various degrees of the hierarchy are superimposed levels or stages of recapitulation. This is where we must find the principal reason for the institution of the episcopate and the papacy: they are at the service of Christ the Recapitulator: they bring mankind, human societies, the material universe and time "into him". The bishops and the popes of every age bring human activities and men themselves, to the twelve apostles, the essential gates of the City, leading them to salvation through the gate of infallibility: *Si quis per me introierit* (Jn 10:9). Salvation is to be found in recapitulation. May Christ recapitulate mankind, the material universe and time! Apart from him there is no salvation for anything. The mystical dimension of his mystery belongs to the cosmic as well as to the spiritual order. He will be all in all (1 Cor 15:28).

The Church incorporates human communities, and in doing this she recapitulates them into Christ. She incorporates the flow of time through the celebration of Christ's mysteries in the course of the liturgical year. She incorporates the material universe by collaborating with men in accepting the work of human culture and civilization, and also by making her own, at a higher level, that of sacramental recapitulation, certain created things: water, wheat, oil. She brings man himself to a higher level of recapitulation through the two sacraments of marriage and holy orders. She secures the safety and integrity of this recapitulation through the sacraments of penance and extreme unction. She strengthens the subjective ability to carry it out through confirmation.

Many other things are recapitulated "into Christ" by the Church. One has only to think of the use made of materials in the building of Churches, or the employment of human talent in worship, the liturgy and preaching. This is something more than mere utilization; it is a recapitulation that already foretells the eschatological recapitulation when all things will acquire their grandeur in God's glory.

We must also envisage, from this same point of view of recapitulation, the whole typological array of prefigurements and images, whether these are persons as "types" of Mary, Christ, the Church; or of things as "types" — the deeds, functions and powers of the Messiah, the sacraments or the events of salvation, the life of the chosen people in the Old Testament as prefiguring that of the people of God in the New, or, as Origen saw it, the life of the early Church as prefiguring that of the Church in her entirety throughout her historical development, and lastly, the Church's total historical existence as prefiguring her life in that eschatological future when images, symbols, signs, foretellings, prefigurements, prophecies, sacraments and powers will all pass away in the presence of Reality.

The nature of prophetic, apostolic unity is an expression of the nature of recapitulation. The typological network which embraces the Lord and the Church throughout time, the material universe and mankind, is a network of recapitulation. The pope, the bishops and the laity are the means by which, in God's mercy, the world becomes increasingly and finally recapitulated. The period of the early Church was consummated in this way; then followed the barbarian kingdoms, the medieval world, the Renaissance and modern times. They have all passed away and entered into Christ's recapitulation. Some things have been saved to enter it, and others lost. Does this mean that everything done and known in history is what was bound to be? That was the Lord's view. There are also things that were not evident and are known to him alone. The part played by the invisible, mystical influence of the Church in the work of recapitulation is always present. Who except the Lord is able to judge history in terms of recapitulation? True, even now the Church can make judgements that are ratified in heaven, but she will see the *liber scriptus* only when all things end.

Prophecy and recapitulation clearly go together. As divine recapitulation extends, so the area of mystery, in the sense of "prophecy", lessens, for Christ's features become increasingly incorporated in the time process, he marks it more firmly with his seal, makes it more determinate, brings its "potentiality" to his own "act". The secret purpose, hidden in the free decision of eternal wisdom, of leading men to salvation, becomes increasingly manifest to human eyes (Rom 16:25; 1 Cor 2:7—10; Col 1:26; Eph 1:8–10; 3:3–12). An element of secrecy always remains and this demands faith, for, until it is fully accomplished, the mystery always works under the veil of signs. God cannot express it wholly and adequately in history; its complete meaning is reserved for heaven. Its very transcendence makes it impossible for it to be known during the time process, except through prophetic signs, made effective through symbols and sacraments. In its totality it will be the same at the end as it was in the beginning, but the interval between is a time of interrupted vision maintained by symbols: it can be seen without being seen, and heard without being heard (Matth 13:3).

We must realize, therefore, that Christ's mystery operates by way of recapitulation, and that the Church, which shares in the Messianic activity, follows that way also.

5. Abolition or consummation?

The Church on earth and in heaven is one and the same: the conditions of her existence differ, her substance remains identical. Her earthly condition indicates the imperfect hold of the Word of God over man and history. Her perfect condition is the completion, the consummation in the supreme actuality and unity of God's presence. Even on earth her final reality begins to be unveiled, but her perfect condition depends upon the revelation that has become complete.

There is a way of regarding Christ's glorified manhood that is almost Docetist. It remains silent about his present role in relation to the Church militant and his final role in relation to the Church triumphant, and leads to him being considered as an immaterial being, as though he had been incarnate only for a while. In reality, however, he is and will always remain the Word incarnate, and it is through him that the Church will see God. Through him, the unity, holiness, catholicity and apostolicity of the Church will be consummated. Her unity will be absorbed in the glorified unity of his divine and human nature; her holiness in his completely sanctified manhood; her catholicity in the fullness of her incorporation into him as leader of the new mankind; her apostolicity in his, the Father's Apostle. For time and eternity, the Church remains the Church of the Word incarnate. The function of the Holy Spirit, on earth as in heaven, is not to turn us away from Christ's manhood, but to lead us to it and to keep us in it, for it is the only revealed way which, on earth as in heaven, can lead us to the Father.

This is the reason why the ministerial structure of the Church on earth tends to be absorbed, both on earth and in heaven, in the divinity, but not be cast into the fire. The Church's visible communion, together with the signs that accompany it, demands to be made perfect one day, through the light of that City, where all things will become luminous, without obscurity; they will not be suppressed, but consummated. Every prophecy demands to be finally fulfilled in the absolute brightness of the Word with whom every utterance will henceforth harmonize. Faith, as faith, will pass away, but the light already in it will be intensified. Hope will gain its object, and the Church on earth, that prophetic hierophany, will be absorbed in God's all commanding presence.

In the Word incarnate glorified, our supreme Pontiff, our King and our Kingdom, our Truth and our Master, the Church will be handed back to the Father. And it is in and through the Son, that the Church, with those called to her, now all summoned and gathered in, will remind the Father of those words with which his Son's mission began: *Ecce venio* (Heb 10:5–9). The Father's name will be hallowed; his Kingdom will have come, his will done on the earth renewed as it is in heaven.

274

The Problem of Worship: The Impact of the Economy of Salvation on the Church as Worshipping Community

I. DEFINITION OF THE PROBLEM

1. The ecumenical problem considered as worship

Various ways of organizing worship, that is, of understanding and living the religious relationship between man and God, have been suggested to us by the forms of religious architecture. English expresses the full scope of this relationship well by the phrase "way of worship"—which means the general conforming of our life to a certain spirit. The vital expressions of worship designated under the term "ways of worship", in which sociology, psychology, history and concrete pastoral needs coalesce with the understanding of revelation, indeed appear as the most definitive manifestation of each particular way of understanding the Christian religion. Christianity is a way of life, that is, an all-embracing way of living the religious relationship of mankind with God according to the example given to us in the Incarnate Word. It is astonishing to note how many times the word "way" occurs in the New Testament—the new way, way of peace, way of salvation, way of life—all ways that reveal what Christ came to inaugurate. Christ is himself the way (Jn 14:6) and in the beginning Christianity was known by the name of "way"—those who followed Christ followed Christ's way. When, for instance, Paul asked the high priest for letters for the synagogues in Damascus in order to bring back to Jerusalem in bonds the adepts of the sect who followed Christ, it was the term of "way" that Luke the Evangelist used to describe Christianity (Acts 9:2).

Thus the link between worship and Christianity is so close that the word "way" may be applied as much to the one as to the other. In worship every aspect of the reality of man intervenes, whether individual or social. Thus all his being with its concrete roots is expressed in it.

275

Worship is not merely a moment or a function of life. It is the synthetic expression of Christianity.

This implanting of the forms of worship as a way of comprehending Christianity and in the concrete reality of human life means that the ecumenical problem in its aspect of worship is a sphere of conflict. The Christian world is in fact in a state of fragmentation, divided into multiple expressions of worship dependent on the variety of denominations. The expression of the Christian religion could not be uniform, since this liturgical pluralism derives its origin if not explicitly from the apostles, at least from times very close to theirs; moreover, by the dispersal of the apostles it was already a fact. What judgement must we bring to bear on this pluralism when it ceases to be the concerted expression of a single form of Christianity and becomes in fact a plurality of incoherent expressions? Moreover, is it lawful to accept the diversity of forms of worship when this becomes a factor of division? The Lund Conference in 1952 pointed out that the disunion of Christians is most clearly revealed in the field of worship and that it is there that the feeling of separation is most acute. Anyone who has a certain experience of interdenominational relations or who even has contact with groups of varied confessional allegiance knows to what an extent the multiplicity of forms of worship is considered not simply as the manifestation of common riches but as a real obstacle to the unity of Christians. This is found to be the case not only in denominations with very definite liturgical demands, but also in those who admit a certain flexibility in the religious expression of belief. We thus arrive at this situation, strange indeed, that Christians who all recognize the same God and the same Christ exclude each other from the adoration of that same God and from communion in his presence.

The ecumenical problem considered under the aspect of worship is that of recovering unity—unity, not uniformity—of the liturgical expression now disintegrated and dispersed throughout the multiplicity of Christian denominations. What is required is to bring these denominations firstly to a mutual understanding of their forms of worship, then to reintegration, for if the Church is and should be one, she must also be so in that in which she most completely expresses herself on earth, in the worshipping assembly. There must be, in fact, an essential meaning, a fundamental structure in Christian worship. Behind all the forms which have resulted from the adaptation to particular peoples of the essential rites established by Christ himself to express the religion of redeemed mankind, we should surely find these essential rites themselves throughout the whole extent of the Christian world.

Every investigation of the problem of worship that is in any way extensive and every solution offered with the aim of reintegrating the discordant forms must take account of the twofold order of the problems involved, some depending on dogmatic and theological factors, others on non-theological elements. Worship is the expression of a faith. It is also the expression of man, the whole of man, man with his roots. History, sociology, psychology help us to understand the interplay of the varying expressions of worship, in accordance with the different backgrounds, times and places. But above all it is belief that controls at depth both religious behaviour and liturgical forms. Moreover, things are often made all the more difficult because the non-theological factors clash with doctrinal elements. The present chapter will be chiefly concerned with the dogmatic and theological aspect of the question, but it must not be thought that abstraction is a denial.

A considerable dispute, almost a long-standing quarrel, exists among Christians as to the meaning and practical application of the mystery of salvation in time. How is this mystery made manifest to us? How is it communicated to us and how do we enter into its presence? Protestantism considered as a whole offers an interpretation which differs considerably from that of the rest of the Christian world. What is, at bottom, the problem set by the difficult question of the impact of the economy of salvation on the Church considered as a worshipping community? To posit the problem of worship is to posit the mystery of the Presence in the Church—the Lord's presence in the cycle of the liturgical year, in the divine office, preaching and the liturgy, in baptism, the Eucharist and the other sacraments. The divine presence is there, but how is it there and how does it act?

In all Christian communions Christianity is conceived in function of the mystery of the Presence. Worship is the celebration of this Presence acting in the economy of salvation in history. Let us call the acts by which God saves us mysteries and ask how these acts shall be celebrated. Here it is asserted that this must be through preaching and the reading of the Bible, to which must be joined the evocation of the Last Supper in the form of a memorial. Let us call this type a prophetic celebration. Elsewhere God's saving acts will be celebrated both by a prophetic celebration and by sacramental rites wrought by the ministry of the priest. Both celebrations certainly effect a breaking down of the limits of the natural order and bring about an entering into relationship with the divine presence, but they differ profoundly from one another. In the Protestant type the sacrament intervenes as a seal which confirms the Word and makes its content authentic, the Presence remaining transcendent, although in contact with the Christian. Rites and symbols are made use of, but as indicative signs. When the Presence comes, it displaces and substitutes itself for them. In the Catholic celebration, on the other hand, one idea is predominant—that of the Real Presence: in the Eucharist Christ is really present, under the veils of the sacrament, in his body, soul and divinity.

In the other sacraments he is present by the irradiation of his holy mysteries that he makes felt there. In the divine office and the liturgical cycle he is present with a spiritual presence.

The total characteristics of each type could again be established differently. For Protestantism salvation is something acquired and the economy of salvation is an order already realized in the Lord. It is a matter of entering into the salvation hidden in God. The liturgical celebration assumes the aspect of the proclamation of an order perfectly accomplished on one occasion and once for all. For Catholicism Christ the Saviour, the ultimate reality of salvation, makes himself present in a real but mystical manner in the Church, the sacraments, the liturgy and the priestly ministry.

The concept of Presence in Protestantism is one and univocal. In Catholicism it is diversified and analogical. Daily life offers us current examples of the various realizations of a presence. One can be present in person. One can be present through one's influence, one's memory, through and in the instruments one employs etc. The scriptures, moreover, suggest to us many modes of God's presence—in his own person or through his servants; as intimacy conferred or as effect established; as living and present reality or as memorial etc. Thus Catholicism considers that there should be more than representation or proclamation of the past, a prolonging, indeed an accomplishing of the economy of salvation.

It is these doctrinal differences to which psychological, historical and sociological factors have added their own complication that explains the breaking up of Christians into innumerable denominations and worshipping communities. The conflict is obvious. Is a drawing together on the level of worship possible between Christian communities? Is it in the process of coming into being? Can steps which may lead to a reconciliation be indicated? It is these various questions that we should like to examine here.

2. Typology of the forms of worship in the Protestant world

The life of Christianity in the communions which have sprung from the Reformation has for about five centuries past assumed a wide variety of liturgical forms. To the differing expressions of the Reformation in Europe correspond the same number of liturgical principles and from these as many different traditions have come. The Reformation in England adopted as its characteristic to be both Catholic and Reformed. These two features are found in the Anglican liturgy. The Reformation in Germany has assumed as many liturgical expressions as it has provided itself with structures of government. The Reformation in Geneva, which afterwards extended to France, Scotland and the Low Countries, gave rise to a tradition of the Puritan type. Then appeared the liturgical type corresponding to the stream of independent communions—Congregationalists, Baptists, Methodists. The Society of Friends, or Quakers, which is connected with the contemporary spiritual stream of the Reformation in the fifteenth century, also presents a new type, the principle of which could be described as that of sacramental silence and the worship of the inner light.

America presents no fewer liturgical variations than Europe. She received the substance of her convictions and practices from Europe, but in addition has provided herself with new forms, with liturgical characteristics and features which result in the problem of reintegration into the unity of worship being considerably different in America from what it is in Europe. Changes in the matter of worship have been as great as those in the matter of theology and social organization. The old denominations which have lingered on with their imported form of liturgy have not escaped modification. The Episcopalians have introduced some change into the sphere of worship as they have done into the pattern of structure. More considerable variations have been introduced in the case of the Methodists and the Presbyterians. The Lutherans also provide a wide variety of expressions of belief and worship according to their confessional regrouping, extending from simplicity to the most formal ritualism. To these must also be added the type which has emerged from American revivalism of the eighteenth and nineteenth centuries, which developed with the movement towards the West and marked the life of several denominations. American life has finally made its impact on the spirit and on the liturgical forms and traditions imported from Europe. Sociology, and particularly psycho-sociology, can make a valuable contribution to the ecumenical movement by helping to pick out the influences foreign to revelation which have a share of responsibility in certain concrete expressions of liturgy. By virtue of the force of the habit of tradition or education, it happens in fact that a particular liturgical form is considered as coming from one single source, or that all the elements which constitute it are placed on the same footing. The establishment of a typology, the retracing of the doctrinal and historical sources, the analysis of the interfertilization of the various liturgical expressions help to determine the proportion of what is relative and what is permanent in them.

If it is to be complete, any attempt at the establishment of a typology of forms of worship in the Protestant world must take account of both principles and facts, for what the principles command is not always followed in practice.

A typology according to the order of principles would have to follow the main lines of the typology of the forms of communion arising out of the Reformation as established in the chapter on the historical problem.

One would thus see the type of liturgy in the forms of classical Protestantism, and then in the forms of its more radical expression.

A typology in accordance with the order of facts would seek to ascertain between what axes the liturgical currents are evolving at present and what are the currently adopted formulas for them, independently of the denominational frontiers.

The movement of liturgical revision which accompanied the Reformation was produced under the action of Luther in Germany, of Zwingli in Zurich, of Bucer in Strasbourg, of Calvin in Strasbourg and Geneva, of Cranmer in England, and it would surely be necessary to add the names of Anabaptism, Spiritualism and Antitrinitarianism whose influence is clear in the forms of radical Protestantism, both from the point of view of structure and worship.

It must be pointed out in the first place that the liturgical principles involved in the fundamental tenets of the Reformation and the concrete expression of the liturgical changes brought about by the reformers are two distinct things. Just as there is a liturgical substance that can be separated from the various expressions of the Reformation, so the liturgical manifestations of these new communions present an attitude of incompleteness, of hesitation, that still has an impact today on the life of the Protestant communions and explains this movement of research and re-assumption as if so to go beyond original deficiencies. It has already been pointed out that the greatest defect among the Reformers of the continent was the lack of historical knowledge of the origins and principles of worship.[1] Their knowledge of liturgical forms seems indeed to have been limited to the contemporary Roman forms alone. The Gallican liturgy and the oriental liturgies or again early worship were for them practically an unknown world. Now it was in this state of ignorance of the existence of evidence as to what primitive worship was that they launched intrepidly into the great adventure of the restoration of that worship. A very serious *a priori* charge weighs on the liturgical revision brought about by the continental Reformation—the ambition of discovering by itself alone the original form of worship without having gathered together all the elements capable of establishing a judgement. If we except the liturgical reform in England and in Strasbourg, there is no alternative but to state that the Protestant liturgical revision, obsessed by the presence of the Roman liturgy, has in fact led only to an impoverishment of worship. They wanted to reform, but principally applied themselves to cutting out whatever in Catholic worship, and more precisely in a particular form of Catholic worship, clashed most with the new sentiments or appeared superfluous. A conclusion already reached in the investigation

[1] W. D. Maxwell, *An Outline of Christian Worship* (1936), p. 72.

of the structural problem again emerges here—the task of re-thinking the whole order of Christianity was too great to be happily accomplished amid the strong feeling and situations of the times. And to a close degree, in the matter of worship as of structure, the reformers had, so to speak, inherited ancient Catholic frameworks. They tried to introduce new forms into them. The adjustment remained in the last resort impossible. Neither in the matter of structure nor of worship did the Reformation produce anything fundamentally original. It is perhaps there that uncertainty and improvisation emerge most. The Protestant world has felt this clearly and today, thanks to an exact and world-wide knowledge of liturgical forms, it is seeking to provide itself, if possible, with an ecumenical worship along the line of the essential principles of the Reformation.

A. LUTHERAN WORSHIP

Luther always taught that the unity of the Church was not produced by uniformity of worship and that it was not broken by its disparity. It can be said in general that the structural variety that has been found in the Lutheran world as a result of the acts established by Luther himself is also found in its liturgical expression. Luther D. Reed has rendered a valuable service to the cause of ecumenism by his work on the Lutheran liturgy.[2] He shows how the principles enunciated by Luther were applied in the German states and principalities according to the good pleasure of outstanding personalities or according to circumstances. For Germany alone he picks out three determining groups—the Saxon-Lutheran centre, the ultra-conservative party and the radical wing. The first group, by far the most important, covers the centre and the north and worship in Denmark is attached to it. The second, fairly limited in numbers, has sought to retain as much as possible of the forms and ceremonies of the pre-Reformation. To it is attached Lutheran worship in Austria and doubtless in Latvia. The third group, in the south-west of Germany, is deeply marked by the influence of the thought of Zwingli and Calvin. In Sweden, on the other hand, worship is clearly conservative in tone. It has kept the structure of the medieval Latin Mass.

After centuries of atomization of liturgical expression, the world of Lutheran communions is now seeking to bring about on the liturgical plane something analogous to what it has accomplished under the form of international regrouping. The American groups are leading. The formation of the national Lutheran council led, in 1958, to a common liturgy for the United States and Canada.

In England and in Sweden almost the whole nation accepted the

---

[2] *The Lutheran Liturgy* (1947; 2nd revised edition, 1959).

Reformation. The position was not the same in Germany where each state was master of its own destiny. Some accepted the Reformation, others refused it. Luther was opposed to the centralization of authority, but something had to be done to remedy the existing disorder. The Protestant princes and the authorities of the free cities decided to put the principles of the Reformation into operation in their territory. For a certain time Luther showed repugnance to undertake the task of re-organizing worship in a manner in conformity with these principles. It seemed to him that such work would ill fit in with his convictions on the Word. He knew very well the state of his own feelings on the Latin liturgy; the institution of a set form of worship seemed to him a return to the mediational structure of the Church. It was thus quite an undertaking to define what the new worship should be and in what manner it would be necessary to organize it. Luther's rediscovery of the primacy of the Word of God, his confidence in his own justification by faith alone—this seemed to him amply sufficient for worship. What need was there of more than the preaching of the Word whence faith arises? True worship would be to sit down like Mary at the Master's feet and listen to his voice. Why the rest, the rites and ceremonies? Was that not rather a pretext for leaving the more important and giving oneself to the accidental? The first years of Luther's life as reformer ware marked by indifference to the external forms of worship. At this period he saw one thing only—to have confidence in the intrinsic and total sufficiency of the Word. Would God, who is not bound by the sacraments, be bound by the external and organized forms of worship? Why should it be necessary to fall back into the rut of liturgical organization after freeing oneself from it?

Religious disorder in Germany had become intolerable and it appeared evident to the principal leaders of the Reformation that the new tendencies could not remain as a spiritual movement, but would have to be organized. It was not sufficient to protest against the Latin Mass. It was necessary to offer the people something else by which they could express their faith and feel their spiritual unity. Mystical individualism would only lead to anarchy, as the Anabaptist movement had fully proved.

Yet Luther did not move immediately in the direction of the complete establishment of a form of worship. Struck by the people's need of religious instruction, he first of all gave to the Church meetings a form closer to teaching than to prayer. He contented himself with explaining to the faithful the essential elements of belief and morality. His intention was to follow the line of the precursor who announced the way by which the Master who would establish personal contact with the soul, would come. This concern with the didactic aspect is found in the "German Mass" (1525) where the Preface is replaced by an exhortation to the participants. But what is Luther's "German Mass", with its displacement of certain parts, such as the Lord's Prayer being inserted before the consecration of the bread and the Sanctus placed between the two consecrations, but the traditional Mass? The first scheme of reformed public worship as Luther saw it was thus established on the liturgy of the Word and Eucharist. But with the development of the polarization of his thought around the Word, Luther orientated worship towards the primacy of the Word. The Word was what had seemed to him the central institution of his life and of Christianity. Taking the traditional schema of liturgy of the Word and liturgy of the sacrament, he gave priority to the Word and made the sacrament a corollary of it. One could not, however, find in Luther, as one could in Calvin, a collection of principles and rules which fixed the order of worship after the manner of logical conclusions deduced from the primacy of the Word. Calvin's views in his *Institutes* are clearly defined. Luther always showed considerable flexibility. It did not seem to him that the Word could imply an explicit and determined form of worship. Much more, every form which did not seem forbidden by the Word was allowed in principle. This is the explanation of the very wide variety of the particular forms of worship in the Lutheran world.

For Luther, then, worship appeared more and more as the worship of the Word. What is the Word, he asked, but the expression of God's will? It is God who in the secret of his mystery knows how he wishes to be adored. The worship paid to the Word thus implicitly contains the true form of worship that God wills that we should offer to him. Under every form of worship is hidden true worship as fixed by the sovereign will of God who demands to be adored as he understands it and not as we understand the matter. Here we must recall Luther's commentaries on the first commandment of the decalogue. He drew from this commandment the principle of worship as a service, a duty, and not a benefit. What is essential in worship is God's honour. To understand this commandment and to live it seemed to him the essence of worship. In every intervention of worship as a benefit for men he saw the intrusion of the spirit of idolatry and man's will to effect his salvation himself. Was it essential for this reason to refuse the sacraments which the Lord mentions explicitly in scripture? Luther judged that as they are mentioned they should be considered as an expression of the Lord's will and received as such. But he also considered that the Word, being living, is dynamic and active and that it is finally the Word which alone can save man when it re-echoes in his conscience and is received with faith. The Word cannot fail to be received in the sacraments since it is there, but the Word can act sacramentally even outside the sacraments. The sacraments have their value in a religion of the Incarnation, they serve as a setting for the Word, they form part of its vitality, but primarily and before all, he said, it is the Word that is charged with the Spirit of God. When it is heard

God is there, truly, really and in an utterly effective way. It is he who at that moment speaks to man, solicits his response and implants faith in him. Whether it be in worship or outside it then, the Word of God has its own sacramental effectiveness. It even became for Luther *the* means of grace, that which explains all the others and which gives to each one his exact measure. The Eucharist itself became another way of presenting and proclaiming the Word. One principle thus dominated the worship reformed by Luther—the supremacy of God's Word and the direct, immediate effectiveness of its action in the soul that hears it.[3]

B. CALVINIST WORSHIP

In its substance Calvin's liturgical thought is the same as that of Luther which repeats systematically, setting it in a framework corresponding to his own personal vision, namely the transcendence and sovereignty of God. Hence the difference of atmosphere and climate in the two liturgies. The Lutheran liturgy reflects in its hymns the experience, sad but at the same time joyful, of the man who is both justified and a sinner; but the Calvinist liturgy does not forget that this sinner must now associate himself with the good fight for the glory of God. The first recounts how God has become merciful to man; the second reminds man of the austere duty of obedience to God. To adore the sovereign Lord and serve him as revealed in his Word, that is what the worship rendered to God should lead to.

Whatever the case may be as to external differences in architecture or in the concrete expression of worship, Luther and Calvin meet in a common position which emphasizes the frontier between Protestantism and Catholicism. The Reformers, in reaction against a practical focussing of worship on the sacraments, which had overshadowed preaching and the importance of God's Word in the genesis of faith, displaced the axis of worship. They identified it with the Word to the extent of making of it the supreme means of the mediation of grace, while the sacraments became other modes of the proclamation of the Word. These one could strictly speaking do without, but it was good to use them since scripture mentioned them. The sacrament was a sign of the grace received, a promise of a greater future gift, a seal by which Christ confirmed his Word in us, but which in its essence added nothing to the proclamation of the Word which was sufficient, or to the grace that the Word alone conferred. The sacrament was an appendix, a corollary which had no value, except through what it confirmed or sealed.

The Reformers' intention was not to suppress the sacraments or the

[3] Nathaniel Micklem, ed., *Christian Worship* (1st edition, 1936; 3rd edition, 1954).

eucharistic liturgy, but to replace them in the perspective of the Word of God. In principle the Word of God was sufficient for everything; at the same time the sacraments were far from being a negligible quantity. They thus kept baptism and the Eucharist because they were explicitly mentioned in scripture. Luther also retained penance, but in a purely devotional sense, the sacraments, it is true, being so to speak incorporated in the Word.

Protestantism had been a reaction against the sacramental practice of the end of the Middle Ages which had established its centre of gravity on the Eucharist and the sacraments, forgetting that it was the revealed Word that alone explained their meaning. The essential bi-focalism of worship had in fact been reduced to a single centre—the sacraments. The Reformation adopted the contrary position—worship received as its centre of gravity the Word, the rest becoming accessory. The disappearance of the Mass as sacrifice was thus seen as inevitable. It would be replaced by communion in the Lord's Supper. At the same time the role of the Christian people in the liturgy was made more important because in a liturgy centred on proclamation all could be proclaimers. Hence the importance of psalms, hymns and chants in Protestant worship. It even came about that Luther separated the liturgy of the Last Supper from the liturgy of the Word and made a separate service of it. The magistrates of Geneva took upon themselves to draw the logical consequences of Calvin's position in the relationship between the liturgy of the Word and the liturgy of the Last Supper. They forced Calvin to agree that communion should only be given four times a year. Such was certainly not the intention of Luther or of Calvin in reforming worship. If the Word had become the centre of gravity it should in principle be accompanied by the communion which was its normal sequel. Communion had not the same importance as the Word, but it was the Word become visible and on this count it constituted a unity of celebration with the Word. Worship should have only one focus and that should be the Word. In principle, however, the Word could not be without the communion which was its corollary.

The reformed tradition was more obedient to the disciplinary rules laid down by the magistrates than to the principle of unity of worship posited by Calvin. The original principles of Calvin's doctrine in liturgy explain the restoration, now become fairly general, of the practice of communion in the reformed Churches. That was what Calvin had intended. In itself the Word possessed its own sufficiency but it required the seal of the sacrament as its confirmation and the two formed only one, the Word becoming visible in the sacrament.

What, according to Calvin, were the relations between Word and sacrament?[4]

[4] Ronald S. Wallace, *Calvin's Doctrine of the Word and Sacrament* (1957).

In the first place the sacraments were neither valid nor effective independently of the Word. Calvin called the sacraments appendices of the Gospel, seals as it were on a diploma which are nothing in themselves but draw their whole value from what is written on the parchment. Once separated from the Word, the human action in the sacrament had no meaning. But when the symbol became filled with the meaning given to it by the Word, then it became effective. For instance, when Christ breathed on the apostles, it was more than a breath that he conferred upon them; it was his own Spirit, and he declared to them explicitly the meaning of his action.

In the second place the sacraments were the seals of the Word. Through the sacraments God strengthened the power of his call. Man as a being of sense-perception needed these gestures which drew his attention, these symbols by which God made himself visible, by which he attested his presence. Man thus understood better what divine loving-kindness meant. It became perceptible to his eyes and was something more than a verbal declaration.

If the sacraments were visible forms of the Word, were they nothing more than mere seals? Calvin said, following St Augustine, that they were visible words. From the things of the senses man could deduce by analogy what spiritual things were, for if there was no likeness between the symbols used and the things signified, the signs would be deceptive and there would no longer be any sacrament. The sign that God had chosen was used because it already possessed a natural value as a symbol, the Word conferring upon it here and now the remainder of its significance. Why the tongues of fire on the day of Pentecost if not because of the analogy between the power of fire and the preaching of the apostles which was to consume everything as it passed? The sacrament which sealed the Word and represented it thus served at the same time to make it clearer and was a confirmation of it all the stronger for being more accessible.

The sacraments thus given, received and understood are a means of exchange between God and man. Through them God expresses himself to man and man, by the fact that he accepts them, signifies to God that he has understood the pattern of his Word. They serve as the link of a mutual belonging. When we receive them, we manifest to God that his Word is confirmed in us and we signify to the men who see us what the confession of our faith is.

But what is the final reality signified by the sacraments? It is essentially the union of Christians with the Incarnate Word in his humanity. The Gospel reveals to us that the union of Christians with Christ is a relation between Christ the Head and the Church which brings it about that the life of the Head is communicated to the Body which is the Church. Now the Word and the sacraments are the two means by which the mystical union of man with God is effected.

Calvin's teaching agrees with that of Luther as to the mode of this union; we are not dealing with a reality to be effected, but with a reality already effected. All that remains is to proclaim it by our preaching, the effect of which is prolonged and revealed by the sacraments. The preaching of the Gospel explains to us how the union between man and God has been produced, it proclaims its definitive realization. The sacraments are another way, more suited to our human weakness, of proclaiming and explaining the mystical union accomplished. When we receive them we make their value true for ourselves. Our share in the life of God hidden in Christ becomes revealed to us. The continuity between Christ and those pre-destined to salvation existed on the part of Christ, but did not exist as to us. Now what happens when this continuity is revealed to us? Calvin insists that we understand that this is called grace, but grace should not be understood as the participation by man in the divine nature under the forms of a reality of the ontological order conceived after the manner of a substance. Grace is the personal presence of Christ. Grace is, properly speaking, in God, not in us. What is in us, he says, is the effect of grace, namely the promise of salvation, the changing of our spiritual dispositions and the adoption of the Lord's standards.

To the question, is Christ truly communicated to us? Calvin can reply: assuredly, since it is the whole Christ who brings to bear on a dynamic action, with his whole being, humanity and divinity, flesh, blood and soul. Christ is truly given since he establishes a continuity between his substance and ours in a mystical manner. The whole Christ is the whole gift. Christ is in heaven and we are on earth, but between him and us a bond is drawn up and it is the Holy Spirit who is the author of it. The Spirit comes down into our soul and raises it up to give it communion in Christ's humanity. How can that actually come about? Calvin does not claim that we can understand the mystery. Here a miracle is in question and even several. How are we otherwise to explain, we who are on earth, that we can enter into communion with the humanity of Christ who is in heaven, and in this communion accomplish the heavenly action of here and now eating the flesh of Christ in a spiritual manner, of having him really present in us? Calvin wants us to understand that such is the meaning of the real presence of Christ in the Eucharist—it is a question of a real but heavenly presence which makes itself felt by mode of a dynamic presence that leaves the bread and wine unchanged after, as before, the pronouncing of the words of institution. He rejects any other interpretation, for otherwise the sacrifice of Christ on the Cross would appear to him incomplete. Christ died once for all and the whole work of salvation has been accomplished. But he has left us the communion as the symbol of his love and of his perfect gift. To receive it is to enter more deeply into the meaning of the proclamation of salvation through him.

The national Churches which emerged from the Reformation in Germany, England, Scotland, Scandinavia, the Low Countries, Denmark, the Swiss cantons and in Geneva, each established a type of worship which, while it remained proportionate to each nation, kept sufficient traditional elements and links with the generality of Christian worship for us to be able to qualify each of its forms with the name of liturgy of the classical type. With the appearance of the Nonconformist groups in Great Britain a new type of worship began which may be classified as radical.

C. PURITAN WORSHIP

In the rise of the Puritan movement in England must be seen a sequel to the introduction of elements of the Lutheran and Calvinistic reform under Edward VI. When Elizabeth decided to make Canterbury independent of Rome and Geneva and to establish her kingdom upon a religious formula that would take account of the three tendencies that the country had experienced up till then, neither the Catholic party nor the ultra-reformist party was satisfied. The latter, who had remained faithful to the Edwardian reform, worked towards an even purer reform, hence the name of Puritans. In turn the Acts of Uniformity passed by Parliament to unify worship in the kingdom, and the Book of Common Prayer, were gradually thrust aside. The Reformers began by the suppression of certain details of liturgical vestments, then they transferred the altar from the choir to the nave to make a communion table of it, they received the elements of the Eucharist seated instead of on their knees and refused to make the sign of the cross on infants during the administration of baptism. The revolt passed from the disciplinary to the doctrinal sphere and thence to separation. One section of those who were discontented remained in the Established Church, while the rest attacked it from outside. Gradually the separatists had to create their own liturgical substitutes. What were their fundamental claims? A purer worship, a form of ecclesiastical government founded on the Word of God, a religion in conformity with the practice of the apostles. This implied the abandonment of all that remained Catholic in the Established Church. They proclaimed the sufficiency and supremacy of the Word of God and in the matter of liturgy only intended to retain the elements that seemed to them in conformity with the will of God—prayer, praise, preaching, baptism and the sacrament of the Lord's Supper, catechetical teaching and the practice of ecclesiastical discipline. The people as a whole, and not only the choir, were to be associated with the celebration of praise. But, above all, preaching was to occupy the centre of worship because it was the declaration of the truth of salvation to the people of God. They kept baptism and the Lord's Supper, but they celebrated them in a narrative and purely indicative manner and did not make of them sacraments in the Catholic sense. They were opposed to the liberty that the Holy Spirit should retain in men's hearts and they ordinarily practised "prophetism", that is, private interpretation of the words of scripture among themselves.[5]

A difference of method separated Puritans and separatists. The latter were marked off from the rest of the reforming Puritans in that they believed that schism with the Established Church was not too great a price to pay for the attainment of their convictions. The others remained in the Established Church, acting in it as a leaven the strength of which came from the example of the separatists.

The characteristic features of the separatists, whence came Congregationalists, Baptists and Methodists, appeared clearly to the Anglicans those of a sect—opposition to institutional forms, the requirement of personal experience of salvation, the claim of the importance of each layman in the Church.

That which forms the dignity of classical worship, radical Protestantism rejected—that is, the presence of an objective piety valid for a whole Church, the ability to bring to the hearts of men the transcendent realities under a wide variety of symbols, the fullness which unites the richness of the visible gifts to the invisible realities. As to sacraments, it preferred the mediation of scripture alone; as to government, equality of all the faithful, and in the matter of doctrine the personal inspiration of the Holy Spirit who expressed himself freely in the personal conscience. Hence arose the features perpetuated to the present day in the denominations resulting from the Puritan movement—their prophetic and antisacramental character, impatience in bearing with ecclesiastical control and the demand for spiritual liberty.

For the Baptists, for instance, baptism should not be considered as a sacrament which brings the grace of regeneration to man, but as an act of surrender of oneself to God— hence their insistence on the bond between baptism and the expression of personal faith. In baptism, according to them, man is an agent, not a receiver, and no act accomplished by the community can be substituted for the action in which each man clothes his total response to God.

For the Congregationalists, participation in the sacrament of the Lord's Supper is considered as a gesture by which the Christian expresses the faith that is his and the love he has for his brothers.

For the Quakers, who represent the extreme evolution of Puritan principles, the rejection of external forms and tangible signs is considered

[5] Evelyn Underhill, *Worship* (1936, 1957); Horton Davies, *The Worship of the English Puritans* (1948), and *The English Free Churches* (1952).

289

as of the essence of Christian worship. Christians come together in the meeting-house and in silence listen to God's Word in their heart. From this emerges a form of worship of a type unique in the Christian world— a collective expectation of the illumination of the inner light in the mystical contemplation of God's Word and of communal silence. They are sure that the presence of God is in the midst of them since the Lord said that he would be where his followers were gathered together. Worship takes place in silence in order to mark clearly the transcendence of the Wholly Other as well as his immanent presence in the soul. No minister to lead the worship is needed. Why should he be in worship that takes place in silence in which the Word as inner light is separated from the scriptures? If we were to look for a point of comparison with Catholicism, it might be said that a gathering of this kind resembles the contemplative prayer made in silence in a monastery where each soul comes to seek the inner light and express its dependence on God. Quaker religion has made a radical choice between the Word and the sacraments, between a form of worship wholly interior and spiritual and one of which preaching and the sacraments are the tangible structure.

D. BETWEEN WHAT FOCAL POINTS DO THESE FORMS OF WORSHIP EVOLVE?

This general sketch has revealed two common types—an institutional worship characterized by clearly defined rites and ceremonies of which the Word alone, or Word and sacrament, are the centre; and a type of worship which is so to speak the "outcome of events", characterized by the greater or lesser spontaneity of its prayer and liberty in regard to institutional liturgical forms.

This classification must be understood with the necessary elasticity. Clearly the institutional type of worship does not fail to take account of the part played by the free action of the sovereign Word or by individual religious action. The appellation here given refers to a framework, an order of rites and ceremonies. Anglican worship, for instance, is institutional in type. On the other hand, other forms of worship that allow of a large proportion of prayers or exhortations composed for a particular service can even so be classed as institutional.

The second classification which principally marks the charismatic, free and independent character of liturgical expression is not always devoid of all institutional aspect. The Quakers themselves come together in a meeting-house and they do come to accept the offices of a minister.

Up to a certain extent it could perhaps be said that the first tendency corresponds with classical Protestantism, and the second with radical Protestantism, the first type corresponding to characteristics that are more or less objective and the second to more or less subjective elements. It seems, moreover, that the whole history of worship evolves in a tension between several series of focal points—objective expression and subjective expression, community form of worship and individual form of worship, devotion ordered to a pattern and spontaneous devotion. When liturgy becomes too objective, too ritualistic, too formal, it causes the emergence of peripheral zones of the community of the faithful intent upon rediscovering personal, joyous and enthusiastic contact with the principle of their salvation. Many Protestant sects are born of this instinctive tendency to seek for personal experience in religion. Even in Catholicism, have not sects arisen as the will's outlet for a religious expression which no longer found a place in the institutional forms? The birth of a sect or the danger of an outbreak can very well be a sign of the judgement of God. Already analysis of the typology and the conclusions that can be drawn from it show us that a balanced worship should be both prophetic and sacramental, institutional and personal. No names can be instanced of important mystics emerging from systems of worship of the so-called charismatic type. Many can be mentioned who have come from the institutional type, so much does the interior life need an order, an order and a structure. Above all, we must not forget that sects usually originate from a search for personal experience of salvation and in reaction against a form of religion considered too mechanical, too external, too heavy.

3. Anglican worship

The typology of the forms of worship in the Protestant world has shown us that the centre of worship is and remains the Word, even with the contemporary restoration of communion.

Anglican worship could not be classed purely and simply in the category of forms of Protestant worship. It requires to be understood in the logic of the position of the Anglican Communion; Catholic, but Reformed; Reformed but Catholic, incorporating in itself in a way which is peculiar to it both Catholic and Protestant elements.

The Lambeth Conferences throw light on this position. First of all and before all, there is at the heart of the Anglican Communion the Prayer Book, the concrete symbol of Anglicanism and the organ *par excellence* of its tradition.[6] It establishes the character of the liturgical and theological position of the Anglican Communion. It is not surprising that the Eucharist should be called "the summit of Christian worship"[7] because there the

[6] *The Lambeth Conference* (1948), p. 83.
[7] *Ibid.* (1930), p. 82.

Presence is found and there again the barriers between man and God disappear.

Eucharistic worship is not, in the Anglican Communion, an accidental element in its liturgy but an essential part conjoined to the liturgy of the Word with which it forms a unity.

The Anglican liturgical tradition is valuable and it is guarded devoutly. For the Anglican Communion it is *the* means beyond all others of its insertion in the universal Church.

This worship is thus Catholic but it is also reformed, it contains both Catholic and Protestant elements which are maintained according to the unity of dialectic tension. Officially the Anglican Communion rejects the definitions of the Council of Trent on transubstantiation and on the Mass as a sacrifice of propitiation. From this can be seen how many things separate us, although many unite us.

4. The essence of Protestantism interpreted in terms of the Church's worship

Would it be possible to pick out, among the variety of forms and types of worship mentioned, the impact of the principles at the heart of the Reformation? Is there at bottom a common position, very broad indeed, but which it is given to every Protestant to be aware of, in the worship of any denomination originating from the Reformation, which is not in Catholic or Orthodox worship?

In trying to establish this we necessarily risk displeasing every single one of the denominations. None of them will admit that their particular worship is identical with that of any other sect. Let us understand that we are here dealing with the releasing of a common substance which does not exist in the state of abstraction but under different modes of realization. It will, moreover, be possible to make a test of the accuracy of these principles by reclothing them with each of the forms from which they are taken. Do they fit in with Lutheran worship, with Methodist or Quaker worship, etc.? If the reply is affirmative, the point is proved.

A. THE ABSOLUTE PRIMACY OF THE WORD AND OF THE LITURGY OF THE WORD

The crux of the matter here consists in the relationship between Word and Sacrament. In Protestantism primacy of the Word does not exclude the sacraments. Two at least are accepted which are so clearly expressed in scripture that they cannot but be accepted—baptism and the Eucharist.

Protestantism has always protested against any mechanical interpretation of the sacraments that assimilates their effect, for instance, to the automatic production of light when we touch an electricity switch. The protest has been extended to the general interpretation of the role of sacraments in the Catholic Church, which Protestantism classes as magic. The sacraments, it asserts, should be administered in close connection with the preaching of the Word and it is on this condition that they can be received by the faith of believers.

This last assertion can be materially accepted in a Catholic perspective but it is essential to see how it stands apart in relation to a Protestant background. In Protestantism the sacrament is another mode of the Word and it is the Word of God that is the true and great sacrament. Behind every sacrament there is scripture whose word—or the act of God revealing himself—serves to call men, to choose them from the heart of the crowd, to gather them together and unite them. Preaching and the Bible really appear as sacraments of the action of God revealing himself in men's hearts, of the Word that re-echoes there. Protestantism considers that no sacrament can replace this primordial role of the Word and of those sacraments homogeneous to it that it has chosen, namely the scriptures and preaching. Sacramental effectiveness is thus wholly brought back there. It is exercised at the very moment when the Word makes use of it, that is, at the very moment when faith arises in man's heart. It is for this reason that Protestantism is so strict about personal faith as a prior condition for the reception of all the sacraments.

The Word of God is prior to all the sacraments; it is also the perfect sacrament. Among the Reformers we often find the statement that the Word of God is the perfect sacrament, the only one which could exist without the substance of Christianity finding itself changed thereby. This principle that they enunciated without the intention of its being applied has been pushed to its logical conclusion in the later history of the Reformation. It is this that is responsible for the liturgical impoverishment which has for a long time predominated and from which today people desire to free themselves.

The Word of God is in short the central sacrament from which all the others receive their light. What is baptism but a new way of saying what the Word has already declared? The Eucharist but a new way of producing the union that the Word has already wrought? Though a new way, it is substantially the same, the mode alone changing, having regard to the needs of our human nature. No new grace is communicated, it is the same and the sole grace that is sealed, for grace is in God and not in us. The Word of God reveals to us that God is full of grace for us and the sacraments set the seal on God's declaration.

What are the intimate relations uniting Word and sacrament? If we keep to the conclusions that have been drawn from the analysis of the forms of worship in Protestantism, we must come to see that no single answer exists. The one that we choose to give at this particular moment is that which corresponds to the general tendencies at the present time. The *Formula Missae* which is Luther's principal liturgical writing, and his "German Mass", are as it were an ellipse with two focal points—the Word and the Sacrament. Calvin claims a similar equilibrium for worship in Geneva. But, with Zwingli, communion was eliminated from the beginning. Disaffection for the sacrament of the Lord's Supper quickly gained hold of the people and pietism and rationalism confirmed the exclusion of communion.

Today a general reversal of attitude can be envisaged. A new equilibrium of worship is being sought for. It is thus in function of the latter tendency that we want to show how these relations are established.

It is considered that the primacy of the Word of God does not mean exclusivity, as if the sacraments were of no value, nor does it mean dilution of the sacraments in the Word of God as if they were without consistency. What comes after the Word of God retains its value and can even have a certain primacy with regard to order. The Word is first in that it awakens us to faith, in that it establishes the sacraments by conferring on material things a new meaning—an eschatological meaning—and a pneumatic value that the Lord himself assigned to them. The sacraments, for their part, have something more than the Word. They are more of a community element for they integrate believers concretely with their Head and with his Body which is the Church. Worship can in the last resort be maintained without sacrament, the Word can exist without the sacrament and bear fruit, but the sacrament can never exist without the Word. The Word, however, normally only bears its full fruit when it is associated with the sacrament, for then it is incarnate, tangible, concrete, it touches man in his whole being and in his situation. It is more in conformity with the line of the redeeming Incarnation, it manifests to a greater degree that God is Word, action and Incarnation. In other words, the Word attains its greatest expansion when it is united to the sacrament.[8]

In this perspective of organic union of Word and sacrament, the Word appears as a sacrament which can be heard and the sacrament as a Word become visible. Both are linked up to the presence of God by the grace of the Holy Spirit. Scripture, in fact, only becomes Word of God for me in the liturgy if the Holy Spirit lights up its meaning in my heart and the sacrament only possesses its true meaning, that is the eschatological one,

---

[8] Roger Will, "Parole et Sacrement", *Études Théologiques et Religieuses* 22 (1947), no. 3–4, p. 195; See also: Bruce, *op. cit.;* William Nicholls, *Jacob's Ladder: The Meaning of Worship* (1958): Oscar Cullmann and F. J. Leenhardt, *Essays on the Lord's Supper* (1958); O. Cullmann, "La signification de la Sainte Cène dans le christianisme primitif", *Revue d'Histoire et de Philosophie religieuse* (1936), and F. J. Leenhardt, "Ceci est mon Corps", *Cahiers théologiques* 37 (1955).

through the liaison that the Holy Spirit brings about between the material sign and the thing signified.

Several explanations of Protestant worship are today moving in the same direction. One could sometimes have the impression that they come very close to Catholicism, for instance that of Richard Paquier.[9] However, after consideration it will be realized that what separates us is the word Presence. Word and sacrament are considered in relation to the Presence, certainly, and the latter is manifested in worship, but the explanation after all does not leave the orbit of the principles of the Reformation, for the mystery of worship is established in reference to a type of virtual, and not real, presence, which comes infinitely close to man, which establishes with him so to say a contiguity of substance, but finally leaves the contact tangential. It is asserted that the action of the sacraments should not be separated from the Word; in spite of all it does seem that difference between Word and sacrament is only modal. The sacrament is revalued, but something of its complete power is still lacking to it. The Lutheran doctrine of the *companatio*, according to which the real presence of Christ is juxtaposed with the eucharistic elements and the sacraments contain a particular reality, would perhaps be closer to Catholicism.

B. THE IMMEDIACY AND TRANSCENDENCE OF THE RELATION BETWEEN CHRIST, THE HEAD OF WORSHIP, AND THE CHRISTIAN

The first principle of Protestantism—the transcendent and radical primacy of the Word—reveals the first characteristic of Protestant worship. Before all else it is a dialogue. At the origin of all things that have to do with man, there is God who speaks and man who replies. The same holds good for worship. In it God reveals what he is—the supreme and absolute initiator of the dialogue he maintains with man, whence necessarily comes the very great importance given in Protestant worship to everything to do with the Word and with the signs which proclaim it. Man must see that it is not he who must declare the secret of the world, the order of the economy of salvation. It is for God to tell man what he must do and no vain philosophical or moralizing speech must be substituted for the terrible and omniscient Word of God. We must allow God to speak and man must listen. When he replies to God, his gesture is expressed as a proclamation which he seals with those perceptible signs which are the sacraments. The centre of worship is the proclamation of the Word. The sacraments are not rites that effect what they signify, but signs which declare, show and promise a reality already effected by Christ. It is not the rite of baptism that effectively regenerates, but in baptism our

[9] *Traité de liturgie* (1954), chapter iv: "Parole et Sacrement".

295

regeneration is declared, demonstrated. What is accomplished by the sacrament is much more the manifestation of what has happened than an effect which is produced here and now for us and makes us at this very moment participators in supernatural life. Finally, in Protestantism, the sacraments appear as so many other languages of the Word which tell us in another manner what the letter of scripture declares to us. The sacrament of baptism expresses to us that once for all the Church has been purified and justified, made perfect in Christ, while the sacrament of the Lord's Supper tells us that it is every day that the Church needs to be renewed, restored, sanctified in the work that Christ has accomplished vicariously for us. How can this be accomplished? The only way for the Church is to shelter herself and take refuge in the worship that Christ, the High Priest of the new law, offered to his Father. Thus dead, buried and risen again in the vicarious offering of Christ, the Church can move forward towards God and associate herself with the celebration of the worship of which Christ is the sovereign Head and the sole celebrant.

Is the worship that the Church on earth offers to God only a simple memorial of the perfect worship offered by Christ, an announcement of the eternal worship which will be revealed to the eyes of men after the Parousia, or has it indeed a real value of actual Presence?

This is the ever present question of the meaning of the Presence of eschatology while the Church is on earth. Jesus offered perfect worship to his Father. Is the worship the Church offers to God on earth only another way for Christ to proclaim again before men, by his revealed Word and the sacraments, what he once accomplished for us? In a word, is Christian worship to be reduced to a kind of liturgical occasionalism, to a symbolical recall, to a virtual and tangential contact, or is it truly worship celebrated literally by Christ-in-his-Church?

For us and for Protestantism scripture and the sacraments are eschatological institutions and events because they come from the world of definitive realities and with all their being tend to lead us there, but there is a difference of interpretation. Catholic worship is founded on faith in the actual action of the Presence which brings about effectively, by the signs which it employs, what the signs signify according to scripture and tradition. There is thus a commemoration of the mysteries of the Lord, anticipation of their final revelation, and the actual real presence of Christ, Head of Christian worship. The root of the difficulty between Protestantism and Catholicism lies in the interpretation of the Presence, for it is the meaning given to this that determines acceptance or refusal of the visible mediation of the Church. Worship founded on the idea of a Church *simul justa et peccatrix* hidden in the Lord, who clothes her with his justice, necessarily involves impossibility of participation in the priesthood of Christ by man. In such a worship the priesthood of Christ can only be seen exercising itself in a transcendental and immediate manner; Christ is the sole and only celebrant, men are only his witnesses; it is definitely Christ alone who performs the worship and our action is only a witness of the perfect worship which he rendered once to God; it is a reminder, a memorial. It is thus a matter of entering into the worship of Christ—which is true in a certain sense—but as it were into a perfect action accomplished vicariously for us. It is Christ who makes and who has made the perfect act of worship, the Church has only to proclaim it.

The place of the priesthood in Christian worship is a thorny one, so much do Catholicism and Protestantism there engage their fundamental convictions. Our friends the Protestant pastors and ministers pay homage in the priest not to the priesthood but to the person who consecrates himself to the divine and to souls and any priest who frequents ecumenical milieux may well meet with the most utter resistance to his priesthood, even though he will be welcomed with the greatest friendship. We cannot ask our very dear friends of other confessions to accept our priesthood, but they will admit that this is something most dear to us and their kindness will not refuse to let us associate with them what is most dear to us, since they are already in our friendship.

We are thus separated on the point of worship by very serious divisions.

But if our Protestant brethren ask us to weigh the motives of our interpretation well, perhaps they in their turn will agree to reconsider theirs? For us as for them, the vision of Christianity is an organic vision. They reject participation in the priesthood of Christ in the name of one conception of the presence of Christ in his Church while we accept it in the name of another. They reject the idea of sacrifice in Christian worship in the name of a doctrine of the union of the Christian with Christ, while we accept it in the name of another doctrine. And each of the points in dispute could thus be taken up.

The root of the opposition is nothing but the interpretation of the relation between Word and sacrament in conformity with two eschatological doctrines. We believe that in the Catholic priesthood it is the eternal Incarnate Word, mediator between God and men, who makes himself visible; in the sacrifice of the Mass, we believe that it is the Word offered in holocaust on the Cross who makes himself sacramentally visible, today as on Calvary. And it is thus that the Word, who willed to become incarnate, continues to make himself visible through the power of the Holy Spirit.

Let us put it in other terms. In Catholic worship Christ the Eschaton continues to pursue the unfolding of his mysteries according to the schema of the worship which his Incarnation has revealed to us. He continues to make use of the ministry of mankind and of tangible things as he did in the days of his earthly life. He unites these earthly elements to heavenly elements according to the same type of sacramental relation that he adopted, so that the ultimate realities might come down to us and that through them we might rise to God. The Holy Spirit whom he sent to his Church to dwell there permanently remains in the Church to be the link between time and eschatology.

Catholic ecclesiology is founded on the idea of continuity of Presence—Christ was truly present on earth in the days of the Incarnation; we believe he is so still but in a mystical manner. How is this possible? Christ, by his Resurrection-Ascension has become wholly Spirit. He can thus terminate any sacramental or ministerial action which is done in his name. If Christ had not died or risen again or gone up to heaven, the Church would doubtless have been of a different type—its heart would have been the historical presence of the Incarnate Word indefinitely prolonged until the end of time. But the accomplishment of the last eschatological events which are called the Death on the Cross, the Resurrection and the Ascension has allowed Christ to continue to remain really present in his Church under the mode of mystery and sacrament, and Pentecost revealed to the apostles that the presence of Christ in mystery had become the proper manner according to which Christ would remain really present in his Church.

Why the Incarnation and why Pentecost? Can we ignore one or the other mystery? Some hidden link must exist between them, since they come from the same wisdom. The Incarnation is the basis of the presence of Christ in his Church; Pentecost is the completion of the revelation of the Presence in mystery.

A real continuity links the Incarnation to the Death on the Cross, the Resurrection, the Ascension, Pentecost and the final consummation. It is the continuity of the Presence. Jesus is the Eschaton, the final reality. He can thus make himself present in mystery to his Church. He did so, moreover, in this new manner after his Resurrection, in his contacts with his Church; but, with Pentecost, he revealed to the Church the new type of his Presence in mystery and it is that on which we live and that through which all the past acts of the life of Jesus reach us in their particular virtue. Thus we love to see in the eucharistic Presence the real presence of Christ in mystery; in the sacraments the Word who makes himself visible and audible; in the priestly ministry the Presence that fills such men with its power for such and such sacred acts; in the whole Church the Word who makes himself visible to the rest of mankind.

C. THE NATURE OF THE CHURCH AS WITNESS IN RELATION TO THE PRIESTLY ACT OF CHRIST

In order thoroughly to understand Protestant worship, it is essential to see that at the root of it is the idea that it is God and God alone, or Christ alone who makes of it a divine service. Whatever be the Protestant name for the liturgical celebration, "worship" or "divine service", the essential idea is the same. "The divine service of the Church", said Karl Barth, "is in the first place, in its origin and essence, a divine act, in the second place only, in a derived and accidental manner, a human act. Man can and should only serve. God alone and not man makes it a divine service. It is God who wills that this service be celebrated, God who supplies the appropriate means, God who proffers his grace through their intermediary, God who makes use of it to awaken, purify and fortify faith. All along the line, it is God who acts and not man."[10]

The word witness is indeed what in Protestantism characterizes the role of the Church in relation to the action of Christ, Head of Christian worship. How are we to understand this word in function of the Church as worshipping community?

The Church is the effect of the Word who has called men and gathered them together. In it God addresses men. It is the situation of the dialogue between him and the world. God in the Church takes men to witness to himself and makes them his witnesses. The Church is God's great witness. She knows God's plan, his gestures and his marvels. It is the Word who has taught them to her and the sacraments have added to their confirmation. The life of the Church as a whole is thus centred on the Word, who is at the root of her birth, life and action. The liturgical life of this people of witnesses is logically presented under the features of testimony—the Church in worship sets forth her faith, she says over again as a body to God and before men what she knows of God, she corrects herself through adherence to the Word, she proclaims her obedience to God, pledges herself to remain under his sovereignty, seals her communion with the thought and will of God by the sacraments, particulary that of the Last Supper; in a word, the people of God meet as a worshipping community to bear witness to God. They meet together as a witness to the pure and spotless oblation offered by Christ, once only and in a perfect manner, on Calvary, as witness to the permanency of this sacrificial offering in heaven for eternity.

The community gathered together for worship is a community that witnesses to its faith in the great eschatological gestures accomplished by Christ that the Word of God has revealed to it. It is also a community

[10] *Connaître Dieu et le servir*, p. 177.

299

that lives in expectation. The celebration of the Last Supper recalls the necessity of this to it. The Lord has commanded that the acts he accomplished at the Last Supper be done in memory of him and has ordered them to be done over and over again until he returns. By the proclamation of the Word of God the worshipping community lives in the memory of the Lord's Death. Through communion in the Last Supper it lives in expectation of the revelation of the full Presence of him who is signified by the symbols.

As witness of the past and witness of the future, the worshipping assembly commemorates and announces the acts of salvation of the Lord. It refers to the transcendental Presence of the priestly act offered once for all by the Saviour, the virtue of which extends to the assembly through the mediation of scripture which the sacraments come to seal. In this liturgy there is only one priest and that is the Lord, and his priesthood is shared equally by all his witnesses. Protestant worship is precisely the witness to this unique priesthood, the presence of which transcends the Church's worship.

If Protestants ask themselves what is the value of Catholic worship, they can be assured that we ask ourselves the same question about their worship.

What, then, from our point of view is the value of Protestant worship, first of all as regards the liturgy of the Word? Can the Word be preached with supernatural effectiveness in Protestantism?

The choice of the Twelve as official witnesses meant that the revealed message required to be proclaimed in an authentic manner, that is, by a mission coming from God. The apostle is one with him who sends him and consequently the presence of the one who gives him his mission is found again in him. Truth of preaching thus requires authenticity of mission. Now how is an authentic mission for preaching received? According to the teaching of the Catholic Church, it is by apostolic succession. The bishops are the successors of the apostles and the mission of preaching reverts to them in their own right. As they cannot exercise the whole of it by themselves, they are obliged to delegate it.

We know how mission and the authority to preach are understood in the Protestant world. There apostolic succession is understood as independent of episcopal succession. It simply means succession in zeal, in teaching and in apostolic work. It is clear also that a Protestant denomination which confers the function of preaching on a pastor does not intend to give him a canonical mission to preach.

Are we to conclude from this that every Protestant pastor or minister is only a pseudo-preacher, or even a false prophet, at the time when he is preaching? We know to what extent an affirmative answer is a grave insult to Protestants. We must in the first place admit the presence of authentic

300

values and riches of Christianity in Protestantism. The scripture is among these. Now we must recognize, and it is the Word of God itself that says so (Is 55:10–11; Rom 1:16), that it, the Word, possesses an effectiveness of its own for the salvation of every man who believes.[11] Consequently, Protestant preaching, centred on the Bible, possesses by virtue of the Word of God, an effectiveness of its own that must be recognized, unless one wants to insult the Word of God itself. But, it will be said, if the Word of God is explained in the sense of the principles of the Reformation, what becomes of the distinction introduced between the Word of God as such and the confessional framework in which it is delivered? Will not the Word of God make this denomination authentic?

It is certain that, from the existential point of view, preaching and the mode of preaching are one. In a straight road, there is not the straightness and then the road by the side of it, it is the road which is straight or which eventually curves. It is God alone who can sort out where the frontier passes between authenticity and deviation. But we should say that the more preaching is biblical and objective, the more truly the supernatural effectiveness of the Word makes itself felt there, and, therefore, the more it tends to unity and to true apostolicity.

This distinction was made as to the object of the preaching. What is the position now in relation to the minister of the Word?

The Protestant minister receives no canonical mission to preach from any sort of authority and, moreover, he claims none. What are his letters of credence and on what is his authority founded? It rests, on the personal plane, essentially on his quality as servant and witness. He is the servant of the Word in the world. He is the disciple who must bear witness to his Master's teaching. His faith and his baptism, the charismata of evangelization that he may receive from the Holy Spirit and even the ministerial grace that may be given to him on the occasion of his ordination to the ministry, are so many titles to the ministry of preaching in the Protestant world.[12]

The ministry of preaching is situated in the general liturgy of the Word in which the people participate by the responses, hymns and psalms. What we have said of the value of the ministry of preaching is valid analogically for the witness that the congregation renders to the Word of God in the liturgy of the Word.

What is to be said of the liturgy of the sacrament?

Can we not see in the celebration of the Last Supper a vestige of the celebration of the Eucharist such as we understand it? And would not this

[11] A. Béa, "Valeur pastorale de la parole de Dieu dans la liturgie", *Maison-Dieu* 47–48 (1956), pp. 127–48.
[12] Avery Dulles, "The Protestant Preacher and the Prophetic Mission", *Theological Studies* 21 (1960), pp. 544—80.

celebration thereby have a certain objective value, in addition to a value in relation to the personal piety of the participants? We do not there recognize a full valid sacrament, but is there no objective sacramental value? Similarly, in the preaching made by a pastor, although we do not recognize a full and authentic apostolic mission, we do not say that this preaching is thereby denuded of all apostolic value, just as, moreover, in the Protestant denominations, although we do not recognize that they are fully a Church we do not wish to deny them all ecclesial value.

We might conclude with Father Schillebeeckx: "If we have stated with St Thomas that even the pagan 'natural sacraments' have a certain positive value, and if we have seen, again with St Thomas, an implicit reference to the mystery of Christ, it is clear *a priori* that, even more than the Jewish sacraments, the sacraments of the separated Churches have a *certain sacramental* value and are in this measure fruitful in grace. Here we have not only the richness of a human sacramentality in general, but an explicit portion of Christianity."[13]

II. THE MOVEMENT OF CLOSER PROXIMITY ALONG THE LINES OF WORSHIP

1. Between Christian communions other than the Roman

The integration which is going on in the world of communions which have emerged from the Reformation has not made itself felt in the same way or to the same degree in all the aspects of the ecumenical problem. Intensive on the external plane of inter-denomination relations, it is more hesitant in the sphere of worship. It is, in fact, easier to reach administrative agreement than to establish a fundamental understanding on the problem of worship. But any degree of integration, even often of inter-denominational cooperation, inevitably involves repercussions in the sphere of worship. If two groups, whether close or remote in their traditions, decide to establish links, they must immediately foresee also what their links in the sphere of worship will be. Moreover, the problem recurs not only each time union between religious groups is in question, but also on the occasion of an ecumenical work camp, of a study session at the Ecumenical Institute, or on the occasions of meetings of the Central Committee or of the General Assembly.

It is perhaps this difficulty of worship which most hinders the development of the ecumenical movement. Since the question of union is linked to that of communion, one hesitates to plunge into the most

[13] *Le Christ, Sacrement de la rencontre de Dieu*, p. 231.

advanced forms of union because one feels incapable of effecting unity in the matter of worship. Certain formulas, such as, "let us pray together whatever be our form of worship and we shall thus join Christ, the Head of worship, who will indeed know how to straighten out the convergence of our sentiments"; or else, "let us celebrate the Last Supper together and give it interiorly the interpretation of our belief", leave a feeling of disappointment, for this prayer made in these dispositions, which is practically the only eventuality possible, does not express communion in the depths of souls and minds, even when it expresses union of hearts.

Under the typology of the forms of worship in the world of the communions coming from the Reformation are hidden many concrete and personal dramas. The problem of worship is that of prayer; now in prayer each one delivers his whole being as a man in this world. But, one Church believes that worship should rest on institutional forms; others put their confidence in less rigid forms, they have confidence in the prophetic charismata that they consider present in their congregation, which give a character of creative spontaneity to worship. Others also consider that it is good that worship should "turn native" when it takes root in new territories. These different attractions are not merely sentiments of pure preference. They correspond to a particular vision of Christ as Pastor and of the Spirit as inspirer of the Church. The responses of the Churches in the Lund report[14] should be read if we are to realize the depth of the debate involved and its repercussions on the religious life of the denominations.

But it is already wonderful that the denominations emerging from the Reformation have agreed to discuss among themselves a question as delicate and intimate as that of worship. When we look at these men who come from all communions to seek together the ways of obedience to God in the unity of worship, we cannot do otherwise than think that the Lord has put under our eyes something of great value.

It is thus very far from the case that the disparity of forms of worship sets no problem for the Protestant world. It does not consider the matter with indifference. One common conviction stimulates the concern for coming closer together and that is the impossibility of arriving at the proclamation of the visible unity of the Church so long as the liturgical fragmentation persists. Yet what perplexity can we not sense in the search for ways of unity of worship? Some believe that the practice of liturgical communion will lead to unity; the rest maintain that participation in the same eucharistic communion could only be the conclusion of a series

---

[14] *Responses of the Churches to Lund* (1952). See also Paul S. Minear, ed., *Faith and Order Findings. The Report to the Fourth World Conference on Faith and Order, Montreal, 1963* (1963), report of the Theological Commission on Worship.

of preliminary unions. No more than one can very well see what form the visible unity of the Church will take, can one be definite as to the best ways to arrive at unity of worship. Certain people think that the true formula is that of an ecumenical worship, but their enthusiasm falls in the face of tenacious convictions in the matter of confessional liturgy. They become discouraged in finding that a time comes when liturgical *rapprochement* reaches a ceiling that it can no longer get beyond because it clashes with resistance which is all the more vigorously asserted just because it is sincere.

However this may be, the ecumenical movement is set upon a path along which it intends to persevere. Moreover, we can see the remarkable results already achieved.

The first is the liturgical revival. This phenomenon is due on the one hand to the influence of the ecumenical movement, but also to other extra-ecumenical factors, such as the theocentric and christological tendency in contemporary Protestant theology. To some degree everywhere a reaction has shown itself against the "spiritualism" of the past generations who, satisfied with inward devotion, had reduced the tangible acts of worship to the minimum. The sermon has been likewise reproached with falling too often into subjectivism and overpersonal interpretations and with having pushed into the background the universal objectivity of revelation. The experience itself of the indefinite multiplication of the Protestant denominations led to the conclusion that the exclusive preponderance of preaching in worship necessarily encouraged the fragmentation of religious groups. Moreover, by virtue of an authentic religious instinct, a tendency occurred towards a revaluation of the sacramental aspect with the conviction that certain concrete realities are poles eminently capable not only of holding back the slide towards denominational fragmentation, but also of restoring unity.

It is in this way that a reaction has occurred in favour of worship established both on the Word and the sacrament of the Last Supper. One no longer runs the risk today, in the Protestant world, of being taxed with disloyalty to the Reformation if one maintains that the two centres of worship are the Word and the sacrament. The argument is brought forward that the most ancient documents mentioned worship centred on the Word after the pattern of the synagogue worship, and sometimes, joined with it, an *agape* eventually accompanied by the celebration of the Eucharist, on the occasion of which, perhaps frequently, charismata of prophecy or glossalalia were manifested. It is also mentioned that the Didache, written in the sub-apostolic period, gives, in its description of worship in the Christian-Jewish milieux, an example of union of Eucharist and *agape*. From the second century onward, Christian worship would have found its equilibrium between liturgy of the Word and liturgy of the Cenacle, or, of the sacrament of the Last Supper, as the first apology of St Justin bears witness. And one could thus, century by century, as much in East as in West, retrace the two foundations of the unity of Christian worship.

The admission of this fact is a happy event. Do not let us see in it, however, a pure and simple admission of the Eucharist such as we understand it.[15] The words of institution of the Eucharist are repeated and communion is given, but the real presence of the Word Incarnate is not there and the celebration of the liturgy of the sacrament has not the meaning of the sacrament of the sacrifice of the Lord; what it is is a memorial in which Christ is present symbolically, indeed even virtually by the effect it can produce in us. The Protestant Reformation was willed as a return to the true primitive form of worship from which there was a departure in fairly early times, as is evidenced, we are assured, by the *Traditio Apostolica* of St Hippolytus, who in reaction against the Jewish elements in the liturgy supposedly gave the central place to the idea of passion and expiation.

The liturgical revival in the Protestant world is at the present time in conformity with this interpretation. It is to this that the new liturgical books used by the various denominations conform and it is from this that the order of worship in the new communions resulting from inter-denominational unions take their inspiration.

It is remarkably interesting to follow the evolution of the liturgy, especially in the trans-confessional unions, such, for instance, as the United Church of Canada and the Church of South India. In these two bodies we find a wish, let us call it ecumenical, to integrate the liturgical experience of the Church of all time, as much of the East as of the West, trying to join the principle of a fixed form of ceremony with the necessary proportion of religious spontaneity which falls to personal charismas.

It is difficult to pronounce on the value of these two liturgies. That of the United Church of Canada seems indeed rather an outline sketch than the evidence of an important phase; as to that of South India, it will be necessary to see it at work over several years.[16]

The substantial agreement effected in the equilibrium of worship in the process of restoration in the Protestant world has expressed itself in two ways that we shall briefly mention: a certain number of agreements or consensus and the search for inter-communion.

The official report on the third Conference on Faith and Order held

---

[15] Max Thurian, *L'Eucharistie, Mémorial du Seigneur, Sacrifice d'Action de grâce et d'Inter-cession* (1959); J. J. Von Allmen, *Worship: Its Theology and Practice* (1965).
[16] T. S. Garrett, *Worship in South India* (1958).

at Lund in 1952[17] sets out the degree of understanding already arrived at in the doctrinal order and the first ecumenical fruits that have resulted from it. Unity of worship on the basis of Word and sacrament, and the conviction that worship is a work of the community and of the Church which concerns the whole of man, are the main points of agreement reached. But in what way are Word and sacrament to be adjusted to each other? What role must be allotted to the minister of worship? Up to what point must worship comprise a proportion of spontaneous and charismatic expression? How can the elements of creation be incorporated in worship? Finally, can the unique and unrepeatable expiation which Christ offered once and in a perfect manner for man's salvation do without the liturgical celebration? On all these questions opinions remain divided.

The drawing together between the Christian communions has brought about a strength of union called inter-communion. Bishop O. S. Tomkins has pointed out that this word in itself has a strange sound and is a typical product of the divisions, for either we are in communion with one another or else in a state of schism or separation.[18] The word is based on an anomaly, for all the denominations have a distinct communion and claim the right to their own sacramental expression. Liturgical, and in particular, sacramental relations between autonomous communions will thus necessarily be relations of inter-communion. Clearly this situation is strange, since scripture speaks of only one communion and one participation in the Eucharist. Yet there are words that it is essential to forge to express certain new situations and there are stages, sometimes anomalous but ineluctable, that must be passed to arrive at results. It is in this sense that outside Roman Catholicism the development of inter-communion is accepted. Already in Edinburgh, on the occasion of the second Conference on Faith and Order, in 1937, it was declared that sacramental inter-communion was a necessary part of any satisfactory unity.

Should the practice of inter-communion be a means or a conclusion? That is the great problem. If Christians do not meet each other at the Lord's table, it is a scandal. On the other hand, can they share in a sacrament they do not recognize? Various formulas have been tried to resolve the problem:

(a) *Full communion* founded on doctrinal harmony between groups of the same confession. This permits of receiving to communion all their members indifferently, or authorizes ministers to celebrate in one or the other communion.

[17] O. S. Tomkins, ed., *The Third Conference on Faith and Order, Lund, 1952* (1953). See also the *Official Report of the Montreal Conference, 1963* (1964).
[18] *The Church in the Purpose of God* (1st edition, 1950; 2nd edition, 1952), p. 57.

(b) *Inter-communion and inter-celebration* which can be practised between denominations of different confessional families and which authorizes communion and celebration in one or the other Church.

(c) *Inter-communion* which authorizes the members of different confessional families to receive communion in the Churches which have established an agreement to this effect.

(d) *Open communion*, or the general invitation to receive communion.

(e) *Mutual open communion*, or limited invitation.

(f) *Limited open communion*, or admission of members of other Churches to receive communion in urgent or special cases.

(g) Lastly *Closed communion*, that is, restricted to the members of one Church or one denomination alone.[19]

2. *The movement for the drawing together of Protestantism and Catholicism along the lines of worship*

All progress, even incomplete, towards a better equilibrium of the liturgy in the world of the communions which have emerged from the Reformation truly signifies a drawing together. Moreover, this great conviction that is increasing from day to day that the liturgy has something to say for the life of the Church here and now, for the accomplishment of her mission, for the gathering together of the world under the sovereignty of the Lord, meets with similar dispositions in the Catholic Church. We too recognize the value of the renewal of the sense of community in worship and of a greater acceptance of the "realism" of the presence of Christ in the Eucharist, although we are not unaware of all that separates us.

Is there any particular point on which the Catholic Church could—in the order not only of theoretical positions but of concrete realizations—favour and prepare this drawing closer together in the sphere of worship? There is one such point and it is precisely the equilibrium of worship. Worship should be centred on Word and sacrament. But does not our Catholic worship sometimes border on sacramentalism? We have multiplied the number of Masses and have made an effort to make them more accessible to the faithful. But all too frequently a kind of tacit

---

[19] Tomkins, ed., *The Third Conference on Faith and Order, Lund, 1952*, p. 52: see also: Pehr Edwall, Eric Hayman and William D. Maxwell, ed., *Ways of Worship* (1951); Leonard Hodgson, ed., *Second World Conference on Faith and Order, Edinburgh 1937* (1938); Theobald Süss, "The Question of Intercommunion", *The Lutheran World Review* (January 1949), pp. 19–37; William Manson, *Church and Intercommunion: Some Considerations bearing on the Present Problem* (1951); Donald Baillie and John Marsh, ed., *Intercommunion* (1952); T. F. Torrance, "Intercommunion and Union of Church" in *Conflict and Agreement on the Church*, vol. I, pp. 123–34 and vol. 2, pp. 191–202.

understanding exists between priests and faithful—a short Mass in which there is nothing more for the proclamation of the Word of God than what the liturgy of the Word contains. It would be a pity if at a time when the Protestant world is seeking for a better liturgical balance, we should revert to the same liturgical lack of equilibrium which was one of the causes of the Reformation. Where are the sacraments enrooted if not in the Word? A sacramental practice, too much cut off from its source, may well be in danger of becoming mechanical and of wilting, even in spite of the presence of God in the sacraments. Reminding ourselves that the reunion of Christians is a work of the Church in which the parish communities, as much as the ecclesiastical leaders, have a part to play, we can here discover a new contribution of the Christian people, to the movement for *rapprochement* under the form of equilibrium and of integrity of worship.

III. CATHOLIC POSITIONS ON THE MYSTERY OF WORSHIP

1. The mystery of the Church as worshipping assembly

The Catholic teaching on the mystery of worship is linked with the Catholic conception of Christianity as a whole. It could scarcely be otherwise, since the liturgy is at the centre of the Church's life and that life is in conformity with the Church's nature. Moreover, does not an analogous ideological relation exist in the Protestant world? The disassociation between the Church of faith and the Church of history there commands a conception of worship in which the Presence is only there in a symbolic, virtual, or parallel manner.

Christianity is an order in which everything holds together. The directing logic, the interpretation of the nature, mission and unity of the Church, is the same as that which maintains the order of her worship and her structure. Now what is this fundamental scheme if not the type of union of the humanity and the divinity realized in the person of the Incarnate Word through the action of the Holy Spirit? [20]

Christianity is a relation of a specific type between time and eternity, between history and eschatology, and it is the Holy Spirit whose mission it is to construct it. Already in the Incarnation of the Word he united mankind to the divinity. He is pursuing the same work in the Church to unite mankind with the Word Incarnate seated in heaven.

In what way can this fundamental structure of Christianity be found in the worship of the Church?

[20] See Liturgical Constitution of the Second Vatican Council.

Christianity is the mystery of the revealed presence of the ultimate or eschatological realities in the tangible universe under a sacramental form. What is the Incarnation if not the mystery of the Word who becomes tangible, visible, in the world, through the action of the Holy Spirit, or, if you prefer, it is the mystery of the union of the historical, of time, with the eschatological, with eternity. The Holy Spirit seems to possess as his own characteristic the role of link between time and the ultimate realities. Such was his role at the Incarnation and as such the Spirit appeared again at Pentecost where he was given to remain permanently in the Church, with a view to assuring for the succession of the ages the link between time and the eschatological realities. That is to say, in short, to make historical, to actualize in time, in tangible and visible realities, the eschatological events of the salvation accomplished by the Incarnate Word. Through the power of the Holy Spirit, the Word is repeated and prolonged in the Church. It continues to become there tangible, visible, incarnate, it becomes so to speak institutionalized. It is the way of the Word which becomes sacramental through the operation of the Holy Spirit.

The life of the Church and particularly her liturgical life is founded on two essential realities, the Word and the sacraments. They must not be understood as two twin or independent realities, but as a single fundamental reality—the Word which becomes sacramental and corporalized. From Word to sacrament there is inner continuity. The Church's liturgical life thus reveals her very being, which is a Word become tangible. The continuity of the Church's liturgical being with her radical being is thus revealed. If, in fact, the Word and the sacrament, which are at the heart of liturgical life, construct the Church, they bring it about that the Church's being is essentially worshipping being.

The mystery of the Church is that in her heart she is one mighty celebration. For the Church to exist is to celebrate the mystery of salvation and this is true of her ultimate state as it is of her pilgrim state. The Church's life in heaven is one great liturgy which unfolds openly and renders thanks to the Father for the wonderful acts, the initiative of which is his and which he has pursued through Christ's Pasch. The Church on earth is the same liturgy but celebrated in mystery and under tangible signs. The celebration of the Church's liturgy in heaven is headed by Christ, the Word of salvation which has become wholly Spirit in the elect which it has gathered around it. On earth the Church's life is the celebration of the same mystery of salvation but in mystery. On earth as in heaven the Word makes itself present to the fullest possible extent in the Church. On earth it seeks to fill what is earthly with the Spirit of God by the way of mystery. In heaven the Word has become wholly Presence in the Church of men now become full of the Spirit of God.

In heaven the visibility of creation and the Church has been reabsorbed into the spirituality and actuality of the Word. On earth the Word seeks to fill all creation to make of it a sacrament of the invisible realities.

What then makes the heart of the Church's life, and in particular of her liturgical life on earth as in heaven, is the presence in her of eschatology. By the liturgical celebration here on earth Catholicism understands not only the memorial of what Christ has accomplished, or the announcement of what will one day be revealed, but the actual and effective unfolding of the one unique liturgy which is now exercised by the active presence of eschatology in her midst. Christ in his state of Ascension is present in her and he there develops the power of the great eschatological events he accomplished in history.

The life of the Church thus appears in its entirety and not only in her liturgical life as a general celebration of the mystery of salvation. When the Church preaches, teaches, consecrates, what does she do but celebrate the mystery of salvation? She recalls the great past events which have led to the world's liberation. She makes these same acts present and actual, or, if you prefer, Christ-in-his-Church makes his Word become visible, tangible, incarnate. In what manner does the Church accomplish this? Her method is always the same—that of the sacramentalization and incarnation of the Word. In other words, just as the nature of the Church is at bottom a liturgical nature, since it is the celebration of the mystery of salvation by the Word who became flesh, so the essential method of action of the Church in the world is a method of worship, for since the Church is made up of Word and sacrament, the Church cannot do otherwise than act according to a method that may be described as sacramental Word.

Consequently, whether the Church is celebrating the mystery of worship or acquitting herself of the remainder of her mission in the world, her being, her life, her mission, appear marked with the general character of a celebration of the mystery of salvation. The Church is in the world to celebrate the office of salvation. This is not a consequence of her being, it is her being itself, since she is the Body of Christ the Priest. Right from her origin, right from her birth on the Cross, she was marked with the priestly character. How could she ever renounce this? Her being is essentially a priestly being and the mystery she celebrates is that of the Word of salvation, made incarnate, immolated and glorified. The Church's action thus always remains sacramental and liturgical in type. What are called the Church's policy and, moreover the necessary diplomatic relations she has to maintain with States, or the material organization of her mission, all this is and must be finalized by one single purpose—the Incarnation of the Word, and any method that the Church adopts to arrive at this must be consecrated by the sacramental method. Otherwise in what would her action, organization and diplomacy be distinguished from those of the world? There lies and must lie the true centre whence the entire life of the Church, the celebration of the great events of salvation, radiates.

The same law holds good for the life of the Church as people of God. The action of the people of God in the world is like an immense liturgy, with Christ as its head, which liberates the world from sin and consecrates it to God. No one is thus left outside the mystery of the celebration of salvation, laymen have their sacerdotal function in it, just as priests have. To build a factory is clearly not to accomplish a liturgical action, but it is not an action outside the celebration of the mystery of salvation. Every work of the Christian people is situated within the economy of salvation and the perspective of the new heaven and the new earth. In wordly tasks the Word must become incarnate, it must be sacramentalized. Thus the earth is liberated from sin, consecrated and restored to the Spirit of God. And if this Christian vision does not impregnate the atmosphere of the life of the Christian in the world, in what will the action of the Christian be different from that of the man without faith? The secularization of the Christian life is the unavoidable consequence of the loss of the meaning of the celebration of the mystery of salvation in the world, of which by his baptism every Christian is a celebrant. [21]

It is thus difficult to find a more central aspect of the Church's being than this aspect of worship. The Church is built on Word and sacrament. She is the Word become visible. She grows through the power and presence of the Word in her. She acts in the world through the way of the sacramental Word. She is an immense mystery of celebration of salvation. Thus we see how all aspects of the mystery of the Church are linked in her fundamental reality—the presence of the Word which in her is made visible.

2. Pentecost in the life of the Church as mystery of celebration

Deeply rooted at the heart of the Church's awareness there is this sense of her mystery as that of a great celebration. The word *paneguris,* which means a festal meeting and from which panegyric comes, can be just as much applied to the Church as can the Greek word *ekklesia* which has become ennobled in passing from the secular to the religious meaning. The Church is in very truth a great festal gathering and the liturgy is the place of its celebration.

Two extraordinary events which correspond to each other, one in the Old Testament, the other in the New, that is, Sinai and Pentecost, inter-

---

[21] See the Pastoral Constitution of the Second Vatican Council on the Church in the Modern World, part I, chapters iii and iv.

vene to reveal this central aspect of the Church. On the day of Sinai the people had been convened for a celebration; recalling the marvels that God had accomplished for them, they had become conscious of being God's people. What they became then was an *ecclesia*. The significance of their meeting ceased to be secular and became religious. All the elements of the *ecclesia* are there—the word of God was uttered by Moses, God's herald; the law was proclaimed; the sacrifices were offered; the glory of God came down on the sacrifices; the covenant was sealed. And this people became a holy nation, a priestly people whose heart is worship. The constitution of the Jewish people as a people vowed to the worship of the true God was thus accomplished in the midst of the unfolding of a sacred feast.

The phenomenon of Pentecost represents the counterpart of Sinai, for the new *Ecclesia*. In the apostles met together in the Cenacle, all the nations were convened. The Lord himself was the herald of the convocation, for it is he who asked them to remain in Jerusalem. Then, suddenly, a true feast of the glory of the Spirit took place. When the apostles received the Holy Spirit, they became suddenly aware that the wonders that God had accomplished for his people in the Old Law and for Christ in the New Law, especially in raising him from among the dead and taking him up to his right hand, were in view of this people of God whom they were themselves. The convened *Ecclesia* then realized that it was truly the people of God. The design of God which was begun as far back as Exodus was instantaneously revealed in its perfect continuity—the true people of God had not ceased to exist; it had been transformed by its passage into the Lord's mysteries.

Pentecost is thus the revelation to the Church of her being as mystery of celebration. Thanks to her it is revealed to us that Christian worship is the expression by the Church, or rather by Christ-in-his-Church, of the joy and exultation caused by the deliverance from sin, death and hell. In worship Jesus-in-his-Church never ceases to express his divine joy at having brought to its conclusion this great work which his Father had entrusted to him. And it is with his own expressions and his own sentiments that we associate ourselves in the joy of our liberation. It is with the very means he has left to his Church, the Word and the sacraments, to express our liberation and bring it actually to us, that we celebrate the wonders of this accomplishment.

The richness of the gifts at Pentecost did not come to separate eschatology from time, but in order that Christ the Eschaton might be even more present in time; and it is the Holy Spirit, the link between time and eschatology who brings it about that henceforward the two are united.

Our celebration of the great eschatological events already accomplished is thus not merely a memorial of the past or the announcement of events to come. It is the celebration of a real presence in the midst of us.

312

Through the Spirit who forms the link between time and eternity, Jesus celebrates here and now the mystery of salvation in his Church, and he gave so many pledges of his presence on the occasion of Pentecost that we must believe that he is indeed there, in very truth, at the heart of worship.

3. The Church, mystery of Presence

The essence of the Church is the presence of the grace of God. That is the essential link that makes the Church one under various conditions according to the degrees of participation in the Presence. Sovereign and immediate presence of God in the vision of the angels and saints; presence of God in faith, hope and charity, in the discipline of ecclesiastical organization, in scripture, tradition and the sacraments. Heaven, or the Church triumphant is the perfect presence. God is all in all. That is heaven, that is the Church in completed act, for that is the term of the convocation which has gathered together angels and men in a congregation which God in Three Persons penetrates with his presence.

The Church militant and the Church suffering is the Presence rendered imperfect because of the limitations of the subjects—time and sin. When all shall have been absorbed in the Holy Spirit—matter, history, understanding—when the creature shall have been delivered from evil, then the Presence will no longer have any other limits than those that separate the created from the uncreated. God will be all in all. [22]

The presence of God creates its means of expression, its organs of convocation and congregation, according to the different objects to be taken hold of, convened, gathered together—angels, men and things. But it is the presence of God communicating himself that is the essential of the Church—presence of God, presence of the Three Persons. The Church of the Trinity, pre-existent to the Church of men, creates its forms of expression which are the Church and the apostolic hierarchy and the Church of the Word and the sacraments, for the Church comes down from heaven. To speak plainly the Church appears to us as the revealed act of the glorious presence of the Three Persons.

4. Analogous realizations of the concept of Presence

We are setting out from the idea that scripture reveals to us various modes of God's presence—by its direct and immediate action or again by its indirect and mediate action; by images, symbols, signs; by the remem-

[22] *Ibid.*

313

brance of the Presence, by its servants, or again as living and actual reality in the person of the Word Incarnate and of the Holy Spirit.

The Church is the mystery or sacrament of the Presence and this Presence manifests itself and is made actual in the Church in various ways and in various degrees. First of all in the Church taken as the society of the faithful. The Church militant is the place that God has chosen to proclaim his wonders. She is the sign of the presence of God among the nations. There is a focal point of salvation upon earth, a centre of diffusion of revelation, a radiating point where God has left the imprint of his descent, and that is the Church. The Church is full of the presence of God which breaks out under the veil of the signs and the symbols, makes herself visible as much as she can do on this earth, expresses herself as Word in unceasing act of proclamation. Where the Word is, there is the Presence.

Wherever we look, it is always the Presence we find—in the witnesses of revelation such as the apostles: in scripture, in tradition, in the sacraments, in the whole Church as a community of prayer and love. The veils only have to be pushed lightly aside to give access to the heart of the Presence, one has only to make oneself more attentive for a moment to discern the Word which can be heard perpetually. The Presence is there and always in act. Man is invited to betake himself there by a movement of sacramental attention. In the scriptures he can then hear God who speaks, in the sacraments it is again God who meets him. The Church is full of the sovereign Presence.

A single Presence is maintained and revealed in several languages, all of which harmonize in the unique Word. The Presence that is in the Church until the consummation of the world pushes aside for us the veils that hide it and reveals itself as far as our condition can bear it. The hearing of the Word of God is in very truth a revelation, a removal of the veil which prevents us from hearing the voice of the Word which resounds without ceasing and which otherwise we do not hear. The eucharistic celebration and all the other sacraments are similarly a revelation, for the sacramental signs are signs chosen by God to remove from our senses what hinders us from entering the Presence. The same is true of the hierarchical structure which is a kind of revelation as the Lord declared: "He who hears you hears me" (Lk 10:16), "He who receives you receives me, and he who receives me receives him who sent me" (Mt 10:40).

Scripture, the sacraments, the apostolic hierarchical structure have a double effect—to create a zone of release and of liberation by removing from ourselves what prevents us from acceding to the eschatological realities that they make present, and then to allow to escape from them the irradiation of the Presence which created them, which sustains them, which penetrates them with the consciousness of its being and its power.

These two effects are caused by the Word present in them which first of all invites to a certain Exodus and then makes us enter into the Promise.

What separates us, then, Catholics and Protestants, is not faith in the Presence, and fortunately indeed, for it is through this objective Presence that all men in good faith can meet in the same Christ our reconciler, but it is the interpretation of the meaning of the Presence, its mode of manifestation to us and our way of entering into it. To use a term which unfortunately the Protestant world holds in horror, our interpretation is founded on an analogous conception of the Presence, whereas in Protestantism the concept which prevails is univocal.

We say that there is only one Presence and it is the same whether manifested in the Church in her pilgrim state or in her final state. Christ is the same in heaven and in the Eucharist although here under sacramental modality. He is the same in the other sacraments, in scripture, in the Church as the society of the faithful, in each Christian and in each man, but clearly in a different way according to the case.

In Protestantism, on the contrary, this Church, the Body of Christ, could not be the Kingdom of God on earth in the pilgrim state. The Church of faith and the Church of history are incompatible. God can come very close to the Church of history, he can extend its action, he can move the Christian but something is always lacking to the immanence of his Presence.

Let us see to some extent how we understand the sacramentalization of the Word that renders it visible even to us. In the first place what is tradition, if not the Presence perpetuated and always living in the Church of the revealed Word which is preserved in identity throughout the course of the history of the Church to measure and evaluate its development, to identify the truth that the waves of history bring to the Church and to reject what is false. Tradition goes hand in hand with the incarnation of the word. It expresses the self-revelation of the Word in the Church. It is relative to the visible permanence of the Word.[23]

There is in the Church a place where the Word as Word has willed to remain present in the world. It is not the Eucharist, it is not the life of the Church, it is not the hierarchical priesthood, for in all these realities the Word exists under a sacramental mode. This place is scripture, the sign chosen by the Word to remain present among us. Certainly the material book of the scriptures appears as the sacrament of the Word, but this sign in so far as it is material is non-living. More, then, than of the material book we wish to speak of this infinitely wonderful and living world of the mysterious and divine meanings present in scripture, the receptacle of an infinite illuminating power in tension towards souls. The scripture is

[23] See the Second Vatican Council's Dogmatic Constitution on Revelation.

thus the voice of the bridegroom to the bride. It is in a very high degree a bond of life between Christ and the Church. When I read the account of Christ's birth, I enter more deeply into his Incarnation, or rather I allow myself to be grasped by the Word who has become flesh to bring mankind to him. If I continue my reading as far as the account of the Resurrection and of the glorious Ascension, then is realized in me the ineffable work described by St Paul of co-burial, co-resurrection, co-ascension. And if I look at this Christ of the Ascension who judges history, then I receive the grace to submit myself to the Lord's judgement and sovereignty. The soul who submits to the Word of God submits to his judgement. Christ is the master of truth and he has not ceased to be so. His Word is masterly and authoritative. It is on this living magisterium of the Word that all magisterium in the Church is founded.

How regrettable it is that the anti-Protestant reaction should have taken away from scripture its sacramental character to make of it a simple memorial whereas during this time Protestantism was rediscovering the sacramental value of scripture but made of the Eucharist a mere memorial. We have all fallen into some degree of unilateralism—Catholics by acting as if the sacraments alone were the means of grace, forgetting the grace proper to the scriptures, and Protestants by making scripture the only visible mediation.

Our investigation now turns to the Eucharist. Is it not the epitome of the Presence in mystery? What we are dealing with is a thin, transparent film, which, so to speak, holds back the Beyond and prevents it from manifesting itself as a power of judgement and Apocalypse in the Parousia. It is these very faint material signs that mark the frontier of the two worlds and prevent them from crashing one into the other, while at the same time leaving them the possibility of communicating in a way which leaves to God the liberty of the invitation and to man the liberty of the response. If this frontier suddenly disappeared, we should at once be confronted with judgement. And the Lord indeed tells us that the Church is a community in expectation, for he has commanded us to repeat the actions of the institution of the Eucharist until he comes again.

Thus the Eucharist is wholly filled with the eschatological presence. We feel the divine presence in it and through it, we see it as a presence of salvation and judgement. Through these sacred signs it is granted to us to become for Christ mystically "bone of his bone and flesh of his flesh" (Gen 2:23).

With regret it must indeed be said that the eucharistic doctrine constitutes a faithful mirror of our differences in ecclesiology. For all of us the Eucharist is memorial, presence and anticipation, but the word "presence", which is the hyphen between the two others, finds us disunited.

Jesus is the Word of salvation. In him salvation has been accomplished.

But how is salvation granted to man? According to the Protestant teaching on the Eucharist, Christ's eternal sacrifice reaches man by way of the Word of God. This seals the symbol of the Last Supper given as confirmation of the reception of the Word which has engendered faith in us, as communion in the past sacrifice of Christ on the Cross. For Catholicism, on the contrary, the eucharistic celebration on earth is the real and actual participation in the unique sacrifice of Christ who dwells in heaven, a sacrifice perpetual and uninterrupted in its eternal value. The Eucharist appears to us both as sacrifice and sacrament because there is found the Word of salvation and it is present in mystery. Now what is the Word of salvation but Christ immolated and glorified? If then such is the Word of salvation, what difficulty is there in seeing it in the celebration of the holy mysteries, in this act of Death and Resurrection? Does not Christ's sacrifice remain for eternity? The Mass thus appears to us as this Word of salvation rendering himself present to us in his actuality of accomplishment of salvation, that is, through his Death and Resurrection, for there is in the words of institution the saving power of the Word who makes himself sacramentally present, that is, truly flesh and truly blood, as in the Incarnation and on the Cross, under the appearances of bread and wine. There is only one single sacrifice—that of the Cross. Celebrated with bloodshed on Calvary, it is now celebrated without bloodshed on the altar.[24]

Our way of seeing the Mass thus depends on our way of considering the presence of Christ the Eschaton in the Church. The Mass is seen as a revelation. Each time the Church opens her eyes and looks into her soul where she preserves the memory and presence of Calvary, she again finds the mystery which is there and which has not ceased to be there. The Mass is like the child who in the morning lifts his eyelids and opens his eyes to the light which was there waiting for him; thus it is with the Church who lifts up her eyes to the heights which had never ceased to be there.

Lastly, what is the Church? A Word, the Word sown in the world, become blood, flesh and life among men. O the greatness and the depth of the mystery of God that the Word received in me by faith becomes Church! The Church is me, it is you, it is all of us, for you also have become Church since you have been called and gathered up into the unity of the sons of God. The Event of salvation has touched you, reached you, seized hold of you. It has found its response in the correspondence of your full liberty by which you have obeyed God who called you to be freed from your limits, consecrated, reunited to him and to the men who have passed through the same experience as you, who have been called to the recognition, service and honour of God. When the

[24] C. Journet, *La Messe, présence du sacrifice de la Croix* (1957).

Spirit came upon you through the Word, through faith and through the sacrament he opened your eyes and you recognized in the work of Jesus Christ your own reconciliation, a Word manifested and binding, sharing with you your wretchedness and your hope. The Father has come since he is never without the Son. The Son and the Spirit have come because they have been sent. And where have they been received if not in you to make you take the form of Church, for in you they are call and congregation. This the Lord has told you and you could not deny it. In you the Word has become Christian life, in you priesthood, in you holy marriage. You must not forget how the Word came down into the Virgin's flesh and into the water of the Jordan, into the hearts of the apostles and into the mass of men and with what long patience he made the Church germinate in them. He came, he went, he passed and his Word raised up the Church. Every action of Christ was an action of Church.

Why try to seek a particular moment for the foundation of the Church? Over these two or three gathered together in his name, these Twelve, this crowd, he gave utterance and they were converted into Church. He caused to appear in them the Event that he was himself and these men by his power revealed themselves as transported into the knowledge and life of Jesus Christ. Because they had been illumined by glory they had ceased to be only themselves, for in them, born of the will of flesh and blood, a new birth had renewed the old man, and in their astonishment at the marvel accomplished in them, they wondered that the Word should have become Church in them, that it should there accomplish works of Church, that it should make its way through their fleshly condition and thus without ceasing to be transcendent, make itself visible to whoever wished to see it.[25] Jesus said nothing else to men and gave them nothing else to understand except that the Word had come among them and that they had only to open to his passage for the Word to make himself visible in them, for the Church to come into being and remain. The death on the Cross, the Resurrection, the institution of Peter as prince of the apostles, the Ascension, are summits of the Church, but they are so precisely after the manner of fragments that the creative power of the Word allowed to escape from himself like the islands that appear on the surface of the sea. Thus the Word whose presence brushes against the realities of the world has revealed itself by ways humble, or majestic, and has dwelt among us.

Let us honour the Church, she is the visible Word of so great a King. Yes, visible Word of divine grace and Eucharist of praise.

[25] See the Second Vatican Council's Dogmatic Constitution on the Church, article 7.

CHAPTER VIII

The Psychological Problem:
The Formation of the Ecumenical Spirit

I. DEFINITION OF THE PROBLEM

What must be given to Christians at the present day is the feeling, the conviction even, that they are much nearer each other than they think. We are all returning from a long journey into the regions of dissimilarity and are like the sons of the same father and mother who during their youth, for various reasons to do with inheritance, are separated without seeing each other again; thus they lost their family spirit although they retained a certain family likeness. It remains for us to explain to each other what happened to us during the centuries of separation, where we went, what we saw, what we have done, what we have lacked.

If reunion is a question of the integration of men, institutions, and traditions, there will surely be agreement in defining the ecumenical problem from the psychological point of view as the question of those factors which together make for the reunion of Christians or the maintenance of division. Why are we divided psychologically? Why, when we use the same words, are we not talking of the same things? What prevents our reunion? There are reasons which are not the result of prejudice or of bad feeling. Some of them belong to the dogmatic or doctrinal order, others are designated under the term non-theological factors.

Different Christian traditions result in different psychological attitudes. The Eastern Churches, also, are faced with this problem. Orthodox, Greeks, Slavs or Arabs, Copts or Armenians, represent so many traditions which will have to be reconciled among themselves before embarking on a larger scale reunion.

The Protestant world, on the other hand, is divided into two great classes of tradition, the classical tradition and the radical tradition, which includes different traditions and from which, in their turn, others are derived.

319

Doctrinal factors must be taken into account, but the non-theological factors are often as, or even more, important than the doctrinal ones. It may even happen, and this should be no cause for astonishment, that doctrinal reasons, which are quoted as the central cause of dispute, are in fact symbols behind which are hidden obstacles of a primarily psychological nature. Thus discussion can go on for centuries without ever getting near the real reasons. The two parties sidetrack each other and there may be mutual accusations of bad will, whereas each knows, on a final analysis, that he was not ready to enter on discussion of the real motives for division and the real ways to reunion. All sorts of overt and covert reasons, motives used as excuses, symbols used as screens, all these things go to make up a dialogue at several levels whose secret aim is not reunion but to test the sincerity and the evolution of the ideas of the other party.

Must this kind of dialogue be abolished? We must contrive to understand it and decide between the real problem and appearances. Moreover, it may well happen that the real heart of the problem has evolved with the centuries. The real questions, those which are only touched in symbolic form, the real problems, those which are concealed behind screens, will be tackled when adequate guarantees are given and then many dogmatic problems will be rapidly resolved. It should not be said that there is duplicity in this language at different levels. In truth it is in accordance, perhaps, with a certain logic: since neither of the parties confronting each other is ready to listen to the other, they speak in symbols. The experience and practice of ecumenism bestows a spiritual sense allowing one to feel the prominent reasons and motives which crop up in discussions and the reasons for the adoption of attitudes. The respective role of dogmatic and other factors is thus confined within certain limits. Dialogue becomes easier as a consequence, because it is more broadly based. It is possible to leave aside or go beyond what is hurtful.

Such in the aggregate are the data of the psychological problem. It will be seen that the traditions, temperaments, psychologies, failings, Satan himself who excels in making good use of differences, are all factors in a kind of agreement of discord. But we must look also towards a solution. As a rule it is simple enough: it amounts to selecting and promoting those attitudes which favour integration together with the elimination of those which cause disintegration. Certain propositions calculated to create integrating attitudes which will result finally in the healing of the Body of Christ will be put forward here.

1. The authentic type or types of Christianity

There is only one Catholicism, and yet what differences there are between English, French, Spanish, American, German or other forms of Catholicism!

If the faith is one, why is there more than one way of expressing it? It is because men, the subjects of faith, are different from each other. And so there are national modalities of Christianity just as there are different languages through which humanity gives expression to its soul. Twenty centuries of Christian life have created an order of seniority and experience, but not in such a way that the young Churches have only to repeat the language of the old Churches, since it is true that the mission of the Church is to be the constant answer to fresh challenges.

The same principle applies in the case of the Eastern Churches which differ in doctrine and in rites and are distinct by their autocephalous nature and conditions of life. The data of the ecumenical problem in the world of the Eastern Churches, only too easily represented as unchanging, are not the same from one generation to another. The younger Churches and those established among emigrants have introduced new points of view. There, too, attention must be paid to the typological differences as they have been modified by new circumstances. But it is especially in the Protestant world that the differences in type of Christianity must be followed step by step. Is there, for example, an American type of Protestantism? There is, if by that is meant that the Protestant Christianity in the United States is of the co-operative, democratic and conciliar kind. But the special character of each denomination must immediately be noted.

Is there a world type of Lutheran, of Presbyterian, etc.? The existence of the great world denominational alliances should not set us on the wrong track. There is nothing more different from a German or Swedish Lutheran than an American Lutheran, more different from an American Calvinist than a Swiss Calvinist, and so on. It is rather because of these differences of Lutheranism, of Presbyterianism, etc. in their national expressions that the alliances have been set up. To the question whether there is a European Protestantism,[1] an American or Asiatic Protestantism, an affirmative answer can be given, provided that it is pointed out that it is the expression of an abstraction.

Attention both to typological differences and typological likenesses can alone provide concrete and connected knowledge of the elements to be united. Various methods of procedure for effecting the induction and different areas of observation will inevitably lead to different classifications.

[1] A. Keller and G. Stewart, *European Protestantism.*

321

Walter Marshall Horton mentions six major types of different conceptions of Christianity, which can be divided in their turn into subdivisions. These are the types: Catholic, Roman and non-Roman; conservative, fundamentalist and speculative Protestant; liberal, idealist and rationalist Protestant; Swiss, Swedish, American neo-Orthodox; Anglican: High Church (Catholic), Low Church (evangelical), Broad Church (liberal) and, finally, the central position.[2]

And, of course, other classifications could be found. What is required essentially is a certain amount of observation, analysis, and induction. Ecumenism can only realize its true nature and its mission in the Church on condition that it remains in contact with the concrete life of the Church.

2. The influence of the dogmatic factors

A. CATHOLICISM AND THE CLASSICAL PROTESTANT TRADITION

The dogmatic aspect is not the only aspect of the ecumenical problem. But of them all it is the most central. The life, action, prayer and psychology of Christians are the result of its influence. What divides Christians in depth is the conception of Christianity. True reunion will only be possible within a substantial identity of views. Every other form of agreement, however valuable and necessary, particularly in our troubled times, can only be a half-agreement. There is no intolerance in saying this. Or if there is, it is that which consists in saying that the means should be proportionate to the end, unless the end is not desired, which is something quite different.

And why are we divided on the nature of Christianity? Doubtless because, without wishing it, we are divided about Christ. The formula defining Christ defines at the same time Christianity, the Church, the action of the Christian and the renewed order of the world.

At the basis of the Catholic as of the Orthodox conception of Christianity is the great doctrine of Chalcedon (451), which is derived from the Fathers who found it in scripture. The formula which, to the glory of the East, defined at Chalcedon the nature of Christ established for ever a unity which explains how the Western and the Eastern Churches in the Middle Ages were able to produce two great twin Christian civilizations and how, even today, Orthodox delegations, when they state their position at the World Council of Churches, often give expression to what we should say ourselves.

What does Chalcedon say of Christ?[3] Jesus Christ is true God and true

[2] *Christian Theology; an Ecumenical Approach*, p. 26.
[3] Denzinger, *Enchiridion Symbolorum*, no. 148.

man; as true God he has the same substance as God; as true man he has the same substance as men. He possesses duality of nature in the unity of a person. But we must see how this affected Christianity as a whole. Since Christ is consubstantial with the Father and consubstantial with men, and since human nature and divine nature in him constitute only one person, the divinity can be communicated to us. The actual communication of the divine nature to man forms indeed the greatest difficulty between Protestantism and the rest of the Christian world, both Catholic and Orthodox. Does that mean that the relationship of Christ with man as it is understood by Protestantism effects nothing in man? To assert that would be unjust to Protestantism. That man is saved by hope implies a certain communication, for hope is a reality and, obviously, the presence of Christ in man transforms him. It has sometimes happened that in Catholicism the Protestant theology of Christ's action on man has been interpreted in such an external way that if Christ's action had been absent, it would have changed nothing. But that is not the authentic meaning of Protestantism. We must see what it is if we wish to show in what way it parts company from us.[4]

In truth, if in the Bible there are passages which tell of our sins being covered, that our disorders are concealed by the mercy of God, there is also to be found something that surpasses all hope, even the loftiest, and that is the multifarious proclamation of the real and effective gift of God, the sharing in his nature by man. Now it is here that the formulas of Chalcedon achieve their ecclesical significance.[5]

The human and the divine are not merged in the Church. The human remains human, the divine does not change. It is the human factor which enters into a new relation with God. Yet between Christ and the Church there is not mere juxtaposition as if the Head were simply placed on the Body, or moved it from outside, or even tangentially. Sacred history is the witness, repeated over and over again, of the long fidelity and the communication of the substance of life from the bridegroom to the bride. Catholic tradition, Eastern as well as Western, has always seen it as internal continuity and communication.

The formula of Christianity as taught to us by Chalcedon is not Nestorian, or Monophysite, or Docetist, or Arian, or Protestant.

Since Christ is the hypostatic relation of a human nature with the divine nature in one person, in the same way Christianity is the relation of nature to supernature in the person of the Incarnate Word. The essential terms are, on the one hand, the reality of nature and of the order of nature and, on the other, of supernature and of the order of supernature; of a nature

[4] Ph. Maury, *Qu'est-ce que l'eschatologie?*
[5] "Inconfuse, Indivise, Inseparabiliter" in Denzinger, *loc. cit.*

impaired whose supernatural restoration has already begun; of a redeemed nature, already mystically united to the Godhead in the person and on the model of the Word Incarnate.

Catholicism is, therefore, a relational conception of Christianity because it is founded on a whole body of relationships between nature and grace, reason and faith, the profane and Christian worlds, Church and State, disposed in accordance with an order of communication and gift. The Protestant conceptions, both classical and radical, can rightly be classified as radical.[6] There is no intention of stating thereby that Protestantism does not possess its own theory of the great orders of Christianity, but its disposition of them marks a violent reaction, radical is the word, against the traditional order. There ensues from this a different position on the great orders of Christianity.

Catholicism and Orthodoxy are characterized by a relational and hierarchical position; Protestantism by a radical and transcendentalist conception. For Catholicism, redeemed nature can share in the order of grace and it is for this reason that the Church is already on earth the Kingdom of God, although in an inchoative and pilgrim state. In Protestantism, on the contrary, nature is so far corrupt that the Kingdom of God remains tangential to it.

A relational conception and a radical conception — two expressions which well indicate the difference between a vision of the Christian economy deriving from trust in the natural order and its capacity to enter into relationship with God and another which is convinced of the contrary. The first is based on an order of communication and gift, the second, without rejecting all communication and gift, does away with what, in our view, constitutes the internal continuity of the Church, from earth right up to heaven.

One of the keys to understanding the thought of Luther, for example, is his idea of nature. According to Luther, a distinction must be made between fallen nature and true nature: the former is utterly corrupted by man's primitive pride and it is impossible for him to enter into a personal and intimate relationship with God and form a harmony with grace. Everything that comes from this corrupt nature is sin. True nature, on the other hand, is the integral, pure and ideal nature of the original state. It is identical with grace.

The cleavage is, therefore, categorical. From the Catholic point of view there is in this a fundamental ambiguity which can be attributed to the complete assimilation of nature (in the sense of visible, corporal, external) with a certain state of nature, namely that of sin. Nothing has lain more heavily on relations between Catholics and Protestants. Nature and grace

[6] Ernst Troeltsch, *The Social Teaching of the Christian Churches*, vol. II, p. 461.

have obviously in Catholicism a meaning different from that in Protestantism. For the latter grace does not mean the real sharing of the divine nature by man by virtue of which fallen nature is purified and raised to the supernatural order; it means on the contrary a radical hostility to the root of sin as represented by nature held to be totally corrupt. In Protestantism, grace is in God, not in man.

Man is the battleground, in which corrupt nature lives in a state of hostility with grace which hangs over him, with the law which accuses him, with God who judges him. He is the most unhappy being that it is possible to imagine, but also the happiest for, although fundamentally corrupt, he is the object of divine grace and is not left to himself. Accepting what Christ accomplished for him, he knows that his sins are covered before God and he is sure that, so long as he is faithful, his corrupt nature will be changed in the end to that of a true son of God. For the present, he is saved only in hope. Luther expressed this complex situation by the trilogy "always sinners, always righteous, always penitents, and all these at the same time".

This essential structure of the Christian soul was discovered by Luther in his interpretation of the Epistle to the Romans. There appeared to him to be three effects of faith: knowledge of self as a sinner, knowledge of self as saved, knowledge of self as a soldier in the service of the faith.

Knowledge of self in the first place: except for Christ there has never been a holy man on earth. Before him, before God, man is nothing. What merit could he urge which would allow him to live? He is conscious of the immeasurable distance and the moral insufficiency separating him from the Holy and Righteous One.[7] All pride is thus reduced to nothing. Man returns to his true dimension, that of humility. It was this profoundly important insight that in 1517 produced Luther's powerful sermons on the penitential psalms which had such an effect that even during his lifetime they passed through twenty-five editions.

Next came knowledge of self as saved. God's justice is not distributed almost impersonally and mechanically as coming from an impassive and remote master who left the administration of his Kingdom to his officers. God is the living God whose love springs forth in an eternal impulse to make men his children. Living, creative, triumphant justice which experiences the imperious need to spread abroad his holiness, his being, his life. Man must give way to this justice and, in doing so, at the same time that he is justified he justifies God's action.

God's justice is an experience undergone. In contact with God, the Just One, man experiences an indescribable peace. He feels himself surrounded by a goodness, an infinite mercy, by a love that is incomprehensible because

[7] Rupp, *op. cit.*

it is undeserved. He has been touched by the goodness of God who has wiped out the debt for him in his Son. Fundamentally, man is a sinner and yet he is welcomed as the prodigal son; he casts himself wholly into the hands of God who invests him with the mantle of his justice, the pledge of his complete rehabilitation one day. A great hope is born of this assurance: God will complete the work which has been begun. Luther illustrated his thought by the parable of a doctor who promised his patient that he would be cured if he followed the doctor's treatment. The doctor, God, knows that man will be cured. To endow him with hope again is already virtually to cure him. But real and perfect health is for eternal life. It is only then that Christ's glorious victory over sin will reach its full achievement for so long as the world lasts the reign of corrupt nature will endure. For the present man must not compromise the chance of his return to health. God will not impute his sin to him and that will be enough to inspire confidence; in Christ the sinner has already overcome sin, death and hell. This man can, therefore, be at the same time righteous and a sinner. A sinner by nature he can only perform the works of sin and his conviction of this will increase his humility. With no illusions about his state, and since his doctor is helping him, he can set out on the way to that renewal which has lit up his soul with hope.

Nevertheless, man must not remain passive. Knowledge of himself as a sinner and as saved leads normally to his taking part in the good fight of faith. For how could he remain indifferent to God's hate of sin and to the action of divine holiness standing against evil, as was shown by Christ's heroic work on the cross when he was directly engaged against the powers of hell? The Christian can be logical with himself only on condition of entering the ranks of Christ's soldiers. As God's soldier he must fight without respite against the evil in him and around him. The experience of his justification is not something entirely restful, a passive undynamic action. On the contrary, he cannot be anything but deeply moved by the fearful power of God's active and dynamic holiness engaged with all its strength in the fight against evil. The Christian thus deeply stirred with himself is drawn into the divine call to victory. He shows his vocation as a Christian by goodness, generosity, service of his neighbour, spiritual mercy, the freeing of man from evil.

Luther terms this spiritual attitude penitence. The expression does not correspond to the interior feeling of humility. It means rather the new attitude of man renewed in hope, who, in virtue of this conversion, gives signs of the detestation of evil and of his engagement in the service of love in the great combat of faith. For if God has the last word of the victory over the evil which is in man and if the latter is associated with Christ's victory and acknowledges his sin, he will regret the evil and experience the same sentiments as God—the infinite desire for God's justice on earth as in heaven. In this way Christian life seems carried away by the very dynamism of divine holiness.

Thus Protestant ecclesiology is governed by the dialectic of the simultaneity of justice and sin *(simul justus et peccator)*. Imputative righteousness, as revised and corrected by Melanchthon, has been called "forensic justice", that is, the justification of man before the court, the tribunal of God.

Thus Luther, rejecting Catholic tradition, Eastern as well as Western, which proclaims that grace is in man as it is in God, and that nature is not wholly corrupt but impaired, through his experience and interpretation of justification moves towards rejection of a whole part of the Church called by vocation of grace to the supernatural. Once the door was closed on understanding of the Catholic tradition, Luther was able to equate interior religion with religion of the freedom brought by Christ, and external religion with religion of the law from which Christ has set us free. Now according to Luther, Christ having set us free from the law has delivered us also from everything which belongs to the sphere of the law, that is, from everything which in the Church is visible, institutional, hierarchical and even sacramental. It is not without a certain inconsistency that Luther retains the sacrament of baptism and the Lord's Supper. They are well warranted by scripture, but why keep them if the Word suffices for everything? And yet although Luther retains certain visible and institutional aspects, it is in a purely non-essential sense.

The Church, according to Luther, is therefore made up of hidden faith in Christ and is consequently essentially invisible.[8] The Church is the communion of saints, the communion of all those of every race, of every age, of every people, even of the whole Christian body, who have been made righteous by Christ and are known by him as such, for, Luther was fond of quoting St Paul, "our life is hidden in Christ" (Col 3:3). The Christian and the Church are already living an eschatological life, not because they already possess it inchoatively, as Catholic tradition teaches, but because they are now hidden in Christ who is their life, as is promised by the Holy Spirit who raises up hope in us. The true Church is there. Interior and spiritual she gathers together all those who are the true faithful.

The present psychological difficulties between Protestants and Catholics arise precisely from their conception of grace, the Church and faith.

Such a way of regarding and arranging the constituent elements of Christianity governs at a deep level the psychological attitude of the Churches and Christian communions.

[8] G. W. Forell, *The Reality of the Church as the Communion of Saints* (1943).

B. THE RADICAL PROTESTANT TRADITION

The table of the origins of the dissident denominations given above can be seen from different points of view.

It enables us to trace back the history of the denominations, their dogmatic affiliations and their interdenominational relations, their sociological and liturgical evolution. It illustrates the fact that different dispositions of the material and formal principles of Protestantism have resulted in traditions which have their repercussions in the ecumenical problem in its psychological aspect.

The fundamental principles of Protestantism are conditioned and modified by each other. Their relationships give rise to the various forms of Protestantism.

As an illustration of the radical Protestant tradition Congregationalism has been chosen. In this typical instance of the radical position can be seen how the radical bodies simultaneously are a continuation of classical Protestantism, are opposed to it and go beyond it. The formal principle of Protestantism finds expression in two ways. In its positive form it states that the Word of God in scripture provides, as a matter of principle and of right, the only objective authority in doctrine, constitution, worship and discipline.

This same principle includes a negative conclusion. No creed, no human doctrine can form an authority on a par with that of the Word of God in scripture. In short, the confessions of faith, the creeds are not authorities in themselves, but they help to understand the sole objective authority. Up to a certain point they can be called manifestations of the same Spirit that is to be found in scripture and in the Christian conscience; nevertheless, the Word of God in scripture is the only authority in matters of faith and discipline. All the rest has only a human value.

The material principle is justification by faith alone.

How can these principles of the Reformation in the classical tradition be at the same time the principles of radical Protestantism such as Methodism, Congregationalism, Quakerism etc.?

Radical Protestantism holds that classical Protestantism, and still more the Anglican reform, have affirmed only a part, although the principal part, of the truth and, more especially, that they have not drawn all the conclusions. The Lutheran reform, on this view, has stopped half-way, and even, with Melanchthon, retreated from its furthest point of advance. Anglicanism would seem to have eluded the consequences of its principles by a torturous form of exegesis.

Congregationalism shows itself as a systematic effort to take further the application of the formal principle of Protestantism not only in the doctrinal sphere but also in regard to constitution, worship etc. and it is from this that it derives its own characteristics.[9]

In what way does Congregationalism wish to take further the material principle of Protestantism?

The Holy Spirit, we know, is the fundamental principle for the building up of the ecclesial community. A form of teaching about the Holy Spirit and his way of acting on the believer and the Church leads to a corresponding interpretation of the nature of the Church and of Christianity.

Protestantism has a special way of treating the nature of the Church and of placing the Holy Spirit in relationship with the believer and the Church. It is an immediate and transcendent relationship.

Now what is the special doctrine of Congregationalism? The immediacy and fullness of the relationship existing between the Spirit of Christ and the Church of Christ are extended to each congregation of true Christians and to the soul of each true believer.[10] Hence the ideal form of the Church for this denomination is the small Church or local congregation. By emphasizing thus in so radical a manner the principle of the immediacy of the relationship between Christ, the Church and the believer there emerges this new expression of Protestantism which is Congregationalism.

In other words, what distinguishes it from other forms of Protestantism is not so much the formal principle, taken absolutely, as the new way of setting it against the material principle. But the material principle reacts in its turn on the formal principle: the denomination turns to the Bible to seek in it and confirm its special conviction of the revelation of the Spirit of Christ.

This case forms an illustration of the unity and multiplicity of the Protestant denominations: the formal principle is one and the same. But it is the way in which it is turned towards the material principle which causes the variety of denominations. According to whether the formal principle is applied more or less intensely, more or less fully, so there appears one or another form of Protestantism. Then from the special relationship and interaction of the material and formal principles each denomination draws the secondary principles and the corollaries which finally give it its special character. We see here at its root the reason for the psychological attitude of the Protestant denominations, in their origins as in their mutual relations.

If Christian Churches and communions differ at so deep a level by reason of their doctrine on the Holy Spirit, what is the special characteristic of Congregationalism? It seems to amount to a kind of egalitarian and autonomous democratization of the Holy Spirit.

[9] Ladd, *op. cit.*
[10] *Ibid.*, p. 14.

In England the violent reaction of the Congregationalist movement against the hierarchic conception of the established Church is accompanied by a similar reaction at the theological level. And it is not Congregationalism alone which has taken this course, but also the Baptist movement, Methodism and so on. Even today one of the most serious problems is precisely the cleavage between the hierarchical and democratic interpretation of the gift of the Holy Spirit. The importance of this can be seen more clearly if it is remembered that in the United States, which numerically represents a half of the Protestant world, it is the denominations of radical type, the Methodist, Congregationalists, Baptists, which predominate. Now all these are connected by a democratic conception of the role of the Holy Spirit.

Certain sects, difficult to understand at first sight, like the Pentecostal sects which originated in Methodism, or the Adventist sects, which originated from the Baptists, become intelligible when their origins are traced back to this principle of the "democratization" of the Holy Spirit.[11]

Considerable difficulties which are to be found at all levels of the ecumenical problem can be explained by this twofold way of regarding the nature, role and action of the Holy Spirit as the principle on which the community of Christians is built up. If, for example, his role is interpreted according to the "Dissenters" of the seventeenth century, it must be agreed that the true form of Church government is founded on the principle of individual equality and autonomy: in the Church, as in Christ, all men are equal; no one possesses power unless it has been delegated to them by the community; the ministers are the deputies of the congregations and are designated by it to carry out certain functions; the seat of power is the congregation of the faithful to whom the Spirit has been communicated equally and without hierarchic mediation of divine right. And this which is true of local congregations is true also of the worldwide Church.

It is not hard to guess the repercussions of this principle at the ecumenical level and the conflicts which it leads to with other conceptions of the role and action of the Holy Spirit.

C. THE LIBERAL TRADITION

In Protestantism there is a liberal tradition which is not connected closely with any particular denomination.[12] On the subject of this tendency, as

---

[11] Seventh-Day Adventists answer Questions on Doctrine (1957).

[12] Wilhelm Pauck, The Heritage of Reformation, 3rd section: Liberalism (1950); Joseph Barth, Toward a Doctrine of the Liberal Church, The Minns Lectures for 1956 (1956); Frank J. Leenhardt, "Pour une orthodoxie libérale" Revue de Théologie et Philosophie 8 (1958), pp. 161–87; Duncan Howlett, Man against the Church: the Struggle between Religion and Ecclesiasticism (1949).

indeed on many others, it should be carefully noted that spiritual differences are not vertical with clear-cut divisions, as if human life was a forest of separate trees, but rather is it that of the human generation with its horizontal exchanges, cross-fertilization, osmosis and compenetration.

There are currents of liberalism in Anglicanism, Lutheranism and the Calvinist Churches, that is, within the classical tradition, and not only in the anthropocentric and rationalist sects. The fact that these latter are repudiated as Protestants by classical Protestantism does not preclude all affinity, dependence or influence. Liberalism, as a state of mind, knows nothing of denominational frontiers.

To the numerous difficulties of the ecumenical movement is added, therefore, the presence of this tradition whose influence is not to be measured by the numerical importance of the denominations which can be classed as its representatives, but by its often unsuspected interdenominational diffusion. Even a certain idea that one may have of the "future great Church" owes something to its inspiration.

Theological liberalism has both a doctrinal and phenomenological origin. Doctrinally it is situated at the meeting point on the one hand of Socinianism of the sixteenth century and of Illuminism of the seventeenth and, on the other hand, of a Protestant idea of tradition interpreted in the sense of a margin of freedom left to the Churches under the sovereignty and trancendence of the World.

Empirically, it desires to take into account the existence, as Christians, of men very different from each other, but it refuses to measure their ideas against an objective scale of truth. Francis of Assisi, Luther, Calvin, Cranmer, Karl Barth, Tillich, Niebuhr are separated by everything: their ecclesiastical allegiance, temperament, period at which they lived, religious ideas and yet, with admiration and gratitude the liberal Protestant considers them all as his own. In the homage which he pays to his heroes he recognizes no frontiers. This spirit often appears in the stained-glass windows of Protestant universities or seminaries. The University of Princeton, to mention but one, has in its chapel representations of the greatest figures of both the Catholic and Protestant traditions. At Union Seminary in New York in the Lampman Chapel Luther rubs elbows with Francis of Assisi and Teresa of Avila.

What is the principle of liberal theology? It can be characterized by the one word relativism. The path traced by the Reformers leads to no fixed arrival point. It is only the starting point of religion. They have opened the way, and it is for their successors to go further. Religious liberalism does not regard itself as an end in itself but as the driving principle of the undefined religious quest. It is a spirit and a method which enable Christianity to be taught, lived and preached in such a manner that it is always able to free itself, in those who practice it as in every social form, from the historical and institutional shell which instinctively wraps itself round the living heart and quenches the interior and spiritual flame.

Liberalism believes in the religion of the Spirit, of inwardness, of pure witness, of the event. It is opposed to what it calls religion of authority, of exteriority, of visible ministry, of the institution. For this is what, in its eyes, is the cause of decline, regression or limitation.

In theology the liberal is a relativist. He holds that expression of belief which cannot come up to the reality of its object. "Doctrine is thus limited at the outset in its quality by a certain subjectivism of knowledge; and it is limited also in its expression as in its duration by the inevitable symbolism of language, as well as by the religious and philosophical character of the period when it is given expression." [13]

The liberal Christian aware of this gap between belief and doctrine considers that it is incumbent upon him to devote himself particularly to those historical sciences enabling him to bring out, as he thinks, the pure meaning of the Gospel from what is its limited expression. And so he pays special attention to the latest conclusions of anthropology on the mythological function of the human imagination, to setting free the pure message of the Gospel from everything which appears as the vesture of a bygone age. [14]

In ecclesiology the liberal Christian is also relativist. He is attached to his Church but does not regard it, as an institution, as the condition or the means of contact with his Saviour. It can only facilitate this contact. "It is therefore extremely useful, but not indispensable in itself; it could not be the object of faith, nor an end in itself, nor a mystical entity. Relative in its essence, the Church is contingent in its form (constitution, organization) and in its traditional manifestations (teaching, liturgy)." [15]

In a word the liberal Protestant is a man who makes use of Christianity, Catholicism, Protestantism, as so many means of living what he considers to be the authentic Christianity of the Gospel. If his preference goes out to Protestantism as the method it is through affinity of spirit. In truth Protestantism possesses only a relative value for him, for if something were absolute, besides his own actuating idea of Christianity, the liberal Christian would no longer be liberal, for he would no longer be relativist.

A kind of evolutionary prophetism seems to bear liberal Protestantism along. Christianity of the past and innumerable witnesses were only stages in the exploration of the world by Christianity. What counts is not

---

[13] André Richardot, "Positions libérales", *Évangile et Liberté* (October 10, 1960), p. 81.
[14] Hans Werner Bartsch, ed., *Kerygma and Myth: a Theological Debate* (1953).
[15] Richardot, *loc. cit.*

Christianity as it has been presented, but that form which is to come. The Gospel is a form of guidance which is created, transforms and welcomes. No institutional form has ever exhausted its content. Alone the history of humanity will reveal its true stature.

II. THE WORLD COUNCIL, TRADITION AND TRADITIONS

For some time in Protestantism there has been a continual effort to promote the ecumenical movement in all its forms to recover the full meaning and purity of the Word of God. To witness this as it proceeds is to be filled with emotion, admiration and hope.

Indeed, consideration of what has been accomplished since the beginning of the century gives some clue, on the one hand, to the measure of mutual understanding, assistance and patience required for the dialogue between groups of such different traditions, divided between the conviction of a special vocation and, on the other, the evidence that an effective result cannot come from a mere lumping together of traditions.

And so there has resulted an effort towards purification, a movement of disinfection, of self-cure. J. M. Geritsen[16] believes that the World Council of Churches is drawing after it a dead weight of liberal conservatism and that the creation of a European Council has emerged from it as a reaction.

It must be acknowledged that in the course of its short history the Council could hardly have contrived to rid itself of what appears to us, as well as to the Orthodox, as doctrinal and ecclesiological liberalism. One proof among others that there has been some progress in this direction is furnished by the fact that the International Council of Christian Churches was set up at Amsterdam in 1948 with the intention of opposing the influence of the World Council of Churches.

It is an immense task that the non-Catholic ecumenical movement has set itself. Within it all the spiritual traditions are in confrontation with all sorts of differing positions: fundamentalism and modernism, orthodoxy and liberalism and extreme differences in matters of worship, government, belief, evangelization, etc.

The confrontation of traditions goes still further since it is continued with the Eastern Churches represented at the World Council, and the Catholic world also is concerned. What have these traditions to say to each other and in unity? The World Council has assumed the mission of leading the traditions into dialogue and mutual comprehension, moving towards unity in which they will discover each other.

[16] "The Recovery of Episcopacy" in Michael Bruce, ed., *Barriers to Unity* (1959), p. 100.

This work of reform has led to the conviction that these traditions have taken excessive advantage of the margin of freedom left to them by God under the authority of the Word. They have often gone beyond the bounds and set themselves limits of which the Word of God knows nothing. They should be led to align themselves once more under the authority of the Word. May this Word be heard in all its exacting requirements, its reproaches and in its summons to pristine purity of faith. What has adopted too individualist a position must discover once more a view of the whole; what has taken liberties with the Word, the guardian of the faith must again hear what this same Word says to the Churches — and these are bound to remain within its bondage.

The World Council of Churches, even in its commission on Tradition and Traditions of the Faith and Order section, does not claim as its province to determine on its own authority what the nature of tradition is. Its only intention is to raise the problem among the member-Churches. The field of dialogue within the Council, which extends from the Eastern Churches to denominations of the radical type, corresponds in fact with the question: Is tradition Protestant or Catholic in nature? Does it include a measure of freedom? Is it synonymous with immobility and unchangeableness? To what extent must it be followed faithfully? Where does unfaithfulness to it begin?

The object of the ecumenical movement is the renewal of impaired traditions. But from the outset we must realize fully that Christians approach the question with very different religious psychologies.

"Tradition in Protestantism means the margin of freedom left by God to his children."[17] This is what, in the view of the reformers, makes the tradition of each Church legitimate. Here then, is the key to understanding the reason for the differences between Catholics and Protestants in all spheres, but also within Protestantism itself between the classical and radical tendencies.

In Protestantism tradition refers to the "place occupied by choice, tendency and decision necessarily implied by the life of a Christian community possessing no other authority than the sacred Scriptures".[18] Under this sovereign and universal authority each people which accepts the Gospel is urged to develop a special ecclesiastical tradition reflecting its character, habits of thought and action, its tastes and even its feelings.

It is understandable that the criteria of receptivity should differ in Protestantism and Catholicism, yet it would be wrong to argue from this that Protestantism is receptive and Catholicism is not. Are there not in

---

[17] P. Lestringant, "Tradition catholique et Tradition protestante", *Foi et Vie*, 44th year (November-December 1946), p. 756.
[18] *Ibid.*

the Catholic Church eight major liturgical rites and all kinds of liturgical languages? Indeed we have been blamed for being too receptive. From outside the Catholic Church it is claimed that she is always hesitant in making her choice from among the innumerable objects that the thought and life of the centuries lay at her feet.

The radical difference for us lies in the fact that tradition is bound up with the internal origin of faith. "The God of Abraham, Isaac and Jacob" (Exod 3:6) is the God as he is revealed in Christ and transmitted to us in the Church. Tradition implies for us a state of soul turned towards a continuity. The Church in which we receive the faith is herself tradition, a living tradition which on the foundation of her living source, her centre and her origin, takes to herself the external world at the same time as she is influenced by it. That there is a place for freedom is certain and it is clearly shown by history. How much freedom is the Church allowed? To what extent can she let herself be identified with the nation, allow herself to interpret revelation in accordance with prevailing currents of thought, in terms of idealism, Hegelianism, existentialism, anthropology or phenomenology? What is venerated elsewhere as a sign of freedom not seldom appears to us as doctrinal relativism.

Tradition with us is also bound up with a condition of universality in time and space. The place occupied by freedom, the legitimate influence of milieu and peoples must never be such that they divide visible Catholicity from tradition in the course of its history or in its continuity in extension in the world. Catholicity means for us increase in substantial identity. Now of this tradition stands as the pledge. There is community control of tradition, in the first place by its authorized witnesses, the apostles and their successors, but tradition is also borne by the whole body of the faithful.[19]

The original deposit deriving from Christ and the apostles, the very substance of Catholic truth, is the supreme rule of faith. The apostolic hierarchy rules that a certain interpretation is, or is not, in conformity with it in the order of faith and life, of doctrine, morals and customs. Whatever appears that is new—and history and life cannot fail to bring something new to the living Church if men are animated by the Creator Spirit—is judged, approved or rejected to the extent that it agrees with the revealed deposit. The Catholic hierarchy does not confer the status of tradition on what is, of its nature, in conformity with the revealed truth. It merely declares, and with authority, that something is or is not in the same line of continuity with the living tradition of the past and, by this official action of the hierarchical Church, it is brought into the external forum of Catholicity. The way in which it is done varies: it may be after

[19] J. H. Newman, *Essays Critical and Historical*, 2 vols. (1871).

a long period of reserve or by rapid intervention, a judgement on experience or a fundamental decision, a certain pragmatism or a magisterial declaration.

In Protestantism tradition forms only an external complement to the Word of God in scripture. In Catholicism scripture itself appears as tradition, but we do not make of it the sole expression of the Word of God. The magisterial function of the apostolic hierarchy is also an expression of the Word. Scripture is tradition, but tradition is also expressed in other ways.

Whatever is outside the precise Word of God in scripture is, therefore, a matter of freedom for Protestantism. And this freedom, which varies in accordance with temperaments, manners of thought, habits of interpretation, is shaped into tradition. This is regarded by Protestantism as legitimate, good and necessary, provided that it does not go beyond certain limits. If they have obviously been passed, it means that there has been a want of faithfulness to the Word. In the World Council of Churches the primary and immediate end of ecumenical education is to lead back the Churches to these limits, to this moderation. To the extent that this is effected, the survial of the Anglican, Lutheran, Calvinist, Methodist, Congregational and other traditions is seen as legitimate and necessary.

But what are the rules for determining that the limits have not been passed? What will form the indication that there has been no abuse of that freedom constituted by tradition under the authority and sovereignty of the Word? Two rules are given at present. The first is an old one: the Word of God preserves in its truth those who endeavour to live in obedience to it; the second rule, and it is a sign of new maturity, is the consensus of the Christian Churches or communions. This is thus coming near to the Catholic and Orthodox idea, but the principle remains Protestant; it is a matter of a consensus obtained by strictly human deliberation. It possesses an indicative and highly persuasive value, but has no imperative or regulating force. The World Council of Churches would consider that it had fulfilled a large part of its mission if it could induce the Churches to produce a consensus which, in a human manner, would be some contribution to maintaining the Churches within the limits of the pure Word of God while the latter is working to keep them under itself by its own transcendent power. We are well aware of how much the member Churches, except the Eastern Churches, are on guard against everything which could give the impression of some authority of divine right, against any power, which remotely or proximately, would resemble a real episcopal power.

The least that can be said is that the attempt to bring to the fore in all the member Churches the principle of a consensus, and, what is still more difficult, to put it into operation, is a challenge by modern Protestantism to the whole of its history and, on that account, in one sense this principle is greater than the history. This attempt puts us in mind of the conciliar movement which at the Council of Basle endeavoured to point the way in the Catholic Church and did not succeed because the principle was based on the delegation of authority from the bottom to the top. The whole community is, it is true, a witness to the faith; but within the order of witness there exists a hierarchy of guarantees and guarantors of the faith.

It is of importance to see clearly what the aims pursued by the World Council of Churches are—the special and immediate aims and the remote aims deriving from the ecumenical nature of the undertaking. In the immediate future the Council seeks the welfare of the member-Churches which constitute it; as a long term policy it is preparing for the greater benefit of unity. A certain vacillation seems to result from the fact of the difference between its own ends, in conformity with a certain idea of tradition, and the quest for greater unity. Whatever our differences, and even on account of our differences, the improvement in relations that has occurred must go on.

For this improvement the Council is working by the ecumenical education which it has undertaken in order to bring the traditions of its members into contact, to cause them to undertake the work of their own reform and reunite under the authority of the Word of God. In Catholicism ecumenical education will be in conformity with the idea which we have of tradition. Should these two forms of education continue in isolation from each other and, if they do, would they in that case remain ecumenical? There can and must be contact between the two. Certain possibilities will be proposed here.

III. THE FORMATION OF AN ECUMENICAL SPIRIT

1. The action of the World Council

In its essentials Catholic formation is already an ecumenical preparation. By means of certain changes of emphasis and new modifications it can lend itself admirably to the work of drawing Christians nearer to each other. Nevertheless, it remains true that fundamental conditions and those of a more proximate nature constitute two orders of differing realities, especially in the present case in which integrating factors of unity are to be created, made general and extended to the point that all Christian Churches and communions will, by the grace of God, set out together on a general quest for unity.

Fortunately this problem of the formation of an ecumenical spirit is not entirely unexplored territory. Several movements of an ecumenical nature have provided the world over the last century with a rich and varied experience. In particular the World Evangelical Alliance of the Y. M. C. A. (1878) and of the Y. W. C. A. spring to mind, as also the World Federation of Christian Students (1895) and the World Alliance for International Friendship through the Churches (1914). For the most part it is from these movements that the leaders of Anglican and Protestant ecumenism have come. To understand their mentality we have to go back to their spiritual origins. Failure to do so has been the cause of unfortunate encounters between certain Catholics and these men who have received a formation more immediately turned in an ecumenical direction.

A second important factor in the formation of an ecumenical spirit has been the ecumenical movement itself. It has been confronted by a gigantic task in the creation of an ideal, in the definition of aims, in discovering means of action and, at the same time, in enduring itself with an ecumenical spirit. Theory has inspired action, in its turn action has modified the spirit. The movement has become ecumenical by doing an ecumenical task. And as it passed through its decisive phases it has been able to exercise self-criticism of its own activity in order to draw conclusions and lessons from experience. The whole of the present organization of the World Council of Churches thus appears as an immense form of collective education which gradually moulds its members in accordance with a well-defined ecumenical pattern.

It is important to be clear that this ecumenical intention corresponds to an actual decision; it is not enough to be universal in principle, it is necessary to be so in act and endeavour, with a precise and well-defined purpose. Policy for the remote future needs to be made specific by a resolutely ecumenical point of view.

Another lesson that we ought to learn from the activity of the ecumenical movement and, especially, from the Secretariat of the World Council at Geneva, is the ecumenical formation of youth. The reactions of those young people who have taken part in the ecumenical work camps or study sessions show the extraordinary revitalizing power of the ecumenical idea. Youth of today wants to live on a worldwide scale, and this desire must find some response at the religious level. Only an ecumenical formation will fashion them into the men that they must be for the times to come.

What new means can be put into operation to establish an ecumenical spirit in the heart of the Churches?

2. Invitation to new working hypotheses

A. INTERCONFESSIONAL PSYCHOLOGY

The time has come to apply the results, both old and new, of psychology to interconfessional relations. In the present stage of drawing closer together, in addition to a theology of ecumenism, we require a psychology bearing on the soul and spirit of the Christian communions to extricate inter-denominational relationships from their deviations and adherents, to criticize and direct them towards integrating, ecumenical positions. These relationships are of such importance that they cannot be left to chance, improvisation and a summary empiricism. Certain efforts of this kind require to be repeated and prolonged.

The term interdenominational psychology is used. This presupposes, of course, knowledge of confessional or interdenominational psychology. There are here two different aspects: knowledge of the bodies as a whole is one thing, knowledge of the relationships between the bodies is another. The science and art of ecumenical relationships require both. But it is necessary to go further.

Ignorance of the mentality of peoples, of their traditions and languages, has emerged as one of the most decisive non-theological factors in provoking and maintaining divisions. The path of unity, to a great extent, has to be retraced in the opposite direction. For the restoration and future maintenance of the union of Christians we must, therefore, give far greater importance to the psychology of peoples, groups and human relationships than we have done in the past. To reduce the whole ecumenical problem to a question of charity or obedience is really too much of an over-simplification. For what a great distance there lies between charity, the supreme principle of ecclesial communion, and actual ecumenical life!

In addition to the factors making for lack of understanding, which come from human sin and from Satan, the very source of division, there exist, therefore, other reasons which derive from the very nature of humanity.

The human species, which forms the substratum of the Church, exists only in the fragmented state in individuals, in groups and nations. Categories are instinctively established which serve as a spontaneous guide in the adjustment of relationships between individuals and groups.[20] Now, it is around these nuclei of generalization that all new impressions come to join together. Humanity prefers easy to difficult solutions. These elementary categories appear to it as the convenient and satisfying means of resolving the problems which confront it. Thus in terms of mutual

[20] Gordon Allport, *The Nature of Prejudice* (1954; abridged edition, 1958).

339

estimation of Christian bodies the words "Catholic", "Protestant", "Ortho-dox", at the popular level correspond with certain categories of the divisions of the Christian world. These simple and summary categories regulate the attitudes of the various Christian groups among themselves. They are not all of a conceptual nature. Several are infected with emotivity. Others are of a purely irrational kind, and they arise no less easily than the first mentioned by reason of the capacity for absorption belonging to the affective powers.

A preconceived idea is not yet a prejudice. It is the possible subject matter of one. When do our categories become prejudices?

Prejudice begins when love of our own system or scale of values becomes for us a universal criterion of perfection and judgement. It is not necessary that this process should be conscious or that it should apply to matters of importance. There are great as well as little prejudices, those of a club, a clan, a house, a team, a village, a parish, as well as those of a nation, a communion or a Church. Essentially the process is the same.

It is, therefore, the exaggerated love of the excellence of one's own categories which is at the root of prejudices. Love causes us to close our eyes to faults and generalize the good qualities. Something is liked, some-thing else is rejected, not for its merits or its faults but because it is seen as a friend or rival, favourable or threatening, in short, not in virtue of an objective scale of values but in relation to those of one's own categories.

But must every attachment to one's own categories be accused of being *a priori* a manifestation of partiality? Would a sort of vacuity, of indiffer-ence, of indecision in matters of preference be better? We see that another value comes into play, namely, fidelity to one's own denominational group.

At the strictly human level, the family group, then the local, regional groups and the nation provide the basis for man's existence, each according to its own measure. It is the same at the religious level. Every Christian depends for his existence as a Christian on his family, local and denomi-national group. The groups appear therefore necessarily as providers of benefits and security. A corresponding loyalty is the normal response to this. Now it is a matter of experience that loyalty tends to be in proportion to the nearness or remoteness of relationships with the primordial group.

If this principle is applied at the ecumenical level, it will be seen that to leave ecumenical education to take place of its own accord is to be certain that "parochialism" and provincialism will prevail over the universal spirit. The wider the good that is sought the less will the individual experience a spontaneous inclination towards it, unless education can cultivate the innate sense that is in every man to prefer the whole to the part. But a specific formation is necessary and this, at the ecumenical level is called ecumenical education. This is not entirely impossible. Already at the human level, from interest or conviction, men have learned in the last fifty years to think in terms of the whole world. Christians must now be led to think that nothing in the world which is Christian should be foreign to them.

Now it is precisely in the absence of ecumenical education that the root of innumerable conflicts is to be found. Every individual thinks that he is doing well by giving his loyalty to the religious group that is nearest to him, which is the most vital for him and, for the rest, loyalty is measured according to a descending scale. The greatest loyalty to the cause of universal Christianity is thus reduced to very short commons indeed.

There is no question of creating a sort of vague, ethereal, indefinite attachment to universal Christianity, forgetting that it begins quite near to oneself, and with oneself and in one's nearest neighbour; nor is it a question in the name of an ecumenical concern for all Christians and all Churches of adopting indifferentism in the matter of religion. What is at stake is to unite loyalty with and openness towards other Christians which alone can lead to reconciliation and union.

Universalism, catholicity, the ecumenical sense, are not things which are received in their fully developed state together with Christian existence. It is not enough to be born a Christian to be ecumenical. Education to ecumenism is not accomplished without raising unsuspected prejudices nor without methodical formation to answer the positive summons of the Church which, of its nature, is a vocation without limits.

B. THE STUDY OF MENTALITIES AND LANGUAGES

The temperament and psychology of peoples can act in an ambivalent direction: they can be factors for reunion as for division. They can be at the service of the greatest ecumenical development; they can also militate against it, and there can be no better way of ensuring that they do so than to confuse in ecumenical relations one mentality with another or to think that all are alike. All men meet at their final destiny and at their roots, but what wide spaces there are between the two! A kind of intellectual and affective humility is needed in order to listen to other mentalities and other temperaments. The Jewish mentality is not the Greek mentality; nor is the French the English mentality, the Latin the Slavonic, the Slavonic the Asiatic. Ecumenical work cannot be approached in the same way in Anglo-Saxon circles as in Latin circles.

In other words, there are various ways of proceeding from the particular to the general, from the concrete to the abstract, of entering into spiritual possession of an object. For the English mentality, for example, life is wider than knowledge. It is the infinite treasure that science attains only by tiny scraps. What the Cartesian spirit would call British illogicality is merely prudent reaction. The English mentality in its approximations makes allowance for imponderables, accepting that knowledge and action cannot achieve parity in this life. There is awareness of what has been seen, but also of what remains. Reality appears as a great sovereign keeping its plans secret. Etiquette requires that they be held in respect. And what appears to other mentalities as an attempt to reconcile the irreconcilable proceeds from the conviction, or at least the hope, that in some way all will mysteriously fall into place by an arrangement not evident to us but nonetheless real. This kind of illogicality, if it is one, is not the reaction of one who does not know enough, but of someone who is very doubtful whether he does not know too much. Hence the important place given to empirical solutions, for knowledge is doubt and opposition to each other is still a form of sharing.

Giving due respect to the primacy of the principles of faith, we must acknowledge that ecumenism, if it is to succeed, must take into consideration a certain empiricism. If we are awaiting, in order to draw nearer to each other and commence dialogue, a uniform acceptance of the truth held by each party, we are dreaming of an impossibility. If on the other hand, we believe that empiricism is a solution of general application, we shall enter on confusion. For example, it would not be enough to say that if we practice intercommunion full communion will follow. This would be to take phenomenology for the path of faith. Yet would it not be possible, keeping matters in proper proportion, and basing ourselves on our unanimity in the universal mission of Christianity, for us to discover a meeting place on certain points wide enough for us to work together? Thus, without raising the question of principles at the outset, we could make the experiment of mutual adaptation at the level of the various systems as a whole.

So long as we have only entered on a dialogue, or rather a monologue with ourselves, we are unaware of the extent to which our own language is strange to those who hear it. At the ecumenical level we all suffer from the mistaken notion that our own language ought to be understood by all since it is we who speak it. Other people's language is strange to us, but ours should not be for them! Since there are various expressions of Christianity, we ought to study each other's language if we wish to enter on a dialogue.

C. ECUMENICAL EDUCATION

It is not sufficient to be in possession of an ecumenical culture; it is still more important to have an ecumenical education. Education is indeed the appropriate word. It means drawing out from what is already in existence, namely one Baptism in Christ, Christian values, good will and those dispositions which will lead to the greatest unity.

Ecumenical education can only be the result of a combination of the whole body of human powers in which the mind with its ecumenical information, the will, the feelings and control of passions, even the body in its visible service of the ecumenical cause, will lead to the highest result that it is possible to attain and this is the determination in man of unity as a stable disposition whose exercise is accomplished in a noble effort and in joy.

Ecumenical information is the first requisite condition. Understanding of the heart begins through the mind. Knowledge of the facts, of the problems and the needs must thus be made accessible by accurate and objective information in proportion with capabilities and actual needs. In addition, the essentials of the ecumenical question together with its evolution, progress and ideals must be explained to the people. Images, symbols and concrete actions will furnish the most appropriate language. Experience of our divisions has shown what the passions of men are capable of when they are not enlightened by accurate knowledge of other Christians.[21]

Ignorance and inaccuracy are not the only factors which, at the intellectual level, are harmful to ecumenical relations. There is also the ready-made formula.

Every Christian body makes for itself a certain image of the others. Objective knowledge reflects the real characteristics of the various groups, deformed knowledge the characteristics as seen by the ready-made formula. Between the first and the second is the difference which exists in the aggregate between objective reality and its caricature.

Knowledge based on the ready-made formula follows the rule of the least effort. Acquired by means of a defective education, it adopts the characteristics and certitude of habit and becomes established. In terms of the ready-made formula Catholics, for example, will be described as Christians of an authoritarian kind, opponents of birth control, upholders of superstition, mariolatry and pope-worship; the Protestant in his turn, will be seen as a "pope, Bible in hand"; the Orthodox as the eccentric survival of an archaic world, and so on.

Already at the human level the tendency to stereotype the characteristics of other groups is a fact of current experience. No race, no people escapes it. These secular habits are transferred to the religious level. A considerable work of purification, then, is required in the features which Christian denominations are very free in attributing to each other. The character-

[21] *1054–1954. Neuf siècles de douloureuse séparation entre l'Orient et l'Occident*, 2 vols. (1954). Vatican II's Decree on Ecumenism contains valuable advice on ecumenical formation.

istic of the stereotyped formula is that there is a generalization of a specific feature, and then its assertion, without verification on a massive scale, on the strength of appearances or of certain aspects of matters considered in isolation.

What is most serious in these ready-made formulas is their enduring nature. They make people forget that history goes on and individuals evolve. How can real contact at a deep level be possible when the parties meet and look at each other without seeing? When the true likeness is deformed by a distorted image and when beneath the features of the heads of Churches at the present day men discern the features of the heads of Churches at the period when the crises and separations occurred? It is hardly worth asking whether contact of this kind can serve as the starting point of ecumenical relations. It is at the level of the will and the passions that ecumenical education will have to deploy its greatest effort.

Charity is the principal motive for opening oneself to communion with other Christians, for emerging from one's religious isolation, entering on ecumenical relationships and maintaining them despite all obstacles. And when the dialogue reaches deadlock, when positions harden for a time by some return of passion, it is charity which prompts the will not to break off relations on account of differences.

Love which governs reconciliation stands beyond the categories of victory and defeat, for these are profane, non-Christian categories. When reunion comes to pass, there will be neither victors nor vanquished, neither victory nor defeat, of any Church. There will only be the victory of faith, hope and charity under the fatherhood and sovereignty of God.

D. THE PARISH, THE ECUMENICAL COMMUNITY

Up till now the great difficulty encountered by the ecumenical movement and, particularly, the World Council of Churches and the national councils of Churches, for which no adequate answer has yet been found, has been to bring ecumenical integration down from the leaders to the people. At the top there is admirable and fruitful encounter between representatives of the Churches. There is fellowship, open co-operation, exchange of ideas and real spiritual brotherhood. The higher organizations, like the permanent Secretariat of the World Council at Geneva and the National Council of the Churches of Christ in the United States at New York, take care that in their offices there is very wide denominational representation. But the leaders of the ecumenical movement are not unaware that they are far ahead of the members of their respective communions. Such a situation cannot endure indefinitely without leading to a cleavage between them and the people whom they represent.

The World Council of Churches has tried various remedies for this situation. It has shown member Churches that there is a need for ecumenical education, a need which several had not suspected. It has suggested various methods to them and has acted as a centre for the exchange of ideas. It has taken personal steps through the Ecumenical Institute and the Department of Ecumenical Action.

But neither the World Council of Churches nor the national councils nor the local councils of Churches are themselves Churches. They are interdenominational agencies. They do what is in their power, but they cannot accomplish what is not in their nature to do. They lack, by virtue of their very constitution, certain organs of communication by which they could reach the ordinary laity, certain essential links to ensure continuity of inspiration and life between the head and the members.

That, then, is the situation. It constitutes a serious problem for the future of the ecumenical movement, for, without the formation of an ecumenical spirit at the popular level, it will be difficult to create a popular will to union.

The reunion of Christians is a Church matter. It is a question of a community, ecclesial work. The union of Christians cannot consist merely in the reconciliation of heads of Churches, as if it could be attained by a body of treaties, reciprocal concessions or contractual agreements. In actual fact it is a question of the reunion of Churches, of Christian communities and not merely of heads of Churches. A reunion based on the agreement of the heads alone, in which the people had no share, would last no longer than the lifetime of the leaders who brought it about, as the example of the second Council of Lyons (1274) and the Council of Florence (1439) plainly shows us.

Likewise, a union founded on the sole pressure of the common dangers threatening us would last only so long as these dangers. In the fifteenth century fear of the Turks forced the Christians to negotiate a reunion. Nowadays, the Turks have been replaced by Communism. In the same way, a union based solely on social needs would fall apart when they were met. Not opportunism, even in its most legitimate form, not Christian action, even in its noblest form, not the mere agreement of heads of Churches, can serve as the basis for lasting communion. Each individual has his share of responsibility in a work which is Church work, for it is a question of the reunion of Churches. The leaders will be all the more encouraged to go forward to the extent that they feel their communities behind them. In this way their successors will be unable to undo what has been done. They will have to continue it. The faithful must love and desire the union of Christians.

How can we succeed in forming this popular will for union which will be in a position to count on the powerful assistance of the World Council of Churches and the national councils of Churches, since these latter are not fitted to form it themselves. There is only one answer: the work rests solely on the Churches. The solution is in three phases. In the first place, ecumenical education is a Church work, a work for Christian communions. In the second place, the Church and Christian communions must act through their own organs of communication, their natural channels which are the parishes. Lastly, if it is really desired to reach the whole body of the faithful and ensure for them an ecumenical education, the parish, wherever necessary, must be endowed with the spirit of an ecumenical community.

Just as in general the Christian bodies have drawn closer together, so, at the local level, there must be some encounter between the different groups of separated Christians. This work is on an immense scale as a glance at the map of the Christian world will show.

In the Christian East the parish must take on an ecumenical outlook if one day the local communities of different rites and jurisdictions are to meet together in the harmonious unity of the Body of Christ.

In the Christian West the parish must take on an ecumenical outlook if one day the local communities, at present Catholic and Protestant, are to meet together in the harmonious unity of the Body of Christ.

In other words, we must go back over the path which led to the separation between East and West, between the Catholic Church and the Protestant Churches. What is required is a union of the different communities in depth, a well-knit union, one that is expressive, organic and living, capable of resolving forthwith the tensions which may crop up among the leaders; a union capable of subsisting in spite of their disagreements, and one which they will have to take into account before plunging their Churches into some ill-conceived adventure.

Such a movement at the level of the parish, the ecumenical community, is difficult, long and perilous. At the outset it cannot be a generalized movement. In the West as in the East certain more united groups must take the lead and make the experiment for the benefit of the Church as a whole. In ecumenism we need pilot-parishes just as there in liturgy.

In several parishes, in Germany and Alsace for example, there are regular meetings between Protestant pastors and Catholic clergy. These are ecumenical meetings. This can be one of the elements of a parish as an ecumenical community, but it is still not the movement of the community as such making its way towards reconciliation of separated brethren and the repair of injured traditions. More is required.

Take the example of a large city parish in America, England or Germany. It is by no means rare for the same geographical area to contain five or six parishes whose communities respect each other but know absolutely nothing of each other. Thus we can see the distance between this situation at popular level and the degree of understanding existing in ecumenical circles. Local Christian communities, which live closely intermingled while knowing nothing of each other, without trace of hate or rivalry must come to the point of asking what they really are in relation to each other, how far do their mutual acceptance and rejection go and whether it is possible to draw nearer to each other.

When several Catholic, Protestant, Anglican and Orthodox parishes think along the same lines a parochial ecumenical movement will be created. At the local level this will mean the beginning of the reuniting of separated traditions. The unity of Christians can only spring from an indefinite multiplication of a movement of this kind.

In a religiously mixed parish specially chosen elements from each confessional group will act as the central core. And in their turn these groups in association will serve as the kernel for a larger region, and so on. The healing of the wounds in the various bodies will be thus the result of the encounter between the two sides of an effort begun at the highest and at the local level, carried out in combination and causing the value of union together to be felt at the same time as it effects it. And the miracle of the unity of Christians will come to pass. Our role will be to contribute, to bring together the elements over which our Saviour will utter the word of reconciliation.

It is necessary to stress this further to show that the decisive part will be played at the local community level by ecumenical education of the young as well as the adults. The creation of a parochial ecumenical movement, which will act as a connecting link between the multidenominational parochial groups at the pastoral, liturgical, doctrinal and all the other levels is of the highest importance.

In a world in which the democratic sense has undergone considerable development and the laity are claiming their share of responsibility, it is no longer possible for everything to be done by the leaders of the Church alone. In the ecumenical field the laity will thus be able to play their own irreplaceable part in the accomplishment of the mission of the Church.

We are aware of the immense importance of this, but we can see, also, its difficulties and dangers. The necessity to go forward should not be confused with a rash venture, and the urgency of establishing links must not lead to confusion. At the outset it will be necessary to be content with very general trends which will create a climate of courtesy and good will among groups. It will be necessary also that different confessional groups come to an understanding so that they may be transformed into communities of prayer and charity which will form an introduction to the knowledge of ecumenical needs. We must always remember that the ecumenical movement is based on the healing and refashioning of the bodies that form the Churches.

In the whole of the new movement there will emerge pilot parishes which, under the control of the respective superior authorities will carry further the experiment of drawing the various bodies closer together at the local Christian level. It will be their function to discover gestures of Christian solidarity which will furnish the separated communions with the experience and awareness of unity. It is a question of putting up bridges, of common or similar elements especially, of introducing elements of creative dialogue, of throwing the frontiers open.

Several spheres lend themselves to pilot experiments—social action, hospitality, prayer, mutual charity.[22] Very simple concrete actions, whose symbolism is immediately obvious at the popular level, can have an immense effect. If it is true that a Church which is closed in on itself exposes another Church to the temptation of discouragement and schism, it is also certain that by its welcoming attitude it can quickly cause the centuries-old walls of separation to crumble. Now peoples are borne along *en masse* towards the object of their love or their hate. Those who are believers must have under their eyes some imposing spectacles of unity in which they can recognize themselves. And one day, perhaps, some immense tidal wave will carry away the last obstacles.

Christian bodies must learn gradually to pray together. In all the new forms of expression of the last twenty years is there perhaps something which can serve as a meeting point? As a possible suggestion the biblical vigil occurs to the mind;[23] with a certain amount of adaptation it might well be used at parochial level for a united service of different denominations. The essential element of these "para-liturgies" is that of a celebration centred on the Word with chants, Bible readings, the saying in common of the Psalms and a homily. It copies the practice of the synagogue which, in the Christian liturgy has been combined with the sacramental celebration. Paraliturgies which, in Catholic worship, seem to be less used than in the immediate past, and, on the other hand, are to some extent similar to Protestant worship which is wholly centred on the Word, might constitute one of the possible paths leading to inter-Christian encounter.

The schemes suggested from time to time in *Paroisse et Liturgie* all follow a common pattern: I. Introduction or entrance rite: introductory psalm, short prayer by the congregation summed up in the collect by the president or celebrant. II. Liturgy of the Word properly so called: readings from the Old Testament and the letters of the apostles interspersed with chants and meditation (psalms or biblical canticles). Then comes the proc-

[22] Oscar Cullmann, *Un projet de solidarité chrétienne* (1958).
[23] *Veillées bibliques pour tous les dimanches de l'année* (1960).

lamation of the Gospel by the deacon, followed by the homily from the president of the congregation. III. Prayer of the faithful: in the first place individual prayer, following the homily, as meditation in silence; then ecclesial prayer. The deacon announces the principal intentions of the Church to each of which the congregation signifies its assent by a ritual formula. This union of the faithful in common prayer for the same intention of the Church receives its consecration in the president's blessing and concludes with spiritual communion in the collective recitation of the Lord's Prayer. IV. The service concludes with the final blessing and, on occasion, with the recessional hymn.

A slightly different formula, which follows the structure of the Mass, has been suggested for religious services in countries or regions in which there is a shortage of priests, especially in missionary territories.[24] The purpose of this formula is to bring the Christian community as close as possible to the celebration of the mysteries of the economy of salvation when sacramental celebration is impossible or can take place only rarely.

The plan suggested by Fathers H. Höfinger, S. J., and J. Kellner, S. J.,[25] includes two parts called the service of the Word and the service of prayer.

The service of the Word follows this plan: opening: psalm or appropriate hymn; first lesson: the Epistle of the day, psalm or intermediate prayer; second lesson: Gospel of the day, psalm in responsorial form; third lesson: catechism, Apostles' Creed.

The service of prayer includes: prayer of intercession, thanksgiving prayer with the *Sanctus* and the Lord's Prayer; a commemoration of the liturgical day or season; final hymn.

In this scheme there is as full a reference as possible to the official preaching of the magisterium through the intermediary of the instruction given to the faithful by the voice of their official teacher and a spiritual orientation to the Eucharist through associating the community with the eternal priesthood of Christ and the Masses celebrated throughout the world. Taking of the service is entrusted to a layman. Or a deacon could do it.

Could this scheme be adapted in its turn to ecumenical rapprochement through the liturgy? It would be of course a pilot scheme in a suitable parish. Communion between the baptized united under the one Word and in the same prayer could well prepare for a deeper, eucharistic and ecclesial communion.

---

[24] Mgr. C. Cramer, "Service religieux en l'absence du prêtre", *Missions et Liturgie,* report of the first international week for studies in missionary liturgy, Nijmegen-Uden, 1959 (1960), pp. 131–5.

[25] *Liturgische Erneuerung in der Weltmission* (1957).

E. FRATERNIZATION BETWEEN CHRISTIAN INSTITUTIONS

On the basis of this principle of faith, love and hope that one day Christians will be united, an attempt is here made to draw from it some idea of the means which will have led us to that unity. We can observe our present divided state and consider our possible union. We have several Christian bodies in juxtaposition; let us consider them now as ideally united. Now quite certainly they will not have passed from the first to the second state directly without transition. And so we must draw up some working hypotheses.

The secular world, and very often not its best side, has given us Christians important lessons in the last years. We have seen the heads of powerful States, despite the cold war, meeting together and by this very fact, offering some hope that peace was not after all banished from the world.

We have seen cities and associations of the Free World fraternizing with that other world which we consider so utterly different. We should remember the fact and not withhold our admiration that certain of the sons of darkness are wiser than the sons of light.

What has been done from motives of peace, whether genuine or not, like cities adopting a "twin" in another country, institutions and associations fraternizing together, mutual help and so on might well serve us for an example of what we could do. Instead of a secular cause and possibly an equivocal undertaking we have a religious cause, we are Christians together. Such a step, without losing its difficulty or delicacy, could well work for the exaltation of the faith.

An American Lutheran theologian, Yaroslav Pelikan, in the autumn of 1959 suggested that a sort of inter-institutional ecumenical institute should be set up based on the bibliographical resources of the Jesuit Fordham University, the interdenominational Union Theological Seminary and the Anglican General Seminary. To start something new it is not always necessary to put up new buildings in which, on occasion the material elements seem more important than the spiritual. It is often sufficient to forge links where there were none before.

A number of other means of inter-institutional collaboration suggest themselves: for example, fraternization between the great monastic orders of the West and the oriental monasteries. It is unnecessary to rebuild on Mount Athos the Benedictine monastery (founded from Amalfi), which existed there at the beginning of the Middle Ages between Karakallu and the Great Laura. Fraternization in our modern world can be expressed in other ways.

Gestures of this kind are suggested to some extent by the example of the friendship which unites the Abbey of Le Bec-Hellouin in Normandy with the primatial see of Canterbury. Could hospitality become still more ecumenical? Those "invisible monasteries" glimpsed by Abbé Couturier are always necessary, but the time has come, perhaps, for other contacts between visible monasteries. We know that Anglican, Calvinist or Lutheran communities would participate, but they may be waiting for a gesture from their elder brothers. Is there no one who could take our weakness down to the pool, where the waters are today being troubled by the angels, so that our wounds will be healed (Jn 5:7)?

And if some great Catholic capital of the Western world established links, at the specifically Christian level, with some great city of the Protestant, Anglican or Orthodox world, what a wonderful symbol it would be for the world! If we desire that one day there should be an avowedly Christian international community, we must not imagine that the mere indirect influence of Christianity will be enough. It will be necessary for Christianity as such to have established a network of ecumenical links.

There is another idea that we could make our own. States and groups of States establish funds for the help of less fortunate countries. The World Council of Churches is at work in its own sphere by mutual aid among the Churches. Would it not be possible to broaden this idea to include mutual assistance among Christians on a worldwide scale? We are well aware that the charitable activity of the World Council of Churches goes beyond the boundaries of the member Churches, just as the papal charitable organizations do not stop at the frontiers of Catholicism. But one would like to see the establishment of a charity which is ecumenical not only in its effects but also in its aims.

F. THE ECUMENICAL DIMENSION IN SPIRITUALITY

Whoever we are, we are Church people because we are Christians and, as such, incorporated in some way in Christ and his Church. In our birth as Christians we find the nature of the spirit which should be ours. In Catholicism there are various "schools" of spirituality—Benedictine, Dominican, Carmelite, Franciscan etc. The Orthodox, too, have their different spiritual trends—Hesychast, communal etc. And then there are well-known types of Anglican piety and the Lutheran and Calvinist types of Protestant piety. We shall only deal directly here with what concerns our own Church.

Various periods of spirituality have followed one another in the history of Christianity down the centuries. A living spirituality must exist side by side with the living soul of the Church; otherwise she makes no progress and does not produce the saints that she ought to produce. And why must spirituality follow the life of the Church? Because the God whom we love, whom we serve, whom we contemplate, is not the God of the philosophers and the learned, but the "God of Abraham, Isaac and Jacob",

351

the Word who was made flesh and dwelt among us, who never ceases to be reborn, to live and grow among us in the hearts of men of all nations until God shall be all in all. No true contemplation of God can be spiritually egoistic or unconcerned with temporal matters; in the most remote of the hermitages of Mount Athos or in the Carmelite's cell, the monk, the nun, encounters the contemporary world not in its own guise, which they do not know, but in the guise of the world to be saved.

A spirituality centred too exclusively on one's own tradition runs the risk of participating in the present life of the Church in an etiolated, shrunken form and, what is more serious still, it is in danger of ignoring Christ in his mystery in the present world, and of forgetting that what has been the greatness of the spiritual masters is precisely that they grasped Christ in the contemporary value of his mystery.

At each period, then, we must listen to what Christ and the Spirit say to the Churches. For a century past under our eyes they have brought out with increasing emphasis the communal and ecclesial dimension of Chritianity. Any spiritual tradition which desires to live the call to perfection, to which Christ summons us once more in this period of the world's history, must enter into this new dimension. And it seems that Christ and the Spirit are calling us to still wider perspectives with the movement for the reunion of Christians.

By an ecumenical dimension of Christian spirituality must not be understood an amplification in the sense of a wider knowledge of the spiritualities of East and West, or a sort of hasty and eclectic amalgamation of the different characteristics of spirituality, taken at random from one source or another.

Christ is one, and if there are periods in which the richness of his mystery is explained in accordance with different traditions, there are also periods in which all spiritual families in seeking to draw nearer to each other to obtain thus a more Catholic integrity, a completeness, desire to recentre their spirituality profoundly in the one mystery of Christ and of the Church which is their spiritual substance.

Invisible but real bonds of brotherly love are established by communion of like souls in Christ, the bond and reconciler of Christians. This is the idea behind Abbé Couturier's invisible monastery.[26]

The whole cycle of the liturgical year becomes impregnated with an ecumenical value.[27] How can we forget that this mystery of Christ, whose phases form the accompaniment of time, is a mystery developing in each and every Christian communion, and that each day shows progress, a halt

---

[26] M. Villain, *Introduction to Ecumenism* (1961).
[27] C. J. Dumont, *Les Voies de l'unité* (1957).

or regression in the accomplishment of the mystery of that unity which is the purpose of the Incarnation (Jn 11:52)?

It is in the depth of love and fidelity to one's own tradition, whose universal roots are to be sought in Christ himself, the one Master (Mt 23:8), that exchanges outside that tradition become possible between brethren. Was this not the rule in the past? Did not the West derive its monastic spirituality from the East? Has the West nothing to offer the East in ascetical and mystical theology? Have we not all wonderful prayers to exchange with each other? [28] Generations of saints have built up for us an extraordinarily rich spiritual heritage. Was it not so that it can be shared out when the time of effective communion arrives? It is sometimes said that it is monks who delay union, but it is certainly not those who go forward in step with the Church.

[28] N. Edelby, *Liturgicon,* and, from the Latin side, for example, *Bible Missal, Layman's Missal* etc. For an example from the Anglican side, Lancelot Andrewes, *The Preces Privatae,* with introduction and notes by F. E. Brightman (1903).

CHAPTER IX

The Sociological and Organic Problem: Disunited or Unitive Catholicism?

I. DEFINITION OF THE PROBLEM

1. Universality and Incarnation

In all ages the problems of the Church and those of the world have been interdependent. The modern crisis of disintegration is a crisis of institutions. Slowly a whole world has collapsed and while humanity was extending its boundaries by means of powerful creations it forgot the narrowness of the old institutions. The crisis was not deliberately provoked by man but occurred through the pressure of the impersonal forces of matter, new technological achievements and the increase of rationalization.

And yet, this same world, with a sure instinct of conservation and balance sought to regain control over its boundaries. The worldwide trend to integration is a law of our times. This world, as a whole, cannot be wrong. The instinct of nature animating it comes from a higher and more remote plane than it thinks. Integration has become a vital need for it. To an agonizing degree it feels the division going through its members. And its memory, derived from the experience of the conflicts of states against states, of one culture against another, of one race against another, of blood against blood, of religions against other religions, does not form the kind of protection which can prevent it from further experience of the same thing.

We do not know how far the mystery of salvation is spread about in history, but we believe and we know that it is still present and that despite setbacks, forces of freedom are at work to lead man through the difficulties of sombre times towards a new unity.

To the era of world revolution and enormous differentiation there corresponds the era of world integration. Firstly, economic integration: thus, the economic organization of the European community; political organization: the United Nations, the Council of Europe, the inter-American organization, the Soviet bloc; social organization: the neighbourhood communities in the great cities, the joint industrial councils, the joint production committees, the labour councils etc.; cultural integration: UNESCO, for example; military integration. And all this leaves out of account many other international organizations in the realm of food, health, reconstruction, integration of refugees and so on.

The present integration has made it inevitable that one day or another the problem of the integration of Christian denominations will arise. The new *Oikumene* awaits from the religious world an answer that shall be in line with modern times.

It is already apparent that the pioneers of the modern ecumenical movement were prophets. At the level of the "practical direction of the life of Christians" God makes use of those prophetical instruments as it pleases him and he does not restrict such gifts to the visible frontiers of his Church.

Christianity is summoned to promote, at its own level, that political, economic, cultural and spiritual integration which the world needs, but not as a faction or as another power, but as the Church, for the benefit of God's plans and in accordance with his spirit, that is, in terms of the history of salvation.

So long as the main bodies of Christendom existed in isolation from each other, they did not feel the acuteness of certain objectively present problems which are now unavoidably brought to the surface as a result of the process of reconciliation. Now when Churches and Christian communions belonging to different traditions enter into ecumenical relations with each other, they regard themselves first and foremost as total institutions and seek to define themselves as such. And then at least one thing is questioned, namely their institutional integrity. Do the existing institutions meet fully the requirements of this new ecumenical age? Or will they have to adapt themselves to be able to cope with the task of Christian unity? And to what degree will they be permitted to make this adaptation?

These questions apply to the Protestant, Catholic, Anglican and Orthodox worlds. They are explicit and call for immediate attention.

Christianity appeared on the human scene as a new type of sociological and religious development, derived from Judaism, but soon to be detached from the parent plant through the latter's very refusal to recognize it as its own. The Jewish religion regarded Christianity as a new sect which could not be reconciled with the sources from which it had sprung. It soon became apparent that the two religions would have to go each its own way, one remaining centred round the temple and the old law, the other displaying its new institutions. Both religiously and sociologically, the Church represented a revolution. It was a worldwide assembly of men, without any culture of its own to support it, an institution without parallel in the world, one that had been totally unforeseen and that would not be followed by any successor.

Having moved away from Jewish culture, Christianity was led to make its home in every part of the world. At an early date the Church took on two major sociological, religious aspects: one Eastern, the other Western. Each of these was characterized by the establishment of forms which were capable of expressing, at the level of faith, order and worship, our Lord's unique institution.

Then in the fifth century the Eastern expression of Christianity split into new sociological and religious groupings: the semitic Syrian world broke away, taking with it other groups in the Middle East and Africa. Then the differences between East and West became increasingly accentuated until finally, in the Middle Ages, there occurred a veritable sociological and religious rupture between the two major expressions of Christianity. At the Renaissance it was the turn of Western Christendom to be split. The Reformation appeared as a new kind of development in Christian thought, and very soon afterwards there began the process of division into an indefinite number of sociological, religious units.

Catholicism, Orthodoxy, Anglicanism and the various forms of Protestantism are so many fundamental ways of living Christianity. And they are opposed to each other as sociological, religious entities, while at the same time they each claim as their authority that unique institution and unique event, which is the Church founded by Jesus Christ.

It is here that the problem lies. To what extent should the Church yield in its capacity of following man in his evolution? Should living Christianity reflect the history of man in proportion as he changes, and should it change its spirit with him? Should the Church show a resemblance to the structural, philosophical and political forms adopted by man in the course of history? To be consistent, it would be necessary in a democratic country, equipped with a federal constitution, to mould the national Church on democratic and federal lines in preference to any others, and in a monarchical State the Church would require a hierarchical form.

Now is it man who assimilates God, or God who assimilates man? Is it the nation which assimilates the religion, or the religion which organically assimilates the nation?

The debate bears on the extent to which the phenomenology category is used as criterion of incarnation in religion, and to which the institution is accepted as a principle of integration. If priority is given to the phenomenology category, the final result is necessarily a disunited catholicity. If, on the other hand, no account is taken of human diversity, then Christianity is by this very fact prevented from developing fully. Christianity is a religion both universal and incarnate. As a universal religion, it must bring all men together, but can only do this if it incorporates them one by one in catholicity. Thus the problem is one of finding a correct balance in the ratio of Universal to Incarnation. At what point does the will to incarnation become disruptive for catholicity? At what point does necessary universality jeopardize the chances of Incarnation? Whatever the answer, what is at stake here is catholicity, either disunited or unitive.

2. The contribution of the ecumenical movement

Since the Edinburgh conference in 1937, the Faith and Order Movement had directed its attention to an examination of the problem of unity in terms of sociology as well as doctrine. However, the efforts made by the movement to explore the sociological aspects did not lead very far, on account of the breadth and vagueness of the subject matter; for many factors, political, historical, psychological, cultural and racial, are included under the heading of non-theological factors. On the occasion of the meeting held at Davos in Switzerland, in 1955, the Faith and Order Permanent Committee decided to set up a commission on "Institutionalism as a factor affecting all the Churches". In particular, the following questions were put to it: to what extent is each Church or communion prompted, as far as its capacity for self-criticism is concerned, to examine, as a result of institutionalism, its own structure from the sociological and theological points of view? To what extent does institutionalism influence the relations between the Churches on the level of ecumenical dialogue? And lastly, how great a part does it play in the kind of Church relations which are expressed in the World Council of Churches as an institution?

A certain amount of tentative research was inevitable in view of the novelty of the undertaking. At the time of the meetings held in Boston in 1958, and Geneva and Tutzing (Germany) in 1959, the Commission on Institutionalism set to work to define the meaning of institution, institutionalism and institutionalization, and to draw conclusions from the analysis of typical cases.

The most appreciable result, apart from that of placing the question before the conscience and responsibility of the member Churches, is probably to have elucidated the different aspects of the problem and their reciprocal connection. The report of the Tutzing meeting in July 1959 drew attention to the fact that if the Church is a creation of God, then it is also a human institution. The word "institution", therefore, lends itself to a certain ambiguity. There is the sociological sense, in which it expresses the element of human activity, and there is the theological sense in which it expresses the element of divine activity. Now the theological and sociological structures of the Church are not only complementary, but are also closely interwoven and often inseparable from each other. They can be distinguished at the analytical level, but they cannot be placed in different compartments. The underlying reality of the Church possesses as a part of its very life factors which have been divinely instituted, such as baptism, the Eucharist, the Word, the ministries and the faith. These theological institutions necessarily give rise to certain social structures in the visible Church, and are connected together in historical forms which develop in proportion as the Church's purpose and task are socialized by various agents and factors in its milieu.[1]

One of the invaluable contributions made by the non-Catholic ecumenical movement will be to have pointed out the influence of sociological factors on the unity and disunity of Christians.

Moreover, as the ecumenical movement spread its net wider, it was logical to raise the question of the relationship between the new ecumenical institution and the existing ecclesial structures and institutions. For example, were the latter still suited to the needs of modern times? Were they not rather, in certain of their aspects, a bar to progress towards reconciliation and unity? And would it be possible to remain satisfied for long with the juxtaposition of denominational and ecumenical institutions? Were not certain institutions seen to be pre-ecumenical? The problem had to be tackled, therefore, all the more because it was obvious that institutionalism affected ecumenical exchanges and the progress towards unity at all levels.

Therefore, the reformed communions undertook, as institutions, the most fundamental revision that they have ever attempted since their origins. At the time of their appearance in the world, the task which they set themselves was that of reforming the whole Church. But they had to split up into national Churches. History, was, however, to bring them one day to a reconsideration of the problem of catholicity. On account of colonial expansion to America, Africa and Asia, the new confessions spread to other continents, some drawn there by missionary zeal, others driven by their desire for liberty. This fact alone caused a fundamental break in the national alliance between a particular form of religion and a certain nation or ethnic group. For example, if Anglicanism became the religion of Africans or Chinese also, and Presbyterianism that of Indians, the question of catholicity returned to the agenda. Missionary expansion over the course of

---

[1] See the documents and studies of the Commission on Institutionalism at the Secretariat of the World Council; Walter G. Muelder, "Institutional Factors affecting Unity and Disunity", *Ecumenical Review* VIII (January 1956), pp. 109–26; Minear, ed., "Institutionalism in Relation to Unity and Disunity" in *The Nature of the Unity We Seek*, pp. 99–102; Nils Ehrenstrom and Walter G. Muelder, *Institutionalism and Church Unity* (1963); see also Minear, ed., *Faith and Order Findings*, and the official report of the Fourth World Conference on Faith and Order, Montreal, 1963.

one or two centuries probably made an infinitely greater contribution towards breaking down narrow national alliances and promoting the search for
catholicity, than the entire body of criticism within the old denominations.
Over the last fifty years, Protestantism and Anglicanism have clearly
evolved towards a stage beyond the alliance between a particular confession
and a particular nation. Perhaps the most interesting aspect of the great
world denominational bodies, such as the Anglican Communion, the World
Lutheran Federation, the Alliance of the Reformed Churches, the International Congregationalist Council, the World Baptist Alliance, the World
Methodist Council, etc., is that they raise, by virtue of their very existence,
the problem of the nature of catholicity. This event may be viewed as a
sign of self-healing.

Whether it was done willingly or not, the Reformation was obliged to
establish itself on the principle of alliance between religion and particular
sociological or national groupings. Anglicanism was first of all a type of
religion intended for the English nation, just as Lutheranism was meant
for the German nation, and Calvinism for the French.

Neither Calvinism, nor Lutheranism, nor even Anglicanism saw their
wishes fulfilled, since numerous other groups coexist alongside them, and
also since dissidents have arisen from within. That, however, is another
question. The problem confronting us here is that of the principle itself
and its consequent effects on ecumenism. To what extent must the will to
meet and rejoin man as he actually exists, and to adopt his temperament,
his national genius, his history and aspirations, give way in the matter of
adapting Christianity to the world, and in the matter of incarnating
Christianity in space and time? Or, to phrase the question differently, is
the break-up of the alliance into disparate forms a return to the kind of
national, restricted alliance that existed in the Old Testament, or else is it
in effect progress? In which direction was the Messianism of the Old
Testament directed? Was it inclined towards a worldwide alliance, or
towards local, partial and multiple alliances, each opposed to the other?
From this point onwards we come to the questions that are central to the
ecumenical problem in its sociological aspect: is it conceivable that the
institution can be incarnated without accepting anything from the sociological environment which receives it? To what extent can the milieu
influence the Church? Can it go so far as to become institutionalized within
the Church? When does the Church-institution become unfaithful to the
intentions of its founder?

Sociology can be of help in this quest. For it shows that every ideal
or abstract form which seeks to be incarnated can do this only by setting
itself up as an institution in the social reality. Sociology also indicates that
in its process of incarnation, the institution must derive part of its substance
from the surrounding milieu. The Word which is made flesh takes on human

nature. Yet God's plan would be thrown completely out of balance if human nature were to supplant the Word. If phenomenology becomes the dominating criterion of Incarnation, the Word and the Church are in danger of disappearing with conscience taking their place. The necessity which impelled them to become incarnate in order to carry out their mission has been thwarted and absorbed by the institutionalizing power of the ambience. Instead of being faithful to its own being, the Church has allowed itself to be lured into the trap of complying with the requirements of the nation, political power, the world and sectarian tendencies. The Church has come to certain arrangements with the culture, power and predominating ideas of its ambience; it has become one vast compromise with the world in which external forms are perhaps respected, but where the original spirit has been emptied out and replaced by another.

All questions now resolve themselves into the following: how is the Church to live in the world without being absorbed by it? How far may the world be received inside the Church? And how can the Church enjoy an infinitely close connection with the world, while still preserving the transcendency of the Kingdom?

Various answers have been given. Several of them, we know, have led to the rupture of the unity of Christians. But ecumenical reconciliation brings us all back to God's original plan.

3. Typology of the sociological forms of religious expression in Christianity

The ecumenical problem as seen from the sociological point of view lies in integrating the Christian groups into a single whole.

Without passing doctrinal judgement on the validity or invalidity of the religious sociological forms that have been manifested within Christianity, especially in the West, though to some extent also even in Eastern Christianity, it must be acknowledged that in fact, if not once more by right, this expression has been characterized by pluralism ever since the Church began to exist.

How are we to establish a typology of the principal forms of sociological religious development which have evolved within Christianity? Will it be necessary to take in the whole vista of Christian history? Will a plan valid for Europe and America have to be devised? A typology that is too particular has the drawback of applying only to these cases which it contains; while a typology that is too general obviously leaves out some part of reality.

We shall seek, primarily, to establish general types, which it will be necessary to state in more precise and complete terms according to the countries. A typology more accurate for America would probably be: Church—sect—denomination—worship. In common with other religions, America has the categories of Church and sect, but denomination and worship, as the latter are understood in Europe, are typically of American institution. The fact is that Christian sociological groups are institutionalized in a different way in each country, according to history, temperaments, and exchanges between persons and groups.

The most general and essential typology has the advantage of reducing everything to the most decisive sociological and theological differences. The problem stands out more clearly in its central element. It will be expressed differently, according to time, place and culture, but the heart of the matter will be clearly stated once and for all.

Another difficulty is that of vocabulary; it crops up, indeed, wherever it is a question of typology. It is easy to notice the cohesion of certain characteristics, but not simple to find the most inclusive nomenclature. Are the words: Church, sect, denomination, mysticism, the best ones for defining the characteristic features common to certain sociological religious groups? What better suggestions are there? It seems very difficult to do without them. It is important then to determine clearly the limits within which they are to be employed, and the wholly external point of view from which they are to be considered.

There arises another difficulty which we could well do without: it happens that the theologian, in regarding his theological point of view as the only valid one, cannot see that a certain kind of classification of Christian groups belongs to the sociological point of view. If he is asked to observe that it is a question of different viewpoints, he will see that there exist three main forms of religious development: Church, sect, mysticism.[2]

It is a well-known fact that in societies separated by differences, the various groups tend to display differences on the level of doctrine, worship and organization. This conclusion is the result of research made in the most thoroughly explored field of sociology. The distinction made by Troeltsch and Weber between Church and sect is based largely on the observation of this fact.[3]

The "sect" tendency has developed within Christianity ever since the first appearance of multiform gnosticism down to the large number of modern sects. Thus, the primitive Millenarians in both the East and West have their present-day counterpart in the contemporary Adventist sects;

[2] Troeltsch, op. cit., vol. I, chapter ii, section 9, pp. 331–43; vol. II, chapter iii, section 4, pp. 691–805, 993.

[3] Milton J. Yinger, "The Present Status of the Sociology of Religion", The Journal of Religion XXXI (July 1951), p. 198; Religion, Society and the Individual, An Introduction to the Sociology of Religion (1957); Elizabeth K. Nottingham, Religion and Society (1954); H. Swedner, Sociological Differentiation of Habits and Attitudes (1960).

362

and the Montanist sect with charismatic ambition has its equivalent in the present Pentecostal movement. There are differences, and there is no question here of tracing the origins of recent sects back to primitive ones, but it is difficult to resist pointing out certain constant factors.

The "mysticism" trend has appeared throughout the entire life of the Church, in the form of a tendency towards a religion of inner light, individualistic and pietistic. It was present in ancient times. It occurred in the Reformation, and it still exists today.

The "Church" trend is self-evident. We need only verify it in the title of the World Council of Churches and the National Council of Churches of Christ in America. Since very ancient times there has existed a tendency to what might be called ecclesial institutionalization. We can leave to one side the question of criteria of legitimacy, and simply state the fact.

A "Church" may be described as a religious association which considers itself equipped with the means of grace and salvation, and which provides itself with certain institutional means, the scale of which can be infinitely varied.

A "sect" is seen as a voluntary association made up of believers, who have, so to speak, followed a course of their own, and who are joined together by a common experience, namely, that of a new birth. This experience is, as we know, the main force behind the virulence of present-day sects, and also the reason why they hold attraction. They claim to give the believer a personal experience which the ancient Church institutions are said to be incapable of giving.

"Mysticism" shows itself as a tendency that is characterized by an appeal made to the inner light, not so much from the intellectual aspect as from the affective. Associational bonds may be present, but are simplified as much as possible, and the same is true of everything in the nature of institutions. The focal point is the individual, standing apart from other men in his unutterable experience of God.

Now two facts should be noticed: first, almost all the denominations call themselves Churches today, not merely by way of embellishment, but Churches in effect; that is, possessed of the means of grace and salvation. Secondly, we must note the general tendency of sects to "up-grade" themselves, that is, to become Churches after having been for a certain period of time merely sects.

An even more concise typology could perhaps be proposed by taking the institutional type and the associational type as the basic classification. Thus all the existing institutions—Churches, communions and sects—would belong to one or other of these two types.

Nevertheless, this classification is itself not without risk, for sects show institutional features, and the voluntary aspect cannot be excluded from the religious groups belonging to the institutional type. If it is to be used, it must be taken as an arrangement in which institution and association are considered as two poles attracted to each other.

Fundamentally, beyond this use of the classification, there sometimes emerges a different idea, in which attraction is replaced by opposition and uncertainty. Institutional would then correspond with authoritarian, structural and juridical and associational would correspond with voluntary and contractual. Some denominations base their foundations and essentials on the notion of an alliance freely agreed upon by their members, while others are said to impose themselves upon their members by their institutional apparatus. To the associational type belong the Quakers, Baptists and Congregationalists; the institutional type includes Catholicism, Anglicanism, Orthodoxy and Lutheranism in the Scandinavian countries, etc.

Thus, there appear to be two basic ways of living Christianity: one being founded upon liberty, the other upon authority; one is said to rest on the personal element, and the other on transpersonal or suprapersonal elements; the first on the biblical idea of covenant, the second on an institutional mediation.

The quest for the typology of the Christian groups that are to be integrated, now brings us to the question which is encountered many times in the present work: is there a conflict or dilemma in the relationship between Protestantism and Catholicism? Conflict and dilemma have certainly existed in the past, and from the point of view of immediate, concrete reality, allegiance must be given to either one or the other. But have not the antagonisms become so firmly fixed that they prevent us from seeing where the common ground lies? Does incorporation in the institution replace or destroy the voluntary, personal side to a Christian's adherence to the Church, the reply which he as an individual must give to the summons addressed to him by God? On the other hand, does man's personal reply to God's call go directly from man to God without passing through the institution?

The vast problem concerning the relationship of the institution to the believer lies here. Is there some continuity between the latter and the former? Could the Christian life of the believer be itself impregnated in some way with institution, and not simply fitted into the institutional framework or provided with an institutional external structure? In brief, is the Christian life of the believer inseparably and intimately a life inside the Church, at the same time as a life within Christ?

Catholicism, the Orthodox Church, and Anglicanism all give the same answer: as a "way of life" and as a religious form which takes possession of the whole of life and reforms it, Christianity has no other meaning.

Several answers have been supplied by Protestantism, and they have institutionalized themselves into so many different sociologico-religious units. It is with these "ways of life" that we are now concerned; they are to be reunited and integrated by freeing them of all that is not in conformity with the essential way of Christianity, such as it has shown itself in Christ, the way of truth and life. For this purpose, the ecumenical movement will not proceed without an ecumenical reformation and a renovation of the form of the Church.

4. Theology and sociology
before the problem of integrating Christian groups in the Una Sancta

Two points of view, both of them correct and necessary, arise on the problem of integrating the Christian groups.

The fact that the Church is a society of men, like them occupying a place in time and space, leads necessarily to a sociological assessment of its nature. However, since the Church is also the "new creation" which descends from heaven, it goes beyond the limits of sociology and, by the mystery which permeates and composes it, reveals its heart to faith alone. We recall the homily of St Gregory the Great on the incredulity and faith of St Thomas the Apostle "aliud vidit et aliud credidit";[4] it was a man that Thomas saw at first, but it was to a God that he afterwards made his confession of faith. He saw a man, but he knew and believed that it was a question of two worlds.

How are the points of view linked? Let us look at the Church from every angle and on each occasion we encounter the human dimension. For is this not the "Church of men"? If we examine the Church in relation to the apostles and their successors, the human element emerges. And if we compare it to Christ, we see humanity once again in the Church of the Word Incarnate. Lastly, if we situate it in relation to the Three Persons, we shall see that the work of the Trinity is directed towards man and creation.

But the fact that the Church's true sphere is the society of the Three Persons does not mean that the Church is such an inaccessible society as to exclude any sociological consideration of its nature and unity. Wherever it comes into contact with this world, the Church is not such a stranger that only faith can grasp some notion of it and only theology speak about it. Although the vision of faith and the ecclesiological evaluation are primary, it is not right to say that sociology as applied to the Church

---

[4] *Homilia in Evangelia,* Bk. II, Hom. 26, no. 8, *PL* LXXVI, col. 1202.

can never provide anything more than a picture that is distorted by the tools employed.

To the sociologist, doctrinal conflicts are not the chief factors in the division of the Churches, any more than it is agreement on the objects of faith that decides for him the unity of the Church. He does not deny it, but as a sociologist it is not his own standpoint, for he approaches faith from the outside, by way of the phenomenological signs of faith and its perceptible conditioning factors. For the theologian, on the other hand, the crux of the ecumenical problem belongs to the order of faith. It follows then that the sociologist considers primarily the non-theological factors in the disunity as well as in the integration of Christian groups. The process by which Christian groups are integrated, like those by which unity is disintegrated, are accessible to sociologists and theologians alike; it is of the greatest importance that they should exchange their information, for the non-theological factors, which are detectable properly by the sociologist, exert a certain influence on division as well as on union, since faith is found in men. The sociologist has the right to tell the theologian that there are certain social states which are harmful to the faith and unity of Christians. He possesses the necessary competence to point out the social signs of disintegration and integration in the union of Christians. The ecumenical quest cannot do without the services of sociology.

The two standpoints are complementary to each other. The problem of the union of Christian groups in the Una Sancta, considered by the sociologist, is seen as a social process of integration. As seen by the theologian, it appears as the problem of healing the Body of Christ.

The relations, or absence of relations, between the various Christian groups (Churches, denominations and sects), although the subject of theology and motive for prayer, lend themselves nevertheless to sociological observation. Indeed, sociology comes to the aid of theology and faith by providing a fresh means of objectifying the ecumenical problem. The bishop, the theologian and the ordinary Christian are thus in a better position to trace the evolution of the disintegration and the reintegration of Christian unity.

II. THE PURSUIT OF UNITY FROM THE SOCIOLOGICAL POINT OF VIEW

Sociology has made a very thorough study of what happens in society when ancient and new forces come into conflict, and how resistance to change has the effect of impelling the most progressive elements to secede. It also explains the nature of the shortcomings found among the conservative elements, the struggle for total control of the movement, and lastly the settlement that is gradually reached by both parties—those who hold back and delay, and those who increase speed and go ahead. With its knowledge of the nature of division and integration, and the conditions for and against group cohesion, sociology possesses instruments of analysis which are useful to the ecumenical movement. Churches, denominations and sects are social bodies and their integration is a question of union or division among social groups composed of Christians. It is not for sociology to assume the role of faith and state whether Christians should be integrated in this particular way or that, or whether such and such an institution is the true one and the best. According to H. P. Douglass, sociology is in a position to offer competent judgement in the field of problems of unity from five different angles.[5]

(i) Sociology can assess the objections raised by the anti-institutionalists, who treat the question of unity as a matter of small importance, because they do not look upon the Church as an important organ of religion. (ii) It is also able to measure the accuracy of the hypothesis of certain stable psychological types or varieties of categories of human nature, which appear to demand in an absolute manner expressions set apart from organized religion, and which for this very reason constitute an obstacle to unity. (iii) Sociology can render more explicit and develop the concept of Church unity by defining the characteristic unifying elements which are basic to the constitution of all societies. (iv) Sociological analysis helps to identify and differentiate the various possible degrees and kinds of integration, and shows their relationship to each other. (v) Lastly, it clarifies the process of social change, enabling us to foresee the possible and even probable stages of the movement towards unity.

The first two aims assigned to sociology in its role of serving ecumenism relate to answering certain objections that are voiced against the ecumenical movement; the other three represent its positive contribution.

1. The negative contribution made by sociology

A. EXAMINATION OF ANTI-INSTITUTIONAL AND ANTI-CHURCH ATTITUDES

Anti-institutional attitudes harmful to the ecumenical movement are the work of individualists, who belittle Christian regrouping because the question of institutional organization of religion is of no interest to them. There is first of all the individualist by temperament, who regards religion essentially as a private matter between himself and God; then, there is the practical individualist who, for what are often solid reasons, acts as a

[5] *Church Unity Movements in the United States*, p. 148.

free-lance; next there is the individualist, acting on principle and in the name of liberty, who sees in integration only an increase in the weight of organization. There is even the semi-mystical individualist, who places himself above the institution and beyond integration, because God is not bound to the institution in his action and his bestowal of grace. If these attitudes continue to be maintained, they finally reduce the institutional system of religion to a position of little importance.

After the anti-institutionalist group there is the anti-Church group. It is not that these people are unaware of the Church, but they treat it as something subordinate in their desire to give greater emphasis to the Gospel. Or else they lay down the principle that religious unity is a matter of good relations, which should confine itself to the purely personal level. They still assert that their sole interest lies in promoting a spirit of Christian ideal and understanding; and they place this spirit of free brotherhood above all other structurally endowed forms of reconciliation, which in their eyes are inevitably associated with the idea of rigidity, constraint and Church. The notion underlying all this is obviously that the institution of Christian groups could only come about at the expense of spiritual union.

These tendencies are extremely widespread not only among Christians who do not belong to any particular denomination, but also even among those who are actually official members of a communion.

A critique of anti-institutionalism and of the anti-Church standpoint can be formulated in precise terms from a sociological point of view. Indeed the tendency to set up institutions is shown by sociologists to be a natural one in men. The latter, acting in a common purpose to satisfy certain needs, make their attitude rigid in the form of social customs. It is from these that natural organizations grow up. The religious need obeys a tendency such as this. It is normal that it should find expression in appropriate institutions. Social habits that have been contracted by man in the pursuit of his deepest interests are adopted consciously, once they have been tested in the light of experience and sanctioned by the authority of a collective conscience. They are then called institutions, that is, permanent forms of collective behaviour.[6]

Speaking solely from the sociological point of view, religion logically contains certain institutional aspects. After completing a vast amount of research on Protestant institutions, H. P. Douglass established the fact that "all mature versions of religion must inevitably find institutional forms".[7] It is impossible to keep up a dynamic religious force on the pre-institutional

[6] Richard T. Lapiere, *Sociology* (1946), p. 71; John F. Cuber, *Sociology: a Synopsis of Principles* (1st edition, 1947; 2nd edition, 1951), pp. 311–13; John W. Bennett and Melvin M. Tumin, *Social Life: Structure and Function* (1952), pp. 69–79, 167–9, 545.

[7] H. P. Douglass and E. de S. Brunner, *Protestant Church as a Social Institution* (1935), p. 33.

level. A certain reaction is touched off when to the religious relationship between individuals is added missionary zeal; groups are formed and inevitably inter-group relations spring up.

Objections to the institution and the Church probably do not arise from a conviction that the institution as such has no place in religion, but rather from other causes. Certain of the latter are subjective, while others are objective. Among the latter, "institutionalism" must be mentioned.

We must not confuse the following terms: "institution", which is a type of permanent collective behaviour, set up in response to certain vital needs; "institutionalization", the process by which the social custom, that is, the institution, becomes established; and "institutionalism", an ambivalent word, which in the negative sense means the corruption of the institution. Institutionalism of this kind exists wherever the original intention has been forgotten or is clearly incapable of meeting subsequent requirements. When this happens, the institution reproduces itself mechanically by using force to ensure its continued acceptance. The negative aspects of institutionalism are well-known: bureaucracy, red tape, the gap between the high administrative circles and the lower echelons, an unawareness in high places of the actual problems and requirements, incapacity to hold dialogue, imposition of unreal or too general solutions, struggle for power and the consolidation of advantages that have been won, the institution's complacency with its own image and its unwillingness to re-examine it, its tendency to perpetuate itself, and so on.

Institutionalism, especially in a Church, may certainly cause separatist groups to arise. Methodism, for example, a revivalist movement, had no intention originally of setting up a new Church, but desired merely to revive the art of preaching. But through the unbending attitude of the Church of England it was obliged to transform itself progressively into an independent Church. Methodism and other denominations of the independent kind constitute as many new sociological types of religious group. It is a question here of a new socio-religious tradition with new institutions, which themselves are exposed to the danger of institutionalism.

Of course, institutionalism is not the only social reason why new denominations appear. Mention must also be made of other causes: for example, cultural levels: voodoo in Haiti and Brazil clings to a certain level of culture; economic differences: several denominations belonging to the Baptist and Methodist family have been formed in the United States specifically for negroes; the frontiers of civilization: the schism that occurred after the Councils of Ephesus and Chalcedon can be put down largely to historical or political causes, for the Syrian and Semitic group of civilizations refused to be merged in the Empire. The refusal of the Jews to be converted to Christianity is likewise partly explained by the hostility between Jewish culture and Hellenism. Differences occurring in the wake of immigration are also a social cause of division, each group bringing with it its own religion.[8]

Now what makes the sociological problem all the more difficult is that all these social factors of division institutionalize themselves. The Churches, sects and denominations add to their institutional vigour by force of circumstances and through being faithful to themselves. Churches perpetuate themselves; sects and denominations all tend to become Churches. The purest and, in its origins, most fiery sectarianism must choose either to disappear or to acquire institutional customs.

We are now sounding the problem in all its depth and difficulty. What is it in the institution of Christianity, wherever it exists, that corresponds with God's intention? Does institutionalization express a natural inclination alone? What is there then to prevent us from saying that the Church is of natural origin, willed by God just as living and breathing are willed by him, and not something of specifically divine origin? How is the institution to be brought back universally to its origins, and brought back to the divine institution, if indeed God desired that there should be one only? How are the outbreaks of institutionalism, which prevent Christian groups from becoming integrated, to be cured?

Sociology makes a valuable contribution by making us aware of the scale of the problem. It even helps us to come to a solution, by offering an explanation of its own of the sociological processes of institutionalization. Through it we are shown the formative agencies that are at work between an ideally conceived institution, striving to take shape, and the surrounding environment, which reacts upon and so influences the institution. Lastly, sociology is useful in helping to draw the dividing-line between fidelity and infidelity, when it is a question of determining whether the original institution has been preserved or whether it has been lost, and what reasons there are for this.

Among such reasons, sociology points out the institutionalizing force of certain ideas, which not only take root in social life, but also are sufficiently powerful to control existing institutions and even dictate the main lines of development for future ones. It must be realized how heavily the notion of religious liberty has hung over Christian divisions, and the extent to which the ecumenical movement has had to take this notion into consideration in matters of policy and in the formulas for unity. In wide sectors of the Christian world, liberty has become institutionalized in religion itself. This goes to explain in part the great numbers of denomi-

---

[8] L. Lambinet, *Das Wesen des katholisch-protestantischen Gegensatzes* (1946); C. H. Dodd, C. R. Cragg and Jacques Ellul, *More than Doctrine Divides the Churches, Social and Cultural Factors in Church Division* (1952); J. Obendiek, *The Social and Cultural Factors in Church Divisions* (1953).

nations that have arisen within categories which go back to specific racial or ethnic origins, or which are confined to certain cultural, economic or social frontiers. One of the greatest ecumenical problems will assuredly be that of reconciling liberty and authority in the context of religion.

Sociology makes its contribution towards solving the problem by indicating the part played by history and social conditions in the development of the notion of liberty. For historical reasons, the United States has stood out pre-eminently as the land of freedom. It was there that social and religious groups, cramped and confined in Europe, came to found a new nation. Liberty took on the appearance of a creed, the very fabric of the nation, almost a criterion of loyalty to the nation. To be American is to be free. Emphasis on authority has something foreign about it, and is not far short of signifying lack of loyalty. One of the difficulties encountered by Catholicism in the United States has indeed arisen out of its authoritarian character, while the rest of the country regarded the belief in liberty held by all the "Free Churches" as being a criterion of Christian orthodoxy. The main body of the population has given its allegiance mainly to those denominations which offered sufficient guarantees of liberty. We are obviously here faced with a case in which a temporal idea has reacted on to the religious institution itself: an idea, which has become institutionalized in the customs of a nation, is institutionalized at a second stage on the level of Christian belief.

Another idea, possessing a vast institutionalizing capacity, has also extended its influence throughout the Christian world. This is the idea of nationalism, and it cannot be said that its power is diminishing. The various occasions when it has occurred could form the subject of a very thorough typology, beginning with the national Churches, taking in the autocephalous Churches, and ending with the type of Church that seeks to be independent while at the same time remaining within the Catholic Church. Both ancient and recent cases are well known.

How many other ideas seek to become institutionalized in the Church? There is, for example, the prestige attaching to a particular form of government; a denomination adopts a federative, unitarian or representative system in imitation of the constitution of a State.

Or again, a denomination or group of denominations transfer on to the religious plane a particular organizational form, which predominates in the life of the nation. It is certain, for example, that American Protestantism has been widely influenced in its social and ecumenical aspects by the form characterized by organizational efficiency and co-operation, for in addition to its being representative in style, it stands out as a co-operative type of Christianity. The most dangerous aspect of the institutionalizing power of some ideas is that their influence is both too subtle and too massive to be appreciated.

The institutionalizing force behind certain attitudes is now less powerful than that of some ideas.

From a sociological point of view, it is worth emphasizing here the institutionalizing power in the pragmatic attitude. The present, truly ecumenical tendencies are powerfully thwarted by the "co-operative Christianity" style which, let it be said without wishing to underrate its great merits, is not prepared to go further than a certain "conciliar" ecumenism. That is to say, in the case of American Protestantism, the practical union of interdenominational co-operation under the control of the Church Councils, a little after the manner of the large federations or the board of directors who run a large business enterprise, except of course that here it is a religious enterprise.

B. CRITICAL EXAMINATION OF THE EXISTENCE OF CERTAIN SPECIAL PSYCHOLOGICAL TYPES

The second service rendered to us by sociology is to examine critically the supposed existence of psychological types, which are said to require completely different religious organizations. The idea that denominationalism is part and parcel of the natural order is much more widespread than is realized. To put it in plain terms, it would appear that some men are cut out to be Quakers, others Lutherans, and others Anglicans, and so on. The same notion is responsible for the opinion that Catholicism is suited to the Latin races, and Lutheranism for the Nordic; the list could be extended to include the peoples of Africa and Asia. In other words, human nature is supposed to be composed of different types of temperament: mystical, authoritarian, sacramentarian, pietist, and aesthetic, which, it is said, find their equivalents in the various forms of religion or denomination.[9] Consequently, every ecumenical programme should manifestly be able to include them all.

Sociology shows much scepticism over such differences, and points out that they are far more the result of different traditions, customs, cultural influences and acquired or inherited habits, than of radical differences in character. Furthermore, it proves that there is nothing more adaptable than human behaviour. What is considered to be a fixed predilection for one particular form of worship is reduced to a practice passed from generation to generation which has taken on the appearance of a sacrosanct tradition. There is no evidence that collective practices are so ingrained that they cannot be changed within the space of one generation by means of appropriate factors. History and sociology both bring forward the

[9] William Adams Brown in *Christian Unity: Its Principles and Possibilities* (1921), pp. 175–6.

obvious case of Catholic nations which have become Protestant. These facts prove that religious practices expressed in the forms of dogma, traditions of worship and ecclesiastical structure, are much less stable and instinctive than is believed. The intransigence of traditions and institutions in relation to each other is often explained by the absence of any contact or dialogue between them.

2. The positive contribution of sociology

What positive contribution can sociology make to the cause of integrating the Christian groups in the Una Sancta?

The Church is of divine institution, that is, the Lord himself laid down the fundamental archetypes of its practices and customs, when he gave it faith, hope and charity, an apostolic structure and the essence of its worship. Is sociology able to throw some light on Church unity, in view of the fact that one part of the Church remains a human institution? In other words, are division and integration in the ecumenical context completely different from division and integration in the context of profane society?

A. THE EXAMPLE OF SOCIAL UNITY

If there is one idea which sociology may venture to assert, it is that the ultimate aim of society is to procure enough liberty for each individual to live without excessive pressure, enough unity for the whole body to be maintained, and enough supervision of that liberty in order to keep the members united. A society can claim to have achieved its aim when, without suppressing the proper identity of the various parts, it is able to lead them to unified action, which preserves both liberty and the contribution of everyone to the common good. The secret of unity in diversity seems to lie in respecting each individuality rather than alienating it, and in the incorporation of each individual in the whole body, and not in imposing uniformity. In the realm of politics there are unitarian and federative systems. Each country must judge which system suits it best. But it is difficult to belive that the most suitable unity formula for the ecumenical assemblage of Christians is the unitarian formula. This is not to say that the most suitable one would be that of a federation or a kind of "common-wealth" of Churches in contradistinction to an imperial formula of the Church.[10] The inappropriateness of the terms "imperial Church" and

---

[10] Sermon given by the Archbishop of Canterbury, Dr Geoffrey Fisher, in All Saints' Anglican Church, Rome, on 1 December 1960, reported in the *Daily Telegraph*, London, on 5 December 1960.

373

"commonwealth of Churches" arises from their profane origin, and their very vagueness and inconstancy. The Church is the Body of Christ. It will find the most suitable formula for Christian reunion in its own nature and past.

B. GENERAL TYPOLOGY OF ASSOCIATIONAL RELATIONS

The second positive contribution which sociology can bring to the ecumenical task consists in a general typology of the positions which groups may adopt in relation to each other, as well as the possible degrees and forms of integration.

We can distinguish two opposite categories: that of groups completely isolated, and that of groups in contact with each other.

Isolation may be unintentional, depending on physical or cultural circumstances, that is, on physical separation or on differences of total outlook on life. Or it may be deliberate when, for example, a particular Church or denomination regards the other groups as sectarian, schismatic or heretical, and ignores them completely.

This absence of mutual contact and any kind of association can be defined as a state of non-adjustment. It cannot, however, be absolute in the world of today, where social groups live increasingly mixed together. Sooner or later, these groups exert an influence on their neighbours.

The description of the second category, that of groups in contact with each other, is complicated in a different way.

Two possibilities can be distinguished: opposition and accommodation. Opposition may take the form of conflict and lead either to elimination or subjection; it may also take the form of rivalry and finish up in compromise. Elimination signifies dissociation and, obviously, any collective action is impossible. Subjection appears at the inter-group level as inequality, and nothing can result here as far as collective action is concerned, unless it is by means of coercion. Rivalry finds expression at the inter-group level in a sliding scale of equality or inequality, and its result at the collective level is unrelated action.

Accommodation assumes two main forms: combination and full integration. Combination is represented at the inter-group level by alliance, and it leads to co-operation as far as collective results are concerned. Full integration appears at the inter-group level as fusion, and its result in the sphere of collective action is corporate or organic action.[11]

Under this abstract, logical system we may place the entire history of the relations between the Christian Churches and communions: the long periods of isolation; the deliberate attitude of indifference; the antagonisms

[11] Douglass, *Church Unity Movements in the United States*, p. 162.

which turn into conflicts and which aim at either eliminating or crushing rebel groups; the rivalry and emulation which end in tacit, uneasy and uncertain compromises; lastly, the search for adjustment between the groups.

Only in the latter case does ecumenical enterprise begin. Everywhere else, the relations are dominated by the idea of the refusal of the "others". Thus we must ask ourselves sincerely what we really desire in the depths of our hearts: deliberate misunderstanding of the rest; elimination; subjugation; compromise which is half bitter, half glad; alliance; or fusion?

One of the most difficult tasks which falls upon the shoulders of Church leaders and leaders of the ecumenical movement is that of judging the state of relations existing between the various Christian groups. Are the latter still at the isolation stage? Have they passed through the opposition stage, and how far have they come in the stage of accommodation? How much further are they prepared to come? And what steps can be taken to prevent the groups which have already reached an advanced stage in their relations, from sliding backwards?

In the light of this plan, we must also give attention to certain constant factors in the history of Christian groups: integration effected through the complete loss of individual identity has always been one of the principal factors, if not the principal factor, responsible for division and the continuance of division.

C. ATTENTION TO THE PROCESSES OF SOCIAL CHANGE

Lastly, sociology draws our attention to certain aspects which are inherent in the process of social change.

The principal aspect is the survival and even the stubborn retention of the ancient within the new, for a variety of reasons: social inertia, ignorance, resistance on the part of certain interests concerned with perpetuating the status quo, a certain feeling of loyalty to established form, and so on. It is difficult to burn one's former idols. Our Lord said that it was wrong to put new wine into old bottles. So it is that the new order is accepted, but secretely something of the old is retained.

In other words, sociology suggests a critical reassessment of Church institutions. The sacred character attached to every religious-type institution impels men to perpetuate in a formalistic way all the things that have been done already; and they fear to make any new appraisal of them, because they think that to do so would amount to lack of respect for them. Some customs, traditions and institutions, which look very well on the surface, may well have lost their *raison d'être*, meaning and vitality. They continue to hold out until the day the clarion call of change rings out and shows them to be no stronger than were the walls of Jericho. If the institutions were given such a revaluation, a clear distinction could be made between what is to be removed and what is to be retained.

3. Ambivalence of the institution

We shall save ourselves much unnecessary confusion and many false problems if we avoid thinking that the word "Church" denotes the Christian religious phenomenon, let us say the "event", the object of theological consideration, while the word "institution" belongs, as a social phenomenon, to sociology alone. This method of distinguishing and opposing institution and event produces two separate worlds. The most that remains then is that the institution is a sign or consequence of the divine, while the Church-event appears tangential to the Church-institution. The true Church would seem to be the first, that of the communion of saints; the other would appear to be a make-shift, an inevitable condition in our human situation and not a humano-divine reality.

The Catholic method of considering the institutional within the mystery of the Church is to place it in the perspective of the Christological doctrine of the Council of Chalcedon. In accordance with this model, in which the human and the divine represent two aspects of a single reality, which are distinguishable by analysis but inseparable on account of reality, concrete existence and especially on account of the mystical manner of their union, we say that in the Church there is the human, which God has endowed with supernatural virtue by positive institution, such as the hierarchical mediation and the magisterium; there are created elements which God has instituted as efficacious signs of salvation, such as the sacraments; there are also natural bonds which God has elevated to the ecclesial level, such as man's natural inclination to join together, live in communion and obey the summons to assembly together. The Church presents itself to the world and to profane or pagan society as an immense sacrament. The world that is blind to faith does not perceive the mysterious essence of the Church's bonds. In its eyes, the Church is an association similar to so many others; there is of course a religious goal, but these men united to fulfil their religious duties would be united just as well for another purpose. The nature of the mystical Body thus escapes their notice. The vision of faith alone enables the Christian to say that the visible bonds of the Church are in reality the expression of the inner mystery, which unites Christians among themselves. They are signs, and effective signs, of the inner reality. They express it and bring it into being.

The institutional in the Church is not the entire reality of the Church. This reality integrates the two planes, that is, the internal and the external, the internal communion of Christians and the natural external communion;

the latter is, however, elevated by means of grace to serve as a support and a sign of the internal communion, and is able to do so all the more because it is already suited to this by its natural symbolism. Christ, the universal principle of the new humanity, takes possession of the natural form which binds men together, and out of this he makes the ecclesial sacrament. The institutional and the mystery are linked by an appropriate bond, the model for which is the one that linked together the divine nature and the human in the Word Incarnate. The Church is in itself institutional, and the institutional is in itself ecclesial. Institutional cannot be correlated exclusively with human, for there exists in the Church some institutional element which is of divine origin. We are entitled to call the Church the "Church of men" (*Ecclesia ex hominibus*) because the human community bond has been raised by God to the dignity of a sacrament. The human ecclesial community is the interpreter to the profane world of the supernatural community of men among themselves and with God.

Thus we must refuse to say: Church is the equivalent of institution, and Christianity is the true essence of the Christian religion. The truth is rather that Christianity is the Church, and is itself institutional. The event and the institution are not separated. The world takes Christian form by means of the institution of ecclesial bonds.

The viewpoint which relegates to the sphere of purely human creation the institutional, as it is seen in the Church in the sacraments, the form of government, the liturgy, the creeds and confessions, has never been accepted everywhere in Protestantism; for it is obvious that according to scripture there is an element of the institutional in the Church, which is there by divine institution. Anglicanism places the Church-institution on a humano-divine plane; classical Protestantism does not go as far in the scope of its acceptance; and the thought of radical Protestantism is even more restrictive. In liberal Protestantism very few things are retained. And yet, certain institutional aspects remain inalienable. Can the very theory of a "charismatic" Church do without the Bible, which is humano-divine and the sacrament of the holy scriptures, the mediator in its action?

The debate centres not so much round the question of whether there is an element of the institutional in the Church or not, as round the question of how large this element is, and what position it occupies in relation to Christ and salvation.

But is everything that is institutional within the Church of divine origin, and does it have the same value throughout all parts of the Church? Are there not grounds for defining one institutional element as being of human origin, and another as being of divine origin?

III. THEOLOGY OF THE INSTITUTIONAL ASPECT

It does not fall within the scope of the present work, which is confined specifically to the question of unity, to develop here a sociology of the Church, considered as a religious institution. But would it be enough to deal only with institutional factors which have an ecumenical bearing, that is, which promote or impede unity?

Some theological exposition seems necessary here, for the simple reason that not all of us have the same view concerning the nature and extent of the institution and its role with respect to the event of Christianity. The two terms of the comparison are Church and institution. It is necessary, therefore, to trace the broad outline of our theology of the institution and the role of institutional factors in the Church.

The importance of this aspect is due to the position it occupies in the Churches, denominations and sects, a position which does not cease to grow as time goes on and as Christianity expands in the world.

We must also look at everything which is institutional in interdenominational relations and which increases as the latter evolve. As soon as the various religious groupings meet and desire to enter into continuous contact, they feel the need to set up certain institutions for the purpose of dialogue, negotiation, co-operation and union. Local, parochial and urban councils, regional, national Church councils, the large international denominational unions, and the World Council of Churches are all institutions relating to ecclesial affairs.

Institutional factors are seen similarly in the doctrinal order, the laying down of creeds, dogmas, confessions, in the forms of government and organization, in the worship, the sacraments and the variety of liturgies, and even in the accomplishment of the Church's mission in the world. They inspire the psychological behaviour of the Churches, communions, sects, and of each individual. There is no aspect of the ecumenical problem which is not affected by them in some degree. The question is central, therefore, to the task of integrating Christian groups. Are the chances of union increased as the institution decreases, or are they increased in proportion to an institution which shows itself to be truly universal? The Catholic Church, the Orthodox Churches and the Churches of the Anglican Communion have always believed in the need for the institutional aspect in the Church: and the evolution of the Protestant world, especially since the beginning of the century, indicates that the institutional has its place in the Church. But what exactly is this place? When does the institutional become a factor of division or reconciliation? What will lead to the integration of the Christian communions within the Church? Will it be a Christianity freed from the institutional, or will it be a Christianity which accepts the institutional?

1. The institutional factor in the structure of Christianity

The action of the Three Persons, the initiative principle and supreme agent, causing the event of predestination, convocation and congregation, must be seen as the primary factor in the foundation of the Church as an institution. The supra-temporal initiative of the Three Persons, when it appears on earth, takes the form of a placing apart, an election, vocation and covenant—a covenant between God and his people, like the covenant between husband and wife.

The covenant is instituted. Thus we have as the elements of institution a divine, unrevoked and stable initiative, which is God's will for salvation extended over mankind; and secondly, the alliance between God and man through the intermediary of the call and the choice of one section of humanity, gathered together in a category, and integrated and consecrated by the bond of mutual dependence.

The divine act is an instituting one, that is, it establishes a permanent order within mankind in the form of a link between mankind and God, and this link rests on a permanent, fundamental structure: convocation-congregation. Moreover, we are invited to see how the process of institution and what is to be instituted are joined together. Institution is the institution of something. It is not merely an inner quality. It is concerned with an incarnate reality. There is not on one side situation, that is, man in the world, and on the other side institution; it is mankind which is instituted or reinstituted by virtue of convocation-congregation. In other words, in institution the historical and the supra-historical meet continually.

The institution begins with the Word. It is the Word, the creative, proclaiming and revealing force, which initiates the process of institution by its act of placing reality in being. We explain here the aspect of the Church as coming from God. On the human side, the Church is instituted by the fact that human beings receive and listen to the Word; the latter summons them, singles them out and convokes them, joining them together through the sacraments in the unity of faith and the unity of meaning attached to that faith.

Fundamental to the institution, therefore, is the act of God, instituting by means of announcement, revelation and sacraments.

There is a permanent manner in which God gives himself, a manner that is repeated, taken up again like a first gesture and made time after time, until it becomes indelibly fixed, something to which we are always faithful. It is the first side of the institution, or active tradition, that through which God gives himself. There is a permanent manner in which man receives: this is through received tradition.

There is a fitting way for God and men to seal the covenant initiated by the Word, and it is through the sacrifices which God designates as being acceptable to him and which man performs.

Men are instituted as Christians by these fundamental actions, which are governed by a permanent structure—the economy of the gift of God. The economy of the gift of God is an institutional structure. Its archetype is to be seen in the essential primordial actions of God.

Does this mean that the Church is a reality in God before it becomes a social fact, a kind of celestial order which is then dropped into the world in an empirical, historical form? If we speak of the idea of God concerning the Church, then the latter exists prior to its realization. If we speak of the model of the Church, a society of persons, then the Church exists previously in the society of the divine Three Persons. But the Trinity is anterior to any institution. It is the communication made by the Trinity according to an order, which is coherent with the order of the Three Persons, that establishes the institution. It is this which prompts St Cyprian to say that the Church is "coherent with the divine mysteries". Moreover, if we speak of the actual institution of the Church, then the divine idea and the divine act are one in the Word which convokes, singles out and integrates mankind in a new order of unity. The institution appears profoundly as a legitimate and necessary element in the nature of the Church.

A fundamental protest was made by the Reformation, in the name of the personal element, against this aspect of the Institution which the supra-personal element represents. To the Reformers, the supra-personal element appeared in Catholicism as an element independent of personal bonds, a kind of autonomous continuity between God and man. The Reformers considered that it was impossible for an institution as such to save man, without man giving to it his personal adherence. Catholicism was accused of repeating the error of the Jews in their action of placing their salvation in the automatic observance of the institution of circumcision, independently of the voluntary and personal response which every individual should make to the covenant.

But the Reformation has not succeeded in putting forward a better balance, in spite of its intentions. It accused Catholicism of having developed to excess certain supra-personal elements of the institution. But the Reformation in its turn went to excess by over-emphasizing the voluntary and personal elements.

The great variety of positions adopted by the Reformers concerning the institution prevents any one of them from being taken as the authorized exponent which we would like to find. Their haste to find an answer showed itself in hesitancy, improvisation and incompleteness, from which Protestantism is still suffering today. From classical Protestantism to radical, a persevering quest still goes on. Its purpose is to define the relationship between institution and event in Christianity. This was the great problem that the Reformation set itself at the start, and the course of evolution in Protestantism could be interpreted as a constantly resumed quest for the fitting answer. Anglicanism believes that an answer to the problem has been found in the very large role allotted by it to the episcopal structure, the liturgy, the creeds, and tradition. Lutheranism adopted a radical position which later had to be revised. Calvin himself varied in his doctrine concerning the structure of the Church. Though radical in his initial enthusiasm, he later came round to extending the role of the institutional, which is spoken of in the scriptures in relation to the Church. The Independents and Nonconformists in England came up against the same problem in their turn. In their opinion, the English and continental Reformations had provided no more than an uncertain answer to it.

The perpetual need to redefine the problem of the institution in relation to the essence of the Church and Christianity, is the sign that this problem was not solved by the Reformation.

2. Ecclesial integration and pleromization of the Church

Catholic theology pertaining to the institutional aspect in the Church is governed by the theology of the Incarnation, the ascendancy of the divine and consecration of human nature by the Word. It implies a decision, a setting apart, an act of integration. Already, through the Incarnation, mankind is radically set free and emancipated, and begins from then on to live in communion with God. God's people, drawn out from the rest of humanity, is set apart as the elect of God; they are chosen, convoked, gathered together and bound to God by a covenant.

Through the Church, God continues his plan for the integration of the world and the growth of the Body of Christ until its pleroma, its plenitude, is reached. There is a continuity between the first phase of God's plan in the Old Testament and the second phase. A fundamental pattern of ideas reveals itself under the old law, which is repeated in the new. The essential structures are, as we know, election, convocation and congregation. God chooses his people. And God, through his people, chooses and singles out, summons and convokes, brings together and integrates, unites and catholicizes.

The plan is first given, under the new alliance, to the apostles, who are entrusted with the mission of placing the basic archetypal idea which the Lord has taken up and renewed in his mysteries into the framework of renewed history. Thus from Pentecost onwards they are seen choosing, convoking, separating, distinguishing and integrating. Peter's speech after the coming of the Holy Spirit shows that the apostles considered in a most simple manner and as a matter of course that they had the powers of decision concerning the opportuneness and relevance of the very special action of integrating the Jewish people in the new ecclesia. Of course, the Holy Spirit inspires their words and they feel themselves urged to speak them, but it is obvious that Peter and the Twelve are taking up again the fundamental system which, as we have seen already, is that of God in the economy of salvation. Except in the matter of predestination which belongs to God alone, the apostles are themselves performing the essential actions in this management: initiative, summons, convocation and congregation. In brief, they are carrying out the functions of a Church. Having attended to the Jews, they turn to the Gentiles, and it is Peter who is the first, before Paul, to take this step. We are at the episode relating to the centurion Cornelius. When Peter mentions this matter at the apostolic council in Jerusalem, the magnitude of the powers of initiative which fall to the Twelve by right is seen fully. And, later on, we again see the apostles deciding, under the guidance of the Holy Spirit, as to the exact opportuneness of integrating the various cultures and civilizations of the world into the unity of the Kingdom.

We spoke of the mission to separate and choose, convoke and summon, gather together and integrate, unite and catholicize. This essential model plan was used by God in the Old Testament with the kings, priests and prophets. He follows the same pattern with his Son, the king, priest and prophet. No other one is revealed to the apostles. As the Word has chosen, taken possession of and assumed human nature, so also the apostles have the mission of choosing the world in the manner of God, of summoning it to enter into the divine plan, and of incorporating it therein.

Is there a mission without the corresponding power? The apostles and their successors, who have the mission to take the initiative, clearly possess the powers of initiative regarding the specific and opportune actions that are to be laid down or not laid down. They have the power to invite, to bring to the Kingdom, to decide what is pure and what is not, to separate and exclude; in short, to investigate and organize the case for or against integration. This is the power of jurisdiction.

The power to integrate and consecrate is the power of order, which is expressed in offering, sacrifice and Eucharist.

The Church is thus the mother who receives, chooses out, assimilates and transforms, integrates and unites in the Body of Christ, the work of his hands.

It is obvious that the Church is profoundly, and with its whole being, institution. We say Church: that is, convocation-congregation. We have just seen, moreover, that the activity of God right from the creation, and afterwards in the choice of his people, in the Incarnation and the founding of the Church, keeps always to the same fundamental plan: election, convocation-congregation, or in other words: the act of deciding the relevance of such and such an action with a view to salvation, the act of uniting and integrating. The fundamental structure of the Church as institution is thus revealed. It has a dual function, comprising two acts or two aspects of the same act: separating and integrating, refusing and accepting, excluding and consecrating, freeing and universalizing.

These two aspects of the same act are found in operation in the salvation of the individual through justification and sanctification, which are inevitably bound up together. The justified man is separated from his previous state, his sin is excluded, rejected and effaced. He is set free, liberated and introduced into the universal of God by participating in his nature. And this is the reason why the soul of the Christian is essentially ecclesial: the same structure is found in the constitution of the being of the individual Christian and of the Church.

The application of the same idea is met with on the plane of the Church's structure. The two powers of the hierarchical Church, power of jurisdiction and of order, are the two inseparably linked aspects of the same act; it can never be complete unless it is, on the one hand, the act of investigating and organizing the case for or against integration in the Kingdom, and, on the other hand, the very integration itself by means of offering, sacrifice, celebration and consecration. Furthermore, this explains the eminent dignity of the hierarchy in the ecclesial assembly: the hierarchy represents and performs the fundamental actions in the divine archetypal plan of the economy of salvation.

Lastly, the Church, taken in the sense of the "Church of men" comprising all the faithful, including the hierarchy, shows itself in conformity with the same structure. The Word suddenly comes to men who are joined together by associational bonds in conformity with their nature, and these social bonds are made into something different from what they were before. From being natural and social they become ecclesial, because they are taken again and placed into a religious category. Sociology remains capable of knowing them, but it cannot describe everything about them. There is something in them which eludes this branch of human knowledge, and it is the transforming quality of the word of God which has summoned them, set them free from the limitations restricting them, and consecrated them. It is the Church, the renewed society. This is also the reason for the eminent dignity of the "Church of men" living in the heart of mankind. The human assembly has been possessed by the Word, the divine form of the renewed creation, and has been fully reshaped. And in this wonderful union there has taken place what might be called the institution of the sacrament of the Church. The new mankind in the Church is truly taken in hand, emancipated from its limits and consecrated by the Word.

It is as it were one great sacrament. All the necessary elements are present. On the one hand stands mankind in its act of gathering together, that is, presenting already the natural symbol from which the Church will emerge by virtue of the Word. On the other, stands the Word which convokes, summons, draws together and unites. From the encounter of the human social bonds and the instituting Word, through the unifying power of the Holy Spirit, there results the Church.

The conclusion is unavoidable that the Church is by essence institution, while at the same time being the event of salvation in history. The event is revealed, it acts and expresses itself in and through the institution. The institution is the reverse side of the event. The institution allows the event to be seen through it. It is clear that their link is a sacramental one. The institution is a perceptible and efficacious sign of grace, not the institution separated from the event—for then where would its effective quality come from?—but the institution which remains thus at every moment only by virtue of the event. For the event, while instituting without ceasing, enables the institution to be filled with the authority from above to liberate, emancipate, integrate and consecrate.

Since the institution is borne in the world by men, there is, of course, the risk that men might seek to impose upon it their own standards and their own rule. There is always the temptation for the institution to materialize, to become a thing in itself, and to fall into decadence. This occurs when the men who bear the institution transform it into something endowed with autonomous power, without realizing that in so doing they are cutting it off from its life line. Instead of being a vast sacrament, the institution now becomes a gigantic machine, whose symbolic sense has been lost. Withered through having been cut off from its creative sources, authority experiences the need to make up for its lack of prophetic appeal, derived from contact with the Word, by a hardening of the juridical element. Authority now becomes oppressive, and its yoke is no longer light. Its subjects no longer see the reason for certain things, since those who ought to explain such things now merely pass them on in a mechanical, automatic fashion. The prophet is silenced by the administrator, contemplation is replaced by repetition. The institution becomes dull and spiritless. It has lost its vigour as the salt of the earth and the light of the world. It is as if man, overwhelmed by the transcendence of the event of the Word, compensates for his own weakness to bear it by subjecting the institution to institutionalism. And the institution may now become a stumbling-block. The worst of it is that the institution, when seen in this deficient state, is confused with the institution it is by right.

Karl Barth once said: "The Church is more or less one vast, energetic enterprise to humanize, temporalize, 'to make a thing of' and to secularize the divine, an attempt to reduce it to a practical system. And all this is done for the welfare of man, who is unable to live without a God or to live with the living God either.[12] In short, the Church represents an attempt to render that difficult, and yet so inevitable path accessible to man. In this, the Catholic Church has certainly had the greatest success, while Protestantism encounters comparatively more difficulties, on account of the fact that man does not ultimately succeed in doing what he would like to do as a Churchman. Clearly, the opposition between the Gospel and the Church is something fundamental and infinite at every point. And so, here we have one point of view pitted against another, here somebody is right and somebody else is wrong." [13]

It is fairly obvious that to Karl Barth the ideal for Christianity and the Church would be the maximum possible amount of spiritual and prophetic fire with the minimum amount of institution.

But is this the point after all? Is it a question of the Church which we would have liked to found ourselves, or of the Church which appears in the scriptures, and which follows the slow, humble, yet realistic paths of the Incarnation, with, of course, the inevitable sharing in the state of personal humiliation and bondage about which St Paul speaks in connection with Christ? What good would it be to envisage a Church other than the one shown to us in the archetypal plan of the economy of salvation, whose pattern was followed by God in history, and whose living incorporation is the Church? If this Church is not the Good News proclaimed to the world, and living and functioning within it, then we ask that a better one be indicated, but we must be sure that it is the right one.

We must not abandon for any other idea of the Church that one which has appeared to us throughout the accomplishment of the plan of salvation in accordance with the scriptures. The actions of separating and consecrating performed by this Church constitute the two aspects of a single act of salvation. These two gestures express the relationship of eternity with time. They are turned simultaneously towards history and eschatology. We must see now how they operate in the sacraments.

In baptism, man is delivered from the world and integrated in the body of Christ. He is separated from sin, which closes him in on himself, and he becomes emancipated, restored to himself, to others and to God, in the sacred bonds of the ecclesial community. From the personal sphere he passes to the supra-personal order, in virtue of which men become members of each other (1 Cor 12:27). It is true that the nature which is common to all men is sufficient in itself to ensure the transition from the personal to the supra-personal order. But the proper role of baptism

[12] Dostoevsky, *The Grand Inquisitor.*
[13] *Der Römerbrief* (1933), pp. 316–17.

consists firstly in ensuring deliverance of nature from the shackles of sin hindering mankind from communicating fully, and secondly in bringing men to supra-personal, intra-Trinitarian communication. In fact, it is by virtue of the latter that the renewed communication between men becomes possible.

In marriage, man and woman are delivered or separated from their own limits as two people confined to their own creative capacity. They now become emancipated in the universality of the bonds which join Christ to the Church, his bride.

In the sacrament of orders, the priest, separated, set apart, is, by virtue of the sacrament, placed at a universal level, as regards both accessibility to God's mystery and responsibility to the community of the faithful. This is even more so in the case of the bishop, a Church structure, in the case of the body of bishops, who are jointly responsible for the universal Church, and also in the case of the pope, who is not merely pope of the Latin or the Eastern Church, but the visible, personal centre of the unity of the Church.

The same is true in the structure of worship. On the one hand, the liturgy by means of appropriate symbols breaks the boundaries of the natural order and, on the other hand, provides an introduction into the realm of the world to come. The Eucharist, in which the substance of bread and wine are changed to the substance of Christ's body and blood, appears in its turn as an emancipation from the confines of matter and, through the consecration, as the transition from the temporal order to that of transcendent reality.

The establishment of the creeds and the formulation of the dogmas and confessions of faith present once again a similar dialectic of separation from the historical and from existential culture, and of deliverance in eschatology, yet without abandoning or rejecting the historical. Salvation is not flight. It is the justification and sanctification of what was previously slavery and unclean.

Faith follows the same pattern. It is an exodus, but also man's entry into the promised land.

This, moreover, is the essential structure of the sacred: first of all it is a transference from familar surroundings, then fascination, a liberation and an engagement.

How could the Church ever fail to be the Church in all its parts? How could Christianity avoid being logical with itself, since in the Incarnation we are shown at first hand from the very source the exemplary plan of the deliverance of mankind from the limitations of his human nature and the exemplary plan also of his union with the divine nature?

The actions of the Three Persons, Christ, the apostles and the Church are faithful to one structure. There is seen the presence of eschatology at work in history, for the constitution and perfection of the Body of Christ and for universal recapitulation. The Word reveals the plan and in so doing establishes it. The Word is faithful to itself in its discourse, that is, the Church. And, by using always the same dialectic, the Word enters into dialogue with man, who has been chosen by it as its interlocutor. The Word obviously possesses special language. Its way of thinking, of conversing with history can be known. In the presence of the Word and under its gaze, the soul and the Church are continually caught up in the dialectic of separation and accomplishment, refusal and fascination, liberation and fullness, which cause them to pass from the sphere of time to that of eternity.

In the continuity of this essential dialectic, in which is found the theological fusion of the two concepts of the Church, one social, the other mystical, occurs one of the greatest difficulties in ecclesiology.[14]

3. The connection, through the Holy Spirit, between the institutional or supra-personal principle and the voluntary principle in the Church

We have had the opportunity on various occasions to see that Catholicism adheres in all respects to the fundamental archetypal plan of the Incarnation, as interpreted in the Chalcedonian sacramental tradition in the Church. Christ is true God and true man. He is the original sacrament. The Church is fashioned in his image.[15] It rests upon two principles, which are united by the Holy Spirit and occur at all levels.

We acknowledge two principles on the historical level: internal continuity and external continuity, united by the Holy Spirit.

At the dogmatic level we find internal and external tradition; the Holy Spirit, sent by Christ, conveys and recalls perpetually to the mind what Christ revealed (Jn 16:13–15). External tradition: the creeds, confessions, dogmatic declarations made by the Councils and the popes, by whom the faith is regulated and preserved from the dangers of subjectivity.

It is the Lord who watches over the handing down of the Christo-apostolic tradition. He does so by sending his Spirit, which protects the internal identity. He also does it by sending forth his apostles as missionaries; they were witnesses to him and they received the Holy Ghost at the first Pentecost, for the purpose of helping them in the life of revelation in the Church and with the regulation of men's thoughts concerning revelation.

[14] Robert Grosche, *Pilgernde Kirche* (1938).
[15] O. Semmelroth, *Kirche als Ursakrament* (1953).

At the structural level, the same duality is again encountered: internal apostolicity and external apostolicity, united by the Holy Spirit. The Church is built on the Twelve. The Twelve are one with Peter. Peter, in his turn, is founded upon Christ, the rock (1 Cor 10:4), and the cornerstone (Acts 4:11), upon whom the entire Church ultimately rests. Christ, the Apostle of the Father, is one with him. We see through this the twofold dimension of apostolicity: the one internal—an internal continuity which connects us to the heart of the Father; the other external, conveyed by the choice of the Twelve and their visible association with the mysteries of Christ and the Spirit.

In the sphere of worship: the Word of God and the sacraments united through the Holy Spirit. In the liturgy scripture is the sacrament of the Word. The Eucharist is the great sacrament, the heart of Christian worship. The perceptible elements, the signs, are appropriated by the act of the presence of God in the outpouring of the Holy Spirit.

In the sphere of the Church's mission: the internal and the external work are united by the Holy Spirit. God is he who transforms the hearts which are in his hand. The first evangelist is God himself in the soul. But the total work of evangelization results also from the part accomplished by the Church's visible organism, the clergy and laity. It is the Holy Spirit who ensures the unity of the work of the Kingdom in the world.

On the psychological level: the interior unitive action of God and the exterior unitive action performed by the clergy and the laity are both united by the Spirit. The Holy Spirit is he who, in the first place, forms among men and in Christian groups ecumenical, communal dispositions; but the action of men is equally necessary. The whole work is for the glory of God who, in the secret places of souls causes hearts to agree and makes the visible efforts of men converge towards each other.

Lastly, at the sociological and organic level, we find the supra-personal element and the personal element united by the Holy Spirit. Upon the first of these elements depends in the Church the continuity of the fundamental dialectic of catholicity which, as we have seen already, is the dialectic of liberation from restrictions and of communion in universality. By this dialectic, man, matter, the community, and time are emancipated at every instant, at every period, in every country and nation, from their limits. They are restored to themselves united in communion, engaged in the vast work of universal recapitulation, carried towards the ultimate joy of perfect eschatological liberation.

The personal element is responsible in the Church for the indispensable aspect of personal response to the summons and convocation which the Three Persons, Christ, the apostles, the bishops, and all men, address to mankind that all may be one. It is the Holy Spirit who unites the personal element with the supra-personal element between the historical and the supra-historical, between the eschatological and the temporal. It is in this way that he revealed himself at Pentecost. In this we see the fullest and deepest significance of Pentecost. To attach any lesser importance to it would be to fail to do justice to it.

It is often said that doctrinal firmness is synonymous with intolerance and rigidity. Such firmness is supposed to be unable to listen or accede to anything. Closed to all points of view, but its own, doctrinal firmness is said to seek to extend its domination without regard for the desires of others. And the absence of definite structure, principles and defined ideas is asserted to be the most genuine basis for openness of mind, readiness to entertain the views of others, and tolerance.

On the contrary, paradoxical as it may seem, it is doctrinal firmness and fullness alone which are able to provide a basis for genuine tolerance and willingness to listen, for the excellent reason that within such firmness there exist reference points and principles of integration.

The same is true on the institutional plane. It is not the absence of institution, or its weakness, that can really act as a principle of integration for the Christian groups.

By what standard shall we measure the extent of the institution, if not by its relation to the mystery of Christ? A universal, ecclesial institution, linked with the mystery of Christ, is unitive and integrating. An ecclesial institution which remains in juxtaposition to the mystery of Christ, by refusing to accept fully the transformation of human nature by means of grace, will certainly be able to accomplish noble and fruitful works of integration, but it will not be able to reach the most universal catholicity. It will always remain in danger of being adopted by ethnic groups, or restricted by nationality, as history reveals.

Likewise, there will always be a certain lack of decisiveness about the idea of a "Commonwealth of Churches", which is advanced as a formula for bridging the gap between the Churches. The same is true of the concept of "Evangelical Catholicity" and "Conciliar Catholicity", despite their value, which must be acknowledged. This lack of decisiveness will prevent them from attaining authentic universality and truly unitive catholicity, which always remains incomplete and fallible as long as it lacks the principle of the infallible communion of bishops, united around the primacy of Peter and his successors.

However, it is not to be thought from all this that the way in which Roman Catholicism has evolved since the time of the separation between East and West and the Reformation period, does not suffer from a certain unilateralism. When the various parts of Christendom cut themselves off from each other, it was inevitable that they should become strangers to each other.

But it is another thing altogether to infer that this unilateralism affects the Catholic Church in its substance and renders it completely closed to the most articulate, and at the same time most coherent, ecclesial expression.

4. *The essential dialectic of Christianity at the ecumenical level*

This is none other than the one that has already been established, concerning the liberation of the groups from their limitations, and their accession to liberty and universality in the Catholica.

Christian reunion cannot be the result of the fitting together, pure and simple, of a great number of broken fragments, which only need rearranging in order to produce catholicity in all its fullness. In other words, it is not enough to integrate all the existing Churches, sects and denominations of every description, in order to rebuild Christian unity. Each one of these bodies has evolved since the separation, with the result that universal adjustment is impossible without correction, healing and further growth.

The principle of reconstruction by bringing the broken pieces together again is excluded. The only adequate principle is that of vital growth. The Church is the Body of Christ, a living organism. Of all created beings, it is the most perfect and thus the most highly articulated and differentiated. It is normal that the laws governing the growth and everyday life of living beings should be found in it. Now, when is the unity in a living body in danger, if it is not when one part of it cuts itself off, so to speak, and starts to follow an autonomous development? The correct balance of the body is not independent of the permanent dialectic between the parts and the whole. The process of integrating the Christian groups must, therefore, be carried out in the same manner. Each of the parts must strive for catholicity, that is, a greater catholicity in the sphere of faith, thought and life.

History can furnish us here with useful lessons. The relations between the apostles and between the apostolic sees reveal to us the existence of a typical formula for these relations. It was that of a dialectic of dialogue between the Churches, as between the constituent principles of unity. Those who argue from this dialectic of dialogue that unity never existed in the Church and that division has been the rule ever since the early days, should realize that in depriving this primitive structure of communion relationship of its significance, they are condemning themselves to wander endlessly in search of some other model for Christian unity.

Moreover, those who say to return to the ancient style is to fall into archeologism, lay themselves open to confusing the historical material forms and the formal lessons of history. It is certain that the dialectic of dialogue, by which the parts of the Church, the Churches and Church leaders free themselves from their limits and come to a communion of the whole, could not be practised today in the same way that it was practised eighteen or nineteen centuries ago. The apostolic model is the ideal pattern for these relations. It is the principle. The application must be new. History never repeats itself in its actual materiality; but there is nothing to prevent a fundamental plan from being expressed in different ways.

Historians who record the story of the relations between the Eastern Churches and the Western Church, view them principally in terms of diplomatic or jurisdictional conflicts, which have occurred between the papacy and chiefly the patriarchate of Constantinople. If these relations are nothing more than a chaos of mutual distrust, thwarted ambitions, cunning battles and vigorous claims, then Christianity would appear to have had a sad history for many centuries. But is this the full story of the history of Christianity? Surely the desire to trace back as far as possible the causes of the separation between East and West has led to an excessively negative view of these relations. Surely the history of the Church, as seen through Western eyes and coloured by our notion of papal supremacy, has had a retrospective influence on the way in which the past has been interpreted. That is to say that we have been led to confuse the dialectic, between East and West, the quest for balance and compensation, harmonization of organicity and autonomy, with the signs and effects of separation. After all, unity is not synonymous with uniformity, rigidity or monologue. Unity must be seen as a dialogue, a dialectic, an exchange, such as is proper between the living members of the same body.

Reflecting upon this long history of relations between the East and West, we must draw certain formal lessons from what we see. Our conclusions are all the more urgent because the young Churches of Africa and Asia stand before us as organizations based on new worlds that are just as different from the West and the Latin Church as was the Eastern world in ancient times. The Latin Church and the Catholic Church are faced with the need to make certain choices. It is difficult to believe that we could pursue, generally speaking, different policies with respect to Asia, Africa and the East. Are we not to move in the direction of the formula of pluralism within unity, even if this is an infinitely delicate matter? The Holy Spirit and the resources of the Church will enable this to be accomplished. It should not be considered temerity to repeat Cardinal Costantini's view: "We have tried to force a foreign hierarchy and the Latin language upon the East, and the East refused them."[16] Much has been accomplished with the establishment of native hierarchies. The most

[16] Memorial address in honour of Mgr Francis Pallu, published in the *Osservatore Romano*, 25 January 1940.

difficult, the most delicate and probably the most dangerous task is yet to come. Or at least it is the time when the great decisions have to be taken; that is, the decisions which determine the future.

We see that the fundamental question concerning the significance of the dialectic of liberation from limitations and communion in universality, which we have raised in the Catholic Church in connection with Christian reunion, has become the object of a similar quest among other Christians.

Related denominations are forming groups, and denominational families are forming national and international alliances; it has become a sign of maturity for a denomination to state how it conceives its role within the "Great Church" of the future.

Would it be too much to suggest that all the denominations might well be in the process of rediscovering and formulating in their own way an idea traditional within the Church, namely the principle of the dialectic or dialogue between the main bodies and between the constituent parts, the principle of balance and compensation, the law of liberation from limitations and of communion in the whole? The parts are liberated, emancipated, they are entering into communion with each other and they remain thus by virtue of the dialectic of dialogue which liberates and unites them.

5. The fundamental dialectic of catholicity at the national level

The Church, taken in its complete sense of Christ the Head united with his mystical Body or, if it is preferred, Christ in his Church, liberates and unites nations.

The fundamental dialectic which we have seen in operation at the level of the individual person, is the same that regulates and inspires Catholicism at the level of nations, and at the ecumenical level: the dialectic of conversion: progress from darkness to light, from slavery to emancipation, from the limitations of the individual to the highest and broadest communion.

Christ in his Body does for nations what he does for individuals. He liberates and unites on the national plane as much as he does so on the individual plane. His action on the national plane is completed by the incorporation of the world in catholicity as much as his action at the individual level is completed by integration in the Church.

Now from what does God deliver us at the individual level? From self-justification, from disobedience and pride of mind: this he does by means of baptism; he delivers us from schism in the soul — this time by means of penance; he delivers us from the sterility of separated men and women—by means of marriage; he delivers us from limitation in the sphere of the sacred: he does this by means of the sacrament of holy orders; and so on.

But at the same time that he emancipates, he integrates and unites. Man is restored to himself for having reached a level of total communion, in which he transcends his former state thanks to the redemption brought by Christ the liberator. Man finds once again the spiritual unity which he lost through original sin. From now on he communicates fully and truly with God and with men through the sacred bonds of Christianity.

The same essential dialectic operates at the level of nations. Christ-in-his-Church rescues nations from the tendency to self-justification, that is, from the inclination to seek within themselves their salvation in the form of national gods, or the false gods of blood, race, the State, progress, history, technology and achievement, violence and death. He delivers nations from the intoxication of victory, power and denomination.

Liberation is the first aspect and the first moment in the unique act of the salvation of nations. What has been liberated must be united. Nations are united under God's judgement and sovereignty, which is proclaimed by the Church; they are united by the action of listening to the Word of God, which convokes and gathers them together; they are united by the holy bonds of the renewed community, of mutual service, and by the universal mission of spreading the good news.

The fundamental dialectic of catholicity is one. It extends from the individual to nations and to the whole world. The purpose of the institution is to integrate this world in God.

The institution must perform for nations the service which it performs for each individual: namely, that of bringing them out of themselves, out of their sacred egoism, from the sin of schism and withdrawal into self, the propensity to excess, from the intoxication of victory, and to set them free and emancipate them in Catholicity.

So long as a Church or a communion remains inseparably tied to an ethnic group, a nation, a country, a race, or culture, or civilization, without coming to universality, it must be concluded that it has not yet been sufficiently freed and emancipated in Christ. The justification of individuals, in the dogmatic sense, and also, analogically, that of nations, lies precisely in this transition, this deliverance or passover of individuals and of nations. It is this liberating dialectic which makes a man, when he is a Christian, greater than his humanity; this same dialectic makes a nation, when it becomes Christian, transcend itself as a people; and it also makes humanity, when it is united in catholicity, assume a new dimension of universality. We are now in the domain of meta-history, in which everything is governed by laws of an appropriate order. Here forgiveness is practised without reckoning or reason, because it is situated beyond the laws governing gifts;

it goes beyond gift. Without this dialectic of emancipation, a child who is weeping would be nothing more than his pain, a happy soul would be no more than its pleasure, a vengeful soul no more than its vengeance, the sinner no more than his sin, and a nation no more than its temporal successes.

The institution is merely a kind of legalism to those who are unable to see anything else in it.

The institution is universally at the service of integration, at the service of the highest event. It should never be forgotten that the institution is itself event. It is the event in its dialectic of election, convocation and congregation. We see that it is thus at the service of redemption and salvation, that it is in unbroken connection as a mission with the mission of Christ, and that it is bound to him mystically. The highest significance of the event as regards its institutional value is that everything in the Church which is situated on the plane of external communion is completed by internal communion in its highest reality. External catholicity in its visible links is completed by internal catholicity, which causes every man and every nation to see that they possess "one heart and soul" (Acts 4:32), which they exchanged among themselves, a common soul which grows and develops in the identity of the same spiritual substance. National differences continue to exist since they are a part of the present time, but at the same time they are transcended in the new order. In this renewal "there is no more Gentile and Jew, no more circumcised and uncircumcised; no one is barbarian or Scythian, no one is slave or free man; there is nothing but Christ in any of us" (Col 3:11). By virtue of integration, men and people are emancipated from the disintegrating force of sin, and they gain access to growth in the Body of Christ. The multiplicity of races, cultures, nations and civilizations ceases to be a dividing factor. The richness of each of them remains as a multiple expression of the Incarnation. Universal recapitulation becomes a possibility which enters into history, and ceases to be too wide a plan to be put into practice. The highest significance of the integration of nations and Christian reunion in catholicity is that of the preparation, by means of sincere fraternal co-operation between individuals and nations, for liberty and perfect eschatological communion, in which the misery of men, Christians and peoples has come to an end.

CHAPTER X

The Place of the Eastern Churches in the Una Sancta

I. DIVERGENT TRADITIONS

1. The fundamental division: Christian East—Christian West

It is frequently stated that there is very little dividing the Catholic Church from the Orthodox and other Eastern Churches. There is mentioned, for example, the question of the primacy and infallibility of the pope, the celibacy of priests, the *Filioque* question, and it is often added that with a certain amount of goodwill reunion could prove easy.

The eight hundred years of separation previous to the proclamation of the primacy and infallibility of the pope, and the two Councils of Union—Lyons (1274) and Florence (1453)—which lasted a very short time, should arouse our suspicions that there are far deeper valleys between us. Certain peaks very near to us seem to move away or prove difficult to climb once we approach them.

Bishop G. K. Bell in his preface to Leo Zander's book, *Vision and Action*,[1] wrote that the fundamental division of Christianity is not the division between Protestants and Catholics, nor between Protestants and Catholics on one side and the Orthodox on the other, but rather the division between the Christian East and the Christian West. For the East Catholicism and Protestantism are two aspects of Western Christianity which have many things in common despite their differences.

This may appear to be a paradox, but if it had been true that the breach between Catholicism and Orthodoxy was less serious than that between Protestantism and Catholicism, there is no doubt that the former would have been healed long ago. It is not enough, therefore, to have the same Eucharist, the same episcopal structure, the same origin, in order to be so close together as appearances would lead one to believe.

---

[1] Published in 1952.

In the eyes of the Christian East what is representative of Christianity is not Roman Catholicism of the Latin rite; nor is it the Eastern Churches in union with Rome, even if their members are Eastern and their liturgy is celebrated in the national language and if, externally, almost nothing separates these Easterns in union with Rome from other Christians of the East.

It must not be said, of course, that the whole question can be reduced to that of primacy. There is more to it than that. It is a question of theology, spirituality and psychology.[2] It is a question of the whole. In this field the Eastern Orthodox finds it hard to stop at half-measures. He believes that it is impossible to be really Eastern if one has not passed through the East, that is, by means of a patristic formation and a theology whose presentation comes primarily from theologians of the East and not of the West.

In addition, he believes that the training in canon law of the clergy should be in accordance with the position of the law in oriental tradition. It is quite wrong to think that canon law and canonical tradition have no place among the Eastern Orthodox. Does not Latin canon law owe much to Roman law which followed the transfer of the capital of the Empire from Rome to Constantinople? And for centuries was it not at Constantinople that canon law developed. There is a juridical foundation common to both the Catholic and Orthodox Churches. But subsequently canon law in the Catholic Church became increasingly an autonomous branch of knowledge, formulated for the Church as a society, while in the Eastern Churches canon law remained less free from and more impregnated with theological and mystical considerations but less precise. The traditions, decisions and jurisprudence of each patriarchate would seem to offer the possibility of considerable codification.

If our canon law seems to the orientals as the counterpart of the law governing States, canon law, as practised in the Eastern Churches, is not entirely irreproachable. One part of the legislation of imperial origin would seem to have been incorporated bodily in legal practice. The allusion here is precisely to the various grounds for divorce which did not all originate with the Churches themselves.

It should also be noticed that the history of the Church has been different in the East and the West. We have had our problems. The East has had its own. Both have passed through a different spiritual evolution, and the result has been that the theological formation has reflected the actual life of each Church. The East did not undergo the influence of

---

[2] *1054—1954. L'Église et les Églises. Neuf siècles de douloureuse séparation entre l'Orient et l'Occident;* C. Korolevski, *L'Uniatisme* (1927), vol. II, pp. 1–64; C. Korolevski, Theodore Haluscynsku and J. Skruten, *Réflexions sur l'uniatisme* (1929), vol. II, pp. 223–61. Cf. Vatican II's Decree on Eastern Catholic Churches.

St Augustine; the consequences of this can be judged solely from the effects that this dominant presence has produced in Catholicism as in Protestantism. And thus, to take but this point alone, oriental anthropology is different from Western. The East was not influenced by St Anselm and we know what his teaching has meant to soteriology. The East was not influenced by St Thomas Aquinas; the methodology of the East is, therefore, different from that of the West. The East has known schisms and heresies, but it was never torn by the crisis of the Reformation. Now it is asserted that our conception of the Church has been dominated for centuries by an apologetic approach to the prejudice of an ecclesiology illustrative of the mystery of the Church. If we take all these factors together, making due allowance for omissions, we shall see how much there is that divides us.

After all, East is East and West is West. It will be possible for them to be united, it will always be impossible for them to be amalgamated. The whole problem is to act in such a way that the differences become the elements of unity instead of being causes of division.

What we know of the ecumenical problem obliges us to allot an important role to the cultural, sociological and anthropological factors through which Christianity is given expression. The differences by which the Christian bodies are distinguished can turn into separating walls just as easily as they can form great assets for Christian unity. It should not be said that every legitimate difference is a divergence. Christianity possesses too much breadth to be confined to one expression of itself. It is only in the symbiosis of various expressions that it discovers the power and fullness of its catholicity. Christianity needs to be Eastern as well as Western for it to be adequately itself. The everlasting problem is that each culture claims to have adequately expressed Christianity and wants to make this expression the universal norm. That is why the East knows little of the West and the West knows little of the East, instead of both being the expression of one and the same Christianity.

2. Two kingdoms divided against themselves

When the East and the rest of the world look at the West they cannot avoid seeing it as a kingdom divided against itself into Roman Catholicism, Anglicanism and Protestantism. The Reformation is a strictly Western phenomenon by the problems which it raises, the way in which it is defined and expressed. It did not appear in Asia, Africa or the East and it did not oppose the Nestorian, Monophysite or Orthodox Churches, but, specifically the Catholic Church.

Now during these four centuries of separation Catholic thought found no other solution to the Reformation than the Counter-Reformation. Despite its breadth and coherence the Tridentine synthesis itself was a reformulation of Catholicism in terms of Western tradition. At the period when the Council was held, the renewal in exegesis and patristic studies had not sufficiently penetrated the Church for the doctrinal presentation to be modified. Councils, it is true, are not intended as syntheses in theology, but in thinking of the orientation that they give to theological speculation and to the image of the Church which they present to the rest of the Christian world, one is obliged to acknowledge the supreme importance of their particular approach. The Council of Trent had a particular aim in view: the re-establishment of Catholic truth in the face of Protestantism and to that it confined itself.

Was the theological horizon of the Reformation any wider? Anglicanism remained open to tradition. But the English Reformation and the continental Reformation were, after all, a reformulation in biblical terms of the doctrine of Christianity but limited to its Western expression.

The tragedy which the Christian West suffered appears like an internal struggle in a kingdom without on either side the introduction of new elements which could change the balance of theological forces facing each other. The Reformation and the Counter-Reformation were both still too closely connected with the immediate theological, sociological and psychological heritage of the dying Middle Ages for it to be possible to replace the examination of the problem of Christianity on a wider basis by admitting the plurality of its aspects, as at the Vatican Council.

The Catholic world has long felt that its interests are not bound up with those of the Protestants and the converse is equally true. Nevertheless, it is of importance to know the judgement of the world about us, and this is that the West presents the picture of a Christian world divided against itself.

Is the picture offered by the Christian East any better?

The Nestorian Churches now have left to them but a fraction of the immense influence which was formerly theirs as far afield as China and Indonesia. On the other hand, it must be pointed out that in the Monophysite Churches some sort of renewal has occurred. This heresy seems to have faded into the background, and indeed has disappeared under the influence of the Orthodox Churches of Greece and Constantinople. It is possible indeed that the desire to use the name Monophysite is to be explained by non-theological factors. Certain Ethiopian bishops have recently protested against the conclusions of a thesis put forward by an Ethiopian Coptic Catholic asserting that Monophysism is no longer a characteristic of the Ethiopian Church.[3] But it seems reasonable to suspect

[3] Mario de Abiy-Adoli, *La Dottrina della Chiesa Etiopica dissidente sull'Unione Ipostatica* (1956).

that the desire of the national Church not to be confused in the minds of the people with the Catholic Ethiopians has been an important factor in this affair. Moreover, the Copts are increasingly anxious to be known as Orthodox. It seems, therefore, that the Orthodox Middle East, Coptic Orthodox Africa, and Orthodox Europe of the South East and East are in general doctrinal agreement.

Yet this agreement, which is considerable, stops there. In jurisdiction and administration we are faced with a fragmentation of Churches all equally jealous of their own autonomy. Antioch, which for some time possessed three Catholic Patriarchs,[4] has also an Orthodox Patriarch and a Syrian Jacobite Patriarch. Alexandria has a Coptic Patriarch and a Greek Melkite Patriarch of Antioch and all the East.[5] The primacies of honour are also the more easily recognized in that they are closely confined within their own boundaries. The jurisdictional primacies do not always find it easy to exercise their functions.

There are many reasons for the great number of autocephalous Churches of Eastern rites—historical reasons, national, sociological and psychological reasons. In principle, the autonomy of the Church has followed autonomy of the nation or nationality. The institution of synodal Churches, of autonomous archbishoprics and patriarchates was intended to facilitate relations between the Churches. But many factors came to interfere with this desire for communion. The demographic importance of the Churches deriving from the ancient patriarchates is one of them. Whose is to be the predominant influence? The prelate with the real power and means of action or the one to whom there remains only the venerable titles of seniority? How far is the authority of a patriarchate to be extended when, on account of political factors, it finds its zone of religious influence enlarged? Moscow and Constantinople are often in conflict on this subject, and a frequent cause of such difficulties is provided by emigration. Political and patriotic convictions never fail to have their repercussions on the question of the division of jurisdiction. Lastly, the survival of the ancient refusal of Syrian society to allow itself to be absorbed by Hellenic society, as well as the resistance of the Christian Arab and the Slav worlds to the Greek element, makes reconciliation between the Eastern Churches a difficult matter. There is plenty of goodwill but it is faced by complex and longstanding difficulties.

All this amounts to an image that in reality is much diminished from the one that would seem to emerge from the principle of autocephalous Churches and the sacred nature of traditions in communion.

[4] The titular Latin Patriarchs of Eastern sees were always anomalous; in future they are to be allowed to lapse.
[5] C. J. Dumont, *Églises orientales unies et dissidentes, tableau de la filiation, et de la répartition des divers rites, confessions, et hiérarchies* (1937).

3. The claims of the Orthodox Church

It would be useful to know definitively how the Orthodox world is to be defined in the general body of the Christian world. The supreme authority which alone could give an infallible declaration on the subject is a general council. Now since the separation between East and West no council of this kind has met. Could not the Orthodox Churches themselves have summoned one if it is true that in them is to be found the Church of Christ, from which Roman Catholicism, in their view, separated itself in the Middle Ages? After the Councils of Ephesus and Chalcedon, when the Nestorian and Monophysite Churches left the undivided Church, were not councils held in which East and West took part without the presence of these Churches, and yet these councils were recognized as general councils?

We need to know the common doctrinal and infallible positions of the Orthodox Churches on the nature of the Church, her unity, catholicity and mission in the world. Now it is really difficult to obtain this information since no general council held in the Orthodox East gives it to us. Are we then to seek it from one group of Churches, from the Greek Orthodox Church, from the Orthodox Church in Russia or from the Orthodox Churches scattered about in the West?

One way remains possible, though it would not have the authority of a general council; this would be to discover what could be called the eternal heart of Orthodoxy. Authors that can be qualified as representing their Churches have endeavoured to do so. We can take as examples Paul Evdokimov [6] and Hamilcar Alivisatos. [7] But their conclusions, on certain points at least, can be contradicted by testimony from other Churches.

Are the Eastern Churches which are not in communion with the Catholic Church to be designated by the term Greek Orthodox or by the term Orthodox alone?

Greek Orthodox, according to Hamilcar Alivisatos, is much more accurate than Orthodox alone; this last word, since it is used by all the Eastern Churches, can cause confusion. Orthodoxy cannot be understood if there is left out of account the fact that in its theology and its history its principal characteristic is Greek. Even the liturgical structure of the Greek Orthodox Church is entirely Greek. The fundamentally Greek character of Orthodoxy makes it the exact contrary of the Roman Communion. Greek Orthodox theologians of Churches whose language is not Greek tend to avoid the adjective "Greek". And when its use appears

---

[6] *L'Orthodoxie* (1960).

[7] "The Holy Greek Orthodox Church" in Flew, ed., *The Nature of the Church*, pp. 41–53.

to be absolutely necessary they use the term "Byzantine". This intentional elimination of the term "Greek", from other than scientific motives, leads to the conclusion that this Church, by reason of its numerical composition, is Slav and not Greek. But the divine liturgy, translated into several languages, remains almost throughout of Greek origin. It is incorrect, and it is a cause of confusion, Hamilcar Alivisatos concludes, to leave out the word which shows the very substance of the Greek Orthodox Church.[8]

On this basis he proceeds to elucidate in broad outline a consensus of the autocephalous Greek Orthodox Churches on the nature of the Church, her origin, composition, unity and her manifestation in the world. He tells us that the Church is of divine institution, for our Lord Jesus Christ, her only Head and Leader, founded her and formed her in a mystical Body by the ties of true living faith. He revealed the truth of salvation to the Church which he confirmed and established for all eternity by his death, resurrection and the guiding mission of the Holy Spirit. God's plan for the Church is the salvation of man by the acceptance and appropriation of revealed faith.

Hamilcar Alivisatos goes on to explain that the Church, although she is a divine organization, does not cease to be at the same time a human organization not only because she is made up of men of all sorts and conditions (Mt 13:47–50), but also because she pursues her ends among men, through men and with human means, even if it is the Holy Spirit who is guiding her. Jesus himself did not reveal and propagate the truth in a miraculous form. He, and the men whom he chose as helpers in his mission, made use of human means (word and sacraments), endowed, it is true, with a spiritual character (Mt 28:19; Mk 16:16; Rom 10:17) accessible to human nature. And so the Church possesses a divine and a human nature. This corresponds with the twofold nature in Jesus, her founder, true God and true man, who through her continues to carry on his saving work among men.

From the twofold divine-human nature of the Church and her mission almost naturally there derives the oneness of the Church. The Church is and must be one. She has one sole founder, and one sole truth was revealed to the Church. There is only one tie between the members of the body of the Church, their common faith and mutual love. The Church has only one end which is the salvation of every individual in human society. It is, therefore, clear that a body with these origins, endowed with this substantial nature, with this function, can only be one.

Hamilcar Alivisatos concludes that to this one body is granted by God the supreme authority, administered by men who are charged to maintain it and are sent to continue Christ's mission in the world (Acts 20:28). The

[8] *Ibid.*, p. 41.

Church is the body of Christ and he is her Head. The Church is his creation. She is founded on the faith of the apostles who organized her by means of the truth revealed to her alone and under the guidance of the Holy Spirit. The Church is, therefore, the only means willed by God for the salvation of man and, as a consequence, outside her there is no salvation—*extra Ecclesiam nulla salus*.[9]

In its totality this ecclesiology is not that of a juridical society but of an organic and mystical one. The mystery of the Church is asserted to be based on the mystery of Christ and the Holy Spirit. The apostles and Christians are kept within the circle of their presence and activity. There is also stated the conviction that the Church is the Church by virtue of the mysteries on which she is founded and that the Christian, who lives in the Church, is Christian by virtue of his faith. The apostolic role in the upholding of the truth is recognized, but the emphasis is laid on the inner essence of the Church and not on her conditioning. In a word, the visible Church is founded exclusively on faith and love and she is upheld by the guidance of the Holy Spirit. Such is the very substance of her existence.

This teaching must now be seen alongside the fact of the division between the Churches.

There are four theories to be considered: the one Church has been lost in the plurality of Churches; the one Church has been broken into several fragments, the present Churches preserving some essential part of the one Church; the one Church can be identified in several Churches of the present which, although separated, can have kept the elements of the authentic Church; lastly, among all the Churches of the present one alone has preserved the revealed truth unchanged and entire.

The Protestant and Anglican Churches between them hold the first three theories; Roman Catholicism and the Greek Orthodox Church the last.

Hamilcar Alivisatos, in the previously mentioned essay, affirms that the one Church established by Jesus Christ still exists, whole, undivided and entire, unchanged and uncorrupted. For those who have lost sight of her the question is to seek her and find her again, although she is not very far from them and it would be fruitless for them to endeavour to re-establish her. It is natural that members of the Church, for good or bad reasons, should have left the ecclesial communion, and that they find it difficult or almost impossible to retract by accepting principles and theories on the Church contrary to their own. But the oneness of the Church is absolute. No modification of this principle can be the subject of discussion.[10]

[9] *Ibid.*, p. 42.   [10] *Ibid.*, p. 44.

What is this Church? It is the Greek Orthodox Church alone, for she alone has preserved unbroken historical continuity with the undivided Church. It is beyond all doubt that, at least until the ninth century, the undivided Church was the continuation of the apostolic Church. The quarrel between East and West, in Hamilcar Alivisatos's view, led to the formation of the Roman Catholic Church as a new Church whose innovations were repudiated by the Greek Orthodox Church while she herself remained basically unchanged. The Western part, in separation from the Greek Orthodox Church, formed a new, separated Church; and the subsequent secession, from the latter, of considerable sections by reason of the Reformation, led to the formation of new Churches which, paying no attention to the true Church which continued to exist unchanged, went further still than the Roman Catholic Church along the path of innovation.[11]

But what reasons are given for asserting the historical continuity of the Greek Orthodox Church with the undivided Church?

In substance they amount to this: 1) The unchanged recognition of Jesus Christ as the one Head of the Church; 2) Faith and love as the sole basis of ecclesial life from the outset; 3) the identity of the ecclesial order with the primitive order; 4) the enduring fullness which results from the encounter of the governing authority and the faithful who are governed in the unity of tradition; 5) liturgical life, an essential factor in the life of the Church from the outset, by which the believer makes his own the very power of the risen Christ; 6) the law of love of the Lord as the primary rule standing above all legislation of the life of the Church as a society; 7) the Church's intention, her heritage from the first centuries, not to depart from her original mission, namely, to be the Church and form Christians and not allow herself to be led into performing a political function in human affairs.

The preservation of the primitive Christian spirit is most certainly an important criterion in regard to the continuity of the Church of the present with the early Church. How does the Greek Orthodox Church give evidence of this in Professor Alivisatos's view?

She does so by her democratic and federative system of the Greek Orthodox Churches and, still more, by the position of the Greek Orthodox Church on the matter of summoning an ecumenical council.

Although in the course of centuries several pressing reasons might well have urged the Greek Orthodox Church to summon the eighth general council, she has refrained from doing so. It would be wrong, in Professor Alivisatos's view, to assert that this can be accounted for by decadence, leaving out of account the historical and political factors which for

[11] *Ibid.,* pp. 47–48.

centuries caused the oppression of this Church. The principal reason is to be found in her preservation of the spirit of true and ancient Catholicity. Since the Great Schism immense portions of the Christian world, the Roman Catholic Church, the Protestant Churches, have broken away from the Mother Church. And yet she has never wished to pass an official judgement on their case while they, adding innovation to innovation, completely forget the existence of the Greek Orthodox Church and leave her in isolation. If the Greek Orthodox Church does not desire herself to summon a general council, it is because she does not desire a council that will be hers. She desires only a council of union. Were not the first seven councils the councils of the undivided Church and not the councils of one communion alone? The summoning of a council must appear to all as the synod of the whole and undivided Church. When the Churches separated from the Greek Orthodox have returned to her fold, only then can it be a question of summoning the ecumenical general council in which all the Churches will take part with equal rights. The Greek Orthodox Church is waiting for other Churches and has no desire to go forward without them. That is the explanation of her immobility. Recovered unity will be the signal for renewal and development, this time not in anarchy and independence but in the combined action of all the Churches.[12]

These propositions are not without clarity and optimism. But, from the ecumenical point of view, do they increase or lessen the gulf between the various traditions?

4. Constantinople and ourselves

It is sometimes thought that ecumenical deadlocks once established do not change. It is forgotten that problems, like ideas, possess a life of their own. Difficulties change. Certain aspects disappear and it even happens that the heart of the matter at issue is transformed. In any situation which has lasted for some time careful observation must be made of what has remained or changed of its original factors. It happens that a conflict which was non-theological at the outset assumes dogmatic implications. But it can also become non-theological again.

The exact terms of the division between Catholicism and Orthodoxy have changed considerably since the separation of 1054 and still more since the fall of Constantinople in 1453. Nowadays, the principal official cause of the separation is given as the conflict between theological and liturgical traditions. Nevertheless, it was very different from that in the Middle Ages. The principal reasons then appeared to be political rather than

[12] *Ibid.*, pp. 51–52.

404

theological and liturgical. It was chiefly the struggle between two empires, the Roman Empire of the West and the Roman Empire of the East which was at the heart of the separation. The Churches of the East and West were caught between the two and dragged into the conflict. It was only subsequently that the theological and liturgical differences, which had existed for centuries without anyone ever thinking them abnormal or wrong, were introduced into the struggle as reasons supporting the division.

The Greek world has always blamed Rome that, with the crowning of Charlemagne as Emperor of the Romans in the year 800, she took the first step in the separation between Rome and Constantinople, between East and West, which was to lead to very serious consequences for the unity of the Church and for the *Oikumene.*

There are a certain number of facts, stronger than mere sentiment, which governed Pope Leo III's gesture.

Constantine's immense plan of establishing the capital of the Roman Empire on the promontory dominating the Sea of Marmara and the Bosphorus is some measure of his genius.[13] In doing for the Empire what younger countries were later to do by moving back their frontiers towards new lands, Constantine intended to ensure for the Empire a new beginning.

Situated at the junction between Europe and Asia in the heart of the hinterland where North and South, the inland seas of the West and the commercial routes of the East all meet, Constantinople, from the geopolitical point of view seemed worthy of a masterstroke of the kind. In an advanced position and yet protected, the city, while founded on the Latin and Greek worlds, the centuries old bases of the Empire, was able to open itself to the new kingdoms conquered by Rome in the Balkans and Asia Minor.

Was Constantine's plan beyond the political, administrative and military means of the times? For centuries we see his successors at grips with the immense problem of holding or reconquering an empire whose parts continually fell away under the pressure of distance or the Barbarians. Sometimes it was the East and sometimes the West. The unity regained under Leo I and Justinian was again lost.[14]

Now the principal fact governing the new direction of pontifical policy was the definitive substitution at the beginning of the Middle Ages of a duality of culture in place of the former difficult unity of imperial civilization.

In the eighth century it had become quite obvious that Constantinople

---

[13] L. Voelkl, *Der Kaiser Konstantin* (1959).
[14] Ch. Diehl, *Justinien et la civilisation byzantine au VIe siècle* (1901); *Byzance, Grandeur et Décadence* (1919).

was less and less able to effect unity between East and West. In the West the Empire had collapsed under Barbarian pressure and new nationalities had appeared which Constantinople could no longer take in hand. Some of these, like the Frankish nation, had been converted to Christianity, and had no feelings about the Empire. The idea of the State, as it was accepted in ancient Rome or Constantinople, was foreign to them. On the other hand, Constantinople was holding Ravenna, the residence of the Byzantine exarchs responsible for the protection of the papacy, only with difficulty, and was increasingly assuming the character that was to be special to it under the name of Byzantium.[15]

What was the papacy going to do? It was obliged on the one hand to think of its own security and independence which were continually threatened by the Barbarian peril that Constantinople was increasingly unable to contain. It had also to forge Christian links capable of uniting these Barbarian nations which had surged up in anarchy. And on the other hand, Rome and the Latin West could hardly forget what Constantinople stood for—an immense tradition to be venerated both as the Empire and the Christian Empire. Indeed until the beginning of the eighth century the popes dated their official documents after the year of the imperial reign and not after that of their pontificate. Could the pope allow himself to do something which might disrupt the Christian Empire?

Was Pope Leo III a great politician? Did he measure the consequences of certain of his actions, actions indeed that were inevitable and that another pope would one day have been obliged to carry out, for both experience and history pointed clearly to their necessity?

What secured his adhesion was possibly a factual judgement of the situation: the impossible is not to be demanded of certain historical situations. In the West the horde of Barbarian nations rendered any return to political unity between East and West unthinkable. In the East, Constantinople was beginning to feel that pressure from Islam which was to be her fate until the end. What was to become of the Roman world? For centuries Christian universalism had been so to say incarnated in Constantinople, and it now appeared that less and less could aid be counted on from that quarter. Was it necessary to resign oneself to choosing a new Empire to be the mouthpiece and protector of Christian universality? Pope Leo III probably believed in the possibility of reconciling the two Christian Empires, for whatever the sporadic difficulties between the Pope and the Patriarch of Constantinople had been for a long time past, there was nothing that allowed Leo to foresee the separation which occurred two centuries later. The Byzantine Empire, in Leo's view, would remain Christian and a new Christian empire would go forward by its side.

History proved this policy to be largely right. The two greatest Christian civilizations that the Church has produced subsequently developed at about the same time in both East and West. But it must be acknowledged that by Leo III's choice, which was unavoidable, for centuries history entered on a twofold course: the Western world was to become increasingly Latin and the Eastern world increasingly Greek. Henceforward there would be two Roman Empires, one of the East and the other of the West. And on the day when the papacy began to appear as the future overlord of Europe, Constantinople preferred to take the path of separation rather than submit to its domination. Lastly, Constantinople, the seat and centre of Roman influence for centuries, the guardian of Roman law, the imperial city where Latin was spoken at the court until the seventh century, by the force of circumstances was led increasingly to lose its character of universality and progressively to identify itself with the Greek or Hellenized world. The patriarchs of Constantinople came to act as the spiritual leaders of the East as if the Church of Christ was a diarchy founded on the Pope as Patriarch of the West and the Patriarch of Constantinople as the religious leader of the capital and empire of the East.

The fate of these two great bodies shows the immense part played by non-theological factors in the division. It seems that it was the interference of the political sphere with the religious which, more than anything, led to the break. Cultural and sociological differences strengthened the opposition. The faith itself and differences of tradition were later invoked to explain and justify a state of affairs in which passions played a large part. Christians began to call each other schismatics and heretics. Were there any favourable results to the Crusades? They postponed for two centuries the capture of Constantinople by the Turks, but it must be recognized that at least the fourth Crusade was diverted from its course by the ambition of Venice to crush the commercial power of Constantinople. Thus the West dealt her a mortal blow from which she had not recovered when the Turks came to complete the destruction. To mention but one matter: how many treasures and relics from Constantinople still even nowadays remain in the West! Sacred loot! And when we feel inclined to emphasize the weakness and sometimes the spiritual poverty of the Eastern Churches, do we ask ourselves if we have not played our part in the weakening of these Churches?

Are there many in the West nowadays sufficiently open-minded to claim Constantinople as their own and to give it a place among the historical sources of their culture and civilization? For the immense majority, it must be admitted unfortunately, Constantinople is a city which, with many others, was Greek and for a long time past has been dead so far as the West is concerned.

A certain deep-rooted antagonism which persists in the subconscious of the Christian East is explained if we go back in history. Should we indeed be surprised when the finest appeals for unity leave them distrustful? Perhaps in this case, as in that of our relations with the Jews, the real reunion will take place when side by side we return together to the impartial reading of history.

There is no question in our day of the Roman Empire of the East or the West. The last occasion in modern times that the idea of the Roman Empire of the East made its reappearance was, it appears, after the great victory of the Russians over the Ottoman Empire in the Russo-Turkish war of 1768–74 when Catherine II at one moment thought of re-establishing the Eastern Roman Empire.[16]

Constantinople is now an essentially Turkish city with a tiny Greek minority always under the threat of expulsion or extermination. The great majority of the faithful subject to the Patriarch of Constantinople are to be found not in Constantinople or the neighbourhood but in America where there are about two millions of them (as compared with 200,000).

For her part the Catholic Church is placing her trust not in a new Charlemagne but in an international order of societies ruled by the natural law, valid for the East as for the West of the world.

With the Crusades and the foundation of the Roman Empire of the West another thorny subject has deep-rooted memories in the East; it is one that explains the extremely violent reaction on certain matters like that of the Eastern Churches in union with Rome, reactions indeed more violent than the subject would seem likely to warrant. The issue is that of the two thousand year old struggle between East and West for the control of the Balkans.

Are the Balkans oriental or occidental? Are they to be Catholic or Orthodox? For two thousand years a veiled struggle, sometimes exploding into violence, has been going on between East and West to tip the scale to one side or the other. It continues with alternating success or retreat, first for one party then for the other, and if on occasion calm prevails, it only flares up again as if it were quite fresh.

The Roman Empire had struck deep into the Balkans. When Constantine transferred the seat of the Empire to the shores of the Bosphorus, the Balkans were caught between East and West. With the separation of the Roman Empire of the West from that of the East and with the increasing political power of the Catholic Church in the Middle Ages as compared with Constantinople, the struggle between East and West for control of

[16] A. Toynbee, *A Study of History* (4th edition, 1948), vol. II, p. 225.

intervening territories, which had been principally political, was complicated by the interference of religion in the political sphere as both East and West sought to establish a zone of politico-religious influence.

There occurred the fall of Constantinople followed by the Turkish invasion of the Balkans. The Turks adopted for their own account the policy pursued by the Byzantine Empire. The West offered vigorous resistance to their advance into Austria and Hungary. When in the nineteenth century the liberation of the Balkans from the Turkish yoke began, these nations, Orthodox in religion, sought to retain their position between the Austro-Hungarian Empire and what remained of the Turkish Empire. After the Second World War it was Moscow this time which, making her own the policy of the Byzantine Empire, extended her influence into the Balkans.

A considerable fear complex on the subject of the Western policy of expansion to the East underlies certain actions and positions of the Orthodox Church in relation to the Catholic Church; it is to be discerned, also, in the action of the Patriarchate of Moscow, after the Second World War, of forcing the Eastern rite Catholics within the new Soviet frontiers to go over to Orthodoxy. Political fears and religious fears, political influences and religious influences are all mixed up in this centuries-old struggle between East and West for the control of the Balkans. The same must be said of the little interest on the part of the Serbian Patriarchate in entering into an ecumenical relationship with the Catholic Church. Religious motives are added to political motives.

The same distrust prevails with regard to Eastern Churches in union with Rome. They are seen as political and religious aggression against the East and Orthodoxy.

It will not be easy to get rid of these causes of disagreement which, as we have seen, are very long-standing and involve very complex factors. Hostility towards the West and the Catholic Church is not merely our own responsibility. We shall have to do our part and Orthodoxy will have to do its own. From the religious point of view it will be for our idea of the Church and her mission in the world to be seen more accurately by the Orthodox Churches. The Catholic Church appears to them as a kind of highly centralized State, a sort of spiritual empire. They find difficulty in understanding the Church as a perfect society, independent of the State and in a position of complete freedom of action in relation to the world, with juridical means at her disposal analogous with those possessed by the State. The idea of the Church in Orthodoxy corresponds with the image of the soul—it is the nation and the State which form the body.[17]

[17] Cf. the decree of the Second Vatican Council on the Eastern Churches, promulgated on 21 November 1964.

To banish memories of the past and replace them with new images will be difficult to accomplish at a speed different from that of history, that is, at the usual slow rate. Of the greatest assistance will be facts, real changes, the actual modification of a situation, not declarations of principle or intention. The annulment of mutual excommunication between Constantinople and Rome on the 7th of December 1965 can be viewed as a bright omen.

Now that certain reasons of political origin which led to the separation no longer exist, a way could be contrived, surely, of reconsidering more calmly the theological and liturgical differences which were not at the origin of the separation but, with the Churches, have been dragged into the conflict between two political worlds, two cultural worlds and two psychological worlds.

Perhaps much will be accomplished for reconciliation on the day when we agree on acceptance of a development that could be qualified as unilateral on one side and the other. History has shown it to be so in the political sphere and it can do so for us in the theological sphere also.

II. THE DIALOGUE OF TRADITIONS

1. The interconnection of the problems of reunion

The ecumenical question is one of the integration of Churches, communions and all Christian bodies in the Una Sancta, but some anxiety remains about the meaning and method of integration. Does it mean purely and simply a return to the status formerly that of the denominations and dissident Churches before the division, or even assimilation and uniformity? We must take into account two classes of facts. The first is that the Reformation occurred in the only apostolic see in the West while the separation between Eastern and Western Christianity was a separation between apostolic sees. The second is the possibility that, as a consequence of a certain rigidity in the Catholic Church following the Reformation, we have closed the door to certain authentic aspects whose development has occurred outside Catholicism.

It is hardly possible not to take these facts into account. It appears that integration purely and simply by imposing uniformity must be excluded not only so far as the Orthodox Churches are concerned, but also the Protestant communions and the Churches of the Anglican Communion. Are these all identical cases? Certainly not. In the case of the bodies originating at the Reformation it is a matter arising within the communion centred on the apostolic see of the West; in the case of the Orthodox Churches it is a matter between brotherly apostolic sees of which Peter's stands first in authority.

410

Are these two series of difficulties independent of each other? Is it possible to solve the ecumenical problem in relation to the Protestant communions by leaving aside the ecumenical problem in relation to the Orthodox Churches? Nowadays these problems are considered together. But it is one thing to approach them simultaneously and quite another to demonstrate their connection.

One of the basic convictions of this book is that these questions are interdependent. The consequence of this is that our view of the place of the Orthodox Churches in the Una Sancta might well, with due allowance being made, serve as our rule and guide for the very definite case of the communions originating at the Reformation. This principle is put forward as a hypothesis of ecumenical work. It remains wide and flexible, but its application would necessarily call for various methods in order to take into account the variety of cases.

A general rule must be our guide: Catholic communion requires that all parts of the body grow in a uniform way, though that is not to say that they should be identical in composition or function. The first principle endowing a person with unity is the soul. And so it is with catholicity— a common soul informing similar bodies though with diversities of expression.

2. Limits of integration

But if integration at the ecclesial level is essential, to what extent should it go? Will the ideal of Catholicity and the *Oikumene* be realized when there is only one universal Church, highly centralized and uniform, of which the Churches will form homogeneous parts and their heads will act as vicars of the supreme authority? Or, on the contrary, will the ideal be realized when there exists on earth only one universal Church whose unity will be held together in dialogue, communion and plurality of a body of brothers presiding over their Churches, in the East as in the West, and who find in a central see the bond of their vocation according to the regions in which God has placed them?

There are several problems underlying the question. Here one of them in particular will be examined, that of the relationship between the power of the pope and of the bishops; its examination occupied a place of exceptional doctrinal and historical importance at the Second Vatican Council, especially at the second and third sessions. It will be necessary here to examine briefly its principal points, referring the reader to other works for more extensive treatment of the subject.[18]

[18] See, for example, Y. Congar and B. D. Dupuy, *L'Épiscopat et l'Église universelle* (1962); Y. Congar, *Report from Rome II, The Second Session of the Vatican Council*

Is episcopal jurisdiction received directly from Christ, the pope designating the bishops and enrolling them in the college of the Twelve after which Christ bestows on them directly special and ordinary authority? Or is episcopal jurisdiction conferred directly by the pope who, having received the fullness of episcopal authority shares it out by the election and designation of a bishop?

Both theses were founded on solid arguments. The first was held particularly in the East in the Orthodox Churches and in the Eastern Churches in union with Rome, but it was also accepted in the West. It was emphasized that the episcopate is of divine right, each apostle having been instituted by Christ; it was added that the real jurisdiction of the bishops of the Orthodox Churches could not come from the pope save by a canonical artifice that was thought to be casuistical: according to this, the pope tacitly granted jurisdiction to every Orthodox bishop, but it was made clear that oriental tradition knew nothing of this thesis and, in the last place, an overemphatic intervention of canon law in this question was suspected, to the detriment of proper consideration being given to the mystery of the Church.

The other thesis, which was held only in the Latin Church, was based on the growing preference of the Roman Pontiffs in its favour as can be seen from certain pontifical documents, especially since the last two centuries: Benedict XIV, [19] Pius VI, [20] Leo XIII, [21] Pius XII. [22] The text of Pius XII lays down that "although (the bishops) enjoy ordinary power of jurisdiction they receive it directly from the Sovereign Pontiff himself". And Leo XIII: "The bishops would lose the right and power of governing if they knowingly separated themselves from Peter or his successors." The fundamental reason adduced by Leo XIII is that "nothing was conferred on the apostles independently of Peter; several things were conferred on Peter alone and independently of the apostles ... He alone indeed was designated by Christ as the foundation of the Church. To him was given all power to bind and to loose; to him alone was entrusted the power of feeding the flock. On the other hand, everything received by the apostles, whether function or authority, they received conjointly with Peter." [23] And Leo XIII quotes St Leo the Great: "If the divine bounty had desired that the other princes of the Church should have something in common with Peter ... it would never have given it save through

(1964); and by the same author, *Le Concile au jour le jour, troisième session* (1965); Bernard Lambert, *De Rome à Jérusalem. Itinéraire spirituel de Vatican II* (1964).

[19] *De Synodo Diocesana*, Bk. I, chapter iv, no. 2.
[20] Decree against Febronianism, 28 November 1786, Denzinger, *op. cit.*, para 1500.
[21] *Satis Cognitum*, 29 June 1896, text in Cattin-Conus, *op. cit.*, p. 368, n. 656.
[22] *Mystici Corporis*, text in Cattin-Conus, *op. cit.*, p. 452, no. 786.
[23] Leo XIII, *Satis Cognitum*, text in Cattin-Conus, *op. cit.*, p. 368, no. 655.

him . . . He alone received many things, but nothing was granted to anyone without Peter also sharing in it." [24]

In the same sense Innocent III wrote to the Patriarch of Constantinople: "What was said to Peter was addressed to him personally, to the exclusion of others; what was said to others was addressed to them in their union with Peter. In consequence power was given to him in such a manner that it could not be the prerogative of others without him by reason of the privilege which was conferred on him and of the fullness of power which was granted him." [25]

The teaching of St Thomas Aquinas is no less clear than that of St Leo the Great. According to him the fullness of power in the Roman Pontiff is rooted in the unity of the Head of the Church *cujus vicem in Ecclesia gerit plenarie Summus Pontifex*, [26] that is, in the vicarial function of the pope in the Church of Christ. Elsewhere St Thomas says: "If anyone says that the one Head and one Shepherd is Jesus Christ, who is the one Bridegroom of the one Church, this answer is insufficient. For it is clear that it is Jesus Christ himself who effects the sacraments in the Church; it is he who baptizes, who forgives sins; he is the true priest who offered himself on the altar of the cross and it is by virtue of this that his body is consecrated everyday upon the altar; and nevertheless as he was not to remain with all the faithful by means of his bodily presence he chose ministers through whom he could dispense to the faithful those sacraments of which we have just spoken, as we mentioned above (c. 74). In the same way because he was to withdraw his bodily presence from the Church it was therefore necessary for him to designate someone to undertake in his place the care of the universal Church. That is why he said to Peter before his ascension: 'Feed my sheep' (Mt 16:17)." [27]

The papacy is placed then as the primary external vicarial source of unity, corresponding to the internal source of unity, which is God, its supreme and sovereign source.

Cajetan, who repeats this teaching, establishes a distinction between the power of jurisdiction received directly from Christ without Peter as intermediary, but as a gratuitous prevenient grace—and this was the case with the jurisdictional power of the apostles—and the normal way of bestowing power, namely, by the pope. Normally, everything ought to come from Peter. "In Peter, indeed, and with Peter, begins all power in the Church and thence it flows into the whole Church as by a normal channel; and yet certain of those subject to Peter received several

[24] *Sermo* IV, chapter ii, *P. L.* XIV, col. 150.
[25] Letter *Apostolicae Sedis*, *P. L.* CCXIV, col. 758.
[26] *Summa Theologiae*, IIa–IIae, qu. 39, art. 1; qu. 88, art. 12, ad 3.
[27] *Contra Gentiles*, Bk. IV, chapter LXXVI.

powers directly from Christ, as an anticipatory grace, which otherwise they would have received from Peter." [28] And in the same sense Cajetan declares that the Church is not greater than the pope in authority, but only numerically and by extension; [29] "that the Church united to the pope has not more power than the pope alone, because the power contains in itself all the other powers and he is their universal cause. There is no power of jurisdiction in the Church that is not vested in the pope". [30] And likewise: "The power of the pope is the total power of the universal Church of which the others are participations." [31]

In the Orthodox Churches the distinction between the direct and privileged collation of power by Christ on the apostles and the ordinary regular collation through Peter and his successors is rejected. According to primitive oriental tradition preserved since then, bishops are chosen by bishops, and there is no clear reason for them to think that their jurisdiction does not come to them directly from Christ.

In these same Churches it has always been feared that the extension and definition of the doctrine by which all power of jurisdiction comes directly from the pope would lead to the bishops becoming mere papal vicars, mere cogs of the central administration and that the mystery of the episcopate would all but disappear in a certain conception of the universal Church regarded as a juridical, administrative and uniform totality. [32]

It can be pointed out, nonetheless, that the mission, power or honour of Peter do not render the mission, power and honour of the episcopal order useless. "And although the authority of the bishops is not full, universal or sovereign they are not to be regarded as mere vicars of the Roman Pontiffs, for they possess their own authority and in all truth they bear the name of ordinary prelates of the people that they govern." [33] And St Gregory the Great said: "My honour is the honour of the universal Church. My honour is the full vigour of the authority of my brethren. I do not feel myself truly honoured save when each of them is given the honour that is his due." [34]

The solution of this difficulty is to be found in the nature of apostolicity.

A distinction is made between interior and exterior apostolicity. The first designates the permanent interior mission of Christ the Apostle

---

[28] Caietani, *Scripta theologica*, ed. by V. M. Jacobus Pollet, vol. I: *De Comparatione Auctoritatis Papae et Concilii* (1936), p. 27, no. 34.

[29] *Ibid.*, no. 209, 580.

[30] *Ibid.*, p. 45, no. 75.

[31] *Ibid.*, p. 69, no. 137.

[32] N. Afanassief, *L'Église qui préside dans l'amour* in *La Primauté de Pierre dans l'Église orthodoxe* (1960), pp. 61–64.

[33] Leo XIII, *Satis Cognitum*, text in Cattin-Conus, *op. cit.*, p. 367, no. 653.

[34] *Epistolarum*, Bk. VIII, *Epist.* XXX, *ad Eulogium*, P. L. LXXVII, col. 933.

coming from the Father, and the second the visible and temporal continuity of the mission entrusted by Christ to the apostles. Christ is the Apostle of the Father, but the whole plan of the economy of salvation requires that he is not without the apostles. The question amounts to this: do the bishops receive their jurisdiction directly from the pope or from God?

The Orthodox conception of the Church is based on an order of objective realities which ensure that the essence of the Church is to be found with them. These objective realities are the mysteries of Christ, the Word, the sacraments, the hierarchical ministry. There can indeed be no question of denying the name of true Church in the strongest sense of the word to the Orthodox Churches, any more than the validity of the priesthood, Eucharist or episcopate in them could be denied. But in the Orthodox conception, the role of Peter's mission, as it is understood in the Catholic Church, finds no place.

In reality, is it not necessary to distinguish two levels, two aspects of the question? One occurs at the level of objective realities, of the structure of Christianity, and there it is impossible that Christianity, genuinely professed in the Orthodox Churches, should not have some objective reference, independent of all human will, with the total structure of the Church in which the apostolate of Peter, as understood by the Catholic Church, is found to be included. And at another level, the level of personal conscience, for various reasons whether psychological, cultural, or educational, there may be denial or refusal of something which nonetheless must exist. For example, the repudiation of one brother by another, the repudiation of a mother by her son, destroys the bonds of brotherhood or filial affection but not those of blood. There is only one way to go right to the end of the logic of repudiation and that is suicide. But so long as a Church does not commit suicide it means that she, therefore, accepts surreptitiously certain bonds even if she denies doing so.

Christ ensures interiorly the charism of jurisdiction for all bishops, Orthodox or not, provided that their consecration is in accordance with the reality of the sacrament. In this sense jurisdiction comes interiorly from God. At the level of external apostolicity it is difficult to exclude at least an objective if not a subjective reference, independent of the will of any individual, to the specific role exercised by Peter. For the Church, at the level of apostolicity, is constituently founded on Christ the Apostle and on Peter, though the fact of Peter's role causes no prejudice to the foundation of the Church on the apostles. There is no real apostolicitiy without the conjunction of these two lines. Wherever, therefore, there is a true bishop, there is an objective reference to Peter, whether it is desired or not. It is the question of a sphere in which the realities are stronger than the psychological refusals.

Rather than consider the question on the basis of the pope's tacit or explicit agreement by which in some way or other he grants jurisdiction to Orthodox bishops, we prefer here to deal with it on the basis of objective realities. In this way, moreover, it seems possible to explain more easily the practice of the early Church. Nowhere in the Gospel is it shown that there was an agreement between Peter and the other apostles on the subject of the possible successors of his colleagues, to whom Peter and his successors would tacitly grant jurisdiction, for if it is said that all jurisdiction is derived directly from the pope, that must have been true formerly as well as today. In the Church of the first centuries the question was regarded no doubt not in terms of law but at the outset on the basis of the mystery of the Church, of communion in those same constituent objective realities of Christianity. When bishops were chosen in the East without Peter or his successors having knowledge of it, implicitly the reference to Peter functioned automatically, if it is true that everything that the apostles received collectively was received in their union with Peter. It was enough, therefore, that the consecrating bishops were acting as witnesses of the whole communion—in which Peter was included according to his function—for the implicit objective reference to Peter to be there. The same consideration is valid in the Orthodox Churches at the present day and they should no longer be termed formally schismatic.

By declaring the sacramentality and collegiality of the episcopate the Second Vatican Council has achieved several results. It has provided the necessary complement to the First Vatican Council; it has restored the primacy of the mystery over the law; it has once more rooted jurisdiction in the Order; it has brought back the definition of the Church to its most ancient and biblical conception, namely, that the universal Church is a communion of local Churches ruled by the communion of bishops under the primacy of the pope, the head and a member of the episcopal college. This notion alone can serve as a basis for reunion, not that of a Church conceived as one whole which can be divided into parts. With the doctrine of the sacramentality of the episcopate it is impossible to go back to a certain idea of it in which episcopal consecration appeared as a sacramental and the bishop could seem to be the delegate of a higher jurisdiction. An idea which does not see in the episcopate a sacrament leads logically to the position of making all jurisdiction depend on the pope. On the other hand, if the episcopate is the sacrament of order in its fullness, its character forms the foundation of jurisdiction. The fullness of the order provides, ontologically, the power of exercising the episcopate, since the bishop is chosen for a people and the episcopal character is an active character of official witness of Christ the Apostle, of personal representative of Christ as High Priest and of source of unity of the communion of his people. The canonical mission, which in the Latin

Church in its present structure is derived from the pope, is meant to guide a certain bishop elect, a certain consecrated bishop towards a certain people. It corresponds with the function of the pope as the bond and head of the communion of bishops. That is the juridico-canonical aspect. It confers, therefore, in its fullness the collegial intention of handing on the apostolic powers.

It can be seen, therefore, that there are profound links between the Catholic Church and the Orthodox Churches. Nevertheless, they are incomplete links. There is a valid hierarchical communion on the level of sharing in the same sacramental nature of the episcopate, even despite the incompleteness at the level of juridico-canonical communion. The canonical mission crops up here as a question of licitness not of validity. So it must be asserted that in the Orthodox Churches the hierarchy as a sacramental jurisdictional office exists radically and effectively by virtue of the consecration, but the hierarchy as a juridico-canonical office, in our point of view, is lacking. Since Paul VI's pilgrimage to Jerusalem it has clearly emerged that insistence on the sacramental bonds in the same episcopate, bonds which ensure in depth even jurisdictional union, serves to emphasize what unites and greatly transcends what still keeps us apart.

Diversity of needs in the course of history has led to emphasis being placed on one side or the other. We must not forget what we owe to the centuries during which, in the Latin portion of the Catholic Church, centralization and uniformity were accentuated, not that the Eastern part also did not benefit. Thus we can be thankful for the uniform and careful training of the clergy, the safeguarding of Christian doctrine, the harmony between Churches of various nations, missionary efficacy in evangelization, and so on. In other words, it must be admitted that historically the system of centralization has worked for the good of the Church in so far as unity, holiness, catholicity and apostolicity are concerned and that it is at this level that must be determined what form can render the greatest service to the Church according to the needs of the times.

On the other hand we can observe how in other Churches and Christian communions the training of clergy and pastors has been carried out, how the quality and security of teaching has been safeguarded together with peace and concord between Churches and the efficacy of missionary zeal.

Perhaps we ought, therefore, to approve the age-old wisdom of the Church and acknowledge that a times of crisis and change—and how can we fail to recognize the long crisis of the modern world?—only what is strong and united can hold out and struggle on, keep the message intact and proclaim it.

The life of the Church thus proceeds with alternate flexibility and firmness, openness and retrenchment, development and renewal. The style of government existing in the Church of the apostles was obviously different from that prevailing today. It would be anachronistic to wish to justify some later form of government by claiming that it was identical in every way with an earlier form.

Are we on the threshold of another period—and of what length—in which we can imagine a new form of government characterized by decentralization, plurality, increased dialogue between the various traditions, not to the prejudice of the primacy but in connection with it? In a word, will there be a different way of exercising the primacy and collegiality?

Has a certain critical period of history which required a certain mode of action come to an end? Are we only in a period of transition to other times for which we must now get ready? The signs of this transition seem clear enough; their state of maturity must be assessed and the stages of their evolution must be judged. The Second Vatican Council has clearly opened new ways in government and in ecumenical relations.

Neither centralization nor decentralization are panaceas. There are occasions when only the central government of the Church can save a Church whose catholicity is in process of becoming eroded, narrow or inactive. There are occasions when only the central government can re-establish peace between hierarchies while Christian people run the danger of losing their faith. There are occasions when only the central government can preserve intact the faith threatened by a spirit of compromise with a national philosophy or bondage to a government. Lastly, there are occasions when only the central government of the Church can infuse new life in a Church that has perished in turmoil and misfortune.

On the other hand, it is certainly true that usually the leaders of a Church are those who know best the problems and actual needs of their Church.

Archeologism, too, is no panacea. It is not enough to prescribe a thoroughgoing return to what was done in the primitive Church, or at the period of the first seven councils, or at the time when St Gregory sent St Augustine to England.[35] To act in this way would be to forget that history has progressed, on all sides, and the present time and times to come clearly cannot be the same, in their historical identity, as times past. Yet it remains for us to profit by the lessons of history, remembering that certain causes lead normally to the same effects.

[35] Dom Lambert Beauduin, "L'Église anglicane unie, non absorbée" in Lord Halifax, *The Conversations at Malines, 1921–1925* (1930), pp. 241–61.

3. The twofold image of the Church: East and West

In the end history is always right. This phrase should be understood in its proper sense. It does not mean the primacy and infallibility of a certain interpretation of history over the faith. It is purely and simply the equivalent of the traditional maxim formulated by St Thomas Aquinas which lays down that grace does not destroy nature.

There are historical constants, factual data, inalienable human, geographical, cultural and sociological characteristics. What is ignored, or what there is pretence of ignoring, has a way of avenging itself by the very fact of its absence. Nothing suffers more than the perfection of the work in hand.

Christianity is one faith. There is "one Lord, one faith, one baptism" (Eph 4:5). Now the faith which is received by men is received in history and in space. It cannot be received otherwise than after the manner of men. It is the coming down of eternity into time, but time which is in movement gives various ages to the faith. Faith is the presence of the ultimate society in humanity, but humanity, which is complex, is the cause of faith having various modes of expression according to cultures and civilizations. Faith is the sign of absolute realities, but earthly space, by reason of its very complexity, obliges faith to assume forms of expression which are not simple.

Faith is inspired by a great plan which is called catholicity. It sees the universe made one in God and, to the extent that the material upon which it works lends itself, it is concerned with the recapitulation of the order of creation in its Head and Lord.

At a period of considerable renewal Christian faith always looks to the practice of the apostles for its inspiration. Already in the lifetime of the apostles the fundamental organization of Christianity had emerged, capable of being continued afterwards and it cannot be ignored without prejudice to the Church.

From Jerusalem Christianity spread from city to city, into Judaea, Samaria, Galilee and Syria. It took root in the north of Asia minor, spread to the South towards Africa, to the East towards Mesopotamia and Asia, to the West into Europe. The apostles were missionaries. By means of the commercial and administrative roads of the Empire, through the Jewish and Greek colonies, they reached all regions. This period is designated as that of apostolic missionary expansion. But since it was a work carried out by the apostles under the direct guidance of the Holy Spirit these events are to be interpreted as something more than history: we have here a fundamental structure, the very archetype of the pattern that is to endure until the end of the world to enable Christianity to recapitulate all things in Christ.

It was not by Peter's permission that Mark went to Africa, John to Asia Minor, Paul to Greece, any more than Peter went to Rome by delegation of the Twelve. No doubt the apostles had few opportunities of meeting together. They were sent out collectively by the Lord to the whole world over which each of them had universal jurisdiction. They endeavoured not to encroach on the work undertaken by one of their number. Very simple agreements must have governed their relations. Peter left the East and he appears as the great apostle of the West.

Already in apostolic times the twofold image of the Church stands revealed. In the West an apostolic see emerges and remains: it was that of Peter in Rome, the one apostolic see of the whole of the West which withstood the passage of time, the see called to become the central and primatial see of the whole of catholicity, the most important, in extent and influence, of all the sees of apostolic origin.

The East, on the other hand, is characterized by a number of sees of apostolic origin. Not all cities in which Christianity was preached by the apostles have come down in history as apostolic sees. Several did not endure. Some of them enjoyed a certain importance for some time, for example, Ephesus, Caesarea, Edessa, etc. Through the development of the various rites we can follow the extension of the fundamental organization from its embryonic state in the apostolic era.

The apostles spread out into the world from Jerusalem. Obviously, however, that does not mean that they took with them from Jerusalem a single liturgy, definitively constructed on the basis of our Lord's eucharistic prayer and the prayers in the Temple, which subsequently assumed various slight local differences according to the regions through which they passed. Just as it was only progressively that they came to understanding of the mystery of Christ and the Church, so, possibly, it was only gradually that they were imbued with understanding of the Eucharist.

In what form exactly was the Eucharist celebrated? How long did it take the Church to come to clear understanding of this mystery? Did she in this pass through stages, first eating the bread of Christ, then the body of Christ and finally offering the body of Christ? [36]

So far as can be seen, the liturgy of Hippolytus in the third century stands in an intermediate position between the liturgical traditions of East and West. It was influenced by Justin and the Didache, and the latter also influenced the liturgy of Addai and Mari at Edessa, the first rite used at Antioch, but discarded because insufficiently capable of development.

---

[36] Axel Andersen, *Das Abendmahl in den zwei ersten Jahrhunderten nach Christus* (1904); Hans Lietzmann, *Mass and Lord's Supper* (1958): "The Mistaken Search for Archetypes", pp. 265–7.

Antioch, according to tradition Peter's first see, appears as a centre of liturgical development. With the Antiochian or Syrian rite are connected the Armenian rite with the influence of Caesarea in Cappadocia, the Maronite rite with borrowings from the Roman rite, the Chaldean rite through the intermediary of Nestorianism in Mesopotamia and in Persia, the Byzantine rite which, deriving from Antioch and by way of Caesarea in Cappadocia, in the fifth century developed in an original manner.

The proto-history of the liturgical rites is far from complete. From the resurrection of Christ until the third century the position is very obscure. With the third century the ritual structure begins to assume the definite shape of liturgy of the Word and liturgy of the Eucharist, a Christian synthesis of the prayer of Temple and synagogue and of the Last Supper.

What criterion decided the choice of the patriarchal sees—their apostolic origin, their political or historical importance or their liturgical importance?

Here we wish to emphasize especially the liturgical importance, in the first place because the Eucharist makes the Church and, secondly, because the liturgy is the principal form of the ordinary magisterium of the Church and of her pastoral action.

Jerusalem was an obvious choice because that city is so closely bound up with the very heart of the Christian mystery, Antioch because it was the centre of a whole number of liturgies, Alexandria for somewhat similar reasons in relation to Africa, and, finally, Rome, on account of Peter.

In the case of Constantinople it is difficult clearly to establish its apostolic origin from the Apostle Andrew[37] and it must be remembered that it was only after the departure of the pontifical legates to the Council of Chalcedon, in 451, that the decree was issued giving to the bishops of Constantinople the same privileges as the bishop of Rome. But if the importance of sees is to be measured by their influence on the Eucharist, and therefore on the Church, Constantinople, whose liturgy has spread throughout the world of the Greco-Slavonic Churches, both before and after the separation, in different languages and continents, has largely made good its title of patriarchate.

This principle of the relation between sees and the Eucharist is one of very great importance. Various liturgies all celebrating the same mysteries of Christ constitute so many ways not only of building up, but also of expressing the Church. There is only one mystery of the Church but there are two ways of interpreting it to the world—the western way and the eastern way. And it is also by these two principal ways that profession of the true faith may be made.

[37] F. Dvornik, *The Idea of Apostolicity in Byzantium* (1958).

Has the twofold image of the Church, Western and Eastern, grown out of date on account of the decadence or poverty of the capital cities which had formed the centres of the liturgical and theological expression of the Christian mysteries? Antioch has nowadays become a straggling village of no importance, yet the patriarchal titles of several heads of Eastern rite Churches still remain attached to it—Maronite, Syrian Catholic, Greek Melkite, Syrian Jacobite, and Orthodox. Until recently, indeed, there was also a (titular) Latin patriarch. In the same way Constantinople has fallen far from its former prestige as capital of the Christian Roman Empire. Jerusalem is divided between two countries, neither of which is Christian. Alexandria is no longer the great Greek-speaking capital on the threshold of Africa.

But dynamic populous nations have come to the aid of the Christian East. In Africa, Ethiopia which, since 1958, has a patriarchate at Addis Ababa, while recognizing the Coptic Patriarch of Alexandria as head of its Church, forms the advanced guard in the African world of a liturgy which possesses its own language and characteristic features and is perhaps destined to be important.

In the Balkans there are nations which threw off the Ottoman yoke in the last century, Serbia, Greece, Bulgaria and Rumania, and have obtained from Constantinople autocephalous status to correspond with their political freedom. In Eastern Europe there is, principally, Russian Orthodoxy, autocephalous since the capture of Constantinople in 1453, whose importance for reunion is preponderant. Lastly, there is the whole world of immigrants from the East, scattered all over Europe and especially in America.

All these facts from the history of the apostolic expansion in East and West, from the history of Constantine's empire, now divided, now reunited and broken up again, from the phenomenon of the enduring nature of the eastern expression of Christianity, despite Islam, the Huns, the Tartars, the Turks and the diaspora, are an expression of an existential law of Christianity which is that the expression of Christianity rests on an inalienable plurality. Christianity is contingently Western or Eastern, Asiatic or African. But it is clear that it was in the Mediterranean region that its essential structures were fixed, which subsequently spread out over the world. Just as it is impossible to turn the West into the East, so it is impossible to make the East into the West, or interpret the East by the West; whenever it has been tried, it has led to failure.

There are various ways of accepting the fact; it can be ignored or minimized, one may resign oneself to it, or go forward making concessions or act sternly. There is also frank acceptance and dialogue between traditions. Several papal declarations in the last century or so call on us to adopt this course. Seen in the logic of their continuity they cannot fail

to reveal the gradual realization of a plan intended to prepare the Catholic Church and the Eastern Churches for reunion.

Each pontificate has enabled the ecumenical cause to make progress. But the idea that unity is identical with uniformity or unilateralism or that Eastern Christianity must be assimilated to the Western model has never been put forward.

The popes did not suffer from the illusion that their plans could be realized in the immediate future since there were so many obstacles on one side and the other. Undue haste would have been harmful to all. They showed the way and it is impossible to believe that so many gestures all tending to union were not directed towards their effective realization at a period when they hoped that the time was near. The Catholic Church has chosen the way of dialogue. Other Christian communions have also entered on it.

4. The dialogue between the fifteenth- and sixteenth-century reformed communions and orthodoxy

There is cause for perplexity on the significance of the relations between these Churches. For centuries contact has always been sought by these denominations rather than by the Orthodox. What is it, then, which attracts the Protestant and Anglican worlds to the Orthodox, particularly since the latter is much nearer to Catholicism than to Protestantism or Anglicanism?

Facile explanations occur to the mind at once: the natural affinity between all that is not Catholic, the intention of uniting against the Catholic Church. But this explanation is hardly sufficient to show why these denominations have always sought contact with the Orthodox world rather than with the Catholic world.

A second explanation. The Churches and communions originating with the Reformation are outside the dispute between Orthodoxy and Catholicism, just as the Orthodox are outside the division between the reformed bodies and Catholicism. These are domestic questions. The Protestant and Anglican worlds have inherited the divided state of Western and Eastern Christendom. They took no part in it. Dialogue would be possible, therefore, between the reformed Churches and denominations, intended as a return to the Church of Christ in its primitive form and, on the other hand, the Eastern Churches which assert that they have remained the representatives of Christianity in its original form, while Catholicism was increasingly assuming the appearance of a Christianity of the West.

In fact, for some years Luther and the professors at Tübingen, convinced that they shared the same faith as the Orthodox Church,

423

remained in contact with the Orthodox Patriarch of Constantinople.[38]

This second explanation, although more satisfying than the first, possesses certain disadvantages. It burkes the question of the responsibility, in the division between East and West, of those countries and Churches which accepted the Reformation. It is really far too easy to say, "we lay on Rome, on the countries which remained Catholic, on Catholicism in our own country before the Reformation, the Western share of the responsibility in the separation between East and West."

In addition, the reformed Churches were not long in coming to the conclusion that the Eastern Churches had much more in common with the Catholic Church than had first been imagined. Would the Reformers have gone so far in the Reformation, would they have been so certain of bringing back the Church to her primitive form if they had been aware of the position of the Eastern Churches as heirs of the primitive Church?

In their desire to reform the Church, the only Church that, in practice, they knew, the Reformers acted at the outset as if they knew nothing of the Christian East, and they behaved like men in a great hurry to finish once and for all with what they had under their eyes. They established a radical rule: whatever is not clearly to be found in scripture will not be retained in the actual Church. On that basis they pruned, they cut away, they reformed. Dogma, structure, liturgy, the Church's mission, all was treated alike.

Critical reflection on their method of action enables it to be said that what has been lauded as holy impatience, sacred zeal in the service of the glory of God and the purity of the Gospel is far from deserving such praise, so obvious is the amount of passionate improvisation, one-sided concern, superficiality and violence that went to its accomplishment.[39] At an early date the general body of ideas of the Reformers was fixed. Although they went over them, worked over them again, they never gave them up. Their criteria, their attitudes and their actions were adopted without its ever occurring to them to criticize the origins of their positions. The Reformation and its history was thus committed to paths from which it would prove difficult to depart.

From this it can be seen to what a great degree the Reformation is strictly a Western phenomenon. In a state of undivided Eastern and Western Christendom all this would have been unthinkable, or at least on a much lesser scale, because the Reformers would not have found it

---

[38] Schaff, *Creeds of Christendom*, vol. I, pp. 51–52; Georges Florovsky, "The Orthodox Churches and the Ecumenical Movement prior to 1910" in Rouse and Neill, *op. cit.*, pp. 171, 215.

[39] Congar, *Vraie et fausse réforme dans l'Église*, pp. 306–32.

Alexandria and of every see which was founded on Christ. From Rome Christianity is seen through the primacy and infallibility. From Jerusalem and the East in general it is seen through the Founder from whom we have been given everything.

Is there opposition between the two? The primacy is not Christianity, but the mystery of Peter—that is, his role chosen from all eternity for the accomplishment of the great plan for the salvation of humanity—is included in the mystery of Christianity. Whether in Jerusalem or in Rome, Peter is not far from Christ. In one place as in another he confesses that Christ is the Son of the living God and he leads the whole Church in the profession of his faith. In one place as in another the Lord says to him, "Thou art Peter and on this rock I will build my Church" (Mt 16:18), "Feed my lambs, feed my sheep" (Jn 21:16–18), "Strengthen your brethren" (Lk 22:32). Peter shows the way to Christ, Christ points to Peter. One is inseparable from the other. At Rome, Peter, who declares his belief in Christ, appears always the first in expression of the common faith, the one who speaks in the name of the others, who grasps the solid truths to which the others on occasion are slower to give themselves, who, after brotherly discussion among the apostles, shows in what way the question is to be decided.

The choice of the apostolic body, one and yet diverse, showed the one yet plural form, sealed by the Spirit, under which Christian universalism was to be expressed. All were dispensers of the mysteries of Christ, united in witness to the life, death, resurrection of the Lord and the coming down of the Holy Spirit; and yet it is impossible not to remark among the Twelve sufficiently pronounced characteristics which make primitive Catholic unity a complex unity, characterized by plurality of aspects in the unity of the same mystery. At times of the greatest difficulty the apostles feel the need to discuss together. The line of conduct finally decided on is the result of a synergy in which each apostle with his own characteristics, place and function within the apostolic college makes his contribution. Peter and Paul in turn take the leading role, James acts as mediator between them. On occasion James causes Peter to withdraw or Paul blames Peter for giving way too much. Peter, whose role as leader is not disputed since he is the centre of the discussions, is the one who furnishes the solution; then adjustments are made on both sides. In this apostolic activity there can be perceived a dialectic that is experienced between union together and guidance, organic structure and decision. The apostles need Peter and Peter needs the apostles.

A great step forward will have been taken towards reconciliation between the Catholic Church and the Eastern Churches when it is accepted that in so complex an entity as Christianity certain parts proceed more quickly than others and develop according to a rhythm which is their own. Is it not the same in the human body which develops its organs and limbs in accordance with a rhythm of which it guards the secret? The Church has her period of infancy, adolescence and maturity. She too must grow in age and wisdom. A development whose external appearance causes us astonishment can only be denounced as wanting in balance if unilateralism is present; if there is none, we must have confidence that the soul will bring the new growth into harmony, retaining this or that development, stimulating another.

Christianity is not the primacy. Peter alone does not save the Church. He needs to be upheld lest he sinks into waters. But the primacy has a connection with the essence of Christianity. If the West has come to awareness of this more quickly than the East, the East, on its side, became more quickly and more profoundly aware than the West of the essence of Christianity, as we can see by the role played by the East in the development of Christianity and in the councils. It was the vocation of the West to bring out clearly for the good of Catholicity as a whole the doctrine of the primacy. The East had other graces in the doctrinal order. In the design of the one soul of the Church these graces were to be exchanged and not held in isolation. Development, making greater progress in one place or another, is still not unilateralism. Unilateralism begins with the refusal of union together which, in its turn, leads to the breach in catholicity.

We must explore this explanation further. It seems indeed that one of the reasons which still makes acceptance of the primacy more difficult is derived from the confusion between the actual mode of its appearance and its essential nature.

Now coincidence and causality, the modality of a thing and its essence, silence and negation are not to be confused. That the existence of a single apostolic see in the West may have favoured to a certain extent the development of the primacy, whereas the East, living under a system of several apostolic sees in communion with each other, saw no reason for it; or that the Roman legal spirit may have given a certain impulsion so that the idea cannot be wholly denied *a priori*. For us it is enough that the essence of the question is saved, and this essence is that the doctrine of the primacy belongs to the doctrinal order, before belonging to the canonical or historical order. The primacy appeared in history but its essence belongs to another order than that of history. The primacy bears a certain relationship with the law which rules the Church, but its essence does not belong to the juridical order. It is something beyond law and history. It belongs to the eschatological order like the mystery of the Church herself, because it concerns the mystery of the unity of faith of the Church, communion between the Churches, charity between the Churches, and the presidency of the Eucharist at the level of the universal Church.

When the discussion on the primacy is brought down to the historical, political or juridical levels it becomes endless. The authority of the Fathers of the Church is invoked; the Latin Fathers, who mention the primacy, are set up in opposition to the Greek Fathers, who for the most part do not mention the subject.

It is useless to put into the mouths of the Greek Fathers something that they did not say, but it is equally wrong to infer their opposition from their silence. To disregard a matter is not to lie about it, neither is lack of knowledge a denial. The only conclusion that it is legitimate to draw from the silence of the Greek Fathers, or the statement of the Latin Fathers, is that of the special vocation of East and West in Catholic unity. It remains for us to bring together in one the heritage of the Greek and Latin Fathers for the good of the whole and not for its division.

In a universal Church whose complex unity rests on the organic structure of Churches spread over East and West, a local Church, a body of Churches, can very well, indeed must, make their personal contribution to the development of some aspect of the Christian mystery, while allowing to others a similar concern. The doctrine of the primacy is a contribution by the Christian West to the cause of the organic unity of Christian universalism. The special contribution of the Christian East may well be the insistence on the principle of communion between Churches.

A second step forward will possibly have been taken when we agree that as a consequence of the division a certain unilateralism may well have slipped in on both sides in the development of the truth. On the one hand, partly by reason of the temporal situation of the papacy in the Middle Ages which, under Innocent III, became the overlord of a part of Europe, then on account of the Great Schism and the Reformation there occurred in the West a concentration of the unity of the Church around the papacy, not without a certain reduction of the full meaning of the principle of union, which was considered in juridical rather than in mystical terms. On the other hand, in the East attachment to the mystical importance of each Church has been accompanied by an immoderate reduction of the canonical and juridical bonds between the Churches. We do not say that in the West the bishops have been absorbed by the papacy. To do so would be to misunderstand the meaning of the dogma proclaimed at the Vatican Council in 1870. Pius IX, more than any other, praised the German bishops for having so well expressed the relationship between the papacy and the episcopate in their letter in January 1875. But the anxiety was the sign of a certain danger; and since the Church's growth must be a balanced one, the doctrine concerning the episcopate must be emphasized side by side with that on the papacy.

On the other hand, in the East attachment to the principle that in tradition, the bishop and the Eucharist the essence of the Church is realized, has, as a result of the separation, not been without prejudice to the completely organic nature of the Church. The unity and communion of the Church do not consist merely in sharing the same faith, the same Eucharist, the same structure, nor yet in the mere absence of hostility between Churches. In addition a centre of unity is necessary. Otherwise, in fact if not by right, the Churches are divided in their life.[40] Unity of the Churches is then in existence, but not the unity of the Church.[41] Unity in the Church, indeed, is not a property special to each Church. It can only be unity that is communicated. Unity without effective communion, which cannot be realized without a centre of unity that is above each individual Church, becomes a separated unity, a sort of vassalage of total unity by one Church or another. This Church, knowingly or not—and knowingly means schism—takes its own unity as the universal category of the Church. In a word, attachment to its own special property is such that it becomes the rule in judging the whole Church.

We are here faced by a difficult problem: is it the papacy as a doctrine or the papacy as an institution which is opposed by Anglicans and Orthodox? Is it because they have not grasped the relationship of the papacy with the mystery of the Church, or is it because the historical image of the papacy is repugnant to them that they reject that institution?

To tell the truth, the difficulties urged against the papacy concern both the doctrine and the institution, that is, the relationship of the papacy with the mystery of Christianity both as event and as institution. In this saving act effected by the Word, in this event by which God speaks to me and to the whole Church and expects from me and from the whole Church an answer, what is the role of the papacy?

Only a profound ecclesiological study and an effort to recentre the institutional aspect of the papacy in the mystery of the Church appear as the decisive means to overcome the centuries-old difficulties of the communions separated from Rome against the papacy.[42]

---

[40] A. Schmemann, *Église et Organisation ecclésiale* (1949).
[41] A. Schmemann, "La Notion de primauté" in Afanassief, Koulomzine, Meyendorff and Schmemann, *op. cit.*, p. 132.
[42] *Catholicity, A Study in the Conflict of Christian Traditions in the West* (1947), p. 39.

6. What are the claims of the see of Peter to the primacy?

The first is that of charity. Have not the manifestation and exercise of charity an intrinsic connection with the papacy? Do they not form one of the reasons for its existence? Are they not one of the motives for which it entered into our Lord's actual plan for his Church? Does not this connection between the papacy and love constitute the basis of certain rights of the Holy See in the whole body of Churches which make up the Body of Christ and which can be summed up in the formula, "The Church which presides over love".[43]

Considerable thought is given to charity in the life of the Christian, in social relationships, but little, in short, to charity as the basis of the Church, still less to the Church as God's charity to the world. Yet where charity is, there is the Church. Our Lord's extraordinary insistence, on all occasions, repeated in all sorts of ways, on the connection between the Church and charity with reference to the unity of his disciples, his apostles and of all those who were to believe in him, shows clearly that love is indeed the form of his Church (Jn 13–17).

Now if our Lord established a close connection between love and Church, he established one also between Peter and love. "Simon, son of John, do you love me more than these... Simon, son of John do you love me?" (Jn 21:15–18). And in answer to Peter's assertion of love he says to him: "Feed my lambs, feed my sheep." That is a remarkable connection. Peter in return for his love does not receive a declaration of reciprocated affection; or rather he receives one but in the form of a transference of responsibility to him of the love which our Lord has for his lambs and sheep. Thus are completed our Lord's words to him as the future foundation of the Church. In both cases Peter finds himself allotted a precise role in that charity of God which is the Church. He appears under the lineaments of love, that is, as the unifying principle, the principle of mutual acceptance and exchange, in a word, the visible bond of charity. The presidency, or rather the primacy, which belongs to Peter on the ground of love, is the presidency of ecclesial love. It is natural, of course, that the love of a Church should extend to the whole Church; but Peter's charity stands out for its special characteristic in the service of unity. It is a question of a mission, a responsibility of love which includes taking in charge the love which the Churches must have for each other in order to control its development, to encourage it if necessary, to guide it towards harmonious growth. The see of Peter presides over charity since it is the visible bond of the charity of the Churches among themselves, since it forms their

---

[43] St Ignatius of Antioch, *Epistola ad Romanos, Greeting*, M. G. 5, 685.

connecting link and establishes communication between them, arousing within them potentialities of receptiveness and tender care, causing them to share in a vision of love which extends to the whole of catholicity.

It is natural that this love of him who presides over the charity between the Churches should possess its means of expression and its own language and take those steps which belong to it by right. His function of love in the charity of the Church bestows this right upon him together with the responsibility and the power. But it must be clearly seen that if the primacy includes a juridical aspect, it is not law which forms the basis of love, but love which forms the basis of law. And when violence is done to the exercise of love of the Church, which presides over love, far more than the law it is love which is injured. If it were only a question of law, the normal response of transgressed law would be punishment and castigation. But because in this case the law is rooted in love, justice can always find measures transcending itself.

Peter, like all the apostles, was a witness to the charity of Christ made manifest in words and deeds. In whom more than in our Lord did there ever exist those charismata of charity which are continually reflected in the primitive Church and the Church down the centuries—help given in so many ways, the practice of mercy, the working of miracles, the gift of his life? The apostle continues by his charity to bear witness that he is faithful to our Lord's command to "love one another". He does not do so on the sole ground of spiritual imitation or personal witness. He is the official, deputed, hierarchical witness of the charity of Christ. The first thing that he proclaims is the goodness which alone explains that God should have given his Son to the world (Jn 3:16) and that Christ should have given his life (1 Jn 4:8). The apostle does not proclaim merely the love of God, but still more that "God is love" (1 Jn 4:8), or that Christ has accomplished a work of charity, but that Christ and the Church, which is his body, are the very charity of the Father in the world. Now in this charity which is the Church, the apostle occupies a special place. He is the organic structure of the charity of the Church, the charity which is the Church. He is the *forma caritatis*, the form of charity. Such is Peter's primordial role, of each of the Twelve and of the bishop. The Holy Spirit ensures to the Church the internal form of charity, the apostle its external, visible form. Now in this mission of charity exercised in common Peter performs a special function: he visibly unites to the Church as the Body of Christ the charity inherent in all the Churches.

Through this may be explained a whole host of actions that the see of Peter has always considered as belonging to it of right and which no other Church has ever claimed as its province. On the last analysis it is this right of love which accounts for it. All these actions cannot be reduced to merely juridical operations. Love here is itself the source of right, the right to take charge of the weakest Churches, the poorest, the least fervent, the least open to catholicity, the right of being concerned about their love, their resources, their needs, the right to bring all the Churches into communication among themselves.

It can never be sufficiently emphasized that it is on this basis that we must understand the role of the see of Peter among the others as making easier relationships within the other Churches. A view of the Church dominated by power and right can only lead to conflicts. In that case a Church becomes, unknowingly and inevitably, a sort of religious analogue of modern States in which the trade and professional bodies, the financial groups, are banded together to assert their rights, their interests, to defend their privileges or win others, while the central power strives to keep the balance between the parties. It is difficult to avoid the thought that surreptitiously some notion of this vast modern phenomenon has crept into the Church; the important bodies which compose it, the religious orders, the secular clergy, the teaching brothers, the laity, all feel bound to defend their "interests", to insist on their "rights", to defend their "privileges" with the help of official or semi-official protectors.

One experiences sometimes a certain feeling of embarrassment when someone says with an air of triumph, "We have obtained this or that from Rome" or "everything is going well" in Rome. There is no need to be surprised at the insistence of the laity now to defend their "right" to be represented in the Church. This claim is possibly some retaliation on the part of the laity for the clergy's excessively juridical image of the Church. Once again, the question does not concern the authenticity of power and law, but their ambience, foundation and whole perspective. The Church is the mystical Body of Christ. That is her nature, and it is on this basis that both her laws and customs must be established.

It is difficult not to think that the Orthodox Church, too, in this connection is the counterpart of the too juridical West.[44] Arnold Toynbee in *A Study of History* often points out that the defensive reaction of one civilization against another is evidenced by the use of the very same arms. If we were to change arms, if love were to defend itself against love by love, should we not be very near to unity?

Secondly, the primacy of the see of Peter is founded on the Eucharist. What does the word charity, in Greek *agape,* mean in the greeting "The Church which presides over charity" addressed by St Ignatius of Antioch to the Church of Rome? Is it the Eucharist or love? When St Ignatius uses this word it directly designates the local Church in its

[44] Schmemann, "La Notion de primauté", *loc. cit.,* pp. 145–6.

eucharistic aspect and indirectly the union of all the Churches on a foundation of love.

The see of Peter presides over love, because it is at the centre and possesses the headship. But how can we explain the position of this see in relation to the Eucharist as ensuring it a further title to the primacy? In the first place, we may inquire: what is the real significance of the pope's presiding on occasion at the celebration of the holy mysteries in an Eastern rite? For the Eastern Churches the rite represents much more than a special manner of celebrating the sacred liturgy. Practically, it designates the Church herself, that is, a cultural, canonical, liturgical, theological and institutional whole.

The problem does not occur to us with the same force as a result of the pope's habitual celebration of the Eucharist according to the Latin rite. Celebration in another rite makes us aware of the fact that the pope is not exclusively the pope of the Latin Church—he is the Patriarch of the West—but the bond between all the Churches. Celebration according to various rites makes manifest the meeting in his person and in the one Eucharist of the catholicity of the Church.

The meaning underlying the practice mentioned is that of the union of the twofold principle governing Catholic unity—the principle of union by the primacy and the principle of union by the *res,* the things, the mysteries, the divine Persons who ensure to Christianity its substance. Now in the celebration of the Eucharist, in no matter what rite, the whole Church, all Christianity is there. On the one side, indeed, there is Peter, the foundation of union between the Churches and, on the other, the Eucharist which "makes" the Church. To the image of the eucharistic celebration by the bishop surrounded by his priests in the diocesan Church there corresponds, at a higher level, the eucharistic celebration by the supreme pontiff surrounded by his brethren the bishops. Just as the bishop who presides over the Eucharist in his diocese is the bond of communion in this Church, so the pope, presiding over the Eucharist in the different rites, acts as witness, minister and principle of union between the various Churches represented by their bishops.

Is there opposition between these two types of bond, one realized by the pope, the other by the Eucharist? What, on a final analysis, makes the Church? Is it the pope or the Eucharist?

It is obvious that since Christ both gave Peter his position and instituted the Eucharist, there cannot be opposition between the two. The Eucharist is Christ, whole and entire. Incontestably the Eucharist makes the Church. Where the Eucharist is, there the Church is. But is the Church present whole and undivided where the Eucharist is celebrated in a state of separation between Churches? Is there not something wanting to the Eucharist when it is celebrated in a state of schism? Does not the Eucharist then in some sort suffer violence, a kind of severance between what is essential, namely, liberation from bonds and fellowship with universality, and the state of division or schism in which it is actually in contradiction to its nature and purpose? In short, is there not wanting to it catholicity in its state of completion? The Eucharist under such circumstances remains true but after a diminished fashion, and, so to say, in a state of bondage within the limits of a local Church which denies fellowship to other Churches.

That in the diocesan Church, even in a state of schism, gathered round its bishop celebrating the Eucharist there should really be present the essence of Christianity as institution and event, cannot be denied, since the Eucharist really makes the Church and through it the real foundation is laid of the identity between all the Churches gathered together in their bishop celebrating the Eucharist. But are the basis and the very essence of the identity all that is required for the catholicity of the Church to be really the Church? A certain Church is Church, but it is not *the* Church. The Church only exists fully through him who presides over the Eucharist as witness, minister and principle of fellowship between Churches. Then in each Church in which the Eucharist is celebrated is found the full dimension of the Church and of catholicity. The Eucharist there really actualizes the Church since it can always be said that this local Church, even in its humblest form, is united to the essential realities of the mystery and, by its bond with Peter, to catholicity without partition or division, multiform in its identity.

Peter presides over the Eucharist, but in a sense it is also the Eucharist which makes Peter, just as it makes the bishop. The special effect of the Eucharist is that in it is to be found the bond effected between all the Churches and here appears this special aspect of the primacy: no bishop can be made the bond between all the Churches; that belongs to the pope alone.

So it is not enough to say that at the level of effecting the Eucharist pope and bishops are absolutely equal, any more than bishop and priest are at this same level. The Eucharist possesses an ecclesial dimension which is different in the case of priest, bishop or pope. The relation of each with unity, holiness, catholicity, apostolicity is different in each case. It is the integral role of each in relation to the Eucharist which regulates the differences. And it is on this basis that the position, the relationships, the hierarchy of the different persons who make up the ecclesial society are established. The heart of ecclesial organization is the Eucharist, hence the expression "the sacrament of order". A certain right belongs respectively to the pope or to a bishop according to his role in respect to presiding over the Eucharist. The Eucharist is truly the source of law in the Church just as it is of love.

To the see which presides over charity and the Eucharist belongs the primacy. There is a third title in connection with this; it is that of the bond and centre of fellowship.

It is not enough in fact that the Churches should be in communion with each other in the effective identity of a same Eucharist and the objective identity of a same love; the unity of the Churches in the same realities and the unity of concord between them are not the unity of the Church, but the unity of the Churches. It is no longer the multiplicity of Churches without links, since all are one in Christ, but it is not yet the unity of the Church since all lack a visible centre of fellowship. At the level of the universal Church the pope is the centre and the visible bond of fellowship of the bishops among themselves. If this role is denied to the pope logically, it must be denied to the bishops. The Protestant Reformation was entirely logical on this. It did not wish to keep for the bishops what it denied to the pope. Only the name of bishop has sometimes remained with certain prerogatives, but the substance of the office has disappeared, that substance made up of charity, Eucharist, communion, authority in bearing witness to the faith, which is infinitely more than the mere function of ecclesial administration.

The great, the immense difficulty in the Orthodox Church rests on the seeking of an internal universality that is to form the economy of external universality, possessing it to the largest possible extent, but always excluding the primacy. By internal universality is meant communion in the one same Eucharist, one same faith, one same Lord, in short the fellowship and unity of the Churches in the same Christ. It is asserted, and rightly, that when this unity prevails the Churches' relationship to each other is no longer that of a scattered multiplicity. They possess a genuine interior bond of unity and community which cannot fail to be externally verifiable, at least to some extent. [45]

Nevertheless, it is difficult to deny the primacy to the see of Peter on the title of bond and centre of fellowship between the Churches if the question is regarded from the Christological viewpoint of Chalcedon which, expressed ecclesiologically, never establishes interior bonds without exterior ones also. On this account, as also by reason of the primacy founded on the presidency of charity and of the Eucharist, it must be concluded that with internal universality there must correspond external universality. The Church, which is founded on love, which is "made" by the Eucharist, requires at the level of external organic unity, as well as at that of internal organic unity, corresponding bonds. That is the meaning of the expression "Vicar of Christ". It expresses the special position of

---

[45] Afanassief, *L'Église qui préside dans l'amour, La Primauté de Pierre dans l'Église Orthodoxe*, pp. 9–64.

Peter's role within the apostolic body. All the apostles were chosen to be witnesses and bonds of communion. The apostle is a witness of the unity of fellowship of the Father with Christ and of Christ with the Father, as it was given to him to know by his life with Christ. The apostle also bears witness to his own fellowship with Christ and with all the apostles, and this witness of communion was, we know, of the greatest importance in the primitive Church. Bearing witness to communion appears as one of the most fundamental aspects of the apostle's mission, and by doing so he calls on men to be joined to him so that they "may have fellowship with us; and our fellowship is with the Father and with his Son Jesus Christ" (1 Jn 1:3). The form of fellowship delivered to the apostles by Christ, on the model of the Trinity, is thus expressed between Christ and the apostles, between the apostles themselves, and then between the Churches. Now, it must be carefully noted that fellowship, as it proceeds from the Incarnate Word, has really a visible centre if it has at the same time an invisible centre. Is it not, therefore, necessary that to the universal internal bonds of which Christ is the living centre, there should correspond external universal bonds of which Peter is the centre? Is fellowship perfect without recourse to Peter? The highest sense of the primacy from this point of view is the brotherly leading of the Churches to the unity of fellowship with the see of Peter, so that fellowship of all the Churches may be with the Father and with his Son, Jesus Christ.

It is through this role of the see of Peter, in fellowship between the Churches, that are to be explained the many steps taken for the purpose of fellowship among the Churches. Without going into high theory or furnishing complicated explanations, they have been taken by the see of Peter with the unerringness of him who guides its steps.

The fourth title of the see of Peter to the primacy is the safeguarding of the unity of faith against heresy.

The apostle is witness to the faith. He knew Christ personally, he lived with him, he had experimental knowledge of his person, his life and his mysteries which gave him the objective authority to bear witness to what he had seen with his eyes, to what he had contemplated and what his hands had touched of the Word of life. Still more, the apostle was constituted, officially, by our Lord, as the decisive and fundamental guarantee in the Church of the truth of the revelation and of the meaning of the mysteries of the Lord. The Holy Spirit, who was given to him for the purpose of his ecclesial mission, is the seal of his word and witness. The apostle, therefore, is the rule of faith.

Certainly, the safeguarding of the faith appears in the primitive Church as a responsibility of the apostolic body as such; certainly, too, the presence of the Word of God and the Spirit, the presence of the Eucharist and the episcopate, are so many decisive factors in the safeguarding of the unity of faith. In them the faith finds both its exterior and interior guarantee, the interior guarantee of the Holy Spirit being confirmed by the eminent witness which the liturgy and the bishop bear to the faith.

But the basic reason for the role of the see of Peter in respect of the unity of faith between the Churches is analogically the same as that which establishes the necessity of a visible rule of faith in the diocesan Church in the person of the bishop. This centre of unity of faith does not abolish or replace the special role of the bishops, or of the episcopal body, or, obviously, the other internal and external objective bonds of the faith. What would such a centre be able to do without them? Its place in the unity of the Church is precisely that of presiding over unity, over the harmony of faith among the Churches, this word "preside" being understood not in the democratic and parliamentary sense but in the primatial and community sense.

If it is true that each Church has the right and the duty of concerning itself with the faith of another Church as of the whole Church, of anxiety about the faith of another Church as of the whole Church, this concern, this anxiety, belong to it not by reason of functional but of community responsibility. Only to the see of Peter belongs the functional responsibility of concern for the unity of faith, the harmony of faith among the Churches, of that special anxiety which is the characteristic of the centre of organic unity. The responsibility and the work of each Church are not thereby abolished. Each Church has its own mission in the work of arousing faith, of reviving it where it is failing, of protecting it against dangers, of checking those expressions which threaten it, of promoting and exalting it. The see of Peter intervenes as the visible bond of agreement in the faith, as the regulator of its Catholic expression, as promotor of the faith as the highest guiding principle of the whole Church on the way to salvation. And that is normal, for it is right that the vision of the plan of salvation for all the Church should be the special responsibility of him who is specially responsible for the whole, just as it is right that he should be entitled to carry out his mission by the means appropriate to it.

In the Orthodox Churches and the Protestant communions a distinction is often made between the person of the pope and the Roman curia. That is certainly one of the most difficult points of the ecumenical problem. But would it not be fitting in the first place to reach agreement on a principle, trusting that this agreement can be worked out subsequently in the wisest and most realistic way? A principle of unity is indispensable. Now, quite obviously, the papal office is beyond the physical capacity of one man. The pope, therefore, must arrange and organize his activity in accordance with various means that are homogeneous with his primacy. The code of canon law lays down that "under the name of Apostolic See or Holy See used in the present code there must be understood not only the Roman Pontiff but also, except for indications to the contrary by the nature of things or of context, the congregations, tribunals and offices by which the Roman Pontiff transacts the business of the universal Church" (c. 7).

The pope has a special function in connection with the unity of faith and of fellowship, with the Eucharist and with charity. This is the basic principle. It is, therefore, necessary that certain organizations should help him in carrying out his mission in the sphere of faith and of the sacraments of faith, in the sphere of the propagation of the faith, in the sphere of the fellowship and unity of the Church. In the state of the union of the Churches, or of the division of the Churches, certain means are absolutely indispensable for the pope to discharge his duties. It is difficult to believe that reunion could take place by acceptance of the pope alone without the essential means by which he fulfils his role. For that would be the equivalent of reducing the pope to a symbolic role, leaving him very little effective power.

On the other hand, it is no less certain that the organization of the Roman Curia occurred especially after the separation between East and West. It dates, for the most part, from the time when the papacy was at Avignon, but the principal organizer of the Roman Curia was Sixtus V who, in his constitution *Immensa* (22 January 1587), set up fifteen new congregations. The course of the historical and geographical evolution of this institution seems to show that we are confronted with a purely Latin and a purely Western phenomenon. But a clear distinction must be made between the principle and the way in which it is manifested. The papacy cannot fulfil its function without adequate institutions. Is it required that should reunion of the Churches take place, this role should be exercised exactly according to its present mode? What can be foreseen is that the primacy will be exercised in a way that will give satisfaction to the two-fold image of the Church, Eastern and Western. An immutable principle can be expressed in various forms.

Is reconciliation possible between Catholicism and Orthodoxy on the precise point of the primacy and infallibility of the pope?

On the Orthodox side it seems that the toothing-stones are all in position and ready for this complement to its teaching, that is, on the episcopal structure and the magisterium. Are not these two elements, each in its own way, a manifestation of the Word? In Catholicism as in Orthodoxy there exists this great central doctrine according to which the Word is made visible in the Incarnation, in the Eucharist and in the ecclesial body. Now in the ecclesial body, both for Orthodoxy and for Catholicism, the bishop appears as a certain incarnation of the World and it is the same in the case of the magisterium. The Catholic doctrine of the primacy and infallibility of the pope, which is essentially theological and not canonical, although the interaction of law and theology in the evolution of this doctrine is not denied, is nothing else than the application to the whole Church of a consequence of the doctrine of the Word which is made visible. In the primacy, indeed, is encountered the visible Word at the level of the episcopal structure to the extent that it concerns the organic nature of the Church, and in the doctrine of the infallible magisterium is encountered the Word at the level of the magisterium in its incidence on the faith which is common to the whole Church. The Word which resounds in the soul of every Christian and is made visible in the Eucharist, in the fellowship of the faithful and of the Churches among themselves, is also made visible in the function of the pope within the Church. It is one and the same presence but revealed at different levels.

Is it too much to ask that an effort be made to recognize at least ideally that this evolution in the Catholic Church is not contrary to the common faith of the undivided Church of the first seven councils? We know that although among certain of the Orthodox there exists on the one hand the strange position which holds that with the first seven councils the hand of God was closed over history, so that what is in his hand is Orthodoxy and what is outside the first seven councils is outside the hand of God, and that there is no more to be done than to await the end of time; on the other hand, there are Orthodox who hold that Orthodoxy must find a new starting-point.

7. What do we expect of the Eastern Churches in the Una Sancta?

The simple and fine idea that they should play the part, the whole part that is theirs by vocation. This part is manifold: it is historical, dogmatic, structural, liturgical, missionary, psychological and sociological.

The problem of reunion gains by being considered in the presence of those masters of reality to be found in statistics, geography and history.

Statistics show us that Catholicism is preponderantly a Western phenomenon, preponderantly of the Latin rite, with a population about one third of which is of Latin race. The Catholic population is distributed more or less as follows: Europe, 48,5 per cent; Central and South America, 27,7 per cent; North America, 14 per cent; Asia, 6,3 per cent; Africa, 3 per cent; Oceania, 0,5 per cent. Now Asia, which is already larger than the rest of the world, is scarcely Christian, in Africa the proportion of Christians is hardly 10 per cent altogether and it seems unlikely that this proportion will be exceeded, at least for some time.

Geography, too, reveals the fact that the natural link between Europe and Asia is the East, that is Eastern Europe. The Catholic countries of North and South America are situated between Europe and Asia, but at what a distance!

Then history tells us that it was principally the Christian East which evangelized the East, the greater part of East and South-East Europe and a part of Asia and Africa.

These are simple facts, but they entail many practical consequences, whether for the exclusion of all ecclesiastical racism or imperialism, even when it is unconscious, or for the establishment of a plan for the universalization of the Christian faith.

It is quite normal that the Christian East should claim to have an historic mission to fulfil and that it should have the intention of doing so when it has new means at its disposal. Why could not this role be played in the united Church? Increasingly it must appear that the cause of Christianity is no longer the cause of a single Church, Latin or Eastern, but that of the Church of God. By this is not meant an impersonal, standardized action on the part of the Churches, but the work of each carried out in fellowship.

When we think of the historic role played by such famous Churches as those of Constantinople, Alexandria, Jerusalem, founded by the apostles or their disciples, and of what more recent Churches, with the Russian Church at their head, can accomplish, with all our hearts we must desire the coming of reunion so that in the fellowship of apostolic continuity the Una Sancta may be in a position to fulfil its role as the bond between the Western and Eastern worlds. That day will surely mark a new doctrinal advance as the example of the seven first councils makes clear, when the Church, chiefly in the East, was able to find the Christian answer to the questions of the ancient cultures. And at the present time, in the Near East and the Far East, in the South, the civilizations and cultures of Africa and Asia pose problems to the Eastern Christian conscience, problems to which it will be difficult to provide an answer without the contribution of the Christian West, yet the latter is prevented as a consequence of the separation. Owing to the divisions among Christians substitutes for united action have had to be found, but nothing can take the place of the natural and historic bonds which would fulfil their role all the better if we willingly placed our own means at the service of those who are the natural intermediaries. Who better than the East can understand the East? And the same applies to Africa and Asia. These parts of the world are not absolutely unconnected at the Christian level; in fact they are connected through the oriental sees. By their key position the oriental Churches are well placed to provide that mystical, theological and liturgical interpretation of Christianity for the peoples surrounding them. In the state of division existing between the Catholic and Orthodox Churches, the Catholic Church had established and followed a certain missionary policy. It is normal that another should be followed as a result of the reunion of the Churches.

The Catholic Church and the Orthodox Church need each other. The Latin Church needs the Eastern Churches, just as these need the Latin Church. The most bitter proof of this which we experienced was the loss of the nations at the Reformation, because previously we had lost the East. The Catholic Church will be in a position the better to attract men to her catholicity when, without rejecting any of her acquirements of the past, her essential supranationality shines out in all its splendour. There is a deep sense bound up with the very mystery of the Church according to which all Christians in union with the see of Peter, in East and West, in Asia and Africa belong to the "city of which all are citizens", to quote a phrase of Pius XII's. [46]

> The Catholic Church, of which Rome is the centre, is supranational by its very essence. This is to be understood in two senses, one negative, the other positive. The Church is a mother, *sancta Mater Ecclesia,* a real mother, the mother of all nations, of all peoples, no less than of all individuals; and precisely because she is a mother, she does not belong and she cannot belong exclusively to one people or another, nor even to one people more than to another, but she belongs to all equally. She is a mother, and in consequence she is not and cannot be a stranger in any place; she lives or, at least, of her nature she must live in all peoples. In addition, as the mother together with her husband and her children form a family, the Church, by virtue of a union incomparably closer, constitutes the mystical Body of Christ. The Church is therefore supranational since she is an indivisible and universal whole.

> Today more than ever she must be supranational. This spirit must imbue and penetrate her visible head, the sacred college, all the activity of the Holy See, on whom, especially nowadays, there weigh important duties which concern not only the present but still more the future.

> Here it is principally a question of spirit: it is a matter of having the exact meaning of this supranationality, and not of measuring it or determining it according to mathematical proportions or according to precise statistics on the nationality of each person individually ... in any case the critical conditions of the present time require that special attention should be paid to the safeguarding of this supranationality and this indivisible unity of the Church. [47]

The Eastern Churches (separated from or in union with Rome) remain in the Church as witnesses reminding the whole Church of a primitive

---

[46] *Negli Ultimi,* radio message of 24 December 1945, quoted in E. Marmy, *La Communauté chrétienne selon l'esprit chrétien* (1949), p. 664.
[47] Pius XII. *loc. cit.*

apostolic structure. The Catholic Church has her roots in the arc of a circle which extends from Rome to Asia Minor passing through Greece. Are not the majority of the Churches founded by the apostles to be found in the East? And if the Church is founded on the apostles, this fact is of no small importance in the Church: *Ecclesia ex apostolis*, the Church was founded on Peter and the college of apostles. The role of Prince of the Apostles has never rendered that of the apostles useless, for the latter come from Christ and not from Peter. What should be said is: *Ecclesia ex Ecclesiis apostolicis*. Their permanence, their presence in the Catholic Church, in which more than in all the dissident Churches all rites are represented, is a reminder to the whole Church that the Church, as desired by Christ, is still at the present time, founded on the Twelve, and that she can be the Church of Christ only on condition of being faithful to her origins. The apostles were not the foundation of the Church only at her beginning. In a mysterious way they still are. And this they are by those visible signs of their works represented by the Churches connected with them. The Catholic Church is the Church of the apostolic Churches.

If the Catholic Church values the oriental Churches, if she insists that they be represented as widely as possible within catholicity, if she is anxious that she should so far as possible be present in each rite and language, that is not meant to check the dissident Churches or to enter into competition with them; it is because she has need of them to be Catholic and she cannot be Catholic without being the Church of the apostolic Churches. Merely by their presence they prevent the Church from slipping into some other formula than that of apostolicity. If Peter is the guardian of the unity of the apostolic college, the foundation of unity, the prince of the apostles, he was not chosen alone. The Church is a body, and it is the visible body itself which is the guardian of the visible head. Moreover, the latter has always known and acted in a way to prevent the success of those who desired that the Head should forget it. It is not only by fatherly love, not only by apostolic concern, or by missionary zeal, that the popes have always cherished the oriental Churches. It was still more so from the necessity of catholicity: the Church could not allow herself to be anything less than wholly the Body of Christ. Peter, prince of the apostles, could not be separated from the apostles. The apostolic Church of Rome could not feel herself catholic without fellowship with the other apostolic Churches. These Churches need Rome; Rome, too, needs them. And never has fellowship between the Church of Rome and the Eastern Churches failed, despite those which fell into dissidence, for unity and representation were recovered in another manner.[48]

---

[48] Maximos IV, "Orient catholique et unité chrétienne: Notre vocation œcuménique", *Bulletin d'orientations œcuméniques* 30 (1960), pp. 4–15.

The Catholic Church, therefore, insists on being both of the East and of the West, because since the beginning she has been the Church of the apostles and by remaining so she is the Body of Christ, a body multiple in form united to her Head by many bonds; and the more she is united to Christ, so much the more is Jesus the Saviour of his Body and his peace comes down upon the world.

CHAPTER XI

Israel and the Reunion of Christians: The Church of Jews and Gentiles

I. DEFINITION OF THE PROBLEM

1. Does the problem of Israel fall within or outside ecumenism?

If the aim of ecumenism is the healing of the Body of Christ, the making whole of Christendom, it is not easy to see at once how Israel fits into the picture, and this uncertainty is reflected in the way in which Protestants and Catholics envisage their relations with the Jews.[1]

Up to the present, both in its history and in its activities, the ecumenical movement has been aimed at achieving the union, or the reunion, of the Christian Churches; it has been hardly if at all concerned with the Jews. A change is now taking place, but its form and direction are uncertain and subject to controversy. The World Council of Churches, at Amsterdam in 1948, produced a special report on the relations of the Churches with the Jews.[2] But in 1954, during the second meeting of the World Council, the debate on Israel ended in a fiasco. The reason may have been that up to then the problem had only been looked at from a missionary and proselytizing point of view.

The Church of England long ago established a body to work in England and overseas, under the name of the Mission to the Jews, and long before the first world missionary conference at Edinburgh in 1910, there were many very active missionary societies working among the Jews. In 1927, two conferences were held under the aegis of the International Missionary Council, at Budapest and Warsaw. In 1929 that Council set up, at

---

[1] In this chapter the word "Israel" means the people of the Old Testament, the Jewish world, or Judaism, unless the modern State of Israel is expressly mentioned.

[2] The Protestant Committee for Jewish Relations, *Une Parole pour Israël, Rapport général*, II, pp. 285–99.

Williamstown in the U. S. A., a Council for Action among the Jews (I. M. C. C. A. J.), which began working in 1931, and organized conferences at Vienna in 1937, at Basle in 1947, and at Edinburgh in 1949. National study-groups and conferences followed in England as the joint responsibility of the British Council of Churches and the British section of the I. M. C. C. A. J. An international conference was held at the Bossey Ecumenical Institute, which produced a book on "The Church and the Jewish People".[3] At the same institute, in 1956, a meeting was held of a joint committee of the International Missionary Council, the World Council of Churches and the special committee of the International Missionary Council for relations with the Jews. And from 1952 to 1960, courses were held in various countries on the Church and the Jews.[4]

Christians are thus seeking to define their position with relation to the Jews. But this involves a fundamental question: is their attitude to be missionary and proselytizing, or firmly ecumenical?

As for the Catholics, they are faced with precisely the same problem, and up to now their activity towards the Jews has been of the same kind as that of Protestants and Anglicans. A clear indication of the wavering of the Catholic Church has been manifested during the last Vatican Council. Though it appeared as a latecomer in the schema on ecumenism, a special chapter dealing with the Jews was discussed during the second session, in October 1963. It was, however, finally set out in quite a different frame in the *Declaration on the Relationship of the Church to Non-Christian Religions*, promulgated on 28 October 1965. In this document the ecumenical perspective remains only in as far as a better psychological and moral approach is considered as a pre-requisite to better ecumenical relations. Evidently the question was not ripe.

But is Israel an extra-ecumenical problem? From the missionary point of view of spreading the Gospel, can we put the Jews on the same footing as the non-Christian peoples? The time has now come, in view of the future of ecumenism, for a completely new appraisal of the problem.

Relations between Jews and Gentiles—or, more precisely, between Jews and Christians—have always been somewhat puzzling and paradoxical. Judaism tends naturally towards Christianity; but its complete rejection of the eschatological events shown forth in Christ and the Church constitutes a sort of negative synthesis of all the rejections which separate Christian sects have opposed to the wholeness of Christendom.

Judaism remains outside the Church: yet it never ceases to act on and in the Church. It acts in the Church through the Jewish origins of

---

[3] Gote Hedenquist, ed., *The Church and the Jewish People* (1954).
[4] H. L. Ellison, "The International Missionary Council's Committee on the Christian Approach to the Jews", *The International Review of Missions* (July 1960), pp. 326–31.

446

Christianity. It acts on the Church in virtue of a kind of shared destiny that brings Jews and Christians together at all the great crossroads of history. The Jew cannot lose sight of the Christian, the Christian cannot ignore the Jew. There is something very strange that both brings us together and separates us, as if neither of us can quite pass the other. The relations between us are governed by an odd alternation of rejection and acceptance.

The Gospel gives the Christian the advantage of being able to guess at the true complementarity of these two parts that both seek and flee from each other. It is revealed to us in the great discourse of our Lord after the Last Supper, when Jesus prayed to his Father to bless the oneness of his Church. The literal sense of the passage shows that it is primarily and above all concerned with the oneness of Jews and Gentiles in Christ, which is given elsewhere as the motive for the Incarnation (Jn 11:52) and as the great secret hidden from older generations (Gal 4:28). In God's plan, Jews and Gentiles are seen as one: there is one election, one predestination, one vocation, one covenant, one glorification. And with the birth of the Church, the great design of the Lord has taken actual form.

Jews and Gentiles have become one. But a mysterious law seems to have been fixed governing the actual development in history of the growth of the Body of Christ towards the integration of Jews and Gentiles in unity. St Paul expresses it in these terms, addressed to the Gentiles: "You were once rebels, until through their rebellion you obtained pardon; they are rebels now, obtaining pardon for you, only to be pardoned in their turn. Thus God has abandoned all men to their rebellion, only to include them all in his pardon" (Rom 11:30–32). Jews and Gentiles thus share the same mystery.

So the problem of Israel is not extra-ecumenical. It concerns the reconciliation of the two parts of the *Oikoumene:* the Jews and the Gentiles. For measured by God's plan for man's salvation, this is the fundamental division of mankind: on the one hand, the Jewish people, the people of the covenant; and on the other, the pagans, the Gentiles. Neither the Old Testament nor the New gives us any other division of human society, in the economy of salvation: on one side, so very few—yet from them comes salvation; on the other, the mass of humanity. The question is not one of numbers or of power, but of election and new birth. Abraham was chosen to be the father of all believers, the starting-point of the new humanity moving forward in faith to the promised land, gathering in as many Gentile peoples as it pleases God to lead that way. The Covenant of nature was the root of the covenant of grace.

We cannot, therefore, tackle the problem of Israel as if it were purely and simply a missionary problem analogous to those we meet in non-Christian lands, for between Israel and the pagans there is this gulf: they are God's chosen people, and he has not repented of his choice. Measured against God's plan, the fundamental reconciliation is not between Orthodox, Catholics, Protestants and Anglicans, but between Jews and Gentiles, between Jews and Christians. It is really a matter of the *Oikoumene,* in the two parts that make up its unity; it is really a matter of the economy of salvation in the continuation of the work of God in the world, of the reconciliation of the two aspects of election: election through the bond in flesh and election through grace divulged. An ecumenism which limited itself simply to the relations between Christians would be in principle condemned never to succeed, because it would be established on too narrow a foundation. All things are contained in ecumenism, for the simple reason that all things are contained in true unity, as they are in the breaking of that unity.[5] The ecumenical attitude is the only wholly adequate one, which sets the problem of the reunion of Israel and Christendom in its proper ecumenical perspective, that of the whole economy of salvation and the mystery of the Church.

Ecumenism begins with a positive act of recognition that there *are* "others". In the special case of the Jews, ecumenism tries to understand the part the Jewish people are called upon to play, and the witness they are called upon to bear to the intervention of the absolute and of ultimate realities in history. The Jewish way is not the Christian way. In practice we must recognize the difference. But must this always be a dilemma, on the level of values? Is it not more often simply a conflict? Judaism looks forward to the fullness of its faith in eschatology as it will be manifested in the Parousia, while the Christian believes in the historical realization of that eschatology in Christ, the Messiah. Yet the witness borne by Judaism to the intervention of God, which is already eschatological, through the law and the prophets, through the living Word of God, is nonetheless acceptable.

It is, therefore, the task of an ecumenical view to sort out these relationships and these links, in the whole plan of God. The ecumenical method is thus self-determined: an all-embracing method that looks above all at questions as a whole, not at individuals, and which takes as its starting-point a central intuition and understanding of Judaism in its life and thought. Briefly, it must accept Judaism as an organic reality, at once religious, sociological and psychological; it must think not of the conversion of persons, but first of the mutual relations of whole groups, and of the growth of each to the fullness of its belief; it must think of healing the wounds of old traditions and of reconciliation. It is in its broad outlines

[5] N. Ohnen, "Le Schisme dans le cadre de l'économie divine", *Irenikon* (1st quarter, 1948), pp. 6–31; P. Demann, "Israel et l'Unité des chrétiens", *Cahiers sioniens,* no. 1 (March 1953), pp. 1–24; A. Larocque, "Israël, pierre de touche et l'œcuménisme", *Verbum Caro,* no. 48 (1958), pp. 331–44.

the same method that should be used in the realm of interdenominational relations within the Christian world: a method of enlightenment and understanding, that has one aim, namely, the reunion of all the parts of the heritage which the revealed God has left to men.

There is a special consideration which should encourage us to form the same relations between groups with Judaism as we are progressively making with Christians: the truly religious value, and the value as witness, of Judaism.

Perhaps it would be right to distinguish here two easily confused processes: the abrogation of an old institution by its absorption in and replacement by a higher institution, and its suppression, pure and simple, by abolition. It is a fundamental principle of Catholicism that the appearance of the new law rendered null and void the institutions of the Temple and the Synagogue. But we must notice clearly that in the Old Testament the Temple and the Synagogue have always been considered as signs, as sacred symbols of the Church to come. In what way can Jewish institutions continue to have value after the coming of Christ? Catholic theology recognizes the real, positive value of the natural religious symbols of pagans, called by St Thomas "natural sacraments", which continue to exist and have value even after the Incarnation. Could we then possibly brush aside the value of the Jewish sacraments? If they contained an implicit reference to the mystery of Christ before his coming, could they have lost it after the Incarnation? And if the Synagogue had before Christ's coming some implicit relationship to the Church, could it have lost it now? We ought to remember the words of Christ, that he came not to destroy the law and the prophets, but to perfect them (Mt 5:17). So what is imperfect preserves its relative value as pointing the way, even if it knows nothing of the fullness to which it is ordained in God's plan.

So we have to recognize the true religious value and holiness which Jewish institutions have, even from our point of view, and that we can legitimately enter into relations with them as one group with another. We are not saying that the Synagogue is the Church, and we cannot put them, doctrinally, on the same level. But we cannot refuse to Judaism today that value which it possesses. After all, we recognize vestiges in Protestant denominations of three Messianic functions of Christ, as king, priest and prophet, which were the foundations of the Church. We do not say that those denominations are the Church, but we admit that they have some true value as Churches, and that this is a sufficient basis for group relationships with them. Why should we not say the same for Judaism? Was not that threefold Messianic function prefigured in the Old Testament? We are simply asserting that there is an objective religious value which is implicitly that of a Church, and that this is a sufficient basis for group relationships.

In other words, if we recognize the light of truth in Protestant denominations even in their separated state, why should we not recognize in Israel a survival of the truth of the Old Testament, even after Christ, the light of the world, has come?

But this raises a difficult problem. Christ has come, and he is the light of the world; consequently every other light must be put out or lost in him. But surely not: the great Light of God has appeared, but it has not put out all the light of ancient Israel, any more than it puts out all the light of a dissident Christian communion. Why not? Surely because in neither case does God repent of his gifts. The light God has once lit in the world he never again puts out. The Church is unique, and always will be unique and saved; but beside her, other commuions have value as Churches, as communions, without being the Church of Christ.

Until the coming of Christ, Judaism was the perfect form of revealed religion; with the coming of Christ, Christianity was. The Old Testament is accomplished in the New. The Old Testament without its perfecting is inadequate. This is what we mean by institutions being abrogated. They are abrogated in respect of something more perfect, of that eschatology which has come into the world in person and brought with him all perfection. But they conserve their relative and imperfect value. For a man who has met Christ, they are no longer enough; for one who has not yet seen him, they are the normal way of salvation. Because of the importance of salvation and of the faith of men, and especially because of the covenant, God does not repent of his gifts. His mercy conserves the genuineness of values which are temporarily denied their fulfilment, through and in spite of the culpability of those who were responsible for their being thus kept in exile. So, in Christ, Jews and Gentiles have become one. But how to put this in practice is another question. The Jewish people, not having all become Christians, cannot be said to be schismatic, for there can be no schism except in relation to a previously accepted value; in a way one could talk of those Jews who have become Christians as schismatic. The Israel which does not believe is separated from the Israel which does, and has rejected it. What is the meaning of this schism?

2. Israel's schism in the economy of salvation

It was the ancient Jews who received the promise, and who kept it. Their fruit was in the best of themselves, and this was transmuted into the Church, and passed into the Lord's salvation. Not all Israel so passed over, but that which bore the "root of Jesse" which flowered, and the expectation of which was fulfilled in the Child of Bethlehem and then in the gift of Pentecost. The rest of the Jews fell away from the greatness of their election in Christ, whom they passed by without recognizing. This is the meaning we are giving here to the word "schism". The Jews remain by their nature God's people. But they are as it were pieces broken off in that election, rocks split by the lightning, but always fragments of gold broken from Sinai.

Ancient Israel changed and was transcended in the new Israel, a new People of God, through the mediation of "the few that were left", "the poor of Yahweh", and of Christ, the new Israel, of Mary, the apostles and the Jews who became members of the new faith, through the power of the Lord's Passover. And the Lord, "descending into hell" to set free the souls of the just waiting from the most ancient times for the Messiah, gathered into his kingdom those elect who, together with the angels, became the nucleus of the true community of the chosen people in heaven.

It is in the face of the unity of this divine economy that we must see the tragic condition of that part of Israel which has not passed into the Christian Ecclesia. If the line of continuity in God's plan is the Church, where would Israel ever be able to find its unity? That part of Israel which is transcended in the Church has pursued its unity without failing; the rest has fallen away from unity. It has lost the key to its own destiny. It has fallen into pieces, scattered throughout the world by the great winds of history.

There is left to it the unity of nostalgia, the unity of a collective deprivation, of a movement of the sea which brings back towards Palestine the remnants of the great people of Israel to meet their destiny there again.

What has survived and still survives of Israel that has not passed into the Church needs the Church to find its way, to find the key to its unity, because the Ecclesia has been, quite precisely, the heart of Israel, its true, transcendent blossoming. For Israel today and tomorrow, to come into the Ecclesia is to come into the best of ancient Israel; it is to discover the reality of what was prefigured in the Old Testament; it is to grow in maturity to find oneself where all promise is fulfilled.

Has the Church supplanted the chosen people? No, for the heart of ancient Israel was accomplished in the Church, is still and always will be so accomplished. For us, the Old Testament as a whole, the chosen people as a whole, moved implicitly towards Christianity. The unity of the chosen people in the Old Testament was a dynamic unity, a covenant growing and developing; it was a prophecy, an annunciation, an exodus towards a higher land.

The Old and the New Testaments cannot be opposed as contraries, or set alongside one another as two different things, since our Lord came "not to set aside but to bring to perfection". The New Testament has not stolen the place of the Old, as if the Old were entirely foreign to it. On the contrary, the finest part and fruit of the Old has passed into the New:

the chosen people of God has gone up from the Temple to the Church. The chosen people as represented by the Poor of Yahweh, the true people of God who kept the covenant, entered the Church. The heart of the Church is thus that Israel of which Christ is the heart, for which he is the living, renewed, new covenant. The substance of the old covenant and the heart of the chosen people passed into the Church, taking with them the heart of the ancient election: that hidden grace which now through our Lord's Passover becomes the new election, grace revealed. The heart of this new election is that Jewish Israel, the people of God, first by vocation and again by grace, of whom Christ is the centre, and about whom are gathered in union the Lord's converts who have received the tidings of the Kingdom. This is the Jewish stem from which the present Church grew, so that the Church is in this sense fundamentally and deeply semitic. The Gentiles have been "grafted on to the true olive's stock" (Rom 11:24). The truth of the ancient people of God has passed, through Christ, the new Israel, into the new covenant.

Is all value, then, denied to those Jewish institutions which continue the old dispensation as if Christ had not come? Surely not: but with Christ's coming they have been revealed in their relativity and their imperfection. After the Jews' withdrawal from the new covenant, in which they had been included by the death and resurrection of our Lord, their life could no longer be what it had been before, for its essence had been fulfilled in the new covenant. What is left lies in its value as prefiguring the Messiah, but as an unfinished story, lacking the secret of its own unity. It is no longer just the Old Testament, pure and simple, which goes on, for the New Testament has supervened. There now persist vestiges of the old covenant, which continue to give out their light; for if they were before the Incarnation signs announcing the Messiah, their value as signs has not been destroyed, only now it rests on an enigma. The people that was not called the people of God has been called the people of God, those who had not been the beloved have been called the beloved, and "in places where they used to be told, you are no people of mine, they will be called, now, sons oft the living God" (Rom 9:25–26; cf. Osee 1:10).

The whole drama arises from the schism which has divided the new Israel ransomed by the blood of the Saviour. Christ told us that the new covenant which he was establishing was destined to bring together all men, Jews and pagans, therefore, into the unity of one house, one family, one fold under one shepherd. By his death that unity was established, for as the Church was brought into being on the cross, there was also the true source of the unity of Jews and Gentiles. Henceforth, in God's sight, there was but one Israel, as St Peter declared on the day of Pentecost. But gradually the apostles perceived that the mass of the Jewish people would pass by the new covenant of grace without recognizing it, without letting the old covenant be transfigured into the new covenant. Only a very small fraction accepted it. The tidings of the new covenant were rejected as had been the person of the Messiah. Such is the condition of the Jews, who are in a state of schism without ever having formally recognized it, just as would have been the case, had the mass of the people accepted Christianity and subsequently separated from it.[6]

3. A religion of expectation

The history of Israel, as it is presented in the Old Testament, and as the Jews themselves confess, is a history of an expectation. It contains beginnings, initiations, projections, but none has any definite end. As we read the books of the Old Testament, we discover a development of the eschatological meaning which is expressed in an increasingly apocalyptic style, to such a point that the first theology to appear in the Church was a theology Semitic in structure expressed in the forms of contemporary Judaism, that is, in apocalyptic form.[7] The Old Testament moves with all the strength of its Messianic hope towards a reality, a person who will fulfil the expectation of Israel. Now, at a certain point, this religion seems to hang in the air, with no conclusion. It had been taut with tension, but that tension is not resolved.

The Christian Apocalypse reveals to us that it was only the Lamb that was slain who could open the book with the seven seals. This is the essence of the Christian faith: in Christ the eschatological order of events is already present. The tension of the Old Testament leads into the Incarnate Word, and in him finds its resolution.

Does, therefore, the present proclamation by the Jews of their messianic expectation as if it had never been fulfilled lose all its value? The Jews are waiting for the Messiah; the Christians tell us he has come. Is the Jewish expectation thus meaningless? Let us recognize their error, but let us also see the religious value of their witness. St Paul says that "a veil hangs over their hearts" (2 Cor 3:15).

Let us make a comparison: a crowd is waiting for a king to go by, and each is trying to guess which is the king. Now the king, instead of coming before them with the pomp and ceremony that belongs to kings, passes unperceived through the crowd, dressed in the most simple manner, with no procession of glorious soldiery or courtiers. A few people, thanks to a

---

[6] Lanne, *Notes sur la situation d'Israël par rapport aux schismes dans l'Église chrétienne* in *L'Église et les Églises*, II, pp. 67–86. See also Vatican II's Declaration on Non-Christian Religions.

[7] J. Daniélou, *Théologie du judéo-christianisme* (1958).

certain feeling for him, see that this can be no other but the king, but the rest still shout the praise of him who should still be coming, but has already passed. Was the Messiah who has come the one whom people expected according to their dreams and revelations, or the one who had to come as he really did? Jesus passed unrecognized except by a small remnant of Israel, the poor of the Lord. We can see the mistake made by those who did not recognize Christ as he passed but continue to wait in expectation of him as if he had still to come.

The second point in which we can still see Judaism as it were a history in state of suspension awaiting a conclusion concerns the universality of the religion of Israel. We can perceive in the Old Testament a tension between the idea of an essentially universal religion, as monotheism is bound to be, and on the other hand the narrowness of Jewish nationalism.[8] Was the mission of Israel to lose itself in a greater whole, or serve as a centre for a universal true religion? Should the Jews be missionaries to all nations?[9] Or should they wait, like a great lord, until the world came to the Temple of Jerusalem? It was not easy for Israel to discover the true meaning of its future destiny. Under the pressure and sufferings of foreign domination, it was the narrower tendency which won the day. It seemed to the exacerbated nationalism of an occupied country that the preservation of the religion of the prophets was bound to be closely linked with the integrity of the nation. We know how difficult it was for Christ and for the Holy Spirit to make the apostles themselves understand the true meaning of the mission of Israel and the Church. At present, the religious world of the Jews still remains divided between the feeling of a call to a higher universality, to which the diaspora itself bears witness, and the need for national cohesion. The tension that survives between universalism and nationalism has not yet resolved. But does this deprive of its value the witness borne to that universalism by the religion announced by the prophets? Let us recognize the immense sufferings borne by the Jews since their election and pay them homage. And let us also recognize that the Jews, scattered among and mingled with pagan nations and even with Christian peoples too often secularized, have borne and bear witness in their religious life, by their refusal to become completely bound up with the temporal world, to the sovereignty of God and to the eschatological orientation of the created world towards the Kingdom of God.

The relation between the transcendence and the immanence of God is another problem not resolved in Judaism. From the first verses of Genesis, God is seen by Israel as at once infinitely close and infinitely distant. He is

[8] C. H. Dodd, *The Authority of the Bible* (revised edition, 1960), pp. 168 ff.
[9] R. Martin-Achard, *Israël et les Nations, la perspective missionnaire de l'Ancien Testament* (1959).

the creator who sits above the clouds, but he is also the God of the covenant, "the God of Abraham, of Isaac, and Jacob" (Exod 3:6). One can almost feel his passing, yet he remains infinitely mysterious. The deeper Israel's religious experience became, the wider the gap between these two: the transcendence and immanence of God. But how can one reconcile extremes such as these, apparently irreconcilable? Various attempts were made. Why should not God, who is the Most High, also dwell in the soul of the humble? This is a simple answer to which the Blessed Virgin, following the Poor of Yahweh, was to bear witness. Others thought of some intermediaries between God and men: angels? Wisdom? Was this a solution? How could this transcendent and immanent God, who had made the covenant with his people, allow the nations of the wicked to flourish while his chosen people were oppressed, not only in punishment for their faults, but also without any appearance of reason? The further the history of Israel developed, the more full of suffering it became. So a paradox cried out for solution, between the covenant with the Most High and the apparant inefficacy of his justice. And when we look back now at the history of the Jews over two thousand years of existence in a pagan and Christian world, we can see that the paradox is still there, unsolved, for them: how can God who made the covenant with our fathers allow these sufferings, so often inflicted by those who claim to be his and to be inheritors of the Old Testament?

Here we have put our finger on the tragedy of our relations with the Jews. The tension between the transcendence and the immanence of God, which we know was resolved in the presence on earth of the incarnate Word, remains wholly mysterious in their eyes. Nor do they see that it is on the cross of the Saviour that are reconciled suffering and expiation, the sacrifice of the just for the salvation of the world and satisfaction for sin. Incarnation remains for them a stumbling block.

The Word of God and the Law, transcendent as they were, were they not given to the Jewish people to become incarnated in the whole of its life and even in its flesh? Law was essentially orientated towards incarnation. The logical blossoming of the incarnational tendency of the Law is Christ, the Word incarnate in whose flesh the Word and the Law, lived by one people for the whole world, were recapitulated in one man, the Son of God.

The power of grace is equally a source of perplexity to them. One of their clearest and strongest objections is that, if the Messiah had really come, the world would have been more changed than it is. In other words, while recognizing the value of the good accomplished in Christianity, the Jews are not convinced that it is enough to be the wonderful sign that ought to accompany the coming of the Messiah. All the same, they do not solve the problem of the value of the works he himself did.

As the Old Testament moved towards Christ, another tension grew, between the weight of observances prescribed by the law, increased by their minuteness, and on the other hand its inward spiritual significance. What God demanded was not so much holocausts and hecatombs of goats and oxen, but the sacrifice of a contrite heart, in return for which he would show himself benevolent to man, and would enfold him in his justice. Israel was well aware that as its life progressed, the number of its transgressions was increasing. The scriptures were there to remind the Jews of covenants made and broken, of reconciliations sworn and forgotten. In their immense weariness, they were torn between waiting for the heavens to open and taking the control of their own justification into their own hands by multiplying the precepts of the law.

Was a resolution of the tension between these two attitudes possible? We can see a solution appearing at the end of the period of the prophets, in Ezekiel and Deutero-Isaiah, in the form of a vast mercy which, surpassing merit and justice, would spread like a wave which would wash away all the multitude of sins. The way was open to a solution. But Jewish legalism, from a sort of puritanism or from a desire to preserve their religion from any contamination by the surrounding paganism, was not favourable to such an idea. And from the first moments of the public life of Jesus, we can see that the tension between justice and grace was as strong as ever.

What of the works done today by the Jews, under the impulse of that ancient law which rules their hearts and minds: are they wrong? The pious Jew who continues to fulfil the precepts of the law, surely fulfils his duty, and continues to bear witness before pagans, and before over-secularized Christians, to the demands of the justice of God, while waiting for God to reveal to him the fullness of the law, that is, the new justice of God (cf. Rom 13:10). Can Christians help him to resolve this tension, this paradox which still hangs over him?

Lastly, there is one other question to which the Jews await the answer: it concerns the conflict between our present and future existence. Does everything end with the end of life, or is there something beyond, and, if so, what? Should one take the most one can from life, or pass through this world as if making no use of it? Some texts in the Old Testament appear to promise an earthly, material blessedness, a sort of paradise on earth, but others tell us that all that is vanity. What then is the lot of man? Is he endowed with immortality? What sort of immortality? We can perceive in the Old Testament a contrast between a desire, a longing, which grows almost in direct proportion as the Jews are despoiled of their goods and oppressed, and on the other hand the idea that the true messianic blessings are measured by a different standard. But it was not easy then to discern the truth. The prophets expressed the highest realities very often under an earthly symbolism, and on the other hand they clearly made their appeal on other occasions through eschatological forms that surpassed this world. Now the same conflict or tension persists in our own day. On one side, we see Jews waiting for an earthly Messiah, and on the other, there is the same appeal as of old to a spiritual withdrawal in the name of eschatology. Here again we must ask ourselves how Christians can help Jews to resolve an ancient paradox to which Christ has given an answer, by showing that it is by sharing his divine life that we resolve the conflict between belonging both to this world and to the world beyond death. But even if we tell this to the Jews, will they believe us?

Such is a brief account of what faces us when we propose to establish ecumenical relations with the contemporary Jewish world. Leaving aside old attitudes which have made no contribution to Israel, we are trying to understand what the Jews' problems are, and learning to judge the religious values the Jews represent; we want to see how, in the spirit of St Paul, the Church is the Church of the Jews and the Gentiles, that is, how we are together one body.

The integration of which contemporary Jewry dreams, the solution of its eternal conflicts, cannot be realized unless they move upwards and outwards into a universal catholicity in which they will find themselves again, finding also the communion they dream of with other men. But relations between Jews and Christians have always suggested that here are two worlds which pursue each other, draw near one to the other and inspect each other, but never meet; which need each other, but fail each other since each turns aside to get on with its own business.

Christianity, the religious context of whose appearance was Judaism, soon lost its roots in that culture and was spread by God into all countries of the world, to put down new roots there, roots always foreign to its own deepest essence.

During this time, Judaism in its exile pursued a similar course. So these two universal creeds remained tangential to each other. For twenty centuries, Christians and Jews, pilgrims in this world, rubbed shoulders with each other at the great crossroads of the earth, but we are still waiting for the miracle of their true and profound meeting. Perhaps we shall first have to stop, both of us, and try to see how our destinies have been much the same from the beginning.

Catholicism, which belongs to all cultures and exclusively to none, whenever it is tempted to settle down comfortably in this one or that, is pulled out by the hand of the Lord, who chases it forth to go to new lands, forcing it to go through another new exodus. Exactly the same is true of Judaism, ceaselessly settled and dislodged, incarnate and disincarnate, always renewing its paths of exile or threatened with returning.

Christianity and Judaism are seen in history as elements the world cannot assimilate, precisely because both are more universal than the world. Election has set them apart for ever; for the one, election by race, for the other, election by pure grace. Emigrants of any nation assimilate themselves perfectly to their new native land without claiming to set up, in virtue of their old nationality, a sort of supra-national, universal nationality wherever their original fellow-countrymen find themselves. Similarly, the Jew assimilates himself to the country in which he lives, but always with part of himself he surpasses it: because his origin is unique. There is in him an essential universality which forces him to be so, whether he wants to or not. It is a question of origin, of election, of nature and of destiny. Often without being conscious of it, the Jewish element in a country, like the Christian element, poses a crucial question for that country: every national entity seeks completely to contain its members, to be itself their limit, and it is difficult for it to find itself limited in some way. Each seeks to be in some way a universality for its own place. So it is very sure that Judaism and Christianity, because of their own essential universality, are regularly seen as threats defying the self-sufficiency of men's political universalities, for Judaism and Christianity bear witness to revelation, that is, the radical insufficiency of the natural order.

The form of the Church which our Lord revealed to us, and which it was the special mission of St Paul to interpret for us, is that of a single Church of Jews and Gentiles. St Paul's message is the great secret, hidden for centuries, that the pagans inherited the promise along with the Jews. St Paul makes clear to us the real foundations for ecumenism after the revelation: there are Jews and there are Gentiles, and all other ecumenical reconciliations are to be set within the whole that is non-Jewry. And the greatest secret, the root secret of universal catholicity, is not the restoration of understanding and agreement between Christians, but between men born of the old covenant and those born of the new covenant. It is the union of the old and the new covenants, the unity of God's plan, which, in God, transcends all distinction between Jew and Gentile to make but one family, the family of God.

The mistake of the mass of Jews who have not passed under the new covenant is not to have seen that the true time for ecumenism was begun with the appearance in person, in time, of him who is the ultimate reality, the Eschaton who transcends the election of this particular people, who up till then had been the chosen people over against the other peoples of the world. In other words, the mass of the Jews have never realized that the eschatological time has really already begun. The election of the Jewish people was then left behind, and the time had come for a movement towards a greater universality, surpassing the carnal aspect of their election. A new time had begun, the time of the end, the time of the Church, the time of the *Oikoumene* of the Lord. The barriers were down, election was open to all, the promise was fulfilled. The Jew still believes that he is justified by the law. The Christian believes that he is not justified by a rule whose value depends on where and when in this world, but against an eternal, eschatological standard. The Jew still lives in a pre-eschatological time, and that is why the straining within Judaism towards universality, towards eschatology and the grace of God, immortality and transcendence, remains as it were hanging in the air. The covenant, glory, promises, worship, the law—all remain enclosed within limits. The Jew cannot understand that one might be able to explain them otherwise than in a natural and national manner. What Christ brought was a break through the limits of race and of time, wholly and really the fulfilment of the law and the prophets (Mt 5:17).

The Jews await the Messiah. It seems to them that the liberation which Christ brought to the world, great though it is, cannot be the true and incomparable liberation of the Messiah, for too much evil still persists. The kingdom which they wait for, with the Messiah, must be such that evil is dominated and enchained. Could the expected Messiah come through the great pagan religions? Or through an earthly and materialist messianism? Since he is the Messiah, will he not rather use spiritual ways?

Will the Jews accept, at least as a hypothesis to work on, that the Messiah could have already drawn out some signs of his coming in Christianity since, according to them, what Christ has done in Christianity is only a shadow of what must be to come? And who knows but that the Messiah might not appear to them through the roundabout way of their ecumenical relations? For the coming of the Messiah means for the Jews the real coming of the Messiah into this world, and since Jews believe that his coming will be announced in the world by precursory signs of a messianic kind, should they not carefully observe the new things that are happening?[10]

---

[10] F. J. Foakes-Jackson, ed., *The Parting of the Roads: Studies in the Development of Judaism and Early Christianity* (1912); G. A. Yates, ed., *In Spirit and in Truth, Aspects of Judaism and Christianity* (1934); A. G. Hebert, *The Throne of David* (1941); Lev Gillet, *Communion in the Messiah: Studies in the Relationships between Judaism and Christianity* (1942); C. Journet, *Destinées d'Israël: à propos du salut par les Juifs* (1945); Joseph Voode, *The Old Testament in the Church* (1949); Jacob Jocz, *The Jewish People and Jesus Christ: a Study in the Relationship between the Jewish People and Jesus Christ* (1949, 1954); *A Theology of Election: Israel and the Church* (1958); S. Mowinckel, *Ham som kommer. Messiasforventningen i dat Gamle Testament og pao Jesu tid* (1951); *He that Cometh, Survey of the Origin, Development and Content of the Idea of the Messiah* (1956); Joseph Klausner, *The Messianic Idea in Israel from its Beginning to the Mishnah* (1955); Samuel Sandmell, *The Jewish Understanding of the New Testament* (1st edition, 1956; 2nd edition, 1957); R. Aigrain and O. Englebert, *Prophecy Fulfilled* (1958); Solomon Schechter, *Studies in Judaism, Essays on Persons, Concepts, Movements of Thought in Jewish Tradition* (1938); L. Cerfaux, J. Coppens, R. de Langhe, V. de Leeuw, A. Descamps, J. Giblet and R. Rigaux, *L'Attente du Messie* (1958); Frederick C. Grant, *Ancient Judaism and the New Testament* (1959).

II. BRINGING TOGETHER CHRISTIANS AND JEWS

1. A new opportunity to resume relations between Christians and Jews

If we take a general look at the whole history of our relations with Judaism, we can say that three great opportunities have been given us in history for Jews and Christians to meet. The first was in the time of Christ. Jesus, the apostles and the first Christian communities were Jews. More, Christianity did not appear in some distant land of the diaspora, but in a fully Jewish context, at the heart of Jewry. And it was in a Jewish context that it first spread, thanks to the two million or so Jews in the Roman Empire who had already pioneered the way in so many directions through Asia, Africa and the West. Yet in Palestine, as elsewhere, the greater part of the Jewish nation passed Christianity by.

A second opportunity occurred in the Middle Ages through the mediation of Judeo-Arabic thought.

The map of the world we look at today shows us three great cultures at the height of their power: Western Christendom, united by Latin culture under the aegis of the Gospel; the wonderful Byzantine civilization, twin sister of the Western; and the medieval Islamic world lying to the south of the two great Christian civilizations.

It would be a myth to believe that these three worlds always lived in perfect autarchy, completely cut off from and ignorant of one another. Links existed between West and East: on the religious level, Christianity, and on the cultural level, Greek culture. We must not forget that centuries before the flourishing of the Western Middle Ages, the empire of Constantinople had been the repository of hellenic culture. Remember also that the Arabs who in the eighth century conquered the Near East—Syria, Palestine and Asia Minor—were in their turn conquered in spirit by Greek philosophy, which was studied in the Nestorian Christian schools. The Arabs thus received Greek thought several centuries before it reached the Latin West and the first effective contact between Greek thought and the West was in fact through translations from the Arabic. Now, to a large extent it was the Jews who acted as intermediaries in this transmission of the hellenic tradition from one world to another. As happens also in our own times, the Jews enjoyed a double linguistic tradition: Arabic, cultivated by the Jews since the Saracen conquest, and the language of social relations and profane culture, and Hebrew, the language that bound the nation together.

So we have in the Middle Ages the two great Christian civilizations with the vast empire of Islam stretching between them, and the Jews of the diaspora spread from Constantinople to the West through the Islamic world. Jewish culture followed the expansion of the Arabs as it had followed the expansion of the Romans, and as it was later to follow the colonial expansion of the West into the new lands of America and Asia and even as far as Oceania.

We are here referring to a cultural factor of immense scope—a Jewish world, Arabic in expression, which had received the teachings of Greek philosophie, and which kept, through the Hebrew, its contact with the rest of the Jewish world of the diaspora scattered in Sicily, Castile, Aragon, northern Italy, Flanders and England, all this as maker and transmitter of culture. It is no exaggeration to say that the Greek sources of scholasticism came to the Latin West, to a large extent, from Islam, and that they were generally brought from Islam by Jews. The first zone of contact between the Jewish world in its Arabic dress and the Latin West was the ancient Magna Graecia, the south of Italy and Sicily, where from the sixth century onwards there were important Jewish elements. But the most important area of exchange was the Iberian peninsula where there had been Jewish colonies even before Christ. After the death of Avicenna it was in the West, and particularly in Spain, that Arabic and Jewish thought went on developing. A most astonishing symbiosis developed. The names of Avicebron, Averroës, Maimonides, Algazel, etc., are well known. And it was in the later Middle Ages after the deaths of Averroës (1198) and Maimonides (1204) that Jewish thought began to be translated into Latin. The names of some of the first translators are known to us, such as Gerard of Cremona, who came to Toledo at this time.

It could be said that the Jews, because of their ancient dispersion throughout the Roman Empire, and then throughout Europe, because of their role as transmitters of Greek culture from Byzantium to Europe, and because of their personal contribution to medieval thought, can be seen as perhaps the most stable element of continuity in the growth of civilization in Europe.[11]

And yet, despite these contacts, despite the extraordinary effect of Judeo-Arabic thought on the Christian world, we still see these two worlds eventually passing each other by without meeting. Why? Was it because of social or religious prejudices, to a too-proselytic or apologetic attitude? Even St Thomas Aquinas seems typical of his times in his attitude to the Jews.

One might reasonably wonder how, at a time when the Fourth Lateran Council (1215) made its own, in relation to the Jews, the policy of the caliphs in relation to the Christians, compelling them to wear a distinctive sign, a yellow cap or fillet, and forbidding them to come out of doors on Good Friday (canon 68),[12] the Jewish and Christian worlds could have established ecumenical relations?

[11] Charles Singer, "The Jewish Factor in Medieval Thought" in *The Legacy of Israel* (1st edition, 1927; 3rd edition, 1948), pp. 173–283.
[12] H. J. Schroeder, *Disciplinary Decrees of the General Councils* (1937).

From the Middle Ages to our own times, no other historical opportunity could occur for union between Christians and Jews. The end of the Middle Ages saw the decadence of scholasticism and the beginnings of the Reformation. The influence of Judaism on the development of the Reformation within Christendom was beyond question, but what exactly that influence was must be appreciated.[13] Could the Jews have expected better times to come than they had known before?

In their attitude to the Jews, the Reformers were completely at one with the habits of thought of their time. Luther said: "Burn their synagogues and their schools ... If any hold out against the fire, bury them in the rubble ... Break down their houses, forbid their rabbis to teach under pain of death and mutilation. Destroy all their prayer-books and Talmuds, in which are to be found only impiety, blasphemies and profanities.[14]

What the Reformers did want from Judaism was the ability to reach a more accurate text of the Word of God. As for the content of Judaism, they were only interested in it so far as the mystical side of it presented some affinities with the movements of interior mysticism as opposed to visible institutions. In all this, Judaism became the sport of inter-Christian rivalries. The Jews, expelled from Spain after the capture of Granada in 1492, and then from Portugal, had hardly better treatment in the countries where the Reformation was successful.

Immediately after the Reformation, that is, at the time of the Council of Trent, when a brief opportunity was presented to Catholics and Protestants to reconsider the relationship between them in a calmer mood, the Jews might have had a chance to play an historic role in a Christian world revitalized by the renewed science of the scriptures. But very soon the attitudes of Catholics and Protestants became more rigid, which led to a sort of frantic breaking down of bridges, as they entered on centuries of opposition and religious wars.

Relations between Christians and Jews are seen historically as a kind of tragedy indefinitely prolonged, which from time to time explodes with an access of violence which it would not hate been thought possible.[15]

---

[13] L. I. Newman, *Jewish Influence on Christian Reform Movements* (1925).

[14] *Sämtliche Werke* (1826–57), XXV, pp. 261–409.

[15] Max L. Margolis and Alex Marx, *A History of the Jewish People* (1st edition, 1927; 10th edition, 1956); George F. Moore, *Judaism in the First Centuries of the Christian Era; the Age of the Tannaim*, 2 vols. (1927, 7th edition in 3 vols., 1954); Salomon Grayzel, *The Church and the Jews in the 13th Century* (1933); idem, *A History of the Jews* (1947); Claris E. Silcox and Galen M. Fisher, *Catholics, Jews and Protestants, a Study of Relationships in the United States and Canada* (1934); Marcel Simon, *Verus Israël, Études sur les relations entre chrétiens et juifs dans l'Empire romain* (1948), pp. 135–425; Malcolm Hay, *Europe and the Jews. The Pressure of Christendom for 1900 Years* (1950; 2nd

There are elements in Catholicism, in Protestantism, and in Judaism, which struggle courageously to get rid of negative attitudes which have too long prevailed. We can think of the National Council for Christians and Jews of the United States, which, without having a strictly ecumenical aim, nevertheless effectively prepares the ground for bringing both closer together. On its side, the World Council of Churches has been studying since the war in a very precise way its relations with the Jewish world. In the same way, the Secretariat for Christian Unity considers that one of the tasks proper to it is to enter into relations with the Jews.

These firm moves can be seen as explicit signs that a certain period of history is past.

But there are still more steps to be taken before we can arrive at any profound rapprochement with Israel. We must, especially, rid our relations of certain attitudes, relics of the past, which persist just below the level of consciousness and direct our actions whether we will or not. History can here play an excellent cathartic role. It forces us to sort out what has been our traditional line of action with respect to the Jews, and to ask ourselves what it is based on and what it has produced.

After the conversion of the Roman Empire, the policy that prevailed was that of social segregation. We know the legal origin of this. It dates from the civil laws of the Roman Empire such as were passed by Constantine and taken up into the Theodosian Code in 438 and the edicts of Justinian. These prescriptions, which are not without some similarity to pagan laws of the earlier empire concerning the Jews, in their tolerance and their mistrust of an unassimilable element, were modified to take account of the new situation of Christianity as the state religion. It was necessary to make laws to create an exception for the Jews, for the Church was opposed to forced baptism. The Edict of Milan in 313, which authorized liberty of conscience, allowed Judaism to survive. But two years later, Constantine passed a law forbidding marriage between Jews and Christians and Jewish proselytism among Christians. What is certain is that the statute of exception created for the Jews social segregation of Jews and the prohibition of life in common with Christians, even to the taking of meals; the prohibition of Jews from all positions, public or private, giving them any authority over Christians; the tolerance of their religion on condition that it should never appear to be the official religion. This established norms of practice which still exert their influence.

Imperial legislation covered the whole empire, and affected the Jewish

edition, 1960); Rudolph M. Loewenstein, *Christians and Jews. A Psychoanalytic Study* (1951); S. W. Baron, *A Social and Religious History of the Jews*, 8 vols. (2nd edition, 1952–58); Will Herberg, *Protestant, Catholic, Jew. An Essay in American Religious Sociology* (1956); B. J. Bamberger, *The Story of Judaism* (1957).

diaspora, scattered as they were throughout it. It was that law which, during the period of the break-up of the empire, and then during the period of the barbarian States, formed the basis of the laws of the new Christian States governing their attitude to the Jews. The civil and religious legislation of Christian countries was modelled on it, with variations in severity or gentleness according to the times, the places and the peoples concerned. The Catholic Church has often been reproached for having in its general or provincial councils passed severe laws against the Jews. It should be stated, on the contrary, that these laws were often a method of tempering and regulating civil and popular practices which would otherwise have been more severe and were of non-ecclesiastical origin.

But intentions do not wipe out history. From the beginning of the Christian empire, the Jews were victimized by numberless vexatious measures and practices. For example, they could have no authority over Christians and were denied access to a number of professions. By virtue of their social segregation, they could not possess land or real property; they were thus forced by the law into certain occupations which they were afterwards to be reproached with following by choice. Being banned for centuries from dealing in real property, they had to specialize in certain occupations: trade in gold, jewels and clothes. It is not surprising that they came to excel as shopkeepers, tailors, hoteliers, bankers and brokers. Even in the Papal States, the Bull of Paul IV *Nimis absurdum*, 1555, banned them from all commerce save in second-hand goods, old furniture and money-lending.

The prohibition against Jews possessing land or real property had at least one appreciable result: a university career remained open to them. One excellent result of this was medieval Judeo-Arabic philosophy. Since then also, in the university world, in philosophy, science and literature, the Jews have played a part out of proportion with their numerical importance.[16]

A host of prejudices, not only among the mass of the people but among the educated classes, prevent Christians and Jews from coming closer together, because Christians often do not know the Christian roots in law of what they consider to be a way of life of strictly Jewish origin. Christans accuse Jews of restricting themselves to certain professions and trades, namely, the most remunerative; they forget that in ancient times the Jews

[16] Leo W. Scharz, ed., *Great Ages and Ideals of the Jewish People* (1956); Mordecai M. Kaplan, *Judaism as a Civilization; Towards a Reconstruction of American Jewish Life* (1957); Morris U. Schappes, *The Jews in the United States, A Pictorial History, 1654 to the Present* (1958); H. M. Sachar, *The Course of Modern Jewish History* (1958); Louis Finkelstein, ed., *The Jews, their History, Culture and Religion* (1st edition, 1949; 3rd edition, 1960); Nathaniel Ausubel, *A Pictorial History of the Jewish People* (11th edition, 1961).

were forced to restrict themselves in this way. One only has to go today to the State of Israel to see, in the kibbutzim, that the Jew is by no means reluctant to till the land or apply himself to any other profession, provided he is master in his own house and not the victim of laws of repression and segregation. Jews are reproached for their part in the French and Russian Revolutions: we forget that they felt they had the right to attempt to free themselves from social ostracism. Men who have nothing to lose are ready for any revolution.

And what of the attitude of the Catholic Church? Provincial councils were very hard on the Jews. The general councils, which often had to generalize for the whole Church matters treated in provincial councils, were generally more gentle. The first provincial council which passed decrees against the Jews was that at Elvira in Spain, about the year 300. Certain Christians had instituted the custom of asking Jews to come and bless their fields. Faced with the danger of syncretism, the council reacted by forbidding Christians to associate with Jews, and especially to eat with them. The legislation of Theodosius and Justinian could only strengthen the rigour of these rules. The councils of Toledo were remarkable for their severity: the third (582), fourth (633: canons 57–66), sixth (638) and twelfth (681) especially, which last adopted the legislation of the Visigothic king Erwig, which prohibited the observance of the Sabbath and of the Jewish dietary laws, and even forbade the Jews to emigrate. Similar measures were passed elsewhere by Merovingian bishops, as at the synods of Rheims and Meaux, the harshness of which was repudiated by St Gregory the Great.

In the Christian Middle Ages, theologians took the same traditional line as secular opinion in polemics and apologetics against the Jews, and they confirmed the enforced social segregation of the Jews.

With the crusades, people confused in their anger the liberation of the tomb of Christ from the hands of the infidels and the handful of Jews who had accused Jesus, and really thought they were assisting to fight the Muslim in the Holy Land by launching terrible slaughter against "Christ's executioners" in Worms, Mainz, Speyer, Cologne, Prague and Ratisbon. When the crusaders got to Palestine, Jews were treated as slaves.

The third (1179) and fourth (1215) Lateran Councils and the Council of Vienne (1267) made the Jews' ostracized position worse. But were they better treated by the popes? These alternated between kindness and strictness. St Gregory the Great, Leo X, and Sixtus V seem models of tolerance, as opposed to Paul IV, who expropriated the Jews of Rome, created the ghetto, and imposed the wearing of the yellow hat, and to St Pius V, Clement VIII and Benedict XIV, who confirmed the same policy. Pius IX opposed the construction of the Roman synagogue, which was authorized when Rome became the capital of Italy, but he did end the ghetto.

Recent goodwill gestures, as in the prayer of Good Friday for the Jews, have been received with satisfaction, but has not the time come for a deep rethinking of our position with regard to the Jews? Should we not now separate ourselves from the survival, at least at the emotive level, of legislation conceived for another era which has brought down centuries of hatred, persecution and misery on a people called with the Gentiles to form the people of God? For twenty centuries Jews have lived among Christians. Christians have accused them of sinning against the light, without understanding that it is not enough to be present with a thing for that thing to be, thereby, simply by being there, to be obvious to us as there. To become a Christian means for a Jew to go over to the side of the traditional oppressor, to betray his race and his tradition. Christians have also claimed that the fate of the Jews is the result of a divine curse. In doing this, they set themselves up as judges in place of God, and impose on Israel a secular punishment for a kind of second original sin. They have accused the Jews of deicide, thus making all the Jews of the Roman Empire, or even just the Jews in Palestine, or simply all the Jews of Jerusalem, responsible for what was the fault of only some of them. How should the vast majority of the Jews be guilty of deicide, not having known Christ? St Peter says that it was "in ignorance" (Acts 3:17) that his compatriots destroyed Christ. Those who cried out against Christ were no one's representatives; no unanimous vote was taken.

The text produced at the general assembly in Amsterdam, in the name of the Protestant Committee of Witness to the Jews, declares: "For us, the words cursing Christ were surely said in the name of the whole Jewish people, just in the same way as Pilate pronounced his condemnation in the name of all pagans."[17] But is it really so simple? The world of Jewry in its totality cannot be made responsible for the death of Christ before three questions have been clearly answered: how far could the members of the Sanhedrin and the High Priest, who had the decisive influence on his death, speak in the name of the Jews scattered throughout the Roman Empire? Take the noisy handful who shouted for the crucifixion of Christ—how far were they free, and how representative were they of the whole Jewish people? And how far can the iniquity of certain leaders be transferred to a whole nation, to a whole people? That is a question which the Jews must ask themselves, having seen six million of their people disappear into the concentration camps of Nazi Germany. Adam, Abraham, Christ and Mary could speak in the name of mankind, because in some way they contained it. But is this true of the trial of Jesus? The actions of the Pharisees, of Pilate and the Jewish crowd had their consequences for the Jewish people, but a formal sharing of the responsibility is quite another thing.

[17] *General Report*, II, p. 289.

466

If we try for a moment to abstract from two thousand years of Christianity and to become contemporaries at the trial of Jesus, we can see how easy it was to pass by the Messiah without recognizing him. We can today see the immense importance of Christianity in history, and we naturally measure what happened when Jesus was put to death by this standard. We extrapolate back, so to speak, the vast importance of Christianity as it has been progressively revealed in the life of the Church, to those events, which happened on what from exterior considerations was a very small stage, the arrest, condemnation and execution of a Nazarene. We forget this fundamental principle of Christianity: that the Word is not manifested in glory, for then man would have been immediately faced with the end, but in a way that was not clear, in humility, in obscurity. The Word is revealed sufficiently for man to be able to believe, but in such a way that he is not immediately faced with God's last judgement. Jesus indeed said as much during his passion: "Dost thou doubt that if I call upon my Father, even now, he will send more than twelve legions of angels to my side?" (Mt 26:53). For if he had, he would by doing so have set the chief priests and the Roman Empire at once in the presence of God's judgement of man's history. Jesus chose rather the certainty of death. He revealed himself sufficiently for man to believe, but he kept back the manifestation of his person so as not to confront man with the judgement too soon, since he himself was the Eschaton. In a sense the power of ultimate reality had to be the more veiled, the closer it came to man. That is why salvation passed by, and still passes by, many imperceptibly, only perceived by the poor of God. There lies the drama of salvation and of the trial of Jesus.

It is difficult to draw any other conclusion than this: that if a curse lies on the people of the old covenant, it is the same as that which falls on the people of the new covenant when they are faithless to their Lord.

In the Middle Ages, the Jewish and Christian worlds met for a second time in a way not previously possible since the days of our Lord. The opportunity was unique, because of the uniy of Western Christendom and of Christian civilization in the Byzantine empire. The opportunity occurred through the cultural interplay of the two: but Christendom was not ready. Then came the sack of Constantinople, and, at about the same time, the disintegration of Western Christendom. Judaism was the victim of our divisions. Despite their permanent contribution to our culture, the Jews no longer played the role of links and intermediaries. Impelled by spiritual currents in different directions, they could not show all that they were capable of.

A new age then began. What are its constituents? The Jews are still scattered, but now over the whole world. Continuing their medieval role, the Jews are to be found wherever the new civilization is taking on its most characteristic forms, especially in Russia and America. It is impossible to see the diaspora and its spread across the world otherwise than as a foundation stone waiting for some great edifice yet to be built. We do not know what the new State of Israel has in store in the cultural and religious spheres. What we do know is that when the Jewish element in any culture has a chance to express itself it produces results, in that culture, which force themselves on our attention. It brings a new leaven to a foreign culture, and thanks to the national ties which confer on it a special kind of universality, it is a mediator between the greatest cultures.

Two new facts, absolutely new after twenty centuries, have now appeared to make Christians and Jews think again about the problem of the relations between them. They are the emergence of the ecumenical movement, and the foundation of the State of Israel.

The second fact is sufficiently new for Jews themselves to wonder just what it means. Is it simply a political, national fact, or also a religious one? From the point of view of the historian of civilizations, there is here an extraordinary example of integration. The Jews of the diaspora, spread over Western cultures, Germanic, Slav, Latin and Arabic, now organize into a synthesis in Israel elements, of race and culture, borrowed from the Gentiles, and give that synthesis the geographical setting of the land of their forefathers. Jews from Russia, Poland, Hungary, Spain, Italy, Germany, the Yemen and Iraq settle together in the *kibbutzim*, in the centres of popular culture and in the universities. The young people born in Israel are a new Jewish youth. Even if not all Jews are ready to emigrate and settle in Israel, that land is for all of them a sign and a symbol.

Let us try to sort out what all this means. Here we have integration, a political integration which produced the State of Israel, a cultural integration producing an Israeli culture, and also a religious integration, for the World Synagogue Council was formed in the United States in 1959 to link together the synagogues of Israel and other countries.

Christianity must resolve to look at the Jewish world as a whole in an ecumenical spirit. The Jews in Israel have made it clear that Christians would do well no longer to consider them as missionary material, a field for proselytism, and this attitude will have its repercussions among the Jews scattered all over the world, who are supported by the thought of the State of Israel. The Jews ask today to be taken for what they are, with the ideas of their part in the world and their mission as they conceive them.

So first of all we must understand the kind of universality Judaism represents, for it is only then that anything can be done. In other words, only an ecumenical attitude can get us anywhere.

The problem of the place of the Jews in the *Una Sancta* is then one of the place of a universality of its own kind which must be recognized as such, a universality, however, set free from what still limits it overmuch, set free in a higher spiritual universality. We are perhaps now offered another chance to renew relations between Jews and Christians.

2. *Judaism's part in the emergence of Christianity from its present impasse*

What is wanted now for the reconciliation of Christians is not knowledge of their differences, nor of their points of agreement. Centuries of controversy and analysis and observation have shown us what separates us and what joins us together. But the dialogue often looks to us like a blind alley. Each advances from his own position with the best of intentions; the dialogue begins; and then it stops. It can go no further. Our basic approaches to Christianity are still too different from one another. Now it is reasonable to suppose that Jewish thought could have an important part to play in the dialogue between Catholics and Protestants, on the decisive points that separate us, especially on the general ordering of Christendom, the original state of man and the sacraments.

First, the general ordering of Christendom. It is a true synthesis of the natural and the supernatural established on the model of, and by the continuation of, the Word incarnate. For the natural must necessarily be accepted as part of it. Now the Lutheran doctrine of the corruption of man's nature has coloured the whole of Protestant thought down to our own day. The bounds of Christendom are thus essentially defined by grace, and no longer by that relation of nature and grace as it has been understood traditionally in Catholicism and Orthodoxy. The great orders that make up Christendom are, therefore, interpreted in a corresponding way.

The primacy of the Bible in Judaism could prove to be an effective meeting point for Catholics and Protestants. We consider our idea of nature to be common to us and the Jews. The human knowledge Christ had of nature, of the creation, as of human nature, he inherited from the traditions of his people. Our idea of nature is in the same line of ancient biblical tradition, in which the fall and consequent corruption are not seen as total. If our interpretation is rejected as too *a priori*, we can appeal to the people of the Bible. Could they also be mistaken? Luther's strong resentment of institutionalized Catholicism, which he regarded as too "natural", obstructed a true estimation of nature as it was to be seen in the Jewish thought of the Old Testament. Besides, what Luther and Calvin were trying above all to make clear, was how the Word of God was man's salvation. But Luther, by neglecting the doctrine of man as the image of God, and by asserting his total corruption as the basis of the "bondage of the will", isolated the Redemption from its proper context, man in creation.[18] The consequence was a radical pessimism concerning the results of the original fall. The rational nature of man, his capacities for culture and civilization, and his search for a certain justice even on a human level, no longer contained any trace of the lost image and likeness of God, and even in the justified man the image of God was not effectively restored by his justification. Calvin has enunciated a doctrine concerning the place of man in creation and his proper task in the transformation of the world, but shares the idea of the fundamental corruption of human nature. Luther and Calvin drew different conclusions from this, the latter in the sense of the glory of God and the submission of all things to his sovereignty, the former of a retreat from the world. For Luther, man is above all confronted with Calvary. The world has disappeared: there is only a unique revelation, Love crucified. For Calvin, man stands beside the tomb, to feel the power of the Risen One in the first light of dawn. But whether man flees from history because it is fundamentally evil, or seeks to dominate it in order the better to subordinate it to God, in either case he is rejecting something.

What Lutheran and Calvinist Protestantism are still deprived of because of their rejection of natural theology is all that follows from the biblical doctrine of the creation of the world and the position of man both within the created order and in relation to his Creator. They miss also the richness of the Old Testament presentation of the work of the Messiah not only as the redemption of man but as the restoration of the universe; and consequently they lack a sacramental and symbolic vision of the world. They cannot, therefore, give full weight to the sacramental principle implicit in the Incarnation. Hence the supreme importance of the Word, together with the depreciation of the sacramental order, reduced to an accidental role in relation to the Word. It thus becomes difficult to do justice to the basic attitude underlying the relation of man to created things in the Old Testament, an attitude which passed into the New Testament: it is an atmosphere of benediction, of sanctification, of *eucharistia*, which spreads over the whole life of the people of God and regulates the work and action of men. It was not enough for Israel that all things should be subject to the Word in virtue of a kind of interior disposition, but creation, matter itself in its goodness, had to be put at the service of the meaning of the Word. The Church took up into her vision of the world the idea of the sanctification of human life which existed in the national life of the Hebrew people, as it is shown to us in the most concrete provisions of the law as well as in the economic and social order.

The bulk of the exegetical work of Luther and Calvin on the scriptures was from the beginning directed by a certain choice: the fundamental

---

[18] *Catholicity, A Study of the Conflict of Christian Tradition in the West.*

corruption of human nature and new conception of eschatology. They have a doctrine of man in creation, but it needs to be filled with the whole spirit of the Bible. In Luther, it is concentrated on certain religious ideas, such as piety and salvation; in Calvin, it becomes his great doctrine of vocation. But in the first, the impression remains that only man has been ransomed; and in the second, vocation is always in danger of being secularized because it lacks the sacramental principle. Neither one nor the other has grasped the basic biblical doctrine of man-in-creation.

In this field, as in those of the original state of man and of sacramental theology, Jewish thought could make a precious contribution to the bringing together of Protestants and Catholics.

It could easily be objected that this is to ask Judaism to play an impossible role, since the Talmudic interpretation of the Bible is a restrictive one. It is not, in fact, the Bible as such that governs Jewish religious thought, but the Bible as read in the rabbinic or Talmudic tradition. There are in the Old Testament adumbrations of the full revelation of the Trinity, of original sin, and of the Mediator between God and men, but the teaching of the Talmud leaves them out. The substance of Judaism is not purely and simply the Word of God, but that Word interpreted in the rabbinic tradition. Biblical Judaism and rabbinic Judaism are two different things, and not purely and simply one and the same.

A dialogue about the Bible between a Protestant minister, a Catholic priest and a rabbi will inevitably begin by each of the three taking up different positions. But the dialogue only has any chance of succeeding if it does go on. The Word of God has joined us together as it were by a chain, and has bound us in the solidarity of a common destiny. Twenty centuries of struggle and conflict have shown that separation is not a solution. What God is making us learn the hard way is the road to unity. If we accepted at the start that our way of salvation is through unity, we should be ready to understand things that up to now we have rejected out of hand. Can we not see in history several examples of the profit to be derived from the cross-fertilization of several cultures and systems of religious thought? Let us take the example of natural theology in St Thomas Aquinas.

The natural theology which Luther and Calvin rejected was based not simply on Greek philosophy but on the thought of the Old Testament. Greek philosophy was chosen, not because it was Greek, but it was right, and universal. A supreme criterion of truth was its judge, the Word of God in the scriptures. We may truly wonder what prejudice makes the Protestants believe that medieval scholasticism obeyed the primacy of reason and not that of the Word! One is almost ashamed to point out that simply from a scientific point of view it is a grave cultural mistake to think that Catholicism is Christianity as revised and corrected by St Thomas Aquinas. Troeltsch encouraged Protestantism down the wrong path in allowing this misconception to be believed.[19]

No less grave a mistake is made if is imagined that the idea of nature in St Thomas came to him exclusively from Aristotle. This is to forget that what sets the tone of the *Summa Theologiae* in particular is not the theological demonstration contained in the body of each article, but the word of scripture which precedes it. *Philosophia ancilla theologiae:* "Philosophy at the service of theology" and faith. It was the certain possession of the spirit of the Bible which guided him in the choice of his philosophical assistance. Even if the explanation of his idea of nature came to him from Aristotle, the idea itself came to him most from Jewish thought. Nor is that all that St Thomas owed to Jewish thought. He owed a direct debt to that Jewish culture which was spread everywhere throughout Europe in the Middle Ages and which influenced the countless sources he used. He was particularly indebted to Maimonides and to Avicebron.[20]

St Albertus Magnus, who made a complete study of the great work of Maimonides, *The Guide for the Perplexed,* was perhaps the man who made it known to St Thomas. The real pivot of the thought of St Albert and St Thomas was the problem of the relations between reason and faith, knowledge and the Word of God. Now *The Guide for the Perplexed,* which is a sort of Jewish scholastic *Summa Theologiae,* poses the fundamental problem of the reconciliation of the conclusions of the sciences and philosophy with the literal sense of the scriptures. Its inspiration was Aristotelian and biblical. St Albert and St Thomas had a guide and a model in Maimonides of the possible products of the ideas of creation and of nature as they are known in the Bible when they are applied to the knowledge of the world, of which Aristotle provided a pagan example. The least one could say would be that the thought of St Thomas on the creation and on nature is doubly biblical, first because it is read in the light of revelation, and secondly because it is corroborated in its account of things by the framework of a Jewish theology which puts philosophy at the service of the Word of God.

St Thomas's commentaries on the *Sentences* already bear witness to the influence of Maimonides. It is found again in his greatest works.[21] Maimonides gave St Thomas the five reasons for the necessity of revelation

---

[19] *The Social Teaching of the Christian Churches,* II, p. 461.
[20] Alfred Guillaume, "The Influence of Judaism on Islam" in *The Legacy of Israel* (1st edition, 1927), pp. 129–73; Charles Singer, "The Jewish Factor in Medieval Thought", *ibid.,* pp. 173–283.
[21] Leo Roth, "Importance of Maimonides and His School" in *The Legacy of Israel,* pp. 437–48.

and of faith.[22] He passed on to St Thomas the fundamental idea of sacrifice, the general exposition of the old Law, and the explanation of the laws of the Old Testament.[23] In theodicy, St Thomas took from Maimonides the proofs for the existence of God through the necessity for a prime mover, a necessary being, a first cause.

But the major contribution of Maimonides to the Thomist synthesis was to be to serve as a new model of the agreement of faith and reason, of a theology in the service of revelation as it is contained in its sources. Each time St Thomas had to explain and bring together the great themes of the Bible such as the nature of God, creation, genesis, the old law, the hierarchy of being, or the knowledge of God that man could have through revelation, he had before him the model of a synthesis made not by a Gentile, but by a Jew.

We can see how much the Reformation lacked a principle of balance and integrity despite its knowledge of Hebrew! The Judaism which enabled Christianity to begin its progress with a universal breadth worked again in the Middle Ages as a stamp guaranteeing the universality of Christian culture. Such is its historic mission, which it can again perform in our time. But we shall have to behave with regard to it as brothers responsible for one another, not as polemists: as witnesses, not as proselytes. A genuinely welcoming attitude, not secular pressure, even under the contemporary guise of Christian institutions well enough intentioned, but too much like conquerors, could bring about a *rapprochement*. We do not need to hide from ourselves the difficulties lying in store for us. The Jews have a deep mistrust engrained in them by centuries of oppression. Instinctively they suspect a new attack behind the efforts made by Christians to draw closer to them. Perhaps our advances will be received by a recoil on their part. They will wonder how far our friendliness goes, and whether it does not conceal some hidden motive; how far does our acceptance go, and are we not using friendliness as a means, as a manouevre? The Jews feel themselves terribly ill-adapted to the Christian world. We shall have to learn, painfully, to understand. The best attitude will be the simplest: when Israel asks us to explain ourselves to him, we shall say, "Will you tell us in return how you see yourself in relation to us?" But before the dialogue is begun in depth, we shall have to get rid of the vestiges of a considerable number of non-theological factors which hinder the frankness of our new relationship.

The Jews have their own convictions, and they have the right to see that they are heard. We too have ours. Many of them, especially on Christ and on the Church, are unacceptable to a Jew, and we have no intention

[22] *Contra Gentiles*, I, chapter iv, v; Summa Theol. Ia, qu. 1, art. 1.
[23] Ia, qu. 98–106; Ia–IIae, qu. 101, art. 1; 102, art. 3 and art. 4.

of imposing them upon him. But they touch too deeply our lives as Christians not to ask that they be respected. The dialogue can be established on the basis of mutual respect. One of the great wonders of ecumenical relations is that the incompatibility of systems does not prevent the compatibility of persons, for we know in our hearts that there is a secret and mysterious convergence towards the will of God. We must practise right from the start a sort of "moral disarmament". That is, we must come without weapons and simply say what we think. We must leave aside any desire to force the other to our view, and only open our talk to light and amity.

III. THE CHURCH OF JEWS AND GENTILES

1. The mystery of our joint calling

What is the mystery of the Church? It is a vast reality which has been on the move since God created the world, which God leads through lengthy preparation towards the light; God dispersed its seeds in the world in the earliest revelation, prefigured it in the religion of Israel, and accomplished it in Christ; he has made it grow in the world through the riddles and the factions of history, and will one day bring it to its fullness in the Church after the Judgement.

The mystery of the Church can be called the whole design of the Three Persons of God as set forth in the world according to the economy of God's supervention, so as to bring towards the Trinity, through their summing-up in Christ, all those it has pleased God to predestine.

The mystery of the Church belongs to time. It belongs to history. It is before history, on the limit trembling on the brink of the Genesis of all things. It also belongs to the order of the agony of all things when the world will again be covered with the clouds on which the Son of Man will descend to pronounce the judgement.

The Church remembers paradise, the waters of the Flood, the first setting-out made in Abraham. For long she wandered with our forefathers in faith. Her voice was lifted up with those of the prophets; she was by the burning bush and on Sinai. She entered into the covenant with God the first time. She took the road into exile, and was there on the return. Lastly, she believed with Mary, the stem of Jesse, and appeared as "the light to all peoples", the movement of the Old Israel towards the New. For "salvation, after all, is to come from the Jews" (Jn 4:22). They bore the mystery which God sowed when he created the world in a state of grace, which man rejected, and which God took back again and kept until a people should please him, a people built out of suffering and exile, for the religion of the Lord was to be a pilgrim religion; a people of ritual fidelity, for the religion of the Lord was to be a religion of a covenant; a people with a soul open to symbols, for the Lord was to reveal himself in holy signs; a people whose soul was made to come to grips with mystery, at one time to fight against and reject it, at another to grasp it passionately, often to accept it reluctantly, or to deny it without ever utterly forgetting it; a people who in their times of exaltation, the times of the making and the renewal of the covenant, would consecrate themselves to it eagerly; a people of the burning bush as well as of the brazen serpent, of the Red Sea and the Exile as well as of the Temple of Solomon; a people with a soul as changeable as the sea, which would break against the Rock of God, which would be in its midst and which it could never forget. A rock is set in the midst of the ocean of the world; the sea surrounding it is at first called Israel. There is no other rock so set, an obstacle to the sea, which wants to be free, as elsewhere in the ocean. God was to be this rock to Israel, at times beaten against in anger, but also loved with tears.

God has revealed himself to the world in many ways: in fire, in burning, in torment, in passion, in force and power and almost in aggression and violence: like a rock which one night arises in the sea and there stays irremovable to defy the sea that beats against it.

And sometimes God reveals himself in a light that passes by (Exod 33:18–23), in that mysterious banquet of the elders on Sinai where he was and presided in glory (Exod 24:11); in the silent tears of exiles (*super flumina Babylonis*, Ps 136:1); and then in Mary's song for her child Jesus. O voices of God, all of which reveal his mystery!

God came first into the world in the creation, with power, and then at the Incarnation, with gentleness. This double coming of God into the world subsists in the mystery of the Church, as she remembers the Old and the New Testaments.

The Bible is the Book in which the people of God have set down the history of their salvation. The Church, in reading it, finds there the extent of her memory, from Genesis to the Apocalypse. She forgets nothing. She rejects nothing. She is since Adam, since Abel; she includes even the angels. The angels dwell even now in the Church militant. The Church loses nothing. For her, there is no story of a chosen people outside herself, only in herself. She brings forth the story of salvation in grief. She does not merely watch the world, for she is mistress of her own destiny. She grasps, she takes up, she incarnates, she takes on herself, bears and sustains. She labours with her whole heart, with her blood; she lets herself be devoured, and at each instant that she gives herself up she is regenerated. She is that miracle that is motherhood. She takes, and she gives; she conceives and brings forth; she opens herself to the world and is transformed. It is the mystery of the Church to bear so much, to come from so far away, to be at the same time so high and so close.

2. The day of the ecclesia

When the mind contemplates the *ecclesia* (assembly of the people) which was seen in the majesty of Sinai, it is immediately swept on by the impetuous torrent of Pentecost, the celebration of the Harvest and of the God of the Wind; and at once thinks of what is to follow the words, "Come, Lord Jesus" (Rev 22:20).

In this the mind is following the line of a unique plan of salvation, following step by step the church-making activity of God, by which he creates, reveals, fashions, spreads and promotes his Church, in its different forms, until its final realization.

We shall look to the Judeo-Christian tradition to reveal to us, according to the laws of its typology, the successive forms of expression of these beginnings of the Church, which emerges at the heart of the luminous and active presence of God, under the form of the sovereign acts named Sinai, Pentecost and the final consummation.

It is with the greatest reverence that the Christian recalls the day which Moses in Deuteronomy calls the Day of the *Ecclesia* (4:10; 9:10; 18:16); the day which the Lord has made, which he determined, made and formed, when he entered into a covenant with a certain people, when something collective began to be born in the intimacy of the Lord, the covenant of grace, which, from being secret, was to become in Christ Jesus the covenant of grace divulged.[24] It is right that it was at this point that the people, *edah*, became *qahal, ecclesia*, assembly. The change of name reflects the innovation in reality.

The Church appeared after Sinai as that act, that event, which God loved and cherished, that he made his own, like "his Day"; which he thought more of than anything else, which he meditated on when he summoned the creation into the high place of his Trinity, so that he might contemplate it encompassed by his presence. The first characteristic we notice about the birth of the *ecclesia* is the absolute, transcendent and creative initiative of God.

It was he who called Moses and his people to the solemn celebration of the covenant, for which he had chosen this people from among the nations. Moses, who passed on God's call, and the conditions of the covenant, was but the faithful mediator, the official herald, the truth of whose

---

[24] *Summa Theol.* IIa–IIae, qu. 1, art. 7; qu. 2, art. 7.

mission was attested by signs and marvels. The call, the proclamation of the law, the will behind the covenant, the exact terms on which it was to be concluded, all came from God, the supreme authority ruling over his *ecclesia.*

The *ecclesia* is dominated by the transcendent and active presence of God. He was there before the Day of the *ecclesia,* as the present help and protection with which he overshadowed the chosen people from Abraham's time, and as the call Moses heard from the burning bush. Behind and beyond Moses, God saw the whole mass of men he binds to himself by his call. He is there again as sovereign when he descends in majesty when he gives us the law, and his shadow covers the sprinkling of blood on people and altar. The God of Abraham, Isaac and Jacob led his people through the covenant to himself.

From the heart of glory the covenant came, and the covenant is at the heart of the mystery of the Church. So it is by that light that we must understand the Church.

The primitive idea of the glory of God in the Semitic world was associated with the idea of weight, of heaviness. St Paul is proof of this when he speaks of "loading us with everlasting glory" (2 Cor 4:17). In the same way on Sinai the sovereign presence of God was joined with a weight of power, of flashing fire, of light, which made even the physical creation tremble as if animate. God comes in a dense cloud that covers the mountain (Exod 19:9); he is announced by thunder and lightning and the sound of a trumpet (Exod 19:16). When God descended in the midst of the fire, the mountain remained trembling and smoking. God, resplendent and fearful, mysterious and imperceptible, suddenly irrupted into the world, outthundering the thunder. He showed his majesty in incomparable power. He showed that he was infinitely different from man. He showed it still further by setting about the mountain a boundary no man might break through under pain of death (Exod 19:12). He demanded that no one be able to approach it before being sanctified. He was within a sacred circle within which he disclosed his flashing power and majesty. He hid his face in the clouds to hide the violence of his glory. The people who saw it could not understand. Moses himself could not break through the circle of his brightness; he saw only the back, the reflection (Exod 33:17–23), and even so he had to veil his face, so intense was the glory of God.

We have now seen the heart of the day of the *ecclesia,* and of the *ecclesia* itself. This people God called together he called for a purpose: to join with him in mutual agreement: "I, to whom all the earth belongs, will single you out among its peoples to be my own" (Exod 19:5–6).

The Church was born because there had been a meeting and a covenant between God and the people. So long as the two parties to the covenant are separate, there is no Church. God freely makes himself a part of the *ecclesia*. Without the descent of God, without the Day of the *ecclesia*, without the indwelling of glory, there is no Church.

The day of the incorporation of the assembly was at the same time the day of the revelation of God to his people and of his people to himself: it was the day when God revealed himself as creator of the *ecclesia*, at the same time as sovereign partner; it was the day when the eyes of the people were opened to their past, their present and their destiny.

Looking back on their life since they fled from slavery in Egypt, and marching towards the promised land, the people became conscious of God's special presence: a presence of help and protection which now culminated in the presence of the covenant. Why had God set them free? Why had he accompanied them in the desert in the pillar of cloud and the pillar of fire? Why had he made them assemble at the foot of this mountain, trembling under the weight of his glory? The people discovered at Sinai that God would be unfailingly with them as their God. They discovered themselves in this solemn act of God, with his people for ever. On one side, God proclaimed his law (Exod 20) and charged Moses to give it to the people, offering his covenant in return for its acceptance. And the people, remembering the miracles of God on their behalf, accepted and entered into the covenant with him.

Thus the day of the *ecclesia*, the day of the people of God, was manifestly the Day of the Lord: a great act in his plan for salvation. The presence of God, before prevenient and accompanying, was now to be fixed in the *ecclesia* in a stable, personal and exclusive way. This was revealed in this church-making act which made of this people no longer a tribe, a nation, an ordinary assembly, but a people sacred to the revealed Word. God's act of calling them revealed his ultimate intention: there were to be no limits to the call to his Church. The call in the *ecclesia* was as violent as the descent on Sinai. The Church has only to obey the call to be borne into the boundlessness of God. What the people became through the covenant, "a royal priesthood, a consecrated nation" (Exod 19:6), they could become in the practice of their lives. Ceaselessly God calls them, if only the *ecclesia* remain open to the active, urgent vocation of God. On God's side, the call remains ever waiting, ever active. The religious actions of the people are realizations of that call, its passing from a state of possibility to intense actuality. The act and the day of the *ecclesia*, once performed and done, never again pass away; the difference arises from men. This is why the great religious revivals in Israel, as in the Church, have always been returns to the covenant, to the call, renewed agreements, with a deepened awareness of the act by which God took his people to change them to his image and likeness.

478

The *ecclesia* is thus seen to be the action of the luminous and active presence of God. There was an *ecclesia* because there was a special presence of God. The Church was born, the image of his mystery and his glory, as an effect of his splendour. God revealing himself changed man's religion. His self-revelation in this act was creative as well as revelatory. From the moment God commanded Moses to call the people together into the assembly, the moment the people responded to the call, man's religion was changed. The plan of salvation in history was revealed. It was one and the same act which revealed and created the Church.

With the covenant, then, began the great re-assembling of the sons of God scattered since the Fall. God on Sinai called together and reunited his people; Christ Jesus, who came to bring to perfection, not to abolish, was to pursue the same end in his Incarnation (Jn 11:52). The covenant of Sinai revealed the passing and inadequate nature of every other religious form. The religious form of the covenant becomes apparent in man's history as the outline of that adequate form God gives to man. Henceforth, every people had to direct its steps in the same direction as the covenant in order to find the way back in religion towards God. Therein Israel was to find the justification of its proselytism, the Church of Christ its universal mission.

Ancient Israel was at the same time the vehicle, the symbol and the anticipation of that universal plan which God works out in stages with the aim of spreading it to all humanity, to make mankind in the end "a royal priesthood, a consecrated nation" (Exod 19:6; 2 Pet 3:9). God untiringly pursues the design he revealed on Sinai: the gathering together of mankind into the Church according to the religious form of the covenant. "All that survive" of Israel (Is 4:3) were to bear witness on the day of the Incarnation to the ever active survival of that day of the *ecclesia*, preserved in the hearts of those who lived in the purity of the line of the ancient calling of the people, and accepted its purification. That day of the *ecclesia*, which remained a humble flame then, was to set the world ablaze when the sun of the resurrection rose. Jesus on the eve of his death was to tell how much he longed for the day, which was to recall that of Sinai and then, in the mystery of the Redemption, should be consummated in the new and eternal covenant. Jesus on the cross took up, continued and crowned the great work begun by God on the day of the *ecclesia*. When Jesus said, "It is finished", he meant us to understand not only that the wall of separation between God and man was broken down, but that henceforth were gathered together again in one new humanity the two parts of the heritage he asked of his Father: the Jews and the Gentiles.

3. The tradition of the ecclesia

Through the vicissitudes of exile, and the failings of the chosen people slipping back to their pagan origins, God preserved the pure lines of his plan. This divine idea of the *ecclesia* which took material form on the "day of the assembly" on Sinai (Deut 4:10; 9:10; 18:16) continued as an imperishable faith "till the appointed time came" (Gal 4:4). It is in this light that we can see how high in the sight of the Church some are raised who were at first hidden by reason of their humility.

For a long time—indeed, at all times—there persisted in Israel the expectation of the Messiah who should restore in splendour the *ecclesia* of Sinai, which had almost fallen under the weight of its trials. Prophetic minds, who had lived faithfully conforming to the terms of the covenant, knew that the fire which smouldered under the ashes had one day to blaze forth again, and that the glory of God would descend in "this land of ours" (Ps 64:10; Ezek 36:24; Col 1:20).

For those who lived waiting for that flame, what great joy there should have been in the words of the Lord: "It is fire that I have come to spread over the earth, and what better wish can I have than that it should be kindled?" (Lk 12:49)

High in the order of those called, who are the *ecclesia*, we must put those great but humble people whom St Luke sets at the beginning of his gospel: Zachary, Joseph, Mary, Simeon, Anne and John the Baptist. The true line of messianic hope in the ecclesia is set out in the sequence Lk 1:15–17, 68, 75, 77 and 79; and 2:14, 30–32, 36 and 38. It is on these humble, righteous and poor people among the "poor of Yahweh" that the grand plan of the *ecclesia* rested, the silent and imperceptible passing, before God and men, of the old *ecclesia* into the new. They were not alone, it is true; but they are the luminous signs of the way, of the continuity of God's design, the high points of the prophetic waiting that comes in their time towards its realization. Jesus was borne by them: the old man Simeon who took the Child in his arms carried there the Church. These righteous keepers of the covenant, these humble supporters of the new *ecclesia*, they are the precursors, the forerunners of the call which the Lord Jesus become man is to address to those other "poor of Yahweh", the apostles, and then through them to all souls trusting in the grace of God. The account of the calling of the apostles (Jn 1:41 ff.) is among the greatest passage of the Gospel.

The apostles, who lived according to the mind of the Church, vie with one another, so to speak, in setting forth the stages in the genesis of the Church.

St Luke shows us the Church at its birth in Jesus, born of Mary, and in the three holy ones united around Jesus in the same calling. St John and St Mark, on the other hand, begin their gospels with the calling of come to set aside the law and the prophets; I have not come to set them the apostles. They prefer to show the Church not at its first birth but at another essential stage, when it is constituted the Church of the apostles. St Mark, who reports the words of the Father over his Son, shows implicitly that the Father calls men into the *ecclesia* through the Son.

In St John the call to the apostles is set in the perspective of the great prologue which begins his gospel. Having shown us there the Word of God come into this world, he opposes the law given by Moses to the truth given by Jesus. And at once he shows us the Incarnate Word on whom, in his baptism, the Holy Spirit descended (Jn 1:38), at work calling his apostles. He follows up the parallel with the words of the Precursor, "Behold the Lamb of God", a theme which dominated the life of the old *ecclesia*. Andrew tells Simon, "We have discovered the Messiah"; and Philip says to Nathaniel: "We have discovered who it was Moses wrote of in his law, and the prophets too" (Jn 1:45).

We cannot but be impressed by the deep concern of these men for the old *ecclesia* and their hope for the new. We are present at the renewal of the *ecclesia* of Sinai: renewal by Yahweh, who is God the Father, through his incarnate Word, who calls his people into the *ecclesia:* "Come and follow me; I will make you into fishers of men" (Mk 1:17). What was imperfect was fulfilled in a higher calling: "Do not think that I have aside, but to bring them to perfection" (Mt 5:17).

At the same time Jesus is shown in the gospels as having a double genealogy: one divine, the other human (Mt 1:1–2; Lk 3:23–28). At the same time, his Church-building work (Jn 11:52) is shown as the result both of the present creative action of God and as a consequence of the law and the prophets.

Jesus was supported by these poor and righteous men. They belonged to the authentic inspiration of the Mosaic Church. He was to turn naturally to them to spread abroad the ancient and great plan for the *ecclesia*. He made them understand the new calling; to them he addressed the Sermon on the Mount (Mt 5:1–12), which is set purely and utterly in the mystic line of development of the *ecclesia*. The Sermon on the Mount, towards the beginning of St Matthew's gospel, is like a symbol and a rallying point. Jesus showed by it to what tradition he belonged, and in what direction lay his plans for the Church. He was the son of Mary and Joseph. He could not have been introduced in a more perfect manner into the tradition of the Righteous of the Old Testament than by his parents, who possessed to such a degree the spirit of the beatitudes, Joseph, described as "a right-minded man" (Mt 1:19) and Mary, who bears witness to herself in the Magnificat. It was in that spiritual climate, in that tradition, that the features of the physiognomy of the Messiah and of the *ecclesia* to come were preserved whole, while the rabbinical tradition and popular hope rejected them in part as irreconcilable with their own ideas.

So Jesus declared that since "salvation, after all, is to come from the Jews", the kingdom should first be offered to the Jews, and then should be taken from them to be given to the Gentiles, scorned by the Jews. In the Old Testament the Jews had received the mission to lead men to the old covenant; but they had come to believe that their mission would lead them to dominate other nations politically and economically. We can see what meaning could be read into many texts from Isaiah interpreted within a view so narrowly nationalist, earthly and legalistic (Jn 7:31–59; Lk 7:30; 11:37–54).

Christianity grew out of that traditional current of righteousness, the traces of which we can follow from the Old to the New Testament.

4. The Church of Christ and the apostles in the perspective of the old ecclesia

When we look at Catholic tradition in the perspective of the tradition of the apostles, we cannot fail to perceive the breadth of the latter. If we regard it simply as a chronological starting-point, we are mistaken. Apostolic tradition does not simply begin with the apostles: they are already within and part of a tradition. These men thought of Christianity as being born through a plan of salvation working out from the most ancient days of Israel. They were Jews, some of "those who survived", with Mary, Anne, Simeon and the rest of the "poor of Yahweh". They had received the formation of the Word. They were convinced that there was a plan of salvation: perhaps they could not systematize or express their ideas on the subject like the teachers of the law, but they were soaked in it. It was their spiritual life-blood. They had received the message, and had kept it faithfully. They were waiting, going over the prophecies in their hearts. They lived in hope for the Messiah.

Now one supreme fact dominated their spiritual vision of the plan of salvation: the *ecclesia* of Sinai. They knew that God would do other wonderful things for his people. What things? What would the Messiah be like? What would he do with the *ecclesia*? They had a sense of the past, but they also dimly perceived the future through a host of prophetic signs. They waited for what was to come, but their sense of the past was clearer to them than their guesses at the future. The nearer they came, chronologically, to the beginning of the new age, the less they were aware of the light that was soon to arise in the midst of the people. So when it had all happened, the Lord was to say to them: "Too slow of wit, too dull of heart, to believe . . ." (Lk 24:25).

They were only gradually to discover the meaning of the plan of salvation working from the beginning of Israel to their own time. The resurrection opened their eyes, and Pentecost completed their enlightenment. What followed had then only to unfold itself as the Holy Spirit led the emerging Church to trace its own path in history.

We have now to consider the place of the Church in the apostle's outlook. Two ideas are ideas important: first, the idea of the *ecclesia* which Christ proclaimed (Mt 16:18) was not an absolute innovation. They had, like every Jew, like Joseph and Mary, an idea of the *ecclesia*. It matters very little by what name it was called—perhaps the Aramaic *qehala?*—what matters is the fact itself. They possessed a traditional sense of the *ecclesia*. So we cannot understand the mind or the work of the apostles without looking at their sources. It was on this traditional idea of the *ecclesia*, which he possessed along with his apostles, having also received it from the Jewish tradition, that Christ relied to build his Church. The scriptures can only properly be understood in the perspective of the *ecclesia;* otherwise they remain only a confused mass from which treasures can at times be extracted, but which keeps its secret.

The second idea is that once the apostles had discovered the Church of Christ they thereby also discovered the whole synthesis of the Church. The prophetic meaning of the *ecclesia* of Sinai was revealed to them, and the revelation of Sinai was linked with that of the Last Supper. The same continuing glory of God made manifest in both fires. But they were to see with the passage of the years that part of what they had been waiting for was still not come, and that the final consummation would not take place during their lifetime. The Temple was going to disappear. They would be scattered over the world. The *ecclesia* would continue to be pilgrim, it would be a new phase of the Exodus. They would have to meditate anew on the long story of the covenant, but according as the "fact" which the ancient ritual had prefigured was now revealed to them as "the Body of Christ". The true meaning of the Temple would emerge, in its spiritual sense. The last manifestation of the glory of God to the *ecclesia* would be the final consummation in the light of the Lamb which would shine forth, one with the glory which was manifested on the different "days of the *ecclesia*" from Sinai to Pentecost.

The apostles, as children of Israel, sharing in a historic plan carried through in stages with an internal continuity guided by God, naturally thought within a particular typology of actions, prophecy and its fulfilment. It was natural also for them to let their minds, having already received a token, move towards a beyond that extended that token's meaning and scope; and when it was all done, to go back over the past to survey its continuity, to catch again its spirit so as to be drawn into the inner meaning of its movement.

Patristic thought itself was for long deeply in agreement with that apostolic way of thinking. They were the standards of salvation and the first masters of Christian thought, so for the Fathers, to make themselves wholly like them spiritually was to grow in the knowledge of God's plan.

If there are some essential elements of the tradition concerning the *ecclesia* in the New Testament, it is now, therefore, formed in the apostles without the background of the *ecclesia* of Sinai and the survival of that day of the *ecclesia* from then to the time of the apostles themselves. This memory of the old *ecclesia* is of the utmost importance in the formation of the new Church.

We should like to outline at this point how often the New Testament refers implicitly to Sinai. Christ himself, the people, the apostles, the primitive Christian community, all refer to it and continually compare the two forms of the *ecclesia*, that of the old covenant and that of the new.

Jesus, born in a tradition dominated by the idea of the old *ecclesia*, thought quite naturally within the forms of that tradition. He lived in it; he accepted it; he recommended its acceptance. He submitted himself to it in the ritual of circumcision and the presentation in the temple; at twelve, he prefigured his public manifestation by the incident of the finding in the temple. He preached and taught in the temple, and there he gathered his disciples together. He was careful of the respect due to it, and wept over its coming destruction. We cannot but be struck by this insistence on the temple when we remember that in the tradition of the Old Testament the *ecclesia* was always linked with the temple.

The predominance of the temple in the life of Christ was the predominance of the *ecclesia*. He compared himself with the temple (Jn 2:19), because he was himself the *ecclesia* from the beginning.

Jesus was born in a tradition of the *ecclesia*. He agreed to be formed by it, and by taking up in himself all its power and worth he prepared to perfect and surpass it. Need we be surprised that the apostles were also soaked in this atmosphere of the *ecclesia*, not only because they were Jews but because they followed the example of their Master?

The *ecclesia* emerges in the New Testament with a presence and a persistence infinitely clearer than one might suspect from the occasional mention of the word itself. The atmosphere is itself the atmosphere of the *ecclesia*. And if, as we shall see that they did, the apostles called attention to it in ways which are perceptible in their writings—and we know that the gospels are only brief summaries—how much more must this idea have been, potentially or behind the symbolism, in clear or implicit terms, a sort of vital context of all their thinking?

If we gather the various ways together, we are struck by their total force. The evangelists we take them from show us that these allusions are invitations to see the large view that is theirs; for example, St Luke and the idea of the temple, or St John and the idea of the paschal Lamb; or when St John says, as it were in passing, that the aim of the Incarnation was the constitution of the Church (11:52); or St Peter when, on the morning after Pentecost, he recalls the idea of the covenant on Sinai: "You are a chosen race, a royal priesthood, a consecrated nation" (1 Pet 2:9; Exod 19:5–6); or St Paul, in whom more than in the other apostles this comparative theology of the two *ecclesia*, the old and the new (Heb; Gal 3:4), is sometimes even systematically worked out; or St Matthew, in whom the idea of "bringing to perfection" the old covenant is uppermost; and St Mark, the disciple and secretary of St Peter, who in his turn takes up the grand themes of the fulfilment of the messianic prophecies.

But was there anything that the apostles wrote that did not come from Christ himself? Thus we are led to estimate the rich power of Christ's preaching in building his Church. When the apostles composed their writings, they had long proved Christianity in their own experience. They faithfully give us the Church as she then lived before their eyes; but they also show us the Church of Christ as she was on her first appearance behind a veil. We can follow the progressive discovery of the meaning which Christ gave to it, the intimate transmutation of the old *ecclesia* into the new.

So first we must suggest the importance of Sinai in the thought of Christ.

He made his own the key images of the *ecclesia* which surrounded the *ecclesia* of Sinai: those of the temple, of Jerusalem, the kingdom, the spouse, the flock and so on, and related them to his Church.

He took up for himself each of the concrete religious elements that made up the old *ecclesia*, and perfected them as parts of Christianity. The mystery of God in the old *ecclesia* was taken up into the mystery of the Trinity; the sacrificial element into the sacramental character of the Church; the assembly of the people into the new community; and the prophetic element into the eschatological aspect of the Church.

He himself declared that he was the God of Sinai, the supreme lawgiver of the new law he was proclaiming: Moses was but the herald of God. Christ, sent by his Father, is above every herald of second rank. He is the first and greatest in the calling together of the *ecclesia*. Every other only has power, actual or potential, in virtue of his power.

As God chose Moses as herald of the old *ecclesia*, Christ chose Peter as herald of the new. We can better understand the granting of the primacy if we see it in the context of Sinai, and the promise, "I will build my Church" (Mt 16:18) is better understood if the word "build" is seen in the light of the Old Testament.[25]

The calling of Peter to the apostolate and to the primacy before the

[25] A. Thibaut, "Édification", in *Dictionnaire de spiritualité*, fasc. xxv (1958), col. 279–93.

passion of our Lord corresponds to the personal calling of Moses.[26] The collation of the primacy of Peter after the resurrection and his practical exercise of it after Pentecost correspond to Moses's taking charge of the *ecclesia* as a result of the covenant. Moses and Peter correspond as characters, and it is this parallelism which finally gives weight to the classic texts on the primacy of Peter (Mt 16:18; Jn 15:16–18).

The great day of the paschal mystery is clearly seen as the day of Christ: it recalls the day of the *ecclesia* on Sinai. Jesus is the foundation of the final reunion of the *ecclesia*.

To take the parallel further, Christ declares that now is shed for the people the "blood of the New Testament" (Mt 26:28). The Christian people through the Redemption have "passed through the Covenant", have entered into a covenant with God by passing through the blood of Christ, the paschal Lamb.

At Pentecost we again find ourselves brought back to Sinai. It is Christ, the supreme convoker of the *ecclesia*, who commanded the apostles to gather together in Jerusalem, and it is he who sent down upon them the flame of his Spirit.

Now we must look briefly at the importance of Sinai for the chief apostle and for the evangelists.

Let us look particularly at St Peter. St Peter, who after the resurrection had been invested with the power and with the supreme calling of being in the name of Christ the visible head of the whole gathering of mankind in the *ecclesia*, was like a second Moses. He was like Moses in being the leader of the people, the new people that came into being after the resurrection, the *ecclesia* born on the cross. He was to guide it for the rest of its exodus towards the promised land; like him, he was to be the chief declarer of the law of God, the supreme pontiff who should unify the sacrifice of the *ecclesia*.[27]

From the day of Pentecost, Peter revealed his position. His first address is full of the revelation of the meaning of the "day of Christ", the day when the new *ecclesia* was formed: Jesus was dead, had risen, had become Lord: "And now, exalted at God's right hand, he has claimed from his Father his promise to bestow the Holy Spirit; and he has poured out that Spirit, as you can see and hear for yourselves" (Acts 2:33). Peter calls together the people whom he intends to join in the new Church: "Repent, and be baptized, every one of you, in the name of Jesus Christ, to have your sins forgiven; then you will receive the gift of the Holy Spirit. This

[26] Cf. St Augustine, *Contra Faustum*, lib. 22, c. 7a, *P. L.* XLII, 445.
[27] Pedro Tena Garriga, *La Palabra ekklesia, Estudio histórico-teológico* (1958); "Ecclesia dans l'Écriture et les premiers temps apostoliques" in *Dictionnaire de spiritualité*, fasc. xxv (1958), col. 370–84.

promise is for you and for your children, and for all those, however far away, whom the Lord our God calls to himself" (Acts 2:38–9).

He sets the new *ecclesia* in relation to the old *ecclesia* as its prophetic fulfilment, long awaited: "This is what was foretold by the prophet Joel: In the last times, God says, I will pour out my spirit upon all mankind" (Acts 2:16–17).

He established the relationship with the old *ecclesia* still more explicitly in his second discourse: "Moses . . . and all the prophets who spoke to you, from Samuel onwards, have foretold those days. You the heirs of the prophets, and of the covenant which God made with our fathers, when he said to Abraham, Every race on earth shall receive a blessing through thy posterity. It is to you first of all that God has sent his Son, whom he raised up from the dead to bring you a blessing, to turn away every one of you from his sins" (Acts 3:24–26).

And later Peter, having always before his eyes the fulfilment of the covenant in the new *ecclesia,* was to take up again the text of Exodus (19:5–6) when he said: "You are a chosen race, a royal priesthood, a consecrated nation, a people God means to have for himself" (1 Pet 2:9). All the central elements of the parallel between the *ecclesia* of Sinai and the *ecclesia* of Christ are there in these discourses of Peter. Before a people capable of understanding this essential background without it being necessary to spell it all out, he ceaselessly referred to the ideas of the covenant, of calling, of the glorious fulfilment of promises made in ancient days but only fulfilled in "these last days" (Acts 2:17; Joel 2:28–32). "Salvation was the aim and quest of the prophets, and the grace of which they prophesied has been reserved for you. The Spirit of Christ was in them, making known to them the sufferings which Christ's cause brings with it, and the glory that crowns them" (1 Pet 1:10).

St Peter appears as the first to call men to that mystery on which "now the angels can satisfy their eager gaze" (1 Pet 1:12). For him, as for the other apostles, there is a continuity of design in the grant of God, from the beginning up to the end. From the Church of Sinai to the Church of the Cross, there is but one birth of the Church. From the liberation of the people from their slavery in Egypt to the liberation of Christ from the slavery of death, it is the same continuing liberation. Peter calls on all the past, all the previous history, seeing no conflict with the new. The God of Jesus Christ is worthy of praise for having raised Jesus the Nazarene, but he is equally worthy of being celebrated for all those great acts which he performed in ancient times which made possible today's victory. Thus St Peter, in a very simple but absolutely certain way, separates what parts of the old law are to pass away and what is to pass into the new. He discerns the standard, the unity and catholicity of the plan of salvation. He reveals the fulfilment in the Church of the old covenant. But he is not dealing with merely a continuity, even a continuity of progress: this continuity has the characteristics of a liberation.

The Church of Christ is only to be understood if one takes its genesis back to its true beginnings, not merely to the New Testament. In truth, it is the idea of the Church which unifies the two Testaments. In this sense, the Synagogue, understood as *congregatio*, an external, empirical and visible community, brought with it the *ecclesia*, which expressed the reality of the people, chosen in spirit. The Church separated itself from the Synagogue, and what was left became an empty shell devoid of its meaning.

Everything then finds its value in the preaching and actions of Christ. The jumble of characteristics, images, allusions, echoes, events and anticipations relating to the Church are explained by this hidden reference to the idea of the Church kept by Christ and "those who survived": the chosen among the chosen people. The Lord Jesus, the key to the unity of the two Testaments, makes the Church whole.

5. The great law of the oikoumene

The story of salvation is a story of waiting. Judaism, which rests on the Old Testament alone, is seen as an unfinished story. Christianity, in its turn, awaits not only the end of time, but something else before the end of time, something that will bring about the effective realization of the unity of Jews and Gentiles. St Paul says that the defection of the Jews had been permitted and would last as long as the mass of the Gentiles had not entered into the Church; then Israel would enter also. So in spite of the movement of the faithful remnant of the old Israel into the new Church, in spite of the immense development of Christianity over twenty centuries, the Church is still waiting. The event she waits for most eagerly is not the welcoming in of new multitudes of Gentiles from Asia, but reconciliation with this little people among the nations. She is waiting until the Lord, who never ceases to watch over Christians and Jews, Gentiles and Jews, with the same mercy, allows that mysterious dialectic within himself to work again, which governs the unfolding of the story of salvation, the election of individuals, peoples and nations: the law of suffering and of mercy.

He allows the fall of some, so that others may be taken up. The faults of Israel, for which God has condemned them to that blindness which prevents them becoming Christian, are the same as those for which God reproached the Gentiles: idolatry and the seeking after their own justification. He allowed the defection of the mass of the Jews, so that the Gentiles might enter the Church. When man is reduced to nothing before God, he intervenes to save him. It is the Gentile, the object of scorn for the Jew, who has been saved, while the mass of the Jewish people remained blind. How much suffering since Abraham has it cost the Jews to remain the chosen people, the olive-tree which bore the grafted branches, the Gentiles! There is in the mystery of the suffering of Israel an element of vicarious redemption for the Gentiles which must move us profoundly. How far has not the vocation of the Gentiles to salvation been due to the suffering of Israel? Is it not possible that they, against their will, have often borne a fruit which was not for them, a fruit they knew nothing of, which drew from them a bitter sap, tortured them, deprived them of life, and left the olive tree weak and bloodless?

The misery of the Gentiles has been imposed on Israel as a burden to bear through their darkness. Israel has been forced, led to practise a torturing mercy that it neither asked for nor prayed for. The Lord has not spared them, neither when they did well nor when they fell into evil. He made demands upon them which surpassed any he made from other peoples. The most dramatic aspect of their fate is perhaps this character of the enforced bearing of the Gentiles from the womb of Israel, this obligation which God imposed on Israel for bearing and supporting a fruit not their own nor for them, but which Israel will perhaps one day recognize at the end of their exhaustion, the end of their long night, when their eyes are opened to the light.

A law of suffering and of mercy: such seems to be the great law of the *oikoumene,* since that is what has brought about the relationship between its two parts, the Jews and the Gentiles. "Bear the burden of one another's failings; then you will be fulfilling the law of Christ" (Gal 6:2); to take up the misery of one another, to be for each other—Jews, Protestants, Catholics, Orthodox, Anglicans—the ministers of mercy. In turn, all have suffered, all must bear the others in their hearts. It seems there is no deeper law to govern the relations of Christians among themselves, or of Jews and Christians.

CHAPTER XII

Renewal and Unity

I. THE PATHS TOWARDS UNITY

All these issues, all these problems lead up to an urgent and concrete question: what will the future of Christianity be? It was this question that was foremost in our thoughts while we endeavoured to distinguish the various factors involved in the problem of ecumenism, and to estimate the forces confronting each other, and to calculate the direction they will follow.

Will some forms of belief disappear? Will those that remain be unchanged? Some will inevitably expand. Can they do this and yet reject every kind of alliance? Into what forms will the new forces be moulded, and will these be creations of which the past was unaware?

Toynbee tells us that in periods of disintegration, the normal healthy reaction is towards a reconstitution of the separate parts in a new universal order whose standardization makes up for the previous breakdown. Are we to consider the attempt now being made by Christians to regain unity as the prelude of a great new epoch or merely as a moment of return in that rhythm of disunion—unity—disunion—which appears to be the law of historical change?

Christians of all denominations are looking for the source from which the greatest developments may be hoped, not simply those that startle, but those that last. We are trying to hold on to the lessons of the past and to alter our course accordingly, as we steer towards the future. Some of the experience we have gained and an understanding of certain invariable happenings have compelled us to adopt a measure of practical wisdom. Where, does the future of Christianity lie? In something absolutely new? In a reformation? In a renewal?

The great decisions of history take place in the human heart. There, many opposing attractions and callings necessitate harsh decisions. These are well worth living through, but after them there follows a feeling of confidence as the problem opens out into the suggestion of solutions that will govern the future. Particular issues are chosen, and the task then is to secure a general and free adhesion to them. Some issues are excluded, and to these also there must be a free assent. No approach will be easy. Whatever solutions may be accepted as a final goal, they must work out their embodied destiny in experience.

What will the future of Christianity be? This question arises when we compare the fragmental Christian bodies with the world in need of salvation. Does the path to the future lead towards change or conservation? Towards development or immobility? Is there no other solution for Protestantism than to continue its exploratory course and for Catholicism and Orthodoxy to remain the representatives of religious conservatism in the world? Will the future of all Christians show a parallel progress along separate paths, or will there be a mutual approach leading to unity?

1. Conflict or dilemma in the establishment of unity

Since the Reformation there have been three tendencies among those who have sought for Christian unity. Each of these has played an important part, outside Catholicism, in the movements towards reconciliation, and all things considered, it does not seem that the World Council of Churches wishes to sacrifice either one of them; it considers that all three together are necessary for the ecumenical movement. These tendencies are the Erasmian, the institutional and the pietist.[1]

On Erasmian lines, the condition *sine qua non* of unity is agreement on a small number of points of doctrine, considered to be necessary and fundamental. Preference will accordingly be given to the doctrinal pronouncements of the early Church, and later utterances on controversial issues will be shelved. In all matters not belonging to this essential core, there must be the greatest possible freedom, and no detailed confession of faith will be exacted.[2]

The second trend does not lay the emphasis primarily on doctrine, but on God's purpose in his calling of his people. What God intended when he gathered men together into a Church that was to be his Body, was above all to form a community that would glorify him. The task of Christians, therefore, will be to make this unity manifest in the world, a

---

[1] W. A. Visser 't Hooft, "Our Ecumenical Task in the Light of History", *The Ecumenical Review* (July 1955).

[2] Desiderius Erasmus, *Opera omnia emendatiora et auctiora* (1961: reprint of the edition of 1703–1706).

unity of fullness and not of the least common denominator. The Church as institution is central to this point of view.

The third trend puts its stress on individual experience and on Christian living. Christianity, it asserts, is fundamentally a personal experience, and provided the grace of justification has been received, a man genuinely belongs to the one community, whatever his visible allegiance to any particular Church may be. It follows from this that questions about Church and doctrine are of interest only in so far as they contribute to individual conversion, and what essentially matters is unity of action in the part taken in a common missionary work of evangelization.

The ecumenical movement realizes all it owes to each of these three sources of inspiration. It may be said that the movements of "Faith and Order" and of "Life and Work" correspond approximately to these three tendencies in the spheres of doctrine, structure and action.

The crux of the problem is that of integrating and reconciling the nature of the Church with her mission, the community aspect of Christianity with its individual aspect, collective experience with individual life. The constant temptation is to secure an agreement that takes into account only one aspect of the total problem of unity, and to propound a formula that would leave Christendom disunited. The method of "fundamental points" in its crude form has been dropped, but it comes back, travestied, in the following proposition: Let us discard dogmatic definitions—under one aspect or another, these are always exploratory and approximate—and unite in the bond of facts, of "realities". Others say: retain any particular doctrine that may be received in your Church as infallibly defined; for our part, we shall accept it as a theological opinion. And yet a third group suggests: within the unity of the Church, you will represent its organization; we, its prophetic element; and the others, mysticism. Let us realize that we are the Church, and leave to God the task of working it out.

Some indeed consider that theology should be left to theologians, primarily emphasize the pastoral and concrete point of view, particularly the protection of Christianity against materialism and atheism. They are thinking of a pragmatic unity of collective action, or else of a subjective unity in love. Let us love one another, love increasingly, and not bother about anything apart from love. Then we shall be united. Let us work together and leave theological quarrels on one side. Then we shall be united. Let us not impose our own way of expressing our faith upon others. Then we shall be united. Let us allow ourselves to be gripped by those Christian realities that are beyond discussion, and not ask what they effect or how they work, but believe simply that they exist in order to produce a vital achievement. Then we shall be united.

Those who are disturbed by institutional difficulties believe that the solution lies in the distinction between the unity given in Christ and unity in history. They ask: has not the Church always existed in Christ? Most certainly. Therefore, since unity is inseparable from the Church, unity has always existed. "The Church", says Karl Barth, "is as certainly one as God is one".[3] Her visible, external unity, has been broken, fragmented and obscured, but this has not affected the Church's invisible unity. That invisible unity is the original and essential unity, and because it is grounded on and in Christ, it is completely indestructible. Historical divisions have never succeeded and never will succeed in affecting it. Therefore we are able to be one in Christ although at the same time we are divided as Churches. We are at once united and divided, just as we are at once righteous and sinners; united and righteous in the Lord; sinners and divided in the Church as she has existed in history.[4] On this view, through the conviction of invisible unity, we can be consoled for the unity that has been lost. Visible unity is not related to invisible unity by a relationship of continuity, but only as an extrinsic sign or an indication of it.

But this does not mean that visible unity is held to be of little worth. On the contrary, every means is used to exalt it, for if it is true that unity is already possessed in God, must it not be proven by works that exhibit unity? The entire meaning of the movement for ecumenical reconciliation that has matured in Protestantism for a century rests on this conviction. A theology of unity resulting from the fundamental principles of the Reformation, in particular the Lutheran doctrine of the simultaneity of righteousness and sin as modified by Calvin, has become the present theory underlying ecumenical action. This explanation was virtually contained in the original principles of the Reformation, and contemporary theologians have explicitly developed them. Luther and Calvin could not give up the idea of a universal Church. This was too clearly expressed in the Bible. But though they retained the idea, they transferred it from the visible to the invisible Church. The Church of faith is the true Church: she is united, and cannot fail to be united, for she is in Christ, and Christ is the immortal living One. So the Church's unity truly exists even today, in spite of the disunion of the Churches that have a fragmented existence over the earth's surface. It exists and cannot not exist because her being and her unity are transported into the new life with Christ through his death and resurrection. Visible unity does not exist apart from some visible elements such as baptism and scripture, and this is another way of saying that the Church belongs at once to the former and to the new era: in a mysterious and hidden way she lives her renewed existence and her unity

---

[3] K. Barth, *Die Theologie und die Kirche* (1928), p. 289.
[4] Welch, *The Reality of the Church*; J. Robert Nelson, *The Realm of Redemption: Studies in the Doctrine of the Nature of the Church in Contemporary Theology* (1951).

in Christ; but this great reality does not extend its coherence to the situation on earth. Therefore both Christians and their Churches are divided: *Ecclesia simul justa et peccatrix, simul una et divisa*. In this era, condemned to pass away, the Church's life is that of a repentant sinner. Her sin consists in the divided state of her soul and body, but God has promised that one day, the eighth day, she shall be healed. In the meanwhile Christians, through their search for unity, must raise the standard of the coming victory, the victory of unity over division, the victory of which they are certain, as certain as the fact that the dying Christ on the Cross took upon himself all divisions past, present and to come, and in return was given unity in the Holy Spirit by his Father. The new life and the new unity will continue to grow together with sin and division, like the tares and the wheat, in the afflicted ground of the human condition until the harvest. Then division will be cast into the fire and unity will expand over the finally realized epoch of the Parousia.

The Church's unity is thus not something to be achieved: it already exists and has never been interrupted. What remains to be done is to indicate its meaning, proclaim it, manifest it. In spite of our divisions, we are united: invisible unity has been acquired and cannot be taken away. Our task is to show, through works of union, co-operation and reconciliation, that we are already one in hidden unity in Christ. This will be done chiefly through the word of proclamation. The world declares that Christians are disunited. But no: it should realize that we are one in the Lord, and although we are externally divided, this is because we are sinners. Since, however, we know that we are mysteriously one already, we set ourselves to show signs of this. Thus, combating our sin and our natural inclinations, we associate ourselves with the victory that Christ has already won. We express our hope that we may share in it, and keeping in sight the firmly promised goal, we employ all our strength to follow the difficult path of unity. The non-Christian world is not left out of this view of things; in fact it is explicitly invited to look forward to the proclamation of that unity already achieved in Christ. But because our external divisions scandalize the world, we must urgently try to provide a serious manifestation of that grace of unity which in Christ is ours. Certain external conditions will be requisite; there must at least be a large measure of agreement on doctrine, the sacraments and the ministry; doubtless also some permanent body, a council or a conference. But all uniform or centralized forms of government under a controlling authority must be avoided.

The decisive word underlying this standpoint that has now acquired the status of common agreement in Protestant ecumenism is the verb "to manifest". Just as the Church on earth is the sign of the gathering of all men into Christ, the source and origin of the new mankind, so the unity of the Church on earth is the sign of the unity achieved in Christ. The Church in Christ, the Church of faith, the Church as the eschatological reality, can never fail. This is also true of unity, since it belongs to the same sphere. But the Church in history does not enjoy the same privilege. She is not indefectible, and her visible unity has perhaps never existed. The Church of faith and the Church of history are two distinct realities. The Church of history has the importance of a sign of the Church of faith, but no interior continuity connects them. They are divided by a frontier—that of the total corruption of human nature. In the same way, the unity of the Church of history makes manifest the Church's unity as an eschatological reality; it witnesses to it and is an expression of it; it prefigures and foreshadows it. But nothing more.

Everything clearly turns on the great problem of the eschatological reality and its relationship with time. A doctrine originating in that reality is bound to possess extraordinary power. We can see this in the dynamism of Protestant ecumenism. Catholicism, too, has always found the secret of its unity and the decisive motive of its concern for Christian reunion in this same reality. But there is disagreement as to its nature. Protestantism holds it to be transcendent but extrinsic; Catholicism believes that it is transcendent, but that the historical process has a part in it.

Protestantism considers that the Catholic idea of a participation in the divine nature contradicts God's transcendence. And yet what could be more transcendent than the introduction of a new ontology of being, a new way of God's self-communication to men, a new intimate relation of friendship with him? Transcendence does not lose its nature when it gives itself. Is it possible that we could so delude ourselves as to imagine that we have bestowed on ourselves what in reality comes down from above? The eschatological reality, without ceasing to be transcendent, becomes the active presence of grace and unity within the visible Church, that Church of history which is also the Church of faith: one in its visibility and its invisibility. We see that she is historical, but we believe that she is trans-historical. She is a sign of the realities of heaven, but she also brings these to men and she does this effectively, not through her power divorced from the Presence, but through that very Presence which dwells in her. The Church is such, a living body, Christ's mystical Body, only through her actual and vital relationship with her Head and Leader. The indwelling of the Three divine Persons, the gift of the Holy Spirit, the regal Presence of the risen Christ—these are the eschatological realities that govern the efficacy, the unity, and, in fact, the whole being of the Church. There is no magic in all this, for it is the Lord who is acting through his Church. What are we taking away from God? Is it not too obvious that our feeble manhood is lost in the brilliance of his luminous and active presence? Where is the self-sufficiency and pride, since human work in the Church, aiming at renewal, reunion and the regaining of community, is accomplished through the power of the eschatological "energies" present within her?

The mystery of the Church's unity is the mystery of the divine community of the Three Persons transforming men, whom sin has scattered, into a unity restored through the unitive power of the Father, Son and Holy Spirit. The Catholic Church stands out as the universal sacrament of the religious unity of the world, and it could not be otherwise if the Kingdom of God has been really inaugurated on earth through the presence of the ultimate realities: the Holy Spirit, the eschatological gift to the Church; the Lord's body and blood through which the Father's love enters into our souls. In addition, we can, even now, experience a foretaste of that mystery, which we can reach only through the obscurity of faith, clearing a path through the ambiguities and distorting envies of history. Our true being is in the Lord, and the Lord is both in heaven and on earth. He it is who has made the Church of history identical with the Church of faith and ensured that all justified men are visibly or invisibly attached to the Church of history. The Catholic Church has a profound conviction of her maternal responsibility for all men, in whatever religion they may be found.[5]

How can anyone fail to see the dramatic nature of the spiritual conflict in which we are all involved and which awaits a solution in light, love and kindness? The logic of Protestantism demands that the search for unity must mean that the invisible Church shall be delivered (from its confinement) in the visible Churches. For Catholicism, this search consists in delivering Christians from their fragmentation so that they may communicate in the Catholica. The desire for reconciliation is common to all; but for Protestants this would take the form of a unity that transcends all the communions, while for Catholics it would take place within a visible communion whose universality springs from the eschatological realities that dwell within it. Protestants look for the visible unity of the Church as the seal of her invisible unity and the foreshadowing of the final unity of the Church in heaven. Catholics, on the other hand, consider visible unity as indeed the sign of invisible unity, but also as the sacrament of that unity, and they attribute a causal significance to it with reference to the establishment of the invisible unity. Visible unity is not only the confirmation of our spiritual unity in the Lord; it also has the significance of a material and efficacious sign.

[5] C. Journet, *L'Église du Verbe incarné*, vol. II, chapter viii, section iii, "Les membres du Christ et de l'Église" (1951), English translation: *The Church of the Word Incarnate* (1951); Gregory Baum, *That They May Be One; A Study of Papal Doctrine* (1958), chapter iv, pp. 89–91: "The Church, Mother of Dissidents".

And this is why although we both proclaim the invisible and visible unity of the Church, we are still divided! Moreover, the Protestant world feels itself to be freer than we are with respect to the visible forms of unity. In principle, every form that ensures the proclamation of the existence of that invisible unity, already a reality in heaven, seems good to it. Catholicism, however, believes that the relationship between visible and invisible unity is such that it prohibits the acceptance of certain forms.

2. The phenomenon of self-healing

The characteristic of Christianity transmitted by the dissident Churches is not the sin of schism or of heresy: it is the Christian heritage affected by a heresy or a schism. A distinction must be carefully drawn between a doctrine and the way it is held, between a principle in its *de jure* condition, and its concrete existential mode. A proposition may, in itself, be formally heretical or schismatic, and yet in a local Church or in an individual Christian it may not be so, through the absence of culpable obstinacy in holding it. [6]

Conclusions of considerable importance for ecumenism follow from this fact. The first is that of an immense movement of self-healing beginning at the Reformation and the separation between East and West. If we take into account the share of responsibility on the Catholic side, the terrible ambiguities of history during those troubled times and the subjective sincerity of the authors of the withdrawal by the Eastern Churches and by those Churches that changed over to the Reformation, it is difficult not to think that such events could have been produced without a grave objective sin, technically called heresy or schism.

But time passes, traditions take shape, children are born into a Church which they receive as their heritage together with life. The reading of the Bible, the hearing of the Word of God, the life of worship, the fashioning of daily life according to Christian precepts—all these lead to the establishment of a Christian way of living and of intercourse within a communion which, though mutilated, become for their members the normal way of salvation. The sin of schism and heresy steadily recedes, and in the process, the powers of grace present in the mutilated Christian heritage tend to reassert themselves. The grace of Christianity is a reality so powerful that it constantly tends to expand its healing power at the same time as it is transmitting life. [7] A child who grows up in this non-

---

[6] Journet, *op. cit.*, vol. II, chapter vi, section ii, 4th div.: "Heresy", 5th: "Schism".
[7] Baum, *op. cit.*, chapter iii, pp. 67–68.

Catholic communion makes, in good faith, the outlook of his Church his own. Only its most educated members are in a position to ratify personally the decisions taken by their ancestors; and even then it is very difficult for them to reach a decision that will be identical in meaning with that of the initiators of the separation. Education, good faith, habit, loyalty to the received outlook, all contribute to make it a question of conscience to act in this way. A paradoxical situation then results: on the one hand there is a movement towards the fullness of Christian truth, due to the abiding nature of Christian values, and on the other, the justification of the resolve to remain in one's own communion. How can we think that this resolve, even if accompanied by an expression rejecting the Catholic Church, is sufficient to constitute an objective sin? We should say rather that this is a paradoxical, although very common, case of the coexistence of two different planes of value; one of them, on the conscious level, arising from education, good faith and habit; and the other existing in a more hidden region of the soul and dependent upon the objective realities that possess it. These latter have intrinsically, a mark of origin and an end, which lead them to their rightful position, even though, on the plane of explicit consciousness, their outlook may be twisted in a different direction. This Christian, therefore, in tendency belongs to the Church. It is an antithetical and paradoxical situation: two levels of life and two levels of belonging are in conflict: the deeper level with its source in the true Church, and the more obvious level originating in the communion of which he is a visible member. It is also true that, in fact, it is through his belonging to the communion of which he is a member that he is enabled to belong in tendency to the Church of Christ.

We Catholics, therefore, have, outside the juridical boundaries of the Church, a multitude of real brethren in Protestantism, Orthodoxy, Anglicanism, Judaism, as well as in the non-Christian religions. And in a very special way, we may always be sure that there is no self-deception when we call a Protestant, an Anglican or an Orthodox Christian our brother. We know that their belonging to the Catholic Church, although not complete, is real, and that it goes much further than they believe, even though they deny it when it is put to them. They will find our way of interpreting their position in relation to the Catholic Church unacceptable. But this thought of their belonging is one we cherish. The least we ask them is not to take it from us, but to allow us to cherish it, if only to please us. We shall, therefore, always be able to hope that if on all sides within Catholicism an awareness of the infinite network of this belonging became a reality, an immense way of love would sweep away many obstacles.

The ecumenical movement may be rightly regarded as a vast effort at self-healing. Each communion has its own mutilations, and ours are greater than those of Protestantism, Anglicanism and Orthodoxy. The Catholic Church suffers from three world-wide mutilations: the first is the loss of the Jewish world; the second is the secession of the Eastern Churches; and the third is the rupture of the Reformation. Our ills are greater than theirs.

II. RENEWAL AND UNITY

1. Renewal and unity are interconnected

Two facts call for our attention. In contemporary Protestantism renewal has been bound up with ecumenism.[8] In Catholicism, the summoning of the ecumenical council had Christian unity in mind. There is thus a shared conviction: renewal and unity belong together. Does this not suggest that reform and renewal cannot be completely real while the main Christian bodies are in a state of separation? So that the question is not so much what conditions for a satisfactory renewal are necessary within a state of separation, but rather, whether a genuine reform and renewal can fully achieve their purpose if the positive influence of the aim of Christians being reunited throughout the world remains excluded?

If we think of the reformed communions of the fifteenth and sixteenth centuries, we are tempted to ask whether a real reform is possible without getting rid of the spirit of secession. And from a Catholic point of view, is the renewal demanded by a new age a possibility unless it is part and parcel of an ecumenical outlook?

The general explanation of this is obvious. Particular parts deprived of their complements cannot achieve completion. Even if we assert that the visible unity of the Church already exists and that it is to be found in the Catholic Church, must we not admit that she lacks an "accidental" perfection? And in this case the adjective does not mean something merely circumstantial or insignificant—as history amply shows.

We shall never achieve the healing of divided Christendom if we have in mind only the separate healing of Protestantism, Anglicanism, Orthodoxy and Catholicism. Juxtaposed healings are only mental illusions, for healing means the re-integration of scattered members. This is why the second Vatican Council, primarily summoned with a view to renewal of the Catholic Church, necessarily came to include Christian reunion. Its primary purpose was the Church's welfare, but another purpose was associated with it: the unity of all Christians. A second stage developed: the Catholic Church was made ready to engage in the work of reunion.

[8] W. A. Visser 't Hooft, *Le Renouveau de l'Église* (1960).

This procedure offers a programme for the other Christian communions also: each of them should think of the common welfare of its members, but only as a stage in the general purpose of Christian reconciliation.

The problem of reunion must be envisaged as concerned with the healing of whole communions. The questions at issue are too close to the essence and heart of Christianity, and the renewal involved is too highly significant for this universal effort to be able to be reduced to a series of quasi-contractual engagement between Church leaders, a kind of ecclesiastical deal: return to the Catholic Church and we will permit you to keep this and that, or else, admit this point and we will accept you.

May God preserve us from undertaking the work of Christian reunion with a mentality unworthy of the goal being sought. Diplomacy will be necessary, but are we engaged in diplomacy? Concessions will be useful, but is it a matter of concessions? Corporate reunion will entail an element of external relations, but it is not a transaction, not even an ecclesiastical transaction. A false approach will be quickly detected through its unhappy results. Opportunism, superficiality and dubious motivation are guaranteed to wreck ecumenical relations.

Ecumenism, on either side, cannot succeed without a profound effort at renewal. That is the touchstone of genuine ecumenism. If an enquirer feels that an attempt is being made to overcome and change him, but that the person attempting this shows no sign of seeking any deepening or spiritual renewal of his own life, relations will be soon broken off; they will have been unreal from the start because no true dialogue has existed. The foundation of dialogue is the search in common for the fullness of truth; the partners in it must have a lively realization that they are both engaged in that search. It will lead them, through spiritual fellowship, to seek the greatest benefits for each other, and to share them to the extent that they can gain them.

In a dialogue, no good results from bitter criticism of one's own Church or denomination. Whatever its defects or deficiencies may be, whatever its spiritual wealth or poverty, it has been responsible for the upbringing of each of us, and if a man has been born into a denomination, even if it is the oddest denomination, it has been the means of his becoming a Christian. To shirk this fact through embarrassment or to pretend that it does not exist, is of no avail, and such criticism foisted on another in order to display "broad-mindedness" does fundamentally harm mutual esteem. Defects have to be admitted, of course, but the way this is done makes all the difference.

To sum up: our problem is to discover what conditions are essential for a reform that will end separation and for a renewal that will develop into ecumenical proportions.

If we compare the present position with what we hope to reach, we shall discover, through our attempts at mutual conversion and through the common effort to reach the fullness of truth, what conditions are necessary in order to achieve a genuine reform and a successful renewal. And this great prevenient grace that will have awakened every Christian to appreciate what unity means, will have fulfilled its purpose.

2. Conditions for a reform that will end separation and for a renewal that leads towards unity

A. OBEDIENCE TO THE WORD OF GOD

It is not at the discretion of Christian communions to decide whether or not they must take the path of unity. The Word of God has made the decision for us: it has shown that unity is the plan and purpose of God. Did not our Lord desire one Church, one alliance, one familiy, one house, one single body. The present-day explanation of our Lord's great prayer for unity (Jn, chapters 13–17) interprets it in an ecumenical sense. Literally, it may have referred to a union between Jews and Gentiles, but implicitly it refers to unity to its fullest extent. In any case, contemporary ecumenism and even the magisterium of the Catholic Church accepts this wider meaning.

The Word of God has a special grace: it induces obedience to faith. When we accept its authority, we are given the grace to obey it. So long as it has not broken and abolished our resistance, it will have the right to demand our perseverance in submission to its action. Besides, it will not allow us to escape: if it puts forward a plan for unity, it will have the creative ability to carry it through. In any case, is it not the Word of God in our time that has awakened us all to an understanding of what unity means? If, therefore, we believe in it, we cannot avoid obeying it.

B. UNDERSTANDING THE SIN OF SEPARATION

Admittedly we are all sinners. Let us try to be sinners who know the meaning of their sin.

The importance of non-theological factors in producing separation has been sufficiently stressed. We must avoid two pitfalls: that of examining sin without reference to anything that contributes to it; and that of making it a perfectly natural phenomenon to be explained by sociology or psychology. It is, in fact, the result of complex factors and, to understand it, we must try not to neglect any of its aspects. Such knowledge is not required from every Christian, but the Church as such should be aware of it, and its component elements should, therefore, be known.[9] The purpose of this knowledge of sin is union with God and communion with the Church. Separation through schism or heresy is a sin. The Church needs to understand it fully. Knowledge of the sociological and psychological factors involved cannot explain everything, but they do need to be known. A narrowly moralistic or emotional attitude is as incomplete as a purely sociological or psychological explanation. Separation is a sin, and this must not be covered up; but it is also a complex reality and, therefore, calls for an attempt to grasp it as a whole.

If we reflect on the various stages of the ecumenical movement in general, we shall discover all we owe to reconsideration of our past. We know, for example, the considerable part played by the missions in provoking that critical attitude within the Protestant bodies that resulted in the movements "Life and Work" and "Faith and Order", in the general assemblies, in the meetings between pastors and theologians, and which has assumed the proportions of a huge process of self-examination, a new look at every aspect of Christianity. Without critical self-questioning, without a reassessment of customary attitudes and points of view, without a new approach and a reconsideration of the problems involved, no readjustment or improvement is possible. Each communion will remain self-enclosed, convinced of its own perfection, and will merely be waiting for outsiders to come in. Any Church or denomination, which considers that it is those outside who are the separatists, is unconsciously led merely to wait until these outsiders return. The Catholic Church, for instance, has long been content to await the return of the dissidents. Anglicanism is waiting for the Methodists, the Methodists are waiting for those bodies that have broken away from them, and the same attitude is repeated *ad infinitum* whenever a Christian communion has undergone an amputation. But waiting leads nowhere. The door must be opened in a new way; the house must be looked at objectively, and an attempt made to see it as outsiders see it. Has it no defects? Is it unwelcoming? Is not this brother now coming towards us uncommonly like a foreigner?

Heresy and schism are usually considered from a single point of view, that of a lapse from Catholic belief. But since sheer imperfection cannot exist as an entity, must there not be some positive element in the great separatist movements? The breakaway was due to excessive tension. And yet, may not this tension have been caused by a search for compensation and balance? A definitive separation indicates a movement that has gone

[9] Augustin Cardinal Bea, "How University Research and Teaching Can Further Christian Unity", chapter vii in *The Unity of Christians* (1963).

too far and passed all acceptable bounds. At the same time it also indicates that questions have been asked whose significance cannot be dismissed. At least as an hypothesis, we may ask whether the great Protestant return to the Word of God was not an attempt to compensate for the absence of the Semitic element in the Church, and whether its stress on the eschatological realities was not an attempt to re-establish the balance upset by the departure of the Eastern Churches from the Catholic Church. The reaction was doubtless excessive, but may it not have represented an effort to re-establish an equilibrium that had been disturbed? Was it not an attempt to restore at least one aspect of an imbalance? The drama was not sought out; it arose because, after a certain point, the movement got out of control, and as a result, the Churches and communions that changed their allegiance at the Reformation became involved in a unilateralism whose echoes, in spite of every effort to regain a balanced position, can still be heard.

One of the greatest lessons that we learn from the history of unity and separation is that in both unity and separation, all the elements are of a piece. The Jewish, Protestant, Anglican, Orthodox and Catholic problems can be stated as a single issue: how men who have been divided by sin may recapture their unity.

It cannot be affirmed *a priori* that every heresy and schism is a sign of a real lack and deficiency in the Christian communion to which these are opposed. That would be to forget the artifices of Satan, and to by-pass the influence of non-theological factors in producing separation. Even if the greatest care is taken to prevent them, heresy and schism will remain a possibility until the end of the world. However this may be, it seems very difficult to dismiss completely a whole series of interconnected weaknesses to which many historical facts bear witness, and in fact the major separatist movements in history have enough in common to make it necessary now to view them as a single whole, and to approach them with a world-wide strategy, if there is to be a response adequate for the restoration of unity.

Life, growth and healing are organic phenomena; the health of any one part affects the whole; and the whole body fights to sustain or promote the part that is suffering or growing.

In Protestantism, no liturgical renewal has taken place without a reassessment of the ministry, nor any progress in the understanding of either liturgy or ministry, without an increased appreciation of the Church's mission, and that inevitably involves a thorough examination of the nature of the Church herself.

An analogous phenomenon is perceptible in Catholicism. The renewal in biblical studies, in worship, in the doctrine of the Church, has made the concern for ecumenism possible, and this in turn has affected the entire range of Catholic life. The Church will certainly no longer be the same after experiencing the ecumenical movement. She will have a fresh spiritual outlook, and forgotten aspects of her corporate existence, of her mission, and of the Word will have been regained.

C. THE FEAR OF GOD AND HIS JUSTICE

It is a very strange fact that in the quest for unity this sense of awe does not occupy its due position. Before Christians accepted separation, did they ponder at length what the consequences of their action upon the world's salvation would be? Some part of the ineffectiveness of the apostolate that has struck the Christian world may be seen as the result of divine justice. How have we come to forget God's words to the seven Churches of the Apocalypse? And yet these Churches all belonged to the undivided Church. We are meeting immense difficulties in carrying out the Church's mission in both non-Christian and Christian society; we are at grips with secularism, atheism and indifference, and we have never thought that this might well be not only a trial that Christians must undergo, but also a punishment for the sin of separation. Christians are the salt of the earth and the light of the world, but separated, these qualities lose their power. When their unity disappears, their bright light becomes hidden under a bushel. God's visitation of ourselves is to be seen in the unbelief of the world. Of course we do good deeds, but why must we use them to justify our apalling self-righteousness? The rediscovery of the fear of God and his justice is evidently another touchstone of any genuine attempt to restore unity.

So long as Protestants, Catholics, Anglicans and Orthodox live in their own enclosures, they have a feeling that they lack nothing. Behind their frontiers, sure of their possessions, they organize their life in an autarchic way, and not observing the others, never suspect their worth. The idea that they may lack anything never enters their head, and if anyone ventures to suggest it, the indiscretion is met with ostracism. Insufficiency is transformed into a sacred self-sufficiency; personal humiliations heap up into a huge collective pride; and many unselfish actions are merged in a sanctified egoism. The ecumenical movement is a universal and complementary attempt to heal traditions that have been mutilated and to reconcile brethren that have been separated.

The statement that in the Catholic Church nothing is lacking and that through reunion she would receive no benefit as regards her catholicity, and that only the others would benefit, conceals an indefinable and unconscious apologetic concern, a fear of seeming insufficiently orthodox, and ultimately a lack of love for the fullness of Catholic truth. On this view, the Church would need Protestants, Orthodox and Anglicans not for her sake, but for theirs. It is not because their absence constitutes any lack in her; but without them, she is deprived of a sphere in which her catholicity may radiate, and through reunion she could enter zones now closed to her influence.

But this attitude is accompanied by an unconscious sacred egocentricism which can easily become irritating. What do we expect from the ecumenical movement? Is it the healing of those "outside"? Of mutilated traditions? Does it mean that some truths we have neglected are recalled to our minds through the ecumenical dialogue? Does it mean the setting up of a system of religious exchange between the Christian communions? What utter unawareness can suggest that the Church has not suffered when the great movements of separation occurred and that no trace of the amputations she has undergone is perceptible in her body and soul?

After these wounds there followed a long period of numbness. Ecumenism's first task is to make us realize that these wounds are real; its second, that they can be healed.

It is true that it is always possible to find consolation in the fact that the Catholic Church has never ceased to be united in spite of the secession of the Jews, the Orthodox and the Protestants, and that Christ's prayer has already found its fulfilment in Catholic unity. But in fact the unity of the Church of mankind suffers from omissions which contradict the solidarity of the human race; the unity of the Church of the apostolic hierarchy suffers from the omission of other bishops who share the apostolic succession, and who are equally responsible for the world's salvation; the unity of the Church of the Incarnation suffers from the hindrance to the purpose of the Incarnation which is to make all mankind one; and lastly, the unity of the Church of the Trinity suffers from the distortion of the image of that interpersonal communion which is the Christian community's gift to man.

Because Protestant and Orthodox Christians are outside the visible frontiers of the Church, their relationship with Catholics is often envisaged solely in canonical terms, and unconsciously a sound point of view is transformed into a false generalization which amounts to this: everything in the Catholic Church is Christian: everything outside is not. From this it naturally follows that on the one side nothing is lacking, and on the other, everything is defective. It is a picture obviously governed by a narrow legalism. That cannot be the full mystery of the Church. She is a body, a living organism, and the prototype of her unity is that of mystical union. The influence of this unity is not restricted to those who are officially recognized as her members. So she can suffer wherever the mystical area of her influence extends. She genuinely suffers from the mutilation endured by those who have separated from her. Is she not a family, and what familiy of any moral standing fails to make its children's suffering its own, even the suffering of those who have rejected it? So long as a Catholic has not inwardly admitted that the mutilation undergone by the Jewish people through their general dismissal of the apostles' appeal, and those suffered by the Eastern Churches and the Protestant communions, are his also; so long as he has not made their ecumenical problem his own, he has not yet opened his heart to the most universal boundaries of the Church. He remains a man with a legalistic mind: what is inside the Church, he accepts; what is outside, he forgets. He misses that dimension of the Church which admits the fact that Christians may legally be outside official and complete membership and yet be joined to her and be real partakers of her mystery which through times of obscurity, clouded vision and exile, continues its life in circumstances of deprivation and with the need for reconciliation.

If these suppositions are correct, then a definite way of seeking the cure of mutilated traditions becomes obligatory. First of all, and above all, we must admit the reality of these mutilations, put them before our Lord and humbly confess all that his Church lost when the Jewish people as a whole refused to follow the little Jewish and Gentile Church at its beginning, and when later, in Christendom, one separation begot another from century to century. There is something scarcely Catholic in the pretence that the fragmentation of the Protestant world, as the years have passed, has been a series of events solely within Protestantism, in no way affecting us. Nothing Christian should be alien to a Catholic. We have been led unconsciously to confuse the perfection of Christ with the perfection of his Body. Nothing is lacking in Christ, unless it is ourselves for whom he gives himself. But how much is lacking in the Church of mankind? How many cultures, human characteristics and national types that give balance and wholeness to the way Christianity is expressed are missing! Even the Church of the apostolic hierarchy is not without its suffering: consider the relationships between the leaders of the Churches on both sides that might be renewed and developed.

The Church wholeheartedly welcomes every real element of Christ's Body wherever it is found and whatever its shape and intensity. Genuine fragments of the Church remain alive even in exile, and though their light may be dimmed, experience shows that it can be revived. The separated part longs for its position in the whole, and that from which it is separated shares its desire for oneness in unity.

No Church or Christian communion should be afraid of confessing its deficiencies to our Lord. If we say that we are in perfect health, what can we obtain from God's mercy?

D. THE SUMMONS TO HOPE

Unity is a great light. Darkness begins with division. Such is the lesson of experience. We see it verified in the life of the undivided Church. How did Christianity, originating as a sect within Judaism, acquire the force to expand and to conquer the Roman Empire? How did the human mind, at grips with the vast novelty of the revealed mystery, manage to keep together in a single whole all the elements of truth in its universality? How did the undivided Church find the resources for its expansion to Africa, Asia, Europe and the North? These things accomplished by our ancestors in the faith have their explanation in the power of unity. The more the Church was one, the more she was resplendent.

Consider also the experience of Protestantism during the last century. How can anyone fail to be struck by the fact that the light has grown brighter as its various communions have drawn closer together. Significant truths have been rediscovered and restored to a position of honour which would have been undreamt of a century ago. The Protestant world is engaged in a complete revaluation of Christianity. No problem—the nature of the Church and of Christianity, the function of the ministry, the meaning of worship, Christian unity, Jewish and Gentile reconcilia- tion—is outside its scope.

Is there any need for us Catholics to prove that the more united the Church has been (this does not necessarily mean the more uniform), the more light she has given forth?

Why do unity and light go hand in hand? Because being and unity are convertible with truth which is light. Increase in unity leads to an increase in the splendour of being. But imperfection of being is expressed in the poverty of its action. Meagre doctrine, weak activity, an absence of any united front between corporate bodies—these follow inevitably from division. The constitutive elements of truth only give forth their full light when they are integrated into a whole.

Unity also is important as a catharsis: the truth is a deliverance. Its liberating power is in proportion to its wholeness. Disrupted factors on their own tend to excess: when they are united they correct each other, criticize each other, and find their right position. Every communion and every truth which isolates itself is exposed to hypertrophy and self- adulation. Lack of catholicity in an individual, in a truth, in a communion or a Church, is always a seed bed of excess and imbalance. But increase in the spirit of universality brings with it rectification, harmony and peace. Unity is a great light, and light is the indispensable condition for healing.

Unity, furthermore, entails communication, an interchange of life and intercommunion. When each part respects its position within the orbit as a whole, it both receives and gives; it shines with the collective light; it is lost and found again in the communal reality. Great deeds are thus made possible.

If we look beyond the political and religious rivalries that have marked the history of the relationships between East and West, we may note that the great periods of the conversion of the world have corresponded to the great periods of unity, first in the time of the apostles, and later in the era of the undivided Church. Perhaps it may be objected that in spite of the separation of modern times a considerable missionary expansion has occurred. But it was precisely this missionary effort which brought the problem of unity to the forefront, and it has provided a fresh proof that the Church's mission is only perfectly carried out when she is united. The missionary problem among Christians of today can be solved only if they draw together and become one.

The great Christian tragedy does not lie in the fact that its light fails to shine in the world, but that its beams conflict. Our experience of the results of reunion, even if they have been the slightest, must strengthen our conviction that unity bestows a hundredfold increase in the power to give forth light upon every movement that tends towards it. Light fails to yield its full radiance when it does not issue from unity.

Lastly, the importance of unity can be seen if we reflect on the way in which the "notes" of the Church are interconnected. There are four of them and unity is their foundation. Holiness, catholicity, and apostolicity are its modes, reflecting its different aspects.

All progress in unity leads, therefore, infallibly to a corresponding progress in catholicity and apostolicity, that is, in the power to develop anew. We ordinarily think of unity as its own reward. But, in fact, the range of its influence is immense. It cannot be too often repeated that every degree of unity, however minute, is significant. Not an atom of it is lost; it bears fruit in a light that shines over he world.

God's judgements are not ours; even so we may be allowed to think that a world united in religion is a holier world than a world divided, and that, therefore, the world that we experience has increased in holiness through the struggle for unity that has taken place in its midst. We may also believe that God, who judges all things truly, knows that together with those vast forces directly ranged against him, there are Christian forces eager to advance under the banner of his kingly rule.

Hope has no greater sustenance than the preview of a great fulfilment whose attractive power widens in proportion to our acceptance of it. The conversion of the world again becomes meaningful.

E. THE LOVE OF UNITY IN ITS BEGINNING

Are we always certain that we really love unity even when we live within it? May we not forget that there is a wider unity to be loved? Love, in this instance also, demands a beginning.

Christian communions cannot think only of themselves; reunion must also fill their minds. They must seek out meeting points, or rather, they must develop their hidden points of contact, so that the power of reform and healing which motivates them may pass from one to the other and effect a complete reconciliation.

We are unaware of what we already owe to these secret and invisible bonds. Since Christians meet together, at least subjectively, in the same Christ, it follows that in him they are mysteriously indebted to each other for spiritual boons. Not self-healing, but mutual healing would seem to be the correct term for what happens when Christians pray for each other, become responsible for each other, and extend their concern as far as the reunion of all Christians. The visible members of the Church are anxious for the salvation of her unknown members; they hold them in their hearts and spiritually incorporate them in their own visible belonging, in the part they take in worship, in the sacraments and in their hearing of the Word. It is even possible that unknown members of the Church may sustain her visible members. For how many things are we indebted to others without knowing it! This is true of us all, Jews, Catholics, Orthodox, Anglicans and Protestants, and it explains why sometimes we feel so close to others who belong to different denominations. The bonds of ecumenism are already in existence.

There is both mystery and grandeur in the work of the Church, carried out in conjunction with her Lord, work whose full implications will only be disclosed later on. As in the night on the sea, the Church picks up a man without seeing him or knowing his name. What she does has repercussions to infinity. She may have some idea of this, but God alone knows its true extent. She has accepted the position of mother to the human race, but a mother who knows neither the time when her children come to her, nor the mode of their belonging.

Union and reconciliation have their beginning in the human heart, in the love of what already unites us, through the strengthening of those fundamental bonds which provide the sustenance for the ecumenical movement within suffering and divided Christendom. Division begins with a schism in the soul, and it is in the soul that any restoration also must begin.

May the ancient spirit of undivided Christendom, held captive behind the barriers engendered by the conflicts in history, by routine and spiritual enervation, again become self-confident! If the attempt is made, it will regain every Christian, every Christian communion, every Church. The age-long slothful idea that all is lost has now been defeated. The visible unity of the Christian family has become evident. A real understanding has been achieved, and the hidden sources of energy that have sustained it, are not exhausted.

F. REPENTANCE AND A NEW LOOK AT OUR PAST

Cardinal Journet has aptly remarked: The Church is not without sinners; she is without sin.[10] Catholics, therefore, have a definite responsibility with regard to the sin of separation. An official document of the Church bids us admit our own part in this wrong-doing. "They (the bishops) will carefully and emphatically make sure that in narrating the history of the Reformation and of the Reformers, the imperfections of Catholics are not so exaggerated and the misdeeds of the Reformers are not so concealed, or factors that are really accidental brought into such prominence, that what is essential—the departure from the Catholic faith—is no longer seen and realized".[11]

We are advised not to exaggerate, but we are also admonished to admit the truth. The sin of separation and of heresy must be recognized as such, but the share of each side in the responsibility for it must be left to the decision of the supreme Judge. Could we demand repentance from other Christian bodies if we did not add our own to theirs? Should we not be fraudulently confusing the objective judgement on the sin of separation and the collective responsibility involved in this same sin? In this way we allow the whole blame to fall upon the other Christian bodies, and we pray that we may be given the grace of unity, as though it is bound to be granted one day, happily falling into our lap like ripe fruit.

Prayer for unity must be accompanied by penance. Although Christian unity is a "state of justice" given by God, repentance forms an essential part of our turning towards each other, and of our common approach to the fullness of love. Scores of pious wishes and attempts at fraternization might create the impression that unity was growing deeper. But if we apply the test of repentance, we shall be in a position to judge the real depth of these feelings. There must indeed be repentance for the loss of unity, and self-accusation before our Lord, according to the extent of our guilt. Unity will be given as an act of forgiveness. Would God grant it without the admission of guilt? Will Christians be able to forgive each other if they have no repentance, or if it is on one side only? It is not

[10] Journet, op. cit., vol. II, p. 906.
[11] Instruction De Motione Œcumenica, text in Cattin-Conus, op. cit., p. 394. See also Vatican II's Decree on Ecumenism, chapter ii, article 7.

so much lengthy theological discussions that will speed the advance towards reunion as, most often, simple and concrete deeds that speak to the heart. It is up to us to find the symbols that will express our mutual repentance. Its manifestation can have immense ecumenical significance. With particular reference to the Catholic Church, we ought not to say that it would mean a diminution of her authority. Surely not, for the Church herself who is sinless would remain as she is, but since she is not without sinners, she knows that the authority which ultimately counts is that of the saints. Our appreciation of Peter, who at Pentecost stood out like a new Moses, is not lessened because we remember that when the cock crew he wept bitterly, and that once while walking on the water, he was afraid.

G. HATRED OF SEPARATION

If our spirit has heard the Word of God, our mind realized the gravity of the sin of separation, and our will fears God and his justice, if we have appealed to the divine mercy, if our hope has developed into the love of unity and our hearts repent of their error, we shall certainly regard separation with hatred and we shall repel it as energetically as God rejects it.

We must carefully examine the extent of this hatred. In principle it is easy to admit that separation is an evil. In practice, however, we accept it without undue disturbance.

Where in scripture or tradition can any justification be found for even a secretly complacent attitude towards separation? Although there may be no formal revelation that the visible unity of all Christians must be maintained throughout history, two things remain certain: first of all, there is nothing in scripture or tradition that rejects this possibility, and secondly, the positive teaching of them both, in their entirety, is that we should hate separation, and it stirs us up to reject it. Of course, we do not know God's ways. It may be that he has decided that Christian unity will not be achieved before the end of time, and that our efforts will only be a spiritual preparation for the unity to be realized after the Parousia. God's intentions on this point are not explicit. Nevertheless, it remains our duty to go on repeating the petition of the Pater: thy will be done on earth, as it is in heaven, that is, that Christians in this world shall be united as they are in heaven. Is it possible for that which exists in heaven to exist on earth also? Are we not asking for an impossibility? We can only reply that at any rate this is the Lord's prayer.

H. THE NEW LIFE

The mystery of unity comes before us as a mystery of crucifixion. The image that springs to mind is that of the Suffering Servant, wounded, humiliated, penitent, obedient. He heard the call of the vocation to unity—a boundless vocation—and he believes that the situation of Christians is not without its remedy. A new life is awakening and its branches spreading. What must we do in order to create in ourselves interconnected sources of love that will grow in the light? Means of the utmost certainty exist, and their power will gradually develop, provided we determine to make use of them with perseverance.

First of all, there is the ministry of mutual forgiveness. Is it not a great thing that whatever our religious allegiance may be, we can be ministers of Christ's forgiveness to each other? Our Lord made expiation, once and for ever, for all our sins. When, within the influence of the unity of the Church and of the Christian people, we forgive one another our mutual offences, we are extending his forgiveness to each other.

Other expressions of the new life of unity are possible. We can, for example, give each other a word that strengthens. Could not Christian Churches and communions offer encouragement when some courageous or striking deed has been done? Silence is the customary practice when one of them has carried out some work of excellence. Error, it is said, must not be encouraged. What would our people think? Would not the approval of some particular issue look like a recognition of the communion in its corporate existence? This is a real difficulty. Nevertheless, we are bound to reply that in an atmosphere of ecumenism, some things become possible that were not so when the circumstances for forming a judgement were different.

We may go further: a Church or communion that sees another hesitate about which direction to take, might perhaps discreetly offer its moral encouragement. There are Christians who have worked with the greatest sincerity for God's cause within a tradition inherited from their fathers, and they have done their work in isolation, while alongside them, other Christians have watched their labours in silence or even condescendingly ignored them. We agree that the strength-giving word should be uttered with all requisite reservation, but let it be uttered. When it is, then the ordinary people will appreciate the worth of this sign.

There is yet a third possibility: that of the inter-Church diaconate. For all Christians God is the bread to be shared. We must be deacons for each other, serving at tables, especially at the great table of divine charity. The Church has a diaconal function with regard to the world;[12] but each

[12] Herbert Krimm, ed., *Das Diakonische Amt der Kirche* (1953).

Church has also a diaconal function with regard to the others.[13] Several ways present themselves: works of mutual aid and charity; the sharing of observations on the Church's mission and needs; certain concrete deeds of co-operaion, etc. In this way, through this diaconal work, serving his Body, the Church, we are performing a eucharistic activity of praise to God. Did not the first separation within the Church occur when one of the Twelve left the eucharistic meal at the Last Supper? The loss of the understanding of the inter-Church diaconate has brought with it the loss of the understanding of fellowship in unity.

The Christian Churches and communions can also carry out for each other a work of inter-Church admonition. When a Church or a communion is on the point of deviating, or of entering upon a dangerous course, it is the duty of a neighbouring Church to warn her of it. In this way a brother might be saved. But is not this a sphere in which an ecumenical understanding could be developed? Tact and judgement will do the rest.

As we learn to tie the bonds together, we shall see in the restoration of Christianity a work of covenant. The ecumenical method is a method of covenant since its object is the Church and the covenant is at the heart of the Church's mystery. The covenant must be worked for by every means; we must know what the connecting links are, how to promote them, and set in motion the one perfect covenant achieved by our Lord on the Cross which made both Jews and Gentiles the people of the new covenant.

We shall do all this through the power of "the Redemption which is in Christ Jesus" (Rom 3:24). He, the High Priest of the new law, broke down the wall of separation between men and God and between men themselves. In him a "new creature" came into being whose life consists of unity, because it is a reconciliation. Therefore, everything we accomplish for Christian reunion will appear as a sign of the grace of unity existing in our Lord. Thus Christians bear the image of the most holy Pontiff, the bridge-builder, of the bonds of unity.

When we look at the divisions that have endured so long and are so deep, we may well feel lost. But this would be to forget that the Word of God, who disclosed the plan of unity to us, has not left us without the means of preserving, restoring and perfecting it.

The Gospel, the Acts, the Letters of the apostles, the example of the early Fathers, who continued these instructions, show us the way in which the prayer for unity was expressed in the terminology of the Word, so as to become, in visible fashion, an utterance of forgiveness, charity, alliance and redemption. And yet we allowed ourselves to believe that we had no

---

[13] N. A. Nissiotis, "The Ecclesiological Significance of Inter-Church Diakonia", *The Ecumenical Review*, vol. XIII, no. 2 (1961), pp. 1–12.

resources! Or else were satisfied with remote and very limited means, forgetting the ways suggested by the early Church for the maintenance or restoration of unity.

Have we not reached the time when the prayer for unity and the attempt to draw together ought to become more detailed and explicit? Just as purely spiritual ecumenism must now acquire a theological and scientific status, so the prayer for unity must become more committed. We have just seen the most important means for securing this.

It is not our intention to let it be supposed that definite prayers for unity at special periods of the year are now outmoded. We know only too well the immense part they have played during the last two centuries. The Christian Churches and communions need these material signs of their common intercession, but these special prayers must now enter into a fuller dimension.

I. THE TWO DIMENSIONS OF UNITED PRAYER

Prayer for unity has always existed in most of the Christian liturgies and communions. And yet it has only been for a little more than two hundred years that organized movements have existed with the precise aim of endowing the prayer for unity with a centre and a direction.

The initiative began in 1740 among Protestants in Scotland. It was only after another century that it gained a welcome in English Catholicism through the efforts of a convert, Ignatius Spencer. Newman put forward a plan of prayer for union, but it met with scant encouragement from the English Catholic hierarchy.

Until the nineteenth century, prayer for unity was confined to particular denominations. After this period it came to be shared by different communions. At first special days of prayer were set aside, and then particular days, such as New Year's Day, were adopted.

In 1857, in England, as the result of a combined Anglican and Catholic initiative, the first association of prayer for unity, was founded.[14] At first it was blessed by Pius IX, but, later, in 1864, it was condemned in principle, and its Catholic members were compelled to withdraw for the same reasons that had frustrated Newman's programme.

Leo XIII felt obliged to take up again the idea of praying for unity. In the encyclical *Provida Matris* (1895) he gave his approval to special prayers, during the season of Pentecost, for the development of unity, and in the encyclical *Satis Cognitum* (1897), he ruled that the nine days in preparation for Pentecost should be especially devoted to this intention.

[14] Ruth Rouse, "Voluntary Movements and the Changing Ecumenical Climate" in Rouse and Neill, *op. cit.*, pp. 345–9.

When the movement began in 1740, prayer was addressed to the Holy Spirit for the renewal of the Churches. But very soon the intention of the reunion of the denominations was added to it, and then the idea of the reunion of all Christendom.

The octave of prayers for unity, from 18 January to 25 January, was not created all of a piece: it was a development of an earlier trend. It goes back to 1907, and we owe it to the initiative of two Anglican clergymen, Spencer Jones and Paul Wattson, both of them pro-Roman in tendency. The former had proposed that the feast of St Peter should be chosen by pro-Roman Anglicans as the day when the prerogatives of St Peter and Rome as the centre of unity would be proclaimed. Paul Wattson proposed that an octave of prayer should be established which would unite in a twofold symbol St Peter's of Rome and St Paul's of London, and this led to the adoption of the dates of the feast of St Peter's Chair and of the conversion of St Paul. In 1909, Pius X gave his blessing to the plan, and Benedict XV extended the octave of prayer to the entire Catholic Church. But there was still a difficulty in the way this common prayer was expressed. It conflicted with the denominational loyalty of several religious bodies who felt it to be too pro-Roman. It was Abbé Couturier who broadened it to meet the needs of all communions, and this explains its worldwide acceptance. [15]

The suppression of the feast of St Peter's Chair in Rome (January 18) removed one of the liturgical buttresses of the octave of prayer. There had, in fact, been something equivocal in the understanding of this feast. Those who initiated the octave of prayer regarded it as the celebration of the episcopal chair, that is, of St Peter's magisterial and primatial authority. But this was incorrect. Originally it was only a memorial celebration of St Peter at his tomb. In ancient Rome, the memory of a dead person was celebrated by a meal at the family grave, in the presence of a *cathedra* left unoccupied. The early Christians transposed this custom to a celebration in memory of their fathers in the faith, and it was in this way that the word *cathedra* passed from its original meaning to that of the episcopal chair. The feast of St Peter's Chair has now been fixed for February 22, the date historically confirmed as being the most ancient.

There are, therefore, two aspects that stand out in the history of the organized movement of prayer for unity: prayer to the Holy Spirit for the renewal of the Christian Churches and communions; and prayer to the Holy Spirit for the visible unity of Christians. There can be no union of Christian bodies without a world-wide renewal. Renewal will lead to unity. Prayer for unity without prayer for renewal will be incomplete. Since prayers in common are necessary, why should we not return to

[15] M. Villain, *L'Abbé Paul Couturier* (1960).

Leo XIII's idea, remembering that the Holy Spirit is the cause of both unity and renewal and that at Pentecost he was sent to the apostolic body to remain with it until the world's end? In this way we could see more clearly the full proportions of the prayer for unity in a way that would be adequate for a further advance in ecumenical relationships.

3. Christian reunion and the expansion of Christianity

The most difficult problem confronting Christian society today is that of finding the means that will lead to a renewed expansion. The shape of the world as it presents itself in this second half of the twentieth century is that of a developing inter-racial and inter-religious society. It is these characteristics that must govern the way in which Christianity regards its mission, its function and its future.

The Catholic Church is a phenomenon predominantly of the white race, Western culture, and very strongly Latin. A tiny minority exists in Africa and Asia. Protestantism and Orthodoxy are also predominantly white. Protestantism as a whole belongs to the non-Latin culture of the West. Orthodoxy belongs to the culture of the East.

Christian reunion—which in any case has not yet been achieved—would not perceptably alter the fact that Christianity is predominantly a phenomenon of the white race. Most Christians would still belong to Western civilization, although there would be a strong element belonging to the East. The problem, therefore, is how to introduce Christianity to the rest of the world.

Our aim is not to set up a Christian block existing after the fashion of all the others throughout the world. That is the characteristic of earthly politics, not of those of the Kingdom. Our aim is to promote the catholicity of the *Oikoumene* as it now appears to us with its new features. Christian reunion may not by itself provide the solution to the problem of Christian expansion, but it can entail the operation of certain principles which may become the real means for the fulfilment of catholicity. At this point we want to indicate as clearly as possible what the acceptance of pluralism would effect in the Catholic expression of Christianity.

In each age the Church does what it is in her power to do. In a period of division some expressions of belief become obligatory: in a period of reunion they would have to be replaced by others. Cardinal Costantini once made known that it grieved him to reflect that we tried to make Asia submit to the West, with the result that Asia would not submit. Is it not true that some of our difficulties and some of the obstacles we encounter in our attempts to spread Christianity are due to the fact that in practice we have identified unity with uniformity and have established a quasi-monopoly of one expression of Christianity which, though excellent in itself, left little room for others to contribute their own special resources with any ease. Politically, it is unquestionable that the East has no intention of submitting to the West, and religiously the same thing is true. Will Africa continue to submit to the West? Will China, India and Indonesia? And will they accept the Latin version of Catholicism? Are we not bound to admit certain conclusions from 400 years of missionary effort, in which neither zeal, nor means, nor talent were lacking? What means were available to Peter and the Twelve? And yet in a short while they succeeded in establishing the bases for the future expansion of Christianity. They went to Africa, Europe and Asia, and in their tracks a pluralist expression of Christianity appeared which we must regard as the prototype of missionary expansion when unity has been regained. In the early Church there was a moment when the temptation arose of making the rest of the world submit to an excessively narrow ruling. The Council of Jerusalem brought out the correct principle of catholicity. Against the Judaisers who sought to compel converts to come in through a too restricted entrance, the apostles declared that Christianity is a universal religion, which, unlike Judaism, is rooted in no particular part of the world, and that its mission is to be sent to the four corners of the earth, and on each occasion to be incarnated anew. From the administrative point of view, uniformity would seem to be the safest and most effective system. But is this absolutely certain? What ultimately determines the permanency of Christianity anywhere is the existence of its essential principles and their incorporation in the human soil. Without this, juridical bonds are fragile indeed; with it, they are all sufficient.

When the pluralist expression of belief within unity has been accepted, an infinity of risks endangering belief and communion are also most certainly involved. And yet the truth is that whatever the system, such risks exist. Neither uniformity nor pluralism offer any absolute guarantee against the dangers of schism and heresy. These latter occurred equally during the time when the Church was undivided and Christianity was expressed in a pluralistic way, as they did later on in the period of separation, when uniformity and centralization predominated. One has only to reflect on the history of the Catholic Church during the last hundred years: in the Philippines (the Independent Church); in Poland (the Mariavite Church); in the United States (the Polish National Catholic Church, apart from a number of Ukrainians who have changed over to the jurisdiction of the Russian Greek Orthodox Catholic Church of North America); and finally, in Eastern Europe after the Second World War, and in China.

Even with the best possible system, the unity of faith and communion are always in danger. No absolute and abiding guarantee against these two dangers exists, especially as it is not only doctrinal or administrative conflicts that may lead to them, but also a number of non-theological, sociological or psychological factors, against which the Church has no specific remedy.

Even the extension of the pluralistic system already partially existing in Catholicism, together with liturgical and administrative pluralism, to the spheres of the non-Christian cultures of Africa, will not prevent fresh dangers of schism or heresy from appearing some time or other. Even Christian reunion will not necessarily indicate the termination of all division for ever. Control of belief in the Chinese, Hindu or any other expression of Christianity will not be easy, and the young Churches will encounter all the dangers that the older Churches have already met: the danger of being assimilated by their culture and their nation, and that of an internal rupture between reason and faith. We do not mean that this is bound to happen, but the experience of the Church's history shows that the problem of Christianity in the world is substantially the same in Europe, Africa, Asia or America. It is subjected to special temptations which recur with the same regularity as the laws of its own activity. The eternal problem concerns what Christianity must do in order to assimilate the world, while allowing itself to be assimilated by it and yet not lost in it, and what Catholicism must do in order to gather all nations together, really becoming a part of them without splitting up into national Churches.

The Church will, therefore, always be engaged, within every country, culture and race, in the constant effort to provide new definitions of her nature and her mission, and to trace the limits of her assimilation by the world, and at the same time to plan the way in which she may become incarnate in any given region and culture; and when the tension becomes excessive, only the supreme witness is left to her: martyrdom, so that she may not be disloyal to the principles laid down by Christ and the apostles.

At the present moment we have to learn many things in a short while; life forces the pace, and events crowd upon us. We must even now draw lessons from still recent ecumenical efforts, and apply them without delay to the direction we wish to give to the Church. Her experience when she was undivided shows that what was wrong at that time was not the pluralist expression of one and the same Catholicism, but the fact that a gulf was allowed to develop between the Western and Eastern expressions of Catholicism, between two cultures and two spiritual outlooks. We should profit by this experience for our future needs. Should this ancient expression, or African or Asiatic expressions of Christianity appear, it is not their development that will prove dangerous—for that accords with the Catholic spirit—but a failure to attend to the division which might be produced between them and other forms of expression. Pluralism unbalanced by fellowship and unity is wide open to schism and heresy. Hence it follows that if Catholicism becomes more explicit and detailed, it must accordingly watch over the bonds of fellowship and unity. Specific organs of co-ordination must be found—but does not the Church possess ample resources for this purpose?

Is this a Utopian idea? We do not fail to realize what this development represents as regards the meaning of the pluralist expression of Catholicism, and how many obstacles the project has to meet. The difficulties involved are far from being entirely the result of routine, or indifference, or lack of vision. Even the wisest plans must await their hour, and even though they may not be applied, this does not mean that they have not been examined; most often it means that their time has not yet come. As a beginning it is often sufficient if the general trend is settled. In any case, the Church does not lack experience in this sphere: the problem is not so essentially different from the one that she encountered in her early days when she had to leave her place of origin and approach new cultures. The Jewish colonies of the diaspora provided the ground in which to establish herself, and Christianity gradually learnt to develop its own roots. In the divided state of Christendom in which we have lived for centuries, the Catholic Church has been compelled to promote the Latin rite and develop it until it required its own autonomy. This was only common sense. Would other methods have been possible? Attempts were made by men of great foresight in China and India, but these experiments, which would have been normal in a period when Catholicism was expressed in a pluralist form, at that time seemed to the Church, governed by the ideal of uniformity, to be beyond what could actually be done. But, with the opening of the era of ecumensim, we may expect unity to be expressed in diversity. In countries with new Christian communities that have reached a sufficient maturiy, and in which Catholicism has become firmly rooted, it can apply the Church's mission in these regions with the chief responsibility that this entails: make the culture, the soul, the national genius, Catholic, and express perennial Christianity—which can only be universal if its relationship to the world is at once transcendent and immanent—in terms of those realities. There will no longer be Jews, Greeks and Barbarians, not because they will have disappeared, but because all of them will be present in unity.

It may well be, therefore, that some of the conditions without which Christian reunion will not be achieved, are the same as those that will govern the future expansion of Christianity. It will be difficult to reject the one series and accept the other, or to reject them all. On all sides the Church is faced with danger. There is no universal panacea for safeguarding the faith or communion. Risks are to be found everywhere and in all circumstances. It belongs to the Church's wisdom to decide whether the time has come for a development, whether this is the time for new seed to be sown.

4. A second spring for the Church

We are reminded of a prophetic utterance made by Pius XII shortly before his death. He realized that we are at the opening of a new age, and he proclaimed its dawn in terms that throw light upon the future of Christianity. Speaking to Italian Catholic Youth on 19 March 1958, he declared that spring was awakening for Christianity.[16]

> "*Jam ... hiems transiit* (Cant. 2:2). Winter, a long, dark winter, is now over. Few people perhaps—and even still fewer young people—realize what a night had covered the world, what an icy cold had made it barren and destroyed countless seeds of life. It was a long dark winter on account of the errors that darkened so many minds; the mire that troubled so many hearts: the vice that stained so many activities. It was long and dark for persons who had gone astray; for shattered families; for ravaged nations; for the whole world torn by horrible wars. Look back, dear children, at the world behind you. Look at the distant, recent and immediate past. You will be unable to refrain from saying that we are coming out from a long dark winter.
>
> "But if the winter is behind you, the summer lies ahead, summer with its promise, its light, its fertility. *Prope est aestas* (Mt 24:32): summer is nigh ... A thousand modern errors have been punished by their very bankruptcy ... Other errors, young people, will be bound to disappear; other thrones must fall; other wild ambitions collapse in ruin. And the ruin will be the more apalling, the greater the rashness of matching self against God has been. The summer will come, dear sons, and a plentiful harvest ...
>
> "Look around you, dear sons, the whole world is awakening; material life ... the ascending curve of progress ... even the life and activity of the mind ... Clear signs of an awakening are evident also in social life. No other period, of all those that men have lived through since Christ's coming, seems to us to have been so decisive for mankind's development as that in which you are now living ...
>
> "As in every spring, so in the one approaching, strong winds and storms will not be lacking: the Church has not ended her martyrdom ... A summons to renewal is traversing the world. Would you like to hear it? ... Look around you, young people, at the springtide

[16] *La Documentation Catholique*, 13 April 1958.

of mankind, the springtide of life. Make our hope your own and tell all men that we are in a springtide of history. God wants it to be one of the finest springtides that men have ever experienced.

After one of the darkest and hardest of winters, spring is coming, the forerunner of one of the most abundant and sunfilled summers."

A prophet's vision of the end shortens the time and sees its reality as already present. This same great plan had been foreseen by Leo XIII at the end of his pontificate, when he summed up his life's hope in an appeal for unity between the Churches and nations. He warmly urged them to unite, trusting in the grace and mercy of the omnipotent God who alone knows when the time is ripe for his bounty, and in whose hands alone every human will is held, to be directed as he pleases. "Moved by a heart-felt desire, we cannot deny ourselves the sweet hope, that the time is not far distant when the Eastern Churches, so illustrious by the faith of their ancestors and of so ancient a glory, will return to the fold ... With a charity no less heartfelt, we now turn to those nations, who, at a recent period, on account of the blows of extraordinary upheavels in both the times and events, left the bosom of the Roman Church." He then unfolds a splendid vision of unity:

"The Church would regain the position of honour which is her due ... For society this would produce the most happy results ... It would, further, be the means of drawing the nations together ... Internally, the renewal of which we are speaking would provide the most certain and the strongest guarantees for public safety which laws and the armed forces could not give ... While our mind dwells on these thoughts and our heart longs with all its might for their realization, we see, unfolding in the distant future, a new order of things, and we know nothing more consoling than the contemplation of the immense benefits that would naturally result from it. The mind can hardly imagine the powerful impetus that would suddenly inspire all nations and raise them to the peak of greatness and prosperity: peace and tranquility would be assured; the humanities would be fostered through this progress; amongst farmers, workers, and owners of industry, new associations would be set up on the Christian principles we have indicated, able to put down usury and enlarge the sphere of useful work. The power of these benefits would extend not only to the civilized nations; it would cross their frontiers and, like a river of overflowing fertility, travel to far distant climes ...

"We are not unaware of the lengthy and difficult labours required for that order of things whose restoration we desire, and many will no doubt consider that we are leaving too much to hope, and pursuing an ideal more to be wished for than expected. But we put all our hope and trust in Jesus Christ, the Saviour of the human race, remembering the great things that the folly of the Cross and its proclamation were formerly able to accomplish, in face of *the wisdom of this world,* stupified and confounded ... May God, so rich in mercy, who holds the time and the favourable moment in his power, hear our prayer, and in his infinite goodness, may he hasten the fulfilment of that promise of Jesus Christ: *there shall be one fold and one shepherd.*" [17]

Does it not seem that from one pontificate to another the reality has drawn nearer and its shape grown clearer? [18]

5. Ecce Mater tua

The Catholic Church has no wish to use force to make anyone share the convictions she holds. She only desires that those who seek the goal of unity will also accept the means to it. That is the sum of her intolerance.

She also asks for respect for her conviction that the authentic great Church of the future will be that arising from reunited Christendom whose visible centre has never ceased to exist.

The error of looking for the great Church in any other place than where it essentially exists, calls to mind the vehement but most understandable desire of a man to rediscover the light, of which an accident has deprived him, or of an orphan trying to find its mother.

In the universal joy that will ensue when reunion has been achieved, it will be realized that the attempt to rediscover the light was only the result of failing to look for it in the right place, and that the orphan's gesture of despair was only a bad dream.

If the Spirit deigns to make her reality clear to the minds of those who do not now see her, the true Church of Christ will appear as "the woman clothed with the sun" (Rev 12:1). For the mother is still alive. She had never ceased to hope, to watch and to wait, far into the long night. She had pondered in her heart and before God what could have so wounded some of her children that they went away from her to those unlikely regions.

But now in the interval of uncertainty that divides the darkness of the Cross from the light of the Resurrection, many of her children are coming back to her; their hearts have become sensitive to a voice that says to them: Doubt has become impossible. "Behold your Mother" (Jn 19:27).

---

[17] *Praeclara Gratulationis,* 20 June 1894, quoted in Marny, *op. cit.,* pp. 822–38.
[18] John XXIII, *Ad Petri Cathedram,* 29 June 1959, 3rd part, "Unity of the Church"; *Aeterna Dei Sapientia,* 11 November 1961, 2nd part, section 6, "Call to All Christians to the Unity of the Church".

INDEX OF AUTHORS

SUBJECT INDEX

Adventism 82—83, 93, 228

American Protestantism 15—17, 53, 55, 74, 92—93, 112—16, 279, 371—2

Anabaptism 73—76, 83, 93

Anglican Communion: definition 50, 64—74, 92; relationship with Anglicanism as seen in the Church of England 73; relationship with Protestantism 72—73, 92; relationship with Orthodoxy 426; idea of the essence of Christianity 141; idea of the mission of the Church 186; idea of the structure of the Church 241—4; idea of worship 225—6; idea of the unity of the Church 373; ecumenical activity 50—51, 121, 125—30, 251—2

Antioch 54, 420, 421

Antitrinitarianism 78—79

Apostle: function 160—4, 265—74, 381—2; relationship with Jesus Christ 258—90; with Peter 258—9, 389—92, 415—23, 426—30, 443

Apostolic Succession: in Catholicism 259—74; in Protestantism 237

Apostolicity 161—3, 257—8, 261—5, 414—15

Ascension of Christ: in Catholicism 211—15, 257—9, 265—6, 308—10; in Protestantism 168—9

Associations 105, 109—23

Augustine's idea of Church's mission 222—4

Autocephalous Churches 399, 425—6

Baptists 79—80, 83, 89, 93, 230, 288—9

Bible, see Scripture

Bishop: in Catholicism 261—74, 386, 411—18, 431—40; in Anglicanism 241—4; in Lutheranism 236—41; in Calvinism 232—6

Calvinism: in general 65—70, 76—78, 92, 169—81; the mission of the Church 189—92; the structure of the Church 231—5, 245; worship 284—8

Catholicism: origin of the word 37; meaning 38—39, 258; new features in contemporary Catholicism 7—9, 25; the essence of Catholicism 138—43, 335; the Catholic structure of the Church 132, 254—6, 308; comparison with Protestantism and Orthodoxy 186—96, 322—7; the dialectic of catholicity at the individual and national level 385—7, 392—4; the twofold image of catholicity 357, 390, 392, 419—23, 427; catholicity, a note of the Church 258, 508; see also Apostolicity, Chalcedon, Mission, Divine Presence, Primacy of the Pope, Structure of the Church, Tradition, Word of God, Worship

Chalcedon 94, 322—4, 436

Christian: in Catholicism 167—8, 174—5, 181, 211—12, 216, 277, 324; in Protestantism 171—6, 277—8, 323—7; dissident Christians 28—29, 498—9, 506—7, 510

Christianity: in relationship with the Christology of Chalcedon 322—4; authentic type or types of Christianity 321—3

Christian Science 89

Church: in Catholicism: convocation-congregation 57, 210, 425; theandric constitution 256; four fundamental meanings 210—11; the Church from heaven 257—9; the ecclesia of Sinai 476—88; from the Incarnation to the Cross 215—16; Pentecost 311—12; from the Resurrection to the final consummation 215—16, 273—4; identity of the Church of faith and the Church of history 168—9,